Native Texas Plants

Turk's cap and cherry laurel flourish in the shade under an Ashe juniper in this Austin garden. Photo by the authors.

By SALLY WASOWSKI

With ANDY WASOWSKI

Native Texas Plants

 LANDSCAPING

REGION *by* REGION

★

TexasMonthlyPress

Texas Monthly Press
P.O. Box 1569
Austin, Texas 78767

A   B   C   D   E   F   G   H

Library of Congress Cataloging-in-Publication Data

Wasowski, Sally, 1946–
    Native Texas plants.

    Bibliography: p.
    Includes index.
    1. Native plant gardening—Texas.   2. Native plants for cultivation—Texas.   3. Landscape gardening—Texas.   I. Wasowski, Andy, 1939–
II. Title.
SB439.24.T4W37   1988   635.9′51′764   88-20048

ISBN 0-87719-111-5

Book Design by Whitehead & Whitehead

Printed in Singapore by
Singapore National Printers Ltd.
through Palace Press

Contents

To Benny J. Simpson.

It would take another whole book to relate how grateful we are
for his wise counsel, amazing
knowledge, and infinite patience, without which this book simply would
not have been possible.

And to Melissa, our wonderful daughter,
for putting up with our absences,
for tolerating our "discussions" while we wrote this book,
and for understanding and loving us
anyway.

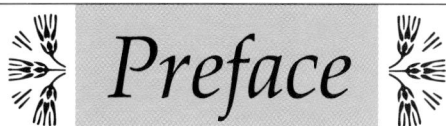

WRITING a first book is a lot easier than writing a second one. At least that's been my experience. True, I'd learned a lot more about the subject since the first effort, but all this newly acquired knowledge just made me painfully aware of how much more I still didn't know—and how little I'd known the first time around. Naiveté and blissful ignorance produced my first book—the second was fueled by fear and humility, with a dash of chutzpah thrown in.

After all, Texas' native plants number almost five thousand species. The subject is tremendously rich in detail and diversity and possibilities. Beyond that, the state itself is a vast and complicated subject. In a sense, Texas is the United States in microcosm. Here, you can find virtually every major type of terrain within the continental U.S., from swamps to deserts to mountains to sunny seashores. As a result, Texas native plants can thrive far beyond our borders, literally from Maine to California.

It's probably impossible to produce a complete book on this subject—at least, one that you could carry around comfortably—and my first book barely scratched the surface. It concentrated on only one portion of Texas—the limestone spine that runs from Dallas–Fort Worth down to Austin–San Antonio. This area had, until then, been largely ignored in landscaping books and by the major nursery wholesalers on both the East and West coasts. That book had been needed, as was evidenced by its immediate and gratifying sales success. Still, I couldn't help but feel a little guilty for having slighted East Texas, El Paso, Amarillo, the Valley, and the entire Gulf Coast.

Clearly, there was need for a second book, one that would cover a lot more ground—literally and figuratively. One that would not only update and expand plant information for the "limestone spine" but would also regionalize the entire state, so that you the reader would know specifically which plants were native to your area and what you could expect from them.

This, of course, meant getting to know Texas more intimately than I'd ever dreamed I'd want to. It meant discovering a lot of new plants that I had little or no knowledge of. And because I can't live everywhere in the state and have firsthand experience with the myriad species and varieties, and all their many quirks and characteristics, I had to rely on local experts.

First I had to find those experts, and then I had to travel around the state to meet them, view their work, see the native plants in their natural habitats, and take photos of both gardens and plants. I needed someone who was a writer, a photographer, a good driver, and a first-class traveling companion. I turned to my favorite partner—my husband, Andy. Together we have traveled more than 35,000 miles in Texas to put this book together.

When all the work was done, we realized one thing above all else: we Texans are extremely lucky. We have such abundant natural beauty all around us. Each region possesses something special that can capture your heart and imagination. In South Texas every leaf you touch seems to be delightfully scented. The air is fragrant on a sunny afternoon with wafts of lemon, spice, or sage. The Hill Country is lovely even in winter with its palette of evergreens, golden grasses, and white limestone. West Texas is a special color feast, combining red soils with foliage ranging from dark green to yellow-green to pale blue and silver. Both our pine forests and our prairies are nothing less than majestic.

If this book does no more than make you aware of the incredible beauty around you, then it was well worth doing.

Sally Wasowski
Dallas, Texas

 *Acknowledgments*

ABOUT midway through our work on this book, we had an unsettling experience. We made a "cold-call" visit at a nursery in an unfamiliar part of the state, hoping to pick up some practical hands-on information about the local native plants.

The owner of the nursery did indeed have valuable data on the region, and since business seemed slow that day, it didn't appear that our chatting would be a problem. But as my questions kept coming, her tone became more and more brittle. She began to show signs of impatience and then irritation. Finally, she suggested rather icily that instead of going around talking to people, I'd be better off "doing some research." I can't imagine what she thought I *was* doing.

Luckily, that was a unique and aberrant encounter, and I mention it only because, when I started out, I honestly feared this would be a typical response. After all, who would want to take time out of a busy day to educate *me*? I had so many questions and so much to learn! I thought that, at best, people would be polite and civil and then shoo me off as soon as they could. If that had been the case, this book could not have been written.

As it turned out, everywhere that Andy and I traveled we met with greater warmth and cooperation than we could have hoped for. We were continually amazed by the generosity shown us, not only in terms of information and access to slide collections but also in that most valuable commodity of all—time. Often our regional contacts would devote an entire workday to helping us in our research. Later, during the sorting-out periods back home and during the actual writing, they were always ready to accept a frantic phone call or respond with detailed letters explaining some fine point on propagation or whatever. Some of these people welcomed us into their homes and allowed us to photograph their gardens. Some provided escort service to unfamiliar parts of the state and introductions to people who might have what we needed. Not once did we detect a note of impatience or disinterest from any of them.

Why were they so helpful? One reason is that they love our Texas native plants. They want native plants to gain greater acceptance and appreciation, and we represented a means to that worthy end. But mostly they helped because, quite simply, that's the kind of people they are. Acknowledging them here is paltry repayment for all their many kindnesses.

Our thanks to Geyata Ajilvsgi, Olivette Beach, Edith Bettinger, Gene Blacklock, W. D. Bransford, Mary Buchanan, Fred Buxton, Marie Caillet, Logan Calhoun, C. W. Carpenter, Judy Black Childress, Wayne Clark, Marvin and Betty Colwill, Paul Cox, Gerald and Rosalie Cyrier, Dallas Museum of Natural History, Walt Davis, David Diamond, James Dick, Stephen K. Domigan, Ted Doremus, Anna Jane Duree, Jim Everitt, Katie Ferguson, Rosa and Charles Finsley, George J. Fix, Jr., Will Fleming, Manuel Flores, Gary Freeborg, Skip Fulton, Robert Gallagher, Linda Gardner, Sue Gardner, Ron Gass, Lorine and David Gibson, Don and Benita Giller, John Gleason, Heard Natural Science Museum, Mike Heep, Martha Henschen, Dan Hinds, Mary Grace Horlock, Agnes Hubbard, Phil Huey, Fred Jones, Margaret Jones, Ed and Margaret Kennedy, Richard Kirkham, John M. Koros, Tom Kramer, Dr. Harold Laughlin, Eric Lautzenheiser, Patty Leslie, Dr. Robert Lonard, Lynn Lowrey, Norma Maddox, Tom Madison, T. J. Marks, Dorothy Mattiza, Norman Maxwell, Janeen McDermott, Lisa McNelis, Denny Miller, Laura Miller, James Stewart Minton, National Wildflower Research Center, Rolf and Anita Nelson, Charlotte Nichols, Jill Nokes, David Northington, Ruth O'Brien, Mary and Carl Owens, Michael Parkey, Michael Passarello, Annie Paulson, Don Perkins, Art Petley, Barbara Pettijohn, Adele Pieper, Bob and Dede Plank, Jack Price, Ray Pulaski, Jim and Chris Ridley, David Riskind, Dr. Chester Rowell, Steve R. Runnells, Santa Ana National Wildlife Refuge, Michael Shoup, Linda Smith, Shannon Smith, Mrs. W. Truett Smith, Dr. Geoffrey Stanford, Alice Staub, Marilyn Stidham, Wash Storm, Harold Stroud, Glenn and Connie Suhren, Dora Sylvester, Kathy Thieleman, John Thomas, Bryan Thompson, Dr. Jimmy L. Tipton, James Turner, Kay Warmerdam, Dr. Barton H. Warnock, Vernon L. and Marie Wesby, John White, Burr Williams, Doug Williams, Tom Wooten. And of course Benny J. Simpson, to whom this book is dedicated.

Special thanks to David Nickel, who did such a wonderful job drawing up my plans for this book (as well as the first one). I'm especially grateful to Ron Nelson, friend and architect, who not only gave me valuable advice but also gave me a quiet refuge away from phones and family where I could complete the plans.

On a more personal note, love and thanks go to those who became substitute parents for our daughter, Melissa, during our many trips away from home. My mother, Sara Hudson, assumed the lioness's share. But also we're grateful to Stephanie Barron Ertel and her daughters, Valerie and Kathleen, and Mary Jane Dietz and her daughter, Stess, for being there for Melissa and for us. And thanks to our neighbors Horace Longino and David Jett for providing a home away from home for our cats so they wouldn't have to be boarded at the vet's.

On the road, we were saved numerous times from motel beds by the hospitality of friends and relatives: cousin Raymond Baber and her husband, Gary, Sheila Taylor and Walter Kennedy, Jacque and Don Stowers,

John Park and Leslie Moore, Genie and Chuck Lindberg, Dody and Bill Spencer, Jill Nokes, Mrs. Una Simpson, Leo and Ida Sims, and, on our trip to Arizona to gather data on desert plants, Andy's folks, Sophie and Frank Roginski.

Want to have nightmares? Write a book and then wonder if somehow you inadvertently left out a very important name in the acknowledgments. If that did indeed happen, please blame it on human fallibility in the face of a rapidly approaching deadline, forgive us, and know that it in no way diminishes our heartfelt gratitude and love.

Introduction

WHAT with Indian raids, droughts, Santa Anna, the Civil War, and assorted other bothersome situations, early Texans had precious little time to think about gardening for pleasure. That changed around the time they discovered oil. The cattle business was thriving, cotton was king, railroad tracks were running in all directions, and the middle class was prospering. Folks realized they weren't living on a rugged frontier any longer. Life was getting civilized.

Those Texans took a look at their homesteads and decided it was high time they planted a few things here and there, to make the old place look more respectable. For the most part they chose plants and landscape patterns they were comfortable with, that is, what they or their parents had known and grown up with before coming to this state.

Texans of Mexican or Spanish heritage enclosed their yards with walls and created patios—a style well suited to our mild climate, which allows us to live outdoors a good deal of the time. They also used the lavishly flowering trees, shrubs, perennials, and vines brought up from below the Rio Grande. These plants are usually drought-tolerant, although they aren't always winter-hardy. If Anglo settlers had followed this direction, Texas gardens would have fared much better.

However, the English and German settlers (as well as French, Poles, Scots, and others) preferred the traditions of northern Europe or of their old homes back East. This is how we got tightly clipped hedges, smooth green lawns, and isolated flower gardens. The plants are not summer-hardy, and the whole style is inappropriate for most of Texas because it requires unconscionable amounts of water. On a square-foot basis, our most basic (and boring) hedge-and-lawn landscape requires more maintenance and watering than some of the most famous gardens of Europe, which, by the way, are usually never watered at all.

Does that mean that we can't have gorgeous gardens? Certainly not. They just have to be designed to suit our conditions. They have to use plants adapted to our soils, rainfall, and temperatures. Of course, one of the best places to find such plants is—you guessed it—right here in Texas.

Do You Have to Go 100 Percent Native?

A close friend once said to me, "I like native plants, but I don't use them because I don't want to give up using other plants in my garden." I was stunned. It had never occurred to me that people would think they had to make an all-or-nothing decision. The idea is to have *more* choices that work well for us, not to give up old favorites—especially plants that have naturalized here and are thriving. My own garden is only 50 percent native. The rest is 25 percent naturalized and 25 percent imports.

How to Use Natives in Landscape Designs

There are two basic approaches. One is to implement classic designs and conventional landscapes—but with native plants, so you'll have less watering to do. The plans in the book that reflect this approach are the Sand Garden, English Mixed Border, Rock Garden, Shrub Garden, Walled Garden, and Water Garden.

The other approach is to imitate nature, using woods and meadows as landscape elements to produce exciting and low-maintenance environments for ourselves. This is not a new idea. The famous English landscape designer Capability Brown transformed numerous grand estates into meadows and woods in the late 1700s. Both the Grass Garden Plan and the Create-a-Woods Plan tell you how to do this—but Texas style. And because I figured most of you were not estate owners, they're on a more modest scale, too.

If you're fortunate enough to have land where nature's landscape has not been destroyed, then natural landscaping is easy. Even a scrubby-looking field can be turned into something special with the addition of a few well-chosen, colorful native plants, along with judicious pruning and an occasional mowing. How to tame a woodland is covered in the regional plans for Post Oak, Blackland, and Valley. How to get the most out of a break or a mesquite wood is covered in the West Texas Plan.

Most natural landscapes need pruning and the addition of flowering plants to enhance them. You want the end result to look as if you were lucky enough to own Eden, when in fact you are demonstrating your imagination and good taste. For this type of landscaping, you must add only those plants indigenous to your region, or you will create a visual faux pas. To help you choose the right plants, the regional plans are strictly indigenous.

You don't want to water your natural landscape, so you'll need to naturalize the plants you add. You do this by getting a plant established and then leaving it completely alone, to do or die. A bit of pruning from time to time is okay. Seedlings establish themselves more quickly and efficiently than larger plants. When you're naturalizing, limit soil preparation to the spot where the plant will go. Also, don't work over the immediate area. Consider it to be already planted.

The Water Crisis: Natives to the Rescue

Conserving water is a steadily growing concern throughout the state. Yet I've driven through countless neighborhoods and seen sprinklers going at high noon, with the sun and wind evaporating a large percentage of the water, and much of the rest running off down the streets and into the sewers—just so people can maintain a Virginia-style landscape.

We can't afford that kind of waste! And tomorrow we'll be able to afford it even less. Our population increases, but our rainfall does not. Our two main sources of water are man-made lakes and reservoirs, and aquifers—natural underground lakes. Both are dependent on rain to keep them full.

The lakes and reservoirs were created after the terrible drought of the fifties. Texas has always had droughts, periods when we get less than 75 percent of our average annual rainfall. We started keeping records on our weather conditions in the late nineteenth century and have listed droughts in the l890s, the teens, the thirties, the fifties, and the seventies. We're due for another sometime in the nineties.

We have six major freshwater aquifers, each with a recharge zone where rainwater filters down and replenishes the supply. Today buildings and parking lots sit atop many of these recharge zones, causing what rainfall we get to run off, not seep down. Then more water is pumped out than can be replaced. It doesn't take an IQ of 200 to see that this is a dead-end policy.

Salt is adding to the water problem in Texas. Lake Meredith, the reservoir for the High Plains, is salty. There is salty water in the coastal aquifers that serve Corpus Christi and the Valley. The Valley also gets salty water from Lake Amistad on the Rio Grande. By the time the Rio Grande reaches the Valley, its waters have been recycled through the public water systems of Albuquerque and El Paso and everything in between, picking up salt all along the way. There is also salty groundwater in the Eastern Cross Timbers and most of the land around Sweetwater, so named because its water was unique in that area.

Since few plants can tolerate salty water, one obvious solution is to use the ones that require little or no supplemental watering. Most water departments are promoting this concept under the term "Xeriscape." The word was coined by the Denver Water Department and comes from the Greek word "*xeros*," meaning "dry." You're going to be hearing it a lot in the days and years to come whenever and wherever responsible landscaping is discussed.

All the plans in this book, except for the Water Garden, are xeriscapic—even the ones for Houston and the Piney Woods. Many people make the mistake of thinking that xeriscapic plants come only from our western deserts. Actually, dogwoods and magnolias are xeriscapic in their native range.

Native plants are ideal for the xeriscapic concept and can make a significant difference in water conservation. For that reason alone they ought to be included in your landscape plan. But of course they have many other valuable virtues.

Blue Northers and Extreme Heat

Texas is famous for its quick changes of extreme weather. Tornadoes, hurricanes, floods, blizzards, and ice storms occur frequently. They are as normal for us as droughts.

I'll admit straight away that Texas native plants are not immune to tornadoes and hurricanes, but our indigenous plants do fare well in blizzards and northers. Cold spells are especially damaging in Texas because our winters are normally mild, except in the Panhandle. This mild weather lulls plants into putting out new spring growth just before they get zapped by a late-spring blue norther.

When this happens, drive around your neighborhood and notice how everything that has been damaged is nonnative. The plants indigenous to the area have become wary of these surprises and hold themselves back, breaking winter dormancy later, when it's safe.

In a severely freakish cold spell, such as that of December and January 1983–84, even native plants that are pushing the northern edge of their native range can be hurt, as the ebonies in Corpus Christi were.

Texas is also prone to hot spells, when temperatures get up to 115° F and stay there for weeks. At night the temperature barely drops into the nineties. Where this occurs, our native plants are ready for it. Their roots are deep, and their leaves are coated with waxes, "fur," oil glands, or other substances that retard evaporation. Some natives even drop their leaves, and releaf when conditions improve.

Why Regional Landscaping?

Because Texas is so big and varied, few plants are native to the state as a whole. We have to break the state down into its many differing geographical, geological, and climatic areas and then address those plants that are indigenous to each region.

A plant that is indigenous to Houston is not likely to be suitable for use in Lubbock, which gets thirty inches less rainfall per year. And a Lubbock native plant would probably be unhappy with the humidity and poor drainage in Houston. However, the regions of Texas stretch far beyond the state's boundaries. A Houston native plant would grow beautifully in Savannah, Georgia, and a Lubbock native plant would feel right at home in Albuquerque, New Mexico.

In a conventional landscape, where you can provide special conditions of extra water or winter protection, experimenting with plants outside your region is fun. Some basic guidelines are helpful, though. First, know where the plant is native. Texas gets drier the farther west you go and colder the farther north you go. If you choose a plant that is native east of you, you know right off that it is accustomed to higher rainfall than you have. So, place it in a swale or where it will get some shade, especially from the hot afternoon sun. When you use a plant that is native west of you, make sure it gets good drainage and lots of sun, even reflected heat, as it is adapted to being drier than is natural for your area.

North-south variations are more difficult to accommodate. Masonry courtyard walls that face southwest, and heavy winter mulches of rocks or organic material, can help protect a plant that is marginally winter-hardy for your area. Moving northern plants south or mountain plants into the low-lands is the hardest of all. Sometimes, no matter how much shade and water you give them in the summer, their roots just can't move the water into their leaves fast enough to keep up with evaporation. And they hate not being able to cool off even at night.

When you are enhancing a natural landscape or planning a conventional landscape that is totally adapted to your soils and climate, it is best to use plants that are native within a fifty-mile radius. They'll be able to naturalize completely and remain healthy.

HOW TO USE THIS BOOK

The Plans

In my landscape design business, I choose from all available adapted plants, both native and nonnative. In this book the plans call for native plants exclusively. I did this, not to discourage integrated gardens but merely to show as many uses for native plants as I could cram into one book. I also wanted to demonstrate that having a 100 percent native landscape is not only possible but also extremely attractive.

There are 21 plans in all. Ten are regional and are found in the chapter on regions. They use indigenous plants only, with a few exceptions that are carefully noted. Using the plants that are native to your region will give you the most maintenance-free garden possible.

Each regional plan reflects the character of the native scenery, but half the plans are suitable for an urban yard, and half are natural landscapes. I tried to give an example of each approach in related regions. For instance, the West Texas Plan is a natural landscape, but the plan for the neighboring High Plains is suitably urban. The Corpus Christi Plan is urban, and the Valley Plan is more natural, except for its small but delightful front court-yard. The El Paso Plan demonstrates both qualities on the same property—natural in front and conventional in back.

In each regional plan, one small portion requires watering to look its best, usually around a patio or up close to the house. But the larger portion of the plan is xeriscapic and can look great with no supplemental watering at all once it's established.

The eleven other plans are theme gardens and are found in the appro-priate plant chapters. The English Mixed Border and the Rock Garden plans are in the perennials chapter, the Shrub Garden in the shrubs chapter, the Water Garden in the water and bog plants chapter, and so on. Everyone should be able to use several of the theme garden plans. Of course, if you don't live on sand, you can't use the Sand Garden Plan in the annuals chapter. On the other hand, the Wildlife Garden Plan offers two or more suggestions for each planting, so it can be used in the whole state.

The theme gardens provide useful groupings of plants. For example, everything in the Water Garden tolerates poor drainage, everything in the Mountain Garden requires cool nights, and everything in the Wildlife Garden is especially attractive to wildlife. There are also helpful groupings within plans. The Walled Garden, for example, provides a list of plants that do well in patio pots.

Individual Plant Descriptions

Several categories are listed at the top of each individual plant description. You should be able to tell by glancing at the headings whether a plant will fit your particular needs and circumstances. The following are some simple explanations of what the headings and terms mean.

Latin Name

Plants have been listed with double Latin names ever since Swedish botanist Carolus Linnaeus started the system back in 1753. The first name signifies the genus; the second name signifies the species. Although these names may change on occasion, they still provide the most precise method of universal identification. For example, if your landscape plan calls for *Salvia greggii* and you buy *Salvia farinacea*, you'll wind up with a blue-flowered perennial instead of a red-flowered shrub.

When a name has been changed recently, I've put the alternate name in parentheses, since some reference books might be using that name instead. (I used Kartesz and Kartesz, and Correll and Johnston.) For example, *Wedelia hispida* used to be called *Zexmenia hispida*. It's still the same plant, and the name might even be changed back to *Zexmenia* someday by the botanical community.

Botanists can generally be categorized into lumpers and splitters. Lumpers lump several varieties together under one name and say the species has variable characteristics. Splitters give each variety a separate species name or divide several species into different genera.

Another reason for a name's being changed is the discovery of new members of a genus. Only a fraction of the world's plants have been cataloged, especially in the tropics. When a new plant is discovered, it sometimes changes the classification of already known plants.

Pronunciation

Now that you know it's better to ask for specific plants by their Latin names, you need to pronounce them. Don't panic. I've provided phonetic guides. The names aren't really hard once you dissect them, and nearly everyone pronounces them differently anyway. Furthermore, after we slap on our Texas vowel sounds, Julius Caesar himself wouldn't recognize his native tongue. I've consulted several books and plant authorities before choosing these pronunciations, but if you already pronounce a name another way, please don't worry about it.

Common Name(s)

Most plants have at least one common name. I've listed only the ones most typically used. Sometimes a common name can refer to more than one species of plant, which really confuses matters. That's when those Latin names can straighten things out.

Usual Height

Here I've listed the height your plant is most likely to achieve. Where relevant, in parentheses I've given the tallest heights recorded in Texas, which your plant might achieve with tender loving care.

Spacing

This measure is the width of the plant or how far apart individual plants should be placed to make a mass planting.

Bloom

If the plant has a noticeable bloom, this category tells you the normal bloom period (which can vary somewhat depending on the temperatures in a given year), color, size of the blooms, and the fragrance (if any).

Fruit

When the fruits of a plant add to its landscaping value, their season, color, and size are listed here.

Winter Foliage

This line lets you know what the plant looks like in winter.

Deciduous means the plant loses its leaves in the winter, but its branches remain intact.

Evergreen in this book indicates that the plant is green both summer and winter. In a strict sense, "evergreen" means that the leaves remain year after year or drop off singly during the year. However, many of our evergreens, such as the live oaks and the southern magnolia, remain green all winter, then lose all their leaves in the spring and grow new ones immediately.

Almost evergreen means the plant is fully evergreen in its southern range but in its northern range loses most or all of its leaves in the winter. You'll know that the plant is getting cold-stressed when the foliage turns bronze or mauve after a hard frost.

Winter rosette refers to a sunburst of leaves at ground level that gradually grows all winter. These rosettes are present in a number of wildflowers. Bluebonnets are called winter annuals because they must winter over with rosettes; the term does not mean they bloom in the winter like pansies. Many perennials and bulbs also winter over this way. If a plant is noted as having an evergreen rosette, that means green leaves are present at all times.

Dormant means the plant disappears by dying back to the roots. New growth appears the next season.

Sometimes, plants become deciduous or dormant in the summer because of drought. When this is the case, it is stated, as are other special dormancies.

Range

The first part of this category describes where the plant is native within Texas. If it grows or is naturalized in other parts of the state, that is indicated in the text below. The second part tells where the plant is native outside of Texas. *Endemic* means the plant is native only in Texas.

Soil

Soil is basically sand, loam, or clay. Sometimes it is mostly rocky, because rocks haven't completely eroded into soil. Rocky soils are most likely to be limestone or igneous. Drainage and pH are other important factors in assessing your soil. Both are affected by the mineral makeup of the soil, and each affects the other. All these characteristics need to be considered when you are choosing a plant to match your soil. Below, these terms are defined as they are used in this book.

Sand is the easiest soil for plants to grow in because the roots don't have to fight their way down. It takes very little rain to moisten sand to a depth of two to three feet. Even when sand is wet, there are plenty of air pockets to hold oxygen. Because calcium and salts are washed through, the pH of sand is usually neutral or acid, although in areas of low rainfall it might be slightly alkaline. *Sugar sand* is a poor, dry soil almost devoid of organic matter. Rain runs through it very rapidly.

Loam is the perfect soil for nearly everything. It is a combination of sand and clay, with lots of rich organic matter mixed in. Sandy loam has a higher proportion of sand; clay loam a higher proportion of clay. Because of the drainage and organic matter, loam is usually neutral to slightly acid.

Clay soils are dense and heavy. It takes a good overnight rain to saturate clay—a sprinkling barely wets the surface. Clay soils have the consistency of glue when wet and are dauntingly hard when dry. Cracks several inches wide and more than a foot deep appear in clay soils during a drought. In Houston this kind of soil is called gumbo. Many plants have developed roots that can cope with these extremes. In fact, clay is the soil of choice for most prairie plants. Clay soils are slightly acid where rainfall averages more than 45 inches annually and are calcareous otherwise. Amended clay or amended gumbo have had sand and organic matter worked in to create loam. To make the soil crumbly enough to work in the amendments, you have to water deeply for two to three hours. Then let it dry for two or three days. When it forks up easily, till in an inch or more of sand and four to eight inches of organic matter. Organic matter is well-rotted plant material such as manure or bark mulch. These amendments usually remain in the soil one to three years. I've found that raking leaves onto clay soils and letting them decompose there over the winter greatly improves the permeability and richness of the soil.

Caliche is a hard layer of calcium carbonate (lime) that forms in areas where rainfall is so low there is not enough water to wash calcium and salts through the soil. It is often crusty, usually one to three feet down, although sometimes it's on the surface. The regions called Corpus Christi, Valley, West Texas, and High Plains in this book are those with the highest concentrations of caliche.

Limestone is also calcium carbonate, but it was formed from the shells of the microscopic sea creatures that gave us oil. Many millions of years ago the central part of Texas was covered by warm shallow seas. The exposed limestone that is so visible in the Edwards Plateau, at Buffalo Gap, around Dallas and Fort Worth, and in the mountains of the Trans-Pecos is the remnant of ancient reefs from these various seas. Austin chalk, from the Lower Cretaceous period, is fairly hard and erodes slowly. Much of the Upper Cretaceous limestone was soft and has already worn away to form limy soils. Limestone layers lie just a few inches to several feet beneath the clay soils of the Blackland and Grand prairies.

Igneous rocks are caused by intense heat, either from ancient volcanoes or from compression within the earth. Granite is an igneous rock. The Llano Uplift and some of the mountains in the Trans-Pecos are also igneous. The soil that results from these rocks tends to be acid.

Acid is the term used for soils with a pH of less than 7. The symbol "pH" stands for the hydrogen ion concentration of the soil, which is measured by a potentiometer or by dyes and is rated on a scale from 0 to 14, with 7 being neutral. Most plants prefer the slight acidity of loam—6.0 to 6.5. East Texas, Houston, the Post Oak Woods, and some very deep sands or igneous rocks in the western part of the state are the areas where acid soils occur in Texas.

Calcareous soils are those containing calcium carbonate: caliche, limestone, and all soils composed of eroded limestone. Calcareous soils are alkaline. "Alkaline" literally means that alkali, a salt, is present, and the word is broadly used to refer to a pH greater than 7.

When I haven't indicated either acid or calcerous, it's because the plant has no known preference.

Often drainage is far more important than pH. *Well drained* means that the plant cannot tolerate standing water. *Poor drainage okay* means that the plant is well adjusted to clay soils and can take standing water for at least a week. *Seasonal poor drainage okay* means poor drainage can be tolerated for less than a week. *Moist* means the soil should be damp at all times. *Moist, well-drained* means the soil should be moist, but poor drainage is not tolerated. *Saline okay* means the plant is known to be tolerant of salty water—a frequent municipal problem—or salty soils.

Light Requirements

Shade means no more than two hours of direct sun or four hours of dappled sun. Few plants do well in this dark environment. If some plants, like

Arkansas yucca, were already established before the shade got this deep, they can hang on but no longer bloom.

Dappled shade is formed by sunlight coming through the leaves of trees. A full day of dappled shade equals about half a day of direct sun. Many shade-loving plants bloom and thrive in a half day or more of dappled shade.

Part shade means a half day of shade and a half day of sun. Most flowers and shrubs that take full sun can bloom in part shade.

Full sun means full, direct sun all day long. *Full sun, a little shade okay* means that a couple of hours of shade is all right, but don't subject the plant to more.

Roots

With most plants, the root system has little if any effect on how they can be used in landscaping. Three exceptions are (1) plants that have a *tap root*, which makes them impossible to dig up unless they are very young, (2) *bulbs* and *tubers*, which must be dug up in their entirety and planted at specific depths, and (3) plants that are aggressive *colonizers*.

Colonizes lets you know at a glance that a plant is likely to travel on its own by rhizomes, stolons, or suckers. This characteristic is a definite liability in many landscape situations but is invaluable in places where ground cover or erosion control is desired. See page 95 in Chapter 2 for more information.

Propagation

Propagation methods are presented here in a simplistic way. If you want more information on exactly how to clean or scarify seed, how long and at what temperature it should stratified, or explicit directions on rooting various types of cuttings, I strongly recommend *How to Grow Native Plants of Texas and the Southwest,* by Jill Nokes. She tells you how to propagate more than 350 species of native trees, shrubs, and woody vines.

Flowers are usually easier to propagate. Annuals germinate quickly from fresh, untreated seed, and perennials are rarely difficult, although some, like blackfoot daisy, can often be grown more easily from softwood cuttings in a mist bench (a process for nurserymen, not laypeople).

A REGIONAL GUIDE TO LANDSCAPING WITH NATIVE TEXAS PLANTS

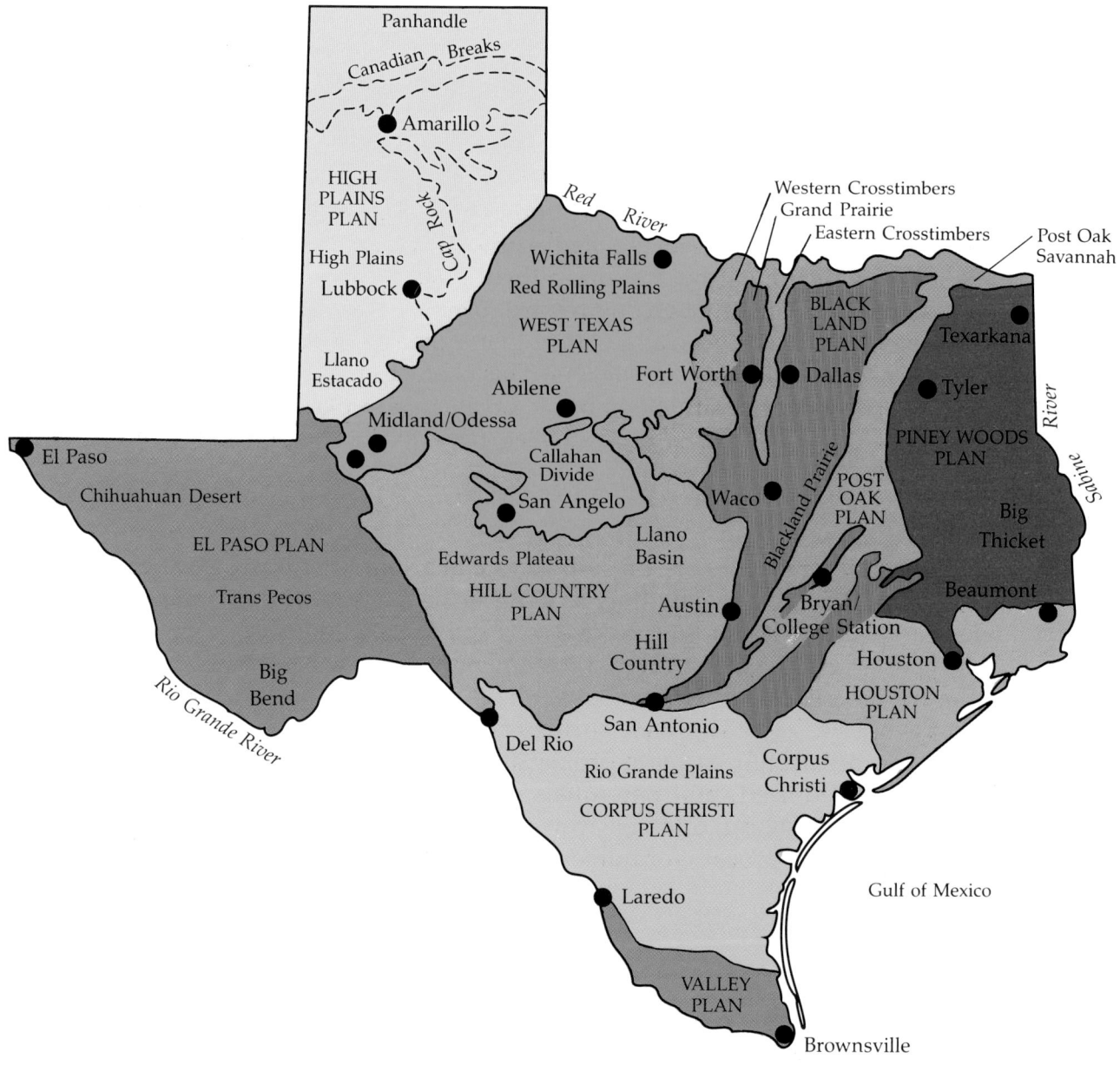

ONE

Regions

BOTANICALLY speaking, life is more interesting when you live "on the edge." That's easy to do in Texas. Most of our major cities are placed right where different soil and vegetational regions meet.

Sometimes the edges are dramatically marked by a great ridge of rock rearing above a plain of vastly different soils, for example, the Cap Rock Escarpment. This sharp edge of the High Plains is only 70 million years old, but the Rolling Plains that abut it are 250 million years old. On the lower terrain of the Rolling Plains are shrubs and small trees, as well as numerous streams, while on the High Plains are shortgrasses and yuccas—and no streams. It's so flat that surface water just sits.

The Balcones Escarpment is a limestone ridge covered with junipers and wildflowers. At its back is the Edwards Plateau, with its exceptional diversity of plants, and at its feet is the Blackland Prairie, which used to be a seemingly endless sea of tallgrasses broken by lines of trees that followed the creeks.

Sometimes the edges of these regions are subtle, as one zone blends into the next, forming a vegetational crazy quilt. Just off the main road between Dallas and Houston I've seen loblolly pines and wax myrtles in moist sands (Piney Woods) give way to post oaks and mesquites in deep, dry sands (Post Oak), followed by less than five miles of grasses and pecans in black clay (Blackland), followed by more sands holding post oaks and huisache (Post Oak)—all in a space of only sixteen miles.

That strip of blackland I just referred to is far away from the main Blackland Prairie that runs through Dallas. This strip is called the San Antonio Prairie, not because it is anywhere near San Antonio (it's actually nearer Bryan–College Station) but because in the 1800s it provided a treeless path for the Old San Antonio Road that came from East Texas.

This is not the only place in Texas where a region has an outlier stuck off someplace else. The Lost Pines of Bastrop, near Austin, are certainly far from the Piney Woods. They exist because sandy, acid soil similar to that in the Piney Woods makes the environment right for them. The Lost Maples in Lost Maples State Natural Area and on the Owl Creek watershed on Fort Hood Military Reservation, as well as other places near Temple, are outliers for a different reason. They are relict populations that hung on after the retreat of the last ice age. The maples are bigtooth maples, and if you want to see more of them, you have to go to the mountains of the Trans-Pecos, more than 150 miles away.

Dr. Terry G. Jordan, a professor in the department of geography at the University of Texas at Austin, cites these out-of-place pockets as evidence that Texas is an environmental transition zone, that is, Texas gathers together many of the major regions of the United States. Coastal prairies, southeastern pinewoods, central hardwoods, tallgrass prairie, Great Plains, and southwestern deserts all funnel into Texas as the stems of a bouquet go into a vase.

The mountains in the Trans-Pecos are a southern extension of the Rocky Mountains, and the Hill Country is connected to the Ozark Mountains, which in turn connect with the Appalachians. And to make things even more interesting, we have the influence of Mexican flora along the entire Rio Grande, which forms our southern border.

Clearly, trying to figure out which region you live in can be a challenge. But don't worry. Read on and see how easy I've made it for you.

Start with the city you live in or live closest to. Every city in Texas with a population of more than 70,000 is listed in alphabetical order in the following chart. There are some exceptions, which I will name right here. If you live in Arlington, Irving, Grand Prairie, Garland, Mesquite, Richardson, Plano, or Sherman-Denison, turn to either Dallas or Fort Worth, whichever is closer to your home. Galveston, Port Arthur, Texas City, and Brazoria should refer to Houston. Those of you in Longview-Marshall should turn to Tyler and those near Killeen-Temple to Austin. All Valley residents should refer to Brownsville or Laredo. Listing all these cities or MSAs (metropolitan statistical areas) in the chart would not help fine-tune your region; it would just make the chart more cumbersome.

Next, read about the possible choices for your area. Then go outside, look at your soil, and match it as best you can to one of those described for your area. The plants listed under your soil description are the ones most characteristic of that region and can serve as indicators.

When looking for indicator plants, check out natural areas by creeks, railroad tracks, and alleys, not someone's cultivated yard. You want to see what is growing natively in your area. If you don't know what the indicator plants look like, look them up in the individual plant descriptions.

Also, consult the map. It shows the ten vegetational regions that are the basis of this book. Each vegetational region is marked by its own set of distinct characteristics—summer and winter temperatures, rainfall amounts, and dominant soil type—and the specific flora that thrive under those conditions.

As an example of how all those characteristics affect vegetation, let's look at Houston and Corpus Christi. Geologically, they have the same soil type (coastal black gumbo) and are usually lumped together on a soils map. Yet their rainfalls and temperatures vary greatly, Houston being wetter and colder. Because of these variations in climate, their soils are also different. In Houston, where rainfall is abundant, the salts and other minerals are washed all the way through the soil, leaving it acid. In Corpus Christi, rain dissolves the minerals and then evaporates, leaving a thick layer of calcium carbonate (caliche), which is alkaline.

These factors determine which plants will feel at home in those regions. Some of our native plants require acid soil, some require alkaline, and some don't seem to care one way or the other. Most plants that require acid soils live in East Texas, Houston, and Post Oak regions, but there are also some in the Trans-Pecos, because the igneous mountain soils are also acid.

Another important thing for you to figure out when you look at your soil is whether it is predominantly sandy or whether it has a high clay content. Some plants can cope with either, but most have a definite preference.

Sand allows water to penetrate deeply and quickly and still leave pockets of oxygen. Under these conditions, roots can easily grow deep enough to keep cool and moist and still breathe. Some plants are found only in sand in the western part of the state but thrive in clay in areas with higher rainfall. They need the sand for moisture, not for air. Some other plants are found only in sand because drainage is so critical; they breathe through their roots and suffocate in clay soils. Clay holds water a long time and then dries out, leaving huge cracks in the ground. Plants that live in clay have to be able to cope with the two extremes of poor drainage and root-cracking drought.

On parts of the Edwards Plateau and other escarpments, the soil has been eroded or is extremely shallow, exposing limestone. This white rock, like sand, retains moisture and oxygen. Many of our most beautiful plants prosper in this inhospitable-looking environment.

Obviously, knowing your soil type is important in determining your region and what will grow there successfully.

For a specific example of how to find your region, let's look at Austin. Looking at the map, you can see that it sits astride three distinct regions: Edwards Plateau to the west, Blackland Prairie right down the middle, and Post Oak Savannah to the east.

If you're an Austin resident, you might walk outside and see white rocks jutting out everywhere. In fact, you seem to have more rocks than soil. What soil there is seems to be crumbled up white rock held together with white clay. This tells you that you're on limestone and/or caliche—in other words, Edwards Plateau—and you need to turn to the Hill Country Plan to see what likes to grow in your limestone.

But suppose you live in the center of Austin, and you look down and see that your soil is black (some people might call it dark gray or dark brown), heavy, gummy clay. This is Blackland Prairie. It doesn't mean you live among neck-high grasses, although that's probably what used to be there a century ago. Turn to the Blackland Plan for the plants that should do especially well for you.

If, in addition to your black soil, you have a limestone creek on your property, don't jump to the conclusion that you must be on the Edwards Plateau. Creekbeds look like this in the Blackland Prairie too. Use the Hill Country Plan only if you are on a limestone hilltop. Hill Country plants like to be well drained, and some of them will rot in blackland clay after a long spell of heavy rain.

If you see neither white rock nor black clay, you will probably see tan-colored soil (sand, sandy loam, or even clay-loam) in your yard. This might mean that you should turn to the Post Oak Plan, but notice that I said "might." There's a good chance the soil on your property was hauled in from somewhere else. You could have two to six inches of sand on top of caliche or black clay, which would put you in the Hill Country or Blackland instead. Be especially suspicious if you are in central Austin, although sandy pockets were left there by ancient meanderings of the Colorado River.

To be absolutely sure you qualify for the Post Oak Plan, you need to find out if the tan soil goes down for at least one foot. If you hit clay or rock, it should be yellowish or reddish. You can always dig down that far, but it's much easier to see if you can find a post oak nearby. Post oaks grow only in tan, acid soils, so they are a good indicator plant. Find a post oak and you can use the Post Oak Plan confidently.

Mesquites are likely to be there too, but mesquites grow nearly anywhere in Texas that is well drained and sunny, so they can never be used as an indicator plant of any particular region.

To be sure you have found the right region for you, read the detailed descriptions that accompany each regional plan.

Regional Identification Chart

City	Region Type	Description	Plan
Abilene	1. Red Rolling Plains	Red to tan sand or clay Mesquite, flowers, sand sagebrush	West Texas
	2. Callahan Divide (Edwards Plateau)	Hilly, limestone Juniper, Texas red oak, Mohr oak, live oak	Hill Country
Amarillo	1. High Plains	Tan sand, clay, caliche, flat Shortgrasses, yucca, no trees, shrubs rare	High Plains
	2. Canadian Breaks	Red sand, clay, broken Sand sagebrush, aromatic sumac, Havard oak	High Plains
Austin	1. Edwards Plateau	Limestone, caliche, hilly Ashe juniper, Texas red oak, escarpment live oak	Hill Country
	2. Blackland Prairies	Dark clay Pecan	Blackland
	3. Post Oak Savannah	Tan sand Post oak	Post Oak
Beaumont	1. Upper Coastal Prairies	Dark gumbo, poor drainage Coastal live oak	Houston
	2. Longleaf Pine Forest	Tan sand, well drained Longleaf pine	Piney Woods
Brownsville	1. Lower Rio Grande Valley	Sand, poor drainage Subtropical, brush	Valley
Bryan– College Station	1. Post Oak Savannah	Tan sand or clay Post oak	Post Oak
	2. Blackland Prairies	Dark clay, acid Pecan	Blackland
Corpus Christi	1. Coastal Bend Prairies and Marshes	Black clay, poor drainage Retama, huisache	Corpus Christi
Dallas	1. Blackland Prairies	Dark clay, alkaline Pecan, tall trees	Blackland
	2. Escarpment	Limestone, caliche, uplands Ashe juniper, short trees	Hill Country
	3. Eastern Cross Timbers	Tan sand Post oak	Post Oak
El Paso	1. Chihuahuan Desert	Sand, dry Creosote brush, pink plains penstemon	El Paso
	2. Franklin Mountains	Igneous or sandy Sotol, goldeneye	El Paso or Mountain Garden
Fort Worth	1. Grand Prairie	Gray clay, alkaline Live oak, Texas ash, Ashe juniper	Blackland or Hill Country
	2. Eastern Cross Timbers	Tan sand to the east Post oak	Post Oak
	3. Western Cross Timbers	Tan sand to the west Post oak	Post Oak

Houston	1. Coastal Prairies	Dark gumbo, poor drainage Coastal live oak, swamp chestnut oak	Houston
	2. Piney Woods	Sand, acid Loblolly and shortleaf pine	Piney Woods
Laredo	1. Rio Grande Valley	Light-colored sand, clay Brush, cenizo	Valley
Lubbock	1. High Plains	Tan clay, sand, caliche, flat Shortgrasses, yucca, trees and shrubs rare	High Plains
	2. Cap Rock Escarpment	Red sand and clay, broken Juniper, joint fir	High Plains
Midland-Odessa	1. High Plains	Tan sand, clay, caliche Agarito, paperflower	West Texas
San Angelo	1. Red Rolling Plains	Red to tan sand, clay Mesquite, prickly pear	West Texas
	2. Edwards Plateau	Limestone Juniper, Mexican buckeye	Hill Country
San Antonio	1. Blackland Prairies	Dark clay, alkaline Pecan	Blackland
	2. Edwards Plateau	Limestone, caliche Ashe juniper, Texas red oak, escarpment live oak	Hill Country
	3. Rio Grande Plains	Tan sand Huisache, guajillo	Corpus Christi
	4. Post Oak Savannah	Tan sand Post oak	Post Oak
Texarkana	1. Piney Woods	Moist loamy sand Loblolly and shortleaf pine	Piney Woods
	2. Post Oak Woods	Dry sand Post oak	Post Oak
Tyler	1. Piney Woods	Moist loamy sand Loblolly and shortleaf pine	Piney Woods
	2. Post Oak Woods	Sugar sand Post oak, prickly pear	Post Oak
Waco	1. Blackland Prairies	Dark clay, alkaline Pecan, tall trees	Blackland
	2. Grand Prairie	Gray clay, alkaline Live oak, Texas ash	Hill Country
Wichita Falls	1. Red Rolling Plains	Red sand or clay Little bluestem, juniper, sand sagebrush	West Texas

Houston

Houston, Beaumont
(Galveston, Angleton, Bay City)

COASTAL PRAIRIES

Regional Description

This coastal area is made up mostly of salt marshes, level slowly draining prairies, and swampy flat woodlands with numerous sluggish rivers,
creeks, bayous, and sloughs. As you enter a coastal prairie, you are struck
by how unrelentingly flat it is. Trees are scarce and short. The sky is immense. As you stand there amid the grasses and the wildflowers, you can
be forgiven for feeling overwhelmed by all this wide-open space.

The prairies were originally populated by tallgrasses, which were kept
in balance by range fires and buffalo herds. Since both are noticeably scarce
these days, this region has been invaded by mesquites and live oaks—at
least those areas that haven't been plowed, paved, or sodded with St. Augustine. A healthy remnant of restored coastal prairie can be seen at Armand Bayou Nature Center, which lies south of Houston.

In the 1800s these prairies were famous for their wildflowers, especially
on ground that had been burned the previous fall. Early travelers and settlers in these parts credited the Indians with firing the prairies. Whether
this is true or mere speculation and, if true, whether the burning was deliberate or the result of campfire accidents, the happy result was that each
spring following a fire the wildflowers were spectacular. Old journals and
letters described vast carpets of color in astonishing variety stretching out
as far as the eye could see.

The major components of the prairie were big bluestem, little bluestem,
Indian grass, switch grass, and eastern gama grass. Beginning in the 1820s,
Anglo-Americans from the southeastern United States ran huge ranching
operations on the prairies, expanding southward until they met up with
the Spanish Mexican ranchers already established in South Texas. The
Stephen F. Austin colonists typically settled in bottom woodlands that bordered these rich prairies. There they built timber homes among the trees,
farmed the bottoms of the creeks, and pastured their livestock on the lush
grasslands.

On May 15, 1837, John James Audubon wrote of landing in Houston to
visit the president of the Republic of Texas, Samuel Houston himself. Audubon described reaching the president's "mansion," a two-room log cabin,

These coastal live oaks, draped with Spanish moss, are growing in poorly drained black clay. Behind the shrubby fencerow, palmettos form a tropical-looking ground cover. Photo by the authors.

by wading across "a level of far-extending prairie, destitute of timber . . . through water above our ankles."

Three years earlier, in May of 1834, Thomas Drummond, an early Texas botanical collector for whom Drummond phlox is named, set off to collect plants from Velasco, on the coast, to Brazoria. On the way the Brazos River flooded, so he finished his journey in a boat over prairies nine to fifteen feet underwater. As evidence of the tremendous wealth of flora of the region, he was able to add 220 species to his list, despite the flooding.

As you can see, the biggest problem faced by Houston, unlike the rest of our state, is too much water. The average annual rainfall in the region varies from 43 inches in Bay City to 55 inches in the Beaumont area. Rainfall is fairly even all year with slight highs in September and late spring. The soils are acid to neutral clays and clay loams called gumbo, heavy soils that do not absorb or release water easily. With low evaporation rates all winter, the land is already soggy, and a spring rain results in water that often stands for two or three days or longer. The land is so flat that the water has nowhere to go. Even with Houston's many concrete bayous, poor drainage is still a problem.

The woodlands on poorly drained black soils are dramatic, almost primeval. They are composed mostly of huge coastal live oaks draped with Spanish moss. Palmettos and other vegetation grow thickly beneath them. The forest is dark, and the sky almost obscured.

On the banks of bayous are sandy loams running like fingers through the gumbo. These lighter soils support deciduous forests of red oaks, willow oak, cedar elm, and American elm mixed with eastern red cedar, a thick understory of yaupon holly, wax myrtle, and the evergreen vine Carolina jessamine. If post oaks or pines are present on your property, you can use either the Post Oak or the Piney Woods Plan instead of the Houston Plan.

Temperatures in Beaumont, Houston, and Bay City are generally mild in the winter and steamy in the summer. On average, you can expect January lows to be in the neighborhood of 43° F inland to 49° along the shore. Average July highs range from 87° along the coast to 93° inland. The lowest recorded temperatures in the region are 4° in Beaumont, 5° in Houston, and 11° in Bay City, which is south of Houston.

In the summer both prairies and forests that were soggy all winter and spring can be baked brick-hard. It's hard to believe that so many plants can take these extremes of flood and drought. The Houston Plan gathers together some of the most popular ones.

Houston Plan
Lot size: 125' × 80'

Gumbo! That's what most of you gardeners in Houston have to contend with. So you need a plan that gives you alternatives to having to live in a swamp occasionally or turning your whole yard into a raised bed. (A fortunate few have lovely loam or sand with pine trees, and if you're in that number, you do have a choice—you can use this plan or the Piney Woods Plan.)

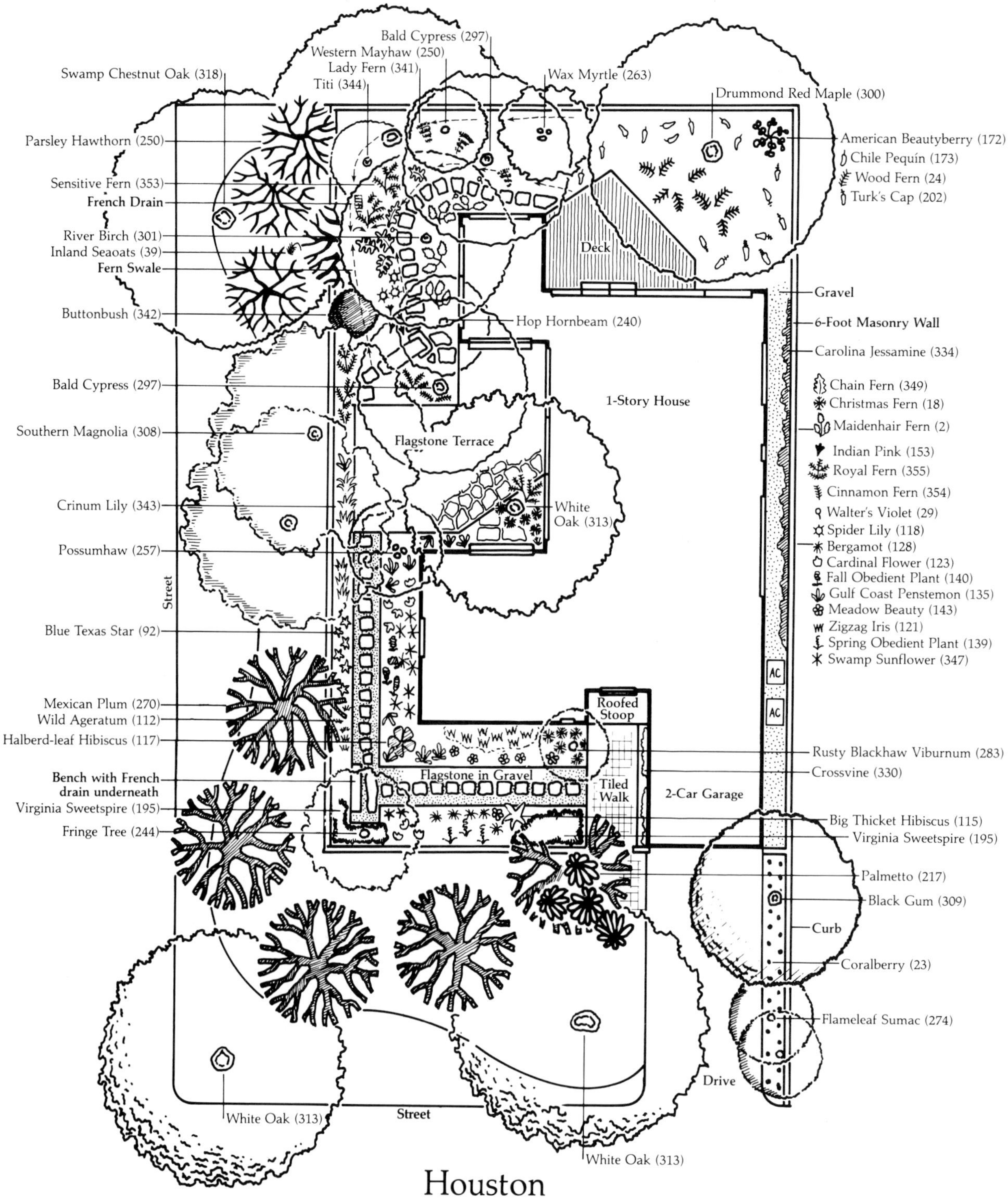

Bald Cypress (297)
Western Mayhaw (250)
Lady Fern (341)
Titi (344)
Wax Myrtle (263)
Drummond Red Maple (300)

Swamp Chestnut Oak (318)

Parsley Hawthorn (250)

American Beautyberry (172)
Chile Pequín (173)
Wood Fern (24)
Turk's Cap (202)

Sensitive Fern (353)
French Drain

River Birch (301)
Inland Seaoats (39)
Fern Swale

Deck

Buttonbush (342)

Gravel

Hop Hornbeam (240)

6-Foot Masonry Wall

Carolina Jessamine (334)

Bald Cypress (297)

1-Story House

Chain Fern (349)
Christmas Fern (18)
Maidenhair Fern (2)

Southern Magnolia (308)

Flagstone Terrace

Indian Pink (153)
Royal Fern (355)
Cinnamon Fern (354)
Walter's Violet (29)
Spider Lily (118)
Bergamot (128)
Cardinal Flower (123)
Fall Obedient Plant (140)
Gulf Coast Penstemon (135)
Meadow Beauty (143)
Zigzag Iris (121)
Spring Obedient Plant (139)
Swamp Sunflower (347)

Crinum Lily (343)

White Oak (313)

Possumhaw (257)

Street

Blue Texas Star (92)

Mexican Plum (270)
Wild Ageratum (112)
Halberd-leaf Hibiscus (117)

Roofed Stoop

Rusty Blackhaw Viburnum (283)
Crossvine (330)

Bench with French drain underneath
Virginia Sweetspire (195)
Fringe Tree (244)

Tiled Walk

2-Car Garage

AC
AC

Big Thicket Hibiscus (115)
Virginia Sweetspire (195)

Flagstone in Gravel

Palmetto (217)
Black Gum (309)
Curb

Coralberry (23)

Flameleaf Sumac (274)

Drive

White Oak (313)
Street

White Oak (313)

Houston

First, look at your situation: clay soil, lots of water, poor drainage. You need a way to channel water off your lot. Don't fight it. Take full advantage of your situation by creating a swale, a shallow dry stream bed in your garden that can carry the water away. It can be filled with ferns, as in this plan, or you can make a water garden. (See the Water Garden Plan in Chapter 11.)

This landscape plan doesn't begin to show all the Texas plants you can use in Houston. Experiment with those of other regions, but remember that everywhere else in the state is drier and better-drained, so the first step in using these plants is to make a raised bed or berm.

This plan takes a different approach. It is designed to show what you can do by using what is naturally already here. These plants are native to the Houston area and are able to thrive on gumbo. Most of them can tolerate at least two or three days of standing water and then survive ground-cracking dryness in the summer.

There are exceptions, though. The ferns in the swale need to be kept moist at all times of the year. The white oak, sumac, coralberry, Mexican plum, fringe tree, and parsley hawthorn can take wet gumbo but will not be happy in standing water for more than half a day. That's why I placed them in the better-drained places. The bed containing the white oak, at the corner of the house by the terrace, is an area that will tend to get wet if not graded carefully. It must drain rapidly into the path that runs down to the French drain hidden under the bench.

The fern garden is lowest at the place where it starts, at the edge of the terrace. There is a two-foot drop here, which then gradually slopes uphill for six inches to the French drain by the titi. The idea is that rainwater running off the terrace will flow into the swale. If the water is more than six inches deep, the excess can empty into the street via the French drain.

Water from the area of the Drummond red maple will flow into the other end of the swale and will also be able to drain. This part of the swale is wider and only about a foot deep, gently dropping six inches. In the summer when there is no rain, water this whole area to keep it moist.

In the winter the wax myrtle is green, as is the titi and the Walter's violets, but for the most part the garden is sleeping. The peach and silver flaking bark of the river birch is particularly noticeable at this time of year when there are few distractions. The first color will be the western mayhaw, which blooms late winter to early spring along with the violets. Next will come the lovely parsley hawthorns—one on the slope and three others visible over the wall. (If you haven't noticed yet, the inner garden surrounding the house is enclosed by a six-foot-high masonry wall.) Following the hawthorns, the garden reaches its climax in May, when the ferns will be fully leafed out and spider lily, with its six-inch white flowers, and titi will both be fragrant and at their peak. The delicate Indian pink adds a touch of brilliant red. The buttonbush, which is also fragrant and white (sometimes pale pink), hits full stride in the summer. In the fall the hop hornbeam and two bald cypresses shower down orange and copper leaves.

The deck area at the head of the swale is quite different. The ground covers under the Drummond red maple—chile pequín, American beauty-berry, and Turk's cap—are amenable to moisture but can also survive on regular rainfall. If they should droop, water them. The wood fern will certainly look fresher with supplemental watering. If you have a sprinkler system, your fern garden should be watered every day during the summer, but the red maple area can be watered once a week or even less, whatever the foundation of your home requires. The overall look here is woodsy—one, two, or three feet tall and delicate rather than lush. The color accents are red in the Turk's cap and chiles and magenta for the fall-to-winter berries of the beautyberry.

The passage down the east side of the house has Carolina jessamine vines to provide an attractive view on the garden walls from the bedroom windows. Gravel is used to cover the ground, as this narrow passage is too dark for most plants and needs to function as a walk.

Going the other way, from the terrace down the flagstone walk toward the front gate, I've located perennial beds. These are not traditional perennial beds described in Chapter 5, which you could certainly use if you lowered the path six inches and sloped the beds for good drainage. These perennial beds are flower gardens that only Houston can use; they are filled with red, purple, pink, yellow, ivory, white, and blue flowers that will not mind if they get inundated once in a while. Gulf Coast penstemon starts blooming in March, as does blue Texas star, rusty blackhaw viburnum, and the Mexican plums seen over the wall. The fringe tree blooms next. Spring obedient plant, zigzag iris, bergamot, and Virginia sweetspire bloom in late spring, while meadow beauty and the hibiscus bloom all summer. Fall is spectacular with cardinal flower, swamp sunflower, wild ageratum, and fall obedient plant.

Near the front door, I've placed evergreens. The Christmas ferns, on the left by the stoop, are an exception to the rule for this plan. They really don't like poor drainage. Give them a very slight slope that starts at the edge of the tiled walk, and keep them evenly moist. The three crossvines at the right of the tiled walk will grow quickly and easily to cover the wall. You can let them cover the ground and spill out over the walk for a lush look, or plant seasonal shady annuals at their feet.

Three trees grow in the front L-shaped flower beds. With the Christmas fern is a glossy-leaved rusty blackhaw viburnum. Near the bench is a fringe tree. It likes fairly good drainage, so it benefits from the French drain hidden beneath the bench. The female possumhaw near the terrace is most adaptable to poor drainage. Its red berries should provide color and warmth to the garden all winter.

In contrast to the intimacy, color, and fine detail of the gardens within the walls, the landscape visible from the street is big and bold. Immediately attracting the eye are the four palmettos that mark the tiled entry to the front gate. Dominating the rest of the scene are two evergreen southern magnolias, which should be allowed to grow large and full all the way down to the ground. On the patio side the branches will extend over the wall and shade

Near downtown Houston, this garden reflects the taste of Alice and the late Dr. Jack Staub, with plant recommendations by nurserymen Lynn Lowrey and Will Fleming. Rusty blackhaw viburnum (left front) is backed by two Mexican plums, their white blossoms fading to a soft pink. Overhead, the bald cypresses have not yet leafed out. The flower garden is a mixture of native perennials, bulbs, and ferns, along with anything else that grows well or looks promising enough to experiment with. Photo by the authors.

the royal fern, as well as the crinum lily, which blooms despite the lack of sunshine.

There's a lot of additional color in this area of the plan, to keep things interesting from spring until after frost. First, there are the five Mexican plums in a sweep against the front wall. Buy these trees in bloom to ensure that they will tend to flower all at the same time instead of a week or so apart. Shading the plums are huge white oaks, while the parsley hawthorns in back are protected by swamp chestnut oaks.

There are several ways to fill the deep bed of ground cover that wraps around the outside of the wall. On the back portion, under the parsley hawthorns, I've shown a mass planting of inland seaoats. This grass takes poor drainage, suckers to form a dense cover, and will do well in the shade that will develop as the trees grow up. It is attractive all year—fresh green in the spring and summer, dancing with seed heads in the fall, and gold to ivory-white in the winter. Sometimes, fresh green growth appears around Christmas, making this grass almost evergreen. Extend it under the magnolias, as there will be lots of bare ground here until they mature.

In the front, under the Mexican plums, I would love to see wood fern for a woodsy look that foreshadows the fern garden in back. This would be a commitment to everlasting watering, though, and could not be used until the trees are large enough to provide plenty of shade. For a more xeriscapic approach, as well as a tropical look, you might consider palmetto. It's evergreen and often covers acres of winter-wet-to-summer-dry low-lying woods. It can also take the hot sun of the early years and then revel in the shade that eventually develops.

Another possibility for the early sunny years is a meadow. Use sideoats grama and mix with it pink evening primrose, winecup, blue-eyed grass, and calylophus for a rainbow of pink, wine, blue, and yellow in the short spring grass. These wildflowers are convenient because, after blooming, they die back without leaving visible dead leaves. The sideoats continues to grow to a height of two to three feet (the drier you keep it, the shorter it will be). By October it will have bloomed and be nodding with delicate seeds that remain all winter.

In the late fall, there should be quite a bit of color. Both the white oaks and the swamp chestnut oaks turn a warm, rich red. In the narrow bed to the east of the driveway, the fruits on the coralberry ripen to a purplish pink. Soon they are joined by the leaves of the flameleaf sumac, which is dependably breathtaking red every year. The black gum is also very good about turning red to dark wine each fall. These plants are all capable of handling the reflected heat off the driveway. I've put in a curb, extending the line of the wall to the street, just in case the neighbors aren't as enthusiastic about having a coralberry and sumac thicket in their yard as you are about having one in yours.

Piney Woods

Tyler, Texarkana, Houston, Beaumont
(Henderson, Longview, Marshall, Palestine)

PINEY WOODS, LONGLEAF PINE FOREST

Regional Description

East Texas is made up mostly of piney woods, with occasional patches and fingers of post oak woods where few or no pines are to be seen. The post oaks indicate less fertile, drier sands. Unlike sandy loam, this "sugar sand" has little organic matter to hold the grains together and runs through your fingers. The river bottoms and floodplains have silty, less acid soils, where sweetgums and other fast-growing swamp trees predominate. Here and there are bogs or seeps, which are often quite acid and support sphagnum moss and water-loving shrubs and flowers.

The Piney Woods is usually equal parts hardwood (oak, maple, magnolia, elm, hickory, and so on) and pines (loblolly and shortleaf). It is the southwest tip of the giant pine-hardwood forests of the southeastern United States.

The pines are tall and straight. Sounds are softened by dense layers of needles. The air is fresh, even on hot summer days, with a deliciously spicy pine scent. Deodorizing sprays offer an almost unrecognizable imitation. This is the only region of the state where the overall natural landscape is not dominated by sky.

Although this habitat has been heavily logged, four national forests have been set aside for preservation and conservation: Angelina, Sabine, Sam Houston, and Davy Crockett. In general, the land in East Texas is gently rolling or hilly, with numerous streams. The soils are mostly light-colored, red, or dark gray sands, or sandy loams with areas of clays. Sandstone or ironstone outcroppings are common. The soils are acid because the calcium has been leached out by frequent rains and generally good drainage.

The average rainfall is 46 inches annually. When it comes to winter temperatures, Tyler has plunged as low as $-8°$ F, although average minimums range from 35° in Texarkana to 45° in Houston. Summer's average is 94°.

There is a very special place in the Piney Woods known as the Big Thicket. Originally it was a large forest with an exceptionally dense understory of yaupon holly, American holly, magnolias, hawthorns, cherry laurel,

A Drummond red maple in full flower stands out against a native woods of pines and still-dormant oaks. In summer, the muddy ground under the maple is carpeted with chain fern and lizardtail, and the banks in front of the wax myrtles are blue and gold with waterleaf and swamp sunflower. Photo by the authors.

and wax myrtle. Then it was extensively logged and drained. The remnants of the various habitats are described in Geyata Ajilvsgi's book *Wildflowers of the Big Thicket*.

The Big Thicket National Preserve is only a fraction of what used to be. Beginning near Woodville, it reaches south almost to Beaumont. Here, stands of stately longleaf pines tower over flowering dogwoods, American holly, big bluestem, and wildflowers on well-drained sands. As you go south, the soil becomes richer and more moist, and the character of the forest changes. Now it is dimly lit and is composed primarily of beech, magnolia, and loblolly pine, with frequent white oaks and red maples. Underneath are beautiful ornamental trees and shrubs such as fringe tree, two-winged silverbell, and azaleas. Scan the forest floor and you will find mayapples, trillium, partridgeberry, and violets.

It is the beauty of this particular forest that the Piney Woods Plan tries to capture. The plan is intended to be used by all who live in the Piney Woods, with alternate choices for those plants that are not universal throughout the region.

Piney Woods Plan
Lot Size: 170' × 107'

The woods in this plan reflects the basic makeup of East Texas woods overall. There are three distinct layers. The canopy, or top layer, consists of pines, oaks, sweetgums, maples, and magnolias. These tall trees tend to space themselves to capture every bit of available sunlight, leaving only dappled light for the understory and the forest floor.

The understory is composed of shorter, shade-tolerant trees: flowering dogwood, fringe tree, plums, hawthorns, viburnums, chalk maple, ironwood, hollies, deciduous magnolias, and so on. The third layer is ground covers, which are ferns and special flowers, such as mayapple and pinewoods lily. Wildflowers and thicket shrubs bloom on the edges of the forest, where they get extra sun. In a landscape, these sunnier environments are created where a street, driveway, patio, or mowed lawn holds the trees at bay.

If you create a woods in your yard, it can be predominantly pine or oak or an equal mixture of both, as in this plan. It all depends on what you have to start with, your taste, and your specific habitat. Which pines you use will also vary. Just north of Beaumont, where the climate is warm and humid, longleaf pines grow. If you live there, strongly consider using them exclusively, as they are especially elegant. In the rest of the Piney Woods, grow loblollies and shortleaf pines. Loblollies are easier to buy; shortleaf pines are more drought-tolerant. The two pines are often found together in nature.

In this plan you will notice that some sand-loving plants have a second label in parentheses. These alternatives are your better choice where you are confronted with clay, poor drainage, and higher humidity. These conditions

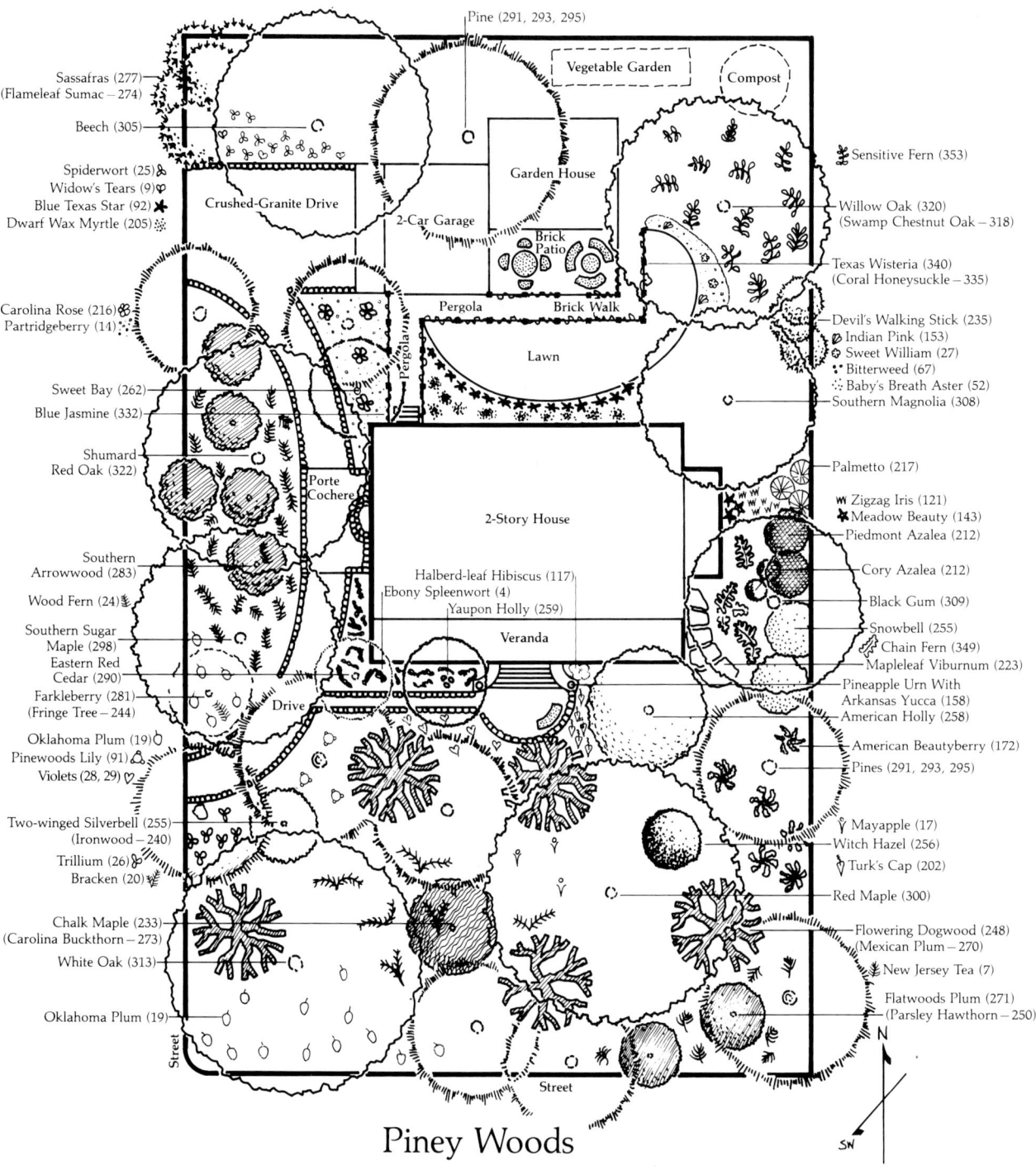

Pine (291, 293, 295)

Vegetable Garden

Compost

Sassafras (277)
(Flameleaf Sumac — 274)

Beech (305)

Garden House

Sensitive Fern (353)

Spiderwort (25)
Widow's Tears (9)
Blue Texas Star (92)
Dwarf Wax Myrtle (205)

Crushed-Granite Drive

2-Car Garage

Willow Oak (320)
(Swamp Chestnut Oak — 318)

Brick Patio

Texas Wisteria (340)
(Coral Honeysuckle — 335)

Carolina Rose (216)
Partridgeberry (14)

Pergola

Brick Walk

Devil's Walking Stick (235)
Indian Pink (153)
Sweet William (27)
Bitterweed (67)
Baby's Breath Aster (52)
Southern Magnolia (308)

Lawn

Sweet Bay (262)
Blue Jasmine (332)

Shumard
Red Oak (322)

Porte
Cochere

Palmetto (217)

Zigzag Iris (121)
Meadow Beauty (143)
Piedmont Azalea (212)

Southern
Arrowwood (283)

2-Story House

Cory Azalea (212)

Wood Fern (24)

Black Gum (309)

Southern Sugar
Maple (298)
Eastern Red
Cedar (290)

Halberd-leaf Hibiscus (117)
Ebony Spleenwort (4)
Yaupon Holly (259)

Snowbell (255)
Chain Fern (349)
Mapleleaf Viburnum (223)

Veranda

Pineapple Urn With
Arkansas Yucca (158)
American Holly (258)

Farkleberry (281)
(Fringe Tree — 244)

Drive

American Beautyberry (172)

Oklahoma Plum (19)
Pinewoods Lily (91)
Violets (28, 29)

Pines (291, 293, 295)

Mayapple (17)
Witch Hazel (256)

Two-winged Silverbell (255)
(Ironwood — 240)

Turk's Cap (202)

Trillium (26)
Bracken (20)

Red Maple (300)

Chalk Maple (233)
(Carolina Buckthorn — 273)

Flowering Dogwood (248)
(Mexican Plum — 270)

White Oak (313)

New Jersey Tea (7)

Flatwoods Plum (271)
(Parsley Hawthorn — 250)

Oklahoma Plum (19)

Street

Street

N

SW

Piney Woods

occur most frequently near Beaumont and Houston, although you can find pockets of clay anywhere in East Texas.

Another reason for giving alternate selections is that some trees become too prolific in one locale. In Tyler and Texarkana, where the sweetgum is sometimes viewed as a pest, residents love the willow oak because it provides light shade and doesn't dump a lot of twigs and old leaves on their property. In Houston, however, the willow oak tends to seed out like mad, so Houstonians prefer the swamp chestnut oak, which turns a soft, rich red in the fall. There are more wonderful choices than you could ever find room for, so there is no sense at all in using something you are not particularly fond of.

The woods in this plan is designed to be low-maintenance, requiring only annual pruning, no leaf raking, and only occasional watering after the plants are established. Most homeowners in East Texas already have several big trees in their front yard. They could develop a full woods quickly and easily by adding understory trees and ground covers.

I have depicted a pine woods here, because I thought that was most typical for East Texas. For a balanced pine forest, you'll want approximately equal numbers of pine trees and hardwoods such as oaks and maples. (If you don't have an existing canopy, see the Create-a-Woods Plan in Chapter 7—Ornamental Trees, for instructions on how to plant a forest.)

If you already have a canopy, you probably lack the understory trees. Even when homeowners or developers are trying their best to preserve a woods, they tend to cut down all the small trees, mistaking them for canopy saplings that are just "cluttering up the place." What they are really getting rid of is flowering dogwood, hawthorn, viburnums, and many other lovely small trees or shrubs such as wax myrtle, yaupon holly, and possumhaw. These understory trees provide color, so you need to plant them if you don't already have them or if you don't have enough. The small trees are used to being shaded by big trees. They have adapted to dappled or part shade and can suffer leaf burn in full sun if they are not well watered.

In this plan the dominant understory tree is dogwood or, if you have clay, the earlier-blooming Mexican plum. Other trees are witch hazel, which blooms in winter; parsley hawthorn and two-winged silverbell, which bloom just before the dogwood; and flatwoods plum, which usually blooms with the dogwood. In the fall the understory is again alive with color. Ironwood, dogwood, chalk maple, and parsley hawthorn display brilliant reds and oranges.

On the edges of the woods near the street are New Jersey tea and Oklahoma plum, both less than two feet tall, making snowy-white masses beneath the dogwoods. Deep in the shade lurk colonies of mayapples, with their twin umbrella leaves and nodding flowers, along with dark red trillium and, much later, pinewoods lily. Fall and winter color is dominated by the purple American beautyberries.

Summer is green and ferny. For easy-care ground cover, use the bracken fern. It's rather coarse and aggressive, so you would never use it in a formal garden, but it's ideal for covering large areas in an unwatered woods. When I say "unwatered," I mean unwatered in a normal summer, when rain falls every two weeks or so. In a dry summer, water if the leaves of the bracken start to brown and turn crisp. Everything in this front woods is drought-tolerant to East Texas, but it might look pitiful in a drought.

To ensure not having to water in a normal summer, let the ground be carpeted with fallen leaves—mulch to keep in moisture and to discourage weeds. Once a year, weed out poison ivy, greenbriar, and other undesirables and remove saplings and deadwood. Prune the trees every other year.

The side by the porte cochere is a continuation of the front, giving you the feeling of being wrapped up in a quiet, secluded forest. The woods is also functional; it shades the house and the driveway from the summer sun. Arrowwood and farkleberry, the understory trees in the woods by the porte cochere, are small trees that flower in the spring and turn from bright red to burgundy in the fall. Underneath them is the low-growing Oklahoma plum, which is continued from the front woods.

The dominant ground cover here is wood fern in dense stands. It serves as the transition to your formal, watered, and manicured back yard. The wood fern will require regular watering to maintain its vitality. That's important, because it's right by the driveway and will be seen up close every day—by you, by luncheon guests, by the delivery boy. Sensitive fern (bead fern) or the small evergreen Christmas fern could be used here also. All three ferns are normally available for purchase.

Notice that the back yard has more sun than the rest of the landscape because the lawn and patio create a clearing. A latticed pergola covered with vines achieves privacy from the street without losing this sense of space. A pergola is a walkway covered by a flat-roofed arbor. In this case the taller and wider main pergola that leads from the garage to the back door is latticed on the side facing the street. The lattice is covered by a delicate little vine called blue jasmine. The other side and top of the pergola are covered by either Texas wisteria or the almost-evergreen coral honeysuckle. These vines continue around the smaller L-shaped pergola.

The small bed in front of the pergola by the drive is a delightful mixture of low-growing evergreen partridgeberry and the fragrant but rampant Carolina rose. This ground-cover-like pink, spicy, everblooming rose will romp through this contained space, giving the grateful partridgeberry a little extra shade during the summer. The sweet bay is placed so that its fragrance can be enjoyed from either the drive or the main pergola, both high-traffic areas.

The back yard, structured by the pergolas, the brick walks and patio, and the oval lawn, presents a formal and elegant scene. To keep the design from becoming stuffy, I've included dwarf wax myrtle, which looks best unhedged. It is evergreen, and the leaves give off a delightful aroma. For spring, the blue Texas star (*Amsonia illustris*) will provide vivid accents, with its star-shaped, sky-blue flowers arranged in large loose clusters.

As we proceed around the rim of the watered lawn, we meet sweet William, Indian pink, bitterweed, and baby's breath aster, providing spring,

The Carl Owens garden near Avinger has evolved over the last thirty years. The bridge, designed by architect Louis Gohmert, spans a narrow spring-fed, sluggish stream bed that empties into a pond (far off to the right). In the stream bed are sensitive fern (locally called sympathy fern) and a naturalized water iris. The trees are shortleaf and loblolly pines, with an understory of flowering dogwood. The stone "cliff" was necessary to prevent erosion. On the hillsides are native and cultivated azaleas. White oak, hibiscus, palmetto, and many native wildflowers also abound in this garden, along with tulips and other nonnative bulbs. Photo by the authors.

summer, and fall blooms. Directly behind these plants is the sensitive fern. Allow it to grow tall, and let the back branches of the oak hang low, so the compost heap and vegetable garden are screened from view. Tucked into the sunny spot, between the oak and the magnolia, is a thicket of the exotic-looking aralia called devil's walking stick. When it blooms in the summer, you'll be delighted by its oddly beautiful foot-long hanging clusters of tiny white flowers. This aralia is like nothing you've ever seen.

The garden on the east side of the house is rather special. This environment, protected from harsh sun and winds, is nestled in a slight hollow, so it is naturally more moist and shady than the rest of the landscape. Primarily viewed from inside the house, the garden faces the sun-room and is not intended for strolling. In the spring it blooms with wild azaleas and iris, and then with snowbell and mapleleaf viburnum. In the summer it is lush and green with low-growing fern and delicate pink meadow beauty. Fall colors come from the bright red foliage of the black gum, and the apricot and oranges of the mapleleaf viburnum.

The driveway and front walk are made of crushed granite, which should be chosen to match the color of the soil as closely as possible. This provides a "gentrified" look. The mortared brick edging gives more of an in-town feeling. The area under the porte cochere, the paths under the pergolas, and the patio are bricked. They can be mortared or unmortared, according to the degree of formality you desire and your budget.

At the rear of the property, next to the driveway, stands a smooth-trunked beech tree. The branches like to hang low and thick. Let them—especially on your property line for privacy. The shade is so dense and the roots are so thick and fibrous that nothing is going to grow here except on the sunny edges near the drive and the street. For the area by the street, I chose a small thicket of sassafras, with its early yellow flowers and vibrant orange, red, and gold fall color. By the driveway, I have used the blue morning-blooming spiderwort and widow's tears. Watering here can range from often to occasional, depending on where you live. Beech trees don't like to be excessively dry.

Post Oak Woods

Bryan–College Station, Tyler, Texarkana
(Grapevine, Irving, Arlington, Weatherford)
Austin, San Antonio, Dallas, Fort Worth, in sandy pockets

POST OAK SAVANNAH, POST OAK WOODS,
EASTERN CROSS TIMBERS, WESTERN CROSS TIMBERS

Regional Description

Savannahs are grasslands dotted with trees. The Post Oak Savannah is grassland dotted with scattered—you guessed it—post oaks. Years ago, when fires were frequent, the Post Oak Savannah was described by explorers as "parklike." Ancient broad-branched trees were spaced widely apart, with little bluestem and other grasses and wildflowers growing beneath. Today fires are rare, so the grasses get shaded out and are replaced by thick undergrowth composed of ornamental trees, shrubs, and ground covers, as in pine and river-bottom woods.

Post oaks thrive wherever the annual rainfall is 30 inches or more and where sand is deep and well drained. Usually sandstone and ironstone are present in small quantities. The land is gently rolling to hilly, with the sand being light-colored and slightly acidic. The sands are separated by clay prairies to form the three distinct identities listed above.

In the big Post Oak Savannah, just west of the Piney Woods and extending to about fifty miles east of San Antonio, the annual rainfall varies from 46 to 30 inches, lessening as you go south and west and with most of it falling in May or June. This area is sometimes called the Oak Woodlands and is the southern tip of the Central Hardwoods of the United States. Scattered peat bogs, like those found in the Piney Woods, are not uncommon in this region. Flowering dogwood and sassafras are also found here, where the rainfall averages 40 inches or more annually.

In the Eastern Cross Timbers, which includes the Mid-Cities (between Dallas and Fort Worth), rainfall is usually closer to 32 inches a year, so dogwood and sassafras are rare if not nonexistent. Greenbriar is an unfortunate dominant part of the understory. Early travelers described the Cross Timbers as an almost impenetrable forest. After the greenbriar is removed, a beautiful understory remains, consisting of rusty blackhaw viburnum, possumhaw, smooth sumac, coralberry, and Arkansas yucca.

The Western Cross Timbers is drier still—with an annual rainfall closer to 30 inches on the average. Because of the reduced moisture, more pockets of prairies occur here, especially where there are clays, and the trees do not grow as close together, except near streams. In Stephenville and Comanche, mottes of live oak are often more evident than post oaks. Here, too, you will be able to use prairie flameleaf sumac, rusty blackhaw viburnum, redbud, Mexican plum, and eastern red cedars.

Because the Post Oak Woods extend so far from north to south, they can handle a wide range of winter temperatures. The record low in Weatherford, which is to the north, is −11° F. Normal winter averages range from 31° to 42°. Summer highs are about 95° everywhere.

To make life a lot easier for you, this plan tries to capture the feeling of the Post Oak Woods with their woody understories as they exist today, instead of as they used to be a century ago with their little bluestem– wildflower understory.

Post Oak Plan
Lot Size: 160′ × 100′

You've just bought a lot where you're going to build your dream home one day. What sold you on this land in the first place was the small but dense forest occupying the lot, and naturally you want to keep that well-wooded look all around your new home. This plan will show you how to go about it.

But before describing the plan, we ought to discuss the first major step: deciding what to keep and what to delete from your lot.

Consider carefully before taking the irrevocable step of cutting down a tree, especially post oaks. They are slow-growing, sensitive to root damage, and not easily replanted.

When you get ready to build your house or office building, tag all the trees you simply must cut down to make room for a house and a driveway. Tie big bows of orange plastic ribbon around the trees you plan to eliminate. Now stand back and look at the woods from all angles. Imagine what it would look like with all the easy-to-spot orange-tagged trees gone. Can you live with their absence? Or would you like to reconsider your building plans? You can wind your driveway around the trees, build a deck with a tree in the middle, or even create an open courtyard in the center of your home to accommodate a special tree—just as long as you don't change the soil level. Trees do not take kindly to that.

Back in 1946, William Randolph Hearst had a hundred-year-old California live oak growing on the very spot where he wanted to add a new wing to his San Simeon castle. But rather than chop the venerable tree down, he had it moved ten feet! Incredibly, as of this writing, it's still alive. I don't recommend trying this with post oaks, though. They can be transplanted, but only with difficulty.

However, planning your house around the post oaks does not guarantee their survival. You need to monitor their treatment both during and after construction to ensure their continued good health. Many people who carefully designed their homes around large and healthy post oaks have watched with growing horror as some of them died in the five years following construction.

This bottomland woods in the Eastern Cross Timbers holds many species not usual in upland sites but does accurately reflect the traditional density of post oak woods held together with that obnoxious native, greenbrier. The Post Oak Savannah, now mostly pastures and farmland, was often open and parklike, as is the driest of the post oak woods, the Western Cross Timbers. Photo by the authors.

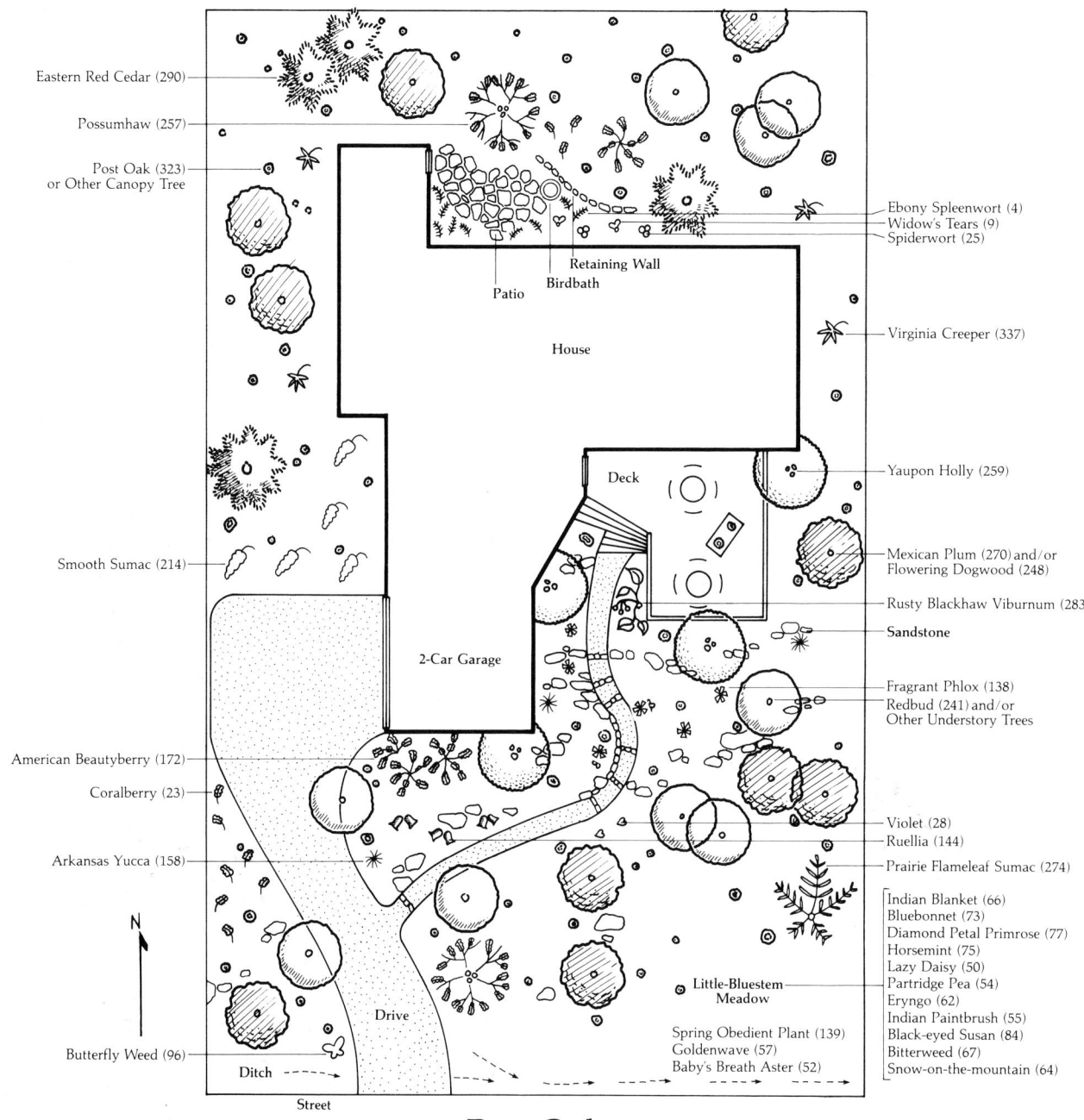

Eastern Red Cedar (290)

Possumhaw (257)

Post Oak (323)
or Other Canopy Tree

Ebony Spleenwort (4)
Widow's Tears (9)
Spiderwort (25)

Virginia Creeper (337)

Retaining Wall
Birdbath

Patio

House

Deck

Yaupon Holly (259)

Smooth Sumac (214)

Mexican Plum (270) and/or
Flowering Dogwood (248)

Rusty Blackhaw Viburnum (283)

Sandstone

2-Car Garage

Fragrant Phlox (138)
Redbud (241) and/or
Other Understory Trees

American Beautyberry (172)

Coralberry (23)

Violet (28)
Ruellia (144)

Arkansas Yucca (158)

Prairie Flameleaf Sumac (274)

Indian Blanket (66)
Bluebonnet (73)
Diamond Petal Primrose (77)
Horsemint (75)
Lazy Daisy (50)
Partridge Pea (54)
Eryngo (62)
Indian Paintbrush (55)
Black-eyed Susan (84)
Bitterweed (67)
Snow-on-the-mountain (64)

N

Little-Bluestem
Meadow

Drive

Spring Obedient Plant (139)
Goldenwave (57)
Baby's Breath Aster (52)

Butterfly Weed (96)

Ditch

Street

Post Oak

Why do post oaks die? Usually because compaction of the soil, overwatering, or jiggling of the roots—or even all three—has made it too difficult for the roots to take in oxygen, which is vital to post oaks. They grow only in predominantly sandy soils because sand leaves lots of air pockets for oxygen. Clay is usually found in the subsoil and is often found in pockets around post oaks, but you will never find a healthy post oak growing in a heavy clay soil. It's just too dense to store enough oxygen.

A three-hundred-year-old post oak can quickly suffocate and die on your property if the subcontractors' trucks packed down the soil so hard that oxygen can no longer percolate in. Surrounding the post oak with a St. Augustine lawn (which needs lots of watering) can have the same effect. Water fills all the air pockets, and the tree slowly drowns. A visible sign of distress is chlorosis, which causes the leaves to turn a sickly chartreuse color.

Post oaks are one of our highest-quality native trees, but you have to do things their way. I have digressed there, but I hope I've made an emphatic point about how important it is to protect your post oaks. Now, how about the rest of the trees?

The best plan is to refrain from clearing out any trees the first year. But there are several plants that you can immediately remove with a clear conscience. Start with greenbriar and poison ivy. Cut the vines off the trunks at ground level. You will be amazed at how this will open up your woods. Often it is all that needs to be done besides pruning out dead branches.

To protect your woods, fence off everything you didn't have to cut down. Build your fence as far out as the drip line (the farthest reach of the branches), if possible. This may seem expensive and unnecessary to you, but take it from someone who has heard her share of horror stories from friends and clients—this is the only way to protect your trees from being attacked and ravaged by bullheaded bulldozer operators, erratic delivery trucks, stacks of lumber and piles of bricks, trash piles, concrete waste, dumped paint thinners, and so on.

Then, as your house is being built, observe and assess your woods. As the trees bloom and leaf out, identify them and mark with blue surveyor's ribbon the ones you definitely want to keep. Add a yellow ribbon to the trees that need pruning to improve their shape.

It's not a good idea to clear out all the trees that are under four-inch caliper (four inches in trunk diameter) on the theory that they're just saplings. A two-inch-caliper rusty blackhaw viburnum is mature, and a four-incher is a fairly old tree. Flowering dogwoods, redbuds, and Mexican plum, as well as Eve's necklace, hawthorns, and farkleberry, are most usually found in the four-inch-caliper or smaller stage. Hercules' club, not featured in this book, is another small tree you might find. It has big thorns all up its trunks, and spines on its aromatic leaves. Hercules' club provides prime bird food and is well worth leaving.

Old woods are naturally canopied at the top and more open underneath.

The ground is heavily mulched with old leaves and rotting logs, with a scattered blooming understory. Invaders from Asia, such as mimosa, ailanthus, chinaberry, and tallow, are usually found only where the woods has been disturbed or at the edge of woods by the road where the environment is sunnier. Unless you are particularly fond of one of these specimens, I would remove all of them. You will end up with a better-balanced and higher-quality woods if you do.

Now, on to the plan. The first thing you need to notice when you look at it is a lot of little irregularly shaped doughnuts. They represent existing shade trees. In this region, a good 50 percent or more will be post oaks. The rest will be other kinds of oaks, especially sand jack (bluejack) and blackjack, and a sprinkling of whatever regional hardwoods abound, such as winged elm and hickory. Eastern red cedar is also common, and in the eastern portions, so are loblolly and shortleaf pines.

This plan assumes that the woods were left essentially as you found them. The treelike circles are understory trees—redbud and Mexican plum being appropriate anywhere post oaks grow, and flowering dogwood being usable in the Post Oak Savannah. If your lot was undisturbed when you bought it, these understory trees will probably already be present in adequate quantity. If your lot was cleared of understory before you bought it, you will need to add them. The tree shapes are spaced on this plan to give a big spring show both from the street and from the deck.

By the driveway and off the back patio are two other small trees—possumhaws, to brighten up a winter scene. They are carefully placed to catch good sun for a bountiful crop of red berries. Also in a sunny spot is the prairie flameleaf sumac, a small hardy tree that turns brilliant red in the fall. If you live in East Texas, use flameleaf sumac instead, as it is more shade-tolerant.

At its feet, in the sunniest place on the lot, is a meadow of little bluestem. Let this meadow extend as far into the woods as sunlight allows. In the Western Cross Timbers this meadow could extend over the whole lot. Little bluestem, the major grass to grow under post oaks, is a beautiful grass that is usually clumpy rather than turflike in Texas. The stems are soft blue in summer and a rich tawny orange after frost. The seeds are white and fluffy and cling all winter, catching the light in lovely ways.

Among the clumps of bluestem grow a variety of wildflowers. Indian blanket, bluebonnets, diamond petal primrose, horsemint, lazy daisy, partridge pea, and eryngo grow well in all the post oak meadows and provide color from earliest spring to frost. In moister sites (or moister years) Indian paintbrush, black-eyed Susans, and bitterweed do well. Snow-on-the-prairie grows in Post Oak Savannah, and snow-on-the-mountain (which is prettier) in the Western Cross Timbers.

Mow your meadow once a year in February just before new growth begins. Do not mow it shorter than four inches, as you don't want to harm the rosettes of the flowers or the clumps of little bluestem. If you have a short dry spring and the meadow looks ratty by June, you can also mow it then.

Gerald and Rosalie Cyrier chose this lot in the Eastern Cross Timbers for its beautiful woods. Post oaks predominate, with blackjack oak, American elm, Texas mulberry, and bois d'arcs. The luxuriant ground cover of Virginia creeper was there when the Cyriers started, and they were wise enough to keep it. I added subtle touches of typical understory—American beautyberry, yaupon holly, coralberry—up near the house. Photo by the authors.

If you have an existing meadow, you will undoubtedly find grasses and flowers not listed here. Even if you install this exact meadow plan, in a few years (if not immediately) other annuals, biennials, and grasses are going to join what you planted. As long as they are attractive, enjoy them. Don't even think about weeding this area, even though it is quite small, unless sandburs, beggar's-ticks, or some other undesirables invade it and make walking in the area a nuisance. (For those of you who might be inexperienced with beggar's-ticks, they're vegetable, not animal. The "ticks" are actually the barbed seeds found on a pretty yellow daisy called bidens. After a one-second stroll through bidens after they set seed, you can spend the next half hour picking the little barbed blankety-blanks off your clothes.)

Rural routes in post oak woods typically have bar ditches by the road. The ditches receive extra moisture, but the county mows them, so they remain a place for grass and flowers instead of bottomland trees and vines. The ditch in this plan runs downhill to the right. Here, masses of pink spring obedient plant and goldenwave can be breathtaking in May. Baby's breath aster in the fall would undoubtedly be joined by bitterweed and snow-on-the-prairie as they seed out from the meadow above.

Above the ditch, just beyond where the county mows but where it can receive runoff and sun—and lots of attention—plant one or more butterfly weeds. These long-lived perennials improve with age and can become very beautiful in a few years.

In the shadier part of the woods nearer the house, the ground starts to rise steeply with outcroppings of ironstone and sandstone. Woodland flowers and ground covers mingle among unraked leaves. The drive is crushed granite in the same soft tan color as the surrounding soil. The path to the front door is also crushed granite and climbs up the slope with occasional groupings of steps. The edges of the steps are faced with the sandstone or ironstone found on the site, while large rocks hold the soil off the walk as it curves on its way uphill.

You should get quite a lot of rocks to play with when the foundation is dug. Be on hand when the work is going on to make your selections of rocks and boulders. If, by any chance, none turn up, you can buy Milsap boulders—lichen-covered sandstone from Parker County.

For quick erosion control on the slope above the main part of the driveway near the garage, use smooth sumac. It gets three to seven feet tall and suckers unbelievably quickly, which is ideal for this situation. Smooth sumac will hold the soil, provide a screen for the back of the house, be brilliant red in the early fall, and attract birds. To the left of the drive, coralberry provides erosion control, fall and winter color, and bird food.

One of the first plants you see to the right of the drive is the Arkansas yucca. I have seen it in deep shade, where it no longer blooms but where the soft evergreen leaves form an attractive two-to-three-foot grasslike clump.

Fall and winter color here is provided by three large American beautyberries. These, with the coralberry and possumhaw already described, should make the entrance cheery in winter.

In the spring, when the flowering trees do their thing, the woodland floor can be carpeted with violets. In late spring and early summer, lavender is still the dominant color. Large lavender bells nod on the spreading plants of ruellia, which are usually well under a foot tall. In this plan they are planted among sandstone boulders near the start of the path. Further up the hill and below the deck are fragrant phlox, also lavender in color.

In this part of the plan you will notice a number of circles with three trunks drawn in the middle. They represent yaupon hollies—abundant in the Post Oak Savannah but naturalized in the Cross Timbers. If you live in the Western Cross Timbers and plan never to water, use eastern red cedars or any native juniper instead. These evergreens provide green in the winter and privacy for the deck.

The deck is redwood, about three and one-half feet above the ground, and large enough to hold two sets of tables and chairs. Note the hole for the existing trees. By the redwood steps is a rusty blackhaw viburnum. This small tree is beautiful in the spring with its large clusters of white flowers, in the summer with its lustrous green leaves, and in the fall when those leaves turn red, purple, and orange. The trunk is evenly checkered, rather like flowering dogwood often is, and the branching is spare and graceful.

The ground cover on the shady east side of the house is Virginia creeper. Keep it off the trees. It would look handsome covering the side of the house, but let it do that only if your house is made of hard stone or well-fired brick. Otherwise it is too destructive.

The back yard really goes back a long way, but there was room on this plan to show only the part immediately around the back door. Because it's on the north side of the house and heavily wooded, this part of the plan gets little sun. The patio is fairly small—slightly less than twenty feet long and ten feet wide. The ground here had to be raised to create good drainage for the house. The soil that was used came from the hole for the foundation.

A small retaining wall protects the original elevation of the nearest existing trees. The patio is built of sandstone laid in the native soil—primitive and natural. If your stone is flat enough, use it; or you can buy Pecos tan paving stones. The patio is a cool, peaceful place to spend a lazy afternoon reading or to watch the fireflies on a summer night.

The plants are small and have lots of space between them—ebony spleenwort (a fern) and widow's tears and spiderwort, two perennials that provide blue morning flowers. An occasional good soaking of these plants will keep them fresh and healthy.

Winter color consists of eastern red cedars, which are dark green. The females seem blue when they are loaded with berries. Against this foil are the reds and purples of coralberry, American beautyberry, and possumhaw. These berries will attract migrating and winter birds for easy viewing from the back windows. There are also flowering trees here for spring beauty. This small bit of the back yard contains all the elements for year-round color and beauty.

Grasslands and woodlands pieced together are a common sight in the Blacklands. This late autumn scene on the Grand Prairie at the Fort Worth Nature Center shows a mixed patch of prairie grasses, already winter russet, accented by paleleaf yucca and surrounded by rusty blackhaw viburnum, prairie flameleaf sumac, mesquite, Texas ash, Shumard red oak, and cedar elm. Photo by the authors.

Blackland

Dallas, Fort Worth, Waco, Austin, San Antonio, Bryan–College Station, (Greenville, La Grange, Paris, Sherman, Temple)

BLACKLAND PRAIRIES, GRAND PRAIRIE

Regional Description

Both these prairies are calcareous, which means the soil is alkaline and limy. You'll find limestone beneath the black waxy clay soil just about anywhere you choose to dig, and exposed where the soil has been eroded in creek beds and on hillsides.

The Blackland Prairies are shaped something like a tornado, with the broad top running from Paris west to Sherman, then narrowing as they run down through Dallas, the east sides of Waco and Austin, and the middle of San Antonio. The Grand Prairie includes Gainesville, Fort Worth, and the west side of Waco.

The soils are mostly clays, and in the Blackland Prairies they are very dark, as you'd expect from the name. Some fields actually resemble black velvet when they are freshly plowed and moistened from a good rain. The Blackland Prairies get an average of 30 to 44 inches of rain annually. During dry spells, the clay shrinks, causing cracks up to six inches wide. The shrinking of the clay also keeps foundation repair companies busy.

These deep black soils historically supported tallgrass prairies. Today it's difficult to imagine how the terrain looked to early travelers—a dramatic 360-degree sweep of horizon, marked only by occasional ribbons of trees growing alongside limestone stream beds.

Little bluestem was the dominant grass and turned the prairie blue-green in the summer and a tawny orange in the fall. Big bluestem, Indian grass, switch grass, and sideoats grama were also important components. The prairie sod was thick, resulting in very deep, very tough root systems. These grasses still exist here, of course, but in small and scattered colonies. The wildflowers here are called forbs, which means that they are not grasses or woody plants but herbs. The autumn flowers grow quite tall in order to reach above the tops of the grasses. Ironweed, pitcher sage, goldenrod, and Maximilian sunflower are some of the most eye-catching.

This rich prairie is all but lost because of plowing and overgrazing. No government protection has yet been extended to any of the remnants, and developers are now destroying them at a terrifying rate.

Blackland bottomland woods are tall, lush, and impenetrable, looking like jungle with thick understory and vines. Where the original vegetation has been disturbed, Japanese honeysuckle and ligustrums from Asia have moved in. The dominant trees are Shumard red oak, bur oak, magnificent chinquapin oak with big leaves, pecan, American and cedar elms, soapberry, hackberry (an unattractive form of the desirable species found in the Rio Grande Plains), and eastern red cedar. Other trees not described in this book are slippery elm, bois d'arc, common persimmon, and locust. The prettiest understory trees found here are redbud, rusty blackhaw viburnum, Mexican plum, and Eve's necklace.

The only other part of this region where woods managed to survive fires and plows was on escarpments. Here the woods are mostly eastern red cedar and Ashe juniper and ornamental trees such as Mexican buckeye, Texas buckeye, Hercules' club, and Eve's necklace.

Below this crest of trees, mesquites and honey locusts are scattered on the thin-soiled limestone slopes. Here too are some of our showiest wildflowers: mealy blue sage, winecup, Barbara's buttons, and greenthread.

The Grand Prairie gets a little less moisture—30 to 35 inches per year. In addition, the soils are generally shallower. This was once a midgrass prairie, with little bluestem dominating. Indian grass and sideoats grama also grew here. But all three were shorter than they were on the Blackland Prairies. On the Grand Prairie you are far more conscious of the underlying limestone; the terrain is more rugged and less gently rolling than the Blackland Prairies.

Before settlers arrived, the trees were limited to the creeks and were the same species found in the creeks of the Blackland Prairies. Today range fires are rare, so woody species are taking over the uplands. Interestingly, the trees are more like what you would find on the Edwards Plateau—Texas ash, escarpment live oak, Ashe juniper, Texas redbud, Mexican buckeye, and short red oaks, so short that they have been mistakenly called Texas red oaks. Benny Simpson, the recognized expert on Texas oaks, has examined the acorns from numerous trees and has found those from Fort Worth north to be Shumard red oaks, the same red oak common to the creeks of the Grand and Blackland prairies. They are smaller because less moisture is available.

These prairies run north-south for almost four hundred miles, so they are subject to wide ranges of temperature. Nevertheless, the native prairie vegetation is basically the same within each prairie. As a result, the plants and grasses I've discussed so far in this section will do equally well in San Antonio and Sherman and all points in between.

Paris, the northernmost city on the Blackland Prairies, has gotten as cold as $-13°$ F, whereas Austin and San Antonio have all-time lows of only (only?) $-2°$ and $0°$, respectively. The average annual lows for these cities range from $34°$ in Paris to $41°$ in Austin and $42°$ in San Antonio. In between are Fort Worth at $35°$, Dallas at $36°$, and Waco at $38°$, where it got as low as $-5°$ at least once. Summer highs for all of these cities average around $95°$.

The Blackland Plan reflects the bottomland woods rather than prairie, on the theory that most people would prefer living beneath shade trees to living in the middle of nose-high grasses. If you live on the Grand Prairie, have deep soil, or plan to water occasionally, the Blackland Plan is appropriate. If you have a lot of white rock showing and don't want to water (or can't), use the Hill Country Plan, which is winter-hardy if you live south of Dallas–Fort Worth.

Blackland Plan
Lot Size: 160′ × 100′

This plan is easy to install because you start with an established woods. After repairing the damage caused by construction (yes, there *will* be damage), maintenance will consist of watering and mowing the horseherb three times a summer, pruning deadwood out of the trees, and keeping vines off the trees where you want visibility. Removal of poison ivy should also be a major concern, as you and your guests may be highly allergic to it.

Many people are currently buying beautiful wooded lots for their new homes. In almost every instance the woods exist not because someone wanted to preserve their beauty but because the topography was too rough for the land to be plowed or grazed. In this plan the cliff that drops from the street to the downstairs level of the house is typical. The drop in this particular plan is sixteen feet, most of it very steep. The dotted lines indicate drop-offs. Bands of limestone are exposed in places. Wherever the rock has crumbled into a gray soil, trees are growing in the usual Blackland density.

The dense growth of large trees, saplings, and ornamentals gives tremendous privacy even in winter if left unpruned. The branches—gray, brown, mauve, and a few even reddish—tangle into a webbing of wood. If you let vines grow in there too, it becomes difficult to see more than thirty to forty feet.

Eastern red cedars are the dominant evergreen, and they can grow right up to the top of the canopy but will be bare-trunked most of their height because the light is so dim. Privet and other ligustrums, photinia, and Japanese honeysuckle are the bird-planted evergreens from Asia that are naturalizing in disturbed woods. You rarely see them in old woods, where all the available niches are already filled, but they are a dominant part of the understory in clearings and woods less than thirty years old.

Where you want privacy, leave the woods totally undisturbed—a jungle of saplings and vines. Where privacy is not the goal, remove the vines and the less interesting saplings, and let most of the small trees remain as blooming understory.

In this plan the large trees (indicated by the larger, darker circles) are bur oak, Shumard red oak, chinquapin oak, cedar elm, American elm, pecan, soapberry (which seems to get twice as big in the Blacklands as elsewhere), white ash, and eastern red cedar. You will have lots of other kinds of trees in your woods, but I've listed those that most people prefer. If, despite your best efforts, you need to replace some shade trees because of construction destruction, these are recommended. If you are on thinner soil or not on a slope over a creek, so that your land is drier, eliminate American elm, white ash, and pecan from the list and add Texas ash and Ashe juniper.

Construction on your lot is usually devastating to the woods. Any time you get a bulldozer on the move, you are likely to end up with only half as many trees as you planned. The power derived from driving a bulldozer must be intoxicating. And giving the plan to the bulldozer operator doesn't mean he can read it or control himself. The only way to protect your trees is to put up temporary fencing around areas that you want that bulldozer to stay out of. Even hanging around while the work is being done, assuming you can spare the time, guarantees nothing. A good friend took time away from his office to oversee the bulldozing on his property. He carefully explained the situation to the driver and never once took his eyes off of him. Then they broke for lunch. My friend returned to find that the enthusiastic driver had started early and had already leveled six desirable trees.

I know that fencing is expensive, but price a few mature trees and decide if it's worth it. Something like snow fencing is quite adequate. The barriers just need to be strongly visual and able to last throughout construction. You might also include in your contract a provision specifying a hefty fine for every desirable tree damaged.

The flowering understory trees are indicated by dots. The best ones are eastern redbud (Texas style, which means it has small thick leaves more like a Texas redbud), Mexican plum, rusty blackhaw viburnum, and Eve's necklace. These trees grow in the woods or on the edges; dappled sun all day is perfect for them. There is a good chance all four will exist on your property, especially if you have at least half an acre of old, uncleared woods. Wherever you have four hours or more of direct sun, you can have a possumhaw or a prairie flameleaf sumac. I have placed one of each by the driveway, which makes the largest clearing in the woods.

I've provided a breathing space around the house—an area averaging about fifteen feet wide. It's very shady and is carpeted with horseherb and the Missouri violet. The horseherb is mowed to make a path among the thinned-out trees from one deck to another, around to the driveway, and on to the glider swing. Horseherb will be thicker and lusher if you water it occasionally. Watering and mowing about three times during the summer should be adequate.

Down near the driveway, I have added Arkansas yucca for the texture of the evergreen leaves and for the white flowers in the spring. Also for spring color, I have put in black sampson, a large pink coneflower. Don't cut back the stems after blooming, because the seed heads look good all summer.

For fall color the Maximilian sunflower is magnificent. This large prairie perennial will gradually expand all the way down the drive. Let it. And turn the hose on it occasionally in the summer so the bottom leaves will not get ratty.

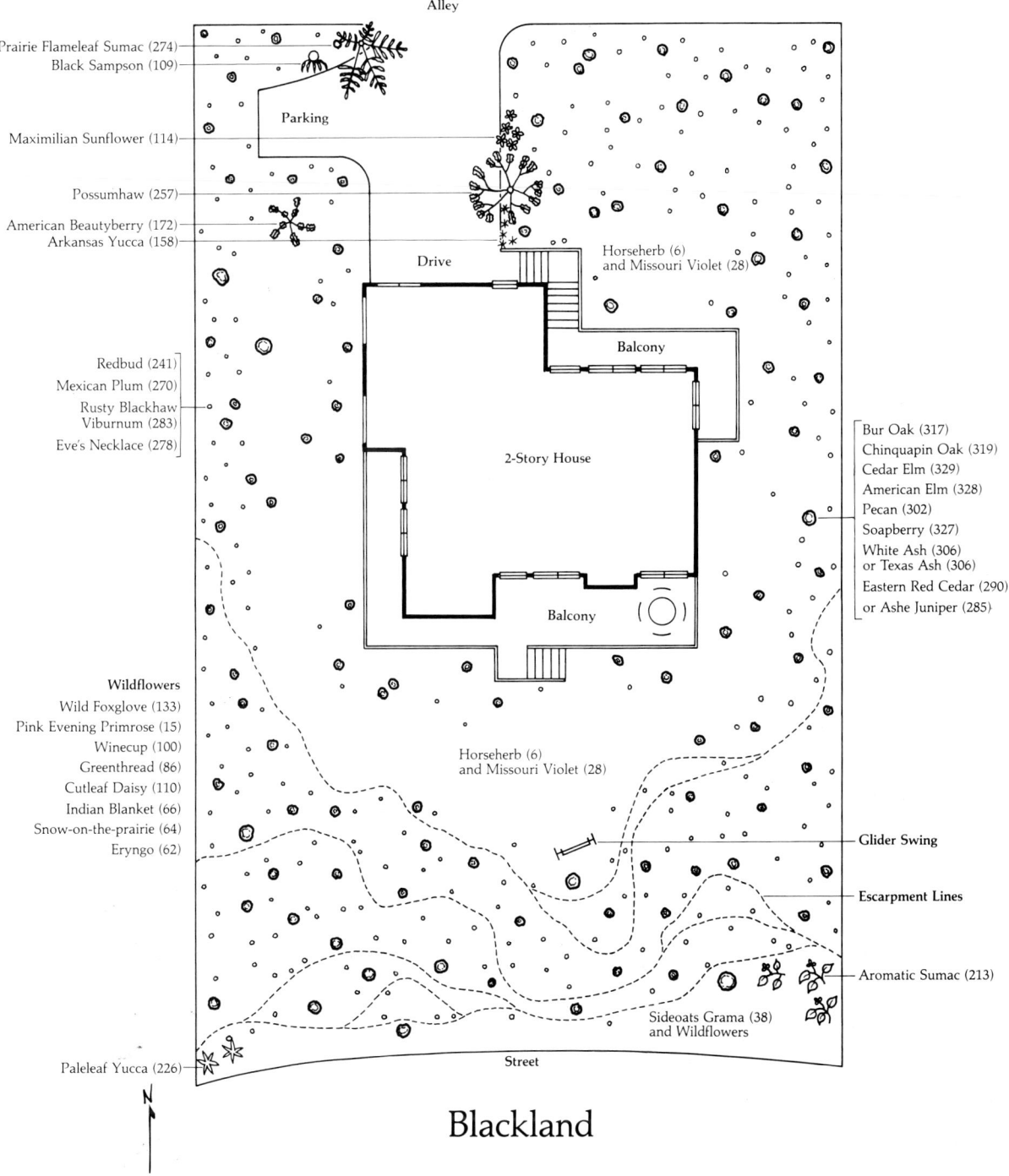

Alley

Prairie Flameleaf Sumac (274)
Black Sampson (109)

Parking

Maximilian Sunflower (114)

Possumhaw (257)

American Beautyberry (172)
Arkansas Yucca (158)

Drive

Horseherb (6)
and Missouri Violet (28)

Balcony

Redbud (241)
Mexican Plum (270)
Rusty Blackhaw
Viburnum (283)
Eve's Necklace (278)

2-Story House

Bur Oak (317)
Chinquapin Oak (319)
Cedar Elm (329)
American Elm (328)
Pecan (302)
Soapberry (327)
White Ash (306)
or Texas Ash (306)
Eastern Red Cedar (290)
or Ashe Juniper (285)

Balcony

Wildflowers
Wild Foxglove (133)
Pink Evening Primrose (15)
Winecup (100)
Greenthread (86)
Cutleaf Daisy (110)
Indian Blanket (66)
Snow-on-the-prairie (64)
Eryngo (62)

Horseherb (6)
and Missouri Violet (28)

Glider Swing

Escarpment Lines

Aromatic Sumac (213)

Sideoats Grama (38)
and Wildflowers

Paleleaf Yucca (226)

Street

N

Blackland

This beautiful Blackland Prairie woods glows on a gloomy fall day. The yellows come mostly from the canopy of cedar elms and a rich understory of redbuds. The late Arthur Berger, a landscape architect in Dallas, started this project in the forties, and owner George Fix has carried on, transplanting in several more eastern red cedars and growing some oaks and other trees from seed. The ground cover is *Vinca major.* Photo by the authors.

Tucked away in the shade off the drive is an American beautyberry. Although seen more often in sandy soils, this shrub is also native to the Blacklands and gives welcome color in late fall and winter.

On the south side of the property, facing the street on the top of the bluff, the environment is hotter and drier than anywhere else on the lot. In one corner are two paleleaf yuccas. In the other I have tucked aromatic sumac under the little bit of shade. In front of that, I have placed a mixture of sideoats grama and wildflowers. This is not an area you ever want to mow or water. Sideoats always looks nice without mowing, and it is especially good with wildflowers because it doesn't begin to grow in the spring until after the flowers are mostly through blooming. Wild foxglove, pink evening primrose, winecup, greenthread, cutleaf daisy, and Indian blanket are the six I would choose. They are tough, easy-to-grow flowers that together give a long blooming season. For fall color, you could add snow-on-the-prairie and eryngo. Don't let that foreign interloper Johnson grass invade here, or it will choke out everything else.

Other wildflowers for the shady part of the woods are ironweed, frostweed (not described in this book but welcome for its late fall color, and likely to turn up without your planting it), wild blue asters, and trout lilies (*Erythronium* spp.—also not in this book). Trout lilies are sometimes called dogtooth violets and in late February are abundant in undisturbed Blackland woods; a stand of these short white flowers can carpet an acre or more.

Suppose you aren't starting out with the woods I described earlier in this chapter but want to emulate this plan anyway. You can plant your own woods. Admittedly, the woods will need a few years to develop into the showplace you have in mind, but it can be done. Refer to the Create-a-Woods Plan in Chapter 7 (Ornamental Trees). Follow the spacing suggested and use the trees recommended in this plan.

If you want to create a native woods that is strictly appropriate to the Blacklands, substitute ornamental trees for some of the shrubs. Blackland woods are unusually dense, but not with shrubs. Shrubs do best on the fringes and not deep inside the woods. Our typical native shrubs are coralberry (well drained or it will mildew), Arkansas yucca, paleleaf yucca, and aromatic sumac.

If you live on the Blacklands and want an entirely different kind of landscape, then use this plan as a shopping list and consult the theme garden plans for one that suits your home and lifestyle.

June found this Hill Country field still in full bloom. Lazy daisy, with touches of coreopsis and thelesperma, provides most of the color on this thin-soiled, well-drained slope. Tephrosia, prickly pear, and a yucca grow under the Ashe juniper, while a young mesquite can be seen farther back among the flowers. Photo by the authors.

Hill Country

Austin, San Antonio
(Del Rio, Fredericksburg, Kerrville, Killeen)
Abilene, Dallas, Fort Worth, San Angelo, Waco,
on escarpments

EDWARDS PLATEAU

Regional Description

The Edwards Plateau is a beautifully rugged land with live oaks, Texas (or Spanish) red oaks, Ashe junipers (which form the eastern "cedar" brakes), mesquites, and lots of wildflowers. Curly mesquite grass and buffalo grass abound. So do deer. In the deeper soils, you'll find little bluestem, Indian grass, and switch grass. I can never decide whether I love the Hill Country better in the winter or the spring. In the winter the grasses are a rich gold, the rocks are white, and the junipers, live oaks, evergreen sumacs, Texas mountain laurels, yuccas, sotols, and agaritos are a welcome green. They create a wonderful combination of colors and textures. In the spring there are two waves of color—our famous bluebonnets come first, followed by everything else in reds, pinks, oranges, purples, blues, and whites and dominated by various kinds of yellow daisies.

Here you can find caliche slopes, limestone escarpments, and thin clay soils barely covering caliche and rock—sometimes all three in a very small area. Limestone is the fossil shell remains of microscopic sea creatures that lived in a massive sea that once covered most of Texas. The escarpments are old reefs, the most famous being the Balcones Escarpment, which runs along the western edge of Austin and the northern edge of San Antonio. Below the Balcones Escarpment is the southern tip of the Blackland Prairies. West of the escarpment, the Edwards Plateau gradually gains in elevation as it extends toward the Pecos River.

This rugged escarpment is what most people think of when they refer to the Hill Country. Several milky-green rivers flow here, lined with magnificent stands of bald cypress and, here and there, towering limestone cliffs. Wood fern (called river fern in this part of the state) grows in the shade and maidenhair fern in the seeps, along with wild red columbines.

Throughout the Hill Country, tucked into protected sites in the valleys, you will encounter Texas madrone, Texas smoke tree, witch hazel, and bigtooth maple—trees normally found far to the northeast in the mountains of Arkansas, to the west in the mountains of the Trans-Pecos, or to the south in the mountains of Mexico.

41

Other trees are found here and nowhere else. Their ancestors were trapped in these canyons long ago and evolved into unique species. Among these are the sycamore-leaf styrax and the Anacacho orchid tree, which occurs at the southernmost edge of the Edwards Plateau.

One chunk of the Edwards Plateau got cut off from the rest. It's called the Callahan Divide, because it divides the Brazos and Colorado rivers. This bit of limestone upland consists of several low mesas entirely surrounded by the Rolling Plains south of Abilene. To see it, go to Buffalo Gap (Abilene State Recreation Area). After seeing nothing larger than a mesquite for miles, you will suddenly find yourself among large live oaks, and then in a good-sized forest.

A peculiar area in the middle of the Edwards Plateau is the Llano Uplift, where ancient granite rock got pushed up from deep within the earth's crust. (Enchanted Rock is the star of the uplift.) There is no limestone here. This area is also called the Central Mineral Region and sometimes the Central Basin. The soils here are mostly sandy, and whitebrush and mesquites are prevalent.

To the north and gradually merging into the Grand Prairie are the Lampasas Cut Plains. Like the Callahan Divide, this area is marked by low mesas on the edge of large stretches of windswept plains. Live oaks and junipers grow on the mesas, both to about the same height.

The western boundary of the Edwards Plateau is the Pecos River. After you cross the Pecos, you are in the Trans-Pecos. The westernmost city connected to the Edwards Plateau is San Angelo, where it is a lot higher, drier, and colder than it is near Austin and San Antonio.

Rainfall on the Edwards Plateau ranges from 29 to 33 inches annually near Austin and San Antonio to just 17 inches in San Angelo. San Angelo and Kerrville are the coldest cities in this region, with an average winter temperature of 34° F. Austin and San Antonio average 41°. Elevation ranges from 1,000 to more than 3,000 feet.

Because so many desirable plants live on the Edwards Plateau, putting them all together in one plan just isn't possible. The Hill Country Plan features only the most desirable plants that grow out of limestone and that are also native to Austin and San Antonio. It leaves out bigtooth maple, madrone, Gregg salvia, skeleton-leaf goldeneye, and many other treasures you might be able to use.

Hill Country Plan
Lot Size: 120' × 80'

Do you live on limestone or on thin soil that barely covers the limestone? Many Texans do. And a number of them, being new to this kind of terrain, assume incorrectly that nothing very worthwhile can grow in these conditions.

Look around your property, as well as at neighboring wild areas. There is a wealth of beautiful trees and flowers growing out of rock or gravel with

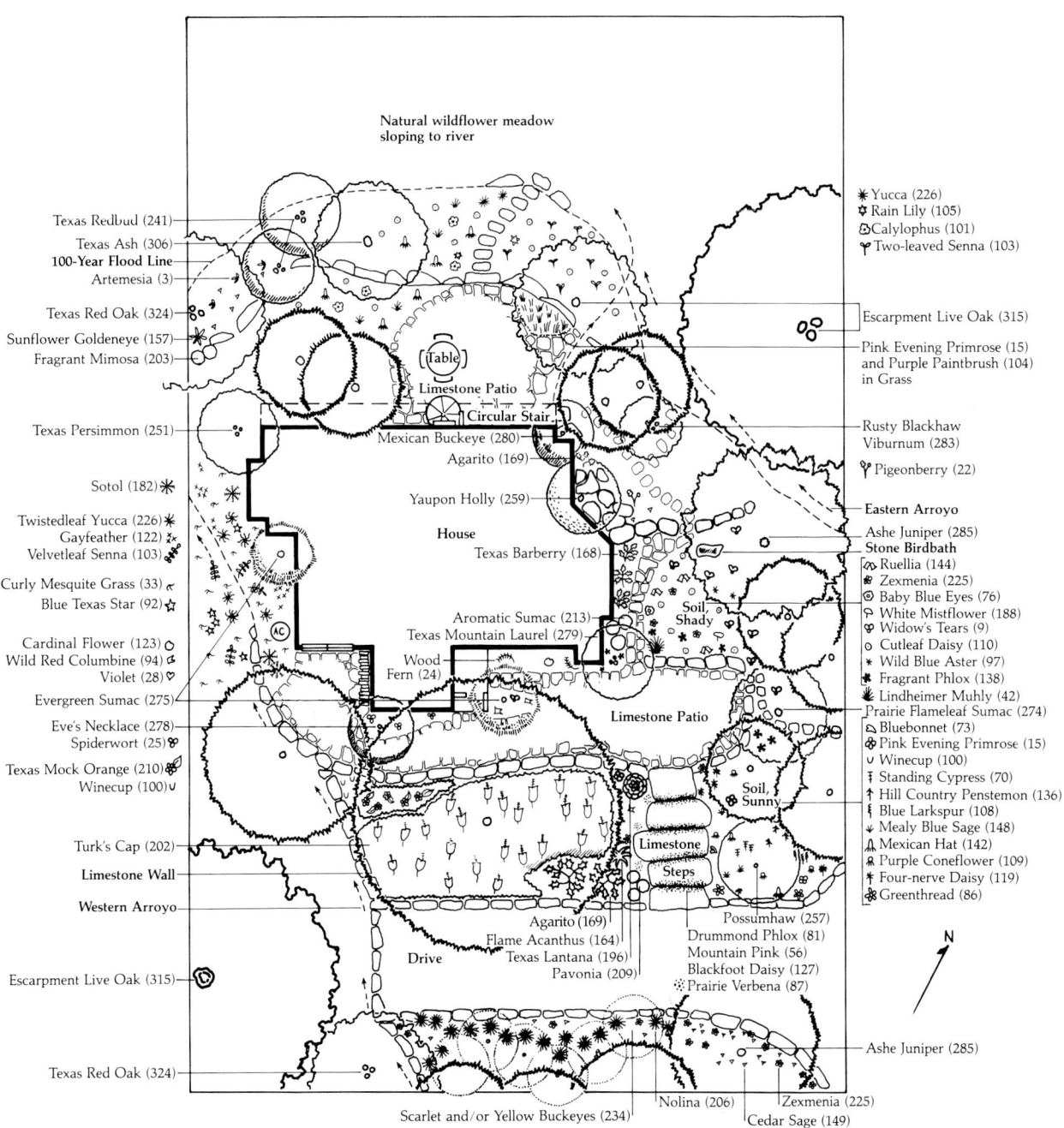

Natural wildflower meadow
sloping to river

Texas Redbud (241)
Texas Ash (306)
100-Year Flood Line
Artemesia (3)

Texas Red Oak (324)
Sunflower Goldeneye (157)
Fragrant Mimosa (203)

Texas Persimmon (251)

Sotol (182)

Twistedleaf Yucca (226)
Gayfeather (122)
Velvetleaf Senna (103)

Curly Mesquite Grass (33)
Blue Texas Star (92)

Cardinal Flower (123)
Wild Red Columbine (94)
Violet (28)

Evergreen Sumac (275)

Eve's Necklace (278)
Spiderwort (25)

Texas Mock Orange (210)
Winecup (100)

Turk's Cap (202)

Limestone Wall

Western Arroyo

Escarpment Live Oak (315)

Texas Red Oak (324)

[Table]
Limestone Patio
Circular Stair

Mexican Buckeye (280)
Agarito (169)

Yaupon Holly (259)

House

Texas Barberry (168)

Aromatic Sumac (213)
Texas Mountain Laurel (279)

Wood
Fern (24)

Soil,
Shady

Limestone Patio

Soil,
Sunny

Limestone
Steps

Agarito (169)
Flame Acanthus (164)
Texas Lantana (196)
Pavonia (209)

Drive

Possumhaw (257)
Drummond Phlox (81)
Mountain Pink (56)
Blackfoot Daisy (127)
Prairie Verbena (87)

Scarlet and/or Yellow Buckeyes (234)

Nolina (206)   Zexmenia (225)
Cedar Sage (149)

Yucca (226)
Rain Lily (105)
Calylophus (101)
Two-leaved Senna (103)

Escarpment Live Oak (315)

Pink Evening Primrose (15)
and Purple Paintbrush (104)
in Grass

Rusty Blackhaw
Viburnum (283)

Pigeonberry (22)

Eastern Arroyo
Ashe Juniper (285)
Stone Birdbath
Ruellia (144)
Zexmenia (225)
Baby Blue Eyes (76)
White Mistflower (188)
Widow's Tears (9)
Cutleaf Daisy (110)
Wild Blue Aster (97)
Fragrant Phlox (138)
Lindheimer Muhly (42)
Prairie Flameleaf Sumac (274)
Bluebonnet (73)
Pink Evening Primrose (15)
Winecup (100)
Standing Cypress (70)
Hill Country Penstemon (136)
Blue Larkspur (108)
Mealy Blue Sage (148)
Mexican Hat (142)
Purple Coneflower (109)
Four-nerve Daisy (119)
Greenthread (86)

Ashe Juniper (285)

N

Hill Country

almost no soil. In fact, many of our state's most attractive plants prefer these conditions.

Many people who live on the Edwards Plateau start out with a naturally enviable landscape that needs nothing but minimal pruning and a willingness to refrain from mowing when the wildflowers are in bloom and seeding out. This plan can help them to identify what they already have and to plan for future growth.

Others of you will use this plan to supplement and enhance what you have by adding some of the flowering trees and shrubs I've listed. This plan shows shady and sunny areas to help you make good choices as to what to add.

And if your property is currently bare, this plan will help you start off right with the most important and rewarding flowers and trees for this part of the state.

Start with small plants, and water them until their roots have grown deep into the crevices where moisture lurks. Planting under the edges of junipers is often a great way to get trees established.

The juniper is probably the single most important tree for the Edwards Plateau. Not only is it absolutely drought-tolerant and evergreen, but it also creates organic matter, provides shade, and captures moisture for the seedlings of more delicate flowering trees such as Texas smoke tree, Texas madrone, rusty blackhaw viburnum, Mexican redbud, Mexican buckeye, scarlet buckeye, and yellow buckeye. The agarito serves some of the same functions as juniper.

There is nothing more jarring in a natural landscape than to see a plant that is entirely out of place—for example, a magnolia among cacti and gravel. It's like wearing a ball gown to a sheep shearing. Many people in Austin and San Antonio live on largely undisturbed escarpment—land that should remain true to its indigenous vegetation. But because of their unfamiliarity with the natural countryside, some people put in bizarre plants to add extra color or simply because they like them.

Since this is not a rare occurrence, I've geared this plan to plants most commonly found on the cedar brakes on the eastern end of the Edwards Plateau. Austin and San Antonio residents who want a coherent wild landscape can choose among these plants for color and accents with no qualms whatsoever.

For people who aren't such purists, there are many lovely Edwards Plateau trees native farther west or south that also grow in limestone: Texas madrone, Texas smoke tree, goldenball leadtree, bigtooth maple, Anacacho orchid tree, and Lacey oak, which is native to the San Antonio area but not Austin. Shrubs are Gregg salvia, damianita, skeleton-leaf goldeneye, and red yucca.

Other desirables were left out of the plan for another good reason: I simply ran out of room! Kidneywood, whitebrush, and numerous flowers fall in this category. Actually, many attractive plants that grow in limestone not only were left out of the plan but also were left out of the book for the same reason. The main thing Texas native plants give us is abundant possibilities.

This particular plan was inspired by the riverfront home of friends in Wimberley. The landscape was created by Olivette Beach, who owns a nursery called Meanwhile Farm in that community. Olivette and her friend Kathy Thieleman, of Nature's Alliance in New Braunfels, were a big help in designing this plan.

The Ashe junipers in the plan already existed, and the house and patio were planned around the huge one in front. The junipers grew where the land was steep and the rock often exposed. They were pruned in some places to allow plantings underneath and were left low in other places to provide screening between adjacent properties.

The live oaks are on slightly deeper soil on either side of the arroyos. Good pruning is essential to the beauty of live oaks, and it should be professionally done every few years.

These two kinds of large evergreen trees join with the limestone rockwork to form the backbone of the landscape. Patios and retaining walls terrace the steep slope around the house into seven levels. Below the hundred-year flood line (which has been reached twice in the last ten years), the land slopes down to the river on its own in a natural meadow of grasses and wildflowers. Several small trees survive the floods here. The wildflowers shift around with the soil, but each year finds a variety ranging from scant to bountiful. Wildflowers grow in this meadow, not because the owners have planted them but because the owners haven't killed them by mowing or spraying herbicides. Maintenance consists of scything the meadow each winter.

The highest terrace is at the other end of the property and can be seen at the bottom of the page on the south side of the driveway. It is bounded on the property line by a screen of junipers. Between the junipers and the driveway is a steep slope of rocks and boulders protected from the hot south sun. This is a good spot for scarlet and yellow buckeyes. In front of them I've placed evergreen nolinas. And among and in front of the nolinas, and hanging over the dry-stack limestone wall, are red-flowered cedar sage, which blooms profusely in the spring and sporadically afterwards, and yellow zexmenia, which blooms all through the summer and fall.

The driveway is packed caliche and gravel. At the west end, on the other side of the retaining wall, is an arroyo that channels water downhill past the house and the gardens into the river below. The land on the other side of the arroyo contains a huge live oak and a juniper. An easy-care meadow is beneath. It could be left entirely to nature and would eventually become thick and brushy, or it could be managed as a meadow.

As you get out of your car and approach the house, you walk on massive stones that form six broad shallow steps down to the first patio, where frogfruit is planted between the limestone flagstones. Between the stone steps seed Drummond phlox and mountain pinks, two annuals for spring color. Blackfoot daisy and prairie verbena could also grow here for perennial color.

Bluebonnets, cutleaf daisies, and a few Drummond phlox grow in terraces created by the immense limestone steps laid by landscape designer Olivette Beach of Wimberley. To the left is a beautiful Ashe juniper with huge spreading limbs like a live oak. Dody and Bill Spencer carefully placed their house to take full advantage of this juniper and the wildflower meadow running down to the river in back. See the Hill Country Plan for more details. Photo by the authors.

The flower bed to the right slopes gently and possesses six inches of real soil. Light shade is provided by the possumhaw, which comes into full glory in the winter when it is covered with bright red berries. The flowers in this sunny flower bed are a mixture designed to bloom from mid-April to frost. Those requiring soil are bluebonnets, pink evening primrose, Mexican hat, winecup, standing cypress, blue larkspur, and purple coneflower. Mealy blue sage, four-nerve daisy, blackfoot daisy, Hill Country penstemon, and greenthread do not need soil, but they grow well in it.

On the other side of the path, where the east sun is strong, are a few of the same flowers, along with pavonia, flame acanthus, and Texas lantana—three shrubs that flower five to seven consecutive months and throughout the summer. Under the shade of the juniper grow masses of Turk's cap. If you have soil here and can occasionally water, American beautyberry and coralberry provide good winter color. If the area is very rocky, use the white honeysuckle bush. In the lower protected corner, use the sweet-smelling Texas mock orange, surrounded by winecups spilling over the low retaining wall.

Up against the house, an Eve's necklace tree and spiderworts provide color for dry shade. Toward the front door, an evergreen sumac marks the entrance and has a mixture of early spring violets and wild red columbine underneath. Against the house, if you care to water, are river ferns (called wood fern in East Texas) and cardinal flower. And in the corner, which gets some good south sun, is a Texas mountain laurel, with fragrant phlox beneath. Along the left side of the limestone path that runs down the east side of the house, I've put shrubs. Aromatic sumac, which turns brilliant red and orange in the fall, will make a low thicket and continue to thrive as the mountain laurel grows larger. Next to the sumac are evergreen Texas barberries, which turn soft shades of plum and coral in the fall and hold their color all winter.

On the right side of the path is a shady flower garden. Here, again, the soil is about six inches deep. Baby blue eyes is a spring annual, followed by widow's tears, cutleaf daisy, and ruellia. Zexmenia blooms all summer, and white mistflower gives cool refreshing color in the fall. Far under the trees here and elsewhere in deep shade grow wild blue asters. The Lindheimer muhly, a grass endemic to the Edwards Plateau, has silvery plumes in the fall, making a striking tall accent. Let the leaves stay on all winter to continue to mark the path.

The path seems to end in a rock garden, which actually marks another terrace. The large plants in the rocks are a yaupon holly tree, a Mexican buckeye, and an agarito. The small plants are cedar sage and pigeonberry, which grow down below on either side of the stepping-stones. These wind through with one path leading down to the river and another to the back steps. This area is shady, and cedar sage, cutleaf daisy, and zexmenia will take up residence here.

At the back steps (a circular stair) is the second patio, also limestone, with frogfruit between the stones. A natural-looking line of big boulders keeps the terrace for this patio from eroding. This patio is carefully graded to help rainwater from the roof run off by the two junipers and down into the eastern arroyo. The arroyos form shallow pathways in dry weather, with the stone exposed and swept clean of vegetation.

The lowest terrace, which marks the last high ground untouched by floods, has a flagstone path leading through flowers, an inviting way to get from the terrace down to the river. The flowers here and around the back patio are growing in grass. As dense as in a garden, they have been planted, weeded, and watered on occasion to prolong blooming and to make a graceful transition from the house to the wild meadow. The grass of choice would be buffalo or curly mesquite grass, as both are naturally short.

Sprinkle the whole area with white rain lilies to bloom in the spring, the fall, or both. Other flowers here are mealy blue sage for blue color in spring, summer, and fall; calylophus and cutleaf daisy for spring yellow, and two-leaved senna for summer yellow; and Mexican hat for red and yellow color all the time. Two yuccas, with spires of white waxy blooms, and a boulder mark the step from this garden to the meadow. Many, many more flowers could be planted here, such as gayfeather, penstemons, blackfoot daisy, prairie verbena—whatever grows in your area that is under two feet tall. Cut off old bloom stalks as in the flower bed to keep a neat appearance.

A special pocket of pink is designed for the moon-shaped bit of grass on the east side of the patio under the young live oak. Plant this area thickly with purple paintbrush and pink evening primrose. The two shades of pink blooming simultaneously in May make a striking picture.

The west side of the house is brutally hot and dry, but there is lots of good easy-care color here. The multitrunked Texas red oak is in a little hollow with cedar sage and silvery artemesia. Its bark is patchy-white and colorful by itself, but the red leaves in the fall are what you will wait for each year—especially when it times itself with the Texas ash, which displays yellow, orange, lime, and mauve all on one tree. Before the leaves turn, usually in October, this area will be ablaze with yellow from one or more sunflower goldeneye. The Texas redbuds provide the spring color—purply-pink blooms in early spring and cherry-red seedpods in late spring. Also, at some point in the spring, usually in late March, fragrant mimosa will cover itself with pale pink puffs.

At the corner of the house is a Texas persimmon. The smooth white trunk makes this tree a lovely sight even when it is bare in the winter. And its purple fruits, ripening all through the summer, are a definite crowd-pleaser as far as birds are concerned.

Between the persimmon and the extension of the front patio by the storage room is one of my favorite gardens. This scene is extremely drought-tolerant and looks good all year, but I love it best when the flowers are in bloom. The ground is covered with exposed limestone and curly mesquite grass. In the corner, to give some height against the stuccoed wall of the house, is an evergreen sumac. Yuccas and sotols provide more evergreens. Use the native twisted-leaf yucca, which has white margins along the twisting leaves. Color accents are velvetleaf senna (yellow in late summer and in fall) and gayfeather (purple and very showy in the fall). Spring color could be blue Texas star (*Amsonia ciliata*), yellow evening primrose, winecup, prairie verbena, blackfoot daisy, calylophus, purple paintbrush, and so on.

These stretches of grassland are what most Northerners think Texas is all about. West Texas is the southernmost extension of the Great Plains. Photo by the authors.

West Texas

Abilene, Wichita Falls, San Angelo, Midland-Odessa

RED ROLLING PLAINS

Regional Description

A. C. Green, in *A Personal Country*, says West Texas begins just past Mineral Wells, on the west side of the Brazos, and ends at the Pecos and Red rivers. That description matches pretty well the area where mesquites are the best candidates for trees—that is, if they get enough moisture to get tall enough to be called trees. Most of this country is known as the Red Rolling Plains. Geologically speaking, Midland and Odessa are actually on the High Plains, but because they get milder winter temperatures than Lubbock and Amarillo, they are in West Texas for the purposes of this book.

The Red Rolling Plains (also called the Permian Red Beds) gets its name from the soil, which is a varied and beautiful assortment of reds ranging from dark rust to pale pink. Not a lot of rain falls here, so the vivid red soils are exposed in places where vegetation cannot completely cover the ground. These reds combine with the silver of sand sagebrush, the whites, yellows, pinks, and purples of the wildflowers, and the greens of low shrubs and spring grasses to create outstandingly lovely landscape scenes.

Together with the High Plains, this region marks the southern end of the Great Plains of the central United States. Once upon a time, hard as it may be to visualize, tallgrasses and midgrasses stretched to the horizon.

The eastern boundary is the Western Cross Timbers, roughly at the 98th meridian, which neatly marks where the rainfall abruptly drops below 30 inches a year. Here woodlands virtually disappear. True, mesquites are everywhere, but they get progressively shorter and scrubbier the farther north and west you go.

The 100th meridian also falls within this area, and it more or less marks where rainfall drops below 25 inches a year. At this line, watering is necessary to get grasses reestablished. From here west the soil is highly visible where the prairie has been overgrazed.

May and September are special months in West Texas—that's when rain is most likely to fall. Summers start at very hot and go on up from there. Drying winds accelerate an already cruel evaporation rate, so rainfall in these parts doesn't do as much good as it does in kinder climates.

It matters a lot whether your soil is sand or clay. Vegetation can get along fine in sand because a small amount of water soaks in quickly and deeply. Tight clays, though, can be as hospitable to plant life as the middle of a concrete patio.

Gaining a little shade and protection from the wind makes the moisture go farther. At natural breaks in the land, several woody species live, including Mohr oak (a kind of live oak), oneseed juniper, and soapberry.

Elevations in West Texas range from 800 feet at Mineral Wells to 3,000 feet at Midland-Odessa. Because of the high altitude, Midland and Odessa are as cold as Wichita Falls, which is much farther north. Their record lows are −11° F and −12°, respectively. Average winter lows are 31° to 33°, Abilene and San Angelo being the warmer cities. Summer averages range from 98° for San Angelo and Wichita Falls to 94° for Midland-Odessa and Abilene. Average annual rainfalls range from 26 inches in Wichita Falls to 23 inches in Abilene to 17 inches in San Angelo and only 13 inches in Midland. Despite the wide range in rainfall, the majority of plant species, predominantly shrubs and flowers, are surprisingly consistent.

The land is beautiful on the breaks but rather fragile. I have designed a plan that shows you how to civilize and augment a natural landscape. For a more formal approach, turn to the High Plains Plan or any of the theme garden plans, especially the Sand Garden Plan in Chapter 4, and then refer to the West Texas Plan for a list of the plants best suited for your needs.

West Texas Plan
Lot Size: 100′ × 150′

The natural vegetation of West Texas often gets a bad rap from folks who aren't familiar with the region. It really isn't flat and boring; it rolls. Everywhere there are hundreds of wildflowers. They're just small; you can't always spot them going by on the Interstate at 65 miles per hour. But jog north or south a bit and ride some of the state highways, and you'll see some truly gorgeous country. In the mesquite woods and particularly on the breaks, the plant life is amazingly colorful and attractive.

This plan is designed for those of you who live in either of these two environments. It shows you how to appreciate and augment your existing vegetation so you'll have a natural-looking, easy-care showplace. If you think the plantings are spaced farther apart than on other plans, you're right; they're reflecting the natural spacing of trees and shrubs in West Texas.

The dotted line shows where the land drops off abruptly. Normally, this drop-off would be called a cliff or an escarpment, but in these parts it's called a "break" because the land is mostly sand and clay and isn't rocky. This environment is extremely vulnerable to damage from wind and water. If you're fortunate enough to own such a piece of land, cherish it. Don't pull out plants you don't like; you risk starting erosion that might threaten the plants you do like. Be extremely cautious about adding anything to the site or taking anything away from it.

On the other hand, there are some plants I would add if I owned such a site and they weren't already growing there. I've indicated some particularly eye-catching ones on the plan. On an actual break, you would see far more variety—tufts of different grasses, many more flowers, and numerous other small shrubs.

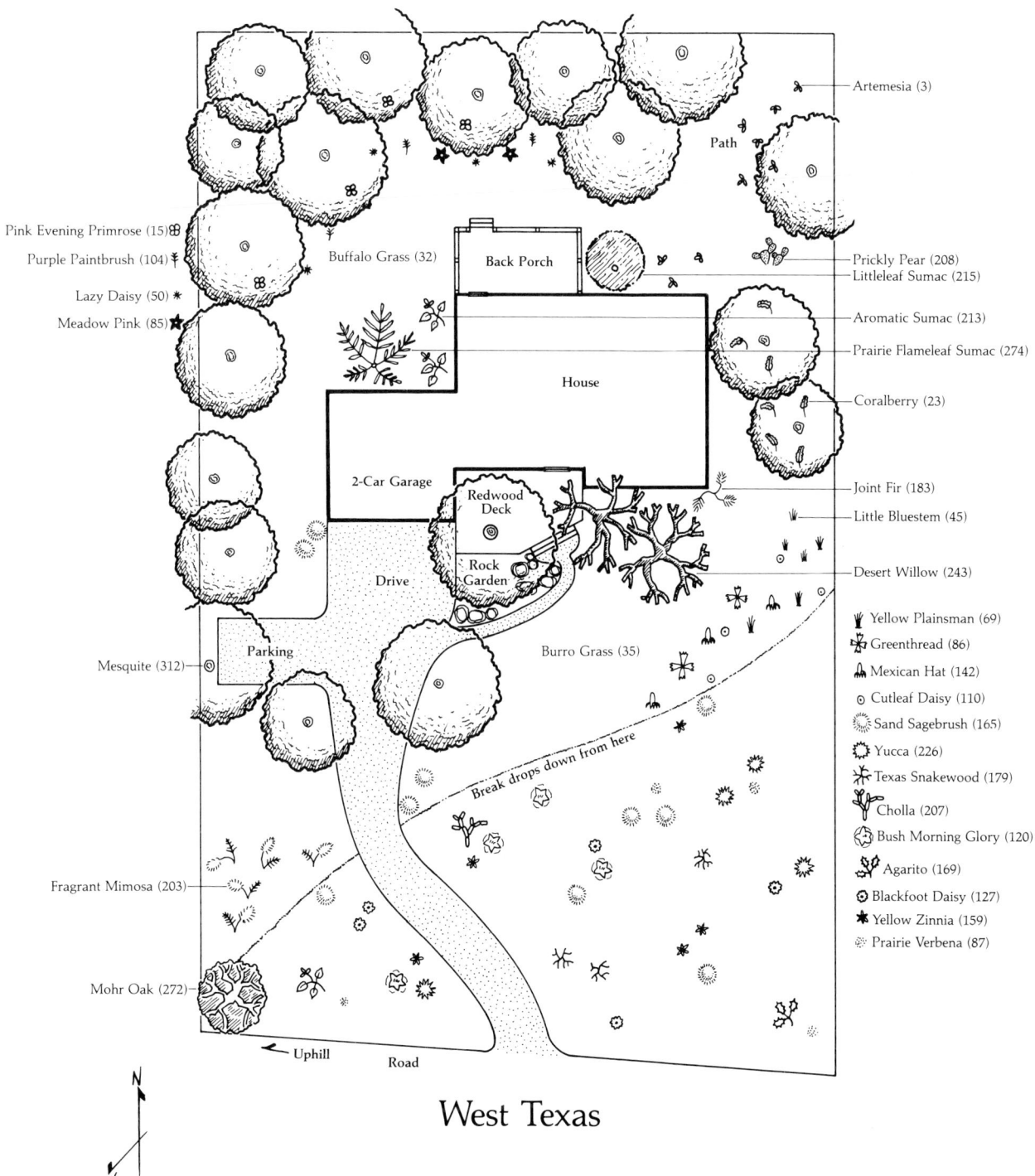

Artemesia (3)

Path

Pink Evening Primrose (15)
Purple Paintbrush (104)

Buffalo Grass (32)

Back Porch

Prickly Pear (208)
Littleleaf Sumac (215)

Lazy Daisy (50)
Meadow Pink (85)

Aromatic Sumac (213)
Prairie Flameleaf Sumac (274)

House

Coralberry (23)

2-Car Garage

Redwood
Deck

Joint Fir (183)
Little Bluestem (45)

Rock
Garden

Drive

Desert Willow (243)

Mesquite (312)

Parking

Burro Grass (35)

Break drops down from here

Yellow Plainsman (69)
Greenthread (86)
Mexican Hat (142)
Cutleaf Daisy (110)
Sand Sagebrush (165)
Yucca (226)
Texas Snakewood (179)
Cholla (207)
Bush Morning Glory (120)
Agarito (169)
Blackfoot Daisy (127)
Yellow Zinnia (159)
Prairie Verbena (87)

Fragrant Mimosa (203)

Mohr Oak (272)

Uphill   Road

N

SW

West Texas

Let me describe what is drawn on the plan. For winter color, I've included the silver-green of sand sagebrush, the dark spiky green of yucca, the blue or green of agarito, the interestingly shaped and marked branches of Texas snakewood, and the cholla. Dependable color from spring to frost is provided by three little flowers: blackfoot daisy (white), yellow zinnia, and prairie verbena (purple). In spring and early summer there will be splashes of big purple flowers from the bush morning glory, and brilliant magenta flowers from the cholla. Also blooming are narrowleaf yucca and fragrant mimosa, a small airy shrub that covers itself with dainty pink flowers.

If all of the plants I've indicated on this break aren't already there, they can be added. It's best to start off with very small plants that have as much root as possible. They should be planted in cool weather and then watched and hand-watered diligently for at least two years. Too much extra water on the whole break could be disastrous.

Trees are somewhat scarce in West Texas, but when you do spot one, most likely it's a mesquite. If you're near a creek, look for soapberries. Mohr oak, a small drought-tolerant live oak, can also be found here, and I've put one on the edge of the break. This isn't exactly an abundance of variety, so for this plan I've cheated and brought in two trees to plant around the house that are not strictly indigenous but do exceptionally well throughout this area. Desert willow, with its narrow-leaved foliage and ever-present flowers, is drought-tolerant and winter-hardy up to the Red River. Prairie flameleaf sumac, native all around West Texas, is another outstanding tree for this area. It has white summer flowers, red fruits for birds, and bright red fall foliage.

All the large circles on the plan are existing mesquites. Near Abilene they can achieve shade-tree height all on their own. But farther west they require slow, deep watering every so often to turn them from shrubs into real trees.

A grove of mesquites embraces the house, providing a windbreak and light shade to prolong the blooming season of the wildflowers that grow in the soft buffalo grass. Pink evening primrose and purple paintbrush, two perennials, should increase and get more lush every year. Lazy daisy and meadow pink are annuals. The color scheme here is delicate—limy-green mesquite leaves and rosy to pale pink flowers, with stars of white lazy daisy in the afternoons. These flowers have a fairly long blooming season, but they'll usually be at their most spectacular in May.

Near the back porch I've placed a littleleaf sumac, a shrub that normally gets quite big. But every so often, I'm told, you'll come across a less ambitious one that reaches only moderate height. Either way, it will fill the corner and attract lots of birds. In the fall it will turn purple, mauve, and red. On the other side of the porch are aromatic sumac, which turns red and orange, and prairie flameleaf sumac, which turns red. For a touch of clear, deep yellow, substitute a soapberry for the flameleaf.

At the back of the plan, you'll notice a gap in the mesquites. This is a path and can be mowed or unmowed. It leads to another part of the prop-

This lovely spring garden, designed by homeowner Mary Buchanan of Abilene, lies in a grove of mesquites. Pink evening primrose, hybrid verbena, and lazy daisy (not yet open; it's early morning) bloom in a sweep of unmown native grasses. Accent shrubs are red yucca, santolina (not a native), yucca, and cenizo. Photo by the authors.

erty that isn't included on this plan. Many properties in this region are fairly large, so it's not unlikely that someone using this landscape scheme might have an orchard, a vegetable garden, or even a horse pasture beyond the confines of this drawing. Since this is my fantasy plan, I envision the path leading to a semiwild pasture. Bordering the path and also under the little-leaf sumac by the porch is artemesia—evergreen, silvery, and aromatic.

There's another natural gap in the mesquites about thirty feet east of the porch. And since one path is enough, I've closed off the gap by placing a prickly pear here. This tends to give the feeling of a private, enclosed back yard.

The next two mesquites, on the east side of the house, are shaded from the west sun by the house. Under them grows a thicket of coralberry. This is also an excellent place to put wildflowers.

To continue the feel of a home entirely enveloped in vegetation, I've planted a patch of little bluestem between the last two mesquites and the break. The pale blue grass echoes the silvery-green sand sagebrush of the break to give coherence to the whole front yard.

Opposite the little bluestem, at the corner of the house, is a plant that is frankly hard to find—joint fir. The firlike texture of this dark green, graceful, evergreen shrub makes it one of my favorites. Animals love it too, so when you manage to locate one, it's usually under prickly shrubs or trees where it won't get nibbled to death. It's also hard to propagate, which accounts for its scarcity in nurseries.

Between the joint fir (also called Mormon tea) and the redwood deck are two desert willows, where their blooms, from spring to frost, can be easily enjoyed.

Underneath them and in a sweep to the edge of the break, I suggest a lawn of burro grass. The sun shining through the pink flowers of this grass, as seen from the deck or house, is incredibly lovely. In the grass are yellow long-blooming wildflowers: greenthread, yellow plainsman, Mexican hat, and cutleaf daisy.

The only part of the entire landscape that requires weeding is the rock garden by the front entrance. It gets a little bit of shade from the big old mesquite that was enclosed in the deck. On a slope held by boulders, this rock garden is approximately 17 feet by 11 feet at its maximum dimensions and can be populated from the enormous selection of small well-behaved flowers available in this area. For ideas, refer to both the Rock Garden Plan and the Sand Garden Plan.

Some rock garden plants native to West Texas are gayfeather (*Liatris punctata*), blackfoot daisy, yellow zinnia, prairie verbena, calylophus, white milkwort, paperflower, Tiny Tim, shrubby skullcap, dwarf germander, abronia, lazy daisy, sleepy daisy, and Tahoka daisy. With a little water and/or winter protection, many others in this book can be used. You can also find lots of possibilities in neighboring fields.

Once established, this kind of landscape can be totally drought-tolerant, but remember that establishing a plant takes two years. The first year, water once a week. The next year, water once every three weeks. After that, watering is optional, but to keep the plants looking fresher and healthier than in nature, water them whenever they stop blooming or about three times a year. The best watering is a slow, deep, overnight soaking.

The breaks along the Cap Rock in Palo Duro Canyon provide shade and wind protection. One-seed juniper, narrowleaf yucca, and clumps of grasses and flowers dot the red soil in this view. Photo by the authors.

High Plains

Lubbock, Amarillo
(Borger, Childress, Muleshoe, Pampa, Plainview)

HIGH PLAINS, ROLLING PLAINS, THE PANHANDLE

Regional Description

The High Plains is a flat plateau 3,000 to 4,700 feet above sea level. Together with the Red Rolling Plains, it forms the southern tip of the Great Plains of the western United States. It is composed of rocks and soils that eroded off the Rocky Mountains. The soils consist of clays and sands over caliche. Midland and Odessa are actually on High Plains soils, but being at the southern end, they are so much warmer in the winter than Lubbock and Amarillo that they have a different range of plants and are included in the West Texas Plan.

The High Plains south of the Canadian River is the fabled Llano Estacado. You can stand here, and on a clear day you can see, as the song says, forever. What you won't see is trees or shrubs. Just buffalo grass, blue grama, and an occasional yucca, or, if the land has been overgrazed, burro grass.

In the sandhills near Muleshoe are tiny Havard oaks. To see other shrubs, you have to go down in the breaks on the Canadian River or just off the Cap Rock or to that little hollow northwest of Amarillo called Bishop Hills. But as soon as you go into the breaks, you are on the Rolling Plains. In other words, you practically have to get off the High Plains and get on to the Rolling Plains to see a woody plant.

The Rolling Plains in the Panhandle are beautiful. You see silvery sand sagebrush, dark clumps of juniper or agarito, and wildflowers, including yellow zinnia, white blackfoot daisy, rose-pink heart's delight, purple prairie verbena, and pale pink, fragrant spectacle pod. Then, as the sun gets higher, the yellow sleepy daisies and white lazy daisies unfold. It's a flower garden set into red soil against a bright blue sky.

Rainfall averages 17 to 20 inches annually on the High Plains, most of it falling in May and June. Many years, this area gets 12 inches or even less. No rivers traverse the High Plains. What rainfall there is collects in playa lakes, depressions that can cover many acres and might contain several feet of standing water just after a heavy rain. Arrowhead, knotweed (*Polygonum* spp.), baby's breath aster, and other flowers grow in the playas as the water slowly evaporates. There are rivers in the Rolling Plains, but they are dry most of the year except for the Canadian River and the Prairie Dog Town Fork of the Red River.

The aquifers of the Ogallala Formation have been providing the bulk of the public water supply for years, but they are running low. Lake Meredith is salty. Obviously, what we want to accomplish here is a first-class landscape that uses as little water as possible.

The High Plains is the chilliest region in Texas. Average winter lows are 20° to 26° F and record lows are −21° in Muleshoe and −16° in Lubbock and Amarillo. Because of their lower altitude, the cities on the Rolling Plains are not quite so bitterly cold, but on the average they are only one degree warmer. The summers in the High Plains average 92° highs—cooler than anywhere else in Texas except in Galveston.

In all other regional plans, the plants I've used have been indigenous to the area. I'm making an exception for West Texas and the High Plains because these regions have almost no indigenous trees. All trees in the High Plains region need some water to remain healthy after getting established, but the ones recommended in this plan will require the least water.

Those of you with land on a break should turn to the West Texas Plan for ideas on how to accommodate the natural beauty of your land. Prune out deadwood, but otherwise keep all vegetation on your property that doesn't stick or sting near a walking area. When you add color, make your selections from the plant list for the High Plains to make sure your choices are winter-hardy.

If you're on flat land or an abandoned farm, examine the Mountain Garden Plan in Chapter 8 (Conifers). It is geared as much to you as to the High Country of the Trans-Pecos. Although half the trees on the plan are not native for your area, alligator juniper, weeping juniper, blue Douglas fir, Rocky Mountain ponderosa pine, bigtooth maple, and chinquapin oak already like your temperatures and just need some watering to be excellent trees for your area.

And for those of you with a regular city lot, the High Plains Plan is my suggestion for an attractive drought-tolerant landscape.

HIGH PLAINS PLAN
Lot Size: 80' × 120'

Talk about a challenge! The High Plains region is cold, dry, and windy. Sun and wind rob the soil of what little moisture it gets. Winters here are the coldest in Texas. This is a hard environment in which to create an elegant landscape with flower gardens, shade, and intimacy, not to mention low water use and easy maintenance. Yet, in spite of all the negatives (or possibly because of them), this landscape turned out to be one of my favorite plans in this whole book.

The key to this design is the use of numerous large stepping-stones, which provide walkways and patios while also creating flower beds. They furnish a cool damp place for roots to grow during hot weather, provide protection for those roots in the winter, cut down on weeding, and prevent erosion.

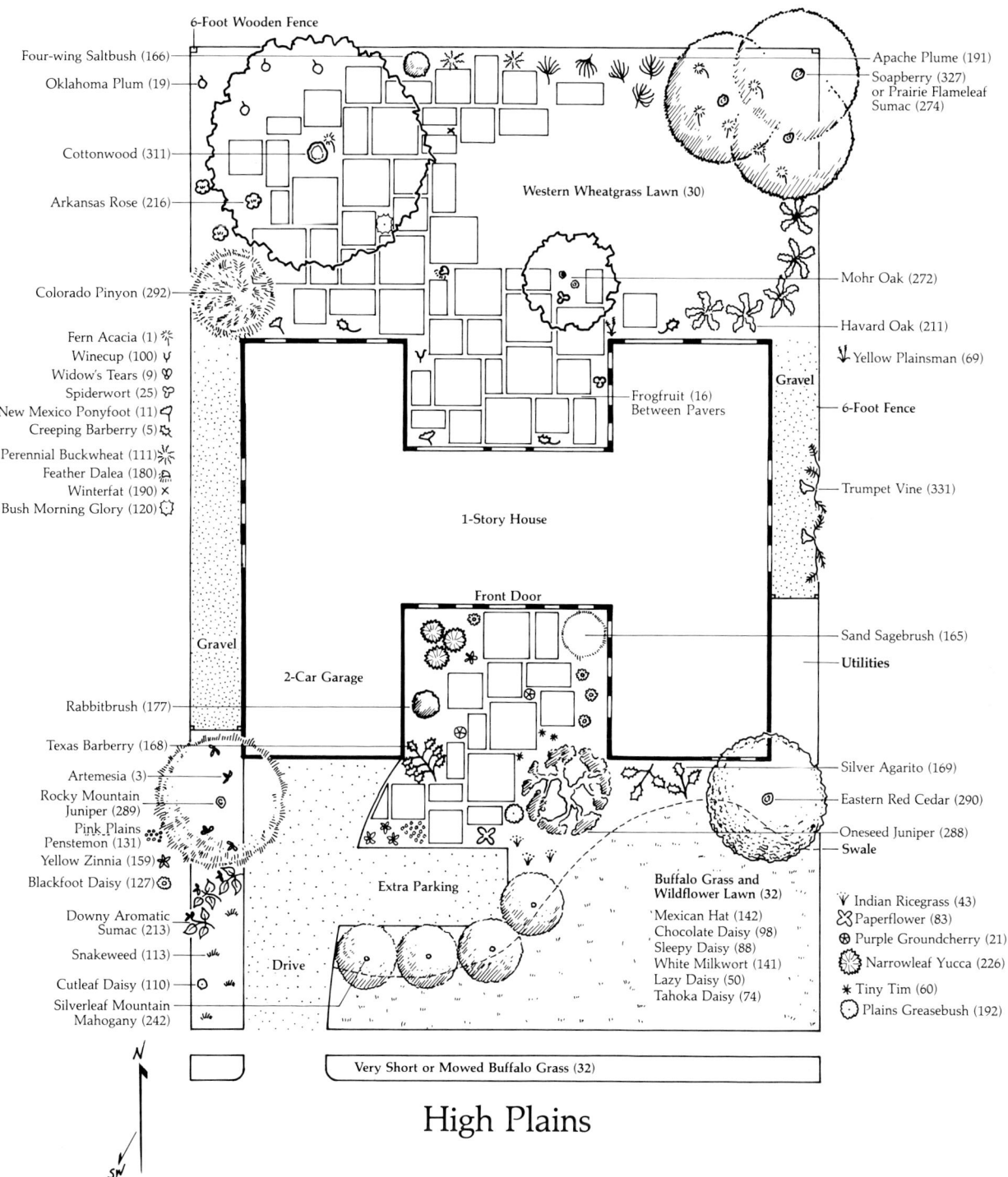

6-Foot Wooden Fence

Four-wing Saltbush (166)

Oklahoma Plum (19)

Cottonwood (311)

Arkansas Rose (216)

Colorado Pinyon (292)

Fern Acacia (1)
Winecup (100)
Widow's Tears (9)
Spiderwort (25)
New Mexico Ponyfoot (11)
Creeping Barberry (5)
Perennial Buckwheat (111)
Feather Dalea (180)
Winterfat (190)
Bush Morning Glory (120)

Gravel

Rabbitbrush (177)

Texas Barberry (168)
Artemesia (3)
Rocky Mountain
Juniper (289)
Pink Plains
Penstemon (131)
Yellow Zinnia (159)
Blackfoot Daisy (127)

Downy Aromatic
Sumac (213)
Snakeweed (113)
Cutleaf Daisy (110)
Silverleaf Mountain
Mahogany (242)

Apache Plume (191)
Soapberry (327)
or Prairie Flameleaf
Sumac (274)

Western Wheatgrass Lawn (30)

Mohr Oak (272)

Havard Oak (211)

Yellow Plainsman (69)

Gravel

6-Foot Fence

Frogfruit (16)
Between Pavers

Trumpet Vine (331)

1-Story House

Front Door

Sand Sagebrush (165)

Utilities

2-Car Garage

Silver Agarito (169)

Eastern Red Cedar (290)

Oneseed Juniper (288)
Swale

Extra Parking

Buffalo Grass and
Wildflower Lawn (32)

Mexican Hat (142)
Chocolate Daisy (98)
Sleepy Daisy (88)
White Milkwort (141)
Lazy Daisy (50)
Tahoka Daisy (74)

Drive

Indian Ricegrass (43)
Paperflower (83)
Purple Groundcherry (21)
Narrowleaf Yucca (226)
Tiny Tim (60)
Plains Greasebush (192)

N

SW

Very Short or Mowed Buffalo Grass (32)

High Plains

These stones are actually poured concrete slabs in four sizes. The large squares are six feet square, the smaller squares are four feet square, and the rectangles are six by three feet and four by two feet. Spaces between the stones are generally from six to nine inches, with some large spaces of one to two feet to accommodate masses of flowers or small shrubs.

Both the front and back yards are contoured so that they will retain rainwater. I don't mean that you are going to create your own playa lake; excess water from a gully washer has a way to drain off. But a few shallow, well-placed swales (subtle hollows) let rainwater and irrigation water soak in slowly and deeply where it is most needed.

The gently curving dotted line in the front yard is a shallow swale that collects water draining from the sidewalk, the house, and the driveway. The extra water retained by this swale makes it possible to grow trees and shrubs on its banks with a minimum of supplemental water.

In the back yard the whole western wheatgrass lawn is slightly lower than the rest of the yard, and everything in the back yard slopes into it. This slope is also subtle. You would not be immediately conscious of this contouring. Western wheatgrass loves to grow in ditches and needs water in the summer to stay as green as it is in winter. To keep it evenly green, the lawn itself should be almost level, draining slightly toward the corner of the house.

The plants surrounding the lawn are drought-tolerant and like to be well drained. There are two reasons why you don't want to give these plants too much water: (1) they don't need it and will only get sickly, and (2) western wheatgrass is very aggressive and will enthusiastically head for the moister soil.

A note on watering: Deep overnight soaking with a drip irrigation system or a soaker hose is most efficient. Because these methods prevent wasteful runoff and evaporation, every drop soaks into the soil. Deep soaking helps the roots grow deep, flushes out salts, and best approximates a good rain. Watering should also be done in the evening or at night, when no sun and low winds cause as little evaporation as possible.

Aside from these points, there are no hard-and-fast watering rules. So much depends on the drought tolerance of the plants, the soil type and depth, the weather . . . you get the idea. As a general rule, plants will need more water during the period when they're getting established, a process that can take up to two years. After the first few weeks of intensive care, water once a week for a year, then every three weeks during the second year. Thereafter two or three soakings a year is generally adequate for trees, shrubs, and grasses. In the flowering areas around the stones, water whenever the blooms slack off.

Everything on this plan is indigenous to the region except Colorado pinyon, Texas barberry, Apache plume, creeping barberry, and trumpet vine. They might need a little more water, especially during the summer, but don't forget that winters can be dry too. Keep an eye on them, and use your own good judgment. Just remember that native plants, once established, are more often harmed by overwatering than by drought.

Now, imagine that this plan has been executed and is looking at its best. Let's walk through the landscape to see what it really looks like. As you drive up, the first thing you notice is a mass of varied evergreens that screen the entrance and the extra parking and provide a richly textured backdrop for the meadow of buffalo grass and wildflowers. One of the swales runs at their feet to get them the extra moisture they need.

The most prominent of the evergreens is the trio of conifers—Rocky Mountain juniper, eastern red cedar, and the shrubbier oneseed juniper. They are normally dark green, but the females will have a bluish cast when in fruit. The Rocky Mountain juniper has to be pruned up the trunk to keep the driveway usable, but the branches of the other two junipers should grow down to the ground. The average height here for many years will be about ten feet, though these trees have the potential of reaching twenty feet.

Among these junipers, I've placed silver agaritos (called algeritas in this region). Unlike the regular agarito, this particular evergreen has leaves that are actually silvery blue. This foliage makes a fine contrast and works well with the silverleaf mountain mahoganies that screen the parking area. Next to them are a few clumps of Indian ricegrass, which dries in midsummer to a pale ivory and holds that color all winter if winds don't beat it up. It grows about knee-high.

The look of the agaritos and mountain mahoganies would be totally ruined if they were clipped into carefully manicured hedges. Instead, they should be allowed to develop and express their own personalities. Some should be allowed to droop low, providing extra screening. Let everything get as tall as it likes. Pick-prune them to keep a graceful shape if they get too dense.

West of the driveway, the silvery evergreen theme is continued with a stand of artemesia planted at the base of the Rocky Mountain juniper. Seasonal color is provided by the downy aromatic sumac (better-behaved than the regular aromatic sumac, at least according to my observations so far). It turns red and orange in the fall and has little creamy-yellow flowers in the spring. The chief color comes from the gutierrezias, commonly called snakeweed, broomweed, turpentine weed, or matchweed, which are about a foot tall and form a sort of billowing lime-green ground cover that turns bright yellow in the fall. In the spring and well into the summer three yellow-flowered cutleaf daisies, planted in a clump, provide a focus of color.

There are always plenty of flowers east of the driveway. This area is what I referred to earlier as the meadow. It is actually a buffalo grass lawn planted thickly with wildflowers. On the parkway, keep the grass mowed. On your property, mow it only after frost or if it grows too tall for your taste. If you barely or rarely water here, it should stay at four to six inches. Blue grama is another nice turf grass that could be used here, and many people plant a mixture of blue grama and buffalo grass.

The wildflowers are mostly yellow: Mexican hat with splashes of orange or maroon, chocolate daisy with its subtle chocolaty aroma, and sleepy daisy, which is a pure, deep yellow. White milkwort and lazy daisy provide a delicate underblanket of white. Tahoka daisy adds touches of lavender. It and the other annuals seed out to keep new plants blooming continually, as long as the weather is warm.

Between the evergreens and the front door, I've created a delightful and intimate courtyard. There are enough evergreens to hold it together in the winter, but it's the masses of flowers during the warm months that will captivate you. Because the courtyard is small, the evergreens in it are all less than five feet tall.

One of my favorites is rabbitbrush, with its feathery silvery leaves. Abundant in Santa Fe, it is also found on the High Plains, where in late summer it displays deep-yellow flowers. When not in bloom, it looks a lot like sand sagebrush, an artemesia that is also present in this courtyard. Both contrast beautifully with the prickly, dark green foliage of the other evergreens.

The most dramatic of these is narrowleaf yucca, often called Spanish dagger, planted in a triple clump to accent the front door. Close to the parking area is the Texas barberry, kin to agarito but softer. Some of the leaves turn mauve and tangerine in the fall and stay that way all winter. Spicy-smelling yellow flowers appear in early spring. Although Texas barberry is not native to the High Plains, it is reported to grow well here. Opposite it is the oneseed juniper. This tree gets two styles of pruning. Inside the courtyard it is pruned up high to show off its gnarled, twisting trunk. Outside, its branches are allowed to grow low to form the eastern wall of the enclosure.

Among and in front of the evergreens, and between the stones, is a riot of dazzling color. It starts in March, when the plains greasebush becomes a cumulus cloud of white flowers.

Nearly all the flowers start blooming in April, and continue until frost. Yellow zinnias, less than a foot tall, are massed solidly in front of a large mound of pale pink plains penstemon. These two plants bloom so thickly that the foliage hardly shows from spring to frost. A yellow paperflower nearby is just as extravagant.

Tiny Tim, a petite plant with miniature yellow daisylike flowers, forms carpets of gold. Several kinds grow in this region, some with green leaves and some with silver. Under the windows and catching the west sun, I've placed a large planting of blackfoot daisy. Like the yellow zinnias, the daisies form a solid mass of everblooming color that spills over and softens the edges of the stones. The flowers are white and smell like wild honey when the sun is strong on them.

Every other inch of ground is carpeted with purple groundcherry, which creeps two to four inches high among the stones and under the shrubs, blooming from early spring to frost.

The backdrop in the back yard is a six-foot cedar (or redwood) fence that

James Stewart Minton, a landscape designer in Lubbock, designed this easy-care, drought-tolerant landscape. Large local rocks form planting areas for pinyon pine, narrowleaf yucca, and two nonnatives—'Wilton carpet' juniper and santolina. In between, he left undisturbed the naturally short-growing buffalo grass with its myriad wildflowers. Photo by the authors.

also protects against winter winds. Here the color will be dictated by the seasons.

Winter foliage is provided by the Mohr oak, which has gray-green leaves, the Colorado pinyon, which is deep olive green, and the four-wing saltbush, which is silvery green.

There are two shady winter ground covers. The first is the charming creeping barberry, which is like the Texas barberry in that its leaves turn mauve, rose, yellow, and tangerine and then hold that color all winter. New growth is also rosy. The other is New Mexico ponyfoot, with wavy-edged, fan-shaped leaves. I've planted both next to the house, where they should be allowed to extend themselves wherever they like. The western wheat-grass lawn is a pale bluish green all winter.

For winter color the star of the winter garden is a little shrub called winterfat. Be sure you get a female; its plumy fruits will cover her in a silvery glow when backlit by the sun. But there must be a male lurking about the immediate neighborhood somewhere to fertilize the female. If there isn't, plant one on the sunny side of the house.

After the weather warms up in the spring, many flowers will fill in the spaces between the stones. One of the dominant ones is frogfruit, a low ground cover that will take moderate amounts of foot traffic. It's a member of the verbena family and is spotted with tiny clusters of white flowers in the spring, summer, and fall.

In shady places, I've indicated blue widow's tears (under the Mohr oak) and lavender spiderwort. Winecups also look magnificent here when they're in bloom. Established ones sprawl out for two or three feet and hold up deep-purple, cup-shaped flowers.

For the sunnier spots, I'd suggest seeding between the stones with sleepy daisy and lazy daisy, two annuals that open in the late morning.

In late spring and throughout the summer, bush morning glory will bloom. This is one of my favorite flowers. Another is the yellow plainsman, which is close to the corner of the house by the Mohr oak. It has silver leaves and deep-yellow clusters of flowers that last well as cut flowers. The back fence is dominated by Apache plume. Nonnative to the Texas High Plains, but very adaptable here, this hardy little shrub displays white rose flowers and pinkish plumes simultaneously all during the warm weather.

For the big shade tree, I'd choose a cottonwood because I like cotton-woods. But I realize that most of you wouldn't, because of its bad reputation for taking advantage of leaky plumbing. You might opt for a chinquapin oak, a bur oak, or even a southern sugar maple, if it can get nonsalty water. These three are not native to the area but should be good choices. Whatever shade tree winds up here, under it are two thickets. The Oklahoma plum, a cloud of pristine white in early spring, is followed by the Arkansas rose, with its display of pink. All summer, the delicate foliage of fern acacia makes soft green masses under both the shade tree and the minigrove in the north-west corner.

The minigrove is a cluster of three smaller trees that can be either soapberry or prairie flameleaf sumac. They both turn color in the fall—the soapberry being a pure yellow, and the sumac bright red.

Other fall color comes from the four-wing saltbush, which has yellow fruits (if female), the perennial buckwheats, and the feather dalea, whose small silver leaves get covered by purple blooms.

The thicket of Havard oak becomes profusely sprinkled with unexpectedly large acorns. The curly-edged leaves, which show furry white undersides, present a coarsely attractive texture.

In the autumn, after all the leaves have fallen, rake them into the thickets and over the flower beds. Cut the stems of the perennials down to about three inches so they can catch the leaves and keep them from blowing away. This blanket will protect the roots from winter cold and will rot away the next spring to form humus for new growth.

McKittrick Canyon is one of the most popular spots in Texas every October when the bigtooth maples turn red, orange, and yellow. Here, in a dry, rocky portion of the limestone stream bed, can be seen the maple, Rocky Mountain ponderosa pine, sotol, and a clump of bull muhly grass. Photo by the authors.

El Paso

El Paso

TRANS-PECOS

Regional Description

Most of the people who live in the Trans-Pecos live in El Paso, the driest city in Texas. Founded on the Rio Grande, it used to have an adequate supply of water from the river, but so many users upstream are diverting water, and the city has grown so large, that water is becoming increasingly precious.

Luckily, there is a great deal of natural beauty in this part of the state, with the most varied and attractive vegetation located on either side of the city itself—along the Rio Grande and in the mountains. The plant life is well adapted to this harsh region and can live and look good on a bare minimum of water.

Most people who live in the Trans-Pecos outside of El Paso live in the mountainous areas. This region got its name from early explorers heading west—it was across (trans) the Pecos River. Elevations range from 2,500 to more than 8,500 feet. The soils are sands, clays, and gravels, always well drained. Rocks might be either limestone or igneous, as both types of mountains exist in this geologically interesting region. The Franklin Mountains above El Paso are both sedimentary and igneous, so the gravel and rocks in El Paso have a wide range of colors and shapes, many of them quartz.

Below the mountains lies the Chihuahuan Desert, which has its own look because its rainfall averages a mere 6 to 12 inches a year, too little to flush salts through the alkaline soils. As a result, they build up in low places called alkali flats, easily marked by four-wing saltbush. Other parts of the desert used to be well covered with tobosa grass, but overgrazing killed it, and the area was overtaken by Torrey yucca and then by creosote bush.

Rainfall improves in the mountains, with the annual average increasing to 16 to 20 inches. Unlike most of Texas, where rains are more likely to come in spring and fall, here the rains come in late summer—July, August, and September. This is when the majority of the flowers bloom.

The mountains are covered with shortgrasses, such as ear muhly and burro grass, among which bloom penstemons, chocolate daisy, and Mexican hat. The shrubs are outstanding here—small, dense, and covered with flowers. Cenizo (three kinds), scarlet bouvardia, daleas (all those found in this book plus others), yellow bells, Gregg coldenia, and skeleton-leaf goldeneye are some of my favorites. Conifers abound: alligator juniper, weeping juniper, Rocky Mountain ponderosa pine, and blue Douglas fir are especially noteworthy. But what draws several hundred people to the mountains of the Trans-Pecos every fall are the bigtooth maple and Texas madrone.

Unfortunately for El Paso, many of these mountain plants cannot take the heat in the city, where summer highs average 95° F. The bigtooth maple refuses to color, probably because there are not enough cool nights to trigger the turning before a freeze hits and kills the leaves. In fact, El Paso really has very mild winters. The average minimum January temperature in El Paso is 32°, usually dipping down to 5° or 10° each winter. It once plunged to −8°. However, these lows last for such a short time that many plants that would freeze elsewhere at the same temperatures are winter-hardy here.

The plan for this region is designed predominantly with El Paso in mind, as that benefits the greatest number of people. Everything I've put into the plan I have, with my own eyes, seen successfully growing down in El Paso, so I know it can take the summers there. I also include the lower slopes of the Franklin Mountains in this assessment.

Those of you who live high in the mountains, where it is appreciably cooler, should consult the Mountain Garden Plan in Chapter 8 (Conifers).

For more information on the plants and geography of this region, read the three books by Dr. Barton H. Warnock, retired professor from Sul Ross State University in Alpine.

El Paso Plan
Lot Size: 125′ × 80′

The El Paso Plan is divided into three basic parts. The front yard is totally drought-tolerant, at least it will be once it gets established. If you never water it, it will look like the Chihuahuan Desert, which is what it is. If you water deeply once or twice a year, it will look fabulous. If you water more, though, you can kill some plants. The garden illustrating this chapter used to have majestic yuccas in the rest of the front yard—magnificent towering specimens over a century old. Seems the neighbors uphill used a lot of water to maintain a back-East-style lawn. A lot of that water ran off their property down to the yuccas and gradually killed off every one.

The back yard around the patio is on a drip system. In it you will find many of the plants I suggested for the front yard. They are the ones that I have been told respond well to regular watering. Once or twice a month during the hot season should be sufficient to keep the flowers fresh and blooming.

The courtyard off the master bedroom is the oasis—the place where you can go and see lush green all year. It is on the east side of the house, protected from hot sun and drying winds. The flower beds are small, so water use is minimal. A corner fountain, with a recirculating pump, provides the soothing, cooling sound of running water.

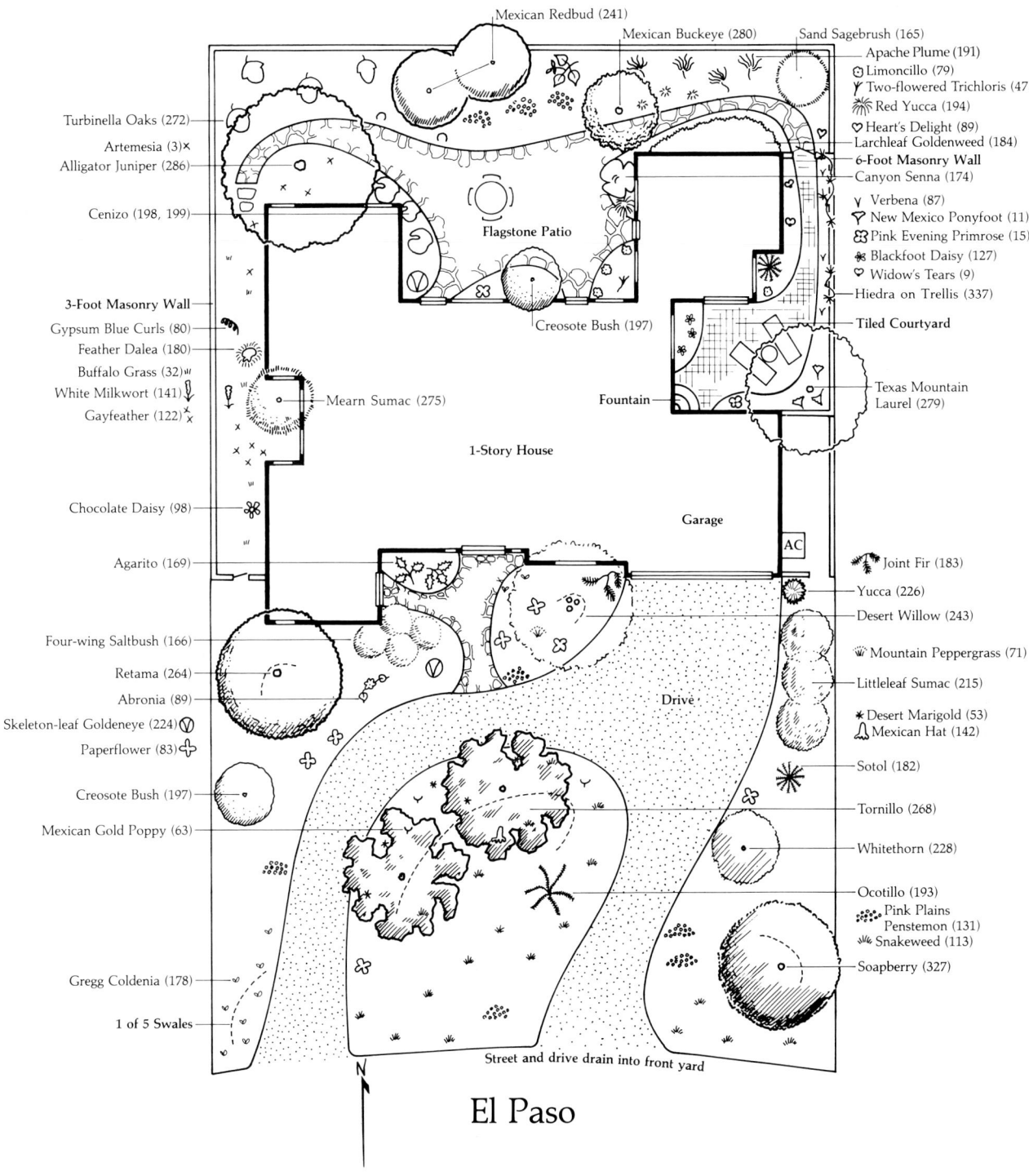

Mexican Redbud (241)

Mexican Buckeye (280)

Sand Sagebrush (165)

Apache Plume (191)
Limoncillo (79)
Two-flowered Trichloris (47)
Red Yucca (194)
Heart's Delight (89)
Larchleaf Goldenweed (184)
6-Foot Masonry Wall
Canyon Senna (174)

Verbena (87)
New Mexico Ponyfoot (11)
Pink Evening Primrose (15)
Blackfoot Daisy (127)
Widow's Tears (9)
Hiedra on Trellis (337)

Tiled Courtyard

Texas Mountain
Laurel (279)

Fountain

Turbinella Oaks (272)
Artemesia (3)
Alligator Juniper (286)

Cenizo (198, 199)

3-Foot Masonry Wall
Gypsum Blue Curls (80)
Feather Dalea (180)
Buffalo Grass (32)
White Milkwort (141)
Gayfeather (122)

Chocolate Daisy (98)

Agarito (169)

Four-wing Saltbush (166)
Retama (264)
Abronia (89)
Skeleton-leaf Goldeneye (224)
Paperflower (83)

Creosote Bush (197)
Mexican Gold Poppy (63)

Gregg Coldenia (178)

1 of 5 Swales

Flagstone Patio

Creosote Bush (197)

Mearn Sumac (275)

1-Story House

Garage

AC

Joint Fir (183)

Yucca (226)

Desert Willow (243)

Mountain Peppergrass (71)

Littleleaf Sumac (215)

Desert Marigold (53)
Mexican Hat (142)

Sotol (182)

Tornillo (268)

Whitethorn (228)

Ocotillo (193)
Pink Plains
Penstemon (131)
Snakeweed (113)

Soapberry (327)

Drive

Street and drive drain into front yard

N

El Paso

Since it rains so rarely in El Paso, street gutter systems aren't needed. By law, each landscape must retain its rainwater. There is normally a swale in the front to catch runoff from the street and driveway, and a masonry wall in back to keep that water from leaving your yard. This is first-rate water conservation. The five swales in this front yard are marked by dotted lines, and in all but one of the swales are trees. This is the only way to have trees in the front because they need more water than rainfall can provide. The swales catch the runoff and remain moist long after other sites have dried out.

The tree near the house is a desert willow. Many beautiful selections are available in nurseries already, and more are coming. The flowers bloom from spring to frost and can be all white, all maroon, or every shade of pink you can imagine, or they can appear in a wide array of combinations of those colors.

Also next to the house is a retama. Retama is probably naturalized rather than indigenous to El Paso. When I'm in this part of the state, I frequently see it growing wild along drainage ditches. Retama's yellow flowers are in bloom as long as the desert willow's, and its branches are always green. However, in a late spring freeze it often loses its branch tips.

In the big swale in front of the circular drive are two mesquites. If you have groundwater near the surface or can let the hose run in this swale a couple of times a year, you can choose the tornillo, the smaller mesquite with the delightful corkscrew beans.

The last tree in front is the soapberry, which turns gold in the fall, even in El Paso. The picture of the soapberry was taken just a few miles east of El Paso. Other fall color comes from the littleleaf sumacs, which turn rose and mauve.

The evergreens in front are agarito, four-wing saltbush, creosote bush, sotol, yucca, and joint fir. The snakeweed is almost evergreen and makes a novel ground cover. It grows up to a foot high and is a fuzzy light green, blooming a brilliant yellow in late summer and fall. Snakeweed is short-lived, so let it seed out and spread freely in the space within the driveway.

Besides the plants already named, all of which flower, those chosen especially for their blooms are skeleton-leaf goldeneye, abronia, paperflower, Gregg coldenia, Mexican gold poppies, pink plains penstemon, ocotillo, whitethorn acacia, Mexican hat, desert marigold, and mountain pepper-grass. All but the Mexican gold poppies, annuals that can form sheets of gold in the very early spring, are long-blooming. Except in the winter, there should always be at least three plants in bloom and usually seven or eight.

It is normal for there to be spaces of bare ground between plants. You don't need to put down black plastic and lava rocks or colored gravel. Beautiful rocks, pebbles, and gravels are endemic to the soil. Let them form the mulch, and let the flowers spread wherever they will. If you wound up with a bounty of splendid blooms, you wouldn't complain, would you?

Chances are that since you're not watering, you won't have to contend

When Anna Jane Duree and her husband bought this house in 1964, they were chiefly attracted to the forty-foot tree yuccas in th front yard. Unfortunately, uphill neighbors watered so much, to maintain a green lawn, that runoff ultimately killed the yuccas. This flower garden, which appreciates a little supplemental water, fared better. Here, in June, you can see a retama (which froze back some in March), pink evening primrose, prairie verbena, yucca, and littleleaf sumac. Nonnatives are vitex, hollyhock, bearded iris, canna, daylily, and several Mexican perennials. Photo by the authors.

with many weeds. It's only during those first two years, when you're watering a lot to get everything established, that you'll have to be diligent about getting rid of the interlopers.

Always give your landscape a long soaking rather than a sprinkle. This encourages deeper root growth and keeps salts in the water from accumulating in the soil. A soaking flushes the salts on through.

The drip-irrigated back yard is more densely planted, more conventional in its design. The patio, approximately twenty by sixteen feet of mortared flagstone, is surrounded on three sides by the house. I love lots of windows, so I gave this house a variety of colorful views from the living room, dining room, and master bedroom. I also put a table and chairs out on the patio so you can eat out there often and enjoy the year-round beauty.

Over in the northwest corner is a grove of turbinella oak. Actually, it will look more like a thicket for a few years, until it gradually grows ten to fifteen feet tall. Turbinella oaks are evergreen with thick, wavy bluegreen leaves. They and the alligator juniper protect your landscape from the west sun and winds.

For height and shade on the north, I've placed two Mexican redbuds and a Mexican buckeye—small pink-flowered trees that bloom, one after the other, in the spring. The shrubs here give fall and winter color, and the flowers in front bloom almost constantly from spring to frost.

By the house are more shrubs and flowers and a bunchgrass. The gorgeous canyon senna is placed next to a red yucca, not native here but well adapted. Benny Simpson first planted these two together, and the combination is so pretty, I couldn't resist passing on the idea here.

The next bed, going clockwise, has two-flowered trichloris, a showy grass, surrounded by the fragrant annual limoncillo. Next is creosote bush, which in this instance should grow thin and graceful, more like a miniature tree. Next to it is a paperflower, whose flowers look good both fresh and dried. Skeleton-leaf goldeneye (another everblooming yellow daisy bush) and cenizos complete the scene. Flower colors are yellow, pink, purple, red, and white. Leaf colors are green, silver, and blue.

The only shade on the west side of the house is cast by the low wall. There is a lot of reflected heat. The alcove with the only windows is shaded by an evergreen sumac, preferably the Mearn sumac. The ground is covered by buffalo grass with white milkwort, chocolate daisy, gayfeather, and gypsum blue curls blooming in it. The only shrub is a feather dalea. Grading into the courtyard under the alligator juniper is artemesia. Occasional watering will be necessary here.

Alongside the path leading to the courtyard is another artemesia—the shrubby sand sagebrush—and rose-colored heart's delight. The mass planting against the house is larchleaf goldenweed, a low-growing pungent shrub that completely covers itself with yellow flowers.

A wooden doorlike gate enters into the courtyard where the walls are six feet tall. The walk and patio are tiled and drain into the beds. The patio is just large enough to hold two lounge chairs and a table comfortably. A small amount of water dribbles from a tiled fountain into a shallow dish attached to the wall, overflows, and then splashes down into the pool, where it is pumped back up behind the wall and recirculated.

The tree is a Texas mountain laurel. It has dark, shiny evergreen leaves and, in early spring, large clusters of fragrant purple flowers. Under its shade grows a ground cover of evergreen New Mexico ponyfoot. In sunnier areas grows pink evening primrose, which I have been told is evergreen in El Paso if watered regularly.

Other flowers here are blackfoot daisy, limoncillo, widow's tears, and prairie verbena, another evergreen. The vine is the western Virginia creeper called hiedra. Its leaves are thicker, wavy-margined, and very glossy, and they also turn red in the fall. The sotol provides texture and anchors the corner by the window.

This courtyard is designed to have large masses of lush color. Although half the plants are not evergreen, the winter view from the windows is mostly green. You should water here more than you would elsewhere on this plan, but not excessively. These plants like good drainage. Observe them, experiment, and adjust your watering with the weather.

After a rain in June, brush along the Rio Grande turns pink, yellow, white, and purple. Here, several acres of cenizo are in full bloom, with skeleton-leaf goldeneye, heartleaf hibiscus, Texas lantana, and Mexican olive close by. Photo by the authors.

Valley

Brownsville, Laredo
(Edinburg, Harlingen, McAllen, Raymondville)

RIO GRANDE VALLEY

Regional Description

The Lower Rio Grande Valley, which is usually defined as Cameron, Willacy, Hidalgo, and Starr counties, contains the only subtropical area in Texas—in and around Brownsville. Here, you'll find a few native species that just barely made it across the border from Mexico and could be classified as dependably winter-hardy only in this southernmost part of the Valley.

Laredo isn't actually in the Valley, but I've included it because its temperature and rainfall are so similar to McAllen's.

Average winter temperatures range from 52° F in Brownsville to 47° in Laredo. Brownsville has recorded an all-time low of 12°, which, believe it or not, is lower than Laredo's all-time low (16°). Rainfall is higher on the coast, which receives 27 inches annually on the average, while Laredo gets 18 inches. Summer highs range from an average of 93° on the coast to 99° in Laredo.

Nearly everything here is drought-tolerant because rainfall, even in Brownsville, is below the amount needed for conventional forest trees. Most of the land that is not being farmed is covered with chaparral or brush. Seen from the road, this landscape looks like a dense thicket of thorny scrub. But when you make your way past the first fifteen feet or so, the brush opens up and looks like a short forest, complete with a top canopy of mesquite, Texas ebony, and huisache, usually only ten to fifteen feet tall but capable of getting over twenty feet high.

Wherever there is enough sun, you'll find a thick understory of smaller trees such as coyotillo, guayacan, paloverde, Mexican olive, guajillo, and blackbrush acacia. There are many others that are thornier and therefore less desirable for a garden but are valuable to wildlife, especially birds. Shrubs growing along with or beneath the smaller trees are cenizo, sometimes in dense masses, and huge prickly pear cactus.

On the inside, where shade is heavy, the understory thins out. It is possible here to maintain a cool, dimly lit forest tall enough to stroll in. The ground cover might be pigeonberry, profusely covered with pink and white flowers and tiny red berries. Scattered here and there might be the showy red blossoms of heartleaf hibiscus. In the subtropical zone you might also find the delightful David's milkberry, thick with white flowers and tiny white egg-shaped fruits. Crushed ebony seedpods make an attractive mulch for the sun-dappled forest floor.

Landscaping for wildlife is critically important and vastly rewarding for Valley residents. One of the four major North American migratory flight patterns for birds funnels through the Valley, and many birds winter here. (See the Wildlife Garden Plan in Chapter 2, Ground Covers, for ideas on how to attract birds and other garden-size creatures.)

Winter temperatures are mild, so rain is what determines when blooms occur and leaves are dropped. More plants are drought-deciduous than cold-deciduous. Peak rains usually occur in May or June and then again in September and October, the latter being the tropical rainy season. Precipitation is scant the rest of the year, but humidity is high near the coast, so Brownsville residents awaken most mornings to heavy dew. The average relative humidity is 88 to 92 percent.

Along the Rio Grande and its floodplains, where there is dependable moisture year-round, you'll find more "conventional" trees, such as the beloved Mexican ash and the cedar elm. These two, along with Texas ebony, create a riparian canopy, with many of the lovely blooming chaparral trees forming the understory. Most of these forests were destroyed beginning in 1937 to make room for agricultural expansion. At Santa Ana Wildlife Refuge near Alamo, Texas, you can walk down by the river on a boardwalk under tall trees draped with Spanish moss and get a sense of what used to be.

The Texas (or Mexican) palm was once plentiful here along the lower Rio Grande, and many small flowering plants, such as the Barbados cherry and David's milkberry, originally grew in palm groves. Near Brownsville, the Rabb Ranch, owned by the Audubon Society, is where you want to go to see the majestic Texas palm in its natural setting.

The Valley is the only place in the United States to see another rare and beautiful tree, the Montezuma cypress. This evergreen cypress, which otherwise resembles the bald cypress, is not yet on protected land, and unless it finds sanctuary soon, its future in the wild is questionable in Texas. It is still abundant in Mexico, however.

Soils in this region are sands to heavy clays. In the resacas (the old meandering paths of the Rio Grande) are clays—and, of course, poor drainage. The southeastern portion of the Valley is essentially the delta of the Rio Grande. Falcon Dam has eliminated cyclic flooding, but drainage is so bad that standing water is a real problem after a heavy thunderstorm.

The land is nearly level, rising gradually to 250 feet above sea level at Falcon Dam and the Bordas Escarpment and continuing to rise to more than 400 feet at Laredo. In the lower portions near Brownsville, salts are a problem for many reasons. Some areas are below sea level, and many areas drain poorly. Municipal water from the Rio Grande is salty because of overuse upstream, a problem that continues all the way to El Paso and beyond. Also, the aquifers near the Valley contain salts in the water. If you use drip irrigation, it is important to occasionally flush the salts through.

The Valley Plan uses plants that are essentially drought-tolerant, requiring little or no watering, and yet create a cool shady space, a colorful garden, and an ideal habitat for birds.

Valley Plan
Lot Size: 120′ × 80′

The principal botanical habitat of the Valley is brush, alias chaparral. "Brush," as described in the Valley Regional Description, is simply a short forest made up of canopy, understory, and ground cover.

If you aren't enthusiastic about landscaping with brush, you need to change your mind. Aside from being very drought-tolerant, brush has profuse and showy blooms, the leaves are usually small, often with a spicy fragrance, and the fruits support some of the best bird-watching in the nation by feeding a wide variety of our feathered friends.

Brush is also versatile. You can shape it into any kind of landscape you want. Depending on its maturity and the amount and style of pruning, brush can be impenetrable or open, shrubby or forestlike, formal or informal.

The quickest and easiest way to get a brush landscape is to buy a lot where brush already exists. Then you have an instant landscape that just needs judicious pruning and a few additions for more color and variety. But you'll need to protect it from bulldozers and workmen while you build your home. (See the Blackland Plan for advice on how to do that.) Your lot will include many plants not in this book. Use and enjoy all of them.

However, if you presently have a cleared lot with nothing on it, or if you have an established lawn with a drought-stricken Mexican ash, and you'd like to use brush in your landscape, then consult this plan for inspiration. Many of the instructions in the Create-a-Woods Plan in Chapter 7 (Ornamental Trees) will be helpful. Use the trees and shrubs listed here, as they are the prettiest and most desirable for you.

Before I describe the plan, you should know a few points about installation: The canopy should go in first. Use mesquite, huisache, and Texas ebony. Notice that they've been spaced out approximately ten to fourteen feet apart on the lower left-hand corner of the plan, in a random, natural pattern and not lined up in rows. After all, we're making a landscape, not an orchard.

Next is the understory—trees or shrubs, such as Mexican olive, paloverde, blackbrush acacia, and brasil. Plant them three to six feet apart where you want the brush to be thick, ten to twelve feet apart for a more open look. Again, do not plant them in a rigid pattern. These trees will need deep watering for the next two to four years, whenever they look thirsty. Once they're established, they'll fend for themselves very nicely.

The ground cover should not be planted until the brush has grown up enough to provide plenty of shade. Sun-loving understory shrubs that naturally grow at the edge of brush can be planted right away.

This type of vegetation shows off to best advantage against smooth,

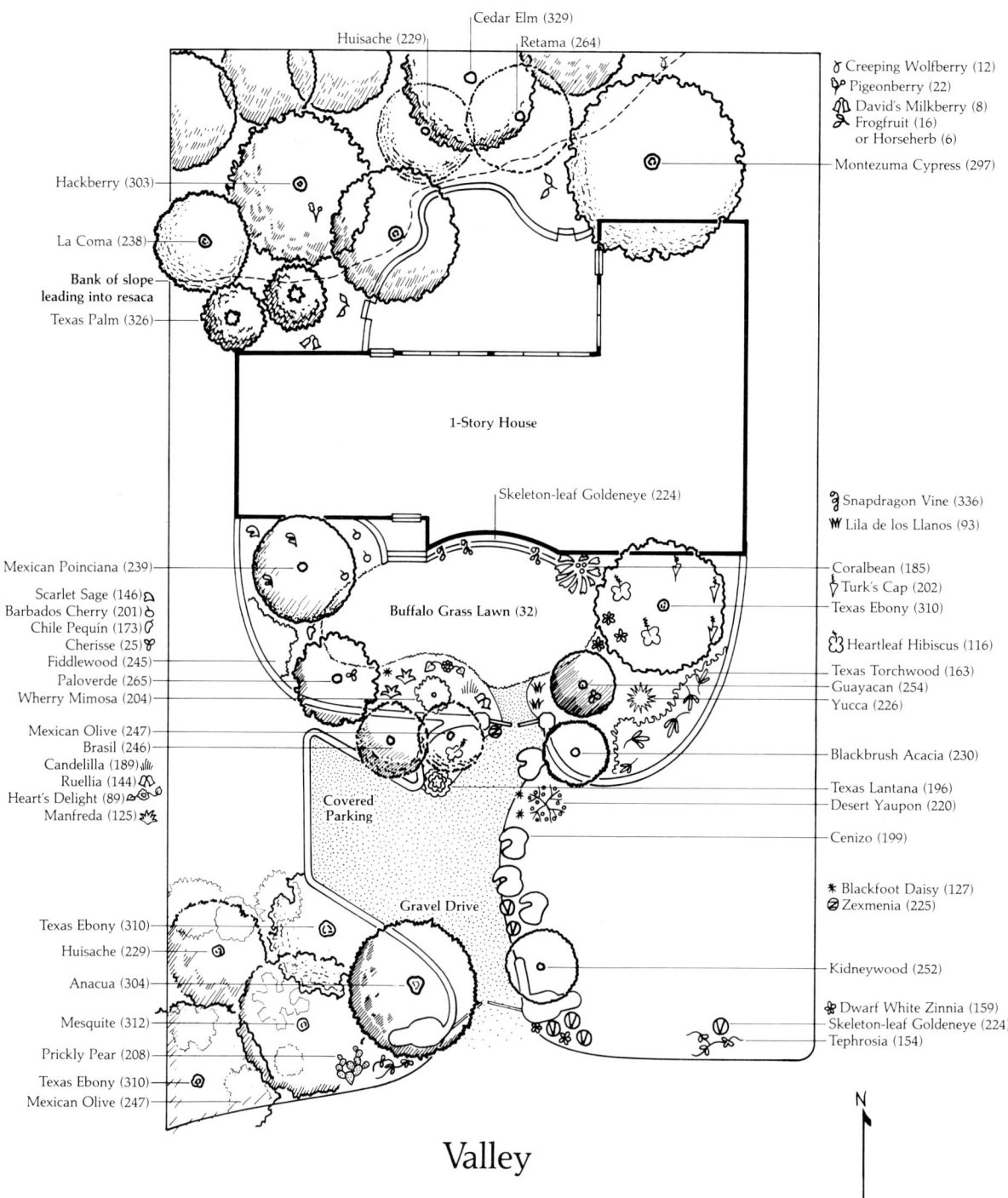

Cedar Elm (329)

Huisache (229)

Retama (264)

Creeping Wolfberry (12)
Pigeonberry (22)
David's Milkberry (8)
Frogfruit (16)
  or Horseherb (6)

Montezuma Cypress (297)

Hackberry (303)

La Coma (238)

Bank of slope
leading into resaca

Texas Palm (326)

1-Story House

Skeleton-leaf Goldeneye (224)

Snapdragon Vine (336)
Lila de los Llanos (93)

Mexican Poinciana (239)

Scarlet Sage (146)
Barbados Cherry (201)
Chile Pequín (173)
Cherisse (25)
Fiddlewood (245)
Paloverde (265)
Wherry Mimosa (204)

Buffalo Grass Lawn (32)

Coralbean (185)
Turk's Cap (202)
Texas Ebony (310)

Heartleaf Hibiscus (116)

Texas Torchwood (163)
Guayacan (254)
Yucca (226)

Mexican Olive (247)
Brasil (246)
Candelilla (189)
Ruellia (144)
Heart's Delight (89)
Manfreda (125)

Blackbrush Acacia (230)

Texas Lantana (196)
Desert Yaupon (220)

Covered
Parking

Cenizo (199)

Blackfoot Daisy (127)
Zexmenia (225)

Texas Ebony (310)

Huisache (229)

Anacua (304)

Mesquite (312)

Gravel Drive

Kidneywood (252)

Prickly Pear (208)

Texas Ebony (310)

Mexican Olive (247)

Dwarf White Zinnia (159)
Skeleton-leaf Goldeneye (224)
Tephrosia (154)

N

Valley

pale surfaces. That's why, in this plan, I've envisioned a low Spanish- or Mexican-style house with thick plaster or stucco walls.

The front is very private. The double-gated entrance is flanked by brush, which should grow thickly along the streets in front and on the east, and by the neighbor on the west to make a visual and physical barrier equivalent to a wall or hedge. Inside, the trees are spaced farther apart and pruned for an open-woods effect you can walk in.

By the edge of the street use two clumps of skeleton-leaf goldeneye, a showy and versatile blooming shrub. It blooms off and on most of the year to give you a strong base of yellow flowers. The purple-pink, low-growing tephrosia looks great at its feet, along with dwarf white zinnias, only six inches tall.

On the far left side of the entrance gate, a large Texas prickly pear firmly marks the boundary of the entrance wall. This wall then sweeps around to a double parking space, roofed in the same style as the house. The gravel drive narrows to a broad footpath lined with more shrubs and flowers.

Here the pink, yellow, and white color scheme is continued. There are three white-blooming trees: an anacua, a kidneywood, and a Mexican olive. More skeleton-leaf goldeneye is mixed with pink cenizo, which has silvery-white leaves. More yellow is found in a zexmenia and a large orange and yellow Texas lantana. The white theme is continued with blackfoot daisies. Over the blackfoot daisies is a desert yaupon, a small shrub brilliant with red berries in the summer. On the shadier side behind the lantana and under the Mexican olive is a cluster of heartleaf hibiscus with its three-inch red flowers.

The reds are introduced to pull your eye immediately to the door-size inner gate, under a plastered archway, which leads into a large private courtyard. The whole front of the house looks out here onto a smoothly mowed, fine-leaved buffalo grass lawn surrounded by flower gardens.

The main color scheme here is brilliant red, found in the coralbean, Turk's cap, heartleaf hibiscus, scarlet sage, and the fruits of the chile pequín, guayacan, and Barbados cherry. There are all sorts of interesting textures too, in the manfreda's soft, fleshy, purple and green mottled leaves, the grasslike leaves of the everblooming and evergreen lila de los llanos, the pale green waxy stems of the candelilla, and the dark green spiky yucca.

The bed directly across from the front stoop is most colorful, with blackfoot daisy, deep-rose-colored heart's delight, violet ruellia, and the sweetly fragrant Wherry mimosa, which is a cloud of creamy yellow in the spring. Another intensely colored area is the raised planter directly across from the arched gateway. Here yellow daisies abound on the skeleton-leaf goldeneye interspersed with the purple and white snapdragon vine, which drapes over the planter wall.

Two masses of shrubs act as a foil for the other colors. One is the Texas torchwood, with its droopy dark green leaves. On the other side is a small planting of fiddlewood, whose leaves turn a brilliant orange when drought-stressed.

Robert Gallagher saved most of the canopy trees and many of the understory trees when he built his home, which backs onto the Arroyo Colorado. In this picture are a thirty-foot Texas ebony, the pale trunk of a hackberry, and sidewalks with brick and wooden terracing designed by the owner. Other native trees on the site include brasil, Texas palm, Texas persimmon, la coma, and cedar elm. Photo by the authors.

The trees are some of my favorites: Texas ebony, fragrant in bloom and striking in fruit; guayacan, purple in the spring and with brilliant orange-red seedpods in the fall; blackbrush acacia, a solid sweet-smelling fluff of creamy white in the spring; paloverde, with delicate lime-green branches; and Mexican poinciana, with lush lime-green leaves and yellow flowers. The brasil, in the shady spot between the carport and the courtyard, is a prime bird tree, producing orange to purple fruits after every rain. Where there are no flowers or shrubs under the trees, I put cherisse, a low-growing evergreen ground cover with cerise flowers scattered over it several times during the year.

The back yard illustrates an entirely different habitat—the resaca, an abandoned oxbow of the Rio Grande filled with alligator gars, catfish, crappies, and, according to a local resident, shopping carts!

The dotted line marks the edge of the high ground. Beneath are sloping banks to the resaca, where water is likely to stand after a heavy rain. The trees here grow taller than they do in the brush. They are a unique mixture of trees found elsewhere in the state along watercourses, such as the hackberry and cedar elm, and the brush trees that are adapted to the moisture and shade, such as the huisache. Retama, la coma, and Texas ebony also grow here, but usually on the banks, where drainage is better.

Two other trees are special to the Valley—the Texas (or Mexican) palm and the evergreen Montezuma cypress. In the plan these trees are placed above the banks by the patio. The palms eventually make tall trees, but they are very slow-growing, so for twenty years their giant fan-shaped leaves will bush out close to ground level. The cypress is fast-growing and will soon provide shade for ground covers.

I've included several attractive ground covers that are suitable to the moist, shady banks. David's milkberry requires more moisture and milder temperatures than rivina, also called rouge plant or pigeonberry. Frogfruit is low-growing—usually under three inches—and will take moderate amounts of foot traffic. It is happy in either sun or shade. Horseherb is ideal where it is too shady for grass and a mowed area for walking is wanted.

In sunny areas on the slope, creeping (or Carolina) wolfberry is perfect because it loves poor drainage and will spread quickly to hold the sides and prevent erosion. It doesn't even object to salty water.

Once established, this plan can be completely drought-tolerant. However, for a lusher look, water the ground covers around the resaca, as well as the flowers in the courtyard. You'll be surprised at how little water they will require. Try watering only when plants first start to droop, and then water deeply. Experiment until you find the right formula for your plants and soil.

In the deep sands at Aransas Pass, wildflowers bloom in front of a backdrop of live oaks. In June, the color is mostly Indian blanket, lazy daisy, and native annual sunflowers. Coralbean, palmettos, and a great fringe of Turk's cap are found nearer to the oaks. Photo by the authors.

Corpus Christi

Corpus Christi, San Antonio (southern side)
(Alice, Beeville, Kingsville, Victoria)

COASTAL BEND PRAIRIES AND MARSHES, RIO GRANDE PLAINS

Regional Description

This region is a unique blend of Houston, the Valley, and the Rio Grande Plains. Average minimum winter temperatures are typically 42° to 48° F. Record low temperatures are 5° along the coast to 0° in San Antonio. Rainfall is 26 to 28 inches annually, too little to support tall trees.

Spring starts in February and summer arrives in May. A flower that blooms in early spring anywhere else in Texas will bloom in February in this region. If it is listed as a late-March-to-April bloomer, it will bloom in early March here. On the other hand, if a fall flower ordinarily blooms from August to October, it might not start until October in these parts, especially if blooming is triggered by cooler weather. First frost will be in November or December inland and in January, February, or not at all along the coast.

This area was settled in the 1600s by the Spanish, who changed it very little. Historical records tell us it was an almost treeless prairie of grasses and spectacular wildflowers, with clumps of mesquite and prickly pear. Inland, on the drier clays, was buffalo grass; on the sands, bluestems.

Trees were found only along creeks and rivers. Mexican ash, cedar elm, retama, huisache, pecan, and bald cypress were some of the more desirable ones. On higher ground were anacua, Texas persimmon, soapberry, live oak, and hackberries. In one area of moist deep sands in Corpus Christi were farkleberry, yaupon holly, and American beautyberry—the Houston contingent.

The Irish came in 1820 and established farms. Prairie fires diminished and grazing intensified, bringing an increase in mesquite and cactus and a decrease in grasses. Prairies and pastures became brushy, like the vegetation already on the caliche uplands. By the time other settlers had plowed the rich black clays and raided the creek bottoms for timber and firewood, the land was more brush than woods and prairies. This brush is an extension of the chaparral in the Valley. Two special Valley trees that are not present in Corpus Christi are Texas palm, which is winter-hardy here, and Montezuma cypress. Texas ebony and Mexican olive are present along the coast, but they occasionally freeze back.

The land is flat and poorly drained. By the time you're as far inland as Beeville, you're still only 200 feet above sea level. The Olmsted brothers, in their book *A Journey Through Texas,* described entering Victoria in the spring of 1853 after a day of rain and seeing water standing "fetlock" deep everywhere. The main road was a quarter of a mile wide because previous ruts became so deep and muddy they had to be avoided.

Soils are alkaline dark clays, caliche, and sands. The sands often have caliche over or under them, except where they occur along streams and bays. Black clays and poor drainage are problems in Corpus Christi and Victoria.

The Corpus Christi Plan picks out the drought-tolerant brush species that are dependably winter-hardy and well adapted to clay and caliche. The courtyard features species that are best adapted to poor drainage.

Corpus Christi Plan
Lot Size: 80' × 12'

In each of these regional plans, I've endeavored to capture the flavor of the area with regard to its native flora. Corpus Christi, frankly, is hard to pin down, because it combines desert acacias, prickly pears, and mesquites with the tropical look of palmettos, anacuas, and hibiscus. With such a wide range of possibilities, Corpus Christi landscapes can be truly exciting and varied.

Corpus Christi uses mesquites with more taste and appreciation than I've seen anywhere else in the state. Because of the warm climate, homeowners also successfully use (except for the occasional freakish winter) imported tropical palms and flowers, such as plumbago, cycads, and bougainvillea. These plants are gorgeous, and if I lived here, I'd use them too, in combination with the natives.

Many appealing natives could be used here but aren't: flowers such as spider lily, Gulf Coast penstemon, heartleaf hibiscus, and violet ruellia, some easy ground covers, and an unusually large selection of beautiful and drought-tolerant evergreens. The point of this plan is to help homeowners (and companies too) stretch out and explore new options.

To show the rich possibilities for Corpus Christi, I've designed a front yard, facing south, that holds drought-tolerant evergreen species that grow on well-drained calcareous clay soils. (These species also do well in sand.) The back yard offers suggestions on how to handle poor drainage.

The two-story Spanish-style house in this plan has a tiled roof, tiled walk and terrace, and wrought-iron balconies. The lot slopes toward the house. The southeast corner is the high point, while the low point is an arroyo (marked by a dotted line) that drains under the side street to the north of the driveway. The front yard is almost flat but drains slowly in a northwesterly direction into conduits under the driveway, where the runoff joins the arroyo.

Guest parking is in a small circular drive off the front street. This entrance is formal. A paloverde, with its startling lime-green trunk and

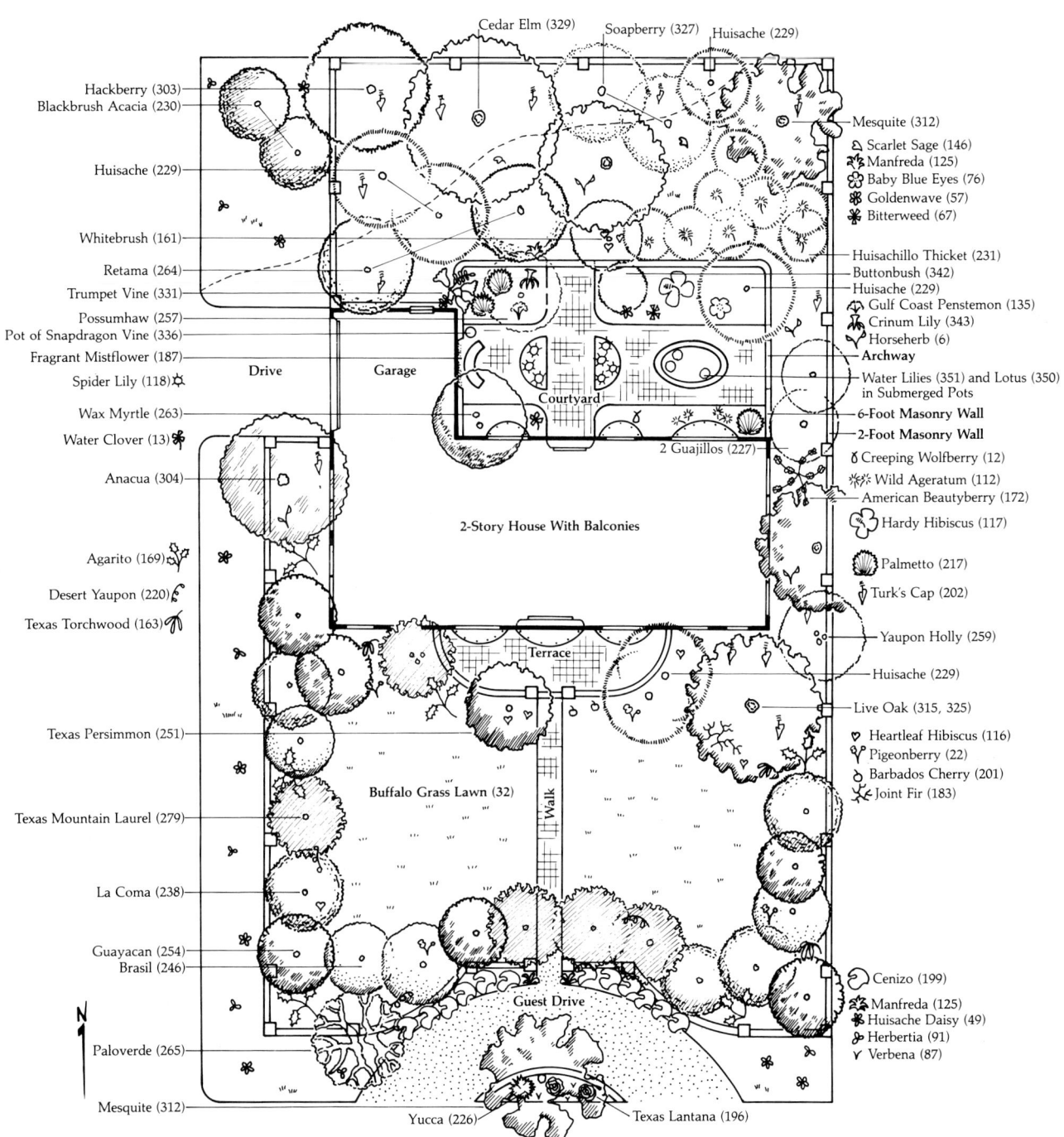

Cedar Elm (329) Soapberry (327) Huisache (229)

Hackberry (303)
Blackbrush Acacia (230)

Huisache (229)

Whitebrush (161)

Retama (264)
Trumpet Vine (331)

Possumhaw (257)
Pot of Snapdragon Vine (336)
Fragrant Mistflower (187)
Spider Lily (118)

Wax Myrtle (263)

Water Clover (13)

Anacua (304)

Agarito (169)

Desert Yaupon (220)
Texas Torchwood (163)

Texas Persimmon (251)

Texas Mountain Laurel (279)

La Coma (238)

Guayacan (254)
Brasil (246)

Paloverde (265)

Mesquite (312)

Yucca (226)   Texas Lantana (196)

Drive   Garage

Courtyard

2-Story House With Balconies

Terrace

Walk

Buffalo Grass Lawn (32)

Guest Drive

Mesquite (312)
Scarlet Sage (146)
Manfreda (125)
Baby Blue Eyes (76)
Goldenwave (57)
Bitterweed (67)

Huisachillo Thicket (231)
Buttonbush (342)
Huisache (229)
Gulf Coast Penstemon (135)
Crinum Lily (343)
Horseherb (6)
Archway
Water Lilies (351) and Lotus (350)
in Submerged Pots
6-Foot Masonry Wall
2-Foot Masonry Wall
2 Guajillos (227)
Creeping Wolfberry (12)
Wild Ageratum (112)
American Beautyberry (172)
Hardy Hibiscus (117)

Palmetto (217)
Turk's Cap (202)

Yaupon Holly (259)

Huisache (229)

Live Oak (315, 325)
Heartleaf Hibiscus (116)
Pigeonberry (22)
Barbados Cherry (201)
Joint Fir (183)

Cenizo (199)
Manfreda (125)
Huisache Daisy (49)
Herbertia (91)
Verbena (87)

N

Corpus Christi

branches (attractive even without its showy yellow spring flowers), gives height and color, along with a mesquite.

Under the mesquite, next to the street, is a colorful planting of yucca, Texas lantana, and verbena. At the entrance is a curving hedge of cenizo. The walk is flanked by two manfredas, fleshy-leaved evergreen rosettes with exotic lily flowers on a tall stalk.

The rights-of-way next to the street are mowable margins of buffalo grass filled with huisache daisy and herbertia, making this a low spring carpet of green, yellow, and purple. These grassy areas back up to a low masonry wall, only two feet high, that encircles the entire property.

In the extreme northwest corner, height is provided by two blackbrush acacias, small trees that bear creamy masses of sweet-smelling blooms in the spring. In the front yard the low wall is surmounted by a dense planting of evergreen shrubs and trees. These evergreens were chosen for their drought tolerance and their willingness to grow in clay and caliche, as well as sandy loams. They make quite an impressive list: agarito, Texas torchwood, desert yaupon, brasil, guayacan, Texas mountain laurel, and la coma. I have arranged them in a thick mixture as they might be found in chaparral.

These evergreens provide far more color than just green foliage. The agarito might have bluish-gray foliage, and the torchwood gets orangy-red when drought-stressed. Blooms appear at different times of year to give sweet-smelling purple or white accents and are followed by berries that are a brilliant shiny red, soft orange, purple, or tawny white. Most of the berries make excellent bird food, and the plants provide nesting sites.

Pruning should be minimal, just enough to keep a soft graceful mass with all deadwood removed. The height will gradually increase over the years, as will the breadth, eventually gaining the shape of a line of small trees. Always let the upper branches grow long and slightly drooping.

Under these shrubs is a ground cover of pigeonberry, which has low-growing pink and white flowers that bloom at the same time the little berries turn bright red. Heartleaf hibiscus, a short perennial with three- to four-inch-wide soft red flowers, is scattered throughout to accent the pink, white, and red of the pigeonberry.

Setting off this chaparral bed is a buffalo grass lawn, which should be kept mowed to highlight the rich textures of the evergreens.

Closer to the house is a live oak surrounded by a great mass of Turk's cap. Like everything described so far, this tree can grow in well-drained clay. However, both the Turk's cap and the live oak require regular watering in the summer, as does the yaupon holly behind them.

On the southwest side of the live oak is a joint fir, an oddly graceful evergreen shrub with spreading firlike branches. The small tree closer to the terrace is a double-trunked huisache. Allow the trunks and a couple of branches to hang low over the ground in that wonderfully artistic way that is so reminiscent of trees in a Japanese painting.

Everywhere else, the usual pigeonberry and heartleaf hibiscus prevail, except for the dwarf Barbados cherry on one side of the steps and the Texas persimmon on the other. Barbados cherry is a charming little shrub that displays pink flowers and cherry-red berries on and off all spring, summer, and fall. It can be hedged, but in this case let it grow naturally into a pleasant evergreen shrub that will not obstruct the steps.

The Texas persimmon is evergreen in a mild winter, but even in a harsh winter it's still beautiful because of its bark. The trunk is a pale gray, almost white, and very smooth. Keep this tree elegantly pruned in an open structure. Never snip off the end of a branch, but cut out interior twigs almost flush with the main trunks and stems.

Where the front yard drains under the driveway and more moisture is present, but drainage is still good, I've put a dark-green-leafed anacua. This tree could have been in the evergreen chaparral mixture, but a large, well-watered specimen of this tree is special. It has a trunk that looks like a bunch of candles tied together. In early spring, when it is covered with sweet white blossoms, it is very impressive. Later, the fruits attract hosts of birds.

The plan described so far is drought-tolerant. After watering to get everything established, you can continue to water occasionally to maintain maximum beauty and health, but that will be necessary only for the live oak, yaupon holly, and Turk's cap.

Beneath the anacua, in its moister, denser shade, I've used horseherb as a ground cover. Horseherb is also present on the east side of the house, which has another drainage path down to the arroyo. In this area of shade, with slightly extra moisture, are a mesquite, its delicate foliage keeping the shade from being too dark, and an American beautyberry, which makes a magnificent view from the house in the fall when the berries turn a rich magenta.

The back yard has two environments, both seasonally moist. One is a formal courtyard that features plants that actually like poor drainage, and the other is an arroyo that can be either wild or tame, depending on whether you prune and mow.

The courtyard will be the first thing to catch your eye. It is surrounded by a masonry wall six feet high. The walk from the door to the arched exit facing the arroyo is six feet wide. The wider portion, from the alcove in the garage wall to the arched exit facing east, is ten feet wide. The surfacing could be tile (as it is here), flagstone, or pea gravel. The half circles next to the house indicate balconies.

The fountain is tiled and in keeping with the architecture of the house. The native blue water lily and the yellow one bloom during the day, and the yellow water lotus perfumes the air at night. These floating water flowers are grown in pots placed at the bottom of the pool, which needs to be at least eighteen inches deep to keep the water cool enough for the plants and the goldfish.

The alcove is decorated with an espaliered fragrant mistflower. This half vine, half shrubby plant has lavender-colored ageratum-like blossoms in the

Bit by bit, Charlotte Nichols of Kenedy built this patio out of antique bricks and cobblestones. Chile pequín and pigeonberry (*Rivina*) lend delicacy to unpaved rectangles. An enormous mesquite and a hackberry provide most of the shade, while anacuas, Texas mountain laurel, and Texas persimmon grow as understory. Agaritos and cenizos mark one edge of the patio, which is mostly unwatered. In September, the only plant drooping and gasping is *Ruellia brittoniana*, a native of Mexico. Photo by the authors.

fall that emit a delightfully sweet fragrance. A curved bench sits in front of the alcove. To the side is a fourteen-inch pot of snapdragon vine, an enchanting little trailing vine with purple snapdragon-like flowers that cascade over the sides of the pot.

The beds in the courtyard are about one to two inches below the level of the walks and are poorly drained. The plants here actively like, or at least tolerate, poor drainage and will look ratty if they dry out too much. When they start to droop, let the hose run into the beds until water is standing in them, and then let it soak in. Doing that once every two to four weeks should suffice.

The north beds, which receive the south sun, are seven feet wide. The shady south beds next to the house are four feet wide. The two half-moon-shaped beds flanking the main walkway are filled with spider lilies. These lilies have big straplike leaves about knee-high. The large white flowers are fragrant and bloom mostly in the spring.

The tree in the west corner next to the house is a wax myrtle, multi-trunked and pruned up high. Underneath is water clover, a low-growing fern with a leaf that resembles that of four-leaf clover. To the right of the back door is creeping wolfberry, a fleshy-leaved ground cover with purple flowers and red fruits. Growing beside it is wild ageratum (also called blue mistflower), a spreading herb that is a relative of fragrant mistflower. In the corner, to furnish the tropical look, is a palmetto, which has evergreen, stiff fan-shaped leaves that eventually get five feet tall and equally broad.

The tree in the northeast corner is a huisache. Underneath it and throughout this bed are three annuals, for spring-to-frost color. One is baby blue eyes, a short, sweet, pale blue flower that blooms a long time in the spring. With it is goldenwave, an annual yellow daisy that blooms in the spring, but with water it will bloom on into the summer and sometimes even into the fall. If you want to ensure late summer and fall color, also plant another annual yellow daisy in this bed—bitterweed.

The height comes from two other plants. One is a six-foot-tall hardy hibiscus. Its large white flowers with dark red centers bloom all summer. Use a local species or one of the hibiscuses described in plant profile 117. The other is a buttonbush, also a summer bloomer with fragrant pale pink or white balls of flowers. The buttonbush will form a short tree with a gnarled, twisting trunk in its old age.

The tree in the northwest bed is a possumhaw. Come winter, its red berries will give the courtyard a bright, festive look. In the corner are two more palmettos. In front of them, under the possumhaw, are the evergreen Gulf Coast penstemon and a clump of crinum lilies. Hanging over the palmettos are the bright orange summer flowers of trumpet vine.

Both arched exits from the courtyard look out onto masses of foliage, increasing the sense of sanctuary inside the courtyard. The east exit faces two guajillos, acacias with ferny foliage and white puffs of flowers, and a massive Turk's cap. You can walk on the horseherb that covers the ground, but you won't get very far. The two-foot wall on the property line is only eight feet away, and when you turn left, you hit the huisachillo thicket. This exit is really for looks, not use.

The main exit is functional and allows access to the garage door (for ease in storing garden equipment) and to the arroyo. The arroyo can be treated in two distinctive ways: it can be a thicket of vegetation forming a wildlife refuge and a total barrier for privacy, or it can be parklike, with a tree-dotted sloping lawn. With either treatment, you'd use the same trees and plant them as shown. You would also plant the same ground covers of buffalo grass, horseherb, scarlet sage, and Turk's cap. The difference would come in the maintenance.

The arroyo, though wet after a rain, is also quite often very dry. Trees that are normally found in arroyos or near streams in this area are cedar elm (which is one of the tallest and broadest trees for Corpus Christi), retama, and huisache. Mexican ash, though not on this plan, is also seen frequently here, but it can get ratty in the summer, so I'm not recommending it. Close by are soapberry, hackberry, and mesquite. On the higher, drier slope is a thicket of huisachillo, a favorite with many, and a whitebrush, a small tree-like shrub of the verbena family with white, sweet-smelling flowers.

To keep the arroyo looking like a park, mow and prune and water occasionally. Mowing is something you should have to do only once or twice a year to discourage new saplings and other woody growth. Where it is sunny, buffalo grass will dominate. Where it is shady, horseherb and scarlet sage will win out. All can be mowed. The sage can be mowed regularly until August, when it should be allowed to bloom freely. If it gets tall and rank, mow it again, being sure you don't take more than half its leaves, and let it start blooming again.

If you want this back area to be a buffer to traffic noise or neighbors, or a refuge for birds and other wildlife, let it go wild. Don't water, don't mow, and prune deadwood and remove poison ivy only if you want to.

I'd like to talk about a few other Texas native plants for this region. They are native only to the Valley but can be used around Corpus Christi. The Mexican olive is a small tree with clusters of large white flowers that bloom almost all the time. It, the Texas ebony, and the Mexican poinciana are usually excellent trees for Corpus Christi, although they proved to be vulnerable to the hard freeze of 1983, which killed them off above ground. I say "above ground" because these trees are root-hardy, and by 1987 I saw evidence that many of them were coming back—as shrubs.

The Texas palm, another Valley native, seems to be perfect for the Corpus Christi tropical look because it is completely winter-hardy. C. W. Carpenter, garden editor for the Corpus Christi Caller Times, says he knows of several specimens in the city that survived the freezes of 1951 and 1983 "without turning a leaf." Texas palm is slow-growing, but every stage of its growth is a visual treat, from a palmetto-like shrub to a towering smoothly trunked tree. Best of all, for children and gardeners, it has no spines.

 # Ground Covers

Y OUR average Texan, especially one who has never lived anywhere else, has a fairly limited outlook on ground covers. If it's not a grass, if it is evergreen, and if it creeps along the ground by runners and never gets higher than six or eight inches, it qualifies. The two that are used most commonly in Texas are English ivy and Asian jasmine—both nonnatives, as you might have guessed from the names. Some people consider these plants a substitute for a grass lawn; they make for easy maintenance, and you can let your lawnmower rust in the garage. They also provide the added bonus of looking a lot more interesting than Bermuda grass.

Europe and Japan and even other parts of the United States have a broader definition of ground covers and don't limit their choices to evergreens, which don't do well in longer cold spells. By necessity, they use a wide array of non-evergreen plants, including woodland flowers such as lily of the valley and yellowroot, and even plants two and three feet high.

Since we have no such limitation, why bother looking for ground cover options beyond the tried-and-true evergreens mentioned? For two basic, and I think very important, reasons: variety and color.

For years landscape architects in the United States as well as other countries have been using masses of shrubs, such as nandinas, Scotch heather, and creeping junipers, as ground covers in sunny spots. If you take this broader viewpoint—and I obviously hope you will—then I believe you will be pleasantly surprised at the number of excellent and rewarding options our own Texas natives provide, for both formal and naturalized (unwatered) uses.

These native ground covers are indeed a varied lot, and you're sure to find at least one that is perfect for your situation. None of them is going to duplicate the look of Asian jasmine, English ivy, or even *Vinca major* or *V. minor.* Most are not evergreen. They tend to be taller or thinner than the stereotypical ground cover that is thick, low, smooth, evergreen, and unchanging all year long. Some naturalize among other ground covers or in a forest floor of fallen leaves. Some are drought-tolerant and take full sun and reflected heat; others must have plenty of shade and water. Most of them give good color at some time during the year. Some are perennial flowers, some are shrubby, and several are ferns. Some are capable of covering large areas, and others are better at filling in more modest spaces.

In early spring, mayapples form a woodland ground cover under oak trees in East Texas. Here, the fat green buds are almost ready to open. Photo by the authors.

In a small area the ponyfoots, partridgeberry, Gregg dalea, or frogfruit are attractive. So is ebony spleenwort (a fern), cherisse (a spiderwort), or the long-flowering purple groundcherry.

Those plants that either prefer or tolerate shade make splendid ground covers in a woodsy situation. Texas does not naturally have evergreen woods. When you see a great deal of green in a woods in the winter, it will most likely be Japanese honeysuckle covering the floor and climbing into and smothering the trees. The prettiest woods are those carpeted with violets and phlox, mayapples and ferns, cedar sage and zexmenia, or little bluestem and meadow flowers, depending on where you live.

Many ground covers form a colorful, shrubby understory—such as coralberry, which gives purple berries in the fall and winter, and Oklahoma plum, which is a fairyland of white blossoms in the spring.

In South Texas the brush can be pruned up to display a ground cover of David's milkberry or pigeonberry, both of which display colorful flowers and fruits most of the year.

Most of the plants in this chapter are capable of forming colonies by suckers, rhizomes, or stolons. For those of you who are not fluent in botanese, allow me to translate. *Suckers* are new plants that come up near the original plant and are attached to it by roots. *Rhizomes* are underground stems, usually thickened, that produce leafy shoots on the upper side and roots on the bottom side. They can produce a linear series of plants or a thicket. *Stolons* are stems that travel above ground and put down roots where they touch the soil. They only root at the tip or at the node. The node is a joint on the stem, usually marked by a leaf. Sometimes stolons are underground.

Plants with roots that like to travel often look awful in a nursery container; having their roots restricted is particularly stressful. Don't worry that you are buying a dying plant. As soon as you get its roots into the ground, it will recover quickly.

When you first plant ground covers, there is always a lot of space in between. Cover these bare spots with a half inch of fine mulch. This helps keep in moisture and discourages weeds. It is important not to use a thick mulch, because then you will make it difficult for the ground covers to spread, especially those that travel by stolons and root at the nodes. For them, lay down the long stems and peg them at the nodes so that they are in contact with the soil, not the mulch.

If you follow the spacings I recommend in the individual plant profiles, the plants should fill in solidly by the second summer, provided you did a good job preparing the soil and were conscientious about watering. Don't expect any ground cover in Texas to provide solid cover without watering and weeding.

The only exceptions are ground covers that are suitable only for naturalizing in a woods. I recommend spacing those farther apart, as that is more in keeping with nature's look.

Some of the plants are slow-growing and will require patience. Mayapple and trillium, for example, take many years to develop into the large beds we see in the forests of East Texas.

Other factors affecting the rate of cover are the weather, your attentiveness, how well you matched the plant to the environment you are planting it in, and so on. Soil is one of the biggest factors. Sand is easier for ground covers to grow in than clay or rocks. Loam is richer and gives more nutrients for quick growth.

At the end of this chapter you will find a list of other plants that can also be used as ground covers, although this is not their primary use. Many shrubs besides the ones listed are low-growing and can be massed to make large-scale ground covers. Also, some of the vines bloom well when used as a ground cover (others bloom only when climbing), and several evergreen perennials can be effective in a small, highly maintained area. If the area is sunny and gets frequent foot traffic, turn to Chapter 3, which discusses lawn grasses.

1. Fern acacia
Acacia hirta
The authors

1. **Latin Name** *Acacia angustissima (A. hirta, A. texensis)*
   Pronunciation ah-KAY-shuh an-gus-TISS-uh-mah
   Common Name FERN ACACIA
   Usual Height 1–3 feet
   Spacing 1½ feet apart
   Bloom Summer; white; ½-inch globes
   Dormant in winter
   Range Widespread throughout Texas New Mexico, Oklahoma, southeastern U.S., Mexico
   Soil Sand, loam, clay, caliche; well drained
   Dappled shade, part shade, full sun
   Colonizes by rhizomes
   Propagation Scarified seed, softwood cuttings

If you have a large north or east slope to cover, this perennial ground cover works well, even in an unwatered situation. Fern acacia looks like a small soft shrub, although its branches are not woody. Best of all, unlike other acacias, its branches have no thorns. The flowers are small and scattered and, frankly, not too thrilling. It's the fine ferny texture of the foliage that makes this ground cover so desirable. Fern acacia can take full sun on a south slope and look fresh all summer, but depending on where you live, it might need several waterings in the summer.

2. Maidenhair fern
Adiantum capillus-veneris
The authors

3. Artemesia
Artemesia ludoviciana
The authors

2. **Latin Name** *Adiantum capillus-veneris*
   Pronunciation ay-dee-AN-tum KAP-eh-lus
   vuh-NEER-us
   Common Name MAIDENHAIR FERN
   Usual Height 1 foot
   Spacing 1 foot apart
   Dormant when dry
   Range Limestone crevices over streams and
   pools in Trans-Pecos, Edwards Plateau,
   Houston, Valley, and Blackland Prairies
   Virginia to South America, Eurasia
   Soil Sand, loam, limestone; well drained
   Shade, dappled shade, part shade
   Colonizes by rhizomes
   Propagation Root division

Although this lovely fern grows from one end of
the state to the other, it is not easy to use. It likes moisture
year-round, which should put it in the Water Garden Plan
of this book, but it must also have good drainage, which
eliminates it from that category. If you're one of the rare
and fortunate few who have your own private limestone
dripping spring, this is an ideal plant for you. Otherwise,
you need to be living in an area of high humidity and high
rainfall like Houston or Beaumont. There, if you have a
sandy wooded slope or a planting bed raised for good
drainage, you can use maidenhair fern as a ground cover.
With watering in the summer, it will be lush and thick.
Without watering, it will go dormant by July.

3. **Latin Name** *Artemesia ludoviciana*
   Pronunciation ar-teh-MEE-zhah
   loo-doh-vee-see-AH-nah
   Common Name ARTEMESIA
   Usual Height 1–3 feet, can be mowed
   occasionally
   Spacing 1 foot apart
   Evergreen if mowed in fall
   Range Throughout Texas except Valley
   Temperate North America
   Soil Sand, loam, clay, caliche, limestone;
   well drained
   Part shade, full sun
   Colonizes by rhizomes
   Propagation Root division

This ground cover has a Spartan constitution. It
takes full sun, reflected heat, any soil, needs no water—
and still stays evergreen. Or should I say "ever-silver"? To
get the thick winter rosettes, you have to mow it in the
fall. Its aromatic leaves have an attractive white fuzziness.
Some people don't like it when it is tall and blooming.
They think it looks ratty. Worse, it is wind-pollinated, and
hay-fever sufferers know what that means. Others love the
shaggy look and use the flowering stalks for sweet-smelling wreaths and winter arrangements. Use artemesia for
its year-round color on a sunny slope with rocks, especially in the western part of the state. In a formal situation,
make sure it is contained, preferably by curbs. This is the
perfect ground cover for sunny parking medians, street
medians, sides of highways, and other tough contained
spots. When mowed, it will bear moderate amounts of
foot traffic.

4. Ebony spleenwort
Asplenium platyneuron
The authors

5. Creeping barberry
Berberis repens
The authors

4. **Latin Name**   *Asplenium platyneuron*
    Pronunciation   ah-SPLEE-nee-um
    plat-ee-NEW-ron
    Common Name   EBONY SPLEENWORT
    Usual Height   9–12 inches, rarely to 16
    inches
    Spacing   1–1½ feet apart
    Dormant in winter
    Range   Stream banks, rotting logs, rocky
    slopes, and thickets from East Texas to
    Fort Worth and San Antonio
    Canada to Florida, west to Iowa and Texas;
    Kansas, Colorado, South Africa
    Soil   Sand, loam, limestone; moist, well
    drained
    Shade, dappled shade
    Colonizes by rhizomes
    Propagation   Root division while dormant

Ebony spleenwort is a small fern, the smallest listed in this book, and one of the most drought-tolerant. This makes it the best one to place in front of small shrubs or under low-growing ornamental trees. It is much shorter and not nearly as aggressive as wood fern. The only condition it must have is good drainage. If you live in the gumbo areas of Houston and have to contend with high rainfall and poorly draining soils, forget this fern. It will grow only on the branches of your live oak. It prefers sand, loam, or a calcareous or gravelly slope. It can be naturalized in the Piney Woods and the Post Oak Savannah, but to form a dense ground cover, it will require some extra watering. Ebony spleenworts are also effective in a shady rock garden, where each fern is isolated to show its individual beauty.

5. **Latin Name**   *Berberis repens*
    Pronunciation   BER-ber-iss REE-penz
    Common Name   CREEPING BARBERRY
    Usual Height   1–2 feet
    Spacing   1 foot apart
    Bloom   Early April; yellow; ¼ inch
    **Evergreen, with some leaves turning mauve,
    dusty rose, rust, and pumpkin**
    Range   Wooded canyons and pine forests in
    Guadalupe Mountains
    Trans-Pecos to California, Rocky Moun-
    tains, and British Columbia
    Soil   Sand, loam, limestone; well drained
    Shade, dappled shade, part shade
    Colonizes by stolons
    Propagation   Fresh, stratified, or scarified
    seed; leafy cuttings in spring

Put this evergreen ground cover in a cool corner of your landscape, sheltered from the afternoon sun and drying winds. It needs to be watered to get it through the heat of summer. This plant does well in a garden setting in and to the north of both Midland and Abilene but is not looking promising in test areas in Dallas. I thought it would do well in El Paso, but Dr. Jimmy L. Tipton of the Texas Agricultural Experiment Station there tells me it has problems in that climate. He even tried it in full shade, and it still succumbed to heat. The leaves are a gentle muted green, larger and softer than our other native barberries. Pastel hues can occur all year—a feature I love. In the wild, creeping barberry makes dense mats six to ten inches high. In a cultivated setting, I've seen it grow up to two feet tall, producing a soft, billowy effect.

6. Horseherb
Calyptocarpus vialis
The authors

6. **Latin Name**   *Calyptocarpus vialis* (*Zexmenia hispidula*)
Pronunciation   kah-lip-toh-KAR-pus vye-AL-iss
Common Names   HORSEHERB, HIERBA DEL CABALLO, STRAGGLER DAISY
Usual Height   8–10 inches, 2–4 inches if mowed
Spacing   1 foot apart
Bloom   Everblooming; yellow; not visually significant
Evergreen to dormant
Range   Eastern two thirds of Texas Gulf states, Mexico, Cuba, Central America
Soil   Sand, loam, clay, caliche; well drained
Shade, dappled shade, part shade
Colonizes by stolons
Propagation   Root division, seed

6. Horseherb
Calyptocarpus vialis
The authors

This plant illustrates how prejudices can cloud the mind. It is described in botanical literature as a "noxious lawn weed." Why? Because it outcompetes grass in the shade. Funny, that's what I thought everyone wants a shady ground cover to do. Admittedly, the rough little leaves and tiny scattered yellow flowers on horseherb are not breathtaking, so I didn't seriously consider it as a candidate for this book until I started doing the plans. I couldn't finish three of them without using this ground cover. What else forms dense mats in the shade with little or no water, can be mowed if desired, and can take moderate amounts of foot traffic? Nothing I can think of. It is evergreen in the Rio Grande Plains and almost evergreen to dormant in Dallas, where it combines nicely with wood violets to keep the area fully green all year. Where it does die back with cold, mow it to take off the dead leaves.

7. New Jersey tea
Ceanothus americanus
The authors

8. David's milkberry
Chiococca alba
The authors

7. **Latin Name**   *Ceanothus americanus*
Pronunciation   see-uh-NOH-thus
   ah-mar-eh-KAH-nus
Common Name   NEW JERSEY TEA
Usual Height   1½–2 feet, can reach 5 feet
Spacing   2 feet apart
Bloom   Early spring to midspring; white;
   2-inch heads
Deciduous
Range   Forests and prairies in East and Central Texas
   Georgia to Iowa, Kansas, and Texas
Soil   Sand, loam, limestone; well drained
Dappled shade, part shade
**Colonizes by grubs (deep, red, burllike
   roots)**
Propagation   Scarified and stratified seed,
   cuttings

I love New Jersey tea naturalized in a woodland landscape. It seems to do best at the edge of woods, usually going no deeper in than ten feet or so. It is often seen blooming in conjunction with Oklahoma plum in the sandy soils of East Texas. It's a grand sight, seeing these two in delicate snowy drifts beneath floating clouds of white flowering dogwood. New Jersey tea is really a subshrub because not all its branches are woody. The upper branches die back each winter, growing anew each year in time to produce blossoms. A very similar shrub, redroot (*Ceanothus herbaceus*), can be found growing out of cracks in limestone rock on the Edwards Plateau, in the Panhandle, and even up into Canada. I have seen this plant naturalized on a limestone slope under Texas red oak with junipers and cedar sage.

8. **Latin Name**   *Chiococca alba*
Pronunciation   kee-oh-KOH-kah AL-buh
Common Names   DAVID'S MILKBERRY,
   CAHINCA, SNOWBERRY
Usual Height   1 foot
Spacing   1 foot apart
Bloom   Everblooming; white (yellow);
   ¼ to ½ inch
Fruit   Hot weather; white; ¼ to ½ inch
Evergreen
Range   Palm groves and brushlands in
   Valley
   Florida, Mexico, tropical America, Brazil
Soil   Sandy loam or clay-loam; moist, well
   drained
Shade, dappled shade, part shade
Propagation   Softwood cuttings

Mike Heep, a nurseryman and landscape designer in the Lower Rio Grande Valley, says this smooth, nonthorny shrub makes a wonderful ground cover for that region. It is not known to be winter-hardy anyplace else in Texas. This is one of those shrubs that can't decide whether its branches want to stand upright, lie down, or climb like a vine. The specimen that Mike selected for propagation has stems that trail out on the ground up to ten feet in length but stay under a foot in height. In a garden with good soil and water, he found that it spreads quickly to make a thick evergreen cover. The tiny white (rarely yellow) drooping flowers are about the same size as the white egg-shaped fruits. Both dangle under the leaves like little bells and show up astonishingly well from a distance. Although David's milkberry stays in flower all winter, its berries are produced only in warmer weather.

9. Widow's tears
Commelina sp.
The authors

10. Gregg dalea
Dalea greggii
The authors

9. **Latin Name**   *Commelina* spp.
    Pronunciation   koh-muh-LEE-nah species
    Common Name   WIDOW'S TEARS
    Usual Height   1–2 feet
    Spacing   1 foot apart
    Bloom   Spring to fall (morning only); blue;
       1¼ inches across
    Dormant in winter
    Range   Woodlands, pastures, and thickets
       throughout Texas
       East Coast to Rocky Mountains
    Soil   Sand, loam, clay, limestone; well
       drained
    Dappled shade, part shade, full sun
    **Colonizes by rhizomes or stolons, depend-
       ing on species**
    Propagation   Seed, tubers

Naturalized in a mass on the edge of a woods, widow's tears is truly a beautiful sight in the morning. I find it most noticeable in the spring and fall, but it will also bloom a little during the summer. It gets its name because the bright blue (true blue, with no hint of lavender) "tears," or petals, dry up by midday. This flower is for woodland or meadow use only; it is too invasive for a flower garden. There are several commelinas in Texas, and one of them is very weedy—smaller-flowered, taller stems, and does it run rampant! Since widow's tears is unlikely to be a nursery product, you will have to propagate your own. Be sure to choose a large-flowered, mild-mannered specimen when gathering seed. Manuel Flores of Native Design Nursery in San Antonio recommends an annual called false dayflower (*Commelinantia anomala*) for open woods on the Edwards Plateau. It is two to three feet tall and green in the winter, has large lavender flowers, and blooms only in the spring.

10. **Latin Name**   *Dalea greggii*
     Pronunciation   DAY-lee-uh GREG-ee-eye
     Common Name   GREGG DALEA
     Usual Height   4–9 inches
     Spacing   1½ feet apart
     Bloom   May to September (big show in fall);
        purple; ½ inch
     Deciduous
     Range   Southeastern Trans-Pecos
        Mexico
     Soil   Sand, loam, limestone, gravel; well
        drained
     Full sun
     Branchlets root at nodes
     Propagation   Fresh seed, semihardwood
        cuttings

Gregg dalea is grown chiefly for its silvery blue-green leaves, although when in full flower it is covered with purple blossoms and abuzz with bees. It tolerates sites with full sun, lots of reflected heat, and porous soil—in a word, dry. But remember, heat in the mountains isn't as intense as heat on a city street corner. A little shade and occasional water is welcome in this situation. Gregg dalea is winter-hardy in most of the state, but keep it dry enough in the fall so it won't keep putting out new growth, which can get hurt in a freeze. Also, keep it dry in the winter so it won't rot. In areas with good fall and winter rains, expect some losses. After first frost, it dies back to the main stem and produces healthy new branchlets the following year. You can either cut away the dead branches, or leave the dense silvery stems all winter—some people think they're attractive. Just be sure to cut them back before the new growth begins, or it will look like a horrible jumble. I've been told that the branches are too wiry to be eaten by deer.

11. Silver ponyfoot
Dichondra argentea
The authors

12. Creeping wolfberry
Lycium carolinianum
var. *quadrifidum*
Vernon L. Wesby

11. **Latin Name** *Dichondra argentea*
Pronunciation dye-KON-drah
ar-jen-TEE-ah
Common Name SILVER PONYFOOT
Usual Height 2–4 inches
Spacing 1 foot apart
Almost evergreen
Range Dry rocky slopes in Trans-Pecos
mountains
Mexico
Soil Sand, loam, limestone; well drained
Part shade, full sun
Colonizes by stolons, mat-forming
Propagation Seed, root division

Silver ponyfoot likes to be well drained. In its native habitat one plant can form a mat thirty inches across. It can cover acres and competes well with shortgrasses, except Bermuda, according to Dr. Barton H. Warnock. In his book *Wildflowers of the Davis Mountains and the Marathon Basin, Texas,* he states that silver ponyfoot also tolerates mowing. Because of the daintiness of its one- to two-inch silvery-gray leaves, this ground cover could be delightful in small areas—in sunny planters or spilling out of patio pots with something equally drought-tolerant, such as damianita or skeleton-leaf goldeneye. You might also like to try it among the flagstones in a patio, or on an embankment held by limestone pavers. Silver ponyfoot has been found to freeze as far north as Dallas, but there is a more cold-hardy ponyfoot native to Texas. *Dichondra brachypoda* (New Mexico ponyfoot) is green, not silver-colored. It is fully evergreen and likes a completely opposite environment—cool, moist, and shady. It can be used in the High Plains or El Paso with supplemental watering.

12. **Latin Name** *Lycium carolinianum* var.
quadrifidum
Pronunciation LYE-see-um
kare-oh-lin-ee-AY-num variety
kwad-ruh-FID-um
Common Names CREEPING WOLFBERRY,
CAROLINA WOLFBERRY
Usual Height 1–3 feet
Spacing 1½–2 feet apart
Bloom April to October; purple; ¼–½ inch,
eggplant shaped
Fruit Red; ¼–½ inch, tomato-shaped
Evergreen with summer watering
Range Ponds, ditches, salt flats, beaches,
marshes along coast
Coastal from Mississippi to Mexico
Soil Sand, loam, clay, gravel; poor drainage
okay; saline okay
Part shade, full sun
Colonizes by stolons
Propagation Fresh seed, semihardwood
cuttings

Mention creeping wolfberry as a landscape possibility to some people and you'll get strange looks. They know it as a large, spiny, drought-tolerant shrub that drops its leaves in the summer. But a selection of this species, grown by Mike Heep, a landscape designer and nurseryman in the Valley, is different. It's a ground cover, and it likes moist places. It even grows in salt flats, so it won't mind if its water is a bit briny. Yes, it *is* spiny, like the other lyciums, but its branches are green and not very woody, so the spines don't get hard and troublesome. The flowers are too small to be showy, but the grayish leaves are thick, and the red fruits give color all summer and fall and provide food for wildlife. Mike really likes it because it covers quickly and densely, making it great for erosion control. Use a line trimmer to trim it to any height you like.

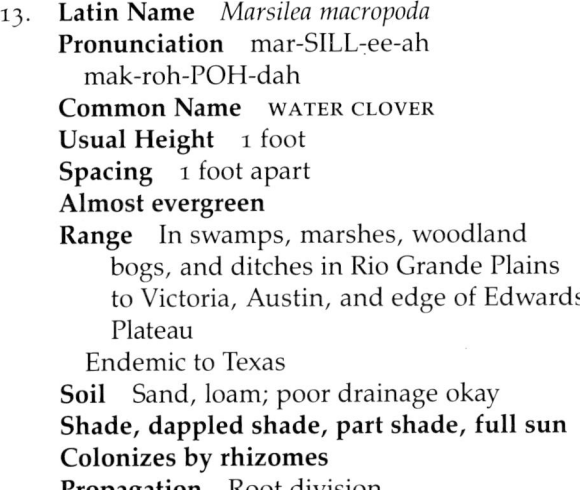

13. Water clover
Marsilea macropoda
The authors

14. Partridgeberry
Mitchella repens
The authors

13. **Latin Name** *Marsilea macropoda*
Pronunciation mar-SILL-ee-ah
mak-roh-POH-dah
Common Name WATER CLOVER
Usual Height 1 foot
Spacing 1 foot apart
Almost evergreen
Range In swamps, marshes, woodland
bogs, and ditches in Rio Grande Plains
to Victoria, Austin, and edge of Edwards
Plateau
Endemic to Texas
Soil Sand, loam; poor drainage okay
Shade, dappled shade, part shade, full sun
Colonizes by rhizomes
Propagation Root division

This water clover adapts well to dry land. It makes a fine ground cover in the southern part of the state and is capable of covering large areas. If you want to see it before you plant it, it's usually on display at the San Antonio Botanical Center. The leaves are clover-shaped but have a downy texture, especially when young. They stay green except for a short time in the winter. As soon as the plant looks messy, cut it back so the new growth will be fresh and uncluttered. The more shade you give it, the less supplemental water it will require. This water clover would love to live at the boggy edge of a water garden, but it is too aggressive. A more suitable water clover for the bog garden is *Marsilea uncinata*. Similar in appearance, it has smoother leaves and colonizes more slowly.

14. **Latin Name** *Mitchella repens*
Pronunciation mih-CHELL-ah REE-penz
Common Name PARTRIDGEBERRY
Usual Height 2 inches
Spacing 9 inches apart
Bloom Summer; white; ¼–½ inch
Fruit Winter; red; ¼-inch berries
Evergreen
Range East Texas woods, dry or moist
Canada to Florida and Texas
Soil Sand, loam; acid; well drained
Shade, dappled shade, part shade
Colonizes by stolons
Propagation Root division

Partridgeberry grows low and evergreen. When conditions are just right, it can cover acres. Trouble is, conditions are rarely just right for it in Texas. Attempt this one only if you live in Houston or East Texas. In the winter it stays dense on its own; during the rest of the year, you'll have to keep it evenly moist. Eric Lautzenheiser, who has done extensive work with native plants in the Houston area, reports that partridgeberry wilts dramatically when it gets thirsty, but it gives you two or three days to come to its rescue before it becomes terminal. Its tiny fragrant white flowers bloom in pairs; they're four-petaled and have fuzzy white silky hairs on them. Sometimes they are tinged with purple. The berries are almost always red (on rare occasions you'll spot some white ones), and although they are not abundant, they do provide touches of color all winter.

15. Pink evening primrose
Oenothera speciosa
The authors

16. Frogfruit
Phyla incisa
The authors

15. **Latin Name**   *Oenothera speciosa*
Pronunciation   ee-NOTH-er-ah or
   ee-noh-THEER-ah spee-see-OH-sah
Common Name   PINK EVENING PRIMROSE
Usual Height   1 foot, can reach 2 feet
Spacing   1 foot apart for cover in a year, or
   ½ pound of seed per acre
Bloom   2–4 months in spring; pink or
   white; 2 inch cups
**Almost evergreen, sometimes dormant in
   summer**
Range   Prairies and open woodlands, road-
   sides, slopes, and ditches throughout
   Texas, but rare in Panhandle
   Kansas to Mexico
Soil   Sand, loam, clay, caliche; well drained
Part shade, full sun
Colonizes by rhizomes
Propagation   Seed sown in fall, root divi-
   sion, cuttings

This wildflower behaves differently in different locales. In Midland and El Paso, it's evergreen as long as it
gets regular watering, and it blooms whenever the temperature is above freezing. In Houston, it's naturally evergreen, but don't depend on it during the summer, when
beetles feed on it and make it thin and ratty. In the rest of
the state the beetles never get a chance; it goes dormant in
the summer, then revives with the fall rains. Team it up
with other ground covers such as Gregg dalea or masses
of lantana—the primrose looks great while they are dormant and vice versa. Near Dallas and the Red River, pink
evening primrose is often thin in the winter, with an occasional red leaf, and doesn't get lush and thick until late
February or March. It looks fantastic planted in a lawn
(don't mow until it's through blooming). I also like it in a
flower bed, but that's definitely a matter of taste. If you
like the inhabitants of your flower bed to know their
places and not go romping around, don't use this primrose. It knows no boundaries.

16. **Latin Name**   *Phyla nodiflora* (*Lippia incisa*,
   Lippia nodiflora)
Pronunciation   FYE-lah noh-deh-FLOR-ah
Common Name   FROGFRUIT
Usual Height   3–4 inches
Spacing   1 foot apart
Bloom   Spring to fall; white; ½-inch heads
Evergreen to dormant in winter
Range   Throughout Texas, including sea-
   shores, woods, and river bottoms
   Southern half U.S. to tropics
Soil   Sand, loam, clay, caliche, limestone;
   well drained or seasonal poor drainage
   okay; saline okay
Shade, dappled shade, part shade, full sun
Colonizes by stolons
Propagation   Root division

Frogfruit is a low-growing ground cover, with verbena-like flowers so tiny they are dwarfed by a bumble-
bee. It is fairly dependably evergreen in the warmer half
of the state. In and around Dallas, if the winter is mild, it
will hold its leaves, although most of them will get reddish or purplish, as Asian jasmine does. In a hard Dallas
winter—or just about any winter in West Texas or the
High Plains—frogfruit would never be evergreen. To maintain it as a thick ground cover anywhere, you must water
it. It will tolerate moderate amounts of foot traffic, so it's
commonly used between stepping-stones or in a parkway.
You can't mow it, though. It hugs the ground as it is, and
if you cut it back any, it seems to resent that a lot. I know
of one instance where it took two years to recover, even
though it had spread quickly when first planted.

17. Mayapple
Podophyllum peltatum
The authors

18. Christmas fern
Polystichum acrostichoides
The authors

17. **Latin Name** *Podophyllum peltatum*
   Pronunciation poh-DOF-eh-lum
      pell-TAY-tum
   Common Name MAYAPPLE
   Usual Height 1–1½ feet
   Spacing 2 feet apart or more
   Bloom April; white (rarely pink); 2 inches
      across
   Fruit May; yellow; 1–3 inches long,
      egg-shaped
   Dormant after setting fruit
   Range Rich hardwoods in East Texas
      Canada to Gulf of Mexico
   Soil Sand, loam; acid; well drained
   Shade, dappled shade, part shade
   Colonizes by rhizomes
   Propagation Seed (blooms third year),
      root division while dormant

Like trilliums, this woodland perennial comes up in March and dies back by June. A three-inch pale finger emerges from beneath the leaves of the forest floor. Two leaves unfurl and form twin umbrellas. The flower appears, usually by April. It is waxy white, or rarely pink, and nods at the vee where the two leaves join. The flower is followed by the pale yellow mayapple. Then, a few weeks later, the plant completely disappears until next year. It's very drought-tolerant in East Texas, but don't try it anywhere else. It is not plentiful in Texas, and it would be a crime to dig any up. They are being grown commercially and can be bought from specialty nurseries in the Houston area. Buy one good thick pot, and divide the roots gently to make several plants. Put them in a small drift, and let them multiply. Don't plant other flowers or ground covers among them; they like to be alone. They prefer to be under oaks or other hardwoods, rather than pines. Mowing will kill them.

18. **Latin Name** *Polystichum acrostichoides*
   Pronunciation pah-LISS-tuh-kum
      ah-kross-teh-CHOY-deez
   Common Name CHRISTMAS FERN
   Usual Height 1–2 feet
   Spacing 1½ feet apart
   Evergreen
   Range Wooded rocky hillsides, sandy
      banks, and thickets in East and South-
      east Texas to Bryan
      Nova Scotia to Wisconsin to Mexico
   Soil Sand, loam; acid to neutral; moist, well
      drained
   Shade, dappled shade
   Colonizes by rhizomes
   Propagation Root division

A ground cover of evergreen fern less than two feet tall . . . Sounds perfect, doesn't it? Well, it is—if you respect its needs and don't force it into an environment it isn't adapted to. To keep Christmas fern happy, plant it in moist soil. Like most ferns, its roots are shallow (six to eight inches deep), so the soil can't be allowed to dry out. But it also likes good drainage, so don't plant it in heavy clay soils. It doesn't like standing water. In addition, it needs cool, deep shade. After all, Texas is the hottest extreme of its natural range. As you can see, this ground cover is a little hard to work with. But if you want a native evergreen fern, it's the only game in town. Just use it in small quantities up close to the house where you can keep an eye on it, and it should reward your care and attention.

19. Oklahoma plum
Prunus gracilis
The authors

19. **Latin Name** *Prunus gracilis*
Pronunciation PROO-nus grah-SILL-us
Common Name OKLAHOMA PLUM
Usual Height 1½ feet, can reach 6 feet
Spacing 1½–3 feet apart
Bloom Midspring before leaves appear; white; ½ inch
Deciduous
Range Open hills and thin woods from East Texas to Panhandle
Oklahoma, Arkansas
Soil Sand; well drained
Dappled shade, part shade, full sun
Colonizes, forms dense thickets
Propagation Stratified seed, cuttings

This is my favorite thicket plum. The ones I see are only eighteen inches to two feet tall and shining white, entirely covered with blossoms. Oklahoma plum blooms at the same time as flowering dogwood, and they make a lovely couple out there in the East Texas woods each spring. Plant this shrub in partial shade, and water it in a drought so it won't get black knot disease. Also give it plenty of room to expand and wander, because that's what thicket plums like to do. Two taller thicket plums are Chickasaw plum (*Prunus angustifolia*), which grows on sands, and creek or hog plum (*P. rivularis*), which grows on limestone soils. Between them, they cover the northern half of the state. In sunny fields they make huge thickets up to twelve feet tall. Under large shade trees, they display graceful clouds of floating white blossoms. Both of these tall thicket plums get webworms, and Chickasaw is usually defoliated in summer because of insect damage. In spite of this, they are popular for their spring beauty and wildlife value.

20. **Latin Name** *Pteridium aquilinum* var. *pseudocaudatum*
Pronunciation tuh-RID-ee-um ak-wih-LINE-um variety soo-doh-kaw-DAY-tum
Common Names BRACKEN, BRACKEN FERN
Usual Height 1–2 feet
Spacing 2–6 feet apart
Dormant in winter
Range Dry woodlands and thickets of East Texas and southern half of Blacklands to Fredericksburg
Florida to Massachusetts
Soil Sand, loam, clay; acid or calcareous; well drained
Shade, dappled shade, part shade, full sun
Colonizes by rhizomes
Propagation Root division while dormant

This large, coarse fern would not be your choice for well-watered areas right up close to your house. It's for those special places where you have large areas of woods— a wood that you cannot or do not want to water, but where you still want to have the wonderful look that only a fern can give. This fern grows all the way south to Fredericksburg, right across the southern half of the Blacklands. I've also seen it in sugar sand in East Texas—and sugar sand can get awfully dry. Not surprisingly, being drought-tolerant, it can also take a lot more sun than other ferns. It's difficult to get established, though, so give it lots of water until it has filled in to your satisfaction. Then let it take care of itself.

21. Purple groundcherry
Quincula lobata
The authors

20. Bracken
Pteridium aquilinum var. *pseudocaudatum*
The authors

21. **Latin Name** *Quincula lobata* (*Physalis lobata*)
Pronunciation KWINK-yoo-lah
  loh-BAH-tah
Common Name PURPLE GROUNDCHERRY
Usual Height 2–6 inches
Spacing 1–1½ feet apart
Bloom Spring to frost; purple, blue, or
  white; 1 inch across
Dormant in winter
Range Western half of Texas
  Western Oklahoma, New Mexico, Arizona,
    Mexico
Soil Sand, loam, clay, caliche; well drained
Part shade, full sun
Colonizes by stolons and rhizomes
Propagation Cuttings

Imagine a carpet of flowers in blue, purple, or white, only about two inches above the ground, and topping green leaves so dense no soil can be seen beneath them. Then imagine having this kind of color starting in spring as soon as the ground warms up and continuing until frost. In well-prepared soil with occasional watering, these plants can fill in solidly in only three or four months. The first year, trailing branches or runners will root at the nodes if you haven't mulched, but the roots don't get aggressive until winter. After frost, the plants go dormant, but the roots get very busy. In the spring new fuzzy, whitish leaves appear where your plants were last year. But they'll also spring up in many new places—like in your lawn. So you might want to use purple groundcherry only where you can surround it with pavement, as in the Sand Garden Plan. There it forms a ground cover in a perennial bed.

22. Pigeonberry
Rivina humilis
The authors

23. Coralberry
Symphoricarpos orbiculatus
The authors

22. **Latin Name**   *Rivina humilis*
Pronunciation   rah-VYE-nah HEW-muh-liss
Common Names   PIGEONBERRY, ROUGE PLANT, RIVINA
Usual Height   1–1½ feet, can reach more than 3 feet
Spacing   1 foot apart
Bloom   Whenever above freezing; pink and white; 2-inch spikes
Fruit   Spring to fall; red berries
Evergreen to dormant in winter
Range   Throughout Texas, but rare in East Texas
Florida, Arkansas, tropical America
Soil   Sand, loam, clay; calcareous preferred; moist, well drained
Dappled shade, part shade
Colonizes by seed
Propagation   Seed, cuttings

Pigeonberry is one of my favorite ground covers. I love it best when it is covered with pink and white flowers and red berries, all at the same time. That happens about seven months out of the year in most of the state. In Corpus Christi and the Valley it is usually an evergreen shrub that blooms almost all winter. It likes best to be tucked up under a larger shrub or, better still, a good shade tree or juniper. Under a mesquite is pure heaven. It also likes moisture and might go semidormant if it gets very dry, so plan an occasional watering for best results. It can establish a solid cover in four months if planted after the weather turns warm. Birds love the red fruits and keep them picked off almost as soon as they ripen, which is continuously. The leaves are not considered good browse, so all but desperately hungry deer may ignore it.

23. **Latin Name**   *Symphoricarpos orbiculatus*
Pronunciation   sim-for-ee-KAR-pus or-bik-yoo-LAH-tus
Common Names   CORALBERRY, INDIAN CURRANT, BUCKBRUSH
Usual Height   1½ feet, can reach 6 feet
Spacing   1½ feet apart
Fruit   Late fall to winter; clusters of ⅛-inch purple berries
Almost Evergreen
Range   Woods, thickets, and along streams in eastern third of Texas
New York, South Dakota, and Colorado to Mexico
Soil   Sand, loam, clay; well drained
Dappled shade, part shade
Colonizes by stolons, forms thickets
Propagation   Firm-wood cuttings of current season's growth

When it's good, it's very, very good, and when it's bad, it's horrid. In October its berries ripen to a bright purple-pink. In February the new leaves come out a luminous lime-green, with the berries still thickly clustered on the branches. The combination of colors is magnificent. The thicket is two to three feet tall, forming solid masses under clumps of mesquites and other short, deciduous trees. That's the good news. The bad news is that coralberry is prone to mildew in heavy soils and to chlorosis on drier calcareous soils, and it can't compete in moist sandy soils. Where it is happy, it provides great erosion control. If yours gets tall and thin, cut it back to the ground when it loses its leaves in the winter. It will come back bushier and with even more berries the next year.

25. Cherisse
Tradescantia micrantha
The authors

25. Spiderwort
Tradescantia sp.
The authors

24. Wood fern
Thelypteris kunthii
The authors

24. **Latin Name** *Thelypteris kunthii* (*Dryopteris normalis*)
Pronunciation thuh-LIP-tare-iss KUN-thee-eye
Common Names WOOD FERN, RIVER FERN, SOUTHERN SHIELD FERN
Usual Height 1½ feet, can reach 5 feet
Spacing 2 feet apart
Dormant in winter
Range Swamps, canyons, creek banks, low woods, and dripping limestone in East Texas, Post Oak Woods, Blackland and Coastal Woods, and southern Edwards Plateau to Big Bend
South Carolina, West Indies, Bahamas, Bermuda
Soil Sand, loam, clay, limestone; moist, poor drainage okay
Shade, dappled shade, part shade
Colonizes by rhizomes
Propagation Root division

Called wood fern in the wooded parts of Texas and river fern in the Hill Country, this is our most versatile and widely used fern. It can be quite aggressive. Katie Ferguson, owner of Lowrey Nursery in Conroe near Houston, uses it to cover huge areas in woodland landscapes. Manuel Flores, a nurseryman in San Antonio, says he has found it to be drought-tolerant in the shade there, but it requires water if it receives a fair amount of sun. He recommends leaving the dead fronds on until Valentine's Day for their soft brown color. But if you prefer, you may cut them off right after first frost. Just be sure to cut them off before the first foliage appears in early spring. Like all ferns, wood fern has shallow roots, so if you have a long drought and can't water it, expect to lose some.

25. **Latin Name** *Tradescantia micrantha*
Pronunciation tray-dess-KAN-shah mih-KRAN-thuh
Common Names CHERISSE (chuh-REESE)
Usual Height 2–6 inches
Spacing 1 foot apart
Bloom April to November; hot pink to fuchsia; ½ inch across
Evergreen
Range Shady places in southern coastal Texas
Endemic to Texas
Soil Sand, loam, clay; well drained
Dappled shade, part shade
Colonizes by stolons, mat-forming
Propagation Root division, seed

In the Valley, nurseryman and landscape designer Mike Heep has been using cherisse as a drought-tolerant, evergreen ground cover under trees and shrubs or on the north side of buildings. Because it is so low-growing, cherisse is especially useful between stepping stones. It roots at the nodes to form a thick mat two to three inches tall with tiny hot pink flowers held above bright green, semi-succulent leaves. Our other native spiderworts (*Tradescantia* spp.) are taller—one to three feet—and have larger flowers and foliage that is more grasslike but are also good ground covers. They are most effective in an informal woodsy situation or as a transition from the formal part of a landscape to a wilder part. Katie Ferguson, a landscape designer in the Houston area, says they look great planted among zigzag and Louisiana iris. Spiderworts grow throughout Texas in a range of colors from purple to white, sometimes two-tone, but most frequently lavender-blue. Most are not aggressive and can be used in perennial gardens.

26. Trillium
Trillium gracile
The authors

27. Sweet William
Verbena canadensis
Edith Bettinger

26. **Latin Name**   *Trillium gracile*
    Pronunciation   TRILL-ee-um gruh-SEEL or
       GRASS-ih-lee
    Common Names   TRILLIUM, WAKE-ROBIN
    Usual Height   8–12 inches
    Spacing   1 foot apart
    Bloom   April; maroon, aging to yellowish
       green or yellow; 2 inches
    Dormant after setting fruit
    Range   Piney Woods in Southeast Texas
       Louisiana, Arkansas, Mississippi
    Soil   Sand, loam; acid; moist, well drained
    Dappled shade, part shade
    Colonizes by rhizomes and seed
    Propagation   Fresh seed planted on site

Trillium is one of our more uncommon woodland perennials that is lovely naturalized in a woodsy area. It blooms in the spring and then disappears, as daffodils do. I've been told that the flowers smell like morel mushrooms. I didn't notice that myself, but maybe I didn't sniff hard enough. The flowers are not showy from a distance. They are for the close-up inspection of true connoisseurs of woodland wildflowers. The leaves are a delicate pale green, mottled with darker green. Although trillum can multiply by the roots, it seems to multiply faster by seed— relatively speaking, that is. We're speaking of glacial "speed." Plant fresh seed on the site. Expect only one leaf the first spring. The next year you should have three leaves. Don't expect a bloom until the third or fourth year. It takes decades for a big stand to develop. *Do not dig trilliums up in the wild!* If you gather seed yourself instead of getting a start from a reputable grower, gather only five to ten seeds so you won't deplete the population.

27. **Latin Name**   *Verbena canadensis* (*Glandularia
       canadensis*)
    Pronunciation   ver-BEE-nah
       kan-ah-DEN-siss
    Common Names   SWEET WILLIAM,
       ROSE VERVAIN
    Usual Height   5–10 inches
    Spacing   1 foot apart
    Bloom   February to April; rose-pink; 2-inch
       clusters; fragrant
    Evergreen, thin in summer
    Range   Fields and woods in eastern half of
       Texas, Austin to Red River
       Illinois to Florida, Colorado
    Soil   Sand, loam; acid; moist, well drained
    Dappled shade, part shade
    **Colonizes by roots and by stems rooting at
       lower nodes**
    Propagation   Seed sown in spring or fall,
       cuttings, root division

Sweet William was named for its sweet fragrance. (I have no idea who William was.) Near a mass planting, the air is heavily scented and swarming with butterflies. Sweet William is capable of forming dense mats, often covering large areas, and is quite low-growing when not in bloom. It needs regular watering in the summer to stay thick and needs mulching in the winter in all but the mildest areas to prevent losses from freezing. (It's considered an annual in its northern range—beyond the Red River.) Besides being used as a conventional ground cover, Sweet William can provide several weeks of spring color when naturalized in a lightly shaded woods or in a sunny meadow. Or, rare for plants in this chapter, it can be used in a flower garden, since it is not difficult to control. This verbena can be quite long-lived. My mother has been admiring a favorite clump near Palestine, Texas, for nearly twenty years. You should know that, given a choice, rabbits will head for the Sweet William first.

28. Missouri violet
Viola missouriensis
The authors

29. Walter's violet
Viola walteri
The authors

28. **Latin Name** *Viola missouriensis*
Pronunciation vye-OH-lah
mih-zoo-ree-EN-siss
Common Names MISSOURI VIOLET,
WOOD VIOLET
Usual Height 2–6 inches
Spacing 1 foot apart or less
Bloom Early spring; purple, lavender, or
white; 1 inch or less across
Green in winter, dormant in summer if dry
Range Woodlands and river forests from
Coastal Bend north to Red River and
west to Western Cross Timbers
Minnesota to Texas to New Mexico
Soil Sand, loam, clay, limestone; well
drained
Shade, dappled shade, part shade
Colonizes by rhizomes and seeds
Propagation Root division (often 20 to 30
plants from one horizontal rhizome), seed
(blooms second year)

Wood violets start blooming in February, and a good-sized stand of them will bloom for about three weeks. Mine are on a dry slope under a Shumard red oak and a bois d'arc tree. They stay green until August and then give up the fight and go dormant until we get the first good fall rain. Then they green up again and remain so all winter. One year it rained in August, and they stayed green that entire year, but I've never achieved the same result with plain old watering. I have all kinds of ornamental trees, bulbs, and woodland flowers planted among my violets, and they coexist easily. All of the purple wood violets are good to use. In East Texas there are several to choose from. Bird's foot violet (*Viola pedata*) is especially charming for the sandy pinelands, but it must be grown from seed. Others, such as lanceleaf violet (*V. lanceolata*) and primrose violet (*V. primulifolia*) tolerate poor drainage and can be found growing in bogs.

29. **Latin Name** *Viola walteri*
Pronunciation vye-OH-lah WALL-ter-eye
Common Name WALTER'S VIOLET
Usual Height 2–6 inches
Spacing 9 inches apart
Bloom Early spring; royal purple; 1 inch
Evergreen
Range Rich oak forests in Southeast Texas
Ohio to Gulf of Mexico
Soil Sand, loam; acid to slightly alkaline;
moist, well drained
Shade, dappled shade
Colonizes by rhizomes
Propagation Root division, seed

This little evergreen violet is too delicate in texture for large stands, but it's ideal for small areas. Like the partridgeberry, it must be kept evenly moist all year, especially in hot, dry weather, to maintain a dense cover. It will tell you when it's too dry, because it will droop dramatically. Besides spreading underground, Walter's violet sends out trailing branches, so it can form solid mats of the little round leaves, which lie flat and are often purply underneath. As a woodland ground cover, it grows well with mayapple, trillium, and partridgeberry in the moist nonpiney woods of East Texas. Unless you have a very small woods in an ordinary-sized front yard, keeping Walter's violet evenly moist probably will not be practical. In that case, it will not grow into a dense stand but will be scattered just as you would find it in the wild.

Wildlife Garden Plan
Lot Size: 40' × 50'

Nearly all of our native plants have some value for wildlife. It's a synergistic relationship, with all of nature interweaving and cooperating. Insects, birds, and mammals depend on plants for food, while at the same time the plants depend on the wildlife to pollinate their flowers and distribute their seeds. This is not news—we all learned about it in school. (Remember the old birds-and-bees routine?) But too often we forget how vital it is that this natural interplay be allowed to continue as undisturbed as possible.

So, if you're interested in creating a wildlife garden, don't think of it only as a source of beauty and pleasure for you and yours. Think of it as a contribution to the ongoing life cycle we're all a part of.

Anyone with a half acre or more of wild area is supporting a lot of wildlife. You don't have to plant, sow, weed, or water. You let nature take care of itself. This plan is for city people who don't have that option because of zoning ordinances, fire laws, and consideration of their neighbors. At a quick glance, this landscape will look fairly ordinary—except that the shrubs have a soft natural shape, and there are a lot more flowers than are normally found in a yard.

On closer inspection, you will see other differences. In a wildlife garden, you can use no poisons or chemicals. Chewed-up leaves often mean that caterpillars are feasting, in preparation for metamorphosing into butterflies. Unwanted infestations need to be taken care of by pruning or handpicking.

I've selected plants that will primarily attract small critters. Not deer and rabbits, who need no encouraging! Not raccoons and opossums, who are quite happy dining on the contents of your trash cans. And not quail and grouse, who are found primarily in grasslands, not around the average home garden. Don't misunderstand me. I like all these creatures, just as I like buffalo, mountain lions, coyotes, and black bears.

But for you and your garden, I have chosen plants and habitats that will attract songbirds, hummingbirds, butterflies, moths, dragonflies, anoles (lizards), toads, fireflies, and bats—little creatures you'll enjoy watching during the day or on summer evenings. (Yes, I include bats. They are probably the most misunderstood animals in the world and are therefore endangered. Aside from the fact that I think they're cute, they are terribly vital to our ecosystem. Just one free-tailed bat, the most common bat in Texas, can eat three thousand insects per night. Think how many of those insects might be mosquitoes!)

In designing this plan,* I wanted to make it usable for everyone in the state, and since our habitats are so diverse, this is an impossible task. You will see two to four names written beside nearly every tree and shrub. The top name is for the Valley and its adjacent areas, which are sometimes east

---

*This garden was designed following the guidelines established by the National Wildlife Federation. For information on how to turn your property into a certified Wildlife Habitat, write to the federation at 1412 Sixteenth St. NW, Washington, DC 20036-2266.

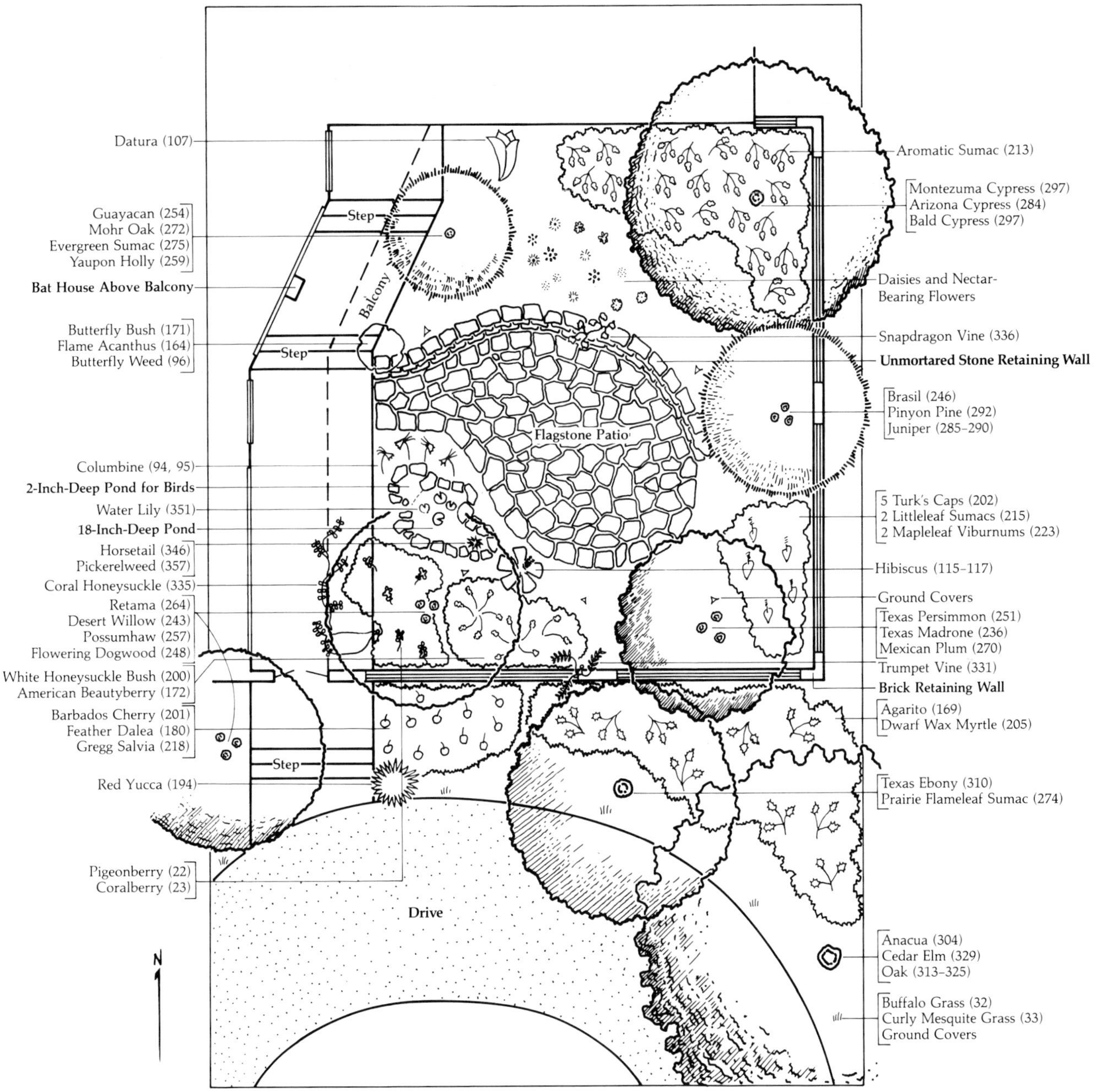

Datura (107)

Guayacan (254)
Mohr Oak (272)
Evergreen Sumac (275)
Yaupon Holly (259)

Bat House Above Balcony

Butterfly Bush (171)
Flame Acanthus (164)
Butterfly Weed (96)

Columbine (94, 95)
2-Inch-Deep Pond for Birds
Water Lily (351)
18-Inch-Deep Pond
Horsetail (346)
Pickerelweed (357)
Coral Honeysuckle (335)
Retama (264)
Desert Willow (243)
Possumhaw (257)
Flowering Dogwood (248)
White Honeysuckle Bush (200)
American Beautyberry (172)
Barbados Cherry (201)
Feather Dalea (180)
Gregg Salvia (218)

Red Yucca (194)

Pigeonberry (22)
Coralberry (23)

Step
Balcony
Step

Flagstone Patio

Step

Drive

N

Aromatic Sumac (213)

Montezuma Cypress (297)
Arizona Cypress (284)
Bald Cypress (297)

Daisies and Nectar-
Bearing Flowers

Snapdragon Vine (336)
Unmortared Stone Retaining Wall

Brasil (246)
Pinyon Pine (292)
Juniper (285–290)

5 Turk's Caps (202)
2 Littleleaf Sumacs (215)
2 Mapleleaf Viburnums (223)

Hibiscus (115–117)

Ground Covers
Texas Persimmon (251)
Texas Madrone (236)
Mexican Plum (270)
Trumpet Vine (331)
Brick Retaining Wall
Agarito (169)
Dwarf Wax Myrtle (205)

Texas Ebony (310)
Prairie Flameleaf Sumac (274)

Anacua (304)
Cedar Elm (329)
Oak (313–325)

Buffalo Grass (32)
Curly Mesquite Grass (33)
Ground Covers

Wildlife Garden

This shallow, easy-to-clean pond, designed by Burr Williams for Bob and Dede Plank in Midland, is ideal for birds. Here they can drink and bathe, surrounded by plenty of nectar flowers, seeds, and berries, with adjacent shrubs and trees for nesting and cover. Photo by the authors.

and sometimes west of the Valley. These plants are exceptionally good for wildlife year-round, but they are not winter-hardy for most of the state.

The last name listed is always for the eastern parts of the state. These plants are not East Texas specialties, like the western mayhaw, but plants that grow over most of the eastern half of the state. They generally require more water than the other choices. Some, like Gregg salvia, are not native there, but in the sun and on a well-drained slope as shown in the plan, they can be successfully grown.

The middle names take care of everyone else, but you are going to have to study the range information in the individual plant profiles to choose the best ones for you. Knowing the most cold-hardy plants will help, so I will do the High Plains for you.

If you live there, choose Mohr oak, possumhaw, feather dalea, agarito, prairie flameleaf sumac, Mexican plum, littleleaf sumac, pinyon pines, and bald cypress. They have the most cold tolerance. Mexican plum, possum-haw, and bald cypress are not likely to be drought-tolerant, so you'll have to be sure to water them. Also, datura and flame acanthus will be only mar-ginally cold-hardy and will need mulching in the winter. They have been placed in the most protected corner of the courtyard just for you High Plains residents.

A wildlife garden has to do more than provide food for all seasons. It also has to furnish water for both drinking and bathing, and cover for court-ing, sleeping, and nesting. Let me walk you around the garden and point out the uses of each plant.

The big shade trees provide nesting and food. The seeds of the cypresses feed many birds, as do those of the cedar elm. Acorns are good for blue jays and squirrels, among others, and the anacua provides nectar for bees and butterflies, fruits for birds and small mammals, and evergreen cover for year-round use.

Evergreens are especially important for birds in Texas, as we have so many that winter over. Evergreens in this plan, besides the anacua, are Montezuma cypress, Arizona cypress, brasil, pinyon pine, juniper, Turk's cap (evergreen only in the Valley), Texas madrone, Texas ebony, agarito, dwarf wax myrtle, Barbados cherry, red yucca, horsetail, guayacan, Mohr oak, evergreen sumac, and yaupon holly. Each one also provides fruit or nectar.

Red yucca is an important hummingbird plant, as are Turk's cap (which everyone can grow with a winter mulch), trumpet vine, coral honeysuckle, flame acanthus, columbines, desert willow, and Gregg salvia.

Butterflies are attracted to butterfly bush, as well as many other sweet-smelling, nectar-bearing flowers, such as verbenas, butterfly weed and other milkweeds, old plainsman, spectacle pod, and bergamot. To see which ones are best for your area, check the individual plant profiles elsewhere in this book. These species can be planted around the pool, in the bed above the rock wall, around the circular drive, and so forth. Geyata Ajilvsgi, author of books on butterflies and butterfly gardens, says that masses of one flower are more effective than a mixture in attracting butterflies.

The pool can be done in one of two ways: It can be completely shallow—two to four inches deep—to serve as a giant birdbath, or one end can slope down to an eighteen-inch depth, as indicated in this plan, to hold two water plants to attract dragonflies. I've given you three to pick from—fragrant water lily, horsetail, and pickerelweed. These have always been particularly loaded down with gorgeous dragonflies whenever I've seen them. You can set them in pots in the edges of the pool so that the tops of the pots are about six inches below the surface. (See the Water Garden Plan in Chapter 11 for more information on how to do this.)

The shallow part of the pool is the most important as far as birds are concerned. They like to wade and frolic or simply perch on the edge to sip water. Make this area only two inches deep in the center and let it gradually slope up.

Line the entire pool with 20 mil black PVC liner, fill it with pebbles, and let some dust and dirt fill in so it looks like a natural spring. Rocks around the edge help with the illusion, and hold the plastic in place. This is the best kind of pool to have out west, so you'll be able to clean it out easily after a dust storm. Also, the pool uses very little water. Make sure the shallow end is shaded, at least in the afternoon, to cut down on evaporation.

The rock wall is unmortared to provide habitat for other small animals: daddy longlegs, garter snakes, anoles, and so on. Of course, scorpions will like it too, so be cautious about lifting stones or sitting on them. Anoles are lizards with lime-green backs and white tummies. The males have pink throats, which they expand to make themselves irresistible to females. Anoles like to spend hot afternoons sunning on a wall or on rocks. They also spend a lot of time lounging in trees and ground covers looking for insects to eat.

Fireflies require rotting wood or moist rich earth under plants in which to lay their eggs. The larvae winter over and then gorge themselves on slugs, snails, earthworms, and soft-bodied insects.

Toads, who eat insects, make their burrows under thick vegetation in loose cool earth. Ground covers are perfect, not just for toads but also for many small ground animals. Use creeping herbs, low-growing shrubs, flowers, or shortgrasses for the areas marked ground covers on this plan. In front, by the circular drive, buffalo grass (mowed only once or twice a year) or curly mesquite grass (never mowed) could be effective by the driveway. Grass seeds also make good food for lots of wildlife.

Insects are the main course for birds during the summer, fresh fruits not being readily available, but you can provide fruits during this period. Aromatic sumac is one of the first to ripen, and agarito ripens by late May. Turk's cap and pigeonberry have flowers and fruits from spring to frost. Other sumacs and barberries ripen during the summer and hold into the fall to feed the migrating hordes. More summer seed is found on the desert willow, anacua, brasil, and Texas persimmon. Fall seeds and berries are produced by guayacan, evergreen sumac, possumhaw, American beautyberry, dwarf wax myrtle, juniper, viburnum, flowering dogwood, and coralberry.

One important source of seeds is daisies. Many of our best flowers are daisies, and if you let the seed ripen instead of cutting off the old stalks, they furnish abundant fresh food all summer and fall.

As you can tell, a wildlife garden is different. Even if you put in all the same plants you'd have in a conventional garden, you'd treat them differently. It can be lots less work if you don't prune, don't remove deadwood, don't cut off old blooms, and don't weed religiously. Your reward will be an ever-changing, always fascinating display of textures, colors, sounds, and sights all year long.

OTHER PLANTS THAT CAN BE USED AS GROUND COVERS

Shade	Sun
Inland seaoats (39)	Snakeweed (113)
Wild red columbine (94), evergreen	Yellow zinnia (159)
Yellow columbine (95), evergreen	Whitebrush (161)
Wild blue aster (97)	Sand sagebrush (165), evergreen
Wild ageratum (112)	Damianita (176)
Flor de San Juan (124)	Larchleaf goldenweed (184)
Gulf Coast penstemon (135), evergreen	Apache plume (191)
Louisiana phlox (137), evergreen	Texas lantana (196)
Fragrant phlox (138)	Cenizos (198, 199)
Fall obedient plant (139), evergreen	Dwarf wax myrtle (205), evergreen
Ruellias (144)	Havard oak (211)
Scarlet sage (146)	Aromatic sumac (213)
Cedar sage (149), evergreen	Smooth sumac (214)
Chile pequín (173)	Gregg salvia (218), evergreen
Starleaf Mexican orange (175), evergreen	Hiedra (337)
Virginia sweetspire (195)	
Turk's cap (202)	
Roses (216)	
Palmetto (217), evergreen	
Zexmenia (225)	
Virginia creeper (337)	

This buffalo grass lawn was broadcast from seed barely a year earlier by Glenn and Connie Suhren of Garland. The raised bed contains winecups, red yucca, and other native and naturalized flowers. Photo by the authors.

THREE

Grasses

GRASSES are the premier ground covers in Texas. That's not surprising, since except for our eastern forests, we are a prairie state. We are also, in case you haven't noticed, a big state, with rainfalls varying from 7 inches to 55 inches and winter temperatures ranging from frost half the year to almost none at all. That creates a tremendous diversity of grasses.

We use our grasses in four major ways: as lawns, as meadows with wildflowers, in pockets of tallgrass prairie, and as garden accents.

I have divided the plant profiles in this chapter into two sections. The first is Lawn Grass Profiles. These grasses are all perennials, and they can all be mowed. They can also take moderate amounts of foot traffic.

For most Texans, buffalo grass is the first choice for a native lawn. It makes a smooth surface, it is naturally low-growing, so mowing is optional, and it grows well all over the state except in the Piney Woods and Houston regions, where there is too much rainfall for it to compete successfully with other grasses and plants.

Buffalo grass was native up to the true Post Oak Savannah, east of the Blackland Prairies, but it was marginal as far east as San Antonio, Austin, Waco, and Dallas until overgrazing destroyed the tallgrasses and allowed the buffalo grass to fill in.

Out west, where scanty rainfall has produced the shortgrass prairies, you have not only buffalo grass but also several other potential lawn grasses to choose from, such as the dainty ear muhly, the pink burro grass, and western wheatgrass, which is evergreen. These lawn grasses, with the exception of western wheatgrass, also make good meadows. Just add wildflowers and mow them only once or twice a year.

The second section of grasses is labeled Bunchgrass Profiles. These grasses make clumps that get bigger each year. Mowed, they would make a lumpy lawn. Furthermore, most of them are sensitive to mowing, except when they are dormant in the winter. Their roots are not as invasive as those of the shortgrasses, so they are often used as accents in a flower garden, like any other large perennial.

The bunchgrasses grow in ever-widening circles, until eventually their middle dies out. If you have one in your garden and this happens, dig it up and divide it, as you would with old perennial flowers, and then plant a vigorous young clump from the edge into the bare spot.

The bunchgrasses range from two to six feet in height and sometimes get even taller. They provide good erosion control and are attractive when used to hold sunny, rocky hillsides or banks. One shade-loving grass, inland seaoats, makes an easy-care ground cover in moist, shady places.

The midheight bunchgrasses provide a variety of textures and colors for meadows. (I am using the word "meadow" to mean a mixture of grasses and wildflowers less than three feet high.) Seep, Gulf, and purple muhly are knee-high and are a lovely soft pink in the fall. Sideoats grama produces seed all summer and into the fall, and it's great for attracting birds. Split-beard bluestem catches the light in its tiny fluffy seeds and almost sparkles with silvery-white puffs. Little bluestem is a beautiful pale blue in late summer and a deep rich brown after frost. It is midheight in low rainfall, and when it gets more water, it joins the tallgrasses.

The big four in tallgrass prairie restoration are big bluestem, little bluestem, Indian grass, and switch grass. Tallgrass prairie is at its southernmost limit in Texas and extends northward through the Great Plains to Canada. If you are interested in creating a pocket prairie, contact the Native Prairies Association of Texas. Its address is listed in Chapter 12, Who's Who in Native Plant Landscaping.

Native grass will not be available in sod until the 1990s. Until then (or if you have more than a half acre), you'll have to plant yours from seed. At this point, let me introduce you to a new term—pure live seed (PLS). This is simply seed that will germinate.

The recommended amount of grass seed for landscape use is one half to two pounds of pure live seed per 1,000 square feet. Ranchers and farmers regularly plant one to two pounds of pure live seed per acre, or 43,560 square feet. When you apply two pounds for just 1,000 square feet, 43 times the density of the ranchers' rate, you are pretty much assured a generous and rapid cover. Personally, I think that a half pound is ample, but that may just be my Scottish heritage. When you buy your seed in large quantities, by law it is required to be tagged with a date showing that the germination test is no more than six months old. In addition, the tag will show percent of guaranteed purity (ideally it should be 95 percent) and guaranteed germination (ideally 75 percent).

For you to apply the seed in the proper PLS-to-area ratio, you need to know your total weight of PLS, and that isn't the total weight of the bag. If only it were that easy.

Inside that bag, along with your PLS, is a lot of other stuff. This is inevitable. It might be unripe seed, other kinds of seed that just happened to be there when your seed was gathered, chaff, and minute bits of this and that. The tag sometimes (but not always) gives you a percentage of PLS, but you need to know the weight, not just the percentage.

To find out how much PLS you have in there, simply multiply the given percentage by the total weight of the bag. Thus, a 70 percent PLS in a ten-pound bag gives you seven pounds of pure live seed. When the PLS percentage isn't on the tag, get out your calculator, take the number given for purity, and multiply it by the number for germination. Class dismissed.

There are many methods for starting a lawn, such as broadcasting and hydromulching, and all of them seem to work. Do exactly as you would for starting a Bermuda grass lawn. The same applies to starting meadows and prairies also. In the fall, grass and wildflower seed may be applied at the same time. Otherwise, start the grass in the spring or summer, and plant the wildflowers in the fall. For large jobs where turf already exists, the best way to sow wildflower seeds is with a newly developed seeding machine, patented by WildSeed, Inc. It can sow several different weights at one pass without disturbing the turf. A landscaper in your area may well own one of these machines, or you can rent one directly from WildSeed.

LAWN GRASS

30. **Latin Name** *Agropyron smithii*
   Pronunciation ah-GROH-peh-ron SMITH-ee-eye
   Common Name WESTERN WHEATGRASS
   Usual Height 1–3 feet if unmowed
   Spacing ½–2 pounds pure live seed (PLS) per 1,000 square feet
   Bloom May to June
   Evergreen with summer watering
   Range High Plains, rare in North Central Texas and moist canyons in the Trans-Pecos
   Western U.S., Kentucky, Tennessee, Arkansas, Ohio
   Soil Sand, loam, clay; moist, seasonal poor drainage okay
   Full sun, a little shade okay
   Colonizes by fragile, easily detached rhizomes
   Propagation Seed, root division

Western wheatgrass stands out because of its handsome bluish-green color. And you get an added bonus—it stays looking that colorful all winter. It prefers cool summers (cool by Texas standards, that is), so it will be used mostly in and around Lubbock and Amarillo. But folks in El Paso, Midland-Odessa, Wichita Falls, and Sherman might also have success with it. A little bit of watering is necessary in the summer to keep it from going dormant. If it gets aggressive, you have given it too much water. Its only drawback is that it cannot be used for a wildflower meadow. The sod is extraordinarily tight, and its vigorous winter growth outcompetes wildflower rosettes. Of course, it outcompetes weeds too. People who have used it describe it as a good, tough turf grass.

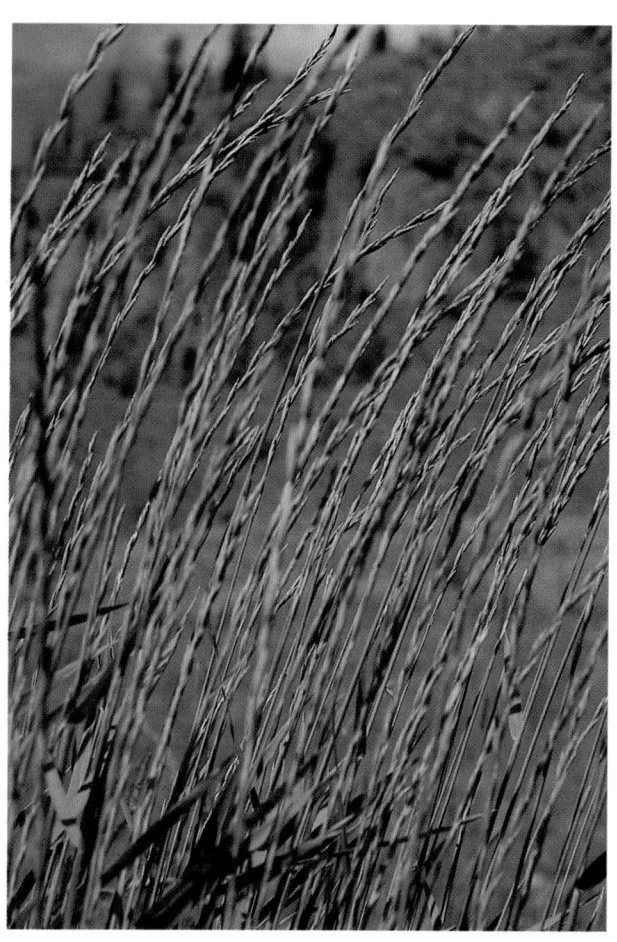

30. Western wheatgrass
Agropyron smithii
The authors

32. **Warm brown winter color of 'Double J Ranch' buffalo grass**
Buchloe dactyloides
John Gleason, National Wildflower Research Center files

31. **Blue grama**
Bouteloua gracilis
The authors

31. **Latin Name** *Bouteloua gracilis*
Pronunciation boo-tuh-LOO-ah grah-SILL-iss
Common Name BLUE GRAMA
Usual Height 1 foot
Spacing ½–2 pounds pure live seed (PLS) per 1,000 square feet
Bloom June to November
Dormant in winter
Range High Plains, West Texas, Trans-Pecos, and western Edwards Plateau Western half of North America
Soil Sand, loam, clay; calcareous; well drained
Full sun, a little shade okay
Sub-rhizomatous, basically a tufted grass
Propagation Seed

Blue grama is a fine-leaved turf grass that gets its name from the blue cast of its seed heads. It's a good choice for a meadow grass, because individual tufts decline within five years, constantly leaving spaces for wildflowers (and more blue grama) to seed out. Blue grama is often mixed with buffalo grass, and together they give excellent cover and provide a lawn so soft and smooth that it satisfies the cravings of people who love to walk barefoot on the grass. Although this type of lawn must be watered to maintain its softness and springiness in the summer, I've been told that the amount of water necessary is a half to a third of that needed just to keep Kentucky bluegrass alive. Because blue grama is nonaggressive, it can also be used as an accent in a perennial garden. It sometimes spreads by rhizomes, but rather timidly, which is why it is called sub-rhizomatous.

**32. Never-been-mown
'Comanche' buffalo grass**
Buchloe dactyloides
Vernon L. Wesby

32. **Latin Name** *Buchloe dactyloides*
  Pronunciation buk-LOH-ee
    dak-till-LOY-deez
  Common Name BUFFALO GRASS
  Usual Height 3–12 inches if unmowed
  Spacing ½–2 pounds pure live seed (PLS)
    per 1,000 square feet, or 4–5 pounds bulk
    seed per 1,000 square feet
  Bloom Whenever not dormant; male and
    female flowers on separate plants
  **Dormant in winter and in drought; soft
  golden brown when dormant**
  Range Throughout Texas except East Texas,
    Houston, and western Trans-Pecos
    Minnesota and Montana to Mexico and
    Peru
  Soil Sand, loam, clay, caliche, limestone;
    well drained
  Full sun, a little shade okay
  Colonizes by stolons
  Propagation Treated seed sown in April to
    mid-September

Everyone I asked said buffalo grass was their favorite native turf grass. It's the toughest and takes the most foot traffic, yet has the softest and most even texture. It covers more quickly than the others, then lives the longest. If you sow it profusely in soil (not caliche), water it three times a day, and arrange for good warm weather, you can have a thick and sturdy stand that can be mowed only one month later. On caliche it takes longer to establish. Just sow extra thickly for a quicker cover.

Those who have established buffalo grass lawns rarely water or mow them. One owner I asked mows his in early February, in time for it to green up, and then again in August. Another has never mowed his at all, and it bends over like a billowing sea. Still another went on vacation and didn't water his all of July and August and returned to find it greener than his neighbor's Bermuda, which had been watered twice a week. Good stuff!

When buffalo grass does go dormant, either after frost or when it gets too dry, it turns a soft golden brown. The male seed heads are the ones everyone loves, and they remain visible even through the winter.

Most of the seed you buy that is acclimated to Texas is either 'Texoka' or 'Comanche.' Both have been bred with cattlemen in mind. The result is that they are both unusually tall—nine to twelve inches—to provide more food per acre. They are great for a meadow and are the kinds WildSeed uses in its meadow mixes. (By 1990 Wild-Seed plans to have sod available.)

Most people with buffalo grass lawns plant either of the two varieties above and mow them as I've indicated. But for a lawn you never have to mow, a three- to four-inch buffalo grass is needed. The kind that grows in bar ditches is perfect. Unfortunately, no one is selling short buffalo grass at the present.

One, named 'Prairie,' is a female strain, for people who don't like the little male flowers. (Takes all kinds!) Apple-green in the spring and golden brown in the fall, it grows only four inches tall. If, as expected, it is released to growers in 1988 and someone decides to grow it, it will be available to the public in the early nineties. Since it spreads by runners rather than by seed, it will be sold as sod or as sprigs.

For those of you who love the dainty male flowers that wave above buffalo grass, you'll have to wait even longer, but help is coming. Several groups of scientists in the United States are working on marketable varieties.

33. Curly mesquite grass
Hilaria belangeri
The authors

33. **Latin Name**   *Hilaria belangeri*
Pronunciation   hye-LARE-ee-uh
beh-LAN-zhur-ee
Common Name   CURLY MESQUITE GRASS
Usual Height   4–6 inches
Spacing   ½–2 pounds pure live seed (PLS)
per 1,000 square feet, or root divisions 1
foot apart
Bloom   Summer to fall
Range   Western half of Texas
New Mexico, Arizona, Mexico
Soil   Sand, loam, clay, caliche, limestone;
well drained
Full sun, a little shade okay
Colonizes by stolons
Propagation   Seed, root division while
dormant

At some times of the year curly mesquite grass looks a lot like buffalo grass, and many people get the two confused. It grows in tufts four to six inches tall and six to eight inches wide. The tufts are always greenish gray with long, silvery, curly hairs. Curly mesquite grass is often used as a lawn, but the tufts make it somewhat lumpy. Also, mowing ruins its rough, shaggy quality. I prefer it as a softly textured ground cover. It looks terrific accented with twisted-leaf yucca and nolina. Add evergreen sumac, blue Texas star (*Amsonia ciliata*) velvetleaf senna, and gay-feather (*Liatris punctata* or *L. mucronata*), and you've got a visual feast of textures and colors unique to the Edwards Plateau and the Trans-Pecos, especially on limestone inclines. This grass provides consistent good looks in full sun with reflected heat and requires no water or care.

34. Ear muhly
Muhlenbergia arenacea
The authors

35. Burro grass
Scleropogon brevifolius
Benny J. Simpson

34. **Latin Name** *Muhlenbergia arenacea*
Pronunciation mew-len-BUR-jee-ah
air-en-AY-see-ah
Common Name EAR MUHLY
Usual Height 4–14 inches
Spacing ½–2 pounds pure live seed (PLS)
per 1,000 square feet
Bloom Summer to fall
Dormant in winter
Range Desert flats and stream valleys in
Edwards Plateau, Trans-Pecos, and Roll-
ing Plains
Colorado to Arizona to Mexico
Soil Sand, loam, limestone; calcareous; well
drained
Full sun, a little shade okay
Colonizes by rhizomes
Propagation Seed, root division while
dormant

This delicate-looking grass can maintain itself in pure stands for acres. When not in flower, it looks a lot like burro grass. Dr. Barton H. Warnock suggested that ear muhly would make an attractive low-maintenance turf grass and showed some to me in the Trans-Pecos. It was late July, during an especially wet period. I instantly loved this grass. It was four or five inches high wherever I saw it. The airy branching of the flowers gives a very different look and feel from any of the other shortgrasses. Mow it normally until the first good rain in late summer or fall. Then stop mowing and let it bloom. When it is through blooming, mow it again.

35. **Latin Name** *Scleropogon brevifolius*
Pronunciation skler-AH-puh-gon
breh-veh-FOLE-ee-us
Common Name BURRO GRASS
Usual Height 4–9 inches
Spacing ½–2 pounds pure live seed (PLS)
per 1,000 square feet
Bloom 1–2 months in July and August;
females pink or white
Dormant in winter
Range Trans-Pecos, western Edwards
Plateau, Rolling and High Plains
Colorado to Nevada to Argentina and
Chile
Soil Sand, loam, clay, caliche; calcareous;
well drained
Full sun, a little shade okay
Colonizes by stolons
Propagation Seed, root division

Burro grass can be extremely aggressive, and ranchers who fight it or cringe when they see it on their land will probably be surprised to think of it as a useful landscape grass. There are both male and female plants, and it is the females that have the pretty flowers. But you have to view them with the light behind them to appreciate the color. Blooms appear after a good soaking rain in July or whenever that rain happens to come. The flower is either pink or white, and I would choose all pink if it were possible. If you need to gather your own seed, you could gather only from pink plants and hope for a high percentage. If you dig and divide to get your start, space your plants about a foot apart. After blooming, the plants turn green in September, provided it rains again. This grass is more drought-tolerant than buffalo grass and looks best with no watering. Mow it like ear muhly.

BUNCHGRASS

36. Big bluestem
Andropogon gerardii
Edith Bettinger

37. Splitbeard bluestem
Andropogon ternarius
The authors

36. **Latin Name** *Andropogon gerardii*
Pronunciation an-DROP-uh-gon jeh-RAR-dee-eye
Common Names BIG BLUESTEM, TURKEYFOOT
Usual Height 3–6 feet
Spacing ½–2 pounds pure live seed (PLS) per 1,000 square feet, or 2 feet apart for garden accent
Bloom August to November
Dormant in winter
Range Low meadows and prairies throughout Texas
Canada to Gulf of Mexico to Mexico
Soil Sand, loam, clay; acid or calcareous, seasonal poor drainage okay
Part shade, full sun
Sometimes colonizes by rhizomes
Propagation Seed, root division while dormant in winter

Big bluestem is an important component of the tallgrass prairie, along with little bluestem, Indian grass, and switch grass. It needs moisture and is not at its best in the dry Panhandle or the Trans-Pecos, where shortgrasses are better adapted. However, in the eastern half of the state, where rainfall is quite adequate, this grass does well, especially if it is placed at the bottom of a slope. Its most recognizable characteristic is the three-toed turkeyfoot shape of the flowering spikelets. Most of the available commercial seed is from north of the Red River, and it does not do well in Texas. It germinates poorly and produces sickly plants. I'd advise you to collect your own seed from a nearby stand. Big bluestem sets seed shortly after flowering, so you can gather it from September on. If you use big bluestem as a garden accent, do not give it too much water and fertilizer or any shade, because it will get top-heavy and can fall over.

38. Sideoats grama
Bouteloua curtipendula
The authors

37. **Latin Name** *Andropogon ternarius*
Pronunciation an-DROP-uh-gon
  ter-NARE-ee-us
Common Name SPLITBEARD BLUESTEM
Usual Height 1½ feet, can reach 4 feet
Spacing ½–2 pounds pure live seed (PLS)
  per 1,000 square feet, or 2 feet apart for
  garden accent
Bloom August to November
Fruit September to November; fluffy white
  seed
Range Open and wooded Central and East
  Texas
  Kentucky to Gulf of Mexico
Soil Sand; well drained
Part shade, full sun
Clumps
Propagation Seed

Splitbeard bluestem is one of my favorite grasses. I love to see it in masses with the autumn sun glowing behind it, showing off its silvery white tufts. Each little feathery seed tuft catches the light and seems to amplify it. With no supplemental watering, this bluestem is usually no taller than two feet. This would make it one of my first choices for a meadow grass in sandy soils and on the edges of post oak woods in the eastern half of Texas. For a neater, greener appearance in the spring, cut back the old stalks in the winter after the seed is all gone and the mellow winter brown has weathered to gray— usually around Valentine's Day. Splitbeard bluestem is often found growing with little bluestem. Flowers that combine well with it are Drummond phlox, old plainsman, scarlet penstemon (*P. murrayanus*), and wild buckwheat.

38. **Latin Name** *Bouteloua curtipendula*
Pronunciation boo-tuh-LOO-ah
  ker-tuh-PEN-dew-lah
Common Name SIDEOATS GRAMA
Usual Height 2–3 feet, can reach 6 feet
Spacing ½–2 pounds pure live seed (PLS)
  per 1,000 square feet, or 3 feet apart for
  garden accent
Fruit June to November
Dormant in winter
Range Throughout Texas except eastern
  forests and Valley
  Canada to Argentina
Soil Sand, loam, clay, limestone, igneous;
  well drained
Dappled shade, part shade, full sun
**Clumps, often rhizomatous, rarely
  stoloniferous**
Propagation Seed, root division while dormant in winter

Sideoats grama is a comfortable size and shape for use as a garden accent. The seed provides excellent bird food all summer and fall and into the winter. Sideoats is frequently found in disturbed sites, that is, bulldozed, overgrazed, or otherwise ravaged places. A garden has also been disturbed, albeit more gently. Sideoats grama can compete well with the short prairie grasses but not with the tallgrasses. It stays low during the spring, so it makes a good grass to use with spring wildflowers and is a frequent choice for meadows. It can be mowed once up to June and again after first frost. If you mow it more in the summer, you risk killing it.

39. Inland seaoats
Chasmanthium latifolium
The authors

39. **Latin Name** *Chasmanthium latifolium*
Pronunciation kaz-MAN-thee-um
lah-teh-FOLE-ee-um
Common Name INLAND SEAOATS
Usual Height 2–4 feet
Spacing ½–2 pounds pure live seed (PLS)
per 1,000 square feet
Bloom Summer and fall
Fruit June to October; ivory seeds
Dormant in winter or winter rosette
Range Moist, shady creek bottoms
throughout Texas except South and West
Texas
Nebraska to Texas
Soil Sand, loam, clay; moist, poor drainage
okay
Shade, dappled shade, part shade
Colonizes by rhizomes
Propagation Seed root division

In moist, poorly drained loams, inland seaoats makes a solid mat. In the fall the big drooping seeds and leaves turn a warm ivory, somewhere between gold and white—very showy in a mass. Cut it back to about four inches when winter weather makes it unsightly, usually in February. New growth typically starts in March, but I've seen it start as early as December, which can give you a green cover all through a mild winter. If the leaves get over two feet tall by spring, cut them in half in May or June. In drier parts of the state such as the Edwards Plateau and the Trans-Pecos, inland seaoats needs almost total shade. It isn't very aggressive in dry areas, so it can even be used as a garden accent. For heavy shade in the Houston area, I have been told that *Chasmanthium sessiliflorum* is a better choice. Inland seaoats does best there with a half day of sun. This plant also does well in a patio pot.

40. Sugarcane plume grass
Erianthus giganteus
Benny J. Simpson

41. Gulf muhly
Muhlenbergia
capillaris
The authors

40. **Latin Name** *Erianthus giganteus*
Pronunciation air-ee-AN-thus
jye-GAN-tee-us
Common Name SUGARCANE PLUME GRASS
Usual Height 6 feet, can reach 10 feet
Spacing 1½ feet apart
Bloom October; red to peach; heads
7–10 inches long
Dormant in winter
Range Moist soils in East and Southeast
Texas
New York to Cuba
Soil Sand, loam, clay; moist, poor drainage
okay
Part shade, full sun
Robust clumps
Propagation Seed, root division while
dormant

Sugarcane plume grass is used best at the edge of a large water garden. It also does well in a bog garden that dries out a little between floodings. And if you're fortunate enough to have a stream running through your property, or if you live on a lake, use it along the banks. This is not a plant for a small pond. Its big feathery tops range in color from dark red to pink to apricot; you'll want to place it in your garden where you can enjoy how it glows when backlit by the sun. If you want to check it out before putting it in your garden, you'll find excellent specimens at the Armand Bayou Nature Center on the south side of Houston. Like all the clump grasses, this one will get bigger each year. If you want to restrain it, dig out part of the roots during its dormant period after frost. If you don't want it to seed out, cut down the stalks after they bloom.

41. **Latin Name** *Muhlenbergia capillaris*
Pronunciation mew-len-BER-jee-ah
kap-uh-LARE-is
Common Name GULF MUHLY
Usual Height 1½ feet, can reach 2½ feet
Spacing ½–2 pounds pure live seed (PLS)
per 1,000 square feet, or 2 feet apart for
garden accent
Bloom Usually mid-October; deep pink
Dormant in winter
Range Prairies and openings in pine forests
of East and Southeast Texas
Massachusetts to Mexico
Soil Sand; well drained
Part shade, full sun
Clumps
Propagation Seed

Gulf muhly grows in the sands of East Texas, while seep muhly (*M. reverchonii*) grows in the limestone of north Central Texas, the Edwards Plateau, and Oklahoma, and purple muhly (*M. rigida*) grows on steep slopes in the Trans-Pecos and in New Mexico, Arizona, and Mexico. As a result, just about everyone in the state can use a muhly successfully. They all look similar—knee-high and a feathery deep pink in the fall. Everyone I asked who knew these muhlies gave them a star rating. They are perfect for a meadow, especially if your meadow is between you and the morning or evening sun—the gorgeous pink really shows off when backlit. Plant flowers in the grass for spring bloom and enjoy the pink in the fall. Mow about Valentine's Day so the new spring growth will be fresh and green, uncluttered by old stalks.

42. Lindheimer muhly
Muhlenbergia lindheimeri
The authors

43. Indian ricegrass
Oryzopsis hymenoides
The authors

42.   **Latin Name**   *Muhlenbergia lindheimeri*
Pronunciation   mew-len-BER-jee-ah
   lind-HYE-mer-eye
Common Name   LINDHEIMER MUHLY
Usual Height   2–5 feet
Spacing   ½–2 pounds pure live seed (PLS)
   per 1,000 square feet, or 3 feet apart for
   garden accent
Bloom   Fall, usually mid-October; silvery
   plumes
Dormant in winter
Range   Limestone uplands near streams in
   Edwards Plateau
   Endemic to Texas
Soil   Sand, loam, clay, limestone; calcare-
   ous; well drained
Part shade, full sun
Clumps
Propagation   Seed

This is a handsome grass for the calcareous soils in the center of the state. Recently some homeowners and landscapers in the Austin and San Antonio area began using Lindheimer muhly as an alternative accent plant to the ubiquitous pampas grass. Both grasses are attractive, so maybe it's a matter of state pride. Lindheimer muhly does have one definite advantage over pampas grass; its leaves are much softer, so when you cut it back, you don't get scratched. If it's planted in a field, it can be mowed as late as June and not be hurt, but it is usually not cut back at all—not even in the winter. After frost, the leaves turn almost white and hold that color until new green leaves appear in the spring. A similar-looking grass is bull muhly (*M. emersleyi*), which grows in the Trans-Pecos.

43. **Latin Name** *Oryzopsis hymenoides*
Pronunciation oh-ree-ZOP-siss
hye-men-OY-deez
Common Name INDIAN RICEGRASS
Usual Height 1–2 feet
Spacing 1–2 pounds pure live seed (PLS)
per 1,000 square feet, or 8–12 inches apart
Bloom Summer
Fruit Fall to winter; ivory
Dormant in winter
Range Infrequent in West Texas, High
Plains, and El Paso area
Western U.S.
Soil Sand, loam, clay; loose, well drained
Part shade, full sun
Propagation Seed, clump division while
dormant

I've heard this plant described as elegant, and after you've seen it, I think you'll agree. It's pretty all year in a garden, but strange as it might sound, I'm especially partial to it in the fall and winter, when it's all dried out. It looks lovely with its airy, ivory-colored seed heads hanging suspended over its wiry straw-colored stems. You can make a truly marvelous dried floral centerpiece out of some cuttings, or you can simply enjoy its delicate look in your yard. If you use Indian ricegrass as an accent in your garden, give it plenty of space so it won't be cramped. Massed, it makes an all-season ground cover—in an area where it can't get crushed. The seeds are eaten by birds and mammals. Germination rates vary, so don't be surprised if it takes two years to get a good stand. Allow a mass planting to renew itself, as individual clumps are not long-lived. Indian ricegrass is at its best in poor, dry soils.

44. Switch grass
Panicum virgatum
The authors

44. **Latin Name** *Panicum virgatum*
Pronunciation PAN-uh-kum ver-GAH-tum
Common Name SWITCH GRASS
Usual Height 3 feet, can reach 6 feet
Spacing ½–2 pounds pure live seed (PLS)
per 1,000 square feet, or 3 feet apart for
garden accent
Bloom Fall
Dormant in winter
Range Throughout Texas, but rare in
Trans-Pecos
Canada to Gulf of Mexico
Soil Sand, loam, clay, limestone; moist,
seasonal poor drainage okay
Part shade, full sun
Rhizomes
Propagation Seed, root division while
dormant

As you can see from the picture, switch grass doesn't mind a little poor drainage. The photo was taken in May, showing the bloom stalk from the previous year. Switch grass always stands out in a tallgrass prairie in the fall because it turns such a deep, rich gold. After frost, this fades to tan, but it's still definitely attractive. This is another bunchgrass that looks fine if you never cut it back at all. Besides being a major component of pocket prairies, it is popular as a garden accent—especially in the Houston area—because it can handle extra water without getting top-heavy.

45. Blue-green summer color of little bluestem
Schizachyrium scoparium
The authors

45. Coppery winter color of little bluestem
Schizachyrium scoparium
Benny J. Simpson

45.   **Latin Name**   *Schizachyrium scoparium*
(*Andropogon scoparius*)
Pronunciation   skih-ZAK-ree-um
skoh-PARE-ee-um
Common Name   LITTLE BLUESTEM
Usual Height   1–2 feet, can reach 5 feet
Spacing   ½–2 pounds pure live seed (PLS)
per 1,000 square feet, or 1½ feet apart for
garden accent
Bloom   Fall
Dormant in winter
Range   Throughout Texas, but rare in ex-
treme west
Southern and central U.S., Mexico
Soil   Sand, loam, clay, caliche, limestone;
well drained
Part shade, full sun

**Clumps, rhizomes along the southern Gulf
Coast**
Propagation   Seed

Little bluestem is probably the most widely dis-
persed bunchgrass in the state. An important part of the
tallgrass prairies, it was also the main grass found under
the post oaks in the Post Oak Savannah and the Cross
Timbers. This is the bunchgrass most frequently seen on
rocky slopes and along highways and is tolerant of a wide
range of moisture or drought. Little bluestem is usually a
compact slender clump less than a foot across and two
feet high. The clumps seem to space themselves a little
distance apart instead of making a dense sod here in
Texas. The color is exceptional year-round: a deep blue-
green in the fall and a warm mahogany-brown with
white, shining seed tufts in the winter.

46. Indian grass
Sorghastrum nutans
Benny J. Simpson

47. Two-flowered trichloris
Trichloris crinita
The authors

46. **Latin Name** *Sorghastrum nutans*
(*S. avenaceum*)
Pronunciation sor-GASS-trum NOO-tanz
Common Name INDIAN GRASS
Usual Height 3–5 feet, can reach 8 feet
Spacing ½–2 pounds pure live seed (PLS) per 1,000 square feet, or 3–5 feet apart for garden accent
Bloom October; bright gold
Dormant in winter
Range Throughout Texas
Canada to Mexico
Soil Sand, loam, clay, limestone; seasonal poor drainage okay
Full sun, a little shade okay
Clumps with rhizomes
Propagation Seed, or root division while dormant

Here's another one of the big four in the tallgrass prairie. Indian grass loves moist rich soils and responds well to fertilizer and watering. It has large, broad blue-green blades and bright golden fall flowers. You have to get right up close to the blooming stalks to appreciate them fully—the deep-yellow flowers are only about as big as your pinky nail, and some of them sport a touch of red, as you see in the picture. As an addition to your garden, Indian grass can be a spectacular accent. It is also magnificent in tallgrass prairie, particularly in North Central Texas. West and south of Fort Worth, Indian grass is best used as a garden accent, unless you have a naturally moist, rich swale.

47. **Latin Name** *Trichloris crinita* (*Chloris crinita*)
Pronunciation trye-KLOR-iss krin-EE-tah
Common Name TWO-FLOWERED TRICHLORIS
Usual Height 2–3 feet
Spacing ½–2 pounds pure live seed (PLS) per 1,000 square feet, or 2 feet apart for garden accent
Bloom May to November; white
Dormant in winter
Range Along streams in Trans-Pecos, rare in Del Rio and West Texas
Arizona to South America
Soil Sand, loam, clay, limestone; calcareous; well drained
Part shade, full sun
Clumps
Propagation Seed

This grass is very showy with its two- to three-inch fingers of white feathery seed heads above blue-green stems. It blooms all summer. Where I saw it in the sands of the public garden at Lajitas, it was seeding out fairly freely, but it was getting watered every night. In his book *Wildflowers of the Big Bend Country, Texas,* Dr. Barton H. Warnock notes that near a watering hole this trichloris was competing quite well for dominance with four-wing saltbush. From these two pieces of information, it seems to me that two-flowered trichloris would do well in a garden, where its long blooming season would be welcome. It would also do well in a small naturalized area that could be watered occasionally. I would love to see it tested in the Austin–San Antonio area, where I also think it would feel at home.

48. Seven-foot-high clump of eastern gama grass
Tripsacum dactyloides
Dr. Geoffrey Stanford

48. **Latin Name**   *Tripsacum dactyloides*
Pronunciation   TRIP-seh-kum dak-till-OY-deez
Common Name   EASTERN GAMA GRASS
Usual Height   2–3 feet, can reach 10 feet
Spacing   ½–2 pounds pure live seed (PLS) per 1,000 square feet, or 3–4 feet apart for garden accent
Fruit   April to November
Dormant in winter
Range   Throughout Texas, but most frequent in east
Eastern U.S., Mexico
Soil   Sand, loam, clay; acid or calcareous; moist, seasonal poor drainage okay
Part shade, full sun
Dense clumps by rhizomes
Propagation   Seed, root division while dormant

Eastern gama grass makes a clump so dense that it is useful as a buffer between a controlled area, such as a lawn or a flower bed, and a wilder area of shrubs, naturalized ground covers, or even a woods. It will tolerate more shade than most prairie grasses, and it gets a rich dark green. Plant it where the soil is usually moist, or on a slope where it gets extra seasonal runoff. Eastern gama grass responds well to fertilizer and extra watering while it is getting established. This long-lived plant doesn't like to be moved. Cut the old leaves back before spring. Like pampas grass leaves, they have sharp edges. The plant is related to corn, so it's not surprising that the seeds form single lines of little hard yellow kernels. Deer love them.

Grass Garden Plan
Lot Size: 90′ × 80′

Admittedly, a garden composed of almost 90 percent grasses—most of them unmowed—isn't your usual approach to landscaping. Most homes are surrounded by a neatly trimmed grass lawn. And even your most conventional neighbors could probably handle some unmowed grasses here and there, as accents or borders. But grasses as the main focus? The principal ingredients? With everything else serving as accents?

Tell your neighbors that you're planning such a grass garden, and they may look at you funny. Show them this plan, and then explain that this grass landscape is remarkably maintenance-free, and they will probably express mild interest. Show them your finished, well-established grass garden—especially in the late afternoon, with the stalks aglow in the sunshine—and they'll be green with envy.

If you're passionate about grasses—and you'd be amazed how much company you have—this plan will show you how to get in the widest possible variety in an area no larger than a normal suburban back yard.

Most of the area in this plan is covered with buffalo grass. Half of it is mowed all the time to create a walk from the driveway to the deck and to create a lawn around the deck and the tallgrass swale. Another section of it is planted with meadow flowers and will bloom from midspring with bluebonnets and Indian paintbrush to June or even later with Indian blanket, horsemint, and greenthread. Then it can be mowed once and allowed to grow again, or it can be mowed regularly along with the path and lawn. Either way, it can be thickly planted with baby's breath aster and bitterweed for white and yellow flowers in the summer and fall.

Another smaller section of buffalo grass (on the far left side) gets mowed only after frost. It contains partridge pea or yellow plainsman, whichever is more appropriate to your region, for yellow summer color. Either will still be colorful in August when snow-on-the-mountain (or snow-on-the-prairie) starts blooming. The result is a two-foot-high field of yellow and white.

Just to the north of this summer and fall meadow is a low thicket of shrubs. Let the buffalo grass grow under the shrubs unhindered. It will help keep out weeds while the shrubs grow. When they are mature, they will shade out the buffalo grass.

There are several thicket shrubs that would be a good height, color, and thickness as a backdrop. Those that colonize are aromatic sumac, smooth sumac, thicket plums, whitebrush, and Havard oak. Plant more closely the noncolonizing shrubs, such as agarito, sand sagebrush, and kidneywood. Make your selections first on the basis of what will grow best for your environment, and then on style. Other considerations are whether you want to attract bees and butterflies or birds and whether you need evergreens to block a particular view year-round. Just be sure that the thicket is far enough to the north or low enough that it does not shade the pink muhly meadow.

The grassy rock garden could be buffalo or curly mesquite grass, which would be my first choice if I lived where curly mesquite grows. The fairly steep slope between the driveway and the deck faces west. I didn't draw in boulders and big rocks, but I sure would want them there. For tall accents, use three white-flowered yuccas or red yucca by the garage, and a nolina or other specimen bunchgrass at the steps. The tree selections I've listed cast very light shade—enough to keep the deck comfortable when the afternoon sun hits it, but not too much for the plantings in the grassy rock garden, which need lots of sun.

Your grassy rock garden should not be cut back at all except in February, and even that's optional. Do cut back old bloom stalks on the yuccas and flowers. There is a profusion of flowers here for spring, summer, and fall. Anything drought-tolerant, low-growing, and long-blooming is suitable. Some suggestions are winecup, pink evening primrose, Barbara's buttons,

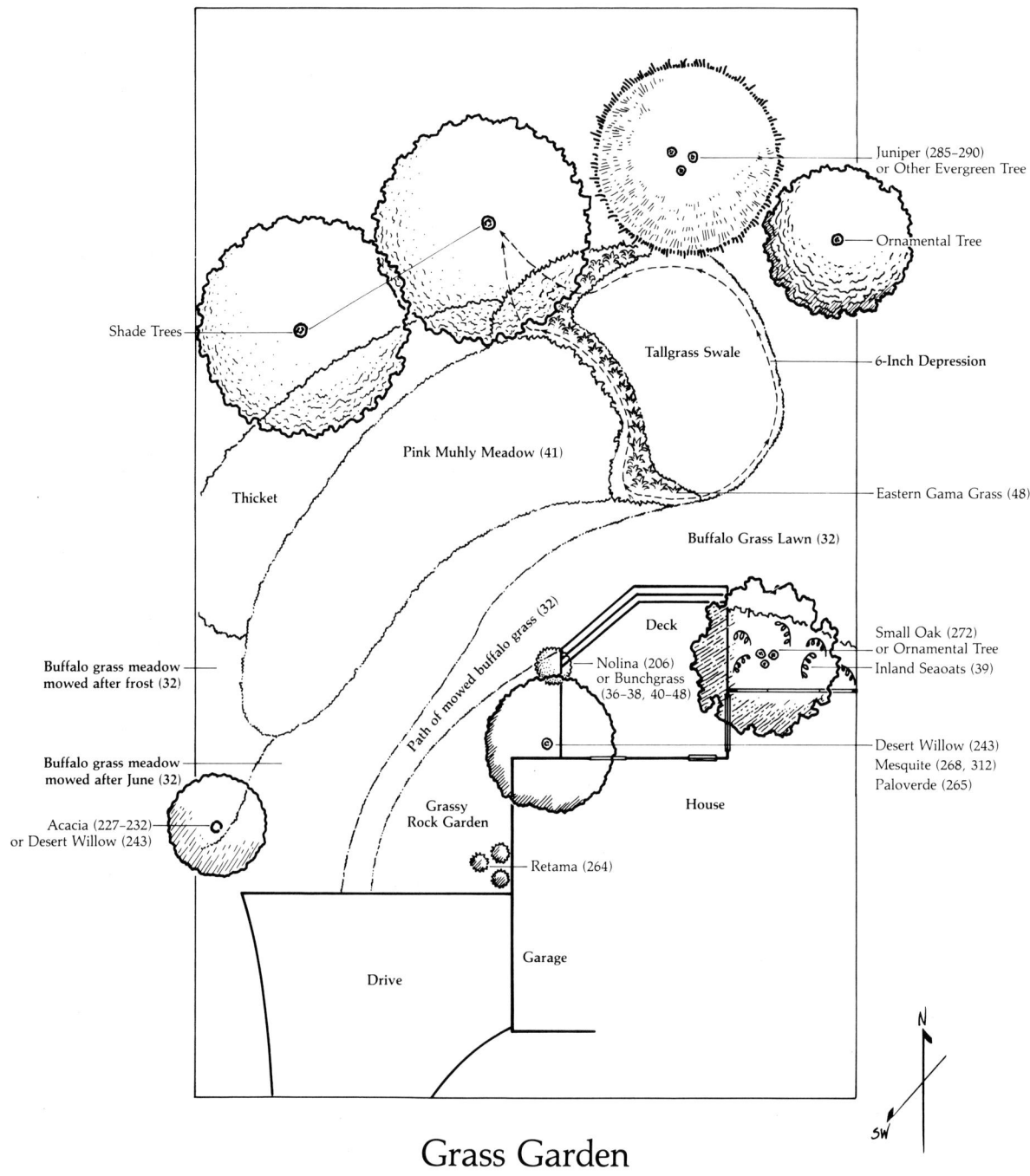

Juniper (285–290) or Other Evergreen Tree

Ornamental Tree

Shade Trees

Tallgrass Swale

6-Inch Depression

Pink Muhly Meadow (41)

Thicket

Eastern Gama Grass (48)

Buffalo Grass Lawn (32)

Deck

Small Oak (272) or Ornamental Tree

Inland Seaoats (39)

Buffalo grass meadow mowed after frost (32)

Nolina (206) or Bunchgrass (36–38, 40–48)

Desert Willow (243)
Mesquite (268, 312)
Paloverde (265)

Buffalo grass meadow mowed after June (32)

Path of mowed buffalo grass (32)

House

Acacia (227–232) or Desert Willow (243)

Grassy Rock Garden

Retama (264)

Drive

Garage

N
SW

Grass Garden

blackfoot daisy, yellow zinnia, dwarf white zinnia, prairie verbena, gay-feather, and mealy blue sage.

The next biggest portion of grass is called the pink muhly meadow. There are three muhlies that grow knee-high and are a lovely pink in the fall—Gulf, seep, and purple. At least one will be right for your area of the state. This meadow will be about twice as tall as the unmowed buffalo grass in front of it and a half to a third as tall as the thicket behind of it. Spring flowers might be cutleaf daisy, chocolate daisy, green eyes, black sampson, and wild blue hyacinth. Summer choices might be velvetleaf senna, two-leaved senna, and Mexican hat.

Many more options are available: after all, the more color, the better. In the fall the main color will come from the grass itself; the tips will be a glorious pink. If heavy spring rains get it too high, scythe it in half (definitely no lower than six to eight inches) after the spring flowers have set seed. I placed this meadow carefully so that as you sit out on your deck on an autumn evening, the late afternoon sun will make your pink grass glow.

So far, everything has been planted on the existing grade of your lot. For a pocket prairie of tallgrasses, a slight swale is advantageous.

The four main tallgrasses are big bluestem, little bluestem, Indian grass, and switch grass. These grasses grow all over the state, but only where the soil is rich and deep and where moisture is present. The swale holds the extra water that these tallgrasses need. You wouldn't want this water on the meadows, as it would make them too tall and rank. Depending on where you live and what the weather is doing (that is, whether it's raining), you might have to let the hose soak the swale overnight one to five times during the growing season.

Besides the tallgrasses, you can have some big prairie perennials. I would start with ironweed, goldenrod, Maximilian sunflower, and bergamot, but there are many other suitable prairie forbs—and other grasses as well. A friend of mine who has a ten-by-ten-foot patch of tallgrass prairie near Dallas found these four perennials too aggressive and prefers cutleaf daisy and fragrant phlox. Once established, his prairie has successfully resisted invasion from Bermuda, Johnson, and Dallis grasses, but he had to weed diligently the first two years.

Another advantage to the swale is that it will help keep the meadow from invading the tallgrasses and vice versa. On the lawn side, mowing will be adequate. On the side next to the pink muhly meadow, I have also put in a barrier of Eastern gama grass, which grows densely and will love the extra moisture on the slope of the swale. It will also tolerate the shade under the trees in the back.

The trees scattered around the plan are optional. What a grass garden chiefly needs is sun. The trees on the south and west side of the plan give light shade—mesquite, desert willow, retama, paloverde, and any of the acacias. On the east and north side of the plan, the shade density doesn't

The Myers house overlooking Lake Travis is landscaped by Skip Fulton, a landscape designer in Austin. The steps from the deck and spa exit onto a path of artfully exposed limestone. Clumps of Lindheimer muhly and little bluestem mingle with zexmenia, white Gregg salvia, and other flowers and grasses planted by Fulton. The trees are prairie flameleaf sumacs and a newly planted Mexican redbud. Photo by the authors.

matter so much as long as the trees are small enough and spaced far enough away that south sun can reach the grasses without interference.

On the east side of the deck, under a tree, is inland seaoats, a grass that loves shade and moisture. It turns ivory in the fall.

There are lots of ways you can play with this plan. If you live in the western parts of the state, you can substitute ear muhly or burro grass for the buffalo grass in spots. You could also substitute either of them for the purple muhly in the pink muhly meadow.

If you live in East Texas or Houston, you will need to use Bermuda grass instead of buffalo grass. Further changes need to be made if you're in this lush part of the state. A grassy rock garden would look out of place here. Instead, plant Gulf muhly on the slope with winecup, pink evening primrose, coreopsis, and black-eyed Susans. You could also use the beautiful splitbeard bluestem. Then, in place of the plants described in the pink muhly meadow, use the tallgrasses, as they don't need a swale to get enough moisture in your area, unless you're on sugar sand. Then you can use the swale as a water or bog garden with sugarcane plume grass and swamp sunflower.

This river-bottom meadow is still ablaze with wildflowers at the end of June. The native plant landscape around the house was designed by Judy Black Childress, a landscape architect with Scherz Landscape Company in San Angelo. The owner, Mrs. W. Truett Smith, consulted with Mark Abbot of Green Horizons in Kerrville on planting the meadow. Horsemint and Indian blanket reseeded while black-eyed Susans and yarrow matured to make this colorful display the second year. Photo by the authors.

FOUR

 # *Annuals, Biennials, and Short-lived Perennials*

OR the most part, plants in these three categories have two basic uses. They can be planted in the grass to make a meadow (a meadow being loosely defined as a short grassland with flowers), and they can be used to fill in spaces in a perennial flower garden.

Yes, it is possible to have a garden composed exclusively of annuals. Many corporations use them in formal, stylized gardens, but they have to hire crews to do the weeding and change out the plantings season by season. That's hard work. And expensive. These companies could save a lot of money by using native annuals in a meadow setting. For one thing, mowing could be a once- or twice-a-year event, not a continuing expense. And it's possible to have glorious color at least half the year, depending on local climate and rainfall. (See the Grass Garden Plan for some ideas on how to use wildflowers in grasses.)

When we see natural acres of wildflowers, they are growing among grasses. Texas has long been famous for the wildflowers that grow in such profusion along its highways. Most of those wildflowers are annuals, and they thrive there because the soil is disturbed. "Disturbed" in this sense means that the ground has been mowed, graded, or otherwise torn up, making it virtually impossible for long-lived plants to get established. (Early explorers found the most spectacular wildflowers in prairies that had been burned the season before.)

Disturbing an area tends to leave a lot of bare soil, which is where seeds of annual wildflowers can find a home and grow. If mowing continues, trees, shrubs, and prairie grasses never have a chance to develop, and the soil remains scantily covered. Of course, indiscriminate mowing can destroy the wildflowers too, if they are cut down while in bud or while blooming and never get to set seed for the next year. Some of the wildflowers that are best adapted to roadside management are bluebonnets, Indian paintbrush, Indian blanket, goldenwave, greenthread, horsemint, and white prickly poppy—all spring annuals. Fall annuals have a harder time because of summer mowing. You usually see them in pastures, and the most visible are eryngo, snow-on-the-mountain, and bitterweed.

Some perennials also survive plentifully along roadsides. A few of the most common are pink evening primrose, winecup, cutleaf daisy, and Mexican hat. Mowing between February and June, when they are showing buds, will kill them. But if you mow earlier (as is done, for example, in the Valley and along the Gulf Coast), they will lie low and then produce a spring-long bounty of flowers.

Hundreds of other wildflowers—annuals, perennials, and biennials—can be spotted as we drive about, and in such variety that it's possible to find as many as thirty species blooming at the same time along a thirty- foot stretch of roadway.

There are two main waves of bloom. The first wave consists chiefly of bluebonnets and Indian paintbrush and is the most celebrated. But the second, dominated by yellow daisies and Indian blanket, is far more interesting. Then you get the great kaleidoscopes of color and variety.

If you don't mow from frost to June, you are more likely to have a varied and abundant harvest of flowers. If you don't mow for another six months after the June mowing, you are likely to have a good crop of fall flowers. But on this regime your grasses will thicken up so much that in three years or so there won't be any more bare soil for seed to settle into. In that event, you'll have to create more bare soil by raking, burning, or thatching.

Don't have a meadow? Use annuals in a garden. They're not only easy but also useful. Because they bloom the first year from seed, annuals can be counted on for quick color—when you're first getting your garden established, and later when another plant dies and leaves you with an empty spot that needs filling.

As a general rule, annuals germinate easily and quickly and bloom constantly until they go to seed. At that time, pull them out and shake out any remaining ripe seed clinging to the plant. Or shake the seed into a paper bag and store it in a dark cool place until the next spring or fall.

Most of the nonnative annual seeds we buy in nurseries should be planted in the spring, as soon as all danger of frost is past (which can sometimes require ESP—how many late March–early April freezes can you recall?). Most of our Texas annuals do best if planted in the autumn, right after the first fall rain. They germinate and grow roots all winter when the soil is generally damper and not likely to lose its moisture to a baking sun. Then, if we have a hot dry spring and summer, they're ready for drought and can perform. Some of our annuals—for example, the bluebonnet—must winter over before blooming and are designated winter annuals.

Then there are some flowers that die after setting seed but are so cautious that they insist on growing roots for a whole year before blooming. They bloom the second spring or summer of their lives and are called biennials. Of course, plants don't read botanical definitions, and sometimes they do things differently. If planted in early fall or brought into a greenhouse, they might bloom their first spring or, in the case of Texas bluebells, their first summer. Also, they don't always die after blooming. Sometimes they live through another winter and bloom again the following spring.

Normally, plants that bloom year after year from one rootstock are called perennials. But here again, real life is not always neat and predictable, and some of our perennials barely live more than one year. Often they are plants that bloom continuously whenever it is above freezing, and they just wear themselves out. Some perennials simply can't be counted on to last even two years, so they're called short-lived perennials. I have included them here with the annuals and biennials because they also usually bloom the first year from seed and self-sow well. You'll like them a lot more if you think of them as annuals that bloom an especially long time rather than as perennials that died way too soon.

Just because these plants individually don't live a long time doesn't mean that they can't have a long-term place in your garden. If they self-sow well (that means, they reseed prolifically on their own), you might have them around for many decades. You can transplant seedlings every fall or winter to a particular spot, or you can let them do pretty much as they please, as long as they don't get too crowded or shade out a valuable perennial. Most of the prettiest and longest-lived gardens are the result of the laissez-faire method. The least work often produces the best results.

Many of these annuals, biennials, and short-lived perennials are not for sale. You'll have to gather seed yourself. It is better to gather seed than to transplant because transplants almost always die, usually before they've set seed. You'd be killing not just that plant but future generations as well. Who needs that on their conscience!

On the other hand, if you gather seed from a good stand of plants, you can get a generous handful of seed without risking future populations in the wild. That handful should give you enough plants to keep your private population going for years. *How to Know and Grow Texas Wildflowers*, by Carroll Abbott, is available through Green Horizons, the mail-order native plant business he founded in Kerrville. The book has many good ideas on how to collect your own seed.

Because some seed must have light to germinate and some must be covered, I always scratch the ground a little, scatter on the seed, and cover about half of it. Also, because some winters are dry and some are glacial, I always save half the seed when planting small amounts in a flower garden, so I can replant in February or March if my seedlings don't come up or don't make it through the winter.

49. Huisache daisy
Amblyolepsis setigera
The authors

50. Lazy daisy
Aphanostephus skirrhobasis
The authors

49. **Latin Name** *Amblyolepsis setigera*
Pronunciation am-blee-oh-LEP-siss
suh-TIJ-er-ah
Common Name HUISACHE DAISY
Annual
Usual Height 1 foot
Spacing 1 foot apart
Bloom February and March in South Texas,
May and June in Trans-Pecos, elsewhere
2 months between these extremes; yellow;
1–2 inches
Range Throughout Texas except across
eastern forests
Mexico
Soil Sand, loam, caliche; well drained
Part shade, full sun
Taproot
Propagation Seed sown in fall or winter

Huisache daisy is an eye-catching two-tone flower—
dark yellow at its center, with creamy-yellow edges. In
small quantities, its scent has been described as new-
mown hay. In masses, you can fairly say it's a little overpowering. It provides lavish color in a meadow or in your
flower garden. In the southern parts of Texas, where it is
most commonly seen, it is often blooming as early as the
end of February. Once it starts blooming, huisache daisy
blooms profusely for about two months, and then, completely worn out, it goes to seed. It really looks ratty at
this point, and you may want to pull it out. But a lot of
ripe seed is still on the plant, so give it a good shake before tossing it, to release that seed for next year's crop.

50. **Latin Name** *Aphanostephus skirrhobasis*
Pronunciation ah-fan-oh-STEE-fus
skeer-oh-BAY-siss
Common Name LAZY DAISY
Annual
Usual Height 2–18 inches
Spacing 9–18 inches apart
Bloom Early spring to frost, in afternoon;
white; 1–2 inches across
Range Sands from Panhandle to Houston
and Corpus Christi
Florida to Oklahoma to Mexico
Soil Sand, including beaches; well drained
Part shade, full sun
Taproot
Propagation Seed sown in fall or early
spring

Lazy daisy is one of our very best annuals for sand
or sandy loam conditions. As you might guess from its
name, it doesn't like to get up with the sun. The white
flowers are closed up all morning, showing us only the
delicate pink veins on the undersides of the petals. By
midday they are open for business and remain that way
for the rest of the day. Planted in good garden soil with
lots of sun and water, lazy daisy makes solid mounds of
blooms, usually about a foot tall and eighteen inches wide
—about twice as wide as it gets in the wild. It's great in a
rock garden, as a border plant, as a ground cover under
roses, and so on. Naturalized in a meadow, it can turn the
area almost pure white in the spring or after a rain.

51. White prickly poppy
Argemone albiflora subsp. *texana*
The authors

52. Baby's breath aster
Aster subulatus
The authors

51. **Latin Name**   *Argemone albiflora* subsp. *texana*
Pronunciation   ar-JEM-uh-nee
   al-beh-FLOR-ah subspecies tex-AN-ah
Common Name   WHITE PRICKLY POPPY
Annual or biennial
Usual Height   1½–2 feet, can reach 5 feet
Spacing   1 foot apart
Bloom   March to June; white; 4–6 inches
   across
Range   Throughout Texas
   Missouri to Texas
Soil   Sand, loam, clay, caliche, limestone;
   well drained
Dappled shade, part shade, full sun
Taproot
Propagation   Seed sown in fall or early
   spring

White prickly poppy is well named. It doesn't get browsed very often, because its prickles are dense and fierce. I included it because the blooms are big and gorgeous; they even look terrific when it's so dry that the bluebonnets are gray and pitiful. This poppy likes disturbed areas and is frequently seen along railroad tracks. It will stand out in a meadow for the first couple of years, before the perennials get dense. It isn't very competitive. In your flower garden, it'll thrive as long as it gets lots of sun and doesn't have to share its space. It blooms in spring only and should be pulled out (with gloves) by June. Shake out the seed or save it until the first fall rains. Red prickly poppy (*A. sanguinea*) shows a vivid range of colors, from deep red to pink to lavender. It is native to South Texas and adjacent Mexico.

52. **Latin Name**   *Aster subulatus*
Pronunciation   ASS-ter soo-boo-LAH-tus
Common Names   BABY'S BREATH ASTER,
   HIERBA DEL MARRANO, BLACKLAND ASTER,
   BLACKWEED, ANNUAL ASTER
Annual
Usual Height   1½ feet, can reach 3 feet
Spacing   2 feet apart
Bloom   September to November; white to
   pale lavender; ½ inch across
Range   Ditches, swales, and poorly drained
   areas throughout Texas
   South Carolina, Kansas to California
Soil   Sand, loam, clay, limestone; moist,
   seasonal poor drainage okay
Dappled shade, part shade, full sun
Propagation   Seed sown in early spring

I much prefer the English common name to the Spanish version, which is translated as "pig's herb" or "filthy person's herb." There are two ways to use this little aster. One is scattered throughout a flower garden. The tiny blooms float in a fine haze like baby's breath. It visually pulls the fall garden together in a special way. The other way I really like this flower is naturalized in the lawn. It coexists well with any grass except St. Augustine, which grows too densely to allow the delicate asters any elbow room. Mowed only two inches high, it still blooms up a storm, and the grass looks like it has been sprinkled with white stars.

53. Desert marigold
Baileya multiradiata
The authors

53. **Latin Name** *Baileya multiradiata*
Pronunciation BAY-lee-ah
mul-tih-ray-dee-AH-tah
Common Name DESERT MARIGOLD, DESERT
BAILEYA
Short-lived perennial
Usual Height 9 inches
Spacing 1 foot apart
Bloom Everblooming; yellow; 1–2 inches
across
Range Trans-Pecos deserts, rare in Edwards
Plateau
California to Utah to Texas to Mexico
Soil Sand, loam, clay, caliche; well drained
Part shade, full sun
Propagation Seed

Desert marigold is exceptionally well behaved and, best of all, extremely long-blooming—a must for any garden from San Angelo west. It has multilayered yellow petals to make daisies on short slim stems above a mat of woolly gray-green leaves. Abilene is the easternmost point where I'm aware of its being grown successfully outside of its natural range. I haven't heard of any experiments with it farther east. It typically lives only about a year, reseeds easily, and usually blooms from seed within three months. Once it starts blooming, it blooms constantly (whenever temperatures are above freezing) until it wears itself out. It is highly poisonous to sheep.

54. **Latin Name** *Cassia fasciculata*
Pronunciation KASS-ee-ah
fass-KIK-yoo-lay-tah
Common Name PARTRIDGE PEA
Annual
Usual Height 1–3 feet, can reach 4½ feet
Spacing 1–2 feet apart, or 20 pounds seed
per acre
Bloom June to October; yellow; 1–2 inches
across
Range Sandy fields in East Texas, west
to Wichita Falls and Abilene, south to
Corpus Christi
Eastern half of U.S.
Soil Sand, loam, clay, limestone; acid or
calcareous; well drained
Part shade, full sun
Propagation Seed

Partridge pea is a good choice for bright summer color, but you can have it only if you possess well-drained soils. Close-up, the flowers are pretty—thin, fragile petals marked with a splash of red and obviously related to the ornamental trees retama and paloverde. The flowers open at dawn and wither in the hottest part of the afternoon. They are visited by bees, ants, and butterflies. The leaves are light green and finely divided like little feathers. Usually partly closed during the day, they open wide at night. The peas are in small flat bean pods and provide important food for both game birds and songbirds. In fact, partridge pea is sometimes planted to attract game birds. It's also used to rejuvenate fallow fields because its roots, like

54. Partridge pea
Cassia fasciculata
The authors

55. Indian paintbrush
Castilleja indivisa
The authors

those of some of the other legumes, have nitrogen-fixing properties. Don't plant partridge pea in a field that might be grazed, as it has been reported to be toxic to livestock. In a garden setting let it reseed itself where you want bright yellow summer color.

55. **Latin Name**   *Castilleja indivisa*
   Pronunciation   kass-teh-LAY-ah
      in-duh-VEE-zah
   Common Name   INDIAN PAINTBRUSH
   Annual or biennial
   Usual Height   6–12 inches
   Spacing   ¼ pound seed per acre
   Bloom   March to May; orange to red; 3- to
      8-inch spikes
   Range   Fields and roadsides in eastern half
      of Texas and Coastal Plains
      Southeastern Oklahoma

Soil   Sand, loam, clay; well drained
Full sun, a little shade okay
Taproot
Propagation   Seed

Although the opinion is not unanimous, it is widely believed that this beautiful wildflower never learned to feed itself; it feeds off grass roots. Obviously, on that premise you would plant it in your lawn or meadow, where both grass and paintbrush can coexist amicably. However, there is mounting evidence that it might grow as well or better in a flower bed. By itself, it makes a clump nine inches wide. In masses with bluebonnets, pink evening primrose, lazy daisy, and anything yellow, it intensifies all the colors. The seed is very fine and doesn't always bloom the first spring after being sown. Don't try to transplant paintbrush. I know a lot of people who have tried it, but none has succeeded in doing anything other than killing the plant.

56. Mountain pink
Centaurium beyrichii
The authors

57. Goldenwave
Coreopsis tinctoria
The authors

56. **Latin Name** *Centaurium beyrichii*
Pronunciation sen(ken)-TAW-ree-um
    bay-RICH-ee-eye
Common Name MOUNTAIN PINK
Annual
Usual Height 9 inches
Spacing 9–12 inches apart
Bloom Summer; pink; 1 inch across or less
Range Prairies, rocky slopes, and granite
    seepage in North Texas and Panhandle
    Arkansas
Soil Sand, limestone, granite, gravel; well
    drained
Part shade, full sun
Taproot
Propagation Seed

This one is a real bargain—one plant looks like an entire bouquet. If I didn't live on black clay, I would go to a lot of trouble to have it every year. And that's what it would take, I'm afraid: a lot of trouble. The seed has to be hand-collected, and, in the words of Benny Simpson, it is "finer than frog feathers." It must be planted in the fall, in rock or gravel, and on a slight slope where a little extra moisture will run over it. It won't like taller flowers shading it, so it should be at the sunny front of the garden. There is a story about Lady Bird Johnson's planting the seed of *Centaurium texense*, Lady Bird's centaury, in 1966. She had been told it couldn't be done, but as she collected the seed, she observed that the plants were most often growing on rocky disturbed roadsides where they got the runoff from the road. So she planted her seed around her ranch's airplane runway, with gratifying results.

57. **Latin Name** *Coreopsis tinctoria*
Pronunciation kor-ee-OP-sis
    tink-TOR-ee-ah
Common Names GOLDENWAVE,
    PLAINS COREOPSIS, CALLIOPSIS
Annual
Usual Height 1–1½ feet, can reach 4 feet
Spacing 1 foot apart, or 2 pounds seed per
    acre
Bloom Spring (early summer); yellow and
    maroon; 1 inch
Range Seasonally moist soils throughout
    Texas, usually in eastern half
    Canada to Louisiana to California
Soil Sand, loam, clay; acid or calcareous;
    poor drainage okay
Part shade, full sun
Propagation Seed

This coreopsis is one of our most abundant spring wildflowers. It's easy to get it confused with two other yellow daisies: lanceleaf coreopsis and greenthread. Goldenwave can be differentiated because it has much smaller flowers, which appear in greater profusion on multibranching stems. It blooms in early spring in the Valley and Corpus Christi and in late spring around Houston, Dallas, and Abilene. Occasionally, especially if we've had rain, you can see it blooming anytime after that up to frost—but never in the showy masses you see in the spring. You can use it in your garden, but its chief use is in a wildflower meadow. It is called goldenwave because it turns a field into a sea of golden waves. Commonly planted with bluebonnets or paintbrush, it blooms as they start going to seed. Sometimes these three, along with Indian blanket, are all planted together, and the dominant species will vary from year to year, as do the rains. Coreopsis is predominant in the wet years.

58. Spectacle pod
Dithyrea wislizenii
The authors

59. Clasping-leaf coneflower
Dracopis amplexicaulis
The authors

58. **Latin Name** *Dithyrea wislizenii* (*Dimorpho-carpa wislizenii*)
    Pronunciation dith-eh-REE-ah whiz-luh-ZEN-ee-eye
    Common Name SPECTACLE POD
    Biennial or short-lived perennial
    Usual Height 1½–2 feet
    Spacing 1 foot apart
    Bloom Spring, rarely to fall; white to pale pink; 1 inch across, fragrant
    Range Sands in West and Southwest Texas Nevada, Utah, New Mexico
    Soil Deep sand; well drained
    Dappled shade, part shade, full sun
    Taproot
    Propagation Seed (blooms second year and often subsequent years)

Sometimes I consider installing a sandbox in my flower garden just so I can grow the flowers that haven't adjusted to hard life in the clays. Spectacle pod is one of them. The flowers are a pretty pale pink (sometimes white, sometimes lavender) on a spike that blooms from the bottom up. This gives you three inches of clustered flowers above ripening seeds that look like miniature sunglasses. The blooming period can be quite long and can be extended by judicious watering, especially in the winter before blooming. I am always fond of anything that smells good, and these flowers have an innocent and gentle fragrance. The leaves are a pale green, in harmony with the delicately hued flowers. The plant gets tall and thin, so it is best placed behind shorter flowers like mountain peppergrass, lazy daisy, sleepy daisy, or heart's delight. If you cut the first blooms for the house, lateral stems will branch and bloom, making a bushier plant with a bouquet of flowers.

59. **Latin Name** *Dracopis amplexicaulis* (*Rudbeckia amplexicaulis*)
    Pronunciation druh-KOH-pus am-plex-eh-KAWL-iss
    Common Name CLASPING-LEAF CONEFLOWER
    Annual
    Usual Height 2 feet, can reach 3 feet
    Spacing 1 foot apart, or 2 pounds seed per acre
    Bloom April to June; yellow with dark center; 2 inches across
    Range Moist fields, ditches, and sunny bottomlands in eastern two thirds of Texas Georgia to Texas
    Soil Sand, loam, clay; acid or calcareous; seasonal poor drainage okay
    Part shade, full sun
    Taproot
    Propagation Seed

I'm including this plant for those of you who have a field or meadow with poor drainage and would like to fill it with a lot of color each spring. Clasping-leaf coneflower is the most vivid plant I've seen around the state that fills the bill. Team it up with fall-blooming snow-on-the-prairie or snow-on-the-mountain (they also like poor drainage). Clasping-leaf coneflower looks similar to black-eyed Susan and also a lot like a yellow Mexican hat. They are all closely related. You can tell this one for sure by the leaf, which clasps the stem. It's the only one of the trio that can handle poor drainage. This annual will also grow on dry slopes, especially if it gets a little extra moisture running over its feet, as on the sides of a railroad track, but it is not aggressive in these situations.

60. Tiny Tim
Dyssodia setifolia var. *radiata*
The authors

61. Wild buckwheat
Eriogonum multiflorum
The authors

60. **Latin Name**   *Dyssodia* spp.
Pronunciation   dye-SOH-dee-uh species
Common Names   TINY TIM, DOGWEED
Annual or short-lived perennial
Usual Height   4–12 inches
Spacing   9–12 inches apart
Bloom   March to frost, with water in summer; yellow; ½–1 inch across
Range   Trans-Pecos to Texas coast Southwestern U.S., Mexico
Soil   Sand, loam, clay, caliche, limestone; well drained
Part shade, full sun
Propagation   Seed

There are many dyssodias—all horticulturally desirable, all petite, all short-lived, and all the perfect size for a rock garden or a border where you want something low-growing that blooms all the time. Most dyssodias are classified as perennials, but everyone I met who has used them advised me to put them in with the annuals. Expect them to be around only one year, and then be pleasantly surprised if they live longer. Actually, you might be able to keep a bed of them going for years, because they seed out well in dry, loose soil. They have been successfully grown in the Valley, Corpus Christi, Abilene, and El Paso. The leaves are dainty, strongly scented, and usually gray and furry. The oil that gives them a pleasant aroma doesn't taste good to grazers. Deer will feed on dyssodia—but only if they are really hungry.

61. **Latin Name**   *Eriogonum multiflorum*
Pronunciation   air-ee-OG-uh-num mull-tye-FLOR-um
Common Name   WILD BUCKWHEAT
Annual or biennial
Usual Height   2 feet
Spacing   1 foot apart
Bloom   September and October; white to orange; 4- to 6-inch clusters
Range   Pine and oak woodlands and openings in Central and East Texas Oklahoma, Louisiana, Mexico
Soil   Sand, loam, gravel; well drained
Dappled shade, part shade
Propagation   Seed

This buckwheat puts on quite a fall show. The flowers are in a big lacy "plate" that starts out brilliantly white. Gradually the flower cluster turns to a subtle peach color and then continues darkening to coral and finally to a rich burnt orange. In the garden the color is good for two or three months. If you pick the heads just as they start to blush, they will turn to burnt orange in the house and stay that way all winter in a dried arrangement. The blooms appear only at the top of the stalk, so place wild buckwheat behind lower-growing flowers in your flower garden. Or if you have a pine or post oak woods, let them naturalize in the sunnier spots. A short perennial that also turns colors like this is whitlow wort, described in Chapter 5.

62. Eryngo
Eryngium leavenworthii
The authors

63. Mexican gold poppy
Eschscholzia mexicana
Dr. Jimmy L. Tipton

62. **Latin Name**   *Eryngium leavenworthii*
Pronunciation   eh-RING-ee-um
leh-ven-WER-thee-eye
Common Name   ERYNGO (ee-RING-oh)
Annual
Usual Height   1½ feet
Spacing   1 foot apart
Bloom   August and September; purple; 2–3
inches across
Range   Plains and prairies throughout Texas
Kansas to Texas
Soil   Sand, loam, clay, caliche, limestone;
well drained
Part shade, full sun
Propagation   Seed sown in fall as soon as
ripe

Most people think eryngo is a thistle—an easily made mistake, since it has prickly leaves and a fuzzy flower with spiny bracts, and at all stages of its growth it is extremely vicious. I would even go so far as to urge you to wear gloves to weed around it and, of course, when you pull out the dead plants after frost. Naturally, I do not recommend planting it near a walkway. Many people like it in a meadow, but remember, it isn't a lot of fun to walk through. I like it best in the flower garden, with about three plants clustered for a good display. It makes a good cut flower. When dried, it keeps its shape but loses its gorgeous color.

63. **Latin Name**   *Eschscholzia mexicana* (*E. californica* subsp. *mexicana*)
Pronunciation   ess-KOLE-zee-ah
mex-eh-KAH-nah
Common Name   MEXICAN GOLD POPPY
Annual
Usual Height   6–12 inches
Spacing   1 foot apart
Bloom   March to May; orange-gold; 2–3
inches across
Range   Limestone slopes of Franklin Mountains and near Lajitas
Texas to Utah, California, Mexico
Soil   Sand, loam, limestone; well drained
Full sun, a little shade okay
Propagation   Seed sown in fall

This looks so much like the California gold poppy that it's hard for most people to tell them apart. In fact, for years there's been a scurrilous rumor circulating around El Paso garden clubs that the poppies growing on the Franklin Mountains were actually planted (some say by a member) and—even worse—that they're really California poppies. Dr. Jimmy L. Tipton of the Texas Agricultural Experiment Station in El Paso assures me that El Pasoans can sleep easy—the poppies are genuine, 100 percent Texas natives. The foliage is lacy and softly blue-green. A mass planting down a rocky slope is a magnificent sight. After flowering, this poppy goes to seed and dies, just like bluebonnets. To get it started, sow seed in the fall. To get good cover faster, plant seed two years in a row. Or use this poppy in your flower bed as a spring annual. Let it self-sow, or gather and store the seed and plant it after a good fall rain.

64. Snow-on-the-mountain
Euphorbia marginata
The authors

64.   **Latin Name**   *Euphorbia marginata*
Pronunciation   yoo-FOR-bee-ah
mar-jin-AH-tah
Common Name   SNOW-ON-THE-MOUNTAIN
Annual
Usual Height   1–3 feet, can reach 5 feet
Spacing   2 feet apart
Bloom   August to October; white and green
leafy bracts; 2–4 inches
Range   Western half of Texas
Minnesota and Montana to New Mexico
Soil   Sand, loam, clay; poor drainage okay
Part shade, full sun
Propagation   Seed sown in fall—leave
uncovered

Masses of this flower are very showy. Snow-on-the-mountain loves ditches and water but grows well in fields—often quite dry ones. If you want to display it up front in a flower bed, pinch the stalks in the spring to make them full and bushy. Everywhere you pinch, more new branches will emerge. But be careful of the sticky white sap that will ooze out. It is a latex and can cause dermatitis in some people. If you don't pinch the stalks, the spectacular leaves and white bracts surrounding the inconspicuous flowers will stay at the top. In this case, put it in the rear of the bed, with other plantings hiding the bare stalks. Naturalized, it looks best in a meadow of knee-high grasses or at the edge of a pond or stock tank. (Livestock will leave this one alone—latex isn't a bovine taste-treat). The eastern version, snow-on-the-prairie (*E. bicolor*), is native in Dallas and Houston and down the coast. It is not as dense and pretty, but now a dwarf selection is on the market. If you're going to naturalize, go with the species that is native to your area. For a flower bed, I definitely recommend trying snow-on-the-mountain.

65.   **Latin Name**   *Eustoma grandiflorum*
Pronunciation   yoo-STOH-mah
gran-deh-FLOR-um
Common Names   TEXAS BLUEBELL,
LISIANTHUS
Annual or biennial
Usual Height   1½ feet, can reach 3 feet
Spacing   1 foot apart
Bloom   June to October; blue, purple, pink,
white, ivory, yellow; 2–4 inches across
Range   Damp prairies, fields, pond edges,
and banks of Rio Grande in most of
Texas
Oklahoma, Nebraska, Colorado, Mexico
Soil   Sand, loam, clay; poor drainage okay
Part shade, full sun
Propagation   Seed sown in fall or spring,
germinates best in greenhouse

Here's a flower that people love for its big rich blooms. Buy it from the nursery in midspring and it'll bloom for you until frost, assuming you take care of it. It puts on its biggest domesticated show at the same time it is being so conspicuous in the wild. Texas bluebell likes good garden soil, water, and fertilizer, and it's one of those rare flowers that does well in clay, where so many others rot out. I've had several winter over, one for four years (pretty good for a biennial!), but I have yet to have one seed out. So, to keep a big bed of them going, I have had to plant anew each spring. If it does winter over, it stays green. The leaves are thick and pale, with a hint of blue or lime. For salty areas, use catchfly (*E. exaltatum*), native from the southern Gulf Coast to the High Plains. It looks very similar to Texas bluebells and has the same range of colors. Bluebells make long-lasting cut flowers, staying fresh for well over a week.

66. Indian blanket with unusually wide yellow band
Gaillardia pulchella
The authors

65. Texas bluebell
Eustoma grandiflorum
The authors

66. **Latin Name**   *Gaillardia pulchella*
Pronunciation   gah-LAR-dee-yah
pul-KELL-ah
Common Names   INDIAN BLANKET,
FIREWHEEL
Annual
Usual Height   1 foot
Spacing   2 feet apart, or 10 pounds seed per
acre
Bloom   Midspring to frost if watered; red
and yellow; 1–2 inches across
Range   Prairies throughout Texas
Nebraska to Colorado to Arizona to
Mexico
Soil   Sand, loam, clay; acid or calcareous;
well drained
Part shade, full sun
Propagation   Seed sown in fall, transplant-
ing in fall or winter

Whatever the opposite of a green thumb is—if you have it, Indian blanket is for you. It's one of the easiest wildflowers to begin with in a meadow. It blooms just as the bluebonnets are finishing and is often the dominant color in a field of flowers. It and the purple horsemint do well even in dry springs. Indian blanket is predominantly red or orange, with a yellow scalloped edge. Red Indian blanket (*G. amblyodon*), which grows in sand, is pure red and even more vivid. Indian blanket sometimes sports all sorts of color variations: cream with yellow scallops, coral with peach scallops, peach with yellow scallops, and red with white scallops. The fluffy seed must be planted in contact with the soil to germinate. In rich fertile clay soil with water, Indian blanket will get rank and sprawl out three or four feet in every direction. In poorer soils or with better drainage it can be a joy from April to frost. If you collect your own seed, collect it carefully. Some Indian blankets get only six inches tall and make broad, neat mounds. Others make colorful one-foot balls, although most are ungainly.

67. Bitterweed
Helenium amarum
The authors

67.   **Latin Name**   *Helenium amarum*
Pronunciation   heh-LEN-ee-um
ah-MAR-um
Common Name   BITTERWEED
Annual
Usual Height   1 foot, can reach 2½ feet, can
be mowed
Spacing   1 foot apart
Bloom   September (April to frost); yellow;
1 inch across
Range   Prairies, openings, and waste places
in eastern two thirds of Texas
Southeastern U.S.
Soil   Sand, loam, clay, limestone; acid or
calcareous; well drained or poor drainage
okay
Part shade, full sun
Taproot
Propagation   Seed sown in fall or spring,
transplanting in winter

This multiflowered yellow daisy with the yellow center can be mowed regularly and still continue to bloom. This makes it useful for color in a lawn or for summer and fall color in a meadow. In a meadow with spring annuals like bluebonnets and paintbrush, you need to mow out the dead foliage at the beginning of summer. Many of the summer- and fall-blooming perennial flowers, like mealy blue sage and Mexican hat, cannot survive mowing at that stage in their growth. Bitterweed doesn't care. It can also be used in swales with spring obedient plant and fall baby's breath aster. Like all annuals, it can get crowded out by perennial flowers and grasses in later years as your meadow matures. It thrives in pastures because the cows eat its competition. It has gotten a bad name because its thready aromatic foliage is occasionally eaten by hungry cows and makes the milk bitter—hence "bitterweed." I've also been told it can affect the taste of honey. But as long as you don't have a herd or a hive feeding on your property, bitterweed is useful as a nonfussy, long-blooming, low-growing, vibrant yellow cover.

---

68.   **Latin Name**   *Hymenopappus artemisiaefolius*
Pronunciation   hye-men-oh-PAH-pus
ar-teh-meez-ee-ah-FOLE-ee-us
Common Names   OLD PLAINSMAN, WOOLLY
WHITE
Biennial
Usual Height   2–4 feet
Spacing   6–9 inches apart
Bloom   April and May; white and pink;
3-inch heads
Range   Coastal, East, and North Central
Texas
Louisiana
Soil   Sand, loam, clay-loam; well drained
Dappled shade, part shade, full sun
Taproot
Propagation   Seed sown in fall, or transplanting of rosettes in late fall

This flower has a lacy, old-fashioned Victorian look; its names, "old plainsman" and "woolly white," always struck me as unsuitable. The blooms are a translucent white on the outside, while inside they are a blushing pink to deep rose-wine. They have a gentle fragrance that must mean the nectar is sweet, because I always see lots of butterflies hovering about. The leaves, pale bluish green, like artemisia, form a rosette, from which arises

69. Yellow plainsman
Hymenopappus flavescens var. *flavescens*
The authors

68. Old plainsman
Hymenopappus artemisiaefolius
The authors

one long, sturdy bare stem. As you can tell, this means each plant is tall and narrow. Mass five to twelve together at the back of the flower border. Grown from seed, they usually don't bloom until the second spring. Plant seed two years in a row for continuous rosettes and blooms every year, and always let the plants seed out. Then cut the stalks back to the rosettes. Don't pull them out as long as they stay green, because they frequently bloom a second year. Cut the first bloom, and new blooming spikes will develop. Old plainsman makes an excellent cut flower.

69. **Latin Name** *Hymenopappus flavescens* var. *flavescens*
Pronunciation hye-men-oh-PAH-pus flah-VESS-enz
Common Name YELLOW PLAINSMAN
Biennial
Usual Height 1½ feet, can reach 3 feet
Spacing 9–12 inches apart
Bloom May to September; bright, deep, rich yellow; 4-inch heads

Range High Plains and Rolling Plains
  Kansas, Colorado, New Mexico
Soil Sand, loam; well drained
Part shade, full sun
Taproot
Propagation Seed sown in fall, transplanting of rosettes before bolting

This biennial is eye-catching. It is a deep bright yellow that never fails to get your attention. The plants are fuller and better-shaped than the eastern pink and white plainsman. The leaves are pale gray-green, and furry on the bottom. They're found mostly in the rosettes, but a few are up on the stems. Mass yellow plainsman to get good effect in a perennial garden, or scatter it in a plot of unmowed grass. Plant seed two years in a row to get a continuous flowering cycle going that will provide blooms each summer. The rosettes spend their first year growing a long taproot, which makes this plant so drought-tolerant. As long as the rosette is small and flat to the ground, you can transplant it successfully—but dig deep to get the long root. The second year, the rosette will bolt, which means it will grow tall. Then it will flower, set seed, and self-sow. If you can find both small rosettes and seed, and then plant them together, either in early spring or in the fall, you should be all set.

70. Standing cypress
Ipomopsis rubra
The authors

71. Mountain peppergrass
Lepidium montanum
Benny J. Simpson

70. **Latin Name** *Ipomopsis rubra*
Pronunciation eye-poh-MOP-sis
ROO-brah
Common Names STANDING CYPRESS,
RED GILIA
Biennial
Usual Height 2–4 feet, can reach 6 feet
Spacing 6–9 inches apart
Bloom May and June; red (yellow); spires
of 1-inch flowers
Range Fields or edges of woods in Cross
Timbers, Post Oak Woods, and Piney
Woods
North Carolina to Florida to Texas
Soil Sand, loam, gravel; well drained
Dappled shade, part shade, full sun
Taproot
Propagation Seed sown in fall, transplant-
ing of rosettes in late fall

Use standing cypress as you would old plainsman
and yellow plainsman. Plant the seed two years in a row,
because you won't get blooms until the second spring. Always let the flowers go to seed to keep up the cycle. Plan
an area of about four square feet to keep as your standing
cypress spot. It should always have rosettes that are just
starting as well as rosettes a year old. In late fall, transplant rosettes that rooted in other parts of the garden into
places where you want them. They have taproots, so dig
at least six inches deep. Standing cypress responds well to
fertilizer and water and can get quite huge without flop-
ping over. Just be sure it is always well drained. It and the
plainsman can be grown on clay slopes, but don't expect
them to seed out. You would have to buy them as annuals
from the nursery each fall. Use *I. aggregata* in West Texas,
in either limestone or igneous soil.

71. **Latin Name** *Lepidium montanum*
Pronunciation leh-PID-ee-um
mon-TAN-um
Common Name MOUNTAIN PEPPERGRASS
Short-lived perennial
Height 1–2 feet
Spacing 1 foot apart
Bloom March to June in nature, to frost in
garden; 2-inch heads
Range Southwest Texas, Panhandle
New Mexico, Colorado, Arizona
Soil Sand, loam, caliche, limestone; calcare-
ous; well drained; saline okay
Part shade, full sun
Propagation Cuttings, seed sown in early
fall

If you're going to grow mountain peppergrass,
make careful selections. Some plants are low and dense,
dazzling white with blooms. Those are the ones recommended in this book. Others might look so bad you'd call
them scraggly and drab. Most are somewhere in between.
Put your choice in your garden—that's where I like it best,
tucked in with other flowers in a perennial garden, by itself near a rock in a rock garden, or near the front of a
mixed border (annuals, biennials, perennials, and small
shrubs blooming together). Spot it sparingly where its
pure, clean white blossoms will intensify the colors of
other flowers around it. Or mass it for a big snowy show.
Its needs are few: at least a half day of sun, well-drained
soil of any kind, and enough water in the summer to keep
it blooming until frost. An individual plant lives only one
or two years, so let an occasional seedling survive to make
sure you will always have more.

72. Blue flax
Linum sp.
The authors

73. Bluebonnet leaf and flower
Lupinus texensis
Edith Bettinger

72. **Latin Name**   *Linum lewisii*
Pronunciation   LYE-num loo-WISS-ee-eye
Common Name   BLUE FLAX
Short-lived perennial
Usual Height   1 foot, can reach 2½ feet
Spacing   1–1½ feet apart
Bloom   April to October; blue (white);
1 inch across or less
Range   Sandy and rocky slopes of West
Texas, Panhandle, and Trans-Pecos
Alaska to Mexico, western U.S.
Soil   Sand, loam, clay, caliche, limestone;
well drained
Part shade, full sun
Propagation   Seed

Blue flax is a major component of virtually every commercial western wildflower mix on the market. When all the various flowers bloom, this is the one that dominates the show—the first year and often the second year too. There is more than one blue flax. *Linum pratense* is native from central Canada to central Mexico, going through the middle of Texas on the way, and *L. usitatissimum*, a native of Europe, is often found in back-East seed mixes. They all prefer sand but will tolerate other well-drained soils. Our golden flaxes are also popular. *Linum rigidum* is the most widespread, with varieties that range throughout Texas. It also needs well-drained soils, preferring sand. All the flaxes have slender, leafless, branching stems, on which the small, thin-petaled blossoms seem to float. The flowers are open only in the morning. Normally, by noon the satiny petals have dropped. But you'll have new flowers each morning, throughout its bloom period.

73. **Latin Name**   *Lupinus texensis*
Pronunciation   loo-PYE-nus tex-EN-siss
Common Name   BLUEBONNET
Winter annual
Usual Height   1 foot
Spacing   1–1½ feet apart, or 35 pounds
seed per acre
Bloom   2–4 weeks in March and April; blue;
2- to 4-inch spikes
Range   Abilene, San Angelo, Del Rio east to
Paris, Bryan, and Corpus Christi
Endemic to Texas
Soil   Sand, loam, clay, caliche, limestone;
well drained
Full sun, a little shade okay
Propagation   Seed sown in fall, seedlings
planted in fall

The bluebonnet—native nowhere else in the world—is as much a symbol of our state as the longhorn. A field of the flowers, dark blue and smelling divinely of the most subtle and delicious perfume imaginable, is an experience we in Texas look forward to each year. To get your own special field or patch, buy fresh seed, and sow it after the first fall rain. Treated seed germinates right away and requires watering for best results. Untreated seed adapts itself to the weather and will space itself out over the next two to three years. It usually takes that long to get a solid field. The beauty of the crop also depends heavily on winter rains, and some people say that cold weather is necessary to produce a really deep blue. To ensure seed for the next year, don't mow until at least half the pods have started to turn tan.

If you are using bluebonnets in a flower bed, plant either seed or young seedlings in the fall. Bluebonnets must winter over in the ground to bloom well. Setting

73. Texas bluebonnet
Lupinus subcarnosus
Benny J. Simpson

out plants in the spring usually produces disappointingly small, pale flowers.

This is really only one of our state flowers—we have six. They're all bluebonnets, and thanks to our state legislature, if we find any others, they'll get to be state flowers too. The one that was originally given that honor is Texas bluebonnet (*L. subcarnosus*). Along with *L. texensis*, it's the only other bluebonnet that presently has commercially available seed. It grows only in deep sands in South and East Texas. Sky-blue with a touch of white, it is considered by many to be the most beautiful of the bluebonnets.

Another annual bluebonnet is Bajada lupine (*L. concinnus*). This one is most often found on the lower slopes of the Franklin Mountains near El Paso, although it can also be found in grama grasslands in the Davis and Chinati mountains and elsewhere at elevations above 4,500 feet. Unlike all the others, it doesn't come in blue—it's reddish purple, with the obligatory white spot.

The largest of the annual bluebonnets is the Big Bend bluebonnet (*L. havardii*). It is most frequently found from Persimmon Gap to Boquillas and then up to Presidio, especially on gravelly hills along the Rio Grande. This bluebonnet stands three to four feet tall and is a very deep blue. About every ten to fifteen years, after a wet year, the hillsides are covered from top to bottom with these glorious bluebonnets.

Now for our perennial bluebonnets. We have two. One has just recently been proven native to Texas. It was found by Geraldine Watson in the Big Thicket. Sundial lupine (*L. perennis*) is native from Texas to Florida and South Carolina in sand, preferring dappled shade in Texas. It has pale blue flowers on a tall slender stalk. It spreads by creeping underground stems and has been known to bloom again in the fall.

The sixth Texas bluebonnet is the dune bluebonnet (*L. plattensis*). This one is for the High Plains, and its preferred habitat is sand dunes. A handsome plant with dark blue to blue-purple flowers, it is at the southern end of its range here in Texas.

---

74. **Latin Name** *Machaeranthera tanacetifolia*
Pronunciation mak-eh-RAN-ther-ah tan-ah-set-eh-FOLE-ee-ah
Common Name TAHOKA DAISY
Annual
Usual Height 6–12 inches
Spacing 6–12 inches apart
Bloom Spring and summer; purple; 2 inches across
Range Rolling Plains, High Plains, Trans-Pecos
South Dakota to Mexico
Soil Sand, loam, clay, caliche, gravel; well drained
Part shade, full sun
Propagation Seed

Sow Tahoka daisy thickly for continuous bloom. Some individual plants might be in flower for only two months and then expire. You can see a cluster in bloom over a six-month period, but you're seeing a succession of plants—not all the same ones. Often people naturalize them in a shortgrass meadow or on a rocky slope. There the daisies can seed out where they want, with some being in bloom at any given time, the way they are in nature.

74. Tahoka daisy
Machaeranthera tanacetifolia
Benny J. Simpson

75. Horsemint, lemon mint
Monarda citriodora
The authors

They are especially effective growing in among the stones in an uncemented patio, with an almost continual show of flowers scattered about. Shake out the seed when you pull up the dead plants, and allow the new ones to come up where they will. In warm weather they'll be in flower in only six weeks. Good drainage is the chief requirement for success. There are several short yellow machaerantheras that are also good for naturalizing, but to grow them you have to gather the seed yourself. Tahoka daisy seed is, at least occasionally, available commercially.

75. **Latin Name** *Monarda citriodora*
Pronunciation moh-NAR-dah
  sit-ree-oh-DOR-ah
Common Names HORSEMINT, LEMON MINT
Annual
Usual Height 1–1½ feet
Spacing 9 inches apart, or 3 pounds seed
  per acre
Bloom Mostly April to June; purple; 6-inch
  spikes
Range Slopes, prairies, and meadows
  throughout Texas
  Missouri to Kansas to Mexico
Soil Sand, loam, clay, limestone; well
  drained

Part shade, full sun
Propagation Seed sown in fall

For folks who want immediate success in a meadow, select horsemint. You can't miss. I realize that this last remark is like getting directions to someplace from a person who then says, "You can't miss it." I always get lost when someone says that! Nevertheless, this one really is easy. Plant fresh seed after the first fall rain. Water in the winter if it is unusually dry and if you have that option (I don't advise carrying buckets out to your meadow). Your horsemint should come into bloom right after the bluebonnets and continue on into early summer, if there are late spring rains. It seems to seed out quite well. In fact, with water and fertilizer it can become aggressive—or successful, depending on how you look at it. I like it best planted with Indian blanket, because I think the orange and purple make a striking combination. The leaves smell good when you rub them, typical of members of the mint family. The seed heads dry white and are attractive long after the blooms have faded, both in the field and in a dried flower arrangement.

76. Baby blue eyes
Nemophila phacelioides
Edith Bettinger

77. Diamond petal primrose
Oenothera rhombipetala
The authors

76. **Latin Name** *Nemophila phacelioides*
Pronunciation neh-MOH-feh-lah
fah-sill-ee-OY-deez
Common Name BABY BLUE EYES
Annual
Usual Height 6–12 inches
Spacing 9–12 inches apart
Bloom March to May; pale blue and white;
1 inch across
Range Open woodlands, prairies, and
streams in East and South Texas
Arkansas, Oklahoma
Soil Sand, loam, clay; calcareous; moist,
well drained
Dappled shade, part shade
Propagation Seed sown in fall

Naturalized at the eastern or northern edge of woods, or in an opening of dappled light, baby blue eyes can make a lovely carpet of pale blue in the spring. Its stems and leaves are soft and hairy and spill over in a way that makes it seem lush, although its foliage is not dense. Another charming use is on the shady side of a patio, where it can sprawl becomingly over the edges. This plant also does well in a shady flower bed where the main flowers are just breaking dormancy in the spring. Baby blue eyes will have died by summer and needs to be pulled out to maintain a neat appearance. Make sure it's gone to seed before removing it. Although it likes moist soil, it cannot take poor drainage, so if you live on Houston gumbo, use it in a raised bed or on a slope and treat it to a little more sun.

77. **Latin Name** *Oenothera rhombipetala*
Pronunciation ee-NOTH-er-ah or
ee-noh-THEER-ah rom-bye-PET-ah-lah
Common Name DIAMOND PETAL PRIMROSE
Biennial or winter annual
Usual Height 2–3 feet
Spacing 1½ feet apart
Bloom Mostly June (October); yellow;
2–3 inches across
Range Sandy soils in fields and sunny
edges in northern half of Texas
Wisconsin to Texas
Soil Sand, loam; acid or calcareous; well
drained
Part shade, full sun
Taproot
Propagation Seed sown in fall

Just when the big spring show is over, when the rains (if they came) have stopped, and when everything seems to be catching its breath to greet the onslaught of summer—that's when this primrose comes into full bloom. It's so striking that you can spot it half a mile away as you barrel down the highway. There are whorls of flowers (each flower is usually 3 inches wide) on each stem, and each plant has several stems. It can be naturalized in a young meadow, but it is best in the flower garden, where you can water it and coax it to bloom through the summer and into October. This primrose seeds out only in bare places and does poorly in thick, well-established sites. It can be transplanted only in its youngest stages because of the taproot. To bloom, it has to winter over, though it often blooms the first spring. The plant is airy enough to allow seedlings to develop underneath, so you can keep a permanent primrose spot in your garden. Once it has seeded out, cut it back. Don't pull it out—it might bloom next year.

78. Palafoxia
Palafoxia hookeriana
Edith Bettinger

79. Limoncillo
Pectis angustifolia
The authors

78. **Latin Name** *Palafoxia* spp.
Pronunciation pal-ah-FOX-ee-ah species
Common Name PALAFOXIA
Annual
Usual Height 2–4 feet
Spacing 2 feet apart
Bloom Summer and fall; pink
Range
P. *hookeriana*—Deep sands in East Texas, Houston, Corpus Christi, and Rio Grande Valley
Small-flowered palafoxias—Well-drained sand, loam, caliche, or beach shell throughout Texas
Endemic to plains states and/or Mexico
Soil Sand, loam, caliche, limestone; well drained
Part shade, full sun
Taproot
Propagation Seed sown in spring or fall (fresh seed in fall best)

Palafoxia hookeriana has one- to two-inch thickly clustered pink daisies from July until frost. It responds well to moisture and fertilizer as long as it has good drainage. Loam is fine in a raised bed or on a slope. Keep snipping and cutting all summer to thicken it and to prolong the blooms, but be sure to let some of them go to seed. This palafoxia self-sows readily in sand. The other palafoxias are reminiscent of dainty pink baby's breath. They are usually extremely easy to grow from seed. Allow them to scatter themselves throughout a flower bed or plant them in a meadow or rocky slope. Butterflies find them particularly rewarding.

79. **Latin Name** *Pectis angustifolia*
Pronunciation PEK-tiss an-gus-teh-FOLE-ee-ah
Common Name LIMONCILLO
Annual
Usual Height 8 inches
Spacing 9 inches apart for a solid cover, 1 foot apart for rock garden
Bloom Summer and fall; yellow; ½ inch across
Range Calcareous dry uplands in Edwards Plateau and Abilene to Trans-Pecos New Mexico, Arizona, Mexico
Soil Sand, loam, gravel, caliche; well drained
Part shade, full sun
Propagation Seed sown in spring or fall

It's hard to decide which I like better about limoncillo—its looks or its fragrance. When I first saw this plant, I couldn't believe I had spent my whole life up to that point unaware of its existence. The flowers are little yellow daisies that are so thick they nearly cover up the leaves. The leaves are responsible for the tangy bouquet—like fresh lemons. Dotted with tiny aromatic oil glands, the leaves are used extensively for flavoring and hot tea and to make a steam vapor for colds. Very low-growing and tidy in its habit, limoncillo has many uses in the landscape. It can form mats in the rock garden, be used as an edging for a flower bed, or be planted between stepping-stones for a flowery and fragrant walk. It can cascade over low stone or stucco walls or over the rim of a flower pot or planter at the base of a larger plant. Or you can just scatter the seeds throughout your garden. Even weeding these plants out can be an olfactory delight.

80. Blue curls
Phacelia congesta
The authors

81. Drummond phlox
Phlox drummondii
The authors

80. **Latin Name** *Phacelia congesta*
Pronunciation fah-SEEL-ee-ah kon-JESS-tah
Common Name BLUE CURLS
Annual or biennial
Usual Height 1–3 feet
Spacing 9–12 inches apart
Bloom April (March to June), June to October in Trans-Pecos; purple to lavender-blue; 3-inch curls
Range Throughout Texas, except East Texas; Arizona to Mexico
P. patuliflora (Purple Phacelia)—Southern two thirds of Texas to Mexico
P. integrifolia (Gypsum Blue Curls)—West and North Texas to Kansas, Utah, Arizona, and Mexico
Soil Sand, loam, clay, limestone; moist, well drained
Dappled shade, part shade, full sun
Propagation Seed sown in fall

Blue curls is usable throughout the state, and I've seen its distinctive curling spikes of flowers dominating many wildflower gardens in late April and early May. It is just one of three phacelias that are held in high affection across the state. All three respond well to garden culture and tend to grow thickly to make a good display. Gypsum blue curls doesn't have the fancy leaves of the regular blue curls. Purple phacelia does, but the flowers look more like baby blue eyes. Purple phacelia tends to grow more often in woodland settings, and the plants are usually less than a foot tall. All three phacelias are easy to grow from seed if they have good drainage and extra moisture. They do best if sheltered from the west sun. A word of caution: Some people find that the foliage can cause a minor rash.

81. **Latin Name** *Phlox drummondii*
Pronunciation FLOX druh-MUN-dee-eye
Common Name DRUMMOND PHLOX
Annual
Usual Height 6–12 inches, can reach 20 inches
Spacing 1 foot apart, or 10 pounds seed per acre
Bloom Spring; red, pink, white, peach, or lavender; 1 inch across
Range Grasslands and openings in woodlands in East Texas, rare north and west to the Llano Basin
Endemic to above areas, but escaped elsewhere in Texas and similar environments throughout the world
Soil Sand; acid to neutral; well drained
Dappled shade, part shade, full sun
Propagation Seed sown on site in fall or in 2-inch pots in early spring

The Drummond phlox we buy is actually a hybrid of two of the five recognized subspecies of Drummond phlox. Each subspecies is attractive, and we often see the pure red one planted alone. But the immense variety of colors with red or white eyes is found only in the hybrid mix. If you live on sand in the area bounded by Paris, Texarkana, Corpus Christi, and San Antonio, you can let them naturalize. Otherwise, plant the seed in bare spaces in your garden or in grass where you can water occasionally. After they bloom, let them seed out at will. You will be rewarded the next spring. Out of any fifteen plants, you can usually find ten or more different color combinations. The leaves and stems are soft, hairy, and slightly sticky, so the seedlings are easy to recognize. Nearly everyone can grow Drummond phlox in well-prepared garden soil from pots set out in early March. Shelter from the west sun helps to prolong their blooming season.

82. Rio Grande phlox
Phlox glabriflora
John M. Koros

83. Paperflower
Psilostrophe tagetina
The authors

82. **Latin Name**   *Phlox glabriflora*
   Pronunciation   FLOX glab-rih-FLOR-ah
   Common Name   RIO GRANDE PHLOX
   Annual or short-lived perennial
   Usual Height   9–10 inches
   Spacing   1½ feet apart
   Bloom   Late spring; deep pink with white
      eye; 1 inch across
   Range   Coastal Bend and Valley to Atascosa
      County south of San Antonio
      Endemic to Texas
   Soil   Deep sand; well drained
   Part shade, full sun
   Taproot
   Propagation   Seed sown in fall, cuttings

This gorgeously colored phlox must have deep dry sands or it will rot. If you don't give it too much water, it will winter over and bloom a second spring. The luscious color you see in the picture is found between Brownsville and Corpus Christi. In some other places this phlox is pale lavender or pale pink and not nearly as exciting. Blooms usually last about six weeks, and the plant is a well-formed mound of vivid color for that period. After flowering, the leaves shrink down to a small rosette for the summer and do not reappear until after a good cooling fall rain. For summer color, plant the phlox near the annual *Palafoxia hookeriana*, which doesn't bloom until the phlox is finished. You can also plant it in with abronia, which is open enough in its growth to allow the phlox to reseed and grow beside it. Both of these plants also love deep dry sands, so you will not risk overwatering and rotting your phlox. John Koros of Mercer Arboretum in Houston often grows this phlox with moss verbena, one of our excellent naturalized verbenas.

83. **Latin Name**   *Psilostrophe tagetina*
   Pronunciation   sye-loh-STROH-fee
      tah-jeh-TEE-nah
   Common Name   PAPERFLOWER
   Short-lived perennial
   Usual Height   1–1½ feet
   Spacing   1 foot apart for massing, 2 feet
      apart for specimen
   Bloom   February to October; yellow; 1 inch
      across
   Range   Trans-Pecos, Midland, San Angelo
      Arizona, New Mexico, Utah, Mexico
   Soil   Sand, loam, clay; well drained
   Full sun, a little shade okay
   Taproot
   Propagation   Seed (blooms second year)

Paperflower is one of our most impressive wildflowers. Nearly all year the flowers are so thick, you can barely see the leaves. Harold Stroud, a landscape designer in El Paso, says that he has found that very little watering is sufficient to keep it blooming until frost. When blooming has ceased, the flowers hang on, gradually fading to pale yellow and finally to a papery white or tan, at which time they make an excellent dried bouquet. If nurseries grew paperflower to blooming age in quantity, it would be a popular choice for massing in medians and at business complexes, as well as being the mainstay of home gardens. A slightly less showy species is *P. villosa*, which grows on the Rolling Plains and the Rio Grande Plains, from the Trans-Pecos all the way to Corpus Christi.

84. Black-eyed Susan
Rudbeckia hirta
The authors

85. Meadow pink
Sabatia campestris
The authors

84. **Latin Name** *Rudbeckia hirta*
Pronunciation rood-BEK-ee-uh HER-tah
Common Names BLACK-EYED SUSAN,
BROWN-EYED SUSAN
Annual or short-lived perennial
Usual Height 1–2 feet
Spacing 9–12 inches apart, or 2 pounds
seed per acre, scattered among other
flowers
Bloom May or June, to September with wa-
ter; yellow; 2–3 inches
Range Prairies and openings in eastern two
thirds of Texas
Newfoundland to Mexico
Soil Sand, loam, clay; well drained
Dappled shade, part shade, full sun
Propagation Seed sown in fall or spring

Black-eyed Susan is usually the "third wave" in an
East Texas or coastal meadow. Bluebonnets bloom first,
then goldenwave, and then black-eyed Susans. With good
rains, or if you are able to give it deep watering, black-
eyed Susan will be lush. It lasts longer if it is shaded from
the afternoon sun. In fact, you can naturalize the eastern
variety, which is closer to being perennial, in dappled
shade under trees. I've had very good luck with mine in a
shady flower bed. Mixed in among my lanceleaf coreopsis, it bides its time as small rosettes until the coreopsis
has bloomed and I have cut it back. Then, with the extra
sun, it shoots up and blooms all summer. I leave the seed
heads uncut for bird food and to seed out for next year.

85. **Latin Name** *Sabatia campestris*
Pronunciation suh-BAY-shuh
kam-PESS-triss
Common Names MEADOW PINK
Annual
Usual Height 9–12 inches
Spacing 1 foot apart
Bloom March to July; pink to rose; 2 inches
across
Range Sandy prairies and woodland edges
in eastern two thirds of Texas
Kansas to Illinois to Mississippi to Texas
Soil Sand, loam; moist, well drained
Dappled shade, part shade, full sun
Propagation Seed sown in early fall—leave
uncovered

"Dainty" is the perfect word to describe meadow
pink. It has an airy look, yet a mass of this pink flower
with its bright yellow center can be very eye-catching in
the spring. It tends to form large colonies in the short
spring grasses, so that the expanse of green appears to be
covered with pink stars. In his book, *How to Know and
Grow Texas Wildflowers*, Carroll Abbott says that meadow
pink can be mowed and still continue to bloom. The seed
is very fine, like that of mountain pink, and needs light to
germinate. Once you have meadow pink going, it self-
sows well. Planted in a flower garden, it gives you a long
and rewarding season of color. For the most carefree and
enjoyable results, mix it in among perennials and let it
self-seed where it will.

86. Greenthread
Thelesperma filifolium
The authors

87. Prairie verbena
Verbena bipinnatifida
The authors

86. **Latin Name** *Thelesperma filifolium*
Pronunciation theh-leh-SPERM-ah fill-ee-FOLE-ee-um
Common Name GREENTHREAD
Annual or weak perennial
Usual Height 1 foot
Spacing 1 foot apart
Bloom February to December, mostly spring; gold; 1½–2 inches across
Range Prairies throughout Texas except East Texas, rare in Trans-Pecos
Arkansas to Colorado to Mexico
Soil Sand, loam, clay, caliche; well drained
Full sun, a little shade okay
Taproot
Propagation Seed sown in fall or spring

Of all the yellow daisies in our state, greenthread and cutleaf daisy are the most visible. But it's greenthread that you are most likely to remember. It's striking en masse, with a rich golden color that is equal in intensity to goldenwave's. But greenthread is less dependent on rainfall, so it thrives where goldenwave won't. Greenthread grows harmoniously with Indian blanket and pink evening primrose. It got its name because its narrow drought-tolerant leaves are hardly wider than threads. Along the limestone spine of the state, the centers of its flowers are dark red-brown. In the Rolling Plains and High Plains, the centers are yellow. This should be one of our most often used wildflowers, but the seeds are not yet commercially available. Gather your own seeds as they ripen in June, store them, and sow them after the first fall rain. In a garden, greenthread needs lots of sun and good drainage. Watering is necessary to keep it blooming during the summer, and it will often bloom again on its own after fall rains.

87. **Latin Name** *Verbena bipinnatifida* (*Glandularia bipinnatifida*)
Pronunciation ver-BEE-nah bye-pin-ah-TIFF-uh-dah
Common Name PRAIRIE VERBENA
Annual or short-lived perennial
Usual Height 6–12 inches
Spacing 1–2 feet apart, depending on soil preparation
Bloom Whenever above freezing; purple; 1- to 2-inch heads
Evergreen
Range Prairies and fields throughout Texas except most of Trans-Pecos, but does well in El Paso
South Dakota to Mexico
Soil Sand, loam, clay, caliche, limestone; well drained
Full sun, a little shade okay
Propagation Seed, cuttings, transplanting of small plants in winter

Prairie verbena would be the best sunny, low-growing, evergreen ground cover in the world—if only it were long-lived. It's usually called a perennial, but it rarely blooms more than two springs, and not always that much. From my observations, I'd say that it really minds cold winters and freezes easily. Since it reseeds easily and blooms the first year from seed, it survives well as an annual. It seems to prefer limestone and good drainage. The one in the picture was three feet wide and was growing out of a crack in a solid hunk of limestone. I've also seen it get this big by midsummer in rich loam with watering. With no watering or care, it can bloom spring, summer, fall, and even winter—as long as temperatures stay above 32° F. It is appropriate for a rock garden, mixes well with other wildflowers, and looks terrific hanging over the edge of a patio pot or a wall. Butterflies love it.

88. Sleepy daisy
Xanthisma texanum
The authors

88.   **Latin Name**   *Xanthisma texanum*
Pronunciation   zan-THEEZ-mah tex-AN-um
Common Name   SLEEPY DAISY
Annual
Usual Height   1–1½ feet, can reach more than 3 feet
Spacing   1½ feet apart
Bloom   April to December, early afternoon; yellow; 2–3 inches across
Range   Sands from Panhandle and Eastern Cross Timbers to Gulf Coast and Valley Oklahoma
Soil   Sand, loam; well drained
Part shade, full sun
Taproot
Propagation   Seed sown in late winter or early spring

Remember the white lazy daisy I mentioned earlier in this chapter—the one that doesn't open up until afternoon? Well, this is its equally lethargic cousin, sleepy daisy. It is also a superb annual, blooming profusely with big bright yellow flowers all summer long—but not until after lunch. It must be planted in sand or light, well-drained garden soil. Don't try to naturalize it anywhere except in sand. Burr Williams, of the Gone Native Nursery in Midland, says he has found that sleepy daisy germinates in the spring. If there are no spring rains, you'll have to water it to get it going. Sleepy daisy and lazy daisy are a knockout combo of low-growing white and yellow blooms all spring, summer, and fall, for people who live on deep sands.

Sand Garden Plan
Lot Size: 62' × 40'

There are some particularly wonderful plants, especially flowers, that grow only in deep sand. Heart's delight is one of the prettiest. It has big balls of pink fragrant flowers that bloom for a long time in spring and early summer. Lazy daisy, a nice-sized bouquet of large white flowers that bloom from March to frost, is another favorite. These two flowers can be grown anywhere in the state where there are well-drained sands.

Sand can be found all over the state—in the Valley, the Rio Grande Plains, the High Plains, the Llano Uplift, the Red Rolling Plains, in El Paso, in East Texas, and wherever there are post oaks. Even in gumbo cities such as Dallas and Austin, courses of ancient rivers have left sandy, gravelly terraces winding through the prairie clays. These deep sands allow easy root growth, provide plenty of oxygen for the roots, and distribute as little as a fraction of an inch of rain evenly a foot or so deep. With conditions like this, no wonder these plants haven't bothered to learn how to survive in tight, heavy clays. A shower barely wets the top inch of clay soil, and a heavy rain drives out all oxygen.

Gypsum and sandstone accent a flower garden bordering the circular driveway of the Plank land-scape in Midland. In the deep sand of this garden, everything grows quickly with almost no water-ing. Burr Williams, a nurseryman and landscape designer, planted here a goldenball leadtree, Gregg salvia, fern acacia, spectacle pod, sleepy daisy, and Tahoka daisy. This picture was taken in early July. Photo by the authors.

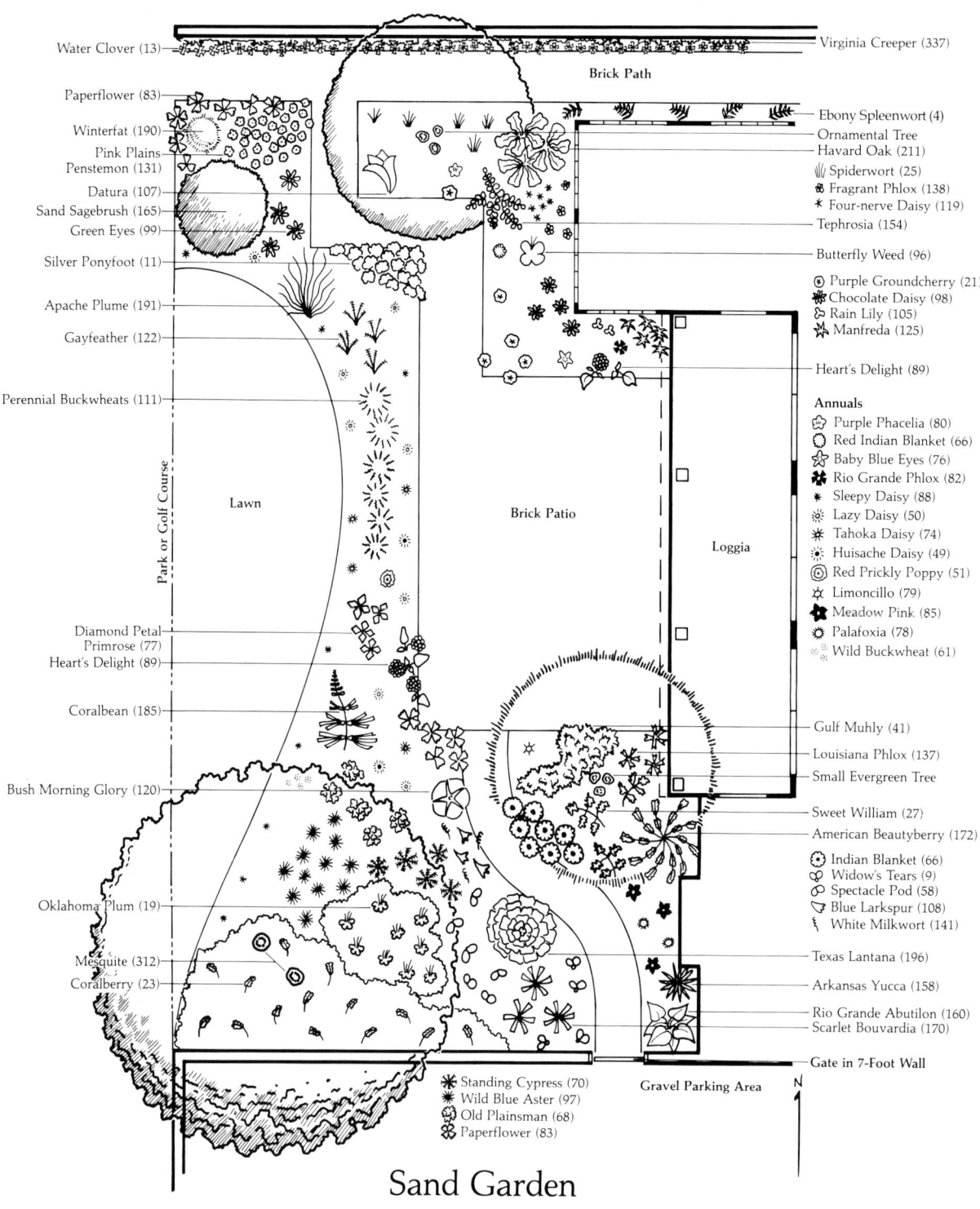

Water Clover (13)
Paperflower (83)
Winterfat (190)
Pink Plains
Penstemon (131)
Datura (107)
Sand Sagebrush (165)
Green Eyes (99)
Silver Ponyfoot (11)
Apache Plume (191)
Gayfeather (122)
Perennial Buckwheats (111)
Diamond Petal
Primrose (77)
Heart's Delight (89)
Coralbean (185)
Bush Morning Glory (120)
Oklahoma Plum (19)
Mesquite (312)
Coralberry (23)

Brick Path

Park or Golf Course
Lawn

Brick Patio

Loggia

Virginia Creeper (337)
Ebony Spleenwort (4)
Ornamental Tree
Havard Oak (211)
Spiderwort (25)
Fragrant Phlox (138)
Four-nerve Daisy (119)
Tephrosia (154)
Butterfly Weed (96)
Purple Groundcherry (21)
Chocolate Daisy (98)
Rain Lily (105)
Manfreda (125)
Heart's Delight (89)

Annuals
Purple Phacelia (80)
Red Indian Blanket (66)
Baby Blue Eyes (76)
Rio Grande Phlox (82)
Sleepy Daisy (88)
Lazy Daisy (50)
Tahoka Daisy (74)
Huisache Daisy (49)
Red Prickly Poppy (51)
Limoncillo (79)
Meadow Pink (85)
Palafoxia (78)
Wild Buckwheat (61)

Gulf Muhly (41)
Louisiana Phlox (137)
Small Evergreen Tree
Sweet William (27)
American Beautyberry (172)
Indian Blanket (66)
Widow's Tears (9)
Spectacle Pod (58)
Blue Larkspur (108)
White Milkwort (141)
Texas Lantana (196)
Arkansas Yucca (158)
Rio Grande Abutilon (160)
Scarlet Bouvardia (170)
Gate in 7-Foot Wall

Standing Cypress (70)
Wild Blue Aster (97)
Old Plainsman (68)
Paperflower (83)

Gravel Parking Area

N

Sand Garden

This plan is composed predominantly of plants that will grow only in sand, although I've included numerous others that grow both in sand and other well-drained situations. When deciding which of these sand-loving plants are suitable for your garden, take into account whether they are summer-hardy or winter-hardy or can adapt to the humidity of your area.

The plan for this garden is on level ground, sheltered on three sides. The west faces onto an open area that might be a golf course, a park, or some other communal green space. Because of the profusion of flowers, this garden is awash with color, perfumes, butterflies, and bees from mid-spring to frost every year.

You would enter the garden through a doorlike gate in a seven-foot brick wall that borders the gravel parking area. This is the way to the front door, which is the middle French door on the loggia. But you would see none of this when you first step into the garden. What you'd see is a path winding to the left of a tree. To your right is a Rio Grande abutilon with soft velvety leaves and a profusion of pumpkin-yellow blossoms. Spilling over either side of the path are flowers in red, yellow, purple, pink, white, and blue.

Meadow pink, palafoxia, sweet William, and Gulf muhly make the right side predominantly pink. Lavender-blue Louisiana phlox intensifies the pinks, while red and yellow Indian blanket and yellow limoncillo form bright accents.

On the left, blue widow's tears surround scarlet bouvardia and Texas lantana. Pale-pink spectacle pod, red standing cypress, old plainsman, and blue larkspur form a dazzling kaleidoscope in May. White milkwort and bush morning glory bloom in early summer, followed by wild blue aster and wild buckwheat.

As the path rounds the tree, a view opens up of the brick patio surrounded by flowers. Pretend for a moment that you are actually in this garden. Pick a sprig of the limoncillo at your feet and sniff the lemony leaves as you look across at the white, yellow, and purple masses of lazy, sleepy, huisache, and Tahoka daisies, backed with splashes of pure-yellow green eyes, Apache plume, dazzling white datura, red prickly poppy, pink tephrosia, and orange butterfly weed, glowing like jewels against the cool blue-green foliage of sand sagebrush, Havard oak, and silver ponyfoot. This is a scene to savor.

The garden still feels intimate and enclosed from here. It is only as you step onto the patio and pass the large shrubby coralbean that you experience the expansive feeling of the park opening out on your left. The flowers between the patio and this vista are all one-foot-high daisies most of the year, so this view is uninterrupted from the loggia. In the fall, two-foot-high buckwheats and gayfeather arise above the still-blooming daisies to produce a particularly vivid scene.

The dining room also has this view from its large floor-to-ceiling windows. They can be opened to let in a cross breeze, which carries exciting scents both sweet and spicy from the fragrant phlox, rain lily, chocolate daisy, and heart's delight placed just beneath the windows.

In the winter this corner between the patio and the dining room is the warmest part of the garden, shielded from the wind and basking in the late afternoon sun. Here are the manfreda, tephrosia, and the tenderest annuals—Rio Grande phlox and red Indian blanket. Here also are baby blue eyes, purple groundcherry, purple phacelia, and four-nerve daisy—all low-growing and long-blooming.

The west wall of the garden is covered with Virginia creeper. Where it gets plenty of sun, it will turn a breathtaking shade of red in the fall. At its feet grows water clover, a fern that looks like four-leaf clover.

Winter color comes from the purple or white berries of American beautyberry (at the base of the loggia), the purple berries of coralberry under the mesquite, and the feathery fruits of winterfat. I've placed this rather unusual shrub among pink plains penstemon and paperflowers so its scraggly summer appearance won't offend. After frost, the stalks of the flowers should be cut back to let the light catch and illuminate the beautiful plumy seeds all fall and winter.

A mesquite, double-trunked, was chosen to be the dominant tree in this plan because it grows so well in sand, it is as drought-tolerant as everything growing beneath it, and it provides light shade so that the flower garden can continue everywhere the wall does not cast heavy shadows.

The ornamental tree can be almost anything you want, as long as it doesn't exceed a sixteen-foot spread when mature. Most trees can grow in a variety of sites, and sand is very hospitable. Flatwoods plum, prairie flameleaf sumac, desert willow, and goldenball leadtree are just suggestions to get you going. Be sure to select a tree that doesn't require excessive moisture. Remember—everything in this plan likes to be well drained. Two or three overnight soakings a year might suffice to keep everything fresh and blooming, and even this small amount of watering might not be needed.

The evergreen tree should also be small. Pinyon pine, yaupon holly, wax myrtle, and Texas mountain laurel are good options.

The shrubs are drawn at their maximum size, which they might achieve in less than five years. If you've previously lived on clay, you'll be amazed how quickly everything grows on sand. Don't make the mistake of bunching things up too closely. Everything will get bigger than usual, so leave plenty of space. The plants you put in will be so small that you may feel silly at first. Just remember that because so many annuals grow well in sand, spaces are easy to fill in completely, even the first year.

The annuals are listed in a chart to the right of the loggia. Lazy daisy and sleepy daisy are the most important, because they provide continuous color (once they open for the day). The limoncillo is next in importance, because it blooms all summer and fall. Wherever flowers are indicated on the plan, that is where seed should be sown the first year, although they might prefer other places in subsequent years. Annuals self-sow extremely well in sand, so be prepared to weed out an overabundance. They can be enjoyed wherever they come up, as long as they don't interfere with a shrub, perennial, or biennial.

Perennials and biennials are drawn in detail like the shrubs. These plants should remain in approximately the same places year after year. Biennials that come up in the wrong places can be transplanted in the fall or early winter. Perennials that seed out should occasionally be moved close to the parent group so that as older plants weaken, fresh ones are ready to fill in.

If you garden in sand, you are fortunate indeed. Everything is easier—preparing the soil, digging the holes, weeding, watering, all the usual gardening chores. The plants also find life easier; they grow quickly and easily into large, healthy specimens. You are especially lucky in being able to use the plants featured on this plan, but they are not the only plants you can use. Nearly anything winter-hardy and summer-hardy to your area should grow well for you.

This English-style mixed border in our front yard combines native and naturalized perennials, shrubs, and ornamental trees. Taken in late May, this photo shows bergamot, naturalized lantana, black-eyed Susan, ox-eye daisy, daylilies, the branch of a vitex, and a crape myrtle in the background. Not in bloom are a spiderwort, wild ageratum, and a large clump of naturalized fall obedient plant. Photo by the authors.

FIVE

Perennials

L IKE death and taxes, perennials are one of those things in life you can count on—at least, once they're established. Like the seeds of annuals, perennial seeds can't germinate unless conditions such as rain and soil are good. And during their first year, growth is slow. But then you can count on reliable color for several years after, because they just aren't as dependent on the vagaries of each year's weather. They can grow their roots down deep to where moisture is always available (except in a terrible drought), store up strength whenever rain falls during the year, and deliver blooms even in a dry spring. They won't be as big and lush in a dry year, but at least they will make an appearance.

Of course, all perennials are not alike, and they display an immense range of differences in terms of longevity and growth habits. These differences are based mostly on what kind of roots the perennial has.

Some roots are so ordinary and unremarkable that no comment is made. But butterfly weed, for example, has a long, single taproot like a giant carrot that goes down several feet. Each year the plant gets larger, but it rarely seeds out and never suckers. It can live at least ten years, and I wouldn't be surprised to learn it can live fifty years. Once this plant is established, all you have to do is enjoy it.

Some other perennials that have taproots are bush morning glory, winecup, cutleaf daisy, the sennas, Mexican hat, Engelmann sage, green eyes, chocolate daisy, four-nerve daisy, blackfoot daisy, whitlow wort, tephrosia, and the two zinnias. Except for possibly bush morning glory, none of these plants is as long-lived as butterfly weed, but most can be expected to live at least five years. Winecups, I know, will live at least ten.

Cardinal flower is just the opposite. It has shallow roots that form small colonies if conditions are moist enough. Individual rosettes live only two or three years, so if you don't let this plant spread, you will lose it. In fact, it is best to bury a couple of stems each fall so they can root over the winter to make new plants. Blue Texas star and lanceleaf coreopsis renew themselves the same way.

Maximilian sunflower displays still another set of habits. It has large fibrous roots that go deep, but they don't form a taproot. They grow outward in concentric circles, a new growth ring each year. A two-year-old plant will send up one flowering stalk. Four years later, the middle stalk is dead, and twenty flower stalks form a circle around it. Needless to say, this can look fairly tacky. The best solution is to divide up the roots every third year. Choose a few young vigorous ones from the periphery and replant them where you want them.

Then there is a host of rhizomatous perennials. Like the cardinal flower and Maximilian sunflower, they spread by the roots, but there is no die-out; the patch just keeps getting bigger. To control these highly successful perennials, you have to dig up the ones you don't want. Usually their roots are fairly shallow; I've found them to be easy to keep in bounds. Some examples of this group are the columbines, wild blue asters, wild ageratum, bergamot, spring and fall obedient plants, and meadow beauty. Two deep-rooted rhizomatous flowers that you must be careful to control are goldenrod and ironweed. They are fall prairie perennials, and I've learned to be wary of putting them in a flower bed. Like an out-of-work in-law, once they make themselves at home, they're hard to get rid of. Irises also travel by rhizomes, but very slowly, and they are tuberous—which brings us to the subject of bulbs.

Bulbs are another whole category of perennials. They are subdivided into bulbs, corms, and tubers. Bulbs look like small onions. The layers are modified leaves. Corms are also rounded, firm, and fleshy—they don't grow in layers like a bulb, because they are actually part of the stem of the plant. Tubers are fleshy, like corms, but are covered with buds and hairy roots. A potato is a tuber.

The bulbs—alliums, pinewoods lily, prairie celestial, herbertia, wild blue hyacinth, and rain lily—like to be planted deep in the earth where temperatures and moisture are fairly stable. They will multiply, but more slowly than you would like. As with daffodils and tulips, they go dormant after the leaves have made enough food to restore the bulb so it can bloom again the next year. They are best planted in ground cover, in grasses, or with summer or fall flowers that are dormant in the spring. The fibrous-rooted blue-eyed grass and fragrant phlox should be used the same way. In spring they can make carpets of color, but by summer they have disappeared.

Gayfeathers are corms. Even while dormant, the stems are usually attached to the corm, so you should never have any trouble deciding how deep to plant. These are long-term, nonaggressive plants. Some grow in poorly drained places in East Texas, but most require perfect drainage.

The tuberous-rooted lila de los llanos and blue larkspur really seem more like ordinary plants. Both have evergreen rosettes in mild winters. Both like their roots to be planted close to the surface of the ground. The tubers on these plants are just fleshy, thickened roots—nothing like a potato at all!

Perennials are mostly used in flower gardens. The plans in this chapter demonstrate two very different but exciting ways to use them. One tells you how to design a flower garden using an English mixed border as an example. The other plan groups together an especially dainty collection for a traditional English rock garden.

89. Heart's delight
Abronia ameliae
Melissa Wasowski

90. Prairie onion
Allium stellatum
The authors

89. **Latin Name** *Abronia ameliae*
Pronunciation ah-BROH-nee-ah
ah-MEEL-ee-eye
Common Names HEART'S DELIGHT,
SAND VERBENA, ABRONIA
Usual Height 8 inches–2 feet
Spacing 1 foot apart
Bloom March to June; deep pink, rarely
paler; 2- to 3-inch heads
Dormant in winter
Range Sandy live oak woods and roadsides
from Rio Grande Plains to Panhandle
east to Centerville
Endemic to Texas
Soil Deep sand; well drained
Part shade, full sun
Long, woody root
Propagation Seed (difficult)

All abronias are of landscape quality, but heart's delight is the best of the lot. It has vivid hot-pink balls of flowers, usually with at least one butterfly in attendance, and indescribably well perfumed. The stems and leaves are sticky and sprawling, with the flowers perched on a stiff stem. *Abronia fragrans* (fragrant abronia), as you might guess by its name, is renowned for its fragrance. This abronia is usually white, sometimes tinged with pink or lavender, and it grows in a more erect stance—one to two feet tall. It blooms from March to August and is native from South Dakota to Mexico. Then there are several annual abronias. Two of the loveliest are *A. angustifolia*, which is a showy pink, and *A. carnea*, which has salmon to pink seedpods that are even prettier than the flowers.

None of the abronias transplants well, and they require perfect drainage at all times to prevent rotting at ground level.

90. **Latin Name** *Allium stellatum*
Pronunciation AL-ee-um stell-LOT-um
Common Name PRAIRIE ONION
Usual Height 1–2 feet
Spacing 8 inches apart
Bloom October; rose-pink; 4-inch ball
Dormant in winter or winter rosette
Range Northeast Texas
Manitoba to Illinois to Texas
Soil Sand, loam, clay, limestone;
calcareous; well drained
Part shade, full sun
Bulb, usually clustered
Propagation Division of bulb cluster, seed

This allium is very showy, and I don't see why it wouldn't do well in well-drained calcareous soils throughout the state. In the fall each bulb sends up one stalk that bears a large sphere of small deep pink flowers. The leaves usually remain green all summer and wither just before flowering. Another attractive Texas species is yellow allium (*A. coryi*), which is golden yellow and blooms in April or May. It is the only yellow onion native to the United States. It is naturally endemic to the Trans-Pecos, but it will also grow in any well-drained soil. Unlike the prairie onion, yellow allium's leaves (eight to twelve inches tall) keep their soft blue-green color during the blooming period. There is also no oniony smell to its leaves or flowers. Space these smaller bulbs six inches apart.

91. **Latin Name** *Alophia drummondii* (*Herbertia
      lahue* subsp. *caerulea*)
     Pronunciation ah-LOH-fee-ah
      druh-MUN-dee-eye
     Common Name HERBERTIA
     Usual Height 4–12 inches
     Spacing 6 inches apart
     Bloom March to May; blue; 1–2 inches
      across
     Green in spring only
     Range Grasslands in South Texas
      Rare in Louisiana
     Soil Sand, loam, clay; well drained
     Dappled shade, part shade, full sun
     Very deep bulb, brown, 1 inch
     Propagation Seed sown in fall

Herbertia is often seen in carpets of color that might bloom for one to two weeks in the spring. It is either blue or purple, is extraordinarily pretty, and has narrow pleated leaves about the same height as the flowers. Individual flowers are usually open between ten in the morning and five in the afternoon, depending on sunshine, for one day only. For this reason, herbertia is often called an ephemeral. It is one of three closely related iris bulbs sharing the above characteristics. The second in this trio is prairie celestial (*Nemastylis geminiflora*), and I've heard it called our most beautiful bulb. It is slightly larger than herbertia and is true blue with no trace of lavender. It blooms in April on clays and limestone soils from South Central Texas and the Edwards Plateau north to Kansas. My favorite of the three is pinewoods lily (*Eustylis purpurea*), which grows in the Piney Woods and in grassy areas in South Texas. It blooms later than the others, usually in June, though rarely as late as October. On all these flowers, the leaves die back as soon as seed is set and the bulb is renewed.

91. **Herbertia**
     Alophia drummondii
     The authors

91. **Pinewoods lily**
     Eustylis purpurea
     Doug Williams

91. **Prairie celestial**
     Nemastylis geminiflora
     The authors

92. Blue Texas star
Amsonia illustris
Melissa Wasowski

93. Lila de los llanos
Anthericum chandleri
The authors

92. **Latin Name** *Amsonia* spp.
Pronunciation am-SOH-nee-ah species
Common Name BLUE TEXAS STAR
Usual Height 1–1½ feet, can reach 4 feet
Spacing 1–2 feet apart
Bloom March to May; blue; 1 inch in a 3- to 4-inch head
Dormant in winter
Range
A. illustris—Eastern third of Texas; southern Missouri to eastern Kansas
A. ciliata—Edwards Plateau, Blackland, Grand Prairie; North Carolina to Gulf
A. arenaria—In sands east of El Paso; Arizona and Mexico
Soil Varies from acid to calcareous, well drained to poor drainage okay, according to species
Dappled shade, part, shade, full sun
Colonizes by stolons
Propagation Root division fall or winter, seed sown in fall

Amsonia illustris (often confused with sand-loving *A. tabernaemontana*) is the least aggressive blue Texas star and is frequently used in flower beds from Houston to Denton. The leaves caress the flowers, which are pale blue stars with lighter centers. After the plant blooms, cut the flower stalk back. The leaves stay green throughout the summer, if watered. *Amsonia ciliata*, one of several blue Texas stars that grow in limestone, is variable according to its habitat. On sunny, rocky slopes, it's less than a foot tall and is scattered. In rich garden soil, either sand or clay loam, it can make quite a display, but you'll need to control it. It is also variable because it hybridizes with two other amsonias that tolerate poor drainage. *Amsonia arenaria*, the best blue Texas star for the Southwest, is the most drought-tolerant and forms large colonies when left undisturbed in dry sands.

93. **Latin Name** *Anthericum chandleri*
Pronunciation an-THER-eh-kum CHAND-ler-eye
Common Name LILA DE LOS LLANOS
Usual Height 1–3 feet
Spacing 1 foot apart
Bloom May to November; soft orange-yellow to lemon; 1–1½ inches across
Evergreen in Valley, dormant in winter elsewhere
Range Chaparral and prairies in Valley and southern coast
Mexico
Soil Sand, loam, clay; well drained
Dappled shade, part shade, full sun
Fleshy tubers
Propagation Seed (easy)

This dainty lily can look quite elegant when massed in a slightly shady location. Its yellow flowers rise on slender stems above grassy leaves, with each plant having several stems and several flowers blooming simultaneously. Mike Heep, a landscaper in the Valley, has found that it blooms continuously and is evergreen as well—a real winner. He says that from seed to bloom takes only six weeks in warm weather. I tried one plant in Dallas. It bloomed a long time in the fall, went dormant at frost, and re-emerged in late April after a mild winter. A similar lily, *A. torreyi*, grows in grasslands in the Trans-Pecos, and sometimes among cedars and oaks on limestone hills both there and on the Edwards Plateau. I don't know of anyone who has tried to grow it, but I would think that it is well worth experimenting with.

94. Wild red columbine
Aquilegia canadensis
The authors

95. Yellow columbine
Aquilegia sp.
The authors

94.   **Latin Name**   *Aquilegia canadensis*
Pronunciation   ah-kwah-LEE-jee-uh
kan-ah-DEN-siss
Common Name   WILD RED COLUMBINE
Usual Height   8–18 inches
Spacing   1 foot apart
Bloom   Early spring; red with yellow;
1½–2 inches
Evergreen, sometimes dormant in summer
Range   On mossy boulders in Edwards
Plateau
Canada to Texas through eastern U.S.
Soil   Sand, loam, limestone; moist, well
drained
Shade, dappled shade, part shade
**Colonizes by rhizomes, but nonaggressive;
self-sows**
Propagation   Seed

Everyone loves this plant. Although it grows native in Texas only on mossy boulders in the Hill Country, it can be grown successfully in gardens where the soil is well drained and rich in organic matter, and where it is watered regularly and receives afternoon shade. There are some exceptions. In East Texas and the sandy parts of Houston, where it has both moisture and good drainage, it struggles against humidity, heat, june-bug grubs feasting on the roots . . . and, the biggest problem, rot! Katie Ferguson of Lowrey Nursery in Conroe (Houston) advises not watering it in the summer but letting it go dormant. Two years is the usual life expectancy here, as it is in San Antonio, where Manuel Flores of Native Design Nursery recommends planting from seed and oversowing. In Dallas it seems to be fully evergreen, and I know of plants that have been around at least seven years. In a patio pot of sand with no saucer, in flower beds, or as understory in moist sloping woods, it can be quite rewarding.

95.   **Latin Name**   *Aquilegia* spp.
Pronunciation   ah-kwah-LEE-jee-ah species
Common Name   YELLOW COLUMBINE
Usual Height   1–3 feet
Spacing   1 foot apart
Bloom   Usually in May, rarely again in fall;
yellow; 3–5 inches long
Evergreen
Range
A. chaplinei, A. hinckleyana—Endemic to
rocky crevices in Trans-Pecos mountains
A. longissima—Trans-Pecos to Mexico
A. chrysantha—Colorado to Mexico
Soil   Sand, loam, limestone, igneous; moist
well drained
Shade, dappled shade
Rhizomes, but nonaggressive
Propagation   Seed

There are four yellow native Texas columbines, and all are gorgeous. When people tend to have a favorite, they don't just like it—they rave about it! Longspur columbine (*A. longissima*) is the most dramatic, with its unusually long spurs. In order to get pollinated and ensure fertile seed, it relies on a moth with an extra-long proboscis to reach the nectar. The other three yellow columbines are *A. hinckleyana*, *A. chrysantha*, and *A. chaplinei*. The differences among them are in size of flower, length of spurs, and shade of yellow. If you plant them all together, they will hybridize. If you plant them with wild red columbine, you'll wind up with red and yellow combinations. Yellow columbines grow best in sand or in rocky soil on slopes, but they can do well in improved garden soil on clays as long as drainage is good enough to prevent crown rot. They are fully evergreen if planted in plenty of shade and are occasionally watered to prevent summer dormancy.

96. Butterfly weed
Asclepias tuberosa
Doug Williams

97. Wild blue aster
Aster sp.
Edith Bettinger

96. **Latin Name** *Asclepias tuberosa*
Pronunciation az-KLEP-ee-as too-ber-OH-zah
Common Name BUTTERFLY WEED
Usual Height 1½–2 feet
Spacing 2 feet apart
Bloom April to September; orange or yellow; 2- to 4-inch clusters
Dormant in winter
Range Prairies, thickets, open woods, and dunes throughout Texas, but rare in west
Eastern half of United States
Soil Sand, loam, clay, limestone; well drained
Dappled shade, part shade, full sun
Taproot
Propagation Seed, root cuttings

The brilliantly colored orange butterfly weed is in the milkweed family, and its nectar is a favorite with butterflies. Its prodigious taproot makes it almost impossible to transplant but also makes it very drought-tolerant and extremely long-lived. It takes three or four years to get big and bushy, adding even more branches and blooms with each passing year—extending its blooming season. Butterfly weed breaks dormancy in late spring, so plant a spring-blooming annual or summer-dormant perennial at its base. The plants sold in nurseries will be small because they do not grow well in pots. They like to concentrate on growing that taproot before even thinking about flowering. Plant a seed directly in the ground and you may have to wait four years to get your first blooms. That happened to me, but then, I'd planted in clay and caliche and didn't water very often.

97. **Latin Name** *Aster* spp.
Pronunciation ASS-ter species
Common Name WILD BLUE ASTER
Usual Height 2–3 feet
Spacing One is enough
Bloom September to December; purple to white; 1–2 inches across
Dormant in winter
Range Throughout Texas except Valley
East of Rocky Mountains
Soil Sand, loam, clay, caliche, limestone; well drained
Shade, dappled shade, part shade, full sun
Colonizes by rhizomes
Propagation Root division, seed sown in spring or fall

Texas has at least six wild blue asters (mostly lavender-blue, sometimes deep brilliant purple). They are apparently difficult to tell apart; my requests for clear identification are usually met with blank stares, embarrassed mumbling, or outright laughter! What is clear is that at least one of them will be at home in most situations. They will also be aggressive. They are best naturalized in the woods or just at the edge of a wood or thicket, where you won't notice if the lower leaves die back—a bad habit most of these asters have. Many homeowners mow them or use a line trimmer on them in spring and summer. If you have one that is well behaved or gets too tall and floppy, you have probably planted an aster that likes good drainage in a moist clay. Most of these wild blue asters flower extravagantly for just a few days in the fall, though sometimes people report weeks of bloom, even into the winter. It is possible to grow perennial asters from seed, but root division is easiest. If you can mark a plant in the fall and transplant one shovelful in the winter, you'll probably get yourself a lifetime supply.

98. Chocolate daisy
Berlandiera lyrata
The authors

99. Green eyes
Berlandiera texana
Benny J. Simpson

98. **Latin Name** *Berlandiera lyrata*
Pronunciation ber-lan-dee-AIR-ah
lye-RAH-tah
Common Names CHOCOLATE DAISY,
BROOCH FLOWER
Usual Height 1 foot, can reach 4 feet
Spacing 1 foot apart
Bloom April to June (to December); yellow;
2 inches across
Winter rosette
Range Panhandle and Trans-Pecos
Kansas to Colorado, Arizona, and Mexico
Soil Sand, loam, clay, caliche; calcareous;
well drained
Part shade, full sun
Taproot
Propagation Seed sown in fall

Yes, chocolate daisy does smell like chocolate—with no calories. Its other name, "brooch flower," describes the fuzzy maroon (sometimes orange) center, which is surrounded, like a gem, by a green setting of leaflike material after the petals drop. The leaves are pale green, a rosette in the winter and fairly dense on the stems during the flowering period. The yellow petals have purple veins on their undersides. This flower can be used in a garden or in a meadow. In a garden, in good soil with water, it can get so tall the stems will flop over and send up branchlets, each of which will bloom. In poor soil, with just enough water to keep it going, it will be a well-formed plant a foot or more tall. In a meadow the flowers will be more single-stemmed than clumpy and will be about a foot tall. It can be mowed in early summer after the first flush of bloom without hurting the plant, but unmowed it will continue to bloom all summer and into the fall, although less brilliantly than it did in the spring. Butterflies are often seen on chocolate daisy.

99. **Latin Name** *Berlandiera texana*
Pronunciation ber-lan-dee-AIR-ah
tex-AN-ah
Common Name GREEN EYES
Usual Height 1–4 feet
Spacing 1 foot apart
Bloom April to November; yellow;
1–3 inches across
Winter rosette
Range Hillsides, woodland edges, and
lightly shaded riverbanks from High
Plains to Corpus Christi
Oklahoma, Missouri
Soil Sand, loam, caliche; well drained
Dappled shade, part shade, full sun
Taproot
Propagation Seed

Green eyes is so named because its center is green or lime-yellow. The veins underneath the yellow petals are also green. This perennial is one of those long-lived ones that can start out in full sun and gradually adapt to light shade. That trait is handy when you are laying out a perennial bed with ornamental trees that are mere sticks when you put them in but will have a twelve-foot spread in only five years. Green eyes blooms splendidly in the spring, sends out new growth and blooms all over again in the summer, and then repeats the process for fall. Although it prefers sand, it adapts to any well-drained soil, and responds positively to watering and fertilizer. *Berlandiera pumila* is very similar but will grow only in the deep sands of East Texas (stretching east to South Carolina). It blooms best in the spring and summer.

100. Winecup
Callirhoe involucrata
The authors

101. Calylophus
Calylophus sp.
The authors

100. **Latin Name** *Callirhoe involucrata*
Pronunciation kal-uh-ROH-ee
in-voh-loo-KRAY-tah
Common Name WINECUP
Usual Height 6–12 inches
Spacing 2 feet apart
Bloom February to June, usually late
spring; wine-red; 2 inches across
Winter rosette
Range Roadsides, open woods, prairies,
scrubland, thickets, and hillsides
throughout Texas
North Dakota and Utah to Texas
Soil Sand, loam, clay, gravel; acid or
calcareous; well drained
Dappled shade, part shade, full sun
Turniplike tuber
Propagation Seed

The more I use winecup the better I like it. Just be sure it's well drained. It looks magnificent cascading over a wall or down a rocky slope. Think of it as an especially long-blooming bulb. Plant it under Texas lantana, butterfly weed, gayfeather, black-eyed Susans, or some other flower that does not get dense or bloom until summer for you. Or let it clamber over a small shrub such as a dalea. Winecup has green rosettes in the winter. In early spring it sends out prostrate stems up to four feet long that bloom throughout April and May in most of the state. It then shrinks back down to small rosettes. In July, if the weather is dry and they are unshaded, they might go dormant altogether until cooler weather and fall rains call them out again. People who water their gardens frequently can keep winecup green and blooming all summer. These people should give each tuber at least four square feet all to itself.

101. **Latin Name** *Calylophus* spp.
Pronunciation kal-ee-LOH-fuss species
Common Name CALYLOPHUS
Usual Height 1–1½ feet
Spacing 1 foot apart
Bloom March to November, mostly spring;
yellow; 2 inches across
Evergreen in mild winters
Range Throughout Texas except Piney
Woods
Colorado to Oklahoma south to Mexico
Soil Sand, loam, clay, caliche, limestone,
gypsum; well drained
Part shade, full sun
Propagation Seed (fall best)

In many ways calylophus is like yellow evening primrose, but calylophus is more upright and bushy. Its leaves are narrower, and the flowers are a little smaller. The soft yellow cups open in the evening about sunset and are moth-pollinated. Then they stay open all of the next day, closing in late afternoon shortly before fresh ones open. The old flowers turn orange or pink. This is an excellent rock garden plant because it loves good drainage and reflected heat and has a dainty appearance. In areas where it is abundant, you might plant masses of it down an unwatered rocky slope. In the garden, pick off old blooms and give it some water in the summer to prolong the flowers. Will Fleming, a nurseryman and landscape designer in Houston, tells me it is evergreen in his part of the state. He advises cutting it back to eight inches in the autumn to get it reshaped for the winter.

102. Wild blue hyacinth
Camassia scilloides
Edith Bettinger

103. Two-leaved senna
Cassia roemeriana
The authors

102. **Latin Name** *Camassia scilloides* (*Quamasia hyacinthina*)
 Pronunciation kah-MAH-see-ah skeh-LOY-deez
 Common Name WILD BLUE HYACINTH
 Usual Height 6 inches–2 feet
 Spacing 4 inches apart
 Bloom March to May; lavender to pale blue; 5- to 7-inch spikes
 Green in spring only
 Range Fields and open woodlands of Edwards Plateau
 North and east to Ontario
 Soil Sand, loam, clay, limestone; moist, well drained
 Dappled shade, part shade, full sun
 Bulb
 Propagation Seed sown in fall

Wild hyacinth is most rewarding in masses, either in a garden or in grasses. You need at least three in a clump for it to be noticeable, because the colors are so subtle—pale lavender, pale blue, or pale pink. Get five or seven in a clump, and they put on quite an elegant display. Also, because the scent is sweet but light, the fragrance is more enjoyable when the flowers are massed. In Houston, wild blue hyacinth needs fairly good drainage and does best in a raised bed or on a slight slope. Farther west, it can be grown in ditches and shallow swales, even in the heavy soils of the Blackland and Grand prairies. As you go farther west and the soils are drier, wild blue hyacinth is naturally found in more shade. If you can water occasionally, plant it where it gets more sun, especially in the spring when it blooms and the leaves photosynthesize. The grasslike leaves die back shortly after the flower sets seed, and the plant remains dormant until the following spring.

103. **Latin Name** *Cassia lindheimeriana*
 Pronunciation KASS-ee-ah lind-hye-MARE-ee-an-nah
 Common Name VELVETLEAF SENNA
 Usual Height 1–2 feet, can reach 6 feet
 Spacing 1–2 feet apart
 Bloom August to October; yellow; 1½ inches across
 Dormant in winter
 Range Edwards Plateau, Trans-Pecos Arizona, Mexico
 Soil Limestone outcrops, thin soils over limestone; well drained
 Part shade, full sun
 Propagation Seed

Velvetleaf senna can grow in a tiny fault in solid limestone. Its leaves are thick and gray and have a velvety texture that makes it hard to pass without stroking it. It provides bright spots of color at the hottest time of year, even in sunny places assaulted by reflected heat. A judicious amount of watering can extend its blooming period. A shorter and equally useful cassia is the two-leaved senna (*C. roemeriana*), which grows in the same areas and up into West Texas as well. It makes a one-foot-by-one-foot mound of yellow all summer, sometimes getting two feet by two feet in good loam. If flowering starts to slack off, water it once to get it going again. In their native areas, both sennas can be used in a flower garden or naturalized in a meadow or on a rocky slope. Elsewhere, use them only in a limestone rock garden with very good drainage, or they will rot.

104. Purple paintbrush
Castilleja purpurea
The authors

105. Rain lily
Cooperia pedunculata
The authors

104. **Latin Name** *Castilleja purpurea*
Pronunciation kass-teh-LAY-ah
per-PER-ee-ah
Common Names PURPLE PAINTBRUSH,
LEMON PAINTBRUSH
Usual Height 6–9 inches
Spacing 6 inches apart
Bloom May; purple, pink, yellow, orange,
or red; 6-inch spikes
Dormant in winter
Range Northern Rio Grande Plains, Ed-
wards Plateau, Blackland Prairies, Grand
Prairie, Western Cross Timbers
Kansas, Missouri, Oklahoma
Soil Sand, loam, clay, limestone; calcare-
ous; well drained
Part shade, full sun
Propagation Seed

Purple paintbrush isn't always purple! There's a yellow one (var. *citrina*) found in the sands of the Llano Basin and Western Cross Timbers; an orange or red vari-ety, which grows on limestone or in the sandy soils of Central Texas; and yes, a purple or pink variety that is usually found on limestone. They all bloom most often in May. The Trans-Pecos has six other perennial paint-brushes, all handsome and all standing six to eighteen inches high. The red, yellow, pink, or purple blooms ap-pear in the summer and sometimes in the fall, depending on the rain. Paintbrushes are suspected of being parasitic on grass roots. (*Castilleja latebracteata* may be an exception. Some believe it is parastic on an agave, the lechuguilla.) I've been told that seed can be successfully germinated in flats, with the seedlings then sold in small pots. But I don't know anyone who has had one that bloomed and grew year after year without having a bit of grass near by. Use a small ornamental grass in the rock garden, or plant paintbrushes in a meadow—in masses they are outstanding.

105. **Latin Name** *Cooperia pedunculata*
Pronunciation koo-PARE-ee-ah
peh-DUNK-yoo-lay-tah
Common Name RAIN LILY
Usual Height 1–1½ feet
Spacing 6 inches apart
Bloom Spring; white; 2–3 inches across;
fragrant
Evergreen by some reports, but mine are not
Range Eastern and Southwest Texas
Mexico
Soil Sand, loam, clay, caliche, limestone;
well drained
Part shade, full sun
Large bulb, black on outside
Propagation Fresh seed

This flower starts out beautiful and gets even bet-ter! It has one large, pure white, heavy-textured fragrant bloom on a slender stem arising from broad grasslike blue-green leaves. By the second day, the flower gets pink at the tips of its petals, and this color gradually spreads as the flower withers, until the petals, which have become papery, are an intense rose-pink. Let the seed form and disperse. After all, you want as much of this loveliness as you can get. The leaves stay green at least until frost, and two people have told me that theirs stay green all winter. They gave me some bulbs, which unfortunately went dor-mant for me. This bulb can be used in a flower bed, in ivy or other low ground cover, or in a meadow. The better-known rain lily is *C. drummondii*. It grows all over the state and usually blooms in October on a leafless stalk. Its tiny bulb naturalizes well in grass, tolerating occasional mow-ing. Both of these bulbs like to be planted very deep, so dig as far as you can, and then let them take it from there.

106. Lanceleaf coreopsis
Coreopsis lanceolata
The authors

106.   **Latin Name**   *Coreopsis lanceolata*
Pronunciation   kor-ee-OP-siss
lance-ee-oh-LAH-tah
Common Names   LANCELEAF COREOPSIS,
GOLDEN WAVE
Usual Height   1½–2 feet
Spacing   1 foot apart, or 10 pounds seed per
acre
Bloom   April to June; yellow with yellow
center; 2–3 inches across
Evergreen
Range   Roadsides, prairies, and edge of
woods in East and Southeast Texas
Most of central, midwestern, and south-
eastern U.S., northern New Mexico
Soil   Sand, clay, loam; acid or calcareous;
well drained
Dappled shade, part shade, full sun
Colonizes by self-layering
Propagation   Seed sown in spring or fall,
division of clumps or offshoots

This wildflower is becoming very popular. No wonder. It establishes so easily, you get almost instant gratifi-
cation. Just prepare the soil and add water, and you have
scads of yellow daisies in late spring and mats of evergreen foliage—and three times as much next year! It
spreads by the stems rooting, but mostly by seed and expansion of clumps. I love it when I'm getting a garden
established, but after the first year I weed out a lot of it.
Individual plants don't live forever, so I always let a few
vigorous seedlings stay. Transplanting is simple. Pull up
a bunch of leaves with a nub of root, stick it in the ground,
and water it. The single daisy with the narrow lance-
shaped leaves and bare stems is the native, but many
hearty cultivars are coming along—some double-bloomed,
some taller, some shorter. Many are of another native, *C.
grandiflora*, which is less drought-tolerant.

107. Datura
Datura wrightii
The authors

108. **Latin Name** *Delphinium carolinianum*
Pronunciation dell-FIN-ee-um
kare-oh-lin-ee-AY-num
Common Name BLUE LARKSPUR
Usual Height 1½–3 feet
Spacing 6–10 inches apart
Bloom April or May; blue to white; 6-inch
spikes
Dormant in summer
Range Northeast Texas, Edwards Plateau;
Illinois to Georgia
D. virescens (White Larkspur)—Throughout
Texas except East Texas; Canada to
Texas
Soil Sand, loam, clay; acid or calcareous;
well drained
Part shade, full sun
Shallow tuber
Propagation Seed

Being a fairly logical person, I used to think that blue larkspur was blue and white larkspur was white. I should've known better! In the plant world, rarely is anything that clear-cut. Blue larkspur is white at least as often as it is blue, and white larkspur can be blue at times. So if you grow either from seed, you might get deep royal blue or ice-white or any shade in between—which is fine, since they're all pretty. If you can find plants to buy in bloom, you can choose your shade of blue (or white). Both larkspurs are attractive and well behaved. Naturalized and unwatered, they will be under two feet on the Edwards Plateau and two feet or more in the Piney Woods. In your garden they will be tall. Since each plant has one straight-up bloom stalk, you'll want to make a thick cluster of them for a good display. They go dormant in the summer, so use them in conjunction with summer and fall flowers, or plant them in your ground cover.

108. Blue larkspur
Delphinium carolinianum
Doug Williams

107. **Latin Name** *Datura wrightii* (*D. meteloides,*
D. innoxia)
Pronunciation day-TOO-rah RITE-ee-eye
Common Names DATURA, ANGEL'S
TRUMPET, WRIGHT JIMSONWEED,
THORN APPLE
Usual Height 5 feet
Spacing 8 feet apart
Bloom May to November; white with
purple; 6–9 inches long, 4–6 inches across
Dormant in winter
Range Floodplains and bottomlands in East
Texas to the Trans-Pecos
California, Mexico
Soil Sandy, loam, clay; acid or calcareous;
well drained
Part shade, full sun
Propagation Seed (easy)

This dramatic night-blooming flower performs constantly from May to frost. The plant dies down to the ground each year but comes back bigger and shrubbier. It blooms the first year from seed and quickly gets as big as three feet by three feet! Datura is popular—despite its being coarse and weedy and poisonous. Although most plants have parts that are toxic if eaten in sufficient quantity, datura's poison is more concentrated. Some people get a rash just from touching the leaves, which are downy on the undersides. The huge flowers are pollinated by hawkmoths. They open in the early evening and perfume the night air, then stay open all day. One of the annual daturas, oakleaf datura (*D. quercifolia*), is also showy and grows in the Panhandle, where *D. wrightii* does not. The double-flowered purple one you often see is *D. metel*—not native, but naturalized here.

109. Purple coneflower
Echinacea purpurea
The authors

110. Cutleaf daisy
Engelmannia pinnatifida
The authors

109. **Latin Name** *Echinacea* spp.
Pronunciation eh-kuh-NAY-see-ah
Common Names PURPLE CONEFLOWER,
BLACK SAMPSON
Usual Height 2 feet
Spacing 1 foot apart for massing,
10 pounds seed per acre for meadow
Bloom April and May; rose, pink, white, or
purple; 2–3 inches across
Winter rosette
Range
E. purpurea (Purple Coneflower)—Extreme
Northeast Texas; Georgia to Michigan
E. pallida (Purple Coneflower)—Piney and
Post Oak woods and prairies in Texas;
Indiana, Nebraska
E. sanguinea (Purple Coneflower)—Sandy
prairies and pine barrens East Texas;
Arkansas
E. angustifolia (Black Sampson)—North
Texas, West Texas, Edwards Plateau;
Canada

Soil Sand, loam, clay, limestone; well
drained
Dappled shade, part shade, full sun
Propagation Seed sown in fall or spring

Purple coneflowers hybridize easily. As a result, if you've seen one, you haven't seen them all! Some display a single bloom atop a single straight stem, while others go in for branch operations, and show off numerous flowers. The petals might make platelike daisies or they might droop like swaying hula skirts. The colors range from dark rose to pale pink to white. The centers are sometimes mounds, but more often full spheres, and come in gold, red, or nearly black. After the petals drop, the centers hold their color and shape for a long time as the seed ripens, and they stay attractive well into fall. Purple coneflowers mostly bloom in late spring or early summer, usually for a couple of weeks, although some populations bloom all summer. Selections and hybrids are now appearing on the market, and in a garden they can be raised successfully far beyond their native range. Everyone who's growing them is raving about them.

110. **Latin Name** *Engelmannia pinnatifida*
Pronunciation eng-guhl-MAHN-ee-ah
pin-ah-TIFF-uh-dah
Common Names CUTLEAF DAISY,
ENGELMANN DAISY
Usual Height 1½–3½ feet
Spacing 1–3 feet apart
Bloom February to November, mostly May,
in morning; yellow; 1 inch across
Winter rosette
Range Fields and roadsides throughout
Texas
Nebraska to Colorado to Mexico
Soil Sand, loam, clay, caliche, limestone;
neutral to calcareous; well drained
Dappled shade, part shade, full sun
Taproot
Propagation Seed

As you drive around Texas in May, from the Rio
Grande Plains through the Edwards Plateau to the Blackland Prairies and across the Rolling Plains, the roadsides
are likely to be continuously adorned with this lovely
daisy. Not even pink evening primrose and white prickly
poppy can be found in such abundance over this range.
Because of its long, stout taproot, cutleaf daisy can bloom
whether it has rained or not. Naturally, given moisture, it
will be lusher and bloom longer. The rosette has large,
fancy-cut hairy leaves, giving this plant its common name
"cutleaf daisy." The stems are strong and don't need stak-
ing. The flowers are lemon-yellow, curling under at the
edges as the day heats up. On a scorcher they are firmly
curled under by noon; if it's raining, they might stay open
all day. In a garden, put this daisy at the back, as it can
get quite tall and broad. In a meadow, it can be mowed
from June on as long as you mow higher than the rosette.

111. **Perennial buckwheat**
Eriogonum wrightii
Benny J. Simpson

111. **Latin Name** *Eriogonum wrightii*
Pronunciation air-ee-OG-oh-num
RITE-ee-eye
Common Names PERENNIAL BUCKWHEAT,
WRIGHT BUCKWHEAT
Usual Height 1–1½ feet
Spacing 2 feet apart, farther in a rock
garden
Bloom July to October; white, cream, pink,
or yellow, fading to pink, then reddish
orange; ¼-inch
Winter rosette
Range Rocky slopes in low mountains of
West Texas and Trans-Pecos
New Mexico, Arizona, varieties along
Pacific coast
Soil Sand, loam, clay, caliche, limestone;
well drained
Part shade, full sun
Propagation Seed

There are several western perennial buckwheats,
three of which are especially attractive: *E. wrightii*, *E.
jamesii*, of similar size and habitat, and *E. correllii*, endemic
to the Panhandle. These handsome buckwheats are completely covered by tiny flowers. The plants make neat
rounded mounds or can cascade down a rocky slope. I've
been told that they provide good erosion control for rocky
cuts. Depending on what species you use, the flower color
might be cream, pink, or yellow, slowly fading to pale
pink, rose, and finally a beautiful coral or burnt orange as
the weather cools. James buckwheat (*E. jamesii*) is creamy
to pink, and Correll buckwheat (*E. correllii*) is brilliant yellow. If you pick the flower heads after they have turned
papery, they will hold all winter in a dried arrangement.
In full bloom the flowers have a sweet nectar that attracts
bees. In spring and summer before blooming, the plants
are matted mounds of pale green leaves fuzzy with whitish hairs.

112. Wild ageratum
Eupatorium coelestinum
The authors

112. **Latin Name**   *Eupatorium coelestinum*
Pronunciation   yoo-pah-TOR-ee-um
   soh-LESS-tuh-num
Common Names   WILD AGERATUM,
   BLUE BONESET, BLUE MISTFLOWER
Usual Height   9 inches–3 feet, usually
   1½ feet in a garden
Spacing   1–2 feet apart
Bloom   April to December, usually August
   and September; purple; ¼ inch
Dormant in winter
Range   Moist woods in East, Southeast, and
   North Central Texas
   New Jersey to the Gulf of Mexico
Soil   Sand, loam, clay; acid or calcareous;
   poor drainage okay
**Dappled shade, part shade, full sun if
   watered**
Colonizes by rhizomes
Propagation   Root division

Described as blue, this flower is really lavender. (Take its picture and it often shows up pink, especially if shot on a sunny day with Kodachrome film.) It looks like a tall ageratum, hence its common name "wild ageratum." Unless you're trying to cover a vast area, one of these plants is usually enough—it spreads quickly. Luckily, it isn't hard to control. The roots are shallow and easy to pull out. I use it in garden areas that have seasonal poor drainage, and it contains itself there quite well, unable to compete with the plants occupying drier sites. About every four years it seems to need to be divided to refresh itself. Palmleaf eupatorium (*E. greggii*) grows in gravelly calcareous soils that get seasonally flooded in the Trans-Pecos, Edwards Plateau, and Rio Grande Plains. It is very

113. Snakeweed
Gutierrezia sarothrae
Benny J. Simpson

similar to the eastern eupatorium in terms of height, forming mats, and seeking shade, but the flowers form puffy two-inch cushions, and the leaves are quite different. As you might guess from the name "palmleaf," they are divided into fancy spreading segments.

113. **Latin Name** *Gutierrezia sarothrae*
(*Xanthocephalum sarothrae*)
Pronunciation goo-tare-EE-zee-ah
sah-ROTH-ray
Common Names SNAKEWEED, BROOMWEED,
TURPENTINE WEED
Usual Height 12–20 inches, can reach 3 feet
Spacing 1–2 feet apart
Bloom Fall; yellow; ¼-inch tufts
Almost evergreen
Range Rio Grande Plains, Trans-Pecos,
West Texas, High Plains
Utah to Mexico
Soil Sand, clay, caliche, limestone; well
drained
Part shade, full sun
Propagation Seed

This plant has great potential. It would make an
effective ground cover in poor, dry soils—especially in
medians, in entrances to industrial parks and airports,
along roadsides, and in other unwatered places. It should
also do well in a rock or flower garden. I say "potential"
because I haven't seen any evidence that anyone is using
snakeweed in any of these ways, and that's a pity. In the
fall it is a breathtaking ball of solid, rich yellow. In the
spring and fall it is a haze of delicate yellow-green foliage.
How green it is in the winter depends on how mild the
temperatures are. Although most broomweeds are annuals, with tiny, scattered, daisylike flowers instead of
tufts, this one is not. The annuals aggressively cover overgrazed land and are a bane to ranchers (all broomweeds
are toxic to livestock). The overall effect is striking en
masse, but their color is not as deep or dazzling as that of
this perennial broomweed. I haven't seen the perennial
broomweed in masses in the wild, so I'm reasonably sure
it isn't as aggressive as the annuals. I could not discover
its life span, but it probably would not live longer than
two or three years in rich soil with supplemental water.

---

114. **Latin Name** *Helianthus maximiliani*
Pronunciation hee-lee-AN-thus
max-uh-mill-ee-AH-nee
Common Name MAXIMILIAN SUNFLOWER
Usual Height 4–6 feet, can be 1–10 feet
Spacing 3 feet apart
Bloom August to October; yellow; 3 inches
across
Dormant in winter
Range Seasonally moist ditches and depres-
sions in prairies in North Central Texas,
Southeast Texas, and Edwards Plateau,
rare in Rolling Plains and Trans-Pecos
Southern Canada to Texas on prairies

114. Maximilian sunflower
Helianthus maximiliani
The authors

Soil Sand, loam, clay, limestone; well
drained
Part shade, full sun
**Colonizes in ever-increasing concentric
circles**
Propagation Root division, seed

This sunflower generates more enthusiasm than
any other. It is truly spectacular in the fall. The flowers
bloom all at once up a stout stem. Each plant has a mass
of stems, and each flower is large, so you might easily
have four square feet of solid gold. Beneath the blooms
the stems usually have leaves that died during the hot
summer—not a terrific sight, so place this sunflower at
the back of your garden. Or, grow it in tallgrasses, which
form its natural habitat. Although it obviously loves moisture, I know of several fine specimens that grow on a limestone knoll. They are only four feet tall and two feet wide,
but they are no less brilliant for their reduced stature. This
habitat also restricts their spread. In good garden soil, divide and replant every three years to keep this sunflower
healthy and under control.

115. Big Thicket hibiscus
Hibiscus aculeatus
The authors

115.   **Latin Name**   *Hibiscus aculeatus*
Pronunciation   hye-BISS-kus
ah-kew-lee-AY-tus
Common Names   BIG THICKET HIBISCUS,
PINEWOOD HIBISCUS
Usual Height   2–4 feet
Spacing   3–4 feet apart
Bloom   June to September; cream; 2–4
inches across
Dormant in winter
Range   Moist pinelands and pine savannahs
in Big Thicket
Louisiana, Mississippi, Arkansas
Soil   Sand; acid; moist, well drained
Dappled shade, part shade
Propagation   Seed

Big Thicket hibiscus does well naturalized under pines in moist but sandy Southeast Texas or in raised beds on the gumbo clays around Houston and Beaumont. It grows quickly to a size roughly three feet high by three feet wide. It has two basic shapes: One has branches fanning out from the ground; the second, and I think more visually appealing, form has a short trunk, with numerous branches emanating from it like a small tree. (This latter version is being propagated in nurseries.) Rather than being dense, both shapes are open and airy, which is better for showing off the stunning flowers. They are a heavy creamy yellow, with a rich, dark red throat that fades to pink. The edges are pinked (as with pinking shears) and frilled. The leaves are variable in shape, one- to five-fingered, and always rough to the touch. This hibiscus is endangered in Texas (its habitat, the Big Thicket, has been largely drained and lumbered), but it is still common in Louisiana. The stems die back to the ground at frost. Cut them off, because new ones come up in the spring.

116. Heartleaf hibiscus
Hibiscus cardiophyllus
The authors

116. **Latin Name** *Hibiscus cardiophyllus*
Pronunciation hye-BISS-kus
kar-dee-OFF-uh-lus
Common Names HEARTLEAF HIBISCUS,
TULIPAN DEL MONTE
Usual Height 1–3 feet, depending on
moisture
Spacing 1–3 feet apart
Bloom Everblooming if no frost; red;
2–3 inches across
Dormant in winter
Range Chaparral and canyons in Rio
Grande Plains to Val Verde and Corpus
Christi
Mexico
Soil Sand, loam, clay, caliche; well drained
Dappled shade, part shade, full sun
Propagation Seed

This hibiscus is different from all of our others because it is small and drought-tolerant. Besides the areas
where it is native, it can be used in San Antonio and
Houston, if planted in well-drained soil—it will rot and
mildew in clay. It can be made more winter-hardy in
Austin if it's well mulched each winter. The solitary flowers bloom at the branch tips and are usually opened out
flat rather than cup-shaped. Shades of color vary from
orange-red to rose-red. In the Valley and along the coast,
where many winters are so mild that it doesn't die back,
heartleaf hibiscus can get woody at the base and look almost like a shrub. If if starts getting too tall and thin—
"leggy"—you can cut it in half in July and let it bush out
again. As long as it's growing, it's producing blooms. Here
in Dallas, where it gets too cold for this hibiscus, I plan to
try it in a patio pot and bring it indoors for the winter.

117. Halberd-leaf hibiscus
Hibiscus militaris
The authors

117. **Latin Name** *Hibiscus militaris (H. laevis)*
Pronunciation hye-BISS-kus
mill-eh-TARE-iss
Common Name HALBERD-LEAF HIBISCUS
Usual Height 3–8 feet
Spacing 3 feet apart
Bloom May or June to October; white or
pink; 4 inches across
Dormant in winter
Range Freshwater marshes and shallow
water in East and North Central Texas,
reported in Panhandle
Ontario to Minnesota to Florida and Texas
Soil Sand, clay, loam; acid or calcareous;
poor drainage okay
Part shade, full sun
Propagation Seed

This is the hibiscus I see most often in the wild. In
water or sugar sand, it gets about three feet tall. In garden
soil, especially on clay, it reaches more than six feet. The
flowers are usually white (rarely rose-pink) with a maroon
center. As with all hibiscuses, young leaves are heart-
shaped, then turn into little daggers with handguards—
not like halberds at all, which are axlike! This hibiscus
grows easily from seed. The first year, it has one stalk and
maybe a few flowers late in the season. By year two it will
have three to five stalks and lots of blooms all summer and
into early fall. The stalks die down each year after first
frost. Cut them back to four inches. When warm weather
returns the next spring, new stalks appear. An equally
tall, winter-hardy species is marshmallow hibiscus (*H.
moscheutos*), usually white and maroon, with heart-shaped
leaves, and now available in dwarf cultivars with huge red
and pink blooms. Give all of these hardy hibiscuses a deep
watering in late summer so they won't go dormant
prematurely.

118. **Spider lily**
*Hymenocallis
liriosme*
The authors

118. **Latin Name** *Hymenocallis liriosme*
(*H. occidentalis*)
Pronunciation hye-men-oh-KAL-us
leer-ee-OZ-meh
Common Name SPIDER LILY
Usual Height 1½–2½ feet
Spacing 1–2 feet apart
Bloom Late spring (to July); white;
4–7 inches across; fragrant
Dormant in winter
Range Piney Woods, Post Oak Savannah,
Houston to Victoria
Mississippi, Louisiana, Arkansas,
Oklahoma and Texas
Soil Sand, loam, clay; acid or calcareous;
poor drainage okay
Dappled shade, part shade, full sun
Bulb
Propagation Division of small bulbs from
base of mature 4- to 5-inch bulbs

Spider lily is one of our most striking flowers. Each of its white blossoms can be as much as seven inches across, and there can be as many as six blossoms in a cluster. The blossom is pure white, except for a touch of yellow in the center, and is exceedingly fragrant. The leaves are two feet long, two inches wide, and a shiny light green. They appear with the flowers, and last until frost. One bulb will eventually multiply to form a dense clump of leaves and numerous flower stems. Lilypons, a waterplant nursery near Houston, sells a Florida-grown spider lily that it says will grow in shallow water year-round. Our

119. **Four-nerve daisy**
Hymenoxys scaposa
The authors

native spider lily, which has the same botanical name, likes "wet feet, dry ankles" and grows only on the edges of water, on tiny islands, or in ditches that dry out in the summer. Ours is adaptable to a bog garden or an ordinary flower bed that receives regular watering. It's a must for Houston's gumbo, and I've even seen it thriving in late summer in a south-facing bed as far west as Dallas.

120. Bush morning glory
Ipomoea leptophylla
Benny J. Simpson

119. **Latin Name** *Hymenoxys scaposa* var. *scaposa*
(*Tetraneuris scaposa*)
Pronunciation hye-men-OX-siss
skay-POH-sah
Common Names FOUR-NERVE DAISY,
HYMENOXYS, BITTERWEED
Usual Height 1 foot
Spacing 9 inches apart
Bloom March to June and September to
October, March to August in Trans-Pecos;
yellow; 1–2 inches across
Winter rosette
Range Throughout Texas except eastern
woodlands
Soil Sand, loam, clay, caliche, limestone;
well drained
Part shade, full sun
Taproot
Propagation Seed

This is a small plant, gracefully elegant in form and habit, perfect for a rock garden or at the front of a border. The leaves are pale gray-green, sometimes furry, usually smooth and shiny. They are somewhat narrow and form rosettes. In the wild the rosettes are commonly four inches wide and are often seen scattered over rocky, sunny slopes. In a garden one rosette might be twice that size, although it's more usual for several small ones to form a clump about eight inches across. The solitary yellow daisies bloom at the top of bare stems. Four veins are easily visible on the petals, giving it its common name—"four-nerve daisy." The leaves smell strong and bitter when crushed, accounting for another of its common names, "bitterweed." ("Bitterweed" is also used to describe heleniums. See plant 67.)

120. **Latin Name** *Ipomoea leptophylla*
Pronunciation ip-oh-MEE-ah
lep-TOFF-eh-lah
Common Name BUSH MORNING GLORY
Usual Height 1½–3 feet
Spacing 3 feet apart
Bloom June and July; lavender to purple;
4 inches long, 3 inches across
Dormant in winter
Range Sandy prairies and roadsides in
Panhandle, Edwards Plateau, east to
Wichita Falls, and southwest to Midland-
Odessa
Nebraska, Colorado, New Mexico
Soil Deep sand; well drained
Part shade, full sun
Tuber
Propagation Seed

This bush morning glory is indeed glorious. It forms large rounded mounds of delicate leaves covered with huge morning glory blossoms. The flowers range in color from almost white (rare) to pale lavender to a rich reddish purple. The centers are always dark red. The tuber stores food and moisture, making bush morning glory long-lived and drought-tolerant but almost impossible to transplant. I've heard that a tuber can weigh up to fifty pounds! If I had sand, I would plant one in a place of prominence and give it several inches of bare soil around the edges, because I like how the feathery branches trail on the ground.

121. Zigzag iris
Iris brevicaulis
The authors

121. **Latin Name** *Iris brevicaulis*
Pronunciation EYE-riss brev-eh-KAWL-iss
Common Name ZIGZAG IRIS
Usual Height 1–2 feet
Spacing 1 foot apart
Bloom April to June; blue, lavender, or white; 3–5 inches across
Dormant in summer if too dry
Range Swamps and damp woods in East Texas
Alabama to Illinois
Soil Sand, loam, clay; poor drainage okay
Dappled shade, part shade, full sun
Rhizomes
Propagation Root division

Zigzag iris is not commonly seen in the wilds of Texas, but you can buy it. It is probably our most adaptable native iris. Use it in a water garden—in the mud just on the edge of the bank, or in shallow water, where it will be evergreen. Or you can use it in a bog garden that is wet in the winter and spring. There it will bloom and then die back as the bog dries up in the summer. If you live anywhere from Houston or East Texas west to Dallas and Austin, you can use it in regular garden soil. There, it might go dormant in the summer if it gets too dry, but it stays green with surprisingly little watering. Zigzag iris gets its name logically—its stems zigzag. The leaves are lax rather than stiffly upright, but there is always a leaf sticking up beyond the flower. This is one of the four irises that have been hybridized to form the beautiful Louisiana iris group, which has flowers up to seven inches across and comes in every shade of blue, purple, copper, pink, and yellow that you can imagine.

122. **Latin Name** *Liatris* spp.
Pronunciation lee-AY-triss species
Common Name GAYFEATHER
Usual Height 1–3 feet
Spacing 1–1½ feet apart, or 10 pounds seed per acre
Bloom 2 weeks in August to December; purple to rose-pink; 4- to 9-inch spikes
Dormant in winter
Range
L. mucronata—Well-drained limestone or sand in Edwards Plateau, North Texas, Corpus Christi; Nebraska to Mexico
L. punctata var. *punctata*—Well-drained limestone soils in West Texas, Trans-Pecos, Panhandle; Canada
L. punctata var. *mexicana*—Well-drained limestone soils in Trans-Pecos; Mexico
L. pycnostachya—Sandy, acid bogs in East Texas, prairies in Kansas north to South Dakota
Soil Varies according to species
Full sun, a little shade okay
Propagation Division of corms, seed sown in spring after wintering over on stalk, stratified seed

These liatrises are just a few of many varieties found in Texas. I've listed these because they are among the prettiest and have the widest range of habitat. All Texans should be able to use at least one of them, although those of us on black clays will have the hardest time. If a liatris that likes good drainage is grown on clay, not only does it get too tall and flops over, but it also writhes—the stems curve like snakes! Each plant should have several stiff stems from the base, each stem being covered one half to one third of its length in flowers. Liatris grows well in a rock garden or naturalized in grass. Individual plants can be fairly long-lived—at least six years and possibly much longer.

123. **Latin Name** *Lobelia cardinalis*
Pronunciation loh-BELL-ee-ah kar-din-AL-iss
Common Name CARDINAL FLOWER
Usual Height 6 inches–6 feet
Spacing 1 foot apart
Bloom May to October; red; 2-inch flowers in spikes, often 8 inches long
Dormant in winter or winter rosette
Range By streams and ponds throughout Texas except Valley
Throughout most of North America
Soil Sand, loam, clay, limestone; poor drainage okay

122. Gayfeather
Liatris mucronata
The authors

123. Cardinal flower
Lobelia cardinalis
The authors

Dappled shade, part shade, full sun
Propagation   Cuttings, layering, division of
   clumps, seed sown in fall

For a dramatic effect, plant cardinal flower in masses in your garden or at the edge of a pond. In garden soil it usually gets eighteen inches tall. Unless it's in naturally moist soils and shaded after midmorning, it needs to be watered. The more shade it gets, the less moisture it needs. The more moisture it gets, the taller it grows. The more sun it gets, the better it blooms. It is actually a water plant, and anyone having a water garden should consider it for its brilliant fall color. Although listed as blooming all summer, the best time to see it is in early fall when the hummingbirds migrate south. This is when the hummingbirds get nectar, and the flower gets pollinated. Cardinal flower is not a long-lived perennial. To keep it going, do a little propagation each year by burying a stem or two still attached to the plant. Hold it down with a rock. New plants will sprout from the leaf nodes. This process is called layering. Every two or three years, in early spring or early fall, dig up an old clump and replant the young vigorous portions that were growing on its edges.

124.   **Latin Name**   *Macrosiphonia macrosiphon*
   Pronunciation   mak-roh-seh-FOH-nee-ah
      mah-KROSS-eh-fon
   Common Names   FLOR DE SAN JUAN,
      ROCK TRUMPET
   Usual Height   6–12 inches
   Spacing   2 feet apart
   Bloom   May to September, evening; white
      (pink); 3- to 4-inch trumpets; fragrant
   Dormant in winter
   Range   Dry rocky slopes in Valley, Edwards
         Plateau, and Trans-Pecos
      Mexico
   Soil   Limestone, gravel; well drained
   Dappled shade, part shade, full sun
   Possibly colonizes
   Propagation   Seed sown in fall, transplant-
      ing in late winter

124. Flor de San Juan
Macrosiphonia macrosiphon
The authors

125. Manfreda
Manfreda sp.
The authors

I have yet to talk to anyone who has used this plant in a garden, but I think it's well worth investigating. Flor de San Juan always grows in the rocks, so give it a rocky incline or plant it above an unmortared rock wall. The dark green leaves wind in and out of the rocks, forming a low-growing mat only six inches tall. Start one plant in an area where it can expand, and let it cover wherever it will and as much as it will. It is probably not aggressive, as no one has reported seeing masses of it. Place it close to where you will be sitting out on summer evenings; that's when its large white trumpets open up wide and fill the air with the scent of gardenias. The flowers rise above the mat on stems that contain a white sticky sap.

---

125. **Latin Name** *Manfreda variegata* (*Polianthes variegata*)
Pronunciation man-FREE-dah veh-ree-ah-GAY-tah
Common Names MANFREDA, TEXAS TUBEROSE, HUACO
Usual Height Leaves 4–12 inches, flower stalks 2–4 feet
Spacing 1 foot apart
Bloom April to July; yellow, aging to coral and orange; 1–2 inches across
Winter rosette
Range Prairies and chaparral in Rio Grande Plains and Valley
Mexico
Soil Sand, loam, clay; acid or calcareous; well drained

Part shade, full sun
Bulbous tuber
Propagation Seed, division of root offsets

This unusual flower is a member of the amaryllis family. The thick fleshy leaves are like those of agaves, but they're soft, even on the tips, and splotched with purple spots. Manfreda looks dramatic when planted singly or in a small cluster next to a rock. Putting mulch around the base is a good way to show off the leaves. The blooms are arranged in an eight-by-five-inch cluster, which sits atop a tall, smooth stalk. It is definitely eye-catching. The flowers have a spicy fragrance. I saw several plants growing rather thickly down a wild rocky, grassy slope in the Valley below the deck of a house, where they made a welcome change from agaves and yuccas. We have several manfredas in Texas. *Manfreda maculosa* has flowers that age to a purplish color. It is endemic to South Central Texas, and I believe it must be the one I saw in the Trans-Pecos. You might be surprised to hear that there are also two that grow in forests in the northern part of the state—one in pinewoods and one in oakwoods. Baby plants, called offsets, sometimes grow at the edge of a mother plant. You can gently detach one to start your own manfreda.

126. Barbara's buttons
Marshallia caespitosa var. *caespitosa*
The authors

127. Blackfoot daisy
Melampodium leucanthum
The authors

126. **Latin Name** *Marshallia caespitosa* var. *caespitosa*
Pronunciation mar-SHAL-ee-ah kass-peh-TOH-sah
Common Name BARBARA'S BUTTONS
Usual Height 8–18 inches
Spacing 3 inches apart
Bloom April to June; white (pale pink); 1½-inch balls; fragrant
Winter rosette
Range Eastern and Central Texas Arkansas, Oklahoma, Mississippi
Soil Sand, loam, clay, limestone; well drained
Part shade, full sun
Propagation Seed sown in fall, root division in fall or winter

Barbara's buttons are dainty balls of white. Occasionally, you will see one tinged with pink or lavender. The flowers are borne on slender leafless stalks arising from a small rosette of narrow leaves. Benny Simpson had his test plants nibbled by rabbits all last winter, and the result was as many as forty "buttons" per plant. This is an extremely well-behaved plant that even the most fastidious gardener can enjoy. It can be used in clumps at the front of a flower garden, in a rock or sand garden, between stones or bricks in those portions of a patio where you seldom walk, along a narrow border, or almost anywhere you have a well-drained space. A bonus is that it has a pleasant, innocent fragrance—sweet but not cloying, rather like perfumed dusting powder. Can you imagine a flower bed of these in varying shades of pastel pink? Or as a floral arrangement on your dinner table? Growers, take note: This perennial should become quite popular.

127. **Latin Name** *Melampodium leucanthum*
Pronunciation mel-am-POH-dee-um loo-KAN-thum
Common Names BLACKFOOT DAISY, ROCK DAISY, MOUNTAIN DAISY
Usual Height 6–12 inches
Spacing 1 foot apart
Bloom March to November; white; 1 inch across
Evergreen in mild winters, almost evergreen or dormant in cold winters
Range Limestone and calcareous soils in West Texas, Panhandle, Trans-Pecos, Edwards Plateau Kansas, Colorado, Arizona, Mexico
Soil Sand, caliche, limestone; well drained
Part shade, full sun
Taproot
Propagation Seed, cuttings in a mist bench

Last year several hundred blackfoot daisies were grown; they were sold within three months. As soon as this daisy hits the market in quantity, it will be one of our most popular perennials. In the wild the plant is small—six inches wide and four inches tall, usually all by its lonesome on a rocky or sandy slope. In a garden, with compost and occasional watering, it will get one foot tall and eighteen inches wide by June and stay that way until frost. It starts blooming early in the spring with the bluebonnets, and throughout the whole warm season it will be magnificently covered by little white flowers with yellow centers. Sunshine releases its strong wild-honey scent. In a rock garden, give it enough room to have bare rock around it. In a flower garden, it can be effectively massed. *M. cinereum*, the blackfoot daisy of South Texas, is equally usable, but it's not winter-hardy north of San Antonio.

128. Bergamot
Monarda fistulosa
The authors

129. Yellow evening primrose
Oenothera missouriensis
The authors

128. **Latin Name** *Monarda fistulosa*
Pronunciation moh-NAR-dah
   fiss-too-LOH-sah
Common Names BERGAMOT, BEEBALM
Usual Height 1½–5 feet
Spacing 2 feet apart
Bloom May to September; lavender, pink,
   or white; 2- to 4-inch heads
Winter rosette
Range Dry open woods, fields, wet
   meadows, ditches, and marsh edges in
   eastern fourth of Texas
   Eastern North America
Soil Sand, loam, clay; acid or calcareous;
   moist, well drained
Dappled shade, part shade, full sun
Colonizes by rhizomes
Propagation Root division, seed

Here's a summer-blooming native you can use in the herb garden. Its leaves are redolent of mint; just brushing past them releases the aroma. In winter, bergamot is a four-inch-high mat of intensely fragrant leaves. It expands each year and is not easily weeded out, so be prepared to gradually acquire more. In spring the flower stalks start to grow. They get branched, leafy, and loaded with buds, while the rosette leaves may completely disappear. The nectar in the flowers smells as minty as the leaves and is known to attract both butterflies and hummingbirds. Bergamot can get mildewed in the shade if the humidity is high. If you have moisture and rich soil, give it full sun and place it at the back of a border with Texas lantana, scarlet sage, Mexican hat, or a eupatorium to hide the bare leggy lower stems. With a dry spring and full sun, bergamot is short and sufficiently leafy, but its roots need to be mulched or partially shaded by other flowers or grasses in the summer, or you'll lose some to drought.

129. **Latin Name** *Oenothera missouriensis*
Pronunciation ee-NOTH-er-ah
   mih-zoor-ee-EN-siss
Common Names YELLOW EVENING
   PRIMROSE, OZARK SUNDROP, MISSOURI
   PRIMROSE
Usual Height 1 foot
Spacing 1½ feet apart
Bloom April to June; yellow; 4 inches
   across
Dormant in winter
Range Exposed limestone and prairies from
   Edwards Plateau north through Black-
   land Prairies, Rolling Plains, and High
   Plains
   Missouri to Nebraska
Soil Sand, caliche, limestone; well drained
Full sun
Propagation Seed

Yellow evening primrose, sporting large, translucent blooms, makes an outstanding addition to a limestone rock garden. Leave plenty of space around it to show off its trailing branches and its flowers, which often extend beyond the ends of the plant. The clear yellow petals form a shallow cup that is enormous in relation to the rest of the plant. The flowers open in the evening, before sunset but after the worst of the day's heat. They stay open all night and probably depend on moths for fertilization. On cloudy spring days the flowers stay open until just about an hour before fresh ones open. On intensely hot days they close by midmorning. The closed flower is pinkish and drooping, as are the buds, which are green and speckled with dark pink. After the blooming season, the rosette shrinks to six inches or less and sometimes goes dormant in the fall, long before frost.

130. Whitlow wort
Paronychia virginica var. *scoparia*
Heard Natural Science Museum

131. Pink plains penstemon
Penstemon ambiguus
The authors

130. **Latin Name** *Paronychia virginica* var. *scoparia*
Pronunciation pare-oh-NIK-ee-ah
ver-JIN-eh-kah variety skoh-PARE-ee-ah
Common Name WHITLOW WORT
Usual Height 6–16 inches
Spacing 1 foot apart
Bloom July to November; chartreuse; 3- to 6-inch heads, which turn yellow to rusty coral in winter
Evergreen to dormant in winter
Range Limestone hills in Edwards Plateau and North Texas
Oklahoma, Arkansas
Soil Sand, loam, clay, caliche, limestone; well drained
Part shade, full sun
Taproot, usually goes horizontal 6 to 7 inches down
Propagation Cuttings, rooting of runners, seed (difficult)

Whitlow wort may not impress you the first time you see it, but it grows on you (figuratively, that is). People can eventually get passionate about it. It's a good choice for the rock garden, and it should be considered for use as a ground cover on dry rocky slopes because of its low height and year-round interest. In the spring it forms a ball of feathery foliage. Older plants might send out a runner or two. In the summer it starts to bloom, a lacy plate of tiny greenish-yellow flowers that gradually change to mustard-yellow, then to orange sherbet, and finally to a deep coral. The foliage might disappear after a hard freeze, but the coral color does not, though it continues to deepen all winter to a rich rusty brown. Cut it down to the ground in February to make way for new leaves and bloom stalks. Don't bury this plant among lush broad-leaved annuals or perennials. Its delicate beauty would be lost, and it might get shaded out.

131. **Latin Name** *Penstemon ambiguus*
Pronunciation PEN-steh-mon
am-BIG-yoo-us
Common Name PINK PLAINS PENSTEMON
Usual Height 1–4 feet
Spacing 1–3 feet apart
Bloom May to October (or above freezing); pink and white; 1 inch across
Evergreen to dormant in winter
Range Trans-Pecos, Rolling Plains, High Plains
Colorado to Mexico
Soil Sand; well drained
Part shade, full sun
Propagation Seed, root division

This is one of my all-time favorite penstemons. It gives masses of color for half a year, or even longer in warm climates. The flowers are white, pale pink, or sometimes pale blue at dawn and fully pink by midmorning. In deep sand with water, pink plains penstemon gets four feet tall and three feet wide, blooming constantly and profusely. In heavier soils it gets only about a foot tall. Experimentation indicates that it will tolerate any well-drained soil, so it doesn't absolutely have to be in sand, although that's the only place where it's likely to naturalize. It looks awful in a nursery pot because it hates having its roots contained—a problem with many of our Texas natives. So when you buy the poor little scraggly thing, plant it in the ground, where it will get bushy and be a pleasure to you inside of a month. In El Paso, it often dies back to the ground. In Midland, cut it back to one foot. In Phoenix, it might bloom all winter.

132. Rock penstemon
Penstemon baccharifolius
The authors

133. Wild foxglove
Penstemon cobaea
The authors

132. **Latin Name** *Penstemon baccharifolius*
 Pronunciation PEN-steh-mon
   bah-kar-eh-FOLE-ee-us
 Common Name ROCK PENSTEMON
 Usual Height 1–1½ feet
 Spacing 1 foot apart
 Bloom June to September; cherry-red;
   spikes of 1½-inch-long flowers
 Evergreen at 20° F and above
 Range Limestone crevices in Edwards
   Plateau and Trans-Pecos
   Mexico
 Soil Limestone; well drained
 Part shade, full sun
 Suckers, taproot
 Propagation Cuttings, seed

Rock penstemon has clustered spikes of cherry-red flowers all summer. The leaves are bottle-green with flexible sawtooth edges. It's a handsome plant, but only when healthy, and it has some exacting requirements. Good drainage is the most critical consideration. Too much moisture will not only bring on root rot but also cause the branches to become brittle and die back. This penstemon also likes to keep its roots cool; mulch and shade from west sun are effective, but piling rocks around it is an attractive way to protect this plant—in the winter, as well. Like pink plains penstemon, rock penstemon is almost shrubby, but I've put it here with the perennials because it dies to the ground in many winters. If it doesn't, it needs to be cut back to regain a dense bushy shape. For those of you who live near hungry deer, you need to know that they, along with sheep and goats, like it.

133. **Latin Name** *Penstemon cobaea*
 Pronunciation PEN-steh-mon co-BAY-ah
 Common Name WILD FOXGLOVE
 Usual Height 1–1½ feet
 Spacing 9 inches apart
 Bloom 2 weeks in April or May; white to
   purple; 2–3 inches long
 Winter rosette
 Range Rolling Plains and Blackland Prairie
   to Gulf of Mexico
   Nebraska, Arkansas
 Soil Sand, loam, clay, limestone outcrops;
   well drained
 Part shade, full sun
 Propagation Seed (blooms second year)

This is our largest-flowered penstemon. It spends most of its life as a rosette, four to six inches broad. Then, about a month before blooming, the rosette swells to at least double its original size, followed by one or more bloom stalks shooting up. In full bloom, opened flowers might cover two thirds of the stalk. Colors range from white to pale pink, lavender, or rosy purple, with contrasting spots in the throats. Truly a splendid sight! Use wild foxglove (no kin to the true foxglove) massed in the middle of a garden where it will be visible while in bloom, but where the shrunken rosettes can get the shade they need from other vegetation in the summer. Individual plants don't live more than three or four years, so I recommend always letting the seed ripen and scatter before you cut off the bloom stalks. This penstemon also does well naturalized in a meadow. A very similar one that blooms in June is *P. jamesii*. It grows in open grasslands

134. Havard penstemon
Penstemon havardii
The authors

on limestone soils in the Trans-Pecos and on the Llano Estacado.

134. **Latin Name** *Penstemon havardii*
Pronunciation PEN-steh-mon huh-VAR-dee-eye
Common Name HAVARD PENSTEMON
Usual Height 2–6 feet
Spacing 1–2 feet apart
Bloom April to June (October); red; 1–2 inches long
Winter rosette
Range Limestone soils in Trans-Pecos
Endemic to Texas
Soil Sand, loam, clay, limestone; well drained
Part shade, full sun
Propagation Seed; does not transplant well

Havard penstemon is the showiest of the scarlet penstemons because, instead of having a single stalk, it has a bunch of stalks. A number of professional gardeners in Austin and San Antonio have been using it and giving it high marks. Keep it on the dry side, because otherwise it can easily get up to six feet tall—kind of overwhelming for most small flower gardens. It spends most of its life as a rosette of thick pale leaves. After it's all done blooming, you'll probably want to cut back the stalks. If you leave them, though, they might bloom again in the fall. The scarlet penstemon from East Texas is *P. murrayanus*. Often six feet tall, it has one straight stem, which goes right through the center of circular pale blue-green leaves. Two

135. Gulf Coast penstemon
Penstemon tenuis
The authors

other tall red penstemons are *P. cardinalis* and *P. barbatus*. All of these penstemons are valuable to hummingbirds. Don't try transplanting any of these penstemons from the wild. I've heard it is almost certain failure to try.

135. **Latin Name** *Penstemon tenuis*
Pronunciation PEN-steh-mon TEN-yoo-iss
Common Name GULF COAST PENSTEMON
Usual Height 1½ feet
Spacing 1 foot apart
Bloom March, April, May; purple (pale pink); 1 inch across
Evergreen or dormant in winter
Range Poorly drained soils in Gulf Prairies and Marshes
Louisiana, Arkansas
Soil Sand, loam, clay; moist, seasonal poor drainage okay
Dappled shade, part shade, full sun
Colonizes
Propagation Seed

If you're getting the idea that all penstemons insist on good drainage, and here you are, sitting on poorly drained gumbo and feeling left out, take heart. Here is the penstemon for you. It has been doing fabulously well in Houston landscapes, and now we are trying it in Dallas

136. Hill Country penstemon
Penstemon triflorus
The authors

137. Louisiana phlox
Phlox divaricata
The authors

with promising results so far. It is a solid mass of blooms for several weeks in the spring, and sometimes it blooms again in the fall. The leaves form a thick mat that can be used as an evergreen ground cover if watered regularly in the summer. It does best in partial shade.

136. **Latin Name** *Penstemon triflorus*
Pronunciation PEN-steh-mon
  treye-FLOR-us
Common Name HILL COUNTRY PENSTEMON
Usual Height 1½–2 feet
Spacing 1½ feet apart
Bloom April and May; red to cherry-red;
  2 inches long
Winter rosette
Range Edwards Plateau
  Endemic to Texas
Soil Sand, loam, clay, limestone; well
  drained
Part shade, full sun
Propagation Seed, cuttings

Benny Simpson says that all penstemons cross-breed easily, and this one seems to be close to another Edwards Plateau endemic, *P. helleri.* Put the two together in a mass planting and you will soon have an exceptionally charming mixture that ranges in color from red to rose to pink. The main bloom time is in late spring, but in a garden you can extend flowering throughout most of the summer by watering sparingly. Allow seedlings to develop at nine-inch intervals to keep a healthy crop going. Cut back the bloom stalks if they turn brown and unattractive. Hill Country penstemon is probably the most brilliant of all our penstemons, considering the intense red color, the largeness of the blooms, and the small bushy stature of the plant.

137. **Latin Name** *Phlox divaricata*
Pronunciation FLOX duh-var-eh-KAH-tah
Common Name LOUISIANA PHLOX
Usual Height 4–18 inches
Spacing 6–12 inches apart
Bloom Late March or April; blue (lavender,
  pink, and white); 1 inch across
Evergreen
Range Rich woodlands along Sabine River,
  rare in Texas
  South Dakota to Florida
Soil Sand, loam, clay; moist, well drained
Dappled shade, part shade
Colonizes by underground stolons
Propagation Root division in February

Texas is too dry for Louisiana phlox to grow well in a naturalized setting, but it does great in a watered landscape. In East Texas it can even be used as a ground cover in small areas. Planted at intervals of one foot, it fills in quickly. By the time you've gotten as far west as the Blackland Prairies, it can be maintained only in patches in a flower garden. Here, unless you are planting in almost solid compost, space the plants six inches apart to get a dense mat right away. Be sure to water it once or twice even during the winter, or you'll have fewer the second year, not more. Louisiana phlox requires at least six inches of soil to maintain the even moisture it prefers. Except in the spring, it is a low-growing creeping mat of small dark green leaves. In March it sends up fragile, almost leafless stalks bearing the pale blue flowers that seem to float above the foliage. The blossoms last about three weeks, timing themselves perfectly most years for flowering among iris or in front of lanceleaf coreopsis.

138. Fragrant phlox
Phlox pilosa
The authors

139. Fall obedient plant
Physostegia virginiana
The authors

138. **Latin Name** *Phlox pilosa*
Pronunciation FLOX pill-OH-sah
Common Names FRAGRANT PHLOX, PRAIRIE PHLOX
Usual Height 8–12 inches
Spacing 1 foot apart
Bloom 4–5 weeks in April and May; pale pink to lavender; 1 inch across; fragrant
Dormant in summer, fall, and winter
Range Post Oak Woods, pinelands, and thickets in eastern half of Texas, grasslands and rocky slopes on Edwards Plateau
Wisconsin to Florida
Soil Sand, loam, clay, limestone; well drained
Dappled shade, part shade
Colonizes by underground stolons
Propagation Stem cuttings, root cuttings, root division, seed

This is one of my favorites, chiefly because of the intense fragrance that sweeps over you when the sun shines full on the flowers. In the evening or on shady days you might have to squat down and sniff to get the full benefit of the delicious scent. Think of this phlox as a bulb to be naturalized in grass, woodlands (where it looks terrific), flower beds, or a rock garden. It is not a bulb, but it blooms and is dormant on roughly the same schedule as many spring bulbs. Let it spread where it will. You can't have too much of it, and it won't hurt or crowd out anything else. I've been experimenting with a fragrant phlox I found in sand under post oaks. I was afraid it wouldn't like limestone and clay, but so far it is multiplying and thriving at a fantastic rate. This phlox usually blooms at the same time as lanceleaf coreopsis and penstemons.

139. **Latin Name** *Physostegia virginiana* (*P. praemorsa*)
Pronunciation fye-soh-STEE-jee-ah ver-JIN-ee-AY-nah
Common Names FALL OBEDIENT PLANT, LIONHEART, FALSE DRAGONHEAD
Usual Height 2 feet, can reach 4 feet
Spacing 1 foot apart
Bloom August to October; pink to lavender; 1-inch flowers in 4- to 6-inch spikes
Dormant in winter
Range Along streams, on moist grasslands in East and North Central Texas, Guadalupe Mountains
Canada to Texas
Soil Sand, clay, limestone; poor drainage okay
Dappled shade, part shade, full sun
Colonizes by rhizomes
Propagation Division of roots, seed (germinates in 20–25 days)

Fall obedient plant is one of those perennials to make black-thumb gardeners rejoice. It is easy to establish and even easier to keep. Also, it stays in bloom a long time in the fall—in Dallas, from late August or early September until frost, and not just for a week or so but solidly the whole time. Place it in dappled shade or on the east or north side of the house. Here it can be drought-tolerant. It spreads aggressively by the roots, but they are shallow and can be easily pulled out, so I haven't found this plant hard to control. Fall obedient plant is often seen in old-fashioned gardens, where it has obviously thrived for years with minimal care. Though it tolerates poor drainage, I have seen it growing in the wild on a limestone knob near Waxahachie.

140. Spring obedient plant in a ditch near Lake Lavon
Physostegia angustifolia
The authors

141. White milkwort
Polygala alba
The authors

140. **Latin Name** *Physostegia* spp.
Pronunciation fye-soh-STEE-jee-ah species
Common Name SPRING OBEDIENT PLANT
Usual Height 2–6 feet
Spacing 1 foot apart
Bloom April to July; pink to lavender;
1-inch flowers in 4- to 6-inch spikes
Dormant after setting fruit
Range Various species in swamps,
marshes, ditches, and bottomlands
throughout Texas except Rolling Plains,
Panhandle, and Trans-Pecos
Illinois to Mississippi
Soil Sand, clay; poor drainage okay
Dappled shade, part shade, full sun
Colonizes by rhizomes
Propagation Root division, seed

These spring (and summer) obedient plants are particularly nice for a water garden. *Physostegia intermedia* can form handsome colonies in shallow standing water. Most of the others do best on the edges of the bank. When they bloom, they are usually the focal point of the whole water garden. But obedient plants also have other uses. Many people in the country have driveways that cross seasonally moist bar ditches. Spring obedient plant is a striking way to dress up the ditch and not have to water, because after it goes dormant, it is drought-tolerant. It also adapts well to a garden, especially in areas of poor drainage where most plants rot. A bonus is that it makes a good cut flower. The name "obedient" came about because you can move an individual fresh flower left or right on the stalk and it will stay right where you put it.

141. **Latin Name** *Polygala alba*
Pronunciation pah-lee-GAY-lah AL-bah
Common Name WHITE MILKWORT
Usual Height 6–12 inches
Spacing 6 inches apart
Bloom April to November; pure white,
rarely lavender; 3- to 6-inch spikes
Winter rosette
Range Mesquite plains, cedar thickets, and
dry washes throughout Texas except
Piney Woods
Minnesota to Washington to Mexico
Soil Sand, clay, caliche, limestone; well
drained
Dappled shade, part shade, full sun
Propagation Seed

White milkwort may not be showy enough for everyone's taste, but it has several distinct advantages. It is well behaved, staying right where you plant it and not wandering off somewhere else. It has an exceedingly long bloom time. It is distasteful, but nontoxic, to deer and rabbits, so it shouldn't get nibbled down to the ground every time you set it out. A thick healthy specimen is a brilliant snowy white. It can be grown in masses, or it can form a well-shaped single specimen in a rock or perennial garden. Also, it can be naturalized in the shade under a juniper tree, along with zexmenia and cedar sage. Or it can be used in a shortgrass meadow in full sun. Those are impressive attributes. Milkwort seems to respond well to fertilizer and water. The rosettes get thick with bloom stalks and make a fan about one foot tall and across.

142. Mexican hat
Ratibida columnaris
The authors

143. Meadow beauty
Rhexia mariana
The authors

142. **Latin Name** *Ratibida columnaris*
(*R. columnifera*)
Pronunciation rah-TIB-eh-dah
kahl-um-NARE-us
Common Name MEXICAN HAT
Usual Height 1½ feet, can reach 3 feet
Spacing 1–2 feet apart, or 2 pounds seed
per acre
Bloom May to frost; dark red and yellow,
all red, all yellow, or splotched with
orange; 2 inches across
Evergreen in mild winters
Range Western two thirds of Texas
Minnesota to Montana to Louisiana and
Mexico
Soil Sand, loam, clay, caliche, limestone;
well drained
Part shade, full sun
Taproot
Propagation Seed (blooms second year)

Mexican hat is normally vase-shaped, but it can vary a lot in size according to its environment. On rocky limestone slopes it is small and well shaped, and it stays fresher and blooms longer with afternoon shade. In rich, moist garden soil in full sun, it makes a luxuriant ferny mound two feet tall and two feet wide, covered with large flowers all through its blooming season. Don't plant it in shade in moist clay soil; it will mildew and get tall with no leaves on the bottom half. Then it is hard to cut back successfully, because if you don't leave half the foliage, you can easily kill the plant. I've found that it will rot in a patio pot if the saucer has standing water for a day or longer. This surprises me, because I've often seen Mexican hat growing in ditches. In August, if it is dying back some with the heat, and rosette leaves are reappearing, you can cut it back or even mow it, but don't hurt the rosette. If it

continues to look fresh, don't cut it back until after frost. I've been told that deer leave this flower alone.

---

143. **Latin Name** *Rhexia mariana*
Pronunciation REX-ee-ah mare-ee-AN-ah
Common Name MEADOW BEAUTY
Usual Height 1–2 feet
Spacing 1 foot apart
Bloom June to early August, morning only;
rose to white; 2 inches across
Dormant in winter
Range Ditches, wet meadows, seepage
bogs in East Texas
Massachusetts to Georgia to Texas to
Illinois
Soil Sand, loam; acid; moist, poor drainage
okay
Dappled shade, part shade, full sun
Colonizes slightly by tubers
Propagation Root division

The chief advantage of this perennial is that it blooms all summer long. The sad thing is that it blooms only in the morning. The four soft-pink petals are distinguished by golden stamens, which pour out of the center of the flower. The stems and leaves are airy, not dense, and lend themselves to the front of a flower bed or to a naturalized area under the edge of trees. This flower is an excellent choice for an East Texas water garden. Its graceful drooping foliage and large flowers act as a foil to the taller, stiffer water plants. However, although it loves moist, rich soil, it isn't in the Water and Bog Plants chapter because it doesn't require poor drainage and constant moisture. It is well adapted to garden situations in Houston and East Texas. Even in these normally moist soils, though, water it regularly during a dry spell.

144. Violet ruellia
Ruellia nudiflora
The authors

145. Pitcher sage
Salvia azurea var. *grandiflora*
Edith Bettinger

144. **Latin Name**   *Ruellia nudiflora*
Pronunciation   roo-ELL-ee-ah
noo-deh-FLOR-ah
Common Names   VIOLET RUELLIA,
WILD PETUNIA
Usual Height   1 foot, can reach 2 feet
Spacing   1 foot apart
Bloom   March to December; violet or
lavender; 2 inches across
Dormant in winter
Range   Pastures, edges of woodland, and
thickets throughout Texas except
Panhandle
Mexico
Soil   Sand, clay, loam, caliche, limestone;
acid or calcareous; well drained
Dappled shade, part shade
Colonizes
Propagation   Root division in February,
seed sown in spring or fall

Violet ruellia is only a few inches tall when it starts blooming in early spring. By summer it can be two feet tall and still blooming. This is usually as high as it gets. It loves good garden soil and is not picky as to type. It adapts well to extra moisture but can be naturalized in dappled shade. Several other, mostly shorter ruellias can be found naturalized at the edges of woodland, often in conjunction with fragrant phlox, violets, baby blue eyes, and other shade-loving flowers. Here ruellias bloom more in spring and fall than in summer. In Corpus Christi I've frequently seen various species of ruellia, including violet ruellia, growing in shady lawns, where they tolerate occasional mowing. The ruellia most people know is Mexican petunia (*R. brittoniana*), a native of Mexico that is naturalized in the southeastern United States. Our native

ruellias are not nearly as tall or aggressive. Although ruellias are often called petunias, they are actually no relation to this family.

---

145. **Latin Name**   *Salvia azurea* var. *grandiflora*
Pronunciation   SAL-vee-ah ah-ZOO-ree-ah
variety gran-deh-FLOR-ah
Common Names   PITCHER SAGE, BLUE SAGE
Usual Height   1½–2½ feet, can reach 6 feet
Spacing   2 feet apart
Bloom   Fall; sky-blue to white; 1 inch across
Winter rosette
Range   Piney Woods, Post Oak Woods,
Blackland Prairies, Edwards Plateau
South Carolina to Nebraska to Mexico
Soil   Sand, loam, clay, limestone; well
drained
Part shade, full sun
Propagation   Seed, cuttings

Pitcher sage is one of those fall prairie flowers that has large, tough, deep roots and strong tall stems, so it can compete with prairie grasses. It is used to having its roots well shaded, so it takes lots of water to get a plant established in a well-weeded flower bed. However, it is easy to grow from seed. A seedling blooms the first year and, being less robust, is often better proportioned than an older, established plant. To make an older plant more manageable in size, and to increase its blooms, cut the stem back to just a few leaves in midsummer. Then it is shorter, and it branches into numerous bloom heads. If you need height in your flower garden, pitcher sage makes a vivid fall display when it's grown with Maximilian sunflower and any of the red sages. If you want to leave it tall, you'll probably need to stake it to keep it from sprawling, especially if heavy spring rains produce fast growth.

**146. Scarlet sage used as a ground cover,
mowed until August**
Salvia coccinea
The authors

147. Engelmann sage
Salvia engelmannii
The authors

146. **Latin Name**   *Salvia coccinea*
Pronunciation   SAL-vee-ah kok-SIN-ee-ah
Common Names   SCARLET SAGE,
  TROPICAL SAGE
Usual Height   2–3 feet, can reach 4 feet
Spacing   1–2 feet apart
Bloom   May to frost (fall best); red, pink,
  rarely white; 1 inch
Evergreen or dormant in winter
Range   East and South Texas
  South Carolina to Mexico
Soil   Sand, loam, clay, caliche; seasonal
  poor drainage okay
Dappled shade, part shade, full sun
Colonizes by seeding out vigorously
Propagation   Seed sown in fall or spring,
  cuttings

This salvia can be grown anywhere in the state, but it will act like an annual in the coldest areas. It will take sun or shade, water or drought, fertilizer or poor soil. But there's a catch. In good conditions you will hate it, because it gets big, coarse, and ugly. So use it in those dry, shady areas with poor soil where you can't get anything else to grow. Water it to get it started, and then leave it on its own unless it looks pitiful. Left entirely to itself on caliche or poor soil, it will make a woodsy two-foot-high ground cover. In better soil or with water, it will get taller. Cut it in half with a line trimmer when it gets taller than you like; that will just make it bushier. For a more formal look, mow it regularly on the highest setting from the time it greens up until August. Then let it bloom until frost, as you see in the picture. After frost, cut back the dead stalks and let leaves collect in the stubble for a winter mulch.

147. **Latin Name**   *Salvia engelmannii*
Pronunciation   SAL-vee-ah
  eng-el-MAHN-ee-eye
Common Name   ENGLEMANN SAGE
Usual Height   1–1½ feet
Spacing   1–2 feet apart
Bloom   April to June; pale blue; 4- to 6-inch
  spikes
Winter rosette
Range   Limestone hills in Central Texas,
  north to Denton
  Endemic to Texas
Soil   Sand, loam, clay, caliche, limestone;
  calcareous; well drained
Part shade, full sun
Taproot
Propagation   Seed, cuttings

Engelmann sage makes a compact mound of pale blue blossoms. The leaves are on the skinny side and have a groove running down the center. They cluster thickly on the fuzzy stems until late fall, when the stems die back and a new rosette forms. In a rock garden, where you don't want it to look hemmed in, plant it in the middle of a two-foot circle. But for a solid cover, place the plants one foot apart. A similar flower is Texas sage (*S. texana*), which grows from Denton to Mexico. The chief difference is in the flowers. Texas sage flowers are dark purply blue, not as profuse, and topped with green buds, so the effect just isn't as striking. But plant these two dwarf blue sages together, especially in a meadow with curly mesquite grass or buffalo grass, add some purple paintbrush, and you have an outstanding scene that'll have you reaching for your camera. A third dwarf blue sage is canyon sage (*S. lycioides*) of the Trans-Pecos. It is shrubby in habit but dies back to the ground some years. Cut it back after it finishes blooming.

148. Mealy blue sage
Salvia farinacea
The authors

149. Cedar sage
Salvia roemeriana
The authors

148.   **Latin Name**   *Salvia farinacea*
Pronunciation   SAL-vee-ah
   fare-eh-NAY-see-ah
Common Name   MEALY BLUE SAGE
Usual Height   2–3 feet
Spacing   1–2 feet apart
Bloom   April to frost; dark blue to white;
   3- to 9-inch spikes
Winter rosette
Range   Calcareous soils throughout Texas
   New Mexico
Soil   Sand, loam, clay, caliche, limestone;
   well drained
Part shade, full sun
Propagation   Seed, cuttings

This popular perennial is used in gardens all over the United States. It is not dependably winter-hardy north of the Red River, so it's used as an annual in many northern landscapes. It's at its best on thin limestone soils, in full sun. Wet clay soils can cause rank growth and weak stems. If heavy spring rains make your plant too leggy, cut it back to only a few leaves and let it branch. The drier the soil, the more shade it can handle. It's excellent in a flower bed, in well drained patio pots (but don't let water stand in the dish), and in massed plantings. It is available in nurseries in bright blue and purple-blue, both of which are more vivid in cool weather, and (my favorite) a stunning white. The leaves come in two styles: soft, wide, and green in South Texas, and narrow and silvery in the northern and western parts of the state. This silver fuzz, covering both stems and leaves, is the "mealiness" that gives this plant its name.

149.   **Latin Name**   *Salvia roemeriana*
Pronunciation   SAL-vee-ah
   roh-mare-ee-AH-nah
Common Name   CEDAR SAGE
Usual Height   1 foot, can reach 2 feet
Spacing   1 foot apart
Bloom   March to August; red; 2- to 3-inch
   spikes
Winter rosette
Range   Edwards Plateau, Trans-Pecos
   Mexico
Soil   Sand, loam, clay, limestone; well
   drained
Shade, dappled shade, part shade
Propagation   Seed, cuttings

Cedar sage is one of our finest flowers for a shady garden. The plant is small and well mannered, with little round leaves that are scalloped along the edges and furry on both sides. Each rosette sends up several stems that bear more leaves and spikes of red flowers that last from four to six weeks. Cedar sage, along with zexmenia, makes a wonderful ground cover under Ashe junipers in the Hill Country. In fact, its name comes from its ability to thrive in the dense shade of these "cedars." Cedar sage also grows under oaks and Texas mountain laurel and in other shady spots. Where you want to establish and maintain a thick ground cover, always allow the seed to ripen and scatter, and then water it periodically. Where cedar sage is naturalized, you can expect the plants to space themselves a foot or so apart, with limestone and juniper needles visible in between.

150. Shrubby skullcap
Scutellaria wrightii
Benny J. Simpson

151. Blue-eyed grass
Sisyrinchium sp.
The authors

150. **Latin Name** *Scutellaria wrightii*
Pronunciation skoo-teh-LARE-ee-ah
RITE-ee-eye
Common Name SHRUBBY SKULLCAP
Usual Height 6–8 inches
Spacing 6–12 inches apart
Bloom June (March to frost); dark purply
blue; ½ inch across
Evergreen
Range Edwards Plateau to Red River and
West Texas
Oklahoma
Soil Sand, loam, clay, caliche, limestone;
well drained
Dappled shade, part shade, full sun
Propagation Seed, cuttings

At a glance, it is easy to get shrubby skullcap confused with Texas sage (*Salvia texana*). The easiest way to
tell them apart is to check the leaves. Texas sage's leaves
are skinny, sometimes toothed; shrubby skullcap's are
rounded. Without trimming or shaping, the whole skullcap plant naturally forms a mound of dark flowers. It
looks outstanding in masses and is ideal for rock gardens.
With water, it will spread as wide as a foot, but even under choice conditions it is unlikely to exceed eight inches
in height. The main period of bloom is in early summer,
but it has been known to flower at other times of year as
well.

151. **Latin Name** *Sisyrinchium* spp.
Pronunciation siss-ee-RINK-ee-um species
Common Name BLUE-EYED GRASS
Usual Height 6 inches, can reach
12–16 inches
Spacing 9 inches apart
Bloom Midspring; purple-blue; ½ inch
Winter rosette, dormant in summer
Range Throughout Texas
North America
Soil Sand, loam, clay, caliche, limestone;
well drained
Dappled shade, part shade, full sun
Bulb
Propagation Seed

Blue-eyed grass is a bulb, a member of the iris
family like pinewoods lily, prairie celestial, and herbertia
(see entry 91). It produces leaves and flowers in the spring
and then lies dormant the rest of the year. In Dallas it
nearly always blooms at the same time as bearded irises,
so consider planting them together; you'll like the look. Its
most effective use is in masses, in short spring grass.
Naturalize it under redbud, flatwoods plum, flowering
dogwood, fringe tree, Eve's necklace, Texas smoke tree, or
other small trees that bloom at the same time it does in
your area. Then, don't mow until it has died back, and
don't spray herbicides on your lawn. It can also be planted
between unmortared flagstones set in sand, or simply
scattered throughout a flower garden.

210

152. Goldenrod
Solidago sp.
The authors

153. Indian pink
Spigelia marilandica
Doug Williams

152. **Latin Name** *Solidago* spp.
Pronunciation sahl-eh-DAY-goh species
Common Name GOLDENROD
Usual Height 2–7 feet
Spacing One is enough
Bloom Fall; yellow; 3- to 9-inch pyramids
Winter rosette
Range Throughout Texas
   North America east of Rocky Mountains
Soil Sand, loam, clay, caliche; seasonal
   poor drainage okay
Part shade, sun
Colonizes by rhizomes
Propagation Fresh untreated seed, root
   division

Goldenrod is gorgeous in the fall, but many people avoid it—unnecessarily. It's unlikely that it causes hay fever, because its pollen grain is too heavy to be windborne. Besides, it is adequately pollinated by bees and butterflies. It probably gets the bad rap because it is so highly visible when ragweed blooms. Ragweed is unnoticeable to untrained eyes but is very noticeable to our sinuses. In spite of all this, I am personally leery of using goldenrod in a garden. It is extremely aggressive and almost impossible to get rid of once you have it. Furthermore, individual plants usually bloom for only one week, and that doesn't make it worth the aggravation. I've been told that *S. rugosa* is short and behaves itself in Houston. Geyata Ajilvsgi, in her book *Wildflowers of Texas*, says that *S. petiolaris* (from the Panhandle to East Texas) has unusually large flower clusters and does not spread from underground runners. *Solidago mollis*, in the sandy prairies of

the Plains Country, is supposed to be another good one. Goldenrods tend to interbreed freely, so propagate yours from the shortest, most contained one you can find.

153. **Latin Name** *Spigelia marilandica*
Pronunciation spye-JEE-lee-ah
   mare-uh-LAN-dee-kah
Common Names INDIAN PINK, PINKROOT
Usual Height 1–2 feet
Spacing 1 foot apart
Bloom 5–6 weeks in late spring; red;
   2 inches across
Dormant in fall and winter
Range East Texas
   Maryland to Missouri to Gulf of Mexico
Soil Sand, loam; acid; moist, well drained
Dappled shade, part shade
Propagation Seed kept dry over winter and
   sown in spring

This unusual-looking flower is for gardeners in East Texas and Houston who have acid, sandy soil and can water regularly. The flowers bloom one at a time on a spike. They are brilliant red outside and smooth yellow inside. The bloom period can be prolonged by removing the flowers as they wither, thus frustrating the plant's need to make seed. The leaves are dark green and glossy and usually die back in August. Indian pink is best used in a moist, partly shaded flower bed or on the sandy banks of a water garden. It combines well with spring obedient plant, partridgeberry, Gulf Coast penstemon, and meadow beauty.

154. Tephrosia
Tephrosia lindheimeri
The authors

155. Dwarf germander
Teucrium laciniatum
The authors

154. **Latin Name** *Tephrosia lindheimeri*
Pronunciation teh-FROH-zee-ah lind-HYE-mer-eye
Common Names TEPHROSIA, HOARY PEA
Usual Height 9 inches
Spacing 3–6 feet apart
Bloom Summer (April to October); hot pink; 3- to 4-inch clusters
Dormant in winter
Range Rio Grande Plains to Llano
Endemic to Texas
Soil Sand, loam; well drained
Part shade, full sun
Taproot
Propagation Seed, root division

The clusters of flowers on this plant remind me of sweet pea. Blooms might appear as early as April, and with a little water and attention in pulling off old blooms, they might still be quite showy in October. The leaves are gray-green, velvety on the upper surface, and silky underneath. The beans are about two inches long and also velvety. The stems are rather tough, arising from a deep taproot and stretching out on the ground about three feet in all directions. They do not root themselves and can be tied to a fence or trellis, if desired, or they can be allowed to drape themselves over a sunny wall. Do not grow this plant where livestock can get at it, because the roots and young leaves contain a poisonous alkaloid.

155. **Latin Name** *Teucrium laciniatum*
Pronunciation TOO-kree-um lah-sin-ee-AY-tum
Common Name DWARF GERMANDER
Usual Height 3–6 inches
Spacing 4–12 inches apart
Bloom May to September; white or cream; 2 inches across; fragrant
Range Edwards Plateau, Trans-Pecos, West Texas, High Plains
Oklahoma, Colorado, New Mexico
Soil Sand, loam, clay, caliche, limestone, gypsum; well drained
Part shade, full sun
Colonizes by creeping roots
Propagation Root division, seed, softwood cuttings

Where conditions are good, dwarf germander forms dense mats—in fact, I seriously considered putting it in the groundcover chapter. It is delightful in an unmortared patio or walkway where it can creep between the stones and release its minty aroma when stepped on. In the rock garden plan, I placed it so it would grow between the stone stairsteps. The blooms are also scented—sweet with spicy overtones. Dwarf germander is extremely drought-tolerant. Unwatered and in full sun, it will remain quite small, often surrounded by several bare inches of sand or gravel. In a flower garden it combines well with blackfoot daisy, yellow zinnia, prairie verbena, shrubby skullcap, chocolate daisy, and heart's delight. It can also be naturalized with shortgrasses and these flowers in places where it is so dry that grasses are thin and hard to establish. Burro grass, blue grama, and buffalo grass are suitable choices.

156. Ironweed
Vernonia baldwinii
The authors

156. **Latin Name** *Vernonia baldwinii*
Pronunciation ver-NOH-nee-ah
bald-WIN-ee-eye
Common Names IRONWEED,
WESTERN IRONWEED
Usual Height 2–5 feet
Spacing One is enough
Bloom July to frost; pink to purple; 6-inch
clusters
Dormant in winter
Range Thoughout Texas except Rio Grande
Plains and Trans-Pecos
Great Plains of U.S.
Soil Sand, loam, clay, caliche, limestone;
well drained
Part shade, full sun
Colonizes by rhizomes
Propagation Root division, seed

Texas has several ironweeds. This one breeds with most of the others and is the most common. I was once very fond of this plant; I'd even used it in a client's garden. My selection grew less than two feet tall and had big fluffy pink flowers that I could keep blooming from August to frost by cutting back the spent blooms. For four years it was a delight. Then it showed why its name is ironweed. The roots took off in all directions. Each one was easily an inch thick, iron-hard, at least a foot underground, and able to travel thirty feet or more, sending up new plants at two-foot intervals. If I had planted my ironweed in prairie grasses, it would have been a gorgeous sight by the fifth summer—a quarter acre of purple, and all one plant. But in that flower bed it was, and still is, a disaster! I can't get rid of it. Maybe when it's not in rich Blackland Prairies clay, it isn't quite so vigorous, but I advise anyone enamored of this plant to use it with extreme caution.

157. Sunflower goldeneye
Viguiera dentata
The authors

158. Arkansas yucca
Yucca arkansana
The authors

157. **Latin Name** *Viguiera dentata*
Pronunciation veh-GWARE-ah
den-TAY-tah
Common Name SUNFLOWER GOLDENEYE
Usual Height 3–6 feet
Spacing 3–4 feet apart
Bloom October; yellow; 1½-inch daisies
Winter rosette
Range Edwards Plateau, Trans-Pecos,
Blacklands
Arizona and New Mexico to Guatemala
Soil Sand, loam, clay, caliche, limestone;
well drained
Part shade, full sun
Colonizes
Propagation Seed, softwood tip cuttings,
root division

Give this perennial plenty of room at the back of a flower border, or naturalize it on the sunny edge of woods or around a drive-in entrance. It's magnificent in full bloom. Extremely drought-tolerant, it prefers dry calcareous soils, where it grows to three feet in full sun and up to six feet under a tree. It branches like a large shrub and completely covers itself with golden daisies. Imagine it in the autumn, beneath the red and orange foliage of a bigtooth maple. Then picture one of the red shrubby salvias—Gregg or mountain sage—at its feet, with purple palmleaf eupatorium in meadow grasses in the foreground.

158. **Latin Name** *Yucca arkansana*
Pronunciation YUH-kuh ar-kan-SAN-ah
Common Names ARKANSAS YUCCA,
SOFTLEAF YUCCA
Usual Height 1–2 feet, flower stalk 3–4 feet
Spacing 1–2 feet apart
Bloom Spring; white to pale green; 2-inch
bells
Evergreen
Range Blacklands, Cross Timbers, Edwards
Plateau
Oklahoma, Arkansas
Soil Sand, loam, clay, limestone; well
drained
Dappled shade, part shade, full sun
Propagation Seed, root division

Arkansas yucca is ideal for a flower garden, being small and more flowerlike than our larger yuccas. The leaves are pale green, curled lengthwise, and sometimes twisted. They are soft and pliable, smoothly white-edged, with fine, curly white hairs, but still having a spine on each flexible tip. In sand, Arkansas yucca grows quickly and easily to form a clump that is typically eighteen inches high and two feet across. On limestone escarpments, it grows more slowly, taking ten years to reach this size. The white spikes of heavy waxy flowers are usually upright—a striking visual effect in a mass planting. This yucca is often seen in deep shade in the Eastern Cross Timbers. It doesn't get enough sun to bloom there, but apparently it can live for years as evergreen understory.

159. **Latin Name**   *Zinnia grandiflora*
Pronunciation   ZIN-ee-ah
   gran-deh-FLOR-ah
Common Names   YELLOW ZINNIA, PLAINS
   ZINNIA, ROCKY MOUNTAIN ZINNIA
Usual Height   6–8 inches
Spacing   8–10 inches apart
Bloom   May to October; yellow; 1 inch
   across
Almost evergreen to dormant in winter
Range   West Texas, High Plains,
   Trans-Pecos
   Colorado to Mexico
Soil   Sand, loam, caliche, limestone, gravel;
   well drained
Part shade, full sun
Colonizes by rhizomes
Propagation   Seed sown in spring or fall
   (50 percent germination), division of
   young plants in spring, transplanting
   (difficult)

Next to blackfoot daisy, this is our most outstanding perennial. It makes a low golden mound of color that
lasts most of the summer and then fades to an ivory hue.
The leaves are tiny, green, and needlelike and form a
mossy mat when not in bloom. In the Panhandle yellow
zinnia is dormant in the winter, but in Austin and El Paso
it is almost evergreen. In loose sand or loam, it spreads by
rhizomes to make a ground cover. Yellow zinnia is ideal
for a dry, gravelly rock garden, for erosion control on
steep sandy slopes, for parkways and medians that have
lots of reflected heat, and in any well-drained flower bed.
I have always seen it loaded down with butterflies. In the
southern half of the state, where summers are very hot,
use the dwarf white zinnia (*Z. acerosa*), which is even
more drought-tolerant but not as winter-hardy. It is native
from the Trans-Pecos to Starr County in the Valley. It
looks just like the yellow zinnia except that its flowers are
white and its foliage silvery.

159. Yellow zinnia
Zinnia grandiflora
The authors

English Mixed Border Plan

Probably the most absolute statement I can make on the subject of landscaping is that the English have the finest flower gardens in the world. We
can learn a lot from them, but we have to develop our own palette of
flowers.

The English have been importing flowers for centuries. It was in Eliza-
bethan times that England achieved a degree of peace and prosperity that
allowed the middle class the luxury of dabbling in their gardens without
worrying about where their next Yorkshire pudding was coming from.

Since then, hundreds of plants from all over the world have been tested.
The ones chosen for English gardens, with few exceptions, do not like our

extremes of heat and cold and drought, although many of them thrive in New England, the Midwest, the Rockies, and the Northwest.

Texans didn't start thinking about flower gardens until after the Comanches were defeated about 1850. Then nurseries started advertising the same flowers the English used—snapdragons and pinks, for example. In Texas we have two to four more months of bloom time. The plants we got from the English (not necessarily native to England at all) that will actually last year after year for us are several kinds of irises, day lilies, red spider lily, ox-eye daisy, and white yarrow. In England they bloom in the summer; here, they bloom in the spring or fall. Our summer flowers come from South America (portulaca and verbenas), Mexico (zinnias and marigolds), and tropical America (cannas and lantanas).

Before the early eighties it was hard to find Texans who used our native flowers in their landscapes. It never occurred to most of them that these hardy "weeds" might also be tameable. Yet, these natives are essential if we want to have beds of color during the summer, as well as spring and fall, without spending a fortune on planting and watering and maintaining exotic annuals.

If you want to try an English-style flower garden, first decide which type you want. The easiest is a mixed garden, often incorrectly called a perennial garden.

A perennial garden is supposed to be composed of only perennials. A mixed garden contains other elements, such as annuals, biennials, bulbs, and small flowering shrubs—with optional ornamental trees. This gives you vastly more material to work with. Also, it is advantageous in Texas to have the shade that ornamental trees provide and to be able to use our exceptionally fine array of flowering shrubs.

But a second option is to plan a theme garden. A perennial garden is a theme garden. So is the White Garden at Sissinghurst, one of the popular gardens in England. It is filled exclusively with white-flowered or silver-leaved plants.

Another example of a theme garden is a fragrance garden, which is a marvelous way to share the pleasures of gardening with the blind. (There is an excellent one at the San Antonio Botanical Center.) Closely related to a fragrance garden is a butterfly garden, which is sure to attract hummingbirds as well. And still another popular theme garden is the herb garden. It can be of the traditional Mediterranean herbs, our native Texas herbs (for example, limoncillo and any of the alliums, salvias, or monardas), or a mixture of both.

Borders are gardens laid out in long lines (straight or curved), usually edging a wall, path, or property line. They are anywhere from six to sixteen feet wide, and as long as you like or have room for. Traditionally, the English slope these gardens for good drainage and for a showier view. The extra soil that makes the slope is heaped against a wall. The viewing side is a path that might be pavement, lawn, crushed caliche (chat), or gravel.

The double border has gardens on both sides of the path. They are from five to twelve feet wide (all rules are made to be broken), and the path is generally six to ten feet wide, although it might be much wider. The path is always at least six feet wide so the plants at the edge can spill out over the walk, leaving a meandering path at least two feet wide that is free of flowers. At the end of a double border there is usually a door, gate, bench, statue, or fountain—some kind of destination that gives you a purpose for walking down the path. As if the flowers weren't reason enough!

Some people think that the border shape is old-fashioned and prefer an island bed, a flower bed surrounded by lawn or walks (but not water). It can be kidney-shaped, square, oval, or some other shape. You can also have irregularly shaped islands around clumps of trees, provided the trees are small enough or pruned up high enough to allow sufficient sunlight for the flowers. Soil is mounded up to form a berm in the center for good drainage. The dotted line indicates the crest of the berm.

Most English gardeners have yards too small and narrow for either an island or a border. So a typical layout is to wrap a border around a central lawn. The simplest way for most Americans to adapt a mixed border to their landscape is to expand the plantings in front of the house, as shown.

If you want good drainage, which means you can have a greater variety of flowers to play with, you might consider constructing a five-degree slope—one inch per foot is about right. If you mound the new soil up to your foundation, be sure it falls below the brick line, or water may leak into the house. Where you have no foundation to hide, the flower bed can come right up to the house.

If you have an old-fashioned high foundation, hide it with shrubs, and lay the flower garden out in front of it. The shrubbery doesn't have to be an evergreen hedge. The back row of the flower garden can be an assortment of shrubs—some evergreen and some with a showy profusion of winter fruit. You could also use an occasional bunchgrass, as bunchgrasses do not get cut back until February, and some don't need to be cut back at all. This way you maintain the variety and rhythm of the flower garden and still conceal your foundation.

After you have determined the basic shape of your flower garden, and its slope, you need to decide which plants are suitable and how to arrange them. The following general directions and the illustration are for a mixed border, but you can adapt this formula to any shape you like.

First, start with a simple sketch (or plan) of the area where you want your flower garden to go. Figure out a scale for your plan—for example, a half inch on your drawing could equal 1 foot in real life. Then draw circles to indicate where you want the ornamental trees. You'll want these trees fifteen to thirty feet apart—don't line them up like soldiers, even in the most formal border. One of the charms of an English garden is that, although carefully planned and laid out, it looks so casual and natural.

Next, draw in one or more large arching shrubs. Where and how many will depend on the size and shape of your garden. If your garden is small, don't use any. If it's large, use several. Place them where you need to have height against the house, to block a view, or to provide shade.

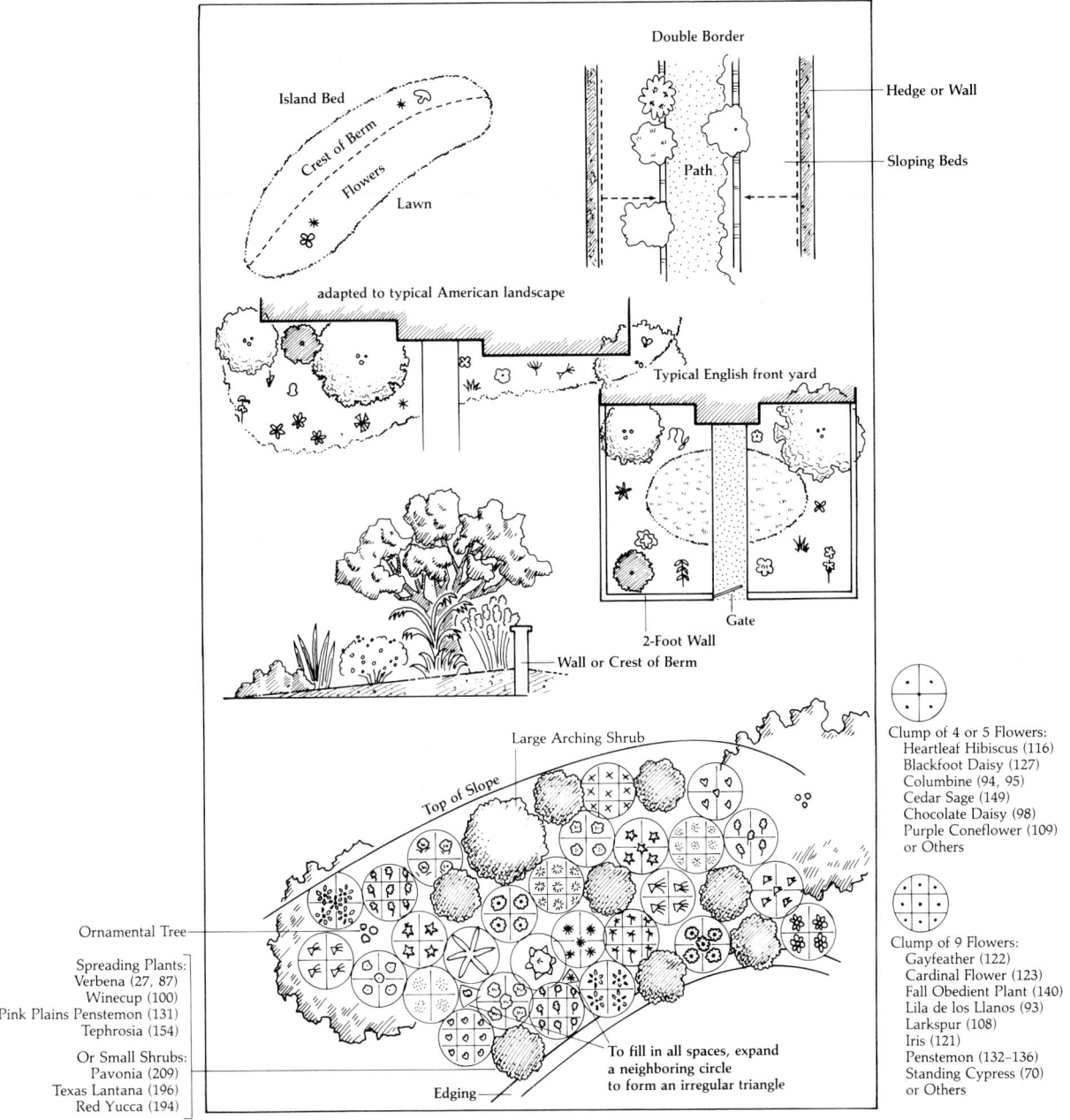

Island Bed

Crest of Berm

Flowers

Lawn

adapted to typical American landscape

Double Border

Path

Hedge or Wall

Sloping Beds

Typical English front yard

2-Foot Wall

Gate

Wall or Crest of Berm

Large Arching Shrub

Top of Slope

Ornamental Tree

Spreading Plants:
Verbena (27, 87)
Winecup (100)
Pink Plains Penstemon (131)
Tephrosia (154)

Or Small Shrubs:
Pavonia (209)
Texas Lantana (196)
Red Yucca (194)

Edging

To fill in all spaces, expand
a neighboring circle
to form an irregular triangle

Clump of 4 or 5 Flowers:
Heartleaf Hibiscus (116)
Blackfoot Daisy (127)
Columbine (94, 95)
Cedar Sage (149)
Chocolate Daisy (98)
Purple Coneflower (109)
or Others

Clump of 9 Flowers:
Gayfeather (122)
Cardinal Flower (123)
Fall Obedient Plant (140)
Lila de los Llanos (93)
Larkspur (108)
Iris (121)
Penstemon (132–136)
Standing Cypress (70)
or Others

English Mixed Border

The flowers you would use should range in height from eighteen inches to three feet. Edging plants can be even lower, although if they can mound up to twelve inches at least, the border looks better. Draw circles on your plan to indicate spaces two feet in diameter that you will fill up with flowers. You don't want to have those plant clusters more than five deep. If you have a very wide border, then use larger clusters—not more of them. You can go as large as four-foot clusters. You always want to maintain a certain proportion.

Divide one third of the two-foot-size circles into quarters. Divide another third of them into ninths. Make dots in the center of each division. These represent individual plants. The circle divided into ninths will contain nine tall, narrow spiky plants, such as gayfeather, cardinal flower, or fall obedient plant. The circle divided into fours will have four clumpy plants (five, if you also use the dead-center spot)—heartleaf hibiscus, blackfoot daisy, columbine, or cedar sage, for example. The individual circles indicate spreading plants, such as verbena, winecup, pink plains penstemon, or tephrosia, or small shrubs such as pavonia, Texas lantana, or red yucca.

You will change your mind twenty times before you've worked out height, shape, color, bloom time, and so forth in a harmonious pattern. Either make several photocopies of your plan to toss away when you mess up (and you will—we all do), or place tissue paper or other see-through paper over your plan and draw on that.

You should now compile a list of flowers that are suitable for your soil and climate. Include flowers that you might harbor some prejudice against—you may actually like them once they're in your garden. I've seen it happen time after time.

Then assess your garden for sun, shade, reflected heat, and drainage. Widely different conditions can sometimes exist only five feet apart. List those conditions, and then list the plants that are best suited to them. (Refer to the plant profiles and plan descriptions for regions that approximate yours.)

Now that you know which flowers are suited to your garden conditions, you need to select the ones that are best for each season. Let's start with winter because it's the hardest season to do. List the flowers that are green or have texture or color, and then place them in a creative pattern.

Consider summer next. This is the longest time period your garden will have to show off. Be sure that summer blooms can carry the garden all by themselves. Repeat two or three particularly dependable plants as a main theme. It often helps to have one color dominate the garden. Texas natives offer an especially nice selection of yellows and hot pinks, both good colors for tying everything together. Use oranges, blues, dark purples, and reds as accents.

Then add in the fall colors—lots of reds, purples, and yellows. Remember that most of your summer flowers will bloom on into the fall.

Fill in whatever circles are still blank with your spring favorites. There should be plenty of these to choose from. Spring is the easiest and most prolific season.

One part of Marvin and Betty Colwill's landscape in Mesquite is a rock garden. Designed by myself, this one consists of a berm with Milsap boulders, as the yard itself has no natural contouring. In this June picture, nonnative yarrow, hybrid verbena, and santolina combine with Texas natives—black sampson, pink evening primrose, black-eyed Susan, and mealy blue sage. The feathery, leafy green stems of gayfeather will bloom in the fall, along with zexmenia. Photo by the authors.

Remember, however, that many spring flowers go dormant in the summer, leaving a big hole where they were lavish in the spring. Combine them with summer flowers that are dormant in the winter and early spring. For example, lantana is dormant in Dallas from frost to mid-April. Pink evening primrose is green all through the winter and blooms all spring. Together these two plants can fill a space with greenery or flowers all year long.

When you have finished filling in all the circles to your satisfaction, you'll notice that there are unfilled gaps between the circles. Since you want your flower bed to be a solid mass of color, extend one of those circles into that gap. The filled-in gaps keep the overall design from being rigid and predictable. Or, instead of extending a circle, you could fill in the gaps with annuals.

Annuals and short-lived perennials play an important role in a successful flower garden. Scatter their seeds liberally over the garden at the time of installation, especially around the slower-growing, long-lived perennials, such as butterfly weed, winecup, hibiscus, and gayfeather. Encourage these annuals to reseed, because no matter how green a thumb you have, your garden will be a little different each year. Although some flowers will do spectacularly well and rapidly outgrow their allotted spaces, others will do unexpectedly poorly or even mysteriously disappear. As a result, each year you'll be confronted with unforeseen bare spaces.

The most successful gardens, year after year, are those that let a few short-lived flowers seed out anywhere they like. In either fall or early spring, you can transplant them and shift them around to where you need them. Coreopsis, black-eyed Susans, cedar sage, verbena, purple coneflower, and paperflower are some that do this especially well. They aren't too aggressive, too tall, or too wide. They bloom a long time and are easily pulled up if in the way. Besides, they give a unity to the garden. Pink evening primrose is another I don't try to restrain in a clay soil.

Watering

A flower garden is an artificial, not a natural, habitat. Unlike a woods or meadow, which can survive on rainfall alone, your garden will require watering. In a flower garden, you have weeded out the grass, which in nature covers the dirt and retains moisture. Even with a thin layer of fine bark mulch, evaporation from the soil is intense. A watering one evening a week in summer is normal, twice a week when high temperatures remain above 100° F. If your garden is sand, you might need to water much less often. Deep soils and afternoon shade can also save on watering. Observe, experiment, and use your own good judgment.

Weeding

The need for this unpleasant task can vary. In my garden there are no fields around and no seeds to blow in. Everything I get is bird-planted or squirrel-planted or is a seedling from the shade trees around me. Ninety-nine percent of my weeding is confined to pulling out small trees. I don't let them get more than six inches tall, but I try to wait for a good soaking rain before attempting to pull them out. Otherwise, I have to dig them out, and that's work.

In one of my client's gardens, the story is very different. He has rich prairie soil. Every year two or three plants we've never even seen before germinate. We let them grow awhile to see how they look. Most are too aggressive or too tall, have insignificant flowers, and so on—in other words, they're weedy, so we pull them out. A few have been uncontrollable for a year and have taken over the whole garden, only to completely disappear the next year. A few have been welcome additions. The two worst pests, however, are Bermuda grass and nut grass. They were brought in by his contractor, who conscientiously spread a thin layer of topsoil over his yard.

Soil preparation

Preparing the soil is the same for a flower garden as for a vegetable garden. Work in lots of organic matter. If you live on clay, work in lots of coarse sand as well. Be cautious when ordering truckloads of such soil amendments. If you see nut grass in the load, don't let the driver dump it. Send the load back. It is possible to find a company that supplies sand, mulch, and manure that's free of nut grass, although it's rare to find someone who will give you a guarantee.

Rock Garden Plan
Planting Area: 20′ × 20′

Our rock garden traditions began in England and Japan long before the Southwest got into the act. In England the concept started because people wanted to grow the miniature alpine flowers they'd found struggling in rocky mountaintops, between tree and snow lines. To duplicate as nearly as possible their natural growing conditions in a warmer and wetter climate, the rock garden was developed. The soil needed to be fast-draining and gritty or gravelly, and the rocks served to keep the roots shaded and cool while they held the light soil in place. Good drainage is important because, what with the rain and high humidity, roots will otherwise rot. And because these plants are smallish, owing to little nutrition, little moisture, and a short growing season, the gardens displaying them are also small.

In Japan the focus is on simplicity. The effect is highly aesthetic—even spiritual. In the Fort Worth Japanese Gardens there is a Zen garden that consists only of raked sand and one carefully placed rock. (Now that's a rock garden!) Usually, however, rocks serve as accents for the native trees, shrubs, and ground covers. The emphasis tends to be on evergreens and the textures of leaves and individual forms rather than on flowers. The design might be very stylized, clipped, and controlled, with the shrubs mounded in careful patterns, or the shrubs might be more natural, but exquisitely pruned into aesthetic masterpieces. Always the garden is immaculate.

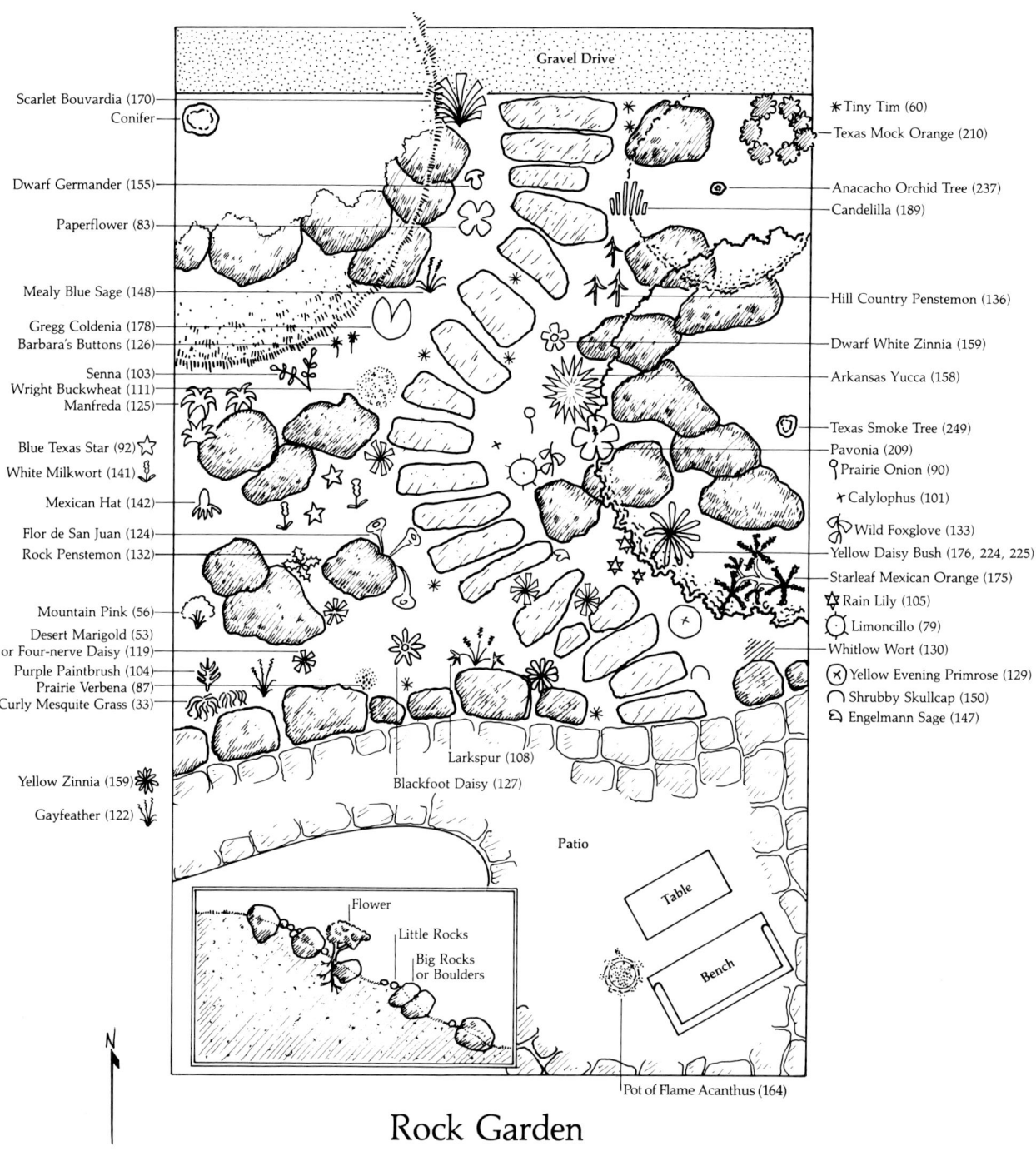

Gravel Drive

Scarlet Bouvardia (170)
Conifer

Dwarf Germander (155)

Paperflower (83)

Mealy Blue Sage (148)

Gregg Coldenia (178)
Barbara's Buttons (126)

Senna (103)
Wright Buckwheat (111)
Manfreda (125)

Blue Texas Star (92)
White Milkwort (141)

Mexican Hat (142)

Flor de San Juan (124)
Rock Penstemon (132)

Mountain Pink (56)

Desert Marigold (53)
or Four-nerve Daisy (119)

Purple Paintbrush (104)
Prairie Verbena (87)
Curly Mesquite Grass (33)

Yellow Zinnia (159)

Gayfeather (122)

Tiny Tim (60)
Texas Mock Orange (210)

Anacacho Orchid Tree (237)
Candelilla (189)

Hill Country Penstemon (136)

Dwarf White Zinnia (159)

Arkansas Yucca (158)

Texas Smoke Tree (249)
Pavonia (209)
Prairie Onion (90)
Calylophus (101)
Wild Foxglove (133)
Yellow Daisy Bush (176, 224, 225)
Starleaf Mexican Orange (175)
Rain Lily (105)
Limoncillo (79)
Whitlow Wort (130)
Yellow Evening Primrose (129)
Shrubby Skullcap (150)
Engelmann Sage (147)

Larkspur (108)

Blackfoot Daisy (127)

Patio

Flower

Little Rocks

Big Rocks
or Boulders

Table

Bench

Pot of Flame Acanthus (164)

N

Rock Garden

The Southwest desert style is a natural arid look. The intent is to have the garden appear as if it had grown there just that way, without any gardener's hand involved. But in fact it is well groomed, as it could never be in a truly natural setting—no weeds, no deadwood, no gum wrappers. Cacti, narrow-leaved multitrunked trees, and rocks are set off in subtle colors and patterns against natural-colored plastered or adobe walls. Bright desert flowers, red tile roofs, and an azure sky are strong elements of the overall design.

This particular plan is in the English tradition—that is, a small, well-drained flower garden—but instead of those diminutive alpine flowers, I've used our own native plants, which can take Texas summers. Our small flowering plants are not dwarfed because of cold and a short growing season. They are small because of drought.

The flowers in this plan are found in rock crevices on the Edwards Plateau, in the rocky mountains of the Trans-Pecos, and in the dry sands of West Texas and the High Plains. They are all small, neatly shaped, and well behaved, although a few like to creep becomingly around rocks. All accept or prefer alkaline soils. They also prefer little or no competition (in nature they are at their best surrounded by bare earth or rocks rather than grasses) and need to be well drained at all times.

The rocks are the core of the garden. They go in first, and if they don't look good all by themselves, then the plants you add later aren't going to help much. The rocks also moderate temperatures, keeping roots cool in the summer and warmer in the winter. They hold in moisture, cutting down on evaporation. They channel rainfall to the plants. And they provide erosion control by holding the slope in place. (See the drawing at the bottom of the plan for a cross section of the hillside.)

The best rock gardens are planted in natural rock formations, but most people don't have this option. If you don't, here are some guidelines on how to construct a rock formation.

First, you must choose a slope. Without drainage, these plants are dead. (If you don't have a slope, proceed to another chapter. Or put in a berm—a man-made mound.)

Second, you must have good sun, a minimum of six hours a day.

Third, choose your rocks with care. A rock garden looks infinitely better if the majority of the rocks are too big for you to handle by yourself. You want boulders! They need to all be the same kind (or color) of rock and preferably locally obtained. Although good drainage is essential, retaining a certain amount of moisture is also important in Texas.

Sandstone holds moisture well. Limestone doesn't hold moisture as well as sandstone, but the soil with it is heavier, is higher in clay content, and does a good job of holding moisture by itself. Sometimes the local limestone crumbles and scales with every freeze. This makes it hard to work with, so if you buy limestone, ask for a hard grade that will hold up. Another native white rock possibility is gypsum (calcium sulfate instead of calcium carbonate, which is limestone). It's found in the Permian Red Beds. For those of you in the Trans-Pecos and the Llano Basin, there are also igneous rocks. In addition, use plenty of smaller stones and gravelsize rocks between the boulders; they act like a mulch. They should be of the same material as the boulders or whatever your local surface rock is.

Sandstone and limestone are both sedimentary rocks. That means that many millions of years ago, ocean sediments settled in layers and then were buried so deep that they were pressed into rock. In sandstone the sediments were, as you might've guessed, sand; in limestone they were composed of the skeletons of microscopic sea creatures. Because every thousand years or so there would be a change in the amount, color, and hardness of other materials that got mixed up in the sediment, there are subtle gradations in the layers today. It's important to get the lines of these layers running in the same direction when you place them into your slope. Otherwise, your rock formation will look outrageously contrived.

Reading about this isn't as good as seeing it with your own eyes. So go study the nearest rock formation in your area. Sketch on paper the position of the rocks buried in the bank and those in the slope. Notice how the tumbled rocks fell. Draw in the sediment lines and faults and how the cracks run. The idea is to duplicate this the best you can in your own garden. It's not easy to do it well, but it is important. The rocks are the chief beauty of the rock garden.

Now look at the Rock Garden Plan. The garden, facing south, extends to either side of a set of stone steps, which then climbs from a patio to a gravel driveway. Because this slope is steep, the steps form a continuous stairway. (On a gentle slope, intersperse the steps with a gravel path, as in the Post Oak Plan.) Between the steps are dainty creeping plants. The line of boulders at the bottom prevents the soil from washing onto the patio. (Within reason, that is. Some soil will always sift through after a heavy rain.)

On to the plants. In the upper northwest corner is a conifer, which shields the garden from winter winds. Conifers look especially good with rocks and are often associated with rock gardens. This is a traditional touch. The other tree, shown here at its mature size of twelve feet in diameter, is a Texas smoke tree, which gives light shade, spring bloom, and fall color. It must have good drainage, like the rock garden flowers. The third tree in the plan is the popular little Anacacho orchid tree. It grows so slowly, it will seem like a shrub for years. These three trees form the northern boundary of the garden.

On the east side, nestled against these trees and the rocks, are several flowering shrubs. The two largest are the Texas mock orange, with its white flowers and shiny dark green leaves, and the evergreen starleaf Mexican orange, which also has white flowers. Other shrubs are a scarlet bouvardia between the juniper and the driveway, a yucca, a pavonia, and one of the yellow daisy bushes (choose from damianita, skeleton-leaf goldeneye, or zexmenia).

Since I told you that the traditional English rock garden was built to show off tiny flowers, you are probably wondering why I stuck in all these trees and shrubs. Well, trees and shrubs are part of the tradition too. After all, a garden needs some density and height to look its best. The above-mentioned woody plants are exceptionally fine and like the exact same conditions as the rock garden flowers.

In placing the flowers, I discovered that yellows, pinks, and whites are the main colors of those plants that bloom for several months throughout the summer. I wanted a good mix and balance of these colors. First, I arranged the yellows—paperflower, Mexican hat, desert marigold or hymenoxys, yellow zinnia, and Tiny Tim. Then the whites—dwarf germander, white milkwort, flor de San Juan, blackfoot daisy, and dwarf white zinnia. Then the pinks, red, and purples—scarlet bouvardia, rock penstemon, prairie verbena, and Hill Country penstemon.

Then I was careful to place the flowers that bloom only a short time in places where they would provide accents against this steady backdrop of color—or continue its main themes. I'll list these seasonal flowers by color. The yellows are calylophus and yellow evening primrose in the spring; manfreda in early summer; two-leaved or velvetleaf senna, limoncillo, and whitlow wort for the rest of the summer and into fall. The pinks are mountain pink, purple paintbrush, and wild foxglove in the spring, Gregg coldenia for summer and fall, and gayfeather and prairie onion in the fall. The whites are Barbara's buttons and rain lily in the spring, and Wright buckwheat in the fall, before it fades to pink and orange. The only spring-to-fall blue color comes from mealy blue sage. The other blues are spring only: blue Texas star, larkspur, shrubby skullcap, and Engelmann sage.

In the winter the flow of rocks is accented by green foliage. The conifer is, of course, the most dominant, but from the top of the slope to the bottom, candelilla, yucca, manfreda, starleaf Mexican orange, and verbena also provide green highlights. If the winter is mild, count on pavonia, Mexican hat, rock penstemon, hymenoxys, and rain lily for still more green. Then, scattered throughout the gravel, will be small rosettes of calylophus, mountain pink, Hill Country penstemon, and desert marigold. The marigold, plus Tiny Tim and verbena, might even bloom if the weather isn't too cold. Some attractive winter seed heads are on whitlow wort, paperflower, gayfeather, and Wright buckwheat.

The west side of the Plank front yard has a windbreak of desert willows, behind which the neighbor's house is visible. Burr Williams planted a mixture of evergreen and flowering shrubs to create a rich, multitextured, and everblooming garden. Flowers such as Tahoka daisy, mealy blue sage, and naturalized *Verbena rigida* fill in the spaces between. The shrubs visible in this photo are a yucca, three red Gregg salvia, a pink plains penstemon, and a silvery-leaved rabbitbrush. Photo by the authors.

 *Shrubs*

IS there anything as misunderstood and misidentified as a shrub? What is a shrub anyway? You can always get a good argument going among plant people about whether or not something or other is a shrub or a tree. Everyone agrees that shrubs have several woody stems that branch out from the ground (or near the ground) and that shrubs are shorter than trees. The trouble is that plants are remarkably oblivious to how we describe them. Often, to aid their survival in the wild, they go off and develop characteristics that don't conform to our neat definitions. Nature has experimented with every possible variation. Most of the plants between herbaceous perennials and giant trees can be safely called shrubs.

One of my hardest tasks in doing this book was to decide whether a "shrub" actually belonged in this chapter. Or was it more accurate to put it in the chapter on perennials or the one on ornamental trees? I consulted books and experts, but ultimately it had to be a matter of personal judgment. Probably no one is going to agree with me one hundred percent. In fact, by the time this book goes to press, I may no longer agree with everything I've written either.

Here's a good example of why shrubs are so much fun. Texas mountain laurel is often classified as a shrub. It is slow-growing, so it stays under five or six feet for many years. It can be seen in thickets. It is multi-stemmed. Sounds like a shrub, doesn't it? Yet it can grow as high as thirty feet, the stems make large trunks, and you can walk under it—and isn't that a tree? I decided to call it a tree in this book.

The other end of the spectrum involves deciding whether a specific plant is a shrub or a perennial flower. Botanists classify a large number of plants as subshrubs, shrublets (a term not even found in most dictionaries) or suffrutescent, which means that only the lower parts of the stems are woody. These plants are not completely woody the way shrubs are supposed to be, but they do have some woodiness, which disqualifies them from being trueblue herbaceous (nonwoody) perennials.

I tried to look at this issue from the viewpoint of a landscaper rather than a botanist. For instance, I put the two zinnias, the perennial buckwheats, and the two "shrubby" penstemons (pink plains penstemon and rock penstemon) in the chapter on perennials.

Then there are the "shrubs" that die back to the roots in the winter—but only in some parts of the state. Coralbean is a good example. Where it is most abundant, along the coast and in the Valley, it is a good-sized shrub or even a small tree. Up near the Red River, it dies to the ground each year but comes back larger each spring. Is it a shrub or a perennial? Rio Grande abutilon, chile pequín, Texas lantana, pavonia, and zexmenia fall into this same category.

Because these plants are shrubby in their main regional habitat, I've included them in this chapter, although I feel a little shaky about the zexmenia, which I have never seen grow larger than an ordinary perennial. Also, it often trails on the ground, which is not very shrublike.

Even with all this winnowing out of the shrubs, they're still a mixed bag, and the second-largest category in the book. There are yuccas and other shrubs in the lily family such as sotol. This is also the most appropriate chapter for large cacti like the prickly pear and cholla. Then there are some evergreen shrubs that fit the popular conception of a shrub—agarito, creosote bush, sand sagebrush, and cenizo. Others are important for their fruits—American beautyberry, winterfat, and desert yaupon.

Several are thicket-forming, perfect for rounding out neglected corners, providing cover for wildlife, or making an effective, easy-care block of color for large-scale plantings. These thicket shrubs are huisachillo, whitebrush, dwarf wax myrtle, Havard oak, aromatic sumac, smooth sumac, and the wild roses.

Lastly, there are shrubs chosen for their magnificent flowers. Some are tall, like canyon senna and yellow bells. Others are best used in mass plantings, like the daleas. Many are used primarily as flowers in perennial gardens. Some of the best for this purpose are scarlet bouvardia, damianita, Gregg coldenia, skeleton-leaf goldeneye, Gregg salvia, and mountain sage.

Because this category is so diverse, I was able to do something fun and unusual with the Shrub Garden Plan. The entire plan is composed of shrubs and nothing else!

161. Whitebrush
Aloysia gratissima
The authors

160. Rio Grande abutilon
Abutilon hypoleucum
The authors

160. **Latin Name** *Abutilon hypoleucum*
Pronunciation ah-BOO-teh-lon
heye-poh-LOO-kum
Common Name RIO GRANDE ABUTILON
Usual Height 4 feet
Spacing 4 feet apart
Bloom Everblooming; yellow to orange;
1–2 inches
Evergreen
Range Woodlands of Rio Grande
floodplains in the Valley
Mexico
Soil Sand, loam; moist, well drained
Dappled shade, part shade
Propagation Seed, softwood cuttings

A large, softly rounded tropical shrub, Rio Grande abutilon blooms every afternoon year-round in its native range. The ones I've seen have flowers of an unusual pale golden-orange tint (a color selection by nurseryman Mike Heep). The lime-green leaves are shaped like elongated hearts and have a soft, velvety texture (sometimes older leaves have a grayish cast). This is one of those rare Valley natives without thorns. Plant it on the north or east side of your house or at the base of a tree. Experimenting with this plant in a protected courtyard in Dallas, I found it to be root-hardy only in a mild winter. It bloomed in the fall, then died back to the ground after the first sharp freeze and broke dormancy in the spring, along with Turk's cap.

161. **Latin Name** *Aloysia gratissima* (*Lippia
ligustrina*)
Pronunciation ah-LOY-see-uh
grah-TEECE-uh-muh
Common Names WHITEBRUSH, BEEBRUSH,
WHITEBUSH
Usual Height 4–8 feet, can reach 14 feet
Spacing 3–4 feet apart
Bloom After rains in spring to fall; white
(violet) with yellow throat; 1- to 3-inch
spikes
Almost evergreen
Range Throughout Texas except
Panhandle, possibly introduced in
eastern part of state
New Mexico, Mexico, South America
Soil Sand, loam, clay, caliche, limestone;
moist, seasonal poor drainage okay
Dappled shade, part shade, full sun
Colonizes, forms thickets
Propagation Fresh seed, softwood tip
cuttings

There are about thirteen Spanish names for this plant, all complimentary and almost all referring to its extraordinarily fresh vanilla scent. The English names are more graphic. "Whitebrush" has obvious meaning after a rain. The rain—and it has to be more than a sprinkle—transforms the brush into a cloud of white verbena-like florets that last for several days. As you can tell from the name "beebrush," this is a bountiful honey plant, always buzzing with bees when in bloom. The flowers are poisonous to horses, mules, and burros, but the fragrant foliage is quite safe. The best use for this shrub is to make a thornless thicket, but it can also be hedged, or even pruned into a slender, graceful small tree. The wood is somewhat brittle. Whitebrush seems to be usable anywhere in Texas south of the Red River.

162. Indigobush amorpha
Amorpha fruticosa
The authors

163. Texas torchwood
Amyris texana
James H. Everitt

162. **Latin Name** *Amorpha fruticosa*
Pronunciation ah-MOR-fah
froo-teh-COH-sah
Common Names INDIGOBUSH AMORPHA,
RIVER LOCUST, FALSE INDIGO
Usual Height 10 feet
Spacing 7–15 feet apart
Bloom Late spring; purple; 6- to 8-inch
spikes
Deciduous
Range Throughout Texas except Valley
Coast to coast; Wyoming; south to Sonora,
Mexico
Soil Sand, loam, clay; acidic or calcareous;
poor drainage okay
Part shade, full sun
Propagation Scarified seed, softwood or
hardwood cuttings

The flowers are unique, and you'll want to get up close to fully appreciate the stunning color combination of deep, rich purple spikes with brilliant orange anthers. It's best use is as a large shrub or small tree in a low area where poor drainage is a problem or at the edge of a water garden. (Look for it in the Water Garden Plan.) But it will also grow well in an ordinary landscape where the lawn is watered enough to keep it green. As a shrub, it has a loose, airy form, with several branches coming off the trunk near the ground. Or you could diligently prune off the lower branches for two years, so that by the third year you'd have a nicely shaped little tree. Indigobush amorpha can also be effective for erosion control along waterways, as it is slightly rhizomatous. Benny Simpson of Texas A&M University has released an especially beautiful selection for nursery production called 'Dark Lance.'

163. **Latin Name** *Amyris texana*
Pronunciation ah-MEER-us tex-AN-ah
Common Names TEXAS TORCHWOOD,
CHAPOTILLO
Usual Height 3 feet, can reach 9 feet
Spacing 3 feet apart
Bloom April to October; white; 1- to 3-inch
clusters, fragrant
Evergreen
Range South Texas brush, north to Victoria
Mexico
Soil Sand, loam, clay; well drained
Dappled shade, part shade, full sun
Propagation Fresh seed sown in spring,
softwood cuttings

Okay, it's honesty time. I think this is a tacky plant, and I didn't want to include it in this book. But so many people whose opinions I trust gave it a star rating that I had to put it in. I've done so with this compromise: I don't have to wax eloquent about it. Texas torchwood is a scraggly, homely plant with droopy, greasy-looking leaves that always look bruised. In the bible for Texas botanists, Correll and Johnston's *Manual of the Vascular Plants of Texas*, it is described as a "rounded shrub" with "shiny leaves." The authors obviously never saw the plants I ran across, and vice versa. This shrub compounds its lack of charm by seeming to lean against fences or other shrubs. To be fair, I should add a few positive things: The white flowers have a sweetly pleasant fragrance, and birds are also positively inclined toward it—they love the fruits. Torchwood is winter-hardy in Houston. *Amyris madrensis* is prettier, with large aromatic leaves and a fuller look, but it's only winter-hardy in the Valley.

164. Flame acanthus
Anisacanthus quadrifidus var. *wrightii*
The authors

165. Sand sagebrush
Artemisia filifolia
The authors

164. **Latin Name** *Anisacanthus quadrifidus* var.
  wrightii
  Pronunciation ah-nee-sah-KAN-thus
  kwah-DRIF-eh-dus variety RITE-ee-eye
  Common Names FLAME ACANTHUS,
  WRIGHT ANISACANTHUS
  Usual Height 3–4 feet
  Spacing 3 feet apart
  Bloom Summer to frost; orange to
  pumpkin-yellow; 2 inches long
  Deciduous
  Range Edwards Plateau
  Mexico
  Soil Sand, loam, clay, caliche, limestone;
  well drained
  Dappled shade, part shade, full sun
  Propagation Fresh seed, cuttings, layering

I usually use this shrub as a flower, because it is so small and it blooms so profusely. Its bright orange blossoms appear steadily all summer and fall, attracting hummingbirds and butterflies to your yard. Flame acanthus is extremely drought-tolerant and does exceptionally well in a patio pot, even with sun and reflected heat beating on it all day. You'll like it in the winter too; the slender branches have pale, shredding bark. Texas has two larger varieties as well: *A. thurberi*, which has red or yellow flowers, and *A. insignis*, which has pink flowers. Benny Simpson has made selections on all three varieties. They appear to have no disease or insect problems and seem to be at least root-hardy as far north as Dallas.

165. **Latin Name** *Artemisia filifolia*
  Pronunciation ar-teh-MEE-zhah
  fill-ee-FOLE-ee-ah
  Common Names SAND SAGEBRUSH,
  SAND SAGE
  Usual Height 3–6 feet
  Spacing 4–6 feet apart
  Almost evergreen
  Range Deep sand in West Texas, High
  Plains, and Trans-Pecos
  Nebraska to Nevada to Mexico
  Soil Sand; well drained
  Part shade, full sun
  Propagation Seed

Wherever you see this shrub growing in nature, you know that the soil has to be sandy. In Midland, where it gets thin in the winter, Burr Williams recommends cutting it back around January. When sand sagebrush is treated this way, you can keep it any height and width you like, and it will always be quite dense. In El Paso, where winters are warmer, this pruning is not necessary. I saw a fine-looking specimen there that had never been pruned; it was about five feet tall and six feet wide and had a feathery free-form look to it. Either way, sand sagebrush can be used as an accent, a boundary planting, or a backdrop. It is also good for erosion control. This shrub should never be hedged. Shearing ruins the thready delicacy of its blue-green foliage. The blooms are insignificant visually, but like those of other artemesias, they release pollen that is quite noticeable to hay-fever sufferers. The leaves have a pleasant fragrance and are used as a sweet-tasting, albeit strong, herbal seasoning, which I've added sparingly to soups on numerous occasions.

166. Four-wing saltbush female in fruit
Atriplex canescens
The authors

167. Baccharis
Baccharis halimifolia
The authors

166. **Latin Name**   *Atriplex canescens*
Pronunciation   AH-treh-plex kan-ESS-enz
Common Names   FOUR-WING SALTBUSH,
CHAMISO
Usual Height   3 feet, can reach 8 feet
Spacing   3–8 feet apart
Fruit   August and September, on females;
yellowish; ¼ inch long and four-winged
Evergreen
Range   High Plains, West Texas, Trans-
Pecos, Valley
Western half of North America
Soil   Sand, loam, clay, caliche, limestone;
calcareous; well drained; saline okay
Part shade, full sun
Colonizes by seed
Propagation   Seed stored over winter to
ripen, sown in early spring; softwood cut-
tings in late summer or early fall

The yellow fall fruits of the female are the most
attractive feature of this silver-leaved shrub—and they
provide food for songbirds. The males release airborne pollen, so keep that in mind if you suffer from hay fever. Use
this shrub as a last resort, when conditions are so dry and
your soil or water is so salty that no other plant in its right
mind would want to live there. You might be tempted to
water a lot at first to encourage rapid growth, but the fresh
new leaves only invite insect damage. This shrub can be
incredibly invasive, but this is a virtue if you need erosion
control.

167. **Latin Name**   *Baccharis halimifolia*
Pronunciation   BAK-ah-rus
hal-eh-mah-FLOR-ee-ah
Common Names   BACCHARIS, GROUNDSEL,
SEA MYRTLE, CONSUMPTION WEED
Usual Height   6–8 feet
Spacing   4–8 feet apart
Bloom and Fruit   September to November
(winter), on females; white; ¼ inch
Deciduous
Range   Piney Woods, Post Oak Woods
Massachusetts to Oklahoma to Gulf of
Mexico
Soil   Sand, loam; acid; poor drainage okay
Part shade, full sun
Propagation   Fresh seed

When the female baccharis is in full bloom, it's
spectacular—as you can see in the picture. It sometimes
starts blooming as early as midsummer and continues
past Christmas. That's half the year! However, the rest of
the time it's not going to be the star of your garden. After
it has lost both flowers and leaves in January, the branches
look pathetic—so cut them way back. It's a bit slow to leaf
out in the spring and can look scraggly during this period
too. Severe pruning, plus water and fertilizer, can make it
bushier. Another baccharis is Roosevelt weed (*B. neglecta*).
It's extremely drought-tolerant and grows in calcareous or
salty soils throughout the state, except in the Piney Woods
and northern High Plains. It's good for erosion control in
dry, disturbed areas. I've often seen Roosevelt weed as
large as a small tree, and I've wondered if it wouldn't be
more attractive pruned that way.

168. Texas barberry
Berberis swaseyi
Benny J. Simpson

169. Agarito
Berberis trifoliolata
The authors

168. **Latin Name**   *Berberis swaseyi* (*Mahonia swazeyi*)
Pronunciation   BER-ber-iss SWAY-zee-eye
Common Name   TEXAS BARBERRY
Usual Height   3–5 feet
Spacing   3 feet apart
Bloom   Early spring; yellow; ½ inch across; spicy fragrance
Evergreen, mauve to wine red in fall
Range   Canyon walls in Edwards Plateau
Endemic to Texas
Soil   Sand, loam, clay, caliche, limestone; well drained
Part shade, full sun
Propagation   Stratified seed

This spiny shrub is useful for its contrasting foliage. Each leaf has five to nine leaflets. The new ones come out rosy in the spring and then turn either yellow-green or a light gray-green. In the autumn the leaves turn muted shades of reds and purples, which last all winter. In early spring the flowers appear, bright golden yellow and fragrant. The fruits are small, amber to bright red, and plump, if there is enough moisture. This is an especially good shrub to use if you need an evergreen that will grow right out of limestone and caliche. It can be allowed to grow in its natural shape, or it can be (ugh) sheared.

169. **Latin Name**   *Berberis trifoliolata* (*Mahonia trifoliata*)
Pronunciation   BER-ber-iss tri-foh-lee-oh-LAY-tah
Common Names   AGARITO, ALGERITA
Usual Height   3–6 feet, can reach 8 feet
Spacing   3–6 feet apart
Bloom   Early spring; yellow; ½ inch across, spicy fragrance
Fruit   May to July; red; ¼ inch
Evergreen
Range   Corpus Christi, Valley, Trans-Pecos, West Texas, Caprock Escarpment, Edwards Plateau
New Mexico, Arizona, Mexico
Soil   Sand, loam, clay, caliche, limestone; well drained
Part shade, full sun
Propagation   Stratified seed

Agarito is widespread and well known to most Texans. Each leaf has three spiny leaflets, usually gray-green but sometimes a beautiful blue-gray—I call this selection silver agarito. Because animals don't tend to browse it, agarito provides a safe haven beneath its branches for vulnerable seedlings, such as Texas madrone and Texas smoke tree, to get established. For this reason, it, like junipers, is known as a nurse plant. It blooms very early in the spring, even before its cousin Texas barberry. The flowers are also golden yellow and strongly fragrant. Its fruits are bright red and supply meals to birds and other wildlife. If you ever see people out in a field hitting the agarito with sticks, they're knocking off the berries to make a delicious jelly. In a landscape, agarito can be used as a specimen or, because of those prickly leaves, as a security hedge.

170. Scarlet bouvardia
Bouvardia ternifolia
The authors

171. Butterfly bush
Buddleja marrubiifolia
The authors

170. **Latin Name**   *Bouvardia ternifolia*
Pronunciation   boo-VAR-dee-ah
tern-eh-FOLE-ee-ah
Common Names   SCARLET BOUVARDIA,
TROMPETILLA
Usual Height   2–4 feet
Spacing   1–2 feet apart
Bloom   May to November; red; 2 inches
long in 4-inch clusters
Deciduous
Range   Trans-Pecos mountains
Mountains of New Mexico, Arizona, and
Mexico
Soil   Sand, loam, gravel, igneous; well
drained
Part shade, full sun
Propagation   Seed, softwood and
semisoftwood cuttings

Scarlet bouvardia is most often used as a flower.
Either massed or singly, it is gorgeous in a perennial border, providing continuous red flowers throughout its season. Snip off old blooms regularly to keep it neat, dense,
and well shaped. You can easily maintain it at a height of
only one to two feet. Its only limitation is its winter-
hardiness—it isn't very, being kin to the tropical coffee
and quinine families. Those of you in the northern fourth
of the state will be glad to know that it does very well in a
patio pot, so you can take it inside in the winter. In early
spring put it back outside where it gets good morning
sun. In Texas, bouvardia is found only in igneous soil, but
it's adaptable to more soils than that. Good drainage is the
important factor. However, I've heard about one selection, grown by nurseryman Tom Dodds in Louisiana, that
can tolerate the humidity and wetter soils of East Texas.

171. **Latin Name**   *Buddleja marrubiifolia*
Pronunciation   BUD-lee-ah
mah-ROO-bee-eye-FOLE-ee-ah
Common Name   BUTTERFLY BUSH
Usual Height   3 feet, can reach 5 feet
Spacing   2–3 feet apart
Bloom   Summer and fall (spring); orange;
½ inch; aromatic
Almost deciduous
Range   Southern Trans-Pecos
Mexico
Soil   Sand, loam, limestone; well drained
Part shade, full sun
Propagation   Seed sown in spring; softwood
or hardwood cuttings

Butterfly bush has small, furry, pale green leaves
that seem to be rimmed in white as the light plays on the
fuzz. The tiny flowers are orange and remind me of Texas
lantana. Yes, butterflies are attracted to this plant each
summer and fall—yet not to such a degree that would explain why it, above all other plants, got its name. In fact,
it more or less inherited the name because it is related to
other buddlejas that really do draw droves of butterflies.
Like scarlet bouvardia, butterfly bush is somewhat tender
for the northern part of the state. If you wish to use it
there, understand that you may lose it every third year
and that you'll have to place it in a protected corner or in
a patio pot that you bring inside every winter. In warmer
parts of the state, in full sun, and with a little care, it can
bloom so profusely that it is appropriate for a flower
garden.

172. American beautyberry
Callicarpa americana
Dan H. Hinds

173. Chile pequín
Capsicum annuum
The authors

172. **Latin Name** *Callicarpa americana*
Pronunciation kal-eh-KAR-pah
ah-mare-eh-KAH-nah
Common Names AMERICAN BEAUTYBERRY,
FRENCH MULBERRY
Usual Height 3–4 feet, can reach 9 feet
Spacing 5–7 feet apart
Fruit Fall and winter; purple (white);
2-inch bunches
Deciduous
Range Piney Woods, Post Oak Woods,
Blackland woodlands, coastal woodlands
Maryland to Mexico, Cuba
Soil Sand, loam, clay; acid or
calcareous; moist, well drained
Dappled shade, part shade
Propagation Seed (stratified or wintered
over in ground), softwood or hardwood
cuttings

The primary use for American beautyberry is as an understory shrub. It is a large shrub that doesn't take kindly to hedging; you must give it lots of space to spread out its long, arching branches. It's at its best in the fall, when bunches of glossy purple fruits weigh down the stems, causing them to arch even more. If these fruits aren't devoured by birds, they remain colorful until new leaves appear in the spring. The leaves are not its best feature; they're somewhat large and coarse in texture and tend to droop in summer. To make up for this poor display, sometimes they try to turn yellow in the fall—but I've never seen them really pull it off. This shrub can probably be used in any shady place in the state, but the farther west you live, the more you'll have to water it. If you have a choice, go with the purple-berried one; the white-berried ones I've seen don't hold up all winter and get brown spots on the berries.

173. **Latin Name** *Capsicum annuum*
(*C. frutescens*)
Pronunciation KAP-seh-kum AN-yoo-um
Common Names CHILE PEQUIN,
CHILE PETIN, BIRD PEPPER
Usual Height 2 feet, can reach 5 feet
Spacing 2 feet apart
Bloom Everblooming; white; ½ inch
Fruit April to November; red; ½–1 inch
**Evergreen in Valley; deciduous to dormant
farther north**
Range Valley, Corpus Christi, Edwards
Plateau, north to Waco
Florida to Arizona and tropical America
Soil Sand, loam, clay, caliche, limestone;
moist, well drained
Shade, dappled shade, part shade
Propagation Seed

This is our original native chile pepper. The birds aren't the only ones who love the spicy fruits; Tex-Mex gourmets use these peppers as seasoning. This shrub has soft thin leaves and green branches. In the Valley it's evergreen and might produce chiles all year. In Dallas it dies to the ground after the first hard frost. It's a pleasant, airy understory shrub, and I've even seen it used effectively as tall woodsy ground cover. Given more sun and a little water, it becomes quite dense. It can seed out quite freely, so if you keep your soil moist and shady and you've got plenty of birds around, you'll have these shrubs springing up everywhere.

174. **Canyon senna with red yucca at Texas Agricultural Experiment Station in Dallas**
Cassia wislizenii
The authors

175. **Starleaf Mexican orange**
Choisya dumosa
The authors

174. **Latin Name** *Cassia wislizenii*
Pronunciation KASS-ee-ah wiz-leh-ZEN-ee-eye
Common Names CANYON SENNA, DWARF SENNA
Usual Height 4–6 feet, can reach 10 feet
Spacing 4 feet apart
Bloom Summer; yellow to gold; 1 inch in 6-inch clusters
Deciduous
Range Trans-Pecos mountains New Mexico, Arizona, Mexico
Soil Sand, loam, clay; acid or calcareous; well drained
Part shade, full sun
Propagation Fresh seed, semihardwood cuttings in late summer

"Dwarf" is a ridiculous label to give our largest senna. I consulted with Benny Simpson, and he suggested calling it canyon senna, as it is always found in little header canyons in the Trans-Pecos. It's a gorgeous shrub and should be given plenty of room to show off its gracefully arching stems. Ron Gass, a native plant grower in Phoenix, told me that he has seen a magnificent specimen of canyon senna that was twenty by twenty feet. I love it planted with red yucca; both bloom all summer. For a dazzling sight in the fall, plant any of the purple daleas at the base of canyon senna.

175. **Latin Name** *Choisya dumosa*
Pronunciation CHOY-zee-ah doo-MOH-sah
Common Names STARLEAF MEXICAN ORANGE, ZORRILLO, FRAGRANT STARLEAF
Usual Height 1–3 feet, can reach 6 feet
Spacing 2–3 feet apart
Bloom June to November; white; 1 inch across; fragrant
Almost evergreen
Range Trans-Pecos mountains New Mexico, Mexico
Soil Sand, loam, caliche, limestone; well drained
Part shade, full sun
Propagation Fresh seed, stratified immediately; semihardwood or hardwood cuttings

I'll tell you how much I like starleaf Mexican orange; I've never even seen one in bloom and I still count it as one of our premier shrubs. The leaves are that gorgeous! They're dark yellow-green and finely divided into a star shape and have a juniper-like texture. The picture doesn't begin to do it justice—and certainly doesn't convey its tangy, citrusy fragrance. This shrub is in the orange family, and I'm told that the flowers have a strong sweet scent. Starleaf Mexican orange is another one of those shrubs that is suitable for a flower garden and can be used in a patio pot. It can also be naturalized under pinyon pines, bigtooth maples, and Texas madrones. Just make sure it is well drained. It will be healthiest in the southwest quadrant of the state. The best time to prune it is right after blooming. And—good news for those of you whose plants are ravaged by wildlife—deer don't like this one.

176. Damianita
Chrysactinia mexicana
Benny J. Simpson

177. Rabbitbrush
Chrysothamnus nauseosus
The authors

176. **Latin Name** *Chrysactinia mexicana*
Pronunciation krye-sak-TIN-ee-ah
mex-eh-KAH-nah
Common Name DAMIANITA
Usual Height 1–2 feet
Spacing 1–2 feet apart
Bloom Late spring to early fall; yellow;
1 inch across
Evergreen
Range Edwards Plateau, Trans-Pecos
New Mexico, Mexico
Soil Sand, loam, caliche, limestone; well
drained
Part shade, full sun
Propagation Seed sown in spring, softwood
cuttings in summer

Although technically a shrub, damianita is one of our best flowers. Low-growing and long-blooming, it's also drought-tolerant; its tiny, narrow aromatic leaves are highly efficient at preventing evaporation losses. Massed, it presents a carpet of vivid golden yellow that can thrive even in median strips or on limestone roadways. Damianita is not in the Hill Country Plan because it isn't native to San Antonio or Austin, yet it thrives there. It is also not native near El Paso, but I suspect it should do well there, especially in a courtyard where it can get some winter protection. We tested one in Dallas and one in Fort Worth, but both died the first winter. Since they were planted in clay, and damianita insists on perfect drainage, poor drainage might have been part of the problem. Often, because of wet clays, roots freeze there at temperatures they could survive if the soils had better drainage.

177. **Latin Name** *Chrysothamnus nauseosus*
Pronunciation krye-soh-THAM-nus
nawz-ee-OH-sus
Common Names RABBITBRUSH, CHAMISA,
RUBBER RABBITBRUSH
Usual Height 2–5 feet
Spacing 3 feet apart
Bloom 2–4 weeks in September and
October; yellow; 4- to 6-inch clusters
Almost evergreen
Range Draws on Rolling Plains in
Panhandle
North Dakota to Arizona
Soil Sand, caliche; well drained
Part shade, full sun
Propagation Untreated seed, hardwood
cuttings in late winter

Rabbitbrush likes cool summers. You see it most frequently in Santa Fe and Albuquerque; it comes into Texas only in the Panhandle at elevations of 3,000 feet and higher. I've included it because it's readily available at New Mexico nurseries. Its aromatic, blue-green, feathery foliage is similar to that of the sand sagebrush. When rabbitbrush blooms in the fall—solid with bright yellow, fuzzy flowers—it closely resembles larchleaf goldenweed. Plant it with wild blue aster or feather dalea for contrast. The color and texture of its leaves work well alongside pinyon pines. If the leaves get thin in the winter, they reveal white woolly stems. This is the time of year to cut it back severely if it has gotten too rangy. It will come back in the spring, thick and bushy. In summer give it a little bit of shade from the afternoon sun so that it won't get overheated. If you're allergic to bees, you should know that this shrub has a reputation for being a good honey producer.

178. Gregg coldenia
Coldenia greggii
Benny J. Simpson

179. Texas snakewood
Colubrina texensis
The authors

178. **Latin Name** *Coldenia greggii* (*Tiquilia greggii*)
Pronunciation kole-DIN-ee-ah
GREG-ee-eye
Common Names GREGG COLDENIA,
HIERBA DEL CENIZO
Usual Height 1–2 feet
Spacing 1½ feet apart
Bloom June to October, in late afternoon;
purple; 1-inch seed head
Almost evergreen
Range Exposed limestone in Trans-Pecos
New Mexico, Mexico
Soil Sand, loam, clay, caliche, limestone;
calcareous preferred; well drained
Part shade, full sun
Propagation Nobody can figure out how to
propagate it!

Everyone loves coldenia. It has tiny, fuchsia-colored flowers that accentuate the lavender of the fluffy seed heads—and the even tinier fuzzy gray leaves. An altogether delightful shrub that can be used as a flower or a mass planting, coldenia is dense and rounded even when very young. As it gets older, it becomes more twiggy but retains its compact shape. Pruning does not seem to be necessary. The only problem with coldenia is that nobody has been able to propagate it commercially. It is included in this book for two reasons: (1) Someday someone is bound to figure out how to grow it, and (2) if you have it on your property, take good care of it, or give it to someone who will. Because coldenia is a native of the Chihuahuan Desert, it needs dry air and well-drained soil.

179. **Latin Name** *Colubrina texensis*
Pronunciation koh-loo-BRYE-nah
tex-EN-siss
Common Names TEXAS SNAKEWOOD,
HOG PLUM
Usual Height 4–6 feet
Spacing 4–6 feet apart
Deciduous
Range Corpus Christi, Valley, southern
Trans-Pecos, north to Abilene and
Midland
Mexico
Soil Sand, loam, clay, caliche, limestone;
well drained
Part shade, full sun
Propagation Stratified seed, semihardwood
tip cuttings

Snakewood got its name because its smooth gray wood, with scaly brown markings, resembles snake-skin. The branches are rigid, joining each other at right angles, and make an overall zigzag structure. The leaves are glossy, one inch long, and not particularly memorable. The yellowish, fragrant blooms aren't too visually exciting either. It's the fruits that are noteworthy, although not what I'd describe as charming. They're about one-half inch in diameter and roughly textured with a black bark-like coat over the tan "nut." It seems that they are popular with javelinas, often called wild hogs, which accounts for this shrub's other common name—"hog plum." The entire shrub, I'm told, makes most landscape architects rhapsodic. Snakewood has proven to be winter-hardy as far north as Dallas.

180. Feather dalea
Dalea formosa
Vernon L. Wesby

181.
Black dalea
Dalea frutescens
Benny J. Simpson

181.
Silver dalea
Dalea bicolor var.
argyraea
The authors

180. **Latin Name** *Dalea formosa*
Pronunciation DAL-ee-ah for-MOH-sah
Common Name FEATHER DALEA
Usual Height 2–3 feet, can reach 6 feet
Spacing 4–6 feet apart
Bloom April to October; purple; 1- to 2-inch clusters
Deciduous
Range Trans-Pecos and High Plains east to Abilene and Laredo
Oklahoma and Colorado to Mexico
Soil Sand, clay, caliche, limestone; well drained
Full sun
Propagation Fresh untreated seed sown in early spring, semi-hardwood cuttings

Feather dalea is the ideal shrub for the lazy gardener. It prefers poor, dry soils, and will only get leggy and weak-stemmed with fertilizer and water. It's also our most winter-hardy dalea. And once it's established, it requires almost no further maintenance, except for an annual whacking back in the spring. It forms large, low-spreading, finely textured mounds—perfect for massive ground covers in sunny, large-scale projects. The silvery leaves are small and grow close together, but when this shrub is in full bloom, its purple flowers almost completely obscure the leaves. All you see are purple blooms and bumblebees. This is another of those photographically frustrating plants—their true color fades to gray in a long shot. Still, the close-up, showing the feathery, silky plumes among the flowers, should inspire you to give it a try.

181. **Latin Name** *Dalea frutescens*
Pronunciation DAL-ee-ah froo-TEH-senz
Common Name BLACK DALEA
Usual Height 1–3 feet
Spacing 4–6 feet apart
Bloom Fall; magenta; ½-inch spikes
Deciduous
Range Trans-Pecos east to Austin and Grand Prairie, north to Red River
Oklahoma, New Mexico, Mexico
Soil Sand, clay, caliche, limestone; well drained
Full sun
Propagation Fresh untreated seed sown in early spring, semihardwood cuttings

Black dalea is similar to the feather dalea, except for two points: Black dalea is more widespread in Texas, and it lacks the distinctive plumes on the flowers. As far as landscape uses and maintenance are concerned, treat the two daleas the same way. Both are considered edible by deer and rabbits, which can be a problem while the plants are getting established. Black dalea gets four-star reviews from landscapers in Arizona, El Paso, San Antonio, Austin, and Dallas, especially for how it works in mass plantings. Another option is silver dalea (*D. bicolor* var. *argyraea*), which gets its name from the fuzzy leaf hairs that catch the light. Its leaves also emit a pleasing fragrance when crushed.

182. Sotol
Dasylirion sp.
The authors

183. Joint fir
Ephedra antisyphilitica
The authors

182. **Latin Name** *Dasylirion* spp.
  Pronunciation day-zee-LEER-ee-on species
  Common Names SOTOL, DESERT PAMPAS
    GRASS, DESERT SPOON
  Usual Height 1½–2½ feet, flower stalk
    9–15 feet
  Spacing 3–4 feet apart
  Bloom May, June, or July; yellowish; 2- to
    3-foot spike
  Evergreen
  Range Western Edwards Plateau to Trans-
    Pecos
    New Mexico, Arizona, Mexico
  Soil Sand, caliche, limestone, igneous; well
    drained
  Dappled shade, part shade, full sun
  Propagation Fresh untreated seed sown in
    spring

Texas has three native sotols, and all of them are used in cultivation. The leaves are the chief attraction. They are dark green, spoon-shaped at the base, then narrow, with spines evenly spaced along the edges. Plant a sotol beneath a window, and those spines will do a marvelous job of discouraging burglars. I particularly like sotol backlit. That's when the marvelous contrast between it and softer-leaved shrubs and flowers really stands out. Always give sotol plenty of elbowroom; it's not visually at its best when cramped. Rocks, curly mesquite grass, buffalo grass, dwarf germander, blackfoot daisy, yellow or white zinnias, and other drought-tolerant, low-growing plants are good choices to plant at the base. Lindheimer or bull muhly, about the same height but very soft, are also effective when planted with sotol. Easy to grow, sotol is successfully used as far north as Dallas and as far east as Corpus Christi. It can also be grown in a patio pot—just keep it well drained.

183. **Latin Name** *Ephedra antisyphilitica*
Pronunciation ah-FEE-drah
AN-tee-sih-feh-LEH-teh-kah
Common Names JOINT FIR, MORMON TEA
Usual Height 3–6 feet
Spacing 3–4 feet apart
Evergreen
Range Southern Panhandle to Corpus
Christi and Valley
Southwestern Oklahoma to Mexico
Soil Sand, loam, clay, caliche; well drained
Part shade, full sun
Propagation Fresh seed, root division

Joint fir is hard to grow, and as far as I know, no one sells it. But I've included it because someone might find out how to grow it commercially after this book comes out, and then you'll be ready for it. There's also the chance that you might have it on your property, and once you know about it, you will want to preserve and cherish it. It looks like a shrubby, squat conifer. The branches resemble fir needles in texture and are capable of photosynthesis. Joint fir has leaves, but they're so teeny, you just might not notice them. The male shrubs have tiny cones, and the females have red berries, neither in great profusion. Deer and cattle consider joint fir mouth-wateringly delicious, and you'll always find it nibbled to a nub in the wild. To survive, it has to hide out under something thorny, like a mesquite. If you have a joint fir, it's probably at the base of a tree. You can prune out deadwood, but let it develop its own shape; it looks best when it's somewhat irregular. Be careful not to overwater it or to change the slope of the land so that you disturb its good drainage.

184. Larchleaf goldenweed
Ericameria laricifolia
The authors

184. **Latin Name** *Ericameria laricifolia*
Pronunciation eh-rik-ah-MARE-ee-ah
lah-riss-eh-FOLE-ee-ah
Common Names LARCHLEAF GOLDENWEED,
TURPENTINE BUSH
Usual Height 1–3 feet
Spacing 1–2 feet apart
Bloom Fall; golden; ¼ inch across
Evergreen
Range Mountains near El Paso and Presidio
New Mexico, Arizona, Mexico
Soil Sand, loam, clay; well drained
Part shade, full sun
Propagation Softwood cuttings

Rub the leaves gently and they emit a tart lemony scent. Rub them harder and they get gummy between your fingers, and they smell like turpentine! There is ac-tually a small amount of rubber in the sap, and you'd think that nothing would browse it. Rabbits do. In fact, they'll eat it down to the ground. In the wild, larchleaf goldenweed forms carpets of dense greenery that turns to solid gold in the fall. Dr. Jimmy L. Tipton, of the Texas Agricultural Experiment Station in El Paso, figured it would make a terrific ground cover or mass planting. In his test garden, where the soil has been loosened and everything gets watered, it has grown taller, but not broader, to make a narrow, upright shrub. Use one in the flower garden, or mass several close together for a big bed. If you want it shorter than three feet, water very, very sparingly, and be prepared to cut it back with a line trimmer one to three times a year.

185. Coralbean
Erythrina herbacea
The authors

186. Strawberry bush
Euonymus americanus
The authors

185. **Latin Name** *Erythrina herbacea*
Pronunciation eh-rith-REEN-ah
er-BAY-shah
Common Name CORALBEAN
Usual Height 6 feet, can reach 15 feet
Spacing 6 feet apart or more
Bloom Spring to frost; red; 8- to 12-inch
spikes
Fruit Dark red; poisonous pods
Deciduous
Range Corpus Christi, Valley, Post Oak
Savannah to Red River
Coastal states from North Carolina to
Veracruz, Mexico
Soil Sand, loam, clay; acid or calcareous;
well drained
Part shade, full sun
Propagation Scarified seed, semihardwood
cuttings, root division

Coralbean is far more winter-hardy and versatile than you might think—if you've seen it only in South Texas. It is actually native to the Red River. The large shrub in the photo grows in McKinney, about fifty miles south of Oklahoma. Furthermore, from its range, you would think coralbean could grow only in sand, but in fact its large, thick, tuberous roots seem quite content in calcareous black clay. However, this far north, coralbean dies back to the ground each winter like a perennial. In the extremely mild winters of the Valley, it goes dormant but never dies back and can get tree-size. Coralbean is often grown for its flamboyant summer flowers and also because many people like to use the seeds for jewelry and other craft projects—in spite of their being very poisonous.

186. **Latin Name** *Euonymus americanus*
Pronunciation YON-eh-mus
ah-mare-eh-KAH-nus
Common Name STRAWBERRY BUSH
Usual Height 6 feet
Spacing 3–4 feet apart
Fruit Fall and winter; red; 1 inch across
**Deciduous, with leaves turning red in the
fall**
Range Moist woods in East Texas
New York to Illinois to Gulf of Mexico
Soil Sand, loam, clay; acid; poor drainage
okay
Shade, dappled shade, part shade
Propagation Stratified seed, semihardwood
cuttings rooted in cold frame, layering,
grafting, budding

Strawberry bush holds its bright red fruits for a long time in the fall. It is an airy understory shrub and shows off best when it's massed in corners or planted at a curve where its height is welcome. It takes lots of shade and poor drainage but is also happy in a relatively dry but shady yard in Houston or East Texas. Just water it a few times during the summer.

187. Fragrant mistflower
Eupatorium odoratum
The authors

188. White mistflower
Eupatorium wrightii
Vernon L. Wesby

187. **Latin Name** *Eupatorium odoratum*
Pronunciation yoo-pah-TOR-ee-um oh-duh-RAH-tum
Common Names FRAGRANT MISTFLOWER, CRUCITA
Usual Height 2–6 feet
Spacing 2 feet apart
Bloom Fall; purple; fragrant
Evergreen in Valley, root-hardy in Rio Grande Plains
Range Valley, Corpus Christi, and elsewhere in Rio Grande Plains
Tropical and subtropical America
Soil Sand, loam, clay, caliche, limestone; poor drainage okay
Shade, dappled shade, part shade
Propagation Seed, softwood cuttings

In places where fragrant mistflower keeps warm all winter, it grows like a shrub, but new growth is in long, leggy shoots, like a woody vine. It does well as a massed planting or tall ground cover. Once a year, cut it back to half its height with clippers or a line trimmer to make it lush. It is at the northern edge of its limits in Texas; in a hard winter it might die back to the roots, but in the Valley it's evergreen. Because of its leggy growth habit, this shrub can be espaliered on a wall, as in the Corpus Christi Plan. You can also put it in a planter box or raised bed where its naturally arching branches can be displayed to best advantage, but even then, I'd recommend cutting it back once a year so it can develop fresh new growth.

188. **Latin Name** *Eupatorium wrightii*
Pronunciation yoo-pah-TOR-ee-um RITE-ee-eye
Common Names WHITE MISTFLOWER, WHITE BONESET, WHITE AGERATUM
Usual Height 1–2 feet, can reach 3 feet
Spacing 1–2 feet apart
Bloom Fall; white to pale pink; 2-inch heads; fragrant
Deciduous
Range Lower slopes of Trans-Pecos mountains
Mexico
Soil Sand, loam, clay, limestone; might tolerate poor drainage
Dappled shade, part shade, full sun
Propagation Softwood or semihardwood cuttings, untreated seed

White mistflower is used best in a flower bed. During a fall in which summer's heat lingers, its cool-white fragrant blooms are welcome. Butterflies and hummingbirds are often found adding to the color. After frost, cut white mistflower back severely so that it will be low, bushy, and full of flowers again the next year. All mistflowers need watering in the summer, but this one seems to be the most drought-tolerant. Giving it afternoon shade will help. Another shrubby white mistflower is *E. havanense*. It is much taller (capable of reaching six feet) than *E. wrightii* and is possibly just as drought-tolerant—I've seen it growing out of limestone in sunny locations in the Edwards Plateau. However, it also tolerates poor drainage.

189. Candelilla
Euphorbia antisyphilitica
The authors

190. Winterfat
Eurotia lanata
The authors

189. **Latin Name** *Euphorbia antisyphilitica*
Pronunciation yoo-FOR-bee-ah
AN-tee-sih-feh-LEH-teh-kah
Common Name CANDELILLA
Usual Height 1–1½ feet, can reach 3 feet
Spacing 1–2 feet apart
Evergreen
Range Along Rio Grande
Mexico
Soil Sand, loam, clay, caliche, limestone;
well drained
Part shade, full sun
Propagation Root division

Candelilla, meaning "little candle," looks like a cluster of slender, pale green, waxy tapers. They are covered with a high-grade wax; the plant was once abundant until heavily harvested for industrial uses. Usually it has no leaves, and it photosynthesizes with these waxy stems. The flowers are inconspicuous—and a good thing, too. They're tiny, black, leathery things, bearing five oblong glands with white concave toothed appendages. Sounds like something in an aliens-from-outer-space movie! Candelilla is evergreen only in mild winters, even in its natural range. It's an effective accent in a desert or rock garden. There its pale color and columnar shape combine well with yucca and sotol and form a foil for softer-looking tropical flowers. North of its range, it will die to the ground in the winter, and if it gets too cold, it will just die. It makes an attractive patio pot plant that can be brought indoors in the winter.

190. **Latin Name** *Eurotia lanata* (*Ceratoides lanata*)
Pronunciation yoo-ROH-shah lan-AH-tah
Common Name WINTERFAT
Usual Height 1–3 feet
Spacing 2 feet apart
Fruit Fall and winter, on females; silvery
white
Almost evergreen
Range High Plains, Trans-Pecos
Western U.S.
Soil Sand, loam, clay, caliche, limestone;
well drained
Part shade, full sun
Propagation Stratified seed, softwood
cuttings

There's one big reason to use winterfat, and that's because it looks absolutely gorgeous backlit by the sun in the fall and winter. So be sure to plant it on the south side of your property. Only the females put on this show, however, but you'll need to include a male somewhere close by or the fruits won't happen. Winterfat will bloom and produce fruits the first year from seed. The leaves are a fuzzy pale blue but sometimes are sparse in a hot Texas summer, so if you don't have winterfat naturalized on a rocky slope, plant it in the middle of a flower bed where it can be surrounded by annuals and perennials in spring and summer. To keep it bushy, prune it back to eight inches in early spring. It doesn't do well outside its natural range because it needs cool nights. Winterfat is no Johnny-come-lately to landscaping; folks have been cultivating it in their gardens since 1895. Because the roots are deep and spreading, it is sometimes used for erosion control. The name came about when it was observed how fat rabbits, elk, and sheep got after munching on it during the winter months.

191. Apache plume
Fallugia paradoxa
The authors

191. **Latin Name** *Fallugia paradoxa*
Pronunciation fah-LOO-jee-ah pare-ah-DOX-ah
Common Name APACHE PLUME
Usual Height 2–6 feet, can reach 10 feet
Spacing 2–4 feet apart
Bloom May to December; white; 2 inches across
Fruit June to December; rose, pink, or silver; 2 inches
Evergreen to deciduous
Range Trans-Pecos, western Edwards Plateau
Texas to California to Mexico
Soil Sand, loam, clay, caliche, limestone; well drained
Part shade, full sun
Propagation Fresh untreated seed, layering, root division

Apache plume has fragile, white, roselike flowers that appear on the plant along with the pink feathery plumes. The color of the seed heads can vary, and the deep-pink ones are definitely the ones to choose. Together, the flowers and fruits give color most of the year, and the tiny dark leaves—where evergreen—are a winter bonus. Apache plume is easy to grow, often blooming the first year from seed. It's invaluable for erosion control and for naturalizing on a slope here, because of its drought tolerance and aggressive seeding-out, especially in sand. On the other hand, these vigorous traits can be a mixed blessing in a watered and weeded flower bed. Apache plume is winter-hardy all over the state and is especially useful in dry places that get a lot of reflected heat.

192. Plains greasebush
Forsellesia planitierum
Benny J. Simpson

192. **Latin Name** *Forsellesia planitierum*
Pronunciation for-sell-EE-zhah plan-ee-tee-AIR-um
Common Name PLAINS GREASEBUSH
Usual Height 2–3 feet
Spacing 2 feet apart
Bloom March; white; 1 inch across
Almost evergreen to deciduous
Range Breaks in High Plains
Oklahoma
Soil Sand, loam, clay, caliche; well drained
Part shade, full sun
Propagation Seed

Plains greasebush is a lot more appealing than its name implies. In early spring, before its new leaves emerge, it bursts into bloom—as pure and white as a miniature plum. The blossoms are five-petaled and profuse on the dense, slightly spiny branches. This is a small shrub, suitable for use in a flower bed or a mass planting. Although sometimes up to three feet tall, it can be kept lower and is sometimes found in the wild in low-growing mats. The leaves are tiny, furry, and nonaromatic. Plains greasebush is drought-tolerant and cold-hardy but is not summer-hardy in most of Texas.

193. Ocotillo
Fouquieria splendens
The authors

194. Red yucca
Hesperaloe parviflora
The authors

193. **Latin Name**   *Fouquieria splendens*
Pronunciation   foo-KWARE-ee-ah
SPLEN-denz
Common Name   OCOTILLO
Usual Height   12 feet, can reach 25 feet or
more
Spacing   6 feet apart
Bloom   May to July; orange-red; 2- to 8-inch
spikes
Evergreen stems
Range   Western Edwards Plateau, Trans-
Pecos
Texas to California to Mexico
Soil   Sand, limestone, igneous; well drained
Part shade, full sun
Propagation   Cuttings, untreated seed

Ocotillo is only for the specialized desert garden. Not only does it need perfect drainage at all times to keep from rotting, but it also will bloom only in dry air. Ocotillo is leafless as long as there's a drought, which is most of the year in the desert. When a little rain occurs (and it doesn't take much) and the humidity rises, leaves immediately sprout. But as soon as it becomes dry again, the leaves drop off and flowers appear. Soon they wither and die too, and the plant sits dormant awaiting the next rain. In Houston, which is always humid, the leaves stay on all the time and it never flowers. Ocotillo looks best as a specimen plant, perhaps used as a substitute for a small tree, with its multistems fanning out. However, because the stems are viciously thorned, you often see ocotillo planted one foot apart as a security fence.

195. **Virginia sweetspire**
Itea virginica
The authors

194. **Latin Name** *Hesperaloe parviflora*
Pronunciation hess-per-ah-LOH-ee
par-veh-FLOR-ah
Common Name RED YUCCA
Usual Height Leaves 2–3 feet, flower stalks
5 feet
Spacing 4 feet apart
Bloom Spring to frost; salmon-pink; 1- to
2-inches across
Evergreen
Range Western Edwards Plateau (Val Verde
County on dry prong of Nueces River)
Mexico
Soil Sand, loam, clay, caliche, limestone;
well drained
Dappled shade, part shade, full sun
Propagation Seed

I don't know why they call this "red yucca." It's not a yucca, and it's pink! The flowers are salmon or coral. Even the stems are pink. Olivette Beach, a nursery owner and landscape designer in Wimberley, calls it deer dessert. Deer love to eat its flowers. Red yucca is found in prairies, on rocky slopes, and in mesquite groves, but to be honest, although I've seen many of them in residential landscapes, I have yet to run across one in the wild. Red yucca is used often in landscapes all over the world. It's evergreen and adaptable to a range of soils and climates across the state (up to the Red River), and the flowers bloom profusely for a long time, almost always with an attendant hummingbird.

195. **Latin Name** *Itea virginica*
Pronunciation eye-TEE-uh ver-JIN-eh-kah
Common Name VIRGINIA SWEETSPIRE
Usual Height 3 feet, can reach 8 feet
Spacing 3 feet apart
Bloom May; white; 4-inch spires
**Deciduous to almost evergreen, with leaves
turning red to purple in fall**
Range Swamps in East Texas
New Jersey to Illinois to Florida to Texas
Soil Sand, loam, clay; acid; moist, poor
drainage okay
Dappled shade, part shade
Colonizes by rhizomes
Propagation Seed, cuttings

In its native habitat, Virginia sweetspire is usually seen growing on a bank beside titi, wax myrtle, black gum, and bald cypress, with perhaps a fragrant white water lily in the water at its feet. Its roots spread, forming thickets that provide great erosion control. It takes poor drainage or can grow on a slope, so it is very versatile for Houston, where it is quite popular with landscapers. The shape is natural and woodsy, not appropriate for a boxy hedge. Let it go soft and natural and just pick-prune if you need to keep it in bounds. The flowers are white spires that droop with the arching branches. They bloom in late spring when the big spring show is over and summer things haven't started. Fall is another reason to love itea— then it is a cheerful bright red! If you don't have it planted in a swamp, give it ample water through the summer.

196. Texas lantana
Lantana horrida
The authors

197. Creosote bush
Larrea tridentata
The authors

196. **Latin Name** *Lantana horrida*
Pronunciation lan-TAN-ah HOR-eh-dah
Common Names TEXAS LANTANA,
CALICO BUSH
Usual Height 1½–3 feet, can reach 6 feet
Spacing 2–3 feet apart
Bloom Spring to frost; orange and yellow;
1- to 2-inch heads
Deciduous
Range Rio Grande Plains, southern
Edwards Plateau
Texas to California to Mexico
Soil Sand, loam, clay, caliche; well drained
Part shade, full sun
Colonizes by self-layering
Propagation Fresh untreated seed,
softwood or semihardwood cuttings, root
cuttings, layering

Texas lantana blooms whenever the weather is hot. Each head is made up of several tiny flowers that start off yellow and turn to orange as they age. The leaves are smaller than those of *L. camara* (which is naturalized through the eastern part of the state), rougher, and slightly crinkly. When you touch them, they give off a sharp aroma that some people think is horrid (thus the name *horrida*), but I happen to love it. I recommend pruning Texas lantana back to the nub each winter to keep it within bounds, but wear gloves! The branches are so prickly that pruning can be an extremely unpleasant chore. Texas lantana is used far north of its native range, but there it dies to the roots in the winter. It's a staple of most Texas flower gardens because it is easy to keep low, has a long and profuse blooming season, and is a favorite hangout for butterflies. Texas lantana is also effective massed in medians or in large-scale landscapes.

197. **Latin Name** *Larrea tridentata*
Pronunciation LAHR-ee-uh
trye-den-TAH-tah
Common Name CREOSOTE BUSH
Usual Height 3–5 feet, can reach 10 feet
Spacing 4 feet apart
Bloom Spring and summer; yellow; ½ inch
across
Fruit Summer and fall; white; ½ inch
Evergreen
Range El Paso to Midland to Valley
Warm deserts of North America
Soil Sand, loam, caliche; well drained
Part shade, full sun
Taproot
Propagation Specially treated seed (process
by Dr. Jimmy L. Tipton)

Creosote bush is the most versatile shrub you can use in the Trans-Pecos. Totally drought-tolerant and without thorns, it can be sheared like boxwood, pick-pruned to a small graceful shrub, or even pruned to make a small tree. One of the pleasures of this shrub is its scent after a rain. The fragrance is light and refreshing. Because of work done by Dr. Jimmy L. Tipton at the Texas Agricultural Experiment Station in El Paso, creosote bush should soon be available in nurseries. Sometimes an established one can be rescued from a building site, but its enormously long taproot makes it difficult to transplant. You'll have more success digging up a small plant in shallow soil, so you can get the whole root. You'll increase your odds if you do it in the spring or fall. Nothing grows under a creosote bush, supposedly because of toxins that it gives off. On one hand, this limits some landscape possibilities, but on the other hand, you'll never have to weed beneath one. Incidentally, it's been said that the oldest living plant in the world is a creosote bush—in the Mojave Desert of California.

198. Violet silverleaf
Leucophyllum candidum
The authors

199. Cenizo
Leucophyllum frutescens
The authors

198. **Latin Name** *Leucophyllum candidum*
Pronunciation loo-koh-FILL-um
kan-DEE-dum
Common Names VIOLET SILVERLEAF,
CENIZO
Usual Height 2–3 feet
Spacing 2–3 feet apart
Bloom Fall (spring, summer); rich purple-
violet; 1 inch across
Evergreen
Range Southern Brewster County (Big
Bend and Black Gap)
Mexico
Soil Sand, loam, clay, caliche, limestone;
well drained
Full sun, a little shade okay
Propagation Cuttings, seed

Violet silverleaf is a naturally dwarfed cenizo with small, furry, silvery-colored leaves. It does best in full sun with perfect drainage and no extra fertilizer. In this situation it forms a soft, dense ball that needs no pruning. If heavy rains or some shade make your plant leggy, you can shear it in early spring prior to the start of new growth. Its big flowering comes in the fall, but blossoms also appear after spring and summer rains. Benny Simpson has released two selections that are obtainable at nurseries—'Silver Cloud' (royal purple flowers) and 'Thunder Cloud' (even more dwarfed and a heavy bloomer). Both can be used successfully in the Blacklands but will freeze back in severe winters. In Houston put it in a raised bed and give it supplemental calcium. A more cold-hardy dwarf cenizo is Big Bend silverleaf (*L. minus*), which can be found from Del Rio to the Guadalupe Mountains, El Paso, and New Mexico. The flowers are an indescribable silvery violet. The selection on the market is 'Rain Cloud,' a hybrid with *L. frutescens*. 'Rain Cloud' is an especially vigorous grower with larger leaves and about the same cold tolerance as 'Silver Cloud.'

199. **Latin Name** *Leucophyllum frutescens*
Pronunciation loo-koh-FILL-um
froo-TEH-senz
Common Names CENIZO, TEXAS SAGE,
PURPLE SAGE, TEXAS RANGER
Usual Height 4–5 feet, can reach 8 feet
Spacing 3–4 feet apart
Bloom Late summer (anytime); violet,
purple, pink, or white; 1 inch across
Evergreen
Range Rio Grande Plains, southern Trans-
Pecos, Edwards Plateau
Mexico
Soil Sand, loam, clay, caliche, limestone;
well drained
Full sun, a little shade okay
Propagation Cuttings, seed

This is the plant usually meant when people say "cenizo." It's also the largest and most widespread cenizo, with blossoms ranging from pure white through all shades of pink and lavender to violet. The leaves are usually silvery white, but one green plant was found by the son of Norman Maxwell, a grower in the Valley. From this one plant came two fast-growing selections: 'Green Cloud,' by Benny Simpson, and 'Green Leaf,' by Norman Maxwell. Another Norman Maxwell selection is 'Convent,' a compact variety with dark purple flowers and silver foliage. Still another compact cenizo, this one with all-white blossoms, is 'White Cloud,' by Benny Simpson. 'Compacta' (under five feet) may be the most widely sold of all cenizos. An unselected specimen from seed you gather yourself might grow to eight feet, especially in cultivation, and attain a silvery twisted trunk. One of these cenizos, loaded with pink flowers and the ground beneath similarly pink with fallen blossoms, is a gorgeous sight. In cold but not killing winters, the leaves will thin out but never entirely disappear. All cenizos are susceptible to cotton root rot.

200. White honeysuckle bush
Lonicera albiflora
The authors

200. **Latin Name** *Lonicera albiflora*
Pronunciation lon-ISS-er-ah
al-beh-FLOR-ah
Common Name WHITE HONEYSUCKLE BUSH
Usual Height 4 feet, can reach 10 feet
Spacing 4 feet apart
Bloom Spring; white; 2- to 3-inch clusters
Fruit Fall; translucent red; 2- to 3-inch
clusters
Almost evergreen
Range Edwards Plateau, Blacklands, Cross
Timbers, West Texas, Trans-Pecos
Oklahoma
Soil Sand, loam, clay, limestone; well
drained
Dappled shade, part shade, full sun
Propagation Softwood or semihardwood
cuttings in summer or fall, cleaned and
stratified seed, layering

In the wild, white honeysuckle bush is usually found clinging to the edges of cliffs or twining up into the branches of trees—botanical gymnastics designed to help it escape from hungry deer. Protect it from browsers, and it will quickly develop into a soft, open shrub. The white flowers are set off by the top leaves, which fuse to form a solid semicircle behind them. The fruits are very noticeable—orange-red, plump, and juicy—in large clusters framed by the same leafy setting, and they attract a number of migrating birds. White honeysuckle bush needs supplemental water in full sun to keep its leaves fresh and unscorched. In shade, under a tree, or against a north wall, white honeysuckle can be drought-tolerant in the eastern half of Texas, but it can really be grown everywhere in the state. Espalier it, shape it into a rounded shrub, or place it above a retaining wall. There let it grow au naturel, with the longer stems gracefully draping over the wall.

201. **Latin Name** *Malpighia glabra*
Pronunciation mal-PIG-ee-ah GLAY-brah
Common Names BARBADOS CHERRY,
MANZANITA
Usual Height 3–4 feet, can reach 9 feet
Spacing 1½–2½ feet apart
Bloom March to December; white to pale
pink; ½ inch across
Fruit May to December; red; ¾ inch
Evergreen above 25° F
Range Brush and palm groves of Valley and
Corpus Christi
South Texas to South America and West
Indies
Soil Sand, loam, clay; moist, well drained
Dappled shade, part shade, full sun
Propagation Fresh seed, softwood or
semihardwood cuttings

Barbados cherry is one of those highly agreeable evergreen shrubs that lets you use it in a wide array of styles. It takes shearing so well that you can use it for topiary or even make a hedge as low as three inches. Or you can allow it to become a large, soft accent shrub. There is a selection available for a dwarf that gets only two feet tall; it is ideal for use in a patio pot, as a flower in a perennial garden, or en masse as a ground cover. Fast-growing Barbados cherry covers itself with pink and white blossoms off and on during the whole warm season in its natural range but is usually most colorful in early fall when far-

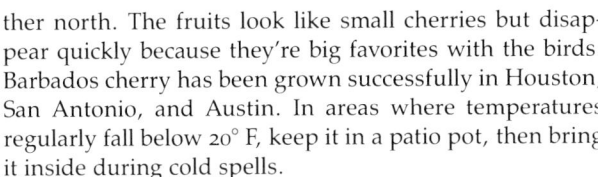

201. Barbados cherry
Malpighia glabra
The authors

202. Turk's cap
Malvaviscus arboreus var. *drummondii*
The authors

ther north. The fruits look like small cherries but disappear quickly because they're big favorites with the birds. Barbados cherry has been grown successfully in Houston, San Antonio, and Austin. In areas where temperatures regularly fall below 20° F, keep it in a patio pot, then bring it inside during cold spells.

202. **Latin Name** *Malvaviscus arboreus* var.
      drummondii
  Pronunciation mal-vah-VISS-kus
      ar-BOR-ee-us variety druh-MUN-dee-eye
  Common Names TURK'S CAP, BLEEDING
      HEART (West Texas only)
  Usual Height 2–3 feet, can reach 9 feet
  Spacing 3–5 feet apart
  Bloom May to November; red; 2–3 inches
      long
  Almost evergreen to dormant in winter
  Range Rio Grande Plains, southern
      Edwards Plateau
      Gulf Coast states from Florida to Mexico,
      Cuba
  Soil Sand, loam, clay, limestone; moist,
      well drained
  Shade, dappled shade, part shade, full sun
  Colonizes by self-layering
  Propagation Fresh untreated seed, soft-
      wood cuttings, root division

Turk's cap can be used all over the state. It's evergreen in the Valley but dies back to the ground in most other regions. Where this happens, don't expect it to get larger than four feet by four feet. It's drought-tolerant as far west as Midland but can also thrive in Houston's gumbo. Turk's cap is especially useful in shady situations, even those that are so dark you'd think that English ivy would be your only option. Here you can use it as an accent or a mass planting, which you can keep to one foot high if you cut it back. When Turk's cap grows in full sun, the branches often lie down like ground cover, but the leaves can get dark and crinkly in a way I find unappealing. Normally its leaves are large, slightly fuzzy, and more tropical than drought-tolerant in appearance. Flowers appear every day in warm weather—all year round in the Valley—and are important to hummingbirds and butterflies. The fruits are small, red cherries that either fall off or get eaten so quickly that they have little ornamental value.

203. Fragrant mimosa
Mimosa borealis
The authors

204. Wherry mimosa
Mimosa wherryana
The authors

203. **Latin Name** *Mimosa borealis*
Pronunciation mye-MOH-sah
 bore-ee-AH-lus
Common Name FRAGRANT MIMOSA
Usual Height 2–3 feet, can reach 6 feet
Spacing 2–3 feet apart
Bloom 7–10 days in April to July; pink;
 ½-inch puffs; fragrant
Deciduous
Range Edwards Plateau, Trans-Pecos, West
 Texas
 Oklahoma, New Mexico, Mexico
Soil Sand, loam, clay, caliche, limestone;
 well drained
Part shade, full sun
Propagation Scarified seed, semihardwood
 cuttings

What most Texans call mimosa isn't a mimosa at all. It's *Albizia julibrissin*, or silk tree, and comes from Persia and China. Fragrant mimosa and the other native mimosa described in this entry are intricately branched, thorny shrubs. Fragrant mimosa is the smaller and the more cold-hardy. It makes a fine accent, but use it only where its hook spines won't snag passersby. It's shown to best advantage when naturalized in a cluster with mesquites as a backdrop. Velvetpod mimosa (*M. dysocarpa*) is more robust, and so are its spines! It blooms in the summer, with two-inch fragrant spikes. In the Trans-Pecos mountains, it normally grows two feet tall, but expect it to be three to six feet tall in your garden. A variety from Arizona, *M. dysocarpa* var. *wrightii*, has longer spikes and is often used in West Texas plantings. These mimosas are useful for their extreme drought-tolerance and ability to take reflected heat. If not naturalized, they look best at the back of a flower bed or in a sparsely planted rock garden.

204. **Latin Name** *Mimosa wherryana*
Pronunciation mye-MOH-sah
 wer-ee-AN-ah
Common Name WHERRY MIMOSA
Usual Height 2–3 feet, can reach 7 feet
Spacing 4 feet apart
Bloom Spring or fall; creamy yellow; ½-inch
 globes; fragrant
Deciduous
Range Rio Grande Valley
 Mexico
Soil Sand, loam, clay, caliche; well drained
Part shade, full sun
Propagation Scarified seed, semihardwood
 cuttings

This little mimosa is gorgeous. It's also quite rare, even in the Valley, and it may not have enough cold tolerance to be usable anywhere else in Texas. Still, when something is as eye-catching and sweet-smelling as Wherry mimosa, you want to talk it up and hope that people will go to the extra trouble to find it and grow it. The one in the photo is two and a half feet tall and four feet wide. Its branching is intricate and dense, and every twig is loaded with blooms or buds. The fragrance is intense, even from several feet away. Its foliage is feathery, and the tiny curved thorns are not as vicious as those on our other mimosas; the one time I tried, I was able to reach in and gather seed without getting stuck. Wherry mimosa grows well with cenizo, kidneywood, paloverde, coyotillo, and desert yaupon.

205. Dwarf wax myrtle
Myrica pusilla
The authors

206. Sacahuista
Nolina texana
The authors

205. **Latin Name** *Myrica pusilla (M. cerifera)*
Pronunciation MYE-reh-kah poo-SILL-ah
Common Names DWARF WAX MYRTLE,
THICKET WAX MYRTLE
Usual Height 2–6 feet
Spacing 1½–2 feet apart
Fruit Winter, on females; pale blue;
⅛-inch berries
Evergreen
Range Moist or dry East Texas pinewoods
and hardwoods
Delaware to Arkansas to Texas to Florida
Soil Sand, loam, clay; poor drainage okay
Dappled shade, part shade, full sun
**Colonizes by stolons and underground
runners**
Propagation Stratified seed, softwood or
semihardwood cuttings

When a landscape calls for a softly shaped, low-growing evergreen shrub, dwarf wax myrtle is one of our most universally acceptable options. It's winter-hardy throughout the state, although it does need supplemental watering outside its natural range. It is strongly thicket-forming and will be hard to control unless you have curbing or can mow the edges. This is an excellent shrub massed in a bed in front of a house or used as a large-scale ground cover for a big public building or on a slope over a parking lot. Maintain the height you want with a line trimmer, or let the shrub develop into an airy, aromatic hedge. The color is light olive-green, but in winter the profuse berries on the females give it a bluish look.

206. **Latin Name** *Nolina texana*
Pronunciation noh-LEE-nah tex-AN-ah
Common Names SACAHUISTA, BASKET
GRASS, NOLINA
Usual Height 1½–2½ feet
Spacing 3–4 feet apart
Bloom May or June (rarely earlier or later);
white; 8- to 16-inch head
Evergreen
Range Trans-Pecos, Rio Grande Plains,
Edwards Plateau
New Mexico, Arizona, Mexico
Soil Sand, loam, clay, caliche, limestone;
well drained
Dappled shade, part shade, full sun
Propagation Seed sown in cool weather,
root division

Sacahuista is the most winter-hardy nolina and the one most commonly grown and cultivated. It is used mainly for its grasslike evergreen foliage, which blends well with flowers and shortgrasses on dry slopes, or fills in shady areas under spreading live oaks. The long, thin leaves trail out on the ground, turning olive-green on the tips in hot, dry summers. The blades are sharp-edged and sparingly toothed—after all, sacahuista is close kin to yuccas and sotols. The flowers are large panicles of creamy blooms hidden inside the foliage. Our other nolinas hold their flowers higher above the leaves, giving the blooms more landscape significance. The prettiest-flowered of them is bear grass (*N. erumpens*). Its flowers are held four to eight feet off the ground in a large rosy cluster. However, this nolina can get too big and aggressive for most sites. Devil's shoestring (*N. lindheimeriana*) has narrow leaves and a narrow spike of flowers and is endemic to the Edwards Plateau. *Nolina micrantha* has pur-

207. Cholla
Opuntia imbricata
The authors

208. Prickly pear
Opuntia phaeacantha
Edith Bettinger

ple tinges on both leaves and flowers, and *N. microcarpa,* I've been told, is the most grasslike and has the softest leaves. Don't plant any nolinas where livestock can graze on them; they're toxic, especially to sheep. Where a nolina is indicated on a plan in this book, any one of these can be used, except *N. erumpens.*

207.   **Latin Name**   *Opuntia imbricata*
   Pronunciation   oh-PUN-shah
       im-breh-KAH-tah
   Common Names   CHOLLA, WALKING-STICK
       CHOLLA
   Usual Height   3 feet, can reach 9 feet
   Spacing   3–4 feet apart
   Bloom   May or June; hot pink; 2–3 inches
       across
   Fruit   Fall; bright yellow; 2 inches
   Evergreen
   Range   Trans-Pecos, High Plains
       Kansas to Colorado to Mexico
   Soil   Sand, caliche, limestone; well drained
   Part shade, full sun
   Propagation   L-shaped cuttings in spring or
       summer

Our two best cacti for landscape purposes are prickly pear and cholla. This particular cholla is the one that most people around the state will be best able to use. Just keep it well drained and give it plenty of elbow-room. It will be a slow grower, but eventually it can become tree-size, with a woody trunk. The blooms appear in early summer, assuming there was rain in May, and when the entire shrub is covered with blooms, the sight is . . . well, gaudy! The fruits start ripening in the fall, going from green to rose and finally ending up in a luminescent yellow. Don't expect to find cholla in your nursery. It's far too prickly for anyone to want to handle. It's easy to root a piece of cholla; just be sure it doesn't get too moist, or it will rot. Take an L-shaped cutting and let it callus. Put one side in the ground, and pat down the soil around it; leave the other side above ground.

208. **Latin Name** *Opuntia* spp.
Pronunciation oh-PUN-shah species
Common Name PRICKLY PEAR
Usual Height 1–2 feet, can reach 6 feet
Spacing 2–4 feet apart
Bloom Spring; yellow to red; 3–4 inches
across
Fruit Fall; red to purple; 2–3 inches
Evergreen
Range Throughout Texas
Southern North America
Soil Sand, loam, clay, caliche; well drained
Propagation Calloused pad rooted in sand,
seed

Prickly pear stems are large, pear-shaped, flattened pads—much different from the cylinders on the cholla. The predominant prickly pear in the southern part of the state is Texas prickly pear (*O. lindheimeri*). Its pads are up to a foot long and profusely covered with two-inch spines. The yellow flowers are sometimes marked with orange or red at the base of the petals. The fruits are juicy and either bright red or rosy purple. One variety of Texas prickly pear is called cow-tongue; it has long, narrow, tongue-shaped pads. Native only near San Antonio, it is widely cultivated. The most abundant prickly pear in the Trans-Pecos and northern Texas is *O. phaeacantha,* which is native as far north as Utah. Its flowers and fruits are as large as Texas prickly pear's, but the plant itself, along with its pads and spines, is half the size. Purple prickly pear (*O. violacea*) is my favorite. Its pads really are lavender-purple, especially in the winter months. Native from Big Bend to Arizona, it froze even there in the terrible winter of '83. These are only a few of the prickly pears native to Texas.

209. Pavonia
Pavonia lasiopetala
The authors

209. **Latin Name** *Pavonia lasiopetala*
Pronunciation pah-VOH-nee-ah
lass-ee-oh-PET-ah-lah
Common Names PAVONIA, ROCKROSE
Usual Height 2–3 feet, can reach 5 feet
Spacing 2–3 feet apart
Bloom Late spring to frost; pink; 2 inches
across
Almost evergreen
Range Edwards Plateau, Rio Grande Plains,
Trans-Pecos
Mexico
Soil Sand, loam, clay, caliche; well drained
Dappled shade, part shade, full sun
Propagation Fresh seed, scarified seed,
softwood tip cuttings

Pavonia is classified as a shrub, because it is woody-stemmed at the base, it branches like a shrub, and it doesn't die back to the roots except in very cold winters north of its natural range. On the other hand, it can be used only as a flower, not a shrub, because it only lives three or four years. It reproduces freely by seed, and you should let a few seedlings survive each year so they'll be ready to replace the mother plant. The leaves are velvety and scalloped and remain on the plant in a mild winter, although they can get rather scattered and scarce. The flowers are obviously related to the hibiscus family; they're clear pink and numerous and open every morning and close every afternoon. I've found that giving the plant shade in the afternoon keeps the flowers open longer, sometimes until dusk. If your pavonia becomes leggy, you can prune it back anytime from February to October. Pavonia can be grown as an annual all over the state and will prove at least root-hardy south of the Red River, although it will need south wall protection and a blanket of mulch.

210. Texas mock orange
Philadelphus texensis
The authors

211. Havard oak
Quercus havardii
Benny J. Simpson

210. **Latin Name**   *Philadelphus texensis*
Pronunciation   fill-ah-DELL-fus tex-EN-siss
Common Name   TEXAS MOCK ORANGE
Usual Height   3 feet
Spacing   2–3 feet apart
Bloom   Spring; white; 1–3 inches across; fragrant
Deciduous
Range   Limestone bluffs of Edwards Plateau
Endemic to Texas
Soil   Sand, loam, clay, limestone; well drained
Dappled shade, part shade, full sun
Propagation   Fresh, untreated, or stratified seed; semihardwood cuttings

Texas mock orange can be completely covered with little blossoms, or it can have fewer but much larger flowers. Either way, when it's in full bloom, this little shrub is a delight. The flowers are silky white and fragrant, and the tiny leaves are dark green and glossy. Prune only after flowering, as the blossoms appear on wood that has grown the previous summer. Texas mock orange has proved adaptable to black clays and is winter-hardy as far north as Dallas. It needs a lot of water to get established and should be placed so it will get shade from the west sun if the soil is dry and rocky. You also need to know that deer love Texas mock orange.

211. **Latin Name**   *Quercus havardii*
Pronunciation   KWER-kus hah-VAR-dee-eye
Common Names   HAVARD OAK, SHINNERY OAK, HAVARD SHIN OAK
Usual Height   2–3 feet
Spacing   2–3 feet apart
Deciduous
Range   High Plains, West Texas
Western Oklahoma, eastern New Mexico
Soil   Deep sand; well drained
Part shade, full sun
Colonizes by rhizomes
Propagation   Acorns fresh off tree

The Havard oak forest stretches from Odessa to New Mexico in what could be the most extensive continuous forest in the world. But since these oaks reach only waist-high, it's difficult to think of them as a forest. Don't expect Havard oak to start suckering right away. It doesn't get established easily, and it may be four years before it takes off. But then, when it does start, it may not have just one sucker—it might have ten! Havard oak makes a coarse-textured thicket in the deep sands of the southern Panhandle. The leaves are a leathery muted green above and furry on the underside, with a silvery fuzz. The acorns produced each year are unexpectedly large for such a little plant. Our other shrub-size oak is the evergreen Hinckley oak (*Q. hinckleyi*), which is even smaller. Everything about it is miniature; the acorns are a quarter inch long, and the leaves are a half inch long. It is very slow-growing, with reddish new leaves. Hinckley oak is so rare that it has been put on the endangered list, which means you mustn't gather its acorns in the wild. However, we can hope that some of the specimens now growing in gardens will produce viable acorns so that this plant can be propagated for landscape use.

212. Piedmont azalea
Rhododendron canescens
Benny J. Simpson

213. Aromatic sumac
Rhus aromatica
The authors

212. **Latin Name** *Rhododendron canescens*
Pronunciation roh-doh-DEN-drun
kan-ESS-enz
Common Name PIEDMONT AZALEA
Usual Height 8 feet
Spacing 8 feet apart
Bloom Early spring; pink; 1–2 inches long;
fragrant
Deciduous
Range Edges of bogs and seeps in East
Texas
Delaware to Ohio to Gulf of Mexico
Soil Sand, loam; acid; moist, well drained
Dappled shade, part shade
Propagation Seed, softwood cuttings in
spring, root division in spring, layering

Our native azaleas (some say we have three, some say four) are for especially moist places in the acid sands of the eastern part of Texas and won't do well anywhere else in our state. Piedmont azalea is the easiest to grow, and it's no cinch! It must be evenly moist and well drained all year. Because our summers are so hot, it has to stay in the shade, where it forms a large yet airy and graceful display. Its pale pink blossoms appear just before the new leaves or with them. It has a wild, woodsy beauty, quite unlike the Asian azaleas. It can be used either singly or massed, at the sandy edge of a water garden, but it doesn't qualify as a water plant because it needs that good drainage. Cory azalea (*R. coryi*—possibly a variety of *R. oblongifolium*) is one to three feet tall and strongly rhizomatous; it's perfect to place in front of piedmont azalea. Its white blooms appear after it has leafed out in the spring, sometimes even as late as July.

213. **Latin Name** *Rhus aromatica*
Pronunciation ROOS air-oh-MAT-eh-kah
Common Names AROMATIC SUMAC,
THREE-LEAVED SUMAC, SKUNKBUSH
Usual Height 3 feet, can reach 8 feet
Spacing 2–3 feet apart for thicket, 6 feet
apart for specimen
Bloom Before leaves; yellow; 2- to 3-inch
spikes
Fruit Late spring; red
**Deciduous, with leaves turning orange, red,
and sometimes yellow in fall**
Range Throughout Texas
Canada to Florida to Texas to Nebraska
Soil Sand, loam, clay, caliche, limestone;
well drained
Part shade, full sun
Colonizes to form thickets
Propagation Scarified and stratified seed,
semihardwood cuttings

Aromatic sumac releases a spicy fragrance when the leaves or branches are bruised. In East Texas the shrubs are always found in thickets. In West Texas, single plants are often found, although long thickets sometimes grow on sandy ridges. Here aromatic sumac is called *Rhus trilobata*. Downy aromatic sumac also grows in West Texas and on the High Plains, but I've seen no evidence that it forms thickets. It is named *R. trilobata* var. *pilosissima*, meaning "very hairy"—a good description. Not only are the leaves fuzzy, but the red berries are too. All three aromatic sumacs often take root at the base of a larger plant, but they achieve their best shape and fall color in full sun. In masses they can be pruned or cut with a brush scythe for even texture and uniform height. Or they can be left au naturel to form soft, fairly dense mounds. The fruits are among the earliest to ripen each year, making aromatic sumac popular with wildlife.

214. Smooth sumac
Rhus glabra
The authors

215. Littleleaf sumac
Rhus microphylla
The authors

214. **Latin Name**   *Rhus glabra*
Pronunciation   ROOS GLAY-brah
Common Name   SMOOTH SUMAC
Usual Height   3–10 feet
Spacing   3 feet apart
Bloom   Late spring or early summer; white; 4- to 6-inch pyramids
Fruit   Fall; red; 4- to 6-inch pyramids
Deciduous, with leaves turning red in fall
Range   East Texas to Bryan, Blacklands, Rolling Plains
Eastern two thirds of North America
Soil   Sand, loam, clay, caliche; well drained
Part shade, full sun
Colonizes by rhizomes
Propagation   Scarified and stratified seed, root division

Smooth sumac is best used for erosion control or in natural landscapes where fall color and wildlife value are desired. Its leaves are among the first to turn in the fall, remain red for several weeks, and are spectacular every year. According to Robert Vines, the fruit is eaten by cottontails, white-tailed deer, and 32 species of birds. All sumacs are fast-growers, but this is the speediest of them all. It is guaranteed to sucker after the first winter, if not after the first month. Although it prefers sand, it does well in any soil and can be grown anywhere in Texas. It requires supplemental water outside its range and during especially hot summers to keep it from looking ratty. Use it on sunny or half-shaded rocky slopes, in medians, or on the edge of woods. It will grow under the trees about ten feet in, but no more—it needs plenty of sun. To keep smooth sumac from spreading where you don't want it to go, mow it several times a year. One mowing, or even a burning, just thickens it up—a useful piece of information if you want a thicker thicket.

215. **Latin Name**   *Rhus microphylla*
Pronunciation   ROOS mye-KRAH-feh-lah
Common Names   LITTLELEAF SUMAC, DESERT SUMAC
Usual Height   4–8 feet, can reach 12–15 feet
Spacing   8–20 feet apart
Bloom   Spring; white; 2- to 4-inch clusters
Fruit   Summer and fall; orange; 2- to 4-inch clusters
Deciduous, with leaves turning muted rose to purple in fall
Range   Western three fourths of Texas
Arizona, New Mexico, Mexico
Soil   Sand, loam, clay, caliche, limestone; well drained
Part shade, full sun
Propagation   Scarified and stratified seed, cuttings

If you think the recommended spacing above is a typo, it isn't. I've been told that one littleleaf sumac can get forty feet wide. Of course, that takes a long time. I've seen many ten-year-olds that are eight feet wide. But don't worry—this shrub takes well to pruning. You can even shape it into a small tree. The fruits are bright orange and fuzzy and remain on the plant a long time; they're eaten by ground squirrels, chipmunks, and birds, but being on the sour side, they aren't a big favorite with the wildlife. It's called desert sumac because it's extremely drought-tolerant. It's called littleleaf sumac because the leaves are less than two inches long; in that space are five to nine leaflets, with tiny wings along the leaf stem (as with prairie flameleaf sumac).

216. Leafy rose
Rosa foliolosa
Edith Bettinger

216. Arkansas rose
Rosa arkansana var. *arkansana*
The authors

216. **Latin Name** *Rosa* spp.
Pronunciation ROH-zah species
Common Names CAROLINA ROSE, LEAFY ROSE, SUNSHINE ROSE, ARKANSAS ROSE, WOODS ROSE
Usual Height 1½–3 feet, can reach 6 feet
Spacing 3 feet apart
Bloom Late spring to July; white to pink; 1–2 inches across; fragrant
Fruit Fall; red; ¼- to ½-inch hips
Deciduous
Range East Texas to Trans-Pecos North America
Soil Sand, loam, clay, limestone; well drained
Dappled shade, part shade, full sun
Colonizes
Propagation Stratified seed, softwood or hardwood cuttings

Our native roses are remarkably hardy; they're disease- and insect-resistant and drought-tolerant and are even able to bloom in shade. However, they also form thickets, especially in sun, so they won't fit into a formal rose garden, where each specimen is allotted three feet and no more. Use them for erosion control, as woodsy understory, and in fencerows. In a pot these roses are likely to look scraggly and show dying shoots. Set them free in the ground, and they will take off. The heaviest blooming takes place in midspring, but they will flower sporadically into the summer.

Carolina rose (*R. carolina*) takes the most humidity, even growing in the Big Thicket without suffering from black spot. Its spicy scent is so intense, you can smell it forty feet away. This rose is only slightly prickly.

Leafy rose (*R. foliolosa*) is one to two feet tall and hardly has spines at all. The flowers are pure white, sometimes tinged with pink, and the leaves are dark green and glossy. It's native to North Central Texas.

Sunshine rose (*R. arkansana* var. *suffulta*), also native to North Central Texas, has one-inch pink flowers and very bristly stems. It blooms more heavily in the summer than the other roses and grows to one to two feet tall.

Arkansas rose (*R. arkansana* var. *arkansana*) displays its pink roses in large clusters but otherwise resembles sunshine rose. I've seen Arkansas rose form an exquisite ground cover under a small grove of trees, where it was less than eighteen inches high, fairly dense, and covered with flowers. You'll find it in the Panhandle.

Woods rose (*R. woodsii*) was named for Joseph Woods (an Englishman who studied roses), not for where you find it. It grows in the Trans-Pecos and is usually three feet tall there, but in rich soil and full sun it will reach six feet, forming a dense, thorny thicket.

See Chapter 10 for a description of the well-behaved climbing prairie rose (*R. setigera*).

217. Palmetto
Sabal minor
The authors

**218. Gregg salvia in red and white
with blue *Salvia lycioides***
Salvia greggii
Richard Kirkham

217. **Latin Name**   *Sabal minor*
Pronunciation   SAY-bahl MYE-ner
Common Names   PALMETTO, DWARF
PALMETTO
Usual Height   3–5 feet, can reach 20 feet
Spacing   4–6 feet apart
Bloom   May and June; white; 1- to 6-foot
clusters
Fruit   Fall; black; 1- to 6-foot drooping
clusters
Evergreen
Range   East Texas along coast to Corpus
Christi, inland to Edwards Plateau
North Carolina to Gulf states
Soil   Sand, loam, clay; poor drainage okay
Shade, dappled shade, part shade, full sun
Propagation   Stratified seed sown in mud

Have a moist, shady spot in your yard? Palmetto would make a dramatic accent there. Its huge palmlike leaves lend a tropical look to a garden, evoking images of pink stucco, balconies, exuberant flowers, and leisure time. It also makes an exotic evergreen ground cover beneath bald cypress or underneath coastal live oaks draped with Spanish moss. If you want a path to wind through your palmettos, keep it comfortably wide, as the edges of palmetto leaves are sharp. Palmetto needs plenty of water to get established, but after that it is fairly drought-tolerant. However, I'd water it in the summer anyway to prevent the lower leaves from dying back. Where it grows in standing water, it forms trunks, often ten feet tall. When a palmetto looks like this, it is often classified as *S. louisiana*, but many botanists argue that such a tree is a product of environment, not genes.

218. **Latin Name**   *Salvia greggii*
Pronunciation   SAL-vee-ah GREG-ee-eye
Common Names   GREGG SALVIA,
AUTUMN SAGE, CHERRY SAGE
Usual Height   2–3 feet
Spacing   2–3 feet apart
Bloom   Spring to frost; red, pink, white, or
coral; 1 inch long
Almost evergreen
Range   Edwards Plateau, Trans-Pecos, Rio
Grande Plains
Mexico
Soil   Sand, loam, clay, caliche, limestone;
well drained
Part shade, full sun
Propagation   Softwood or semihardwood
cuttings, fresh seed sown in spring, root
layering

"Salvia" is the true name for sage. The leaves of most salvias are aromatic, and this one smells good even if you just brush against it. Although it is called autumn sage, Gregg salvia blooms as prolifically in the spring and summer as it does in the fall. If you keep snipping off the tips, it will bloom constantly from spring to frost. It has become one of our most widely used natives, being adaptable everywhere in the state except in Wichita Falls and the High Plains, where it isn't winter-hardy. But it can be enjoyed even there if grown in patio pots. It can be used as a flower in the perennial bed, as a sunny ground cover, or as a hedge, either natural or shaped. To keep it low-growing and dense and to encourage lots of blooms, cut it in half (or even to four inches) in early spring. Most gardeners don't recommend doing this every year, however. The only thing Gregg salvia is fussy about is getting

219. Mountain sage
Salvia regla
The authors

220. Desert yaupon
Schaefferia cuneifolia
The authors

good drainage. If you have clay soil, plant it only on a berm or slope or in a raised bed, and work coarse sand and gravel into the soil.

219. **Latin Name** *Salvia regla*
Pronunciation SAL-vee-ah REG-lah
Common Name MOUNTAIN SAGE
Usual Height 3–5 feet, can reach 8 feet
Spacing 2–3 feet apart
Bloom Fall; red to orange; 1 inch long
Deciduous
Range Chisos Mountains in Trans-Pecos Mexico
Soil Sand, loam, clay; slightly acid to slightly alkaline; well drained
Dappled shade, part shade
Propagation Softwood or semihardwood cuttings, fresh seed sown in spring

Mountain sage cleverly coordinates its blooms to the fall migration of several species of hummingbirds. Then, for nearly two months its glossy, aromatic, heart-shaped leaves are completely covered with masses of flame-red flowers. In fact, you'll still see blooms on this plant right up until frost. 'Mount Emory,' a selection made by Benny Simpson, is winter-hardy down to 10° F and is root-hardy down to 0°. It is extremely drought-tolerant after being established, if you give it protection from the hot west sun. Lone Star Growers is marketing a mountain sage propagated from an even shinier-leaved specimen found in Mexico. It is beautiful, but in Dallas it can't survive even an extremely mild winter. So if you live north of the Rio Grande Plains, be sure the mountain sage you buy is 'Mount Emory.'

220. **Latin Name** *Schaefferia cuneifolia*
Pronunciation shah-FEER-ee-ah kun-ee-eh-FOLE-ee-ah
Common Name DESERT YAUPON
Usual Height 3–4 feet, can reach 6 feet
Spacing 2–3 feet apart, 5–6 feet for specimen
Fruit Late summer to fall, on females; red to orange; ¼ inch
Evergreen
Range Corpus Christi and Valley to southern Trans-Pecos Mexico
Soil Sand, loam, clay, caliche, limestone; well drained
Part shade, full sun
Propagation Fresh seed, root cuttings

The tiny heavy leaves and translucent orange-red berries on the desert yaupon grow close to the stems, just like its unrelated namesake, yaupon holly. Also, like the holly, its luscious-looking fruits are not a big favorite with birds, so they'll last several months. They start ripening in August (I've seen some as early as June) and can still be colorful in the Valley at Thanksgiving. Desert yaupon differs from the yaupon holly in that it is far more drought-tolerant. However, unless it gets rain (or watering), it can't bloom. The flowers are teensy and yellow and usually appear in the May–June rains. If you don't live near a population of desert yaupons, you'll need to buy a male to fertilize the females so they can set fruit. Desert yaupon is often used as a hedge—three to six feet tall. For an accent, let it grow naturally. The stiff branches are slightly spinescent and will arrange themselves in an open, airy fashion.

221. Yellow sophora
Sophora tomentosa
Dr. Robert Lonard

222. Yellow bells
Tecoma stans var. *angustata*
The authors

221. **Latin Name** *Sophora tomentosa*
Pronunciation SOFF-er-ah or soh-FOR-ah toh-men-TOH-sah
Common Names YELLOW SOPHORA, NECKLACE POD, TAMBALISA
Usual Height 3 feet, can reach 5 feet
Spacing 3–4 feet apart
Bloom April to November; yellow; 4- to 16-inch spikes
Evergreen
Range Beaches from Valley to Port Aransas Warm coastal areas of world
Soil Sand, loam; well drained; saline okay
Part shade, full sun
Propagation Scarified seed

Yellow sophora is kin to the purple-flowered Texas mountain laurel (or mescal bean) and to the pink-flowered Eve's Necklace, but it's much shorter and grows only along the coast. There it's at its limit of cold-hardiness in Texas and might freeze down to its roots even in the Valley. Use it as a long-blooming accent in a flower bed with south wall protection. It has a delicate multistemmed shape and chartreuse branches. The leaves (shaped like those of the other sophoras, but with more leaflets) are silvery green and feel like velvet when young, then get leathery with age. The "necklaces"—tawny seedpods— are also velvety and often remain hanging on the shrub for a year or more. Inside are poisonous seeds, fortunately covered by a very hard protective coat. The bright yellow flowers continue to bloom for a long time, with new blossoms appearing on the end of each spike as fresh seedpods form at its base.

222. **Latin Name** *Tecoma stans* var. *angustata*
Pronunciation teh-KOH-mah STANZ variety an-gus-TAH-tuh
Common Names YELLOW BELLS, ESPERANZA
Usual Height 3–6 feet
Spacing 3–4 feet apart
Bloom April to November; yellow; 3- to 5-inch bells
Deciduous
Range Trans-Pecos mountains Florida to Arizona to South America
Soil Sand, loam, limestone; well drained
Part shade, full sun
Propagation Fresh seed sown in sand, semihardwood cuttings

You'll often find yellow bells used in a flower or rock garden or as an accent around a patio. It can be grown as a pot plant, as long as the container is at least twelve inches in diameter. In a large-scale landscape it looks stunning massed in front of larger shrubs. The bright yellow bells are clustered to make a vivid display that appears off and on throughout the blooming season. It would be used more, but it isn't very winter-hardy. In fact, it often freezes down to the ground, even in its natural range in the Franklin Mountains near El Paso. There are various ways to protect it. One is to withhold water after the summer heat abates; that way it won't develop any new growth as winter approaches. Of course, if it rains . . . Another way is to mulch the crown of roots with rocks or some other protection. A gardener in the Trans-Pecos region told me he just cuts it to the ground each winter and doesn't worry about it, as it looks and blooms better the next year when it has all new growth anyway. Down in the Valley you can see a tree-size plant that looks a lot like yellow bells. It is *T. stans* var. *stans*, which is native to the tropics.

223. Mapleleaf viburnum
Viburnum acerifolium
The authors

224. Skeleton-leaf goldeneye
Viguiera stenoloba
The authors

223. **Latin Name** *Viburnum acerifolium*
Pronunciation vye-BER-num
ah-ser-eh-FOLE-ee-um
Common Name MAPLELEAF VIBURNUM
Usual Height 4–5 feet, can reach 8 feet
Spacing 3–4 feet apart
Bloom Late spring; white; 3- to 4-inch
clusters
**Deciduous, with leaves turning apricot, red,
and purple in the fall**
Range East Texas
Eastern Canada to Gulf of Mexico
Soil Sand, loam, clay; acid; well drained
Shade, dappled shade, part shade
Colonizes a little by stolons
Propagation Fresh seed sown in fall,
semihardwood cuttings

Mapleleaf viburnum is a favorite with people in Houston and East Texas who specialize in woodland landscapes. It's drought-tolerant in East Texas but doesn't object to supplemental water as long as it is in sand or loam. It doesn't care for slow-draining gumbo. Clustered in a shady corner or at the edge of woods, it provides snowy blooms during the late spring lull when, normally, Virginia sweetspire is the only other color around. In late summer the blue fruits of mapleleaf viburnum ripen and are eaten by several species of birds. In the fall its autumn shades are nothing less than magnificent. The colors will be brighter and the shrub will be larger if it is given good morning sun—but it cannot endure full sun.

224. **Latin Name** *Viguiera stenoloba*
Pronunciation veh-GWARE-ah
sten-oh-LOH-bah
Common Names SKELETON-LEAF
GOLDENEYE, RESINBUSH
Usual Height 1½–2 feet, can reach 4 feet
Spacing 2 feet apart
Bloom Spring to frost; yellow; 1- to 2-inch
daisies
Evergreen to deciduous
Range Valley to Edwards Plateau to Trans-
Pecos
New Mexico, Mexico
Soil Sand, loam, clay, caliche, limestone;
well drained
Part shade, full sun
Propagation Softwood tip cuttings, fresh
seed

Skeleton-leaf goldeneye is used most effectively as a flower in the perennial garden. It makes a mound of deep-yellow daisies that stays in flower for months. Cutting off old blooms will give it a neater appearance and promote the growth of fresh ones. If it gets too tall for your taste, you can cut it in half once a year to promote new, dense growth and more flowers. It is extremely drought-tolerant and grows well on limestone slopes. Skeleton-leaf goldeneye has proven to be winter-hardy in San Antonio, Austin, and Midland and might be in Dallas as well, if it is brought in from its northernmost range. Good drainage is essential, as the roots are more likely to freeze and burst when they and the surrounding soil are moist. I've been told that it can be used in Houston's humidity and gumbo in a raised bed with good drainage where its gets reflected heat. The leaves are the easiest way to tell this plant from other yellow daisy bushes such as damianita and zexmenia. Skeleton-leaf goldeneye has a narrow groove running down the center of each slender leaflet.

225. Zexmenia
Wedelia hispida
The authors

226. Narrowleaf yucca
Yucca angustifolia
The authors

225.   **Latin Name**   *Wedelia hispida* (*Zexmenia hispida*)
Pronunciation   weh-DEEL-ee-ah HISS-peh-dah
Common Name   ZEXMENIA
Usual Height   1½–2 feet, can reach 3 feet
Spacing   2 feet apart
Bloom   May to November; orangy yellow; 1-inch daisies
Evergreen to dormant in winter
Range   Edwards Plateau, Trans-Pecos, Corpus Christi, Valley Mexico
Soil   Sand, loam, clay, caliche, limestone; well drained
Dappled shade, part shade, full sun
Propagation   Fresh seed, semihardwood cuttings

Zexmenia is classified as a shrub by some botanists and as a perennial by others. I can see both points of view. In its southern range, it is woody-stemmed and evergreen. Farther north it not only loses its leaves but dies to the ground. It's extremely long-lived and well behaved (never aggressive)—in other words, a high-quality plant for the flower garden or a mass planting. It makes a rounded mound of yellow daisies in full sun, where it is fully drought-tolerant. In dappled shade it reclines like a ground cover, blooming steadily, although never brilliantly. I love it mixed with cedar sage under junipers in the Hill Country. Its leaves are slightly sticky, as are those of two of its ground cover kin—horseherb and *Wedelia trilobata*, a sunny Mexican native that is used in the Valley and Corpus Christi.

226.   **Latin Name**   *Yucca* spp.
Pronunciation   YUK-ah species
Common Names   YUCCA, SPANISH DAGGER
Usual Height   Leaves 1–2 feet, flower stalks 2–6 feet
Spacing   2–4 feet apart
Bloom   Summer; white; 2–3 inches on large spikes
Evergreen
Range   Throughout Texas
Only *Y. angustifolia* (*Y. glauca* var. *glauca*) native north of Texas
Soil   Sand, loam, clay, caliche; well drained
Dappled shade, part shade, full sun
Propagation   Fresh seed sown in spring, root or stem cuttings

Yuccas look at home with lush, tropical flowers, in grasslands vibrant with wildflowers, and in desert rock gardens too. I love their white waxy flowers at night, when they release their fragrance to attract the white moths that pollinate them.

Texas yuccas come in an abundance of sizes and shapes. We have twenty in all. The smallest, Arkansas

226. Twisted-leaf yucca
Yucca rupicola
The authors

base again. Most of our yuccas are the sizes listed above. With age they start to clump, sending up several bloom stalks. They have such massive, heavy roots that transplanting old ones often ends in failure. I've heard that nurseries can grow the equivalent of a 150-year-old yucca in only 5 to 7 years, thereby providing good landscape material and also saving our native stands.

Narrowleaf yucca (*Y. angustifolia*) is frequently seen in the Panhandle. It is our most winter-hardy, being native clear to South Dakota. It seems to adapt well as far east as Dallas, as long as it is given sun and good drainage. Its leaves usually stand two to three feet high.

Soaptree (*Y. elata*) is the one that can reach thirty feet. Its leaves are generally three feet high, and it typically forms clumps eight feet wide. With age it develops a trunk, which gives it height. You can't dig up this yucca because it has a taproot eighty miles long.

Paleleaf yucca (*Y. pallida*) is endemic to the Blackland Prairies and adjacent limestone slopes. The leaves are a pale blue-green and only a foot tall. This is one of our smaller yuccas.

Twisted-leaf yucca (*Y. rupicola*) is endemic to the Edwards Plateau. The leaves are under two feet tall and are edged with white or red and covered with thin white curly hairs. New leaves are straight, but older leaves are twisted, giving this yucca its name.

Thompson yucca (*Y. thompsoniana*), native to the mountains of the Trans-Pecos, will slowly grow to a height of seven feet. A grouping of Thompson yuccas makes a good evergreen screen for West Texas.

These are just a few of our yuccas. All have landscape potential. Some even have a pink or purple blush to the flowers.

yucca (*Y. arkansana*), is described with the perennials in Chapter 5. The largest, soaptree (*Y. elata*), develops a big strong trunk and can reach thirty feet, so I could have put it in with the trees, except it takes a century or so to achieve this height. Most yuccas try to make at least a small trunk. If you don't want the height or don't like the look, cut it off at ground level and it will leaf out at the

Shrub Garden Plan
Lot Size: 40' × 60'

Based on my definition of shrubs, given at the beginning of this chapter, it's clear that Texas has an abundant variety of them.

I'm a big advocate of the natural look, that is, allowing plants to grow the way nature intended, with a minimum of help from us. But when I began working out a plan that would best show off these shrubs, I found myself veering toward a garden style I don't usually espouse—a formal, very structured, geometric affair.

Whether or not a garden is formal depends more on the layout than the plants themselves or how they're trimmed. Often the left side exactly balances the right, as at Hampton Court in England, for example. To some people, "formal" means that the shrubs must be clipped and manicured and sculpted to a fare-thee-well, but in fact I've seen formal gardens where the shrubs were left graceful and arching. I've also seen gardens that weren't formal at all, yet still inserted topiary here and there. (Talk about a split personality!)

In this plan I use both sculpted and natural shrubs. Hedges are shown in varying heights, from one that forms a tall garden wall to a parterre—a tiny hedge trimmed in geometric patterns that surround flower beds, which themselves can be trimmed and manicured or left au naturel. The plan also uses topiary—hedges that are sculpted into spheres, spirals, bunny rabbits, elephants, you name it. And there is also a large shrub pruned as a tree and lots of small shrubs used as flowers. Whatever else you can say about it, this landscape is not boring.

When I did this plan, I decided not to specify whether this was a back yard or a front yard. In fact, it could be either. (If that's hedging, what better chapter to do it in.)

The door faces the entrance to the circular terrace. I've made the brick walk flush with the house, but you could insert a hedge or ground cover planting between the walk and the house if you prefer. All the brick walks and straight sheared hedges are symmetrical.

The lawn, which separates the circular terrace garden from the parterre, is a broad walkway of matching rectangles with brick edging between a pair of arches—carved out of the tall hedge. One of the arches is an exit to the driveway. The other is a niche, the same size and shape as the exit arch. The niche is placed to maintain balance and contains a sculpture to provide a focus in line with the exit archway.

As the terrace is a perfect circle, I've tried to make it more visually interesting by splitting it into two levels, both of which are sunken. This split works well with the slope of the land, which drops gently away from the house. The upper terrace is one step below ground level and is surrounded by an eight-inch-high mortared brick wall. Two more steps take you down to the next terrace, which is twelve inches below the first and approximately twenty inches below ground level.

Because the ground is about four inches lower here than it is right next to the house, the brick wall also takes a step down, on a level with the lower step that bisects the circle. It is 22 inches high around the lower terrace. Two grates over French drains are not drawn on the plan but are necessary for this sunken terrace. I'd place them under the two tables, where they would not be visible or in a traffic path.

The terrace garden is unexpectedly exuberant for a formal landscape. Stiff yuccas, sotols, and nolinas mix easily with large unpruned shrubs that sport giant arching stems and with small shrubs that drape themselves over the brick wall. There is color here year-round. In the winter there are evergreens and bright red berries. The rest of the year there is a great variety and profusion of flowers. Nothing here should be sheared; it should be all pick-pruned or lightly topped to take off seed heads and encourage more blooms.

Each part of the state will have a different selection of shrubs to use, so I've indicated only sizes and textures. Because the beds drain into the terrace through seep holes at the bottom of the brick wall, even places like Houston and Dallas can get a good variety of shrubs by working lots of coarse sand and gravel into the clay soil. As long as you provide good drain-

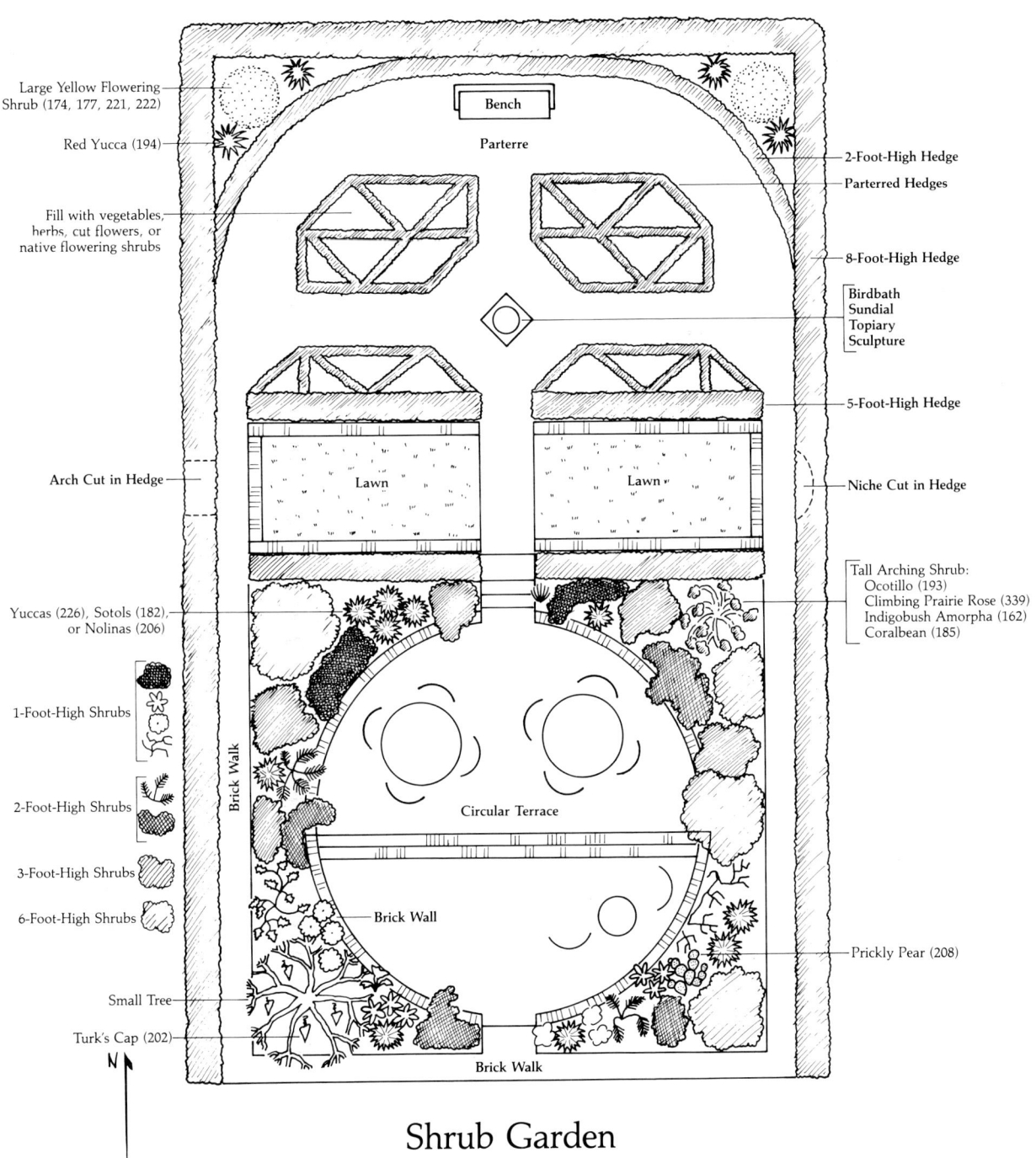

Large Yellow Flowering Shrub (174, 177, 221, 222)

Red Yucca (194)

Fill with vegetables, herbs, cut flowers, or native flowering shrubs

Arch Cut in Hedge

Yuccas (226), Sotols (182), or Nolinas (206)

1-Foot-High Shrubs

2-Foot-High Shrubs

3-Foot-High Shrubs

6-Foot-High Shrubs

Small Tree

Turk's Cap (202)

N

Bench

Parterre

2-Foot-High Hedge

Parterred Hedges

8-Foot-High Hedge

Birdbath
Sundial
Topiary
Sculpture

5-Foot-High Hedge

Lawn

Lawn

Niche Cut in Hedge

Tall Arching Shrub:
Ocotillo (193)
Climbing Prairie Rose (339)
Indigobush Amorpha (162)
Coralbean (185)

Brick Walk

Circular Terrace

Brick Wall

Prickly Pear (208)

Brick Walk

Shrub Garden

James Turner, author, artist, and landscape architect, moved to Austin from Louisiana and created a delightful garden that accurately reflects the rugged beauty of the Hill Country. In the shade under the crape myrtle is a Turk's cap, another shrubby mallow called *Wissadula holosericea*, and chile pequín. In the lighter shade of a mesquite across the drive are Gregg salvia and zexmenia. Annuals, perennials, grasses, and small trees, like kidneywood and Texas mountain laurel, are also tucked into this tiny garden. Photo by the authors.

age, you can pretty much choose what you like, taking into consideration cold- and heat-hardiness. But bear in mind that high humidity seems to adversely affect the blooming of desert plants.

In the lower left-hand corner is a small tree. Any of the choices listed for the tall hedges (keep reading—the list appears shortly) is fine if you want an evergreen, but there are also many options for a small flowering tree. Most of the ornamental trees in this book are classified as either trees or shrubs by botanists. So if you get intrigued with the idea of using only plants that can be technically classified as shrubs in your landscape, you have a big choice.

Some tree-shrubs that are suitable for this sunny spot are acacias, buckeyes, Texas persimmon (evergreen in its southern range, but the trunk is too pretty to think about hedging the plant), kidneywood, fragrant ash, possumhaw, goldenball leadtree, paloverde, Texas pistachio (also semievergreen), tornillo, Mexican elderberry, Eve's necklace, and rusty blackhaw viburnum. If you live in the Valley, a coralbean can make a wonderful little tree.

The planting area around the terrace is bordered on three sides by a two-foot-wide brick walk to provide easy access for maintenance of both the shrub flower garden and the tall clipped hedges, which act as green walls and provide a lush backdrop for the garden.

The eight-foot hedges on the plan are the outer boundaries of the design on three sides. They are drawn here two feet wide, although if you have room, three feet wide or more is better. Because a hedge of this sort tends to get thin at the bottom, you'll want to prune it a bit wider at the base to make it look denser. Do this subtly, however, so that a casual observer might not even notice. When the hedge is first getting started, stretch wires along its length to serve as a guideline for the shearing. Keep in mind that a hedge of this kind takes a long time and needs careful training to be successful.

Evergreen Shrubs 8 Feet Tall or More

Evergreen shrubs or ornamental trees that grow eight feet tall or more and can be sheared into a dense hedge are listed below. These are the evergreens that can also be used as ornamental trees, and most of them are found in Chapter 7. This list is arranged from the most cold-hardy to the least.

Silverleaf mountain mahogany (242)	Texas pistachio (266)
Wax myrtle (263)	Creosote bush (197)
Cherry laurel (269)	Guayacan (254)
Yaupon holly (259)	Texas torchwood (163)
Any live oak (314, 315, 325), turbinella oak (272)	Brasil (246)
Chisos rosewood (282)	Coyotillo (260)
Evergreen sumac (275)	Fiddlewood (245)
Texas mountain laurel (279)	Tenaza (267)
Cenizo, not a compact (199)	Texas ebony (310)

Evergreen Shrubs 5 Feet Tall

On either side of the lawn, forming the visual barrier between the terrace and the parterre, are five-foot hedges. The same shrubs used for the eight-foot hedges can be maintained at a height of five feet, but here are some shorter ones you can use:

Agarito (169)
Texas barberry (168)
White honeysuckle bush (200)

Dwarf wax myrtle (205)
Barbados cherry (201)

Evergreen Shrubs Under 3 Feet

Small shrubs that can be sheared into tiny parterred hedges are in this list, as well as those that can be allowed to develop naturally for a soft-looking hedge that remains low under windows. Again, the list is from most to least winter-hardy least.

Dwarf yaupon, not strictly native
  (259)
Creosote bush (197)
Larchleaf goldenweed (184)
Cenizo, a compact selection or
  cultivar (199)

Violet silverleaf (198)
Big Bend silverleaf (198)
Dwarf Barbados cherry (201)

In this plan, the small shrubs are used as clipped hedges. One hedge, two feet high and a foot wide, forms a long semicircle. It creates two corner beds against the back tall hedge. If you live far enough south to use a silverleaf or one of the other cenizos, make this long, low, sweeping hedge a contrasting color. Another fine choice would be the larchleaf goldenweed, which turns solid gold in the fall.

The corner beds, between the two hedges, are filled with a large, loosely shaped yellow shrub, such as rabbitbrush, canyon senna, yellow bells, or the velvet-leaved yellow sophora. Flanking either side of the yellow shrubs are red yuccas. These choices give several months of color and can be seen down the long brick paths on the sides.

A parterre looks best when it is sculpted in green-leaved shrubs, because the real focus should be on the flowers within them. But there's no need to use flowers. The beds could make classy vegetable gardens. Many people use the beds for herbs or for a cutting garden—a garden of long-stemmed, long-lasting flowers grown just for floral arrangements. The beds are frequently filled with annuals and perennials. Of course, in this plan I'm going to suggest that you fill them with shrubs.

Shrubs to Use as Flowers

Many native Texas shrubs are small in stature, often well under three feet, and bloom so profusely that they are used as flowers. This list is of those that have such a long bloom period that I recommend them for flower gardens and patio pots or for filling a parterre, as in this plan. The list is alphabetical (by scientific name).least.

Flame acanthus (164)	Big Bend silverleaf (198)
Scarlet bouvardia (170)	Cenizo, compact (199)
Damianita (176)	Pavonia (209)
Gregg coldenia (178)	Gregg salvia (218)
Apache plume (191)	Skeleton-leaf goldeneye (224)
Texas lantana (196)	Zexmenia (225)
Violet silverleaf (198)	

Those of you who are not purists can add seven perennials that botanists classify as subshrubs because they get woody at the base, but which landscapers use only as flowers. These subshrubs are yellow and white zinnias, pink plains penstemon and rock penstemon, and the three perennial buckwheats recommended in this book.

The parterre in this plan is nine inches high and six inches wide, a fairly typical height and breadth to work with. The beds inside the hedges are all less than four feet, a comfortable reach for weeding.

The spaces around the parterre are paved with the same kind of brick that is used in the terrace. The bricks could be worked into geometric patterns reflecting the overall shapes of the parterre, or they could be laid in a simple linear pattern.

There is a bench for sitting and contemplating the parterre or some other high-minded subject. It is lined up with the door to the house. Only one thing obstructs the straight-shot view: the diamond shape in the parterre. In the center of this diamond you could place a birdbath, a sundial, a tall, narrow piece of topiary, or a sculpture—anything to provide a focal point and leave the walkways usable.

The sweet-smelling blooms of blackbrush acacia glow with light in front of another acacia—the orange-flowered, larger-growing huisache. Bluebonnets in the short spring grasses complete this late March scene at the San Antonio Botanical Center. Photo by the authors.

 # Ornamental Trees

ORNAMENTAL trees make me think of Hollywood starlets. I imagine one of those gala Hollywood parties (no, I've never been to one) where the movie mogul–host invites a gaggle of sweet young things to mingle with the guests. They aren't there to make witty conversation or offer philosophical insights; they're there because they're beautiful.

Ornamental trees are the starlets of a garden. They aren't there to provide shade or erosion control or to hide the neighbor's ugly fence. They're there because they're beautiful! Every landscape should have at least one.

Ornamental trees are usually understory, residing beneath large canopy trees approximately twice their size. In this dimly lit environment, they tend to grow in a woodsy manner, with the branches well spaced. Put them in full sun, and they fill out into dense, well-rounded small trees with more blooms and fruits.

Size, of course, is relative. Ornamental trees are usually about one third to half the size of large shade trees from the same area. In East Texas they get up to thirty feet at maturity. In West Texas and the Valley (where only shade trees get as high as thirty feet—and not very often) they are typically under fifteen feet.

These smaller ornamental trees are often classified as shrubs or small trees. They can look shrubby in the wild for several reasons. For one thing, many have been browsed by deer or cattle. For another, because they grow in full sun, they are thick and bushy down at their bottoms. They also tend to look even shorter than they are. If you stand next to a ten- or twelve-foot shrub-tree, you perceive it as a tree. But when you see it silhouetted against the sky from a distance of five hundred yards, it looks dwarfed and rounded like a shrub. Pruning is necessary to reveal the multiple trunks and make these trees look graceful.

No tree should be poorly pruned, but doing a good job on an ornamental tree is crucial to showing it off to its best effect. You should begin pruning as soon as the tree is well established. This is when you will determine if the tree will have one or multiple trunks.

If you decide on a one-trunked tree, leave the center trunk and cut off the others at ground level. If you want multiple trunks, keep the ones that are most widely separated from each other. A multitrunked tree will ultimately be a shorter tree than one with a single trunk.

Never prune off the end of a branch, because it will sprout in six different directions and ruin the clean shape of the tree. Always cut off branches almost flush with the trunk or a main branch (leaving the branch collar for faster healing), and prune out all those branches that grow inward, or toward the trunk—you want everything to grow upward and outward. If you're already adept at pruning your yaupon holly or crape myrtle, you'll do fine on any of the other small ornamental trees.

If you're planning to grow flowers underneath the tree, or if you want to preserve a view, prune away all branches from the bottom two thirds of the trunk. Ornamental trees are ideal for flower beds in that they allow just the right amount of sun for profuse flowering.

Ornamental trees are useful in many situations because of their small stature. They are a comfortable size for typical urban yards. You can use two or three ornamental trees around a patio to give yourself variety and visual interest at special times of year. They're ideal around a swimming pool because they don't block all the sun; you can still get your tan. And they won't drop tons of leaves into the water.

In large-scale projects, they are effective planted in drifts for a big splash of seasonal color. As understory in a woods, they give life and drama, making the woods pink and white in the spring, red and gold in the fall.

ACACIAS

After my first botanical excursion into South Texas, I began thinking that every tree I saw must be some kind of acacia. Taken all together, they form the dominant component of brush (chaparral). We have twelve species across the state, and all but two of them live along the Rio Grande. (Worldwide, there are more than six hundred species.) I've put seven of our best in this book. Six are listed as ornamental trees, and one as a ground cover.

All acacias have twice-divided leaves and spines—from prickles to stout thorns, either of which might be straight or curved. The flowers are fluffy, white to yellow, fragrant, and used by bees to make excellent honey. Because acacias are legumes, the fruits are bean pods—dark brown and often remaining on the tree for more than a year.

All acacias prefer full sun and are among the first to invade a disturbed site. Most are fast-growing and relatively short-lived. When young, the tree acacias have a fountain of stems coming up from the base. With maturity, the stems sort themselves out into several small trunks. Huisache can actually get fairly large and is considered a canopy tree of the brush. But because I've seen only two giant huisaches in my whole life, and about 10,000 small ones, I thought it would be of more value to landscapers to put huisache in this chapter.

Since acacias are drought-tolerant and live in subdesert conditions, they are often smaller in the field than what I have indicated—sometimes half the size. The heights given are what you can expect in a landscape where you water one to three times a year.

In winter, acacias tend to get rather thin, although most try to be evergreen in the Valley. The one that's most nearly evergreen is Wright acacia; guajillo is the next most evergreen. Huisache and huisachillo are definitely deciduous. The others are best described as almost deciduous.

227. Guajillo
Acacia berlandieri
The authors

228. Whitethorn
Acacia constricta
The authors

227. **Latin Name** *Acacia berlandieri*
Pronunciation ah-KAY-shuh
ber-lan-dee-AIR-ee
Common Name GUAJILLO
Usual Height 9–15 feet
Spacing 9–15 feet apart
Bloom Early spring and occasionally later;
creamy white; ½-inch globes; fragrant
Deciduous to almost deciduous
Range Dry limestone hills in Rio Grande
Plains and Edwards Plateau west to
Big Bend
Mexico
Soil Sand, loam, clay, caliche, limestone
gravel; well drained
Part shade, full sun
Taproot
Propagation Untreated seed

When guajillo starts to bloom, it does it in style—
with deliciously fragrant, creamy-white puffs of flowers.
Even the ferny light-green leaves are lovely. This tree tries
hard to be evergreen, getting thin or losing its leaves only
for a short time in a hard winter. Of course, I mean a hard
winter by South Texas standards. In a really hard winter,
where it might get down to 10° F, as it did in Austin in the
"big freeze of '83," it will not just freeze down to the
ground; it will die. Also, like most acacias, it has spines,
but in this case they are tiny—prickles really—and straight
instead of barbed. Sometimes the branches are nearly
spineless, and it seems to me that a thornless selection
should be possible.

228. **Latin Name** *Acacia constricta*
Pronunciation ah-KAY-shuh
kon-STRIK-tah
Common Names WHITETHORN, MESCAT
ACACIA
Usual Height 9–15 feet
Spacing 9–15 feet apart
Bloom May to August; dark yellow; ½-inch
globes; fragrant
Fruit After blooms; red; 2- to 4-inch beans
Deciduous
Range Trans-Pecos, rare in South Texas
Southwestern U.S., Mexico
Soil Sand, caliche; well drained
Full sun
Taproot
Propagation Untreated seed

Whitethorn is popular with El Paso gardeners because of its fragrance (it reminds me of roses) and its vivid
color. The tiny deep-yellow balls of flowers cover the plant
so profusely every spring that sometimes you aren't aware
of the foliage. I've seen it in full bloom at other times of
year as well. There are no thorns among the flowers because the flowers are on new growth. But on old woody
branches there are copious thorns—white, as you would
expect from the name, and ominously large. You'll be glad
to hear that whitethorn can be found in the wild with few
or no thorns, so a thornless selection is possible. After the
blooms are gone, beans form and ripen to a bright red.
Then, in the winter, the branches get a distinctly purple
cast, giving whitethorn interest and color all year. It will
look shrubby for the first five years or so. After that, it will
grow into a small multitrunked tree. I think that pruning
it to just a few trunks improves its shape significantly.

229. Huisache
Acacia farnesiana
The authors

230. Blackbrush acacia
Acacia rigidula
Benny J. Simpson

229. **Latin Name** *Acacia farnesiana*
Pronunciation ah-KAY-shuh
far-nee-zee-AN-ah
Common Name HUISACHE (WEE-satch or
wee-SATCH-ee)
Usual Height 15–20 feet, 30 feet in Uvalde
and Brackettville
Spacing 15–20 feet apart
Bloom Before new leaves in spring; orange;
¼ inch; fragrant
Deciduous
Range Coastal Prairies and Rio Grande
Plains to Big Bend
Gulf Coast, Arizona, California, tropical
America
Soil Sand, loam, clay, caliche; poor drain-
age okay
Full sun
Suckers, forms dense thickets; deep-rooted
Propagation Scarified seed

Huisache is better appreciated where it is not so
abundant. In its native habitat, I rarely see it in gardens,
but north of the Rio Grande Plains, people would give
anything if only it were winter-hardy in their area. They'd
love to enjoy it in the spring when it turns a glowing orange and releases its magnificent perfume. In Austin it
appears to grow well, but actually it flowers only once in
seven or eight years because late frosts ruin the buds. In
fact, it blooms so early that that can even happen in Corpus Christi. Other dangers are acacia beetles, which gir-
dle limbs three inches across or less, and inchworms,
which migrant birds obligingly eat each spring. However, huisache is tough. It can handle standing water and
drought even better than a mesquite. Normally fountain-
shaped, its multiple trunks gradually fan out, and long,

limber branches of light green, ferny foliage cascade
down. Huisache has been cultivated in Europe since 1611,
when it was introduced to the Roman gardens of Cardinal
Odoardo Farnese, for whom it was named. Some botanists have now decided to separate ours from the main
group and call it *A. smallii*.

230. **Latin Name** *Acacia rigidula*
Pronunciation ah-KAY-shuh
reh-JID-yoo-lah
Common Name BLACKBRUSH ACACIA
Usual Height 10–15 feet
Spacing 10–15 feet apart
Bloom Before new leaves in spring; pale
yellow, 2- to 3-inch spikes; fragrant
Deciduous to almost deciduous
Range Rio Grande Plains to Austin and
Big Bend
Mexico
Soil Sand, loam, clay, caliche; well drained
Part shade, full sun
Suckers, forms dense thickets
Propagation Untreated seed

Have you ever seen a blackbrush acacia on a bright
blue spring day, backlit by the sun? The little fuzzy spikes
of ivory-colored flowers make the whole tree seem to
glow and shimmer. As you would expect from an acacia,
it also smells sweet, even sweeter than huisache. Blackbrush acacia is slow-growing compared with other acacias, which probably means it is longer-lived. It can also
sucker, so if you want a specimen tree instead of a thicket,
pull off the suckers at ground level and prune the trunks
into a graceful tree.

231. Huisachillo
Acacia schaffneri var. *bravoensis*
Dr. Robert Lonard

232. Wright acacia
Acacia wrightii
The authors

231. **Latin Name** *Acacia schaffneri* var. *bravoensis*
(*A. tortuosa*)
Pronunciation ah-KAY-shuh
shaff-NARE-ee variety brah-voh-EN-siss
Common Names HUISACHILLO,
TWISTED ACACIA
Usual Height 6–12 feet
Spacing 6–8 feet apart
Bloom Spring; deep yellow to orange;
½-inch globes; fragrant
Deciduous
Range Rio Grande Plains
Mexico, West Indies
Soil Sand, loam, clay, caliche; well drained
Part shade, full sun
Propagation Untreated seed

Except for guajillo, this is the smallest of the acacias in this chapter. It looks shrubby for its first few years, but in your yard it will quickly grow to nine feet or more and make a small multitrunked tree. It's called huisachillo because it looks like a little huisache. It's called twisted acacia because the branches are twisted and bent in different directions. In fact, even the black, velvety seedpods are twisted. Pruned with sensitivity, this little tree can be exquisite. Because huisachillo is often seen in thickets, you might think it suckers, but instead it seeds out easily. Outside its native range, it has been found to be winter-hardy in Houston and as far north as Dallas, if it's placed against a protected south wall.

232. **Latin Name** *Acacia wrightii*
Pronunciation ah-KAY-shuh RITE-ee-eye
Common Name WRIGHT ACACIA
Usual Height 6–10 feet, can reach 30 feet
near Uvalde
Spacing 10 feet apart
Bloom Spring; white to pale yellow; 2-inch
spikes
Deciduous to almost evergreen
Range In brush in Rio Grande Plains, along
creeks and in canyons on Edwards
Plateau north to Abilene and Fort Worth
Southern U.S., northern Mexico
Soil Sand, loam, clay, caliche, limestone;
well drained
Part shade, full sun
Taproot
Propagation Untreated seed

The most cold-hardy of all the tree acacias, Wright acacia is native as far north as Abilene. After watching its performance in Dallas during the freeze of '83, Benny Simpson says he is sure it can be used all the way up to the Red River with no trouble at all. Because the northern part of Texas doesn't have other acacias, the delicate foliage, light shade, and small stature of Wright acacia make it a valuable addition to small-scale landscapes. But be careful when handling this acacia—the thorns have tiny hooks.

233. Chalk maple
Acer leucoderme
The authors

234. Yellow buckeye
Aesculus pavia var. *flavescens*
The authors

233. **Latin Name** *Acer leucoderme*
Pronunciation AY-ser loo-koh-DER-mee
Common Name CHALK MAPLE
Usual Height 25 feet
Spacing 15 feet apart
Deciduous, with leaves turning red, orange, or gold in fall
Range Moist soil in Sabine National Forest Southeastern U.S.
Soil Sand, loam; moist, well drained
Dappled shade, part shade, full sun
Propagation Fresh seed

The name comes from the bark, which is supposedly white or pale gray on a mature tree. I say "supposedly" because I don't know anyone who has ever seen a tree that mature. Chalk maple normally has 2 or 3 trunks, but it's not unusual to find some with single trunks. As an understory tree, it can be grown under hardwoods (oaks, elms, and so on) or pines. It's used chiefly for its rich fall color, which can be quite vivid even in shady situations. Give it sufficient moisture and it can also be grown in full sun. The way you can tell this maple from others in the nursery is by looking at the undersides of the leaves—they will be as green as the top side, whereas other maples have lighter undersides. I've been told that chalk maple does not color well as far south as Houston, and it gets chlorotic and drought-stressed as far west as Dallas.

234. **Latin Name** *Aesculus pavia*
Pronunciation ESS-kah-lus PAH-vee-ah
Common Names SCARLET BUCKEYE, YELLOW BUCKEYE
Usual Height 10–20 feet, can reach 35 feet
Spacing 6–12 feet apart
Bloom Midspring; red or yellow; 6- to 10-inch upright clusters
Deciduous
Range
A. pavia var. *pavia* (Scarlet Buckeye)—Piney Woods, Post Oak Savannah, Coastal and Blackland Prairies; southeastern U.S.
A. pavia var. *flavescens* (Yellow Buckeye)—Endemic to Edwards Plateau
Soil Sand, loam, clay, limestone; moist, well drained
Shade, dappled shade, part shade
Propagation Fresh seed, dormant root cuttings

The bright red southeastern buckeye called scarlet buckeye is well liked and often used in landscapes. It is rare in the eastern Edwards Plateau, growing only in good deep soil. Yellow buckeye grows well on rocky limestone slopes and shows an enormous preference for northern exposures. Both are best used as understory trees and should be clustered whenever possible; they make a much bigger impact that way. The leaves each consist of five glossy leaflets, and they have one big drawback: They've all fallen by the end of the summer. Extra watering can gain you only a month at most, as leaf blotch and anthracnose are the real culprits. Texas does have a buckeye that takes full sun, *A. arguta*, called Texas or white buckeye. Actually its blooms aren't white at all; they're pale yellow. Instead of five leaflets, this one might have as many as eleven, and it can grow as tall as fifty feet. It grows in limestone or sand in the northeastern part of the state north to Kansas.

235. **Devil's walking stick**
Aralia spinosa
Benny J. Simpson

236. **Texas madrone**
Arbutus texana
The authors

235. **Latin Name** *Aralia spinosa*
Pronunciation ah-RALE-ee-ah
spye-NOH-sah
Common Name DEVIL'S WALKING STICK
Usual Height 12–15 feet, can reach 20 feet
Spacing 6–8 feet apart
Bloom Summer; whitish; 1- to 4-foot
clusters
Fruit Fall; black; ½ inch
**Dies back to ground in winter, leaves might
turn purple**
Range Moist bottomlands in East Texas
New Jersey to Iowa to Gulf of Mexico
Soil Loam; moist, well drained
Shade, dappled shade, part shade
Taproot and colonizes by rhizomes
Propagation Fresh seed, dormant root
cuttings, transplanting of suckers

This is one of the weirdest trees in the world. Each
spring it breaks ground and shoots up a tall stem covered
with orange prickles. The twice-divided leaves can be
three to four feet long and just as wide. They're also spiny.
Only a few leaves are borne at the top of the stem, along
with flowers in the summer and black juicy fruits each
September. Place this plant in rich, moist loam under a
shade tree, or naturalize it in a clearing. It is often seen
growing with sassafras, hawthorns, or eastern red cedar.
After about four years, devil's walking stick will begin to
form a thicket. Dig out the suckers if you don't want them.
The roots are pleasantly pungent, but some people break
out in blisters after handling them. You can expect your
original plant to live twenty to forty years.

236. **Latin Name** *Arbutus texana* (erroneously
called *A. xalapensis*)
Pronunciation ar-BYOO-tus tex-AN-ah
Common Name TEXAS MADRONE
Usual Height 20–30 feet
Spacing 15–25 feet apart
Bloom Spring; white to pale pink; ½ inch
long
Evergreen
Range Wooded, rocky canyons of Trans-
Pecos and Edwards Plateau
Texas and southeastern New Mexico
through Mexico to Guatemala
Soil Sand, loam, clay, caliche, limestone;
moist, well drained
Part shade
Propagation Fresh or stratified seed,
cuttings

Usually multitrunked, Texas madrone's thin papery bark goes through a lovely metamorphosis each year,
beginning in the fall when the old skin peels away and
reveals the soft cream-colored new bark. The color then
changes to peach to coral to Indian red to chocolate and
then peels away to start the marvelous process all over
again. The leaves are dark green and have a leathery texture. In the spring the blossoms are clusters of little white
or pale pink flowers. The fall fruits look like ripe rasp-
berries, hanging all over the tree in three-inch clusters.
Texas madrone likes moisture, but also good drainage. It
has been exceedingly hard to transplant because its root
system is similar to that of azaleas—not surprising, since
they're in the same family. Unlike azaleas, Texas madrone
doesn't need acid soil; in fact, it grows out of limestone.
However, seedlings are susceptible to black spot and
damping-off. It needs five full years to get established,
and even then it should get supplemental watering.

237. Anacacho orchid tree
Bauhinia congesta
The authors

238. La coma
Bumelia celastrina
The authors

237. **Latin Name** *Bauhinia congesta* (*B. lunarioides*)
Pronunciation baw-HIN-ee-ah
 kun-JESS-tah
Common Names ANACACHO ORCHID TREE,
ORCHID TREE
Usual Height 6–12 feet
Spacing 6–12 feet apart
Bloom March to May (sometimes after fall
 rain); white or pale pink; 1½- to 2-inch
 clusters
Deciduous
Range Canyons of Anacacho Mountains in
 Edwards Plateau
 Northeastern Mexico
Soil Sand, loam, limestone; well drained
Dappled shade, part shade, full sun
Propagation Fresh or scarified seed

Anacacho orchid tree is relatively rapid-growing and usually flowers the second year from seed. It is a single-trunked tree with small, light green leaves that look like cloven hooves. Its best use is as an understory or patio tree in the Hill Country; it seems to prefer limestone soils. Once widely grown in Houston, the original plantings have died off or are declining, and we don't really know why. It could be the lack of limestone, but a few local naturalists I've talked to seem to think that the tree just isn't getting sufficient drainage. If you want to grow this tree north of its native range, be sure to place it against a masonry wall that can absorb the warmth of the south or west sun in the winter. Since it doesn't need the extra heat in the summer, shade it with a deciduous tree.

238. **Latin Name** *Bumelia celastrina*
Pronunciation boo-MELL-ee-ah
 sell-ah-STRYE-nah
Common Name LA COMA
Usual Height 15–20 feet
Spacing 10–15 feet apart
Bloom May to November; white; ¼ inch
 long; fragrant
Evergreen
Range Brush, resaca banks, and gravelly
 hills from Matagorda to Valley
 Peninsular Florida, Florida Keys, and
 South Texas to Venezuela
Soil Sand, clay, caliche, shell; well drained
Part shade, full sun
Propagation Scarified seed

La coma is a tree of the South Texas brush. I'm recommending it because it is fully evergreen, adapts to any soil, and can easily be pruned into a pretty shape. It's also valuable to wildlife, providing nesting sites and purple fruits that are eaten by a number of birds and mammals. I've noticed many people in the Valley using yaupon holly, even though la coma is so much better adapted to that region. La coma's leaves are small and dark green, like those of yaupon holly, and la coma gives you the bonus of fragrant flowers. There are long, sharp spines at the ends of the twigs. How far la coma can be used outside of its native range has not been explored, but the San Antonio Botanical Center has found it to be winter-hardy in that area.

239. Mexican poinciana
Caesalpinia mexicana
The authors

240. Ironwood
Carpinus caroliniana
Doug Williams

239. **Latin Name** *Caesalpinia mexicana*
Pronunciation see-zul-PEEN-ee-ah
mex-eh-KAH-nah
Common Names MEXICAN POINCIANA,
MEXICAN CAESALPINIA
Usual Height 10–20 feet
Spacing lo–15 feet apart
Bloom Spring to fall; yellow; 3- to 6-inch
racemes; fragrant
Deciduous
Range Cameron and Hidalgo counties
Mexico
Soil Sand, loam, clay; well drained
Part shade, full sun
Propagation Untreated seed

When you see Mexican poinciana in fencerows and other places where the ground is cracked with drought, it will usually be less than nine feet tall. But in your courtyard or in a lawn that you occasionally water, it can quickly reach more than twenty feet. It blooms off and on all year, sometimes scantily, sometimes putting on a colorful show. The blooms are bright yellow, fragrant, and often visited by enormous black bees. The leaves are light green. This tree has been planted as far north as Corpus Christi and San Antonio. In Corpus Christi it froze during that terrible winter in '83. The ones I saw had come back from the roots, but they'd lost their trunks and are now multistemmed and shrubby. In ten more years, who knows? They might well develop into multitrunked trees.

240. **Latin Name** *Carpinus caroliniana*
Pronunciation kar-PINE-us
kare-oh-lin-ee-AY-nah
Common Names IRONWOOD,
AMERICAN HORNBEAM, MUSCLEWOOD
Usual Height 15–25 feet
Spacing 12 feet apart
**Deciduous, with leaves turning yellow,
orange, or red in fall**
Range Rich bottomwoods in East Texas
Maryland to Illinois to Gulf of Mexico
Soil Sand, loam, clay; acid; moist; well
drained
Shade, dappled shade, part shade
Propagation Fresh, slightly green seed or
ripe stratified seed

I always remember this tree by its common name "musclewood." Both the branches and the trunk are pale gray and sinewy. The way they form smoothly twisting bulges (not unlike muscles) makes me think that this tree must have been working out. This may not sound appealing, but it is, and you'll want to situate this tree where you can see it often. It is best planted under a shade tree and can be used as understory in woods that don't get too dry. The flowers are green and small, and the fruits are papery; it's the fall color that makes this tree outstanding. Unlike chalk maple, it colors well in Houston. A tree usually mentioned in the same breath—by landscapers, that is— is hop hornbeam (*Ostrya virginiana*). It too is a good fall-coloring understory tree, but it can get larger, and its papery fruits might hang all winter. The bark is also attractive, but in a different way from ironwood's—flaking and peeling on mature trees. Both ironwood and hop hornbeam are slow-growing and difficult to transplant.

241. **Sometimes redbud is available in white.**
Cercis canadensis
The authors

241.   **Latin Name**   *Cercis canadensis*
     Pronunciation   SER-siss kan-ah-DEN-siss
     Common Name   REDBUD
     Usual Height   10–20 feet (eastern redbud can reach 40 feet)
     Spacing   15–20 feet apart
     Bloom   Early spring; rose-pink (white); ½ inch long
     Deciduous, with leaves turning yellow in fall
     Range   Throughout Texas except Corpus Christi and Valley
     Eastern U.S., Mexico
     Soil   Sand, loam, clay, limestone; well drained
     Dappled shade, part shade, full sun
     Propagation   Scarified and stratified seed

241. **Texas redbud**
Cercis canadensis
The authors

We have three native varieties of redbuds: eastern redbud (var. *canadensis*), Texas redbud (var. *texensis*), and Mexican redbud (var. *mexicana*). All bloom spectacularly in the spring before their leaves emerge. They interbreed on their way west, so we probably have more hybrids than pure forms overall. As you would guess, redbuds get smaller and more drought-tolerant the farther west they go. Redbuds in the Piney Woods, Houston, Post Oak Woods, and Blackland woods are essentially understory trees and are either pure eastern redbud or a hybrid cross with Texas redbud. Whichever they are in Dallas, I think that's where they show off best; they bloom three to four weeks every spring, and the leaves turn a clear yellow most falls. Redbuds on limestone escarpment in the central part of the state are called Texas redbuds. Their leaves are rounder, heavier, and very glossy. The seedpods turn a beautiful rosy hue in late spring. Mexican redbuds, which occur in the Trans-Pecos, have small wavy leaves, a feature that assists in drought tolerance. All redbuds are winter-hardy, even in the Panhandle, and I'm sure at least one, and maybe all three, should do well where you live—even in the Valley.

242. Silverleaf mountain mahogany
Cercocarpus montanus var. *argenteus*
The authors

243. Desert willow
Chilopsis linearis
The authors

242. **Latin Name** *Cercocarpus montanus* var. *argenteus*
Pronunciation ser-koh-KAR-pus mon-TAN-us variety ar-JEN-tee-us
Common Name SILVERLEAF MOUNTAIN MAHOGANY
Usual Height 8–15 feet
Spacing 6–15 feet apart
Fruit May to November; white; 2 inches long
Almost evergreen
Range Rocky slopes and canyons in Edwards Plateau, Trans-Pecos, and Panhandle
Western U.S., northern Mexico
Soil Sand, loam, clay, caliche, limestone; well drained
Part shade, full sun
Propagation Scarified and stratified seed, softwood cuttings in spring

Silverleaf mountain mahogany often looks shrubby in nature because it's good deer browse, but in your yard it would make an attractive small tree. The leaves are dark green on top and a fuzzy silver on the underside. It's most lovely when in fruit, which is usually in late summer or early fall. The fruits are silvery white and feathery (some call them silky), and when they're in abundance on the tree and backlit, they can look stunning. (Sorry, we never came across one looking like this when we had a camera handy.) There are two other varieties in the state, but neither comes close to the beauty of silverleaf mountain mahogany. This tree is in the rose family and is slow-growing, with very hard wood.

243. **Latin Name** *Chilopsis linearis*
Pronunciation kye-LOP-siss lin-ee-AIR-us
Common Name DESERT WILLOW
Usual Height 15–25 feet
Spacing 10–15 feet apart
Bloom Spring to fall; white to burgundy; 3 inches long
Deciduous
Range Watercourses and dry streams in Trans-Pecos and West Texas
Texas to California to Mexico
Soil Sand, loam, clay, caliche; well drained
Part shade, full sun
Propagation Fresh seed, dormant cuttings, semihardwood cuttings in late summer

This tree is not a willow, in spite of its name. Actually, it's related to trumpet vine and crossvine. It's a fast-growing, drought-tolerant tree with absolutely gorgeous flowers that bloom whenever the weather is warm. It's one of our best native trees. It doesn't grow as fast or get as tall in the Blackland Prairies, but it is highly resistant to cotton root rot. Benny Simpson has released two new selections (a pure white called 'White Storm,' and a rich burgundy named 'Dark Storm'), both of which are grown by Lone Star Growers, who also grow a pink one named 'Pink Star.' Dr. Jimmy L. Tipton has released 'Marfa Lace,' 'Tejas,' and 'Alpine,' which is notable for its short, wide leaves. Ask for these selections. Desert willow grows well in Corpus Christi and the Valley and, I'm told, will do well in Houston if given very good drainage. It's winter-hardy almost all the way to Amarillo.

244. Fringe tree
Chionanthus virginica
The authors

245. Fiddlewood
Citharexylum berlandieri
The authors

244. **Latin Name** *Chionanthus virginica*
Pronunciation kye-oh-NAN-thus
   ver-JIN-eh-kah
Common Name FRINGE TREE
Usual Height 15–25 feet, can reach 30 feet
Spacing 15–20 feet apart
Bloom 8–14 days in spring; white; 5- to
   10-inch clusters
**Deciduous, with leaves turning yellow in a
   cool autumn**
Range Damp woods and bluffs in East
   Texas
   New Jersey to Ohio to Gulf of Mexico
Soil Sand, loam, clay; acid; poor drainage
   okay
Dappled shade, part shade
Propagation Double-stratified seed, layer-
   ing, grafting, budding, softwood cuttings

There are only two species of fringe tree in the whole world: ours and China's. Ours is taller, with larger leaves and flower clusters. Blooms appear just before or simultaneously with the leaves, usually right after dogwood starts blooming. On one tree, you can find flower clusters with both male and female blooms or all-male blooms or all-female blooms. You can also find a tree that is totally male or totally female. Both sexes are equally striking, but only the females bear fruit—dark blue, juicy, grapelike clusters that ripen in late summer or early fall. The flowers appear on last year's wood, so do your pruning right after blooming. Never prune a fringe tree severely. It grows slowly and can't recover from a big loss of leaves and branches. If you want a single-trunked tree, you have to prune for that feature from the start. Trunks are pale gray with bandings of white, and leaves are dark green and glossy. I've seen it growing in dryish sand where it got west sun, but it looks its best where its roots are protected with ground cover or mulch and where it gets shade part of the day. It also grows as understory, along with two-winged silverbell and redbud. Fringe tree can also tolerate Houston's gumbo.

245. **Latin Name** *Citharexylum berlandieri*
Pronunciation sith-ar-EX-eh-lum
   ber-lan-dee-AIR-ee
Common Name FIDDLEWOOD
Usual Height 10–15 feet
Spacing 8 feet apart, 3 feet apart for hedge
Bloom February to August; white; 1- to
   2-inch pyramids; fragrant
Fruit Winter; orange; spikes of 1- to 2-inch
   berries
**Evergreen, with leaves turning orange in
   drought**
Range Brush in Cameron and Willacy
   counties
   Mexico
Soil Clay, clay-loam; well drained
Part shade, full sun
Propagation Seed

Mike Heep, a landscaper in the Valley, likes to use fiddlewood as a shrub or a hedge. If you don't shear or prune it this way, it will make a small tree that will become more visually interesting as its trunk gets gnarled with age. It requires a lot of water to get established, and if you give it fertilizer too, it will be a fast grower. You can always tell when it's drought-stressed; the leaves turn orange, as in the picture. I don't wish to sound cruel, but I think it looks pretty that way. Fiddlewood blooms several times during the year, followed by autumn and early-winter fruits that are a lot showier than the flowers. The fruits are an orangy red and ripen to black. One of the best features of this tree is that it has no thorns.

246. Brasil's characteristic light green foliage
Condalia hookeri
The authors

247. Mexican olive
Cordia boissieri
The authors

246. **Latin Name**   *Condalia hookeri*
Pronunciation   kohn-DALE-ee-ah
HOOK-er-eye
Common Names   BRASIL, BLUEWOOD
CONDALIA
Usual Height   12–15 feet, can reach 30 feet
Spacing   15 feet apart
Evergreen
Range   Rio Grande Plains, north to Mata-
gorda and Austin
Mexico
Soil   Sand, loam, clay, caliche; well drained
Dappled shade, part shade, full sun
Forms thickets
Propagation   Fresh or stratified seed,
semihardwood cuttings

This is a well-shaped small evergreen that is usu-ally remembered for its vibrant lime-green leaves. It's also memorable because it always seems to be in fruit. Since it flowers regularly, the fruits are always at various stages of ripeness. It's not unusual to find, on the same branch, fruits that range from pale green to yellow to orange to wine-red to blue-black; birds quickly grab the ripe ones. The tiny green flowers are notoriously inconspicuous. The wood is pale gray, yet is known for producing a blue dye (thus its name). The thorns, which are plentiful, are also pale gray (or is that "impale gray"?). The tree is al-most always multitrunked. If you find little bumps on the leaves, they are galls and won't hurt the tree at all, accord-ing to Jim Everitt, USDA research scientist in Weslaco.

247. **Latin Name**   *Cordia boissieri*
Pronunciation   KOR-dee-ah boy-zee-AIR-ee
Common Names   MEXICAN OLIVE, WILD
OLIVE, ANACAHUITE
Usual Height   12–15 feet, can reach 24 feet
Spacing   12–15 feet apart
Bloom   Everblooming; white; 2 inches
across
Evergreen
Range   Brushlands and stream banks of
Valley
Mexico
Soil   Sand, loam, clay, caliche; well drained
Part shade, full sun
Propagation   Fresh or double-stratified
seed, softwood or semihardwood cuttings
in summer

Mexican olive is an absolutely wonderful tree. It should be used everywhere it's winter-hardy—and I'm just sick that I can't have one where I live. It has big, dark leaves, no thorns, and football-size clusters of yellow-throated white blossoms. They appear all year round but are most profuse in spring and early summer. Mexican olive needs lots of water to get started but is very drought-tolerant once it's established. The purple fruits have been known to make deer and cattle tipsy if eaten to excess; I've been told they love it. Unfortunately, this tree is not very winter-hardy. In Corpus Christi and San Antonio, and even as far south as Refugio, Mexican olives were frozen back or killed by the freeze of '83.

248. Flowering dogwood
Cornus florida
The authors

248. Flowering dogwood
Cornus florida
The authors

sonal observations, I think dogwood is more particular about drainage than about the acidity of the soil. I have three dogwoods growing over limestone in my front yard, and they're very healthy, if smallish. Large dogwoods are usually found in deep sandy loam. Besides its aesthetic appeal, the tree is popular with 28 species of birds, as well as squirrels and deer, who all eat the fruits.

249. **Latin Name**　*Cotinus obovatus*
Pronunciation　KOH-ten-us oh-boh-VAY-tus
Common Names　TEXAS SMOKE TREE,
　　AMERICAN SMOKE TREE
Usual Height　15 feet, can reach 30 feet
Spacing　15 feet apart
Bloom　Midspring; purple to pink; 12-inch
　　panicles
**Deciduous, with leaves turning yellow to
　apricot to scarlet in fall**
Range　Rocky woods and limestone slopes
　　in Edwards Plateau
　　Oklahoma south to Alabama and Texas
Soil　Sand, loam, clay, limestone; well
　　drained
Part shade, full sun
Propagation　Fresh seed, root or stem
　　cuttings, layering

　　Texas smoke tree is one of our most outstanding ornamental trees for rocky limestone soils. Its name comes from its ethereal floral clouds. In the spring each emerging leaf is colored both pink and lime, and in the fall the range of hues is fantastic. Even the wood is rainbow-colored with streaks of orange, lime, purple, and rose. Unfortunately, these colors are inside, so we can't see them, but I like knowing they're there. In its natural habitat on a rocky north- or east-facing slope, Texas smoke tree grows so slowly that the wood becomes extremely hard and dense. In a garden, with rich soil and water, it might grow so fast that the wood is weak. So once it is established, ease off the watering. If you are going to naturalize it, and you don't have a north-facing slope, planting on the protected side of an Ashe juniper is equally effective. You'll also be glad to hear that deer do not eat the tender new growth unless famine conditions exist.

248. **Latin Name**　*Cornus florida*
Pronunciation　KOR-nus FLOR-eh-dah
Common Name　FLOWERING DOGWOOD
Usual Height　15–25 feet, can reach 35 feet
Spacing　8–15 feet apart
Bloom　3 weeks in spring; white bracts;
　　3–4 inches across
Fruits　Fall and winter; glossy red; ½ inch
Deciduous, with leaves turning red in fall
Range　Piney Woods and Post Oak
　　Savannah
　　Eastern North America
Soil　Sand, loam; well drained
Dappled shade, part shade
Propagation　Stratified seed, root and stem
　　cuttings, layering

　　Have you ever wondered how dogwood got its name? It seems an extract taken from a related species was once used in England to wash mangy dogs! I like dogwood best when it's planted in masses—great drifts of them under shade trees. You don't need a giant piece of property to have this; five, six, or seven dogwoods can fit nicely into an average-sized yard. Dogwood can be single-trunked but is most often multitrunked. Its lovely, graceful branching seems to display the leaves in distinct tiers, but only when you plant it in the shade. From my per-

250. Parsley hawthorn
Crataegus marshallii
The authors

249. Texas smoke tree
Cotinus obovatus
The authors

249. Texas smoke tree
Cotinus obovatus
Benny J. Simpson

250. **Latin Name** *Crataegus marshallii*
Pronunciation krah-TEE-gus
mar-SHAL-ee-eye
Common Name PARSLEY HAWTHORN
Usual Height 10–15 feet, can reach 25 feet
Spacing 7 feet apart in woods, 15 feet apart
for specimen
Bloom March; white; 1 inch; unpleasant
fragrance
Deciduous, with leaves turning red in fall
Range Sandy woodlands and pastures in
East Texas and Houston
Virginia to Missouri to Gulf of Mexico
Soil Sand, loam, clay; acid; seasonal poor
drainage okay
Dappled shade, part shade, full sun
Propagation Scarified and stratified seed

Parsley hawthorn in full bloom is a dainty, glistening white. It grows well in sugar sand with possumhaw, rusty blackhaw viburnum, cherry laurel, and redbud, under red oaks and loblolly pines. I saw one once with a ground cover of lanceleaf coreopsis and winecups beneath. Surprisingly, parsley hawthorn also does well in Houston's gumbo. Although hawthorns hybridize freely and are often difficult to tell apart, parsley hawthorn is easy to identify; its leaves are parsley-shaped. They look best in May when they're still shiny, new, and unnibbled. By June, caterpillars have obviously been at them. (Like other members of the rose family, hawthorns are considered particularly tasty by many insects.) In September or

250. Fall color of parsley hawthorn
Crataegus marshallii
Doug Williams

251. Texas persimmon
Diospyros texana
The authors

October, the fruits, called haws, ripen to a cherry red and are quickly gobbled up by birds and mammals. Western mayhaw (*C. opaca*) is famous for its fruits, which ripen May to July. It isn't so showy when it blooms in February and is grown chiefly for its haws, which I'm told make a delicious jelly. It grows well in Houston's gumbo and other poorly drained areas. Both of these hawthorns are fairly fast-growing, relatively short-lived, and susceptible to cedar-apple rust. Although most hawthorns are thorny, some specimens are almost thornless, which is important to know when making selections.

251.   **Latin Name**   *Diospyros texana*
   Pronunciation   dye-OSS-per-us tex-AN-ah
   Common Names   TEXAS PERSIMMON,
      MEXICAN PERSIMMON, BLACK PERSIMMON
   Usual Height   10–15 feet, can reach 35 feet
   Spacing   6–10 feet apart
   Bloom   Early spring (fall); white; ⅓ inch
      across; fragrant
   Fruit   Summer, on females; black; 1- to
      2-inch persimmons
   Deciduous to evergreen
   Range   South Texas and Edwards Plateau,
      east to Bryan and west to Big Bend
      Mexico
   Soil   Loam, clay, caliche, limestone; well
      drained
   Might colonize to form a thicket
   Part shade, full sun
   Propagation   Fresh seed

When this tree is in full bloom, you're more likely to smell the tiny blossoms before you spot them; the fragrance is sharply sweet. The black fruits are also sweet but have little edible flesh surrounding the pits. In spite of that, they are an important food for birds and deer. The chief beauty of the tree is the bark. It's thin, smooth, and pale gray and peels off in patchy strips to expose the white trunk. Be sure to prune this tree up fairly high to show off this feature. I've seen some that have single trunks, but most are multitrunked. Down in the Valley and in Mexico, this persimmon is evergreen, changing its leaves in April, like live oaks. North of there, it is deciduous in all but the mildest winters. Although its natural range stops short of Abilene, it seems to be perfectly winter-hardy to the Red River.

252. Kidneywood
Eysenhardtia texana
The authors

253. Fragrant ash
Fraxinus cuspidata
Benny J. Simpson

252. **Latin Name** *Eysenhardtia texana*
Pronunciation eye-zen-HAR-dee-ah
tex-AN-ah
Common Name KIDNEYWOOD
Usual Height 6–9 feet, can reach 15 feet
Spacing 6–8 feet apart
Bloom April to November, after rain; white;
3- to 4-inch spikes; fragrant
Deciduous
Range Rio Grande Plains, north to Killeen,
west to Big Bend
Mexico
Soil Sand, loam, clay, caliche, limestone;
well drained
Part shade, full sun
Propagation Fresh seed, softwood or
semihardwood cuttings in early fall

Most people think of kidneywood as a shrub; in fact, I had originally planned to put it in the chapter on shrubs. But it's not really a dense plant. It's rather open and airy in structure, and with a little pruning, it makes a much more appealing tree than a shrub. The leaves are somewhat finely divided too, although not as much as acacia leaves, and they smell like citrus when crushed. The sweet-scented flowers can be quite profuse and are a favorite destination for bees and butterflies. Kidneywood will grow quickly with extra watering, but as soon as it's established, it can be extremely drought-tolerant. Naturalized, it might lose its leaves in a long dry spell, but that's only temporary. It will green up again as soon as it gets some rain.

253. **Latin Name** *Fraxinus cuspidata*
Pronunciation FRAX-eh-nus
kus-peh-DAY-tah
Common Name FRAGRANT ASH
Usual Height 10–12 feet, can reach 25 feet
Spacing 8–10 feet apart
Bloom Late spring; white to cream; 3- to
4-inch panicles; fragrant
Deciduous
Range Rocky canyon slopes in Trans-Pecos
New Mexico, Arizona
Soil Sand, loam, clay, caliche, limestone;
well drained
Part shade, full sun
Propagation Fresh or stratified seed

Fragrant ash is the western version of the fringe tree—not that they're related, the blooms just look somewhat similar, and fragrant ash can be used in those parts of the state where fringe tree won't grow. Benny Simpson describes fragrant ash in full bloom as looking like a giant white handkerchief. He has been experimenting with it in Dallas and reports that it came through the cold winter of '84 very well. How it might have fared in '83, which was really bad, is not known, since he put out his specimens the following spring. Although drought-tolerant, it grows quickly with watering and doesn't seem to need extra-good drainage. Fragrant ash often forms a large single trunk. Despite its name, it's only mildly fragrant.

254. Guayacan
Guaiacum angustifolium
Benny J. Simpson

255. Two-winged silverbell
Halesia diptera
The authors

254. **Latin Name** *Guaiacum angustifolium*
(*Porlieria angustifolia*)
Pronunciation WYE-uh-kum
an-gus-teh-FOLE-ee-um
Common Names GUAYACAN, SOAPBUSH
Usual Height 8–10 feet, can reach 20 feet
Spacing 15–20 feet apart
Bloom Spring to fall; purple to white;
1 inch across; fragrant
Fruit Early fall; glossy red; ½–1 inch
Evergreen
Range Valley to Big Bend
Mexico
Soil Sand, loam, clay, caliche, limestone;
well drained
Part shade, full sun
Propagation Seed

This tree is a long-lived relative of creosote bush. It's also kin to lignum vitae, the national flower of Jamaica, and in fact they look a lot alike. Guayacan develops one or more well-defined trunks, which are quite smooth when mature. When young, this tree looks like a dense shrub; the tiny leaves grow so close to the wood that one naturalist in Corpus Christi thinks of guayacan as always needing a shave. Whenever it gets water, pale blue flowers engulf the tree. The camera doesn't do justice to the showy display, so we decided to use a close-up here. The red fruits are more photogenic. Although they form after each blooming, they are most visible in the fall. Guayacan is slow-growing in the wild, but in a yard, with occasional watering (but no fertilizer), it can reach its maximum height in just ten years.

255. **Latin Name** *Halesia diptera*
Pronunciation hah-LEE-zhuh DIP-ter-ah
Common Names TWO-WINGED SILVERBELL,
SNOWDROP TREE
Usual Height 15–25 feet
Spacing 15 feet apart
Bloom Early spring; white; 1-inch bells
Deciduous
Range Moist woods and stream banks in
East Texas
South Carolina to Arkansas to Gulf of
Mexico
Soil Sand, loam; acid; moist, well drained
Dappled shade, part shade
Propagation Fresh seed in ground, double-
stratified or cold-stratified seed, layering,
root or softwood cuttings

Each spring this little tree is hung with small waxy white bells. Use it in East Texas only, either massed as understory or as an accent in a small area. The wood is somewhat brittle. A close relative is *Styrax americana* (snowbell), which can be used in Houston because it tolerates poor drainage. Will Fleming, a native plant landscaper in the area, says there's one major point of difference between the two trees; the two-winged silverbell can be enjoyed from some distance off, but to get the most out of snowbell's blooms, you have to sit down right under it and look straight up. Sycamore-leafed styrax (*S. platanifolia*) is endemic to the Edwards Plateau, making it the only one of these three that can be enjoyed on calcareous soil.

256. Witch hazel
Hamamelis virginiana
Benny J. Simpson

257. Possumhaw, female
Ilex decidua
The authors

256. **Latin Name** *Hamamelis virginiana*
Pronunciation ham-ah-MAY-liss
ver-jin-ee-AY-nah
Common Name WITCH HAZEL
Usual Height 10–15 feet
Spacing 8–10 feet apart
Bloom Fall and winter, after leaves have
dropped; yellow; ½–1 inch long
**Deciduous, with leaves turning yellow,
purple, or orange in fall**
Range Woodlands in East Texas, west to
Bandera County on Edwards Plateau
Canada to Georgia to Texas
Soil Sand, loam, clay; acid or calcareous;
moist, well drained
Dappled shade, part shade
Propagation Double-stratified seed,
layering from new wood

Witch hazel distillate was once a standard feature of all good barbershops and was used to dab on nicks and cuts. If you ever smelled it, you wouldn't soon forget it. The tree, from whose bark this astringent was derived, is a small understory plant that is remarkable for its yellow blooms, which appear in the fall, right after most autumn leaves have disappeared. In summer it displays heavy foliage; the leaves are six inches long and wavy-toothed along the edges. The fruits (little brown capsules) take all spring and summer to ripen and are held close to the branches. They open dramatically and suddenly, shooting the seeds out many feet from the tree. Birds eat these fruits—that is, if the birds manage to get to them before they explode. Witch hazel can be used in any well-drained oak woodlands or in any yard within its range where it gets shade. Ozark witch hazel (*H. vernalis*) blooms in spring or late winter. Its flowers are smaller but intensely fragrant on warm days.

257. **Latin Name** *Ilex decidua*
Pronunciation EYE-lex deh-SID-yoo-ah
Common Name POSSUMHAW
Usual Height 12–15 feet
Spacing 12–15 feet apart
Fruit Fall and winter, on females; red
(yellow); ¼ inch
Deciduous
Range Woods and edges of swamps in East
and Central Texas, south to Victoria
Virginia to Illinois to Gulf of Mexico
Soil Sand, loam, clay, caliche; seasonal
poor drainage okay
Dappled shade, part shade, full sun
Propagation Fresh seed, scarified (optional)
and double-stratified seed, semihardwood
cuttings

I use possumhaw a lot because it's so versatile. It's also one of the best trees (native or otherwise) when it comes to winter color. But it will need at least six hours of sun to become fully covered with berries. Since these trees are either male or female, the female flowers must be pollinated to make berries. If you live near a woods where possumhaw is native, there's no problem. But out of its range, you'll have to plant a male as well, although I've heard that nonnative 'Burford' and other berrying hollies can do the job too. The berries stay on until new leaves appear in the spring, unless cedar waxwings, blue jays, robins, and thrashers, among others, get to them first. This is a tree that you'll want to buy in a nursery, as selections have already been made for berries that hold their color all winter. Some people call this tree a deciduous yaupon because its size, shape, and smooth, pale gray multitrunks make it look a lot like yaupon holly in the summer. Possumhaw leaves are larger and thinner than those of yaupon holly.

258. American holly
Ilex opaca
The authors

259. Yaupon holly
Ilex vomitoria
The authors

258. **Latin Name** *Ilex opaca*
Pronunciation EYE-lex oh-PAK-ah
Common Name AMERICAN HOLLY
Usual Height 15–25 feet, can reach 50 feet
Spacing 20 feet apart
Fruit Late fall to winter; on females; red;
⅓ inch
Evergreen
Range Moist woods in East and South
Central Texas
Massachusetts to Wisconsin to Gulf of
Mexico
Soil Sand, loam; acid; moist, well drained
Shade, dappled shade, part shade, full sun
Propagation Fresh seed, scarified (optional)
and double-stratified seed, semihardwood
cuttings

American holly is your traditional Christmas orna-mental holly. It grows best in the Piney Woods, but with supplemental watering, it should do well wherever post oaks grow. In the Houston area use only 'Savannah,' a reputed hybrid or selection. It's better adapted to clay and won't get algae on its leaves from too much humidity. In full sun, American holly is drought-tolerant in its native range and makes a tall pyramidal tree. Like southern mag-nolia, it is most grand when its lower branches are al-lowed to grow right down to the ground. Pruned up, it can be planted in a confined space next to a street. In a mass planting for a large-scale screen, these hollies should be placed ten feet apart. American holly, being an under-story tree, can tolerate a lot of shade; it grows well under pine, beech, oak, and southern magnolia. In this environ-ment it is often multitrunked and not pyramidal. Even un-der the best conditions, it is a slow to moderate grower. Probably the only negative thing you can say about this tree is that its leaves are not glossy.

259. **Latin Name** *Ilex vomitoria*
Pronunciation EYE-lex vah-meh-TOR-ee-ah
Common Name YAUPON HOLLY
Usual Height 12–15 feet, can reach 25 feet
Spacing 12–15 feet apart
Fruit Fall and winter, on females; red;
¼ inch
Evergreen
Range Sandy pinewoods or oakwoods and
bottomlands in East Texas, Houston,
Post Oak Savannah, and scattered
locations on eastern Edwards Plateau
(naturalized in Eastern Cross Timbers)
Virginia to Arkansas to Gulf of Mexico
Soil Sand, loam, clay, limestone; poor
drainage okay
Shade, dappled shade, part shade, full sun
Might colonize to form a thicket
Propagation Fresh seed, scarified (optional)
and double-stratified seed, semihardwood
cuttings

Yaupon holly has become one of the most used na-tive plants all across Texas. It's a small tree, suited to nearly any landscape—residential and commercial—because it's tolerant of both drought and poor drainage and can thrive in full sun or any degree of shade. It's fairly slow-growing, so you rarely find one in a nursery that was grown from seed or cuttings; yaupon holly is abundant in nature and even large specimens are easy to transplant. (Two selections that are nursery-grown are dwarf yaupon and weeping yaupon.) Yaupon holly is multitrunked and has a pale gray bark with white patches. It naturally tends to shrub from the base and get thick and twiggy on the inside, so you have to prune carefully to get an elegantly shaped tree. Although the red berries are eaten by at least

260. Coyotillo
Karwinskia humboldtiana
The authors

261. Goldenball leadtree
Leucaena retusa
The authors

seven species of birds, the birds don't usually start on them until relatively late in the winter, when almost nothing else is left.

260. **Latin Name** *Karwinskia humboldtiana*
Pronunciation kar-WIN-skee-ah hum-bol-tee-AN-ah
Common Name COYOTILLO
Usual Height 6–7 feet, can reach 20 feet
Spacing 15 feet apart
Evergreen
Range Corpus Christi to Davis Mountains and south
Mexico
Soil Sand, loam, clay, caliche; well drained
Dappled shade, part shade, full sun
Propagation Seed

What I like best about this small tree is its fresh spring-green, crisply veined leaves. They are unusually large for the Valley, where most leaves (or leaflets) are well under an inch in length. Coyotillo's leaves are in the two-to three-inch range. Its inconspicuous and uninspiring blooms and its juicy black fruits occur all year except in the winter. This plant is poisonous—probably as toxic as oleander. Children, pigs, chickens, turkeys, and rabbits are definitely in danger from the fruits and leaves. Even deer leave coyotillo alone. Wild birds and coyotes are able to eat the fruits, presumably neutralizing the poison in their digestive systems. As a small tree, it has been seen with a trunk as large as six inches in diameter. As a shrub, it has been found to hedge easily. It is sometimes offered in the nursery trade in the Valley but is often mislabeled fiddlewood. Like fiddlewood, coyotillo has no thorns.

261. **Latin Name** *Leucaena retusa*
Pronunciation loo-SEE-nah reh-TOO-sah
Common Name GOLDENBALL LEADTREE
Usual Height 12–15 feet, can reach 25 feet
Spacing 12–15 feet apart
Bloom April to October; gold; 1-inch globes; fragrant
Deciduous
Range Dry canyons in western Edwards Plateau and Trans-Pecos Mountains
Northern Mexico
Soil Sand, loam, clay, caliche, limestone; well drained
Part shade, full sun
Propagation Fresh seed, semihardwood cuttings in summer

If you have a sunny spot and rocky soil, goldenball leadtree is a great ornamental tree to consider. But, naturally, it isn't adverse to kinder locales. The best thing about it is its orange to yellow balls of sweet-smelling flowers, which are on display throughout the warm season. The foliage is also pretty, being light-green and open enough so that even sun-loving flowers can bloom underneath. Usually multitrunked, this tree can be pruned to a single trunk if you prefer. It's fairly fast-growing. The wood is usually brittle, even when the tree grows slowly, so give it protection from stiff winds. This tree has been found to be winter-hardy as far north as McKinney and Midland and could probably go even to the Red River.

262. Sweet bay
Magnolia virginiana
The authors

263. Wax myrtle
Myrica cerifera
The authors

262. **Latin Name** *Magnolia virginiana*
Pronunciation mag-NOH-lee-ah ver-jin-ee-AY-nah
Common Names SWEET BAY, SWAMP BAY
Usual Height 20–30 feet
Spacing 20 feet apart
Bloom May and June; white; 4–6 inches across; fragrant
Almost evergreen
Range Swamps and low woods in East Texas
Massachusetts to Gulf of Mexico
Soil Sand, loam, clay; acid; poor drainage okay
Dappled shade, part shade, full sun
Propagation Stratified seed, semihardwood cuttings in summer

Seeing them side by side, you'd definitely be more attracted to the southern magnolia than this sweet bay; that big, glossy-leaved giant tends to dominate the scene. But that could be the very reason you'd go with the sweet bay in certain situations. You may want an ornamental that is more understated and won't grab the spotlight from your other plantings. Unlike its bigger cousin, sweet bay allows other plants to grow under its branches. Best of all, it has the same beautiful, lemony-fragrant, velvety white flowers as the southern magnolia—they're just a bit smaller. The leaves are also smaller, paler, and much thinner. In a mild winter, sweet bay will be almost evergreen, the leaves dropping just before new ones come on in the spring. It does well both in Houston gumbo and in East Texas. Like all magnolias, it's slow-growing.

263. **Latin Name** *Myrica cerifera*
Pronunciation MYE-reh-kah ser-IFF-er-ah
Common Name WAX MYRTLE
Usual Height 6–12 feet, can reach 36 feet
Spacing 8–15 feet apart
Evergreen
Range Wet woodlands and grasslands in East Texas
New Jersey to Gulf of Mexico
Soil Sand, loam, clay; poor drainage okay; saline okay
Dappled shade, part shade, full sun
Might colonize to form a thicket
Propagation Stratified seed, softwood or semihardwood cuttings

Extremely adaptable, this fast-growing little multi-trunked tree not only is comfortable in Houston gumbo but also can survive with as little as 25 inches of rain a year. It does require careful watering to get established, though. The leaves are a light olive-green and are spicy and aromatic when crushed. Its pale blue berries cluster on the stems of the females and are eaten by at least forty species of birds. If you have lots of leisure time, you could boil down these berries and make bayberry candles. Wax myrtle is naturally shrubby and, left unpruned, will make a large softly shaped boundary hedge. Or it can be pruned into a multitrunked tree, as in the photo. It's ideal for cutouts in a patio or for median plantings, because its roots don't mind confinement and poor drainage.

264. Retama
Parkinsonia aculeata
The authors

265. Paloverde
Parkinsonia texana
var. *macrum*
The authors

264. **Latin Name** *Parkinsonia aculeata*
Pronunciation par-kin-SOH-nee-ah
ak-yoo-lee-AH-tah
Common Names RETAMA, JERUSALEM
THORN
Usual Height 12–15 feet, can reach 35 feet
Spacing 12–15 feet apart
Bloom Spring to fall; yellow; 5- to 6-inch
clusters; fragrant
Deciduous
Range Rio Grande Plains to Georgetown
and El Paso (possibly naturalized in part
of this area)
Mexico to South America
Soil Sand, loam, clay, caliche; seasonal
poor drainage okay; some salinity okay
Part shade, full sun
Taproot
Propagation Untreated seed, semihard-
wood cuttings

The two most striking characteristics of the retama
are its lime-green branches and its ability to be almost always in bloom—except of course in extreme drought. At
such times, it drops its leaves and, showing great re-
sourcefulness, photosynthesizes with the chlorophyll in
its branches. The flowers, which are on display most of
the year, are yellow. As these blooms get older, an interesting thing happens—one petal (and only one) turns
orange. The leaves are even more curious. The leaf stem
is thicker than the leaflets, which run, evenly spaced,
down both sides. It reminds me of the way railroad tracks
are indicated on maps. About a dozen leaves thrust out
from the flower cluster, creating a dazzling effect. On
the bad side, retama seeds out profusely in moist soils,
and in large groves the fragrance can be unpleasantly
overpowering.

265. **Latin Name** *Parkinsonia texana* var. *macrum*
(*Cercidium macrum*)
Pronunciation par-kin-SOH-nee-ah
tex-AN-ah variety MAK-rum
Common Name PALOVERDE
Usual Height 9–12 feet
Spacing 12–15 feet apart
Bloom Spring (occasionally later); yellow;
1 inch long
Deciduous
Range Eastern half of Rio Grande Plains
Mexico
Soil Sand, loam, clay, caliche; well drained
Part shade, full sun
Propagation Untreated seed,
semihardwood cuttings in fall

Paloverde is similar to the retama, with a few important differences. For one thing, it is more drought-
tolerant and needs super drainage. Most people who live
around both trees prefer the paloverde because its behav-
ior is more sedate and because its trunk is prettier—
smooth and green, like the branches. The retama has a
rough-barked trunk. Paloverde's flowers are similar to retama's—yellow, with ruffled margins and with a red spot
on one petal—but grow in smaller clusters. Also, paloverde has a much shorter bloom period. The foliage of
paloverde is dense and dark, not at all like the airier, more
open look of the retama. In fact, paloverde leaves look
more like acacia leaves—not surprising, since both plants
are in the legume family. Paloverde has short, straight
spines that are not nearly as vicious as the recurved spines
of retama.

266. Texas pistachio
Pistacia texana
The authors

267. Tenaza
Pithecellobium pallens
James H. Everitt

266. **Latin Name** *Pistacia texana*
Pronunciation pis-TAH-shee-ah tex-AN-ah
Common Names TEXAS PISTACHIO,
  MEXICAN PISTACHIO, AMERICAN PISTACHIO
Usual Height 12–20 feet, can reach 40 feet
Spacing 15–20 feet apart
Bloom Late spring and early summer;
  white; 2–3 inches long
Fruit Fall, on females; red; 4- to 6-inch
  clusters
Deciduous to almost evergreen
Range Limestone cliffs near Rio Grande in
  Val Verde and Terrell counties
  Northern Mexico
Soil Sand, loam, clay, caliche, limestone;
  well drained
Part shade, full sun
Propagation Fresh seed, semihardwood
  cuttings in late summer through fall

Texas pistachio is a large, airy, rounded shrub or multitrunked small tree. The foliage is glossy; the new leaves are reddish in the spring, then turn dark green. One of the loveliest sights I've ever seen was a Texas pistachio tree completely loaded down with fresh red fruits, and three pairs of cardinals feeding in the branches. Sadly, it was closing time at the Judge Roy Bean Park in Langtry, and we had to leave without taking a picture. I still get depressed when I think about it. Although Texas pistachio grows on rocky limestone slopes, it is easier to establish in deep, rich soils. With watering, it will grow rapidly. In fact, in Houston, where the rainfall is almost too much for it, it can get top-heavy and fall over in high winds. Manuel

Flores of San Antonio says he has found that it makes an excellent hedge. For the first several years of its life, he recommends cutting it in half in mid-February to stunt and thicken it.

---

267. **Latin Name** *Pithecellobium pallens*
Pronunciation pith-eh-sell-OH-bee-um
  PAL-enz
Common Names TENAZA, APE'S EARRING
Usual Height 10–15 feet
Spacing 10–15 feet apart
Bloom May to August, after rains; creamy
  white; 2- to 6-inch clusters; fragrant
Evergreen
Range Rio Grande Valley to just north of
  Corpus Christi
  Mexico
Soil Loam; well drained
Part shade, full sun
Taproot
Propagation Scarified seed

Down in the Valley, they love tenaza because when it blooms, the entire tree is covered with sweet-smelling, fluffy white blossoms. Unfortunately, the only time we saw one, it had rained the night before and it looked like a wet dog! Unlike the zigzag branches of Texas ebony (another *Pithecellobium*), its branches are long and straight. It has spines on the twigs and branches, but it's rare to find them on the smooth, pale bark of the trunk. The foliage is pale green and loosely spaced. Tenaza is fairly fast-growing and not as drought-tolerant as most of the other Valley species in this book. Besides Valley residents, bees also love the flowers.

268. Tornillo
Prosopis pubescens
The authors

269. Cherry laurel
Prunus caroliniana
The authors

268. **Latin Name** *Prosopis pubescens*
Pronunciation proh-SOH-pus
pyoo-BESS-enz
Common Names TORNILLO,
SCREWBEAN MESQUITE
Usual Height 10–15 feet
Spacing 10–15 feet apart
Bloom May and June; cream to bright
yellow; 2- to 3-inch spikes
Fruit July to August; 2- to 3-inch
screwbeans
Deciduous
Range Trans-Pecos
Texas to California to Baja California
Soil Sand, loam, caliche; moist, well
drained
Part shade, full sun
Propagation Fresh seed, root cuttings

Tornillo is absolutely breathtaking in full bloom. The blossoms vary in color from pale yellow to a vivid, rich yellow. You'll also like the crazy, twisty screwbeans. The tree and its thorns are smaller and the foliage is lacier than that of honey mesquite. It'll be as pretty as your pruning allows. Tornillo is found growing in nature only in spots where the water table is close to the surface or where there is extra moisture from runoff. We found several nice specimens growing in a low place by the side of a road in Tornillo, Texas. (After all, what better place to look for one than in a town named for the tree!) You can't naturalize tornillo in El Paso on a dry site, but you'd be amazed how little extra watering it needs to do well.

269. **Latin Name** *Prunus caroliniana*
Pronunciation PROO-nus
kare-oh-lin-ee-AY-nah
Common Name CHERRY LAUREL
Usual Height 15–20 feet
Spacing 8–15 feet apart
Bloom Spring; white; 1- to 2-inch spikes
Evergreen
Range Fields and woodlands in East Texas
North Carolina to Gulf of Mexico
Soil Sand, loam, clay-loam; moist, well
drained
Part shade, full sun
Propagation Double-stratified seed,
cuttings

Back in the fifties, cherry laurel was used extensively as a hedge throughout East Texas, Houston, and the Blackland Prairies. Everyone was excited about this native evergreen, with its big, glossy, dark green leaves. It soon became obvious that cherry laurel didn't like being hedged and insisted on making itself into a tree. Many fine specimens remain from that period. It's useful as a large-scale screen at the back or side of a big property. Birds love the juicy black fruits that ripen in the fall and persist through the winter until they've all been eaten. After a freeze, the berries ferment, giving the birds a high. Even as far west as Dallas and Austin, cherry laurel appears to be drought-tolerant where its roots are shaded, but if the blackland soil isn't deep and loamy, the tree will get mildly chlorotic. Another drawback is that in old age the trunk can get ugly from borer attacks. A smaller version called 'Compacta' is currently being grown and should be a more manageable size if you want to use it as a shrub.

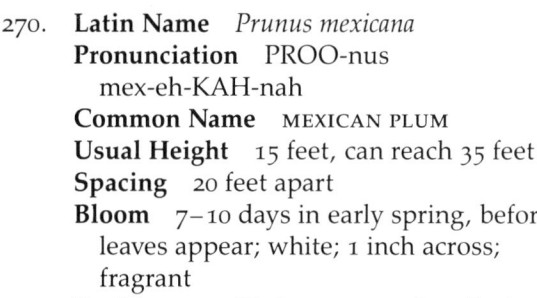

270. Mexican plum
Prunus mexicana
The authors

271. Flatwoods plum
Prunus umbellata
The authors

270. **Latin Name** *Prunus mexicana*
Pronunciation PROO-nus
mex-eh-KAH-nah
Common Name MEXICAN PLUM
Usual Height 15 feet, can reach 35 feet
Spacing 20 feet apart
Bloom 7–10 days in early spring, before
leaves appear; white; 1 inch across;
fragrant
**Deciduous, with leaves occasionally turning
yellow in fall**
Range River bottoms and prairies in Piney
Woods, Post Oak Woods, Houston,
Blacklands, and Edwards Plateau
Northern Mexico
Soil Sand, loam, clay, limestone; well
drained
Dappled shade, part shade, full sun
Propagation Double-stratified seed,
cuttings

This is the star of our native plums. In full sun or
as understory, Mexican plum makes a beautiful wide-
spreading tree. Inside its native range, it's one of the first
ornamental trees to bloom, often joined by redbud. The
scent is quite strong and sweet. Trees in full bloom are
often buzzing with bees. As the blossoms fade, they become pale pink. With age, the trunk of Mexican plum develops more character and becomes handsome—satiny,
blue-gray, with darker striations running horizontally like
fingers, and bits of peeling bark like that of birch. The

plums change color from yellow to mauve to purple as
they ripen. Birds and mammals feast on them. The leaves
sometimes have a feltlike texture on their top sides. Our
smaller plums form thickets, but Mexican plum is well
behaved—a tree to enjoy and treasure for years. It can be
used as an accent in full sun, massed for a large-scale and
dramatic effect, or scattered with redbuds in the woods to
create a vernal pink and white scene.

271. **Latin Name** *Prunus umbellata*
Pronunciation PROO-nus oom-bell-AH-tah
Common Name FLATWOODS PLUM
Usual Height 12–15 feet, can reach 20 feet
Spacing 15 feet apart
Bloom Spring; white; 1 inch across
Deciduous
Range East Texas
Mississippi to Arkansas and Texas
Soil Sand, loam; acid; well drained
Dappled shade, part shade, full sun
Propagation Stratified seed, cuttings

In East Texas they call this the forgotten plum.
Smaller and a later bloomer than Mexican plum, it just
gets upstaged. Otherwise, it is equally beautiful. The later
blooming is actually an advantage if you want a scene that
includes colorful wildflowers beneath its branches—as in
the picture, where the flatwoods plum poses with Drummond phlox. Unfortunately, this plum doesn't seem to
like heavy clay, making it an option only for those of you
with fast-draining soil.

272. Mohr oak
Quercus mohriana
The authors

273. Carolina buckthorn
Rhamnus caroliniana
The authors

272. **Latin Name** *Quercus mohriana*
Pronunciation KWER-kus mor-ee-AY-nah
Common Names MOHR OAK, SHIN OAK, SCRUB OAK
Usual Height 10–20 feet
Spacing 12 feet apart
Almost evergreen
Range Limestone hills and mountains in Trans-Pecos, West Texas, and High Plains
Northern Mexico
Soil Sand, loam, caliche, limestone; well drained
Part shade, full sun
Might colonize to form a thicket
Propagation Fresh acorns

This small live oak is more drought-tolerant than escarpment live oak, but less so than Vasey oak. Its leaves are dark green to gray-green and shiny on the top side, wavy along the edges, and furry white on the underside. If you leave Mohr oak alone, it will form a small grove, but you'll get a bigger tree if you prune off the suckers. In very dry areas Mohr Oak will form thickets only three to four feet high. A similar oak is the turbinella (*Q. turbinella*), which also shares the name "scrub oak." It is completely evergreen in El Paso, and its leaves are similar to those of Hinckley oak—small, hollylike, and blue-green. An ornamental oak for the central part of the state is the Bigelow (*Q. sinuata* var. *breviloba*). This oak doesn't even attempt to be evergreen, but its pale gray, flaking bark is so outstanding, it attracts lots of winter interest. In the limestone near Goldthwaite, it's a beautiful multitrunked tree, eight to ten feet tall. In the sands of the Red River, it gets only three feet tall. Don't ask me why!

273. **Latin Name** *Rhamnus caroliniana*
Pronunciation RAM-nus kare-oh-lin-ee-AY-nah
Common Names CAROLINA BUCKTHORN, INDIAN CHERRY
Usual Height 12–15 feet, can reach 20 feet
Spacing 8–12 feet apart
Fruit Fall; red, turning to black; ½ inch
Deciduous to almost evergreen, with leaves turning bright yellow in fall
Range Bottomlands or along streams in Piney Woods, Post Oak Woods, Houston, Blacklands, and Edwards Plateau
Virginia to Gulf of Mexico
Soil Sand, loam, clay, limestone; poor drainage okay
Dappled shade, part shade, full sun
Propagation Fresh seed, semihardwood cuttings in late summer, dormant hardwood cuttings

Carolina buckthorn is prettiest under the shade of a large tree. There it becomes airy and tiered, like shaded flowering dogwoods. However, in dense shade, it will die because it needs three to four hours of sun a day. In full sun, it is healthy but tends to get dense and shrubby, losing its ethereal quality. Commercially grown selections have the glossy leaves that make this tree so visually special. Carolina buckthorn can be found in seasonally flooded ditches in the Big Thicket. It does well in Houston's gumbo but can't take standing water for extended periods of time. It can also be found on limestone hillsides near Goldthwaite, where it can become drought-stressed. Still, groves of these buckthorns exist there, proving the versatility of this tree. The fruits turn red in late summer and hold this bright color for a couple of months, finally ripening to black in October. As soon as they ripen, they are demolished by several species of birds.

274. Prairie flameleaf sumac
Rhus lanceolata
The authors

275. Evergreen sumac
Rhus virens
The authors

274. **Latin Name** *Rhus lanceolata*
Pronunciation ROOS lan-see-oh-LAH-tah
Common Names PRAIRIE FLAMELEAF
SUMAC, LANCELEAF SUMAC
Usual Height 10–20 feet
Spacing 10–15 feet apart
Bloom Mid to late summer; white; 4- to
6-inch pyramids
Fruit Fall and winter; red; 4- to 6-inch
pyramids
Deciduous, with leaves turning red in fall
Range On limestone and calcareous soils in
North Central Texas, Edwards Plateau,
Trans-Pecos, north to Palo Duro Canyon
New Mexico
R. copallina (Flameleaf Sumac)—Eastern half
of Texas; New England to Illinois to Gulf
of Mexico
Soil Sand, loam, clay, caliche, limestone;
well drained
Part shade, full sun
Might colonize to form a thicket
Propagation Scarified seed, semihardwood
cuttings in late summer

Prairie flameleaf sumac really lives up to its name.
It provides unfailingly vivid red fall color for several
weeks, year after year, no matter what the weather. It is a
nicely shaped tree, frequently single-trunked. And although it can sucker, I haven't noticed its doing so unless
it has been damaged by grazing, mowing, or burning. To
tell it apart from the extremely aggressive smooth sumac
(in Chapter 6, Shrubs), look at a leaf, which consists of a
stem and several pairs of leaflets; if the stem is winged,
you're safe. Prairie flameleaf looks marvelous standing
alone, but it does well clustered for a big fall show, especially when backed by yellow-leaved soapberry. It provides food for bees, mammals, and more than twenty species of birds. Flameleaf sumac is the version that is native
to moister, shadier East Texas.

275. **Latin Name** *Rhus virens*
Pronunciation ROOS VYE-renz
Common Name EVERGREEN SUMAC
Usual Height 8–12 feet
Spacing 8 feet apart
Bloom Late summer; white; 2-inch clusters
Evergreen
Range Gullies and dry hillsides in Edwards
Plateau and Trans-Pecos
Northern Mexico
Soil Sand, loam, clay, caliche, limestone,
igneous; well drained
Part shade, full sun
Propagation Fresh scarified seed

276. Mexican elderberry
Sambucus mexicana
The authors

276. **Latin Name** *Sambucus mexicana*
Pronunciation sam-BOO-kus
mex-eh-KAH-nah
Common Names MEXICAN ELDERBERRY,
TAPIRO, SAUCO
Usual Height 10–15 feet, can reach 35 feet
Spacing 10–15 feet apart
Bloom June and fall; pale yellow to white;
4- to 8-inch clusters
Almost evergreen
Range Along streams at lower elevations in
Trans-Pecos
California to Mexico
Soil Sand, loam, gravel; poor drainage okay
Part shade, full sun
Propagation Scarified and stratified seed,
softwood cuttings

This is one of my favorite evergreens. Like live oak, this sumac isn't a true evergreen; its leaves are green through the winter, then drop, to be replaced within a week by a new crop. The leaves are shiny and tinged with pink when they first come out in the spring. Many people think of evergreen sumac as a shrub, because it is short and takes well to hedging. But I've seen it grow to a height well over my head, with a handsome, long, straight trunk. Its flowers are white and redolent of honey and are a special treat because they appear in August, when most other flowers are barely holding on. Bees and butterflies are especially appreciative. These blooms are followed by orange-red fuzzy fruits that are important food for both birds and small mammals; they usually provide color through Christmas. After frost, the leaves sometimes become tinged with maroon. Evergreen sumac is marginally winter-hardy in Dallas, where it needs a sunny, protected corner. If you're going to use it in Houston, give it good drainage. Mearn sumac (*R. virens* subsp. *choriophylla*) is similar and even more drought-tolerant, growing as far west as Arizona.

Cultivated from El Paso to Del Rio, Mexican elderberry has saucer-size clusters of flowers that can be white, cream, or pale yellow. The fruits that follow look like clusters of blueberries and are eaten by a number of birds. You'll never find a big Mexican elderberry in a nursery container, but it will really take off as soon as you get it into the ground. Like all elderberries, it loves extra water and can grow quite fast. As a result the branches can become brittle and often get frozen back in El Paso. The tree recovers so quickly, however, that it remains popular there. It is fairly drought-tolerant but will drop its leaves in the summer if it gets too dry.

277. Sassafras
Sassafras albidum
The authors

277. Sassafras
Sassafras albidum
The authors

277. **Latin Name** *Sassafras albidum*
Pronunciation SASS-ah-frass al-BEE-dum
Common Name SASSAFRAS
Usual Height 15–20 feet
Spacing 10–15 feet apart
Bloom Early spring; females larger and prettier; yellow; 2-inch clusters
Deciduous, with leaves turning red, orange, peach, and yellow in fall
Range Sandy woods in eastern third of Texas
Michigan to Gulf of Mexico
Soil Sand, loam; acid; well drained
Part shade, full sun
Might colonize to form a thicket
Propagation Stratified seed, root cuttings

Sassafras blooms early in the spring, before its mitten-shaped leaves appear. Both male and female trees flower, but on the males the blooms are small and sparsely distributed. The females put on a much better display, with little bunches of bright yellow flowers scattered profusely over the entire tree. They seem to float, there being no foliage to distract your eye. The fruits don't have time to be decorative; they're gobbled up by birds as soon as they ripen in early autumn. The bark and roots emit a spicy fragrance when bruised. Sassafras grows quickly with fertilizer and moisture but must be well drained. It isn't really drought-tolerant and can't be used outside of East Texas. You can control sassafras as a single tree, or let it sucker into a small grove. Put several of the trees in a sunny corner of your yard, and watch how the blooms and fall colors come even more alive en masse.

278. **Latin Name** *Sophora affinis*
Pronunciation SOFF-er-ah or soh-FOR-ah ah-FIN-us
Common Name EVE'S NECKLACE
Usual Height 15 feet, can reach 30 feet
Spacing 10 feet apart
Bloom Late spring; pink; 4- to 6-inch drooping clusters
Fruit Fall and winter; black; 4- to 6-inch strings of ½-inch beads
Deciduous
Range Fields or woodlands in Blacklands, Cross Timbers, and Edwards Plateau
Oklahoma, Arkansas, Louisiana
Soil Sand, loam, clay, limestone; well drained
Dappled shade, part shade, full sun
Might colonize to form a thicket
Propagation Scarified seed

Eve's necklace puts forth pink wisteria-like blooms in late spring, after it has leafed out. Sometimes they're pale or yellowish, so choose your tree in bloom if possible, to make sure you'll wind up with good color. The winter

278. Eve's necklace
Sophora affinis
The authors

279. Texas mountain laurel
Sophora secundiflora
The authors

necklaces are highly ornamental and don't drop until new leaves appear in the spring. These fruits contain a poisonous substance, which tends to make them a less-than-popular menu item with wildlife. I've often seen groves of Eve's necklace under red oaks and junipers on limestone escarpment. I've also seen this tree growing in full sun in deep sand, and in partial shade on the high banks of streams. It must be well drained, or it gets chlorotic. It will grow from a seed to a six-foot tree in three years. Transplant it from the wild only in the winter.

279. **Latin Name** *Sophora secundiflora*
Pronunciation SOFF-er-ah or soh-FOR-ah seh-kun-deh-FLOR-ah
Common Names TEXAS MOUNTAIN LAUREL, MESCAL BEAN
Usual Height 6–12 feet, can reach 30 feet
Spacing 10 feet apart
Bloom Early spring; purple; 3- to 7-inch drooping clusters; fragrant
Evergreen
Range Brush in Rio Grande Plains north to Austin and west to Trans-Pecos New Mexico, Mexico
Soil Sand, loam, clay, caliche, limestone; well drained; some salinity okay
Dappled shade, part shade, full sun
Might colonize to form a thicket

Propagation Scarified seed, fresh seed still swollen in pod, cuttings from juvenile trees

This beautiful tree, if left unpruned and in full sun, can be used as a large shrub. It also grows well as understory beneath live oaks in the Hill Country. The heavy green leaves are glossy, and the flowers open as deep purple, then gradually fade to pale lavender. The scent is strong—crisp and clean on a cold, windy day, but like icky sweet grape soda on a hot day. The pale tan seedpods have a feltlike texture and aren't very exciting. But the seeds themselves are a vibrant red and are used in making jewelry. They are even more toxic than those of Eve's necklace. But as with Eve's necklace, the seed coat is so hard that it is difficult to release the poison. Although naturally slow-growing, Texas mountain laurel can be forced to grow more speedily, but then its tender new leaves get gobbled up by *Uresiphita reversalis*, which everybody simply calls "the worm"!

280. Mexican buckeye
Ungnadia speciosa
The authors

281. Farkleberry
Vaccinium arboreum
The authors

281. Farkleberry
Vaccinium arboreum
Benny J. Simpson

280. **Latin Name**   *Ungnadia speciosa*
Pronunciation   ung-NAH-dee-ah
  spee-see-OH-sah
Common Name   MEXICAN BUCKEYE
Usual Height   8–12 feet, can reach 30 feet
Spacing   8 feet apart
Bloom   Early spring; pink; 1 inch; fragrant
Deciduous, with leaves turning yellow in fall
Range   In canyons and on rocky slopes in
  Rio Grande Plains, Trans-Pecos,
  Edwards Plateau, and northeast to Dallas
  and on bayous near Houston
  New Mexico, Mexico
Soil   Sand, loam, clay, caliche, limestone;
  well drained
Part shade, full sun
Propagation   Untreated seed

Mexican buckeye is one of our most beautiful ornamental trees—yet it's virtually impossible to photograph it flatteringly in the spring. You see it in full flower and imagine what an award-winning picture it will make. Then you see the results, and the pink blooms seem to have disappeared. The light green leaves start unfolding with the flowers and turn a clear golden yellow in the fall. The seeds, which are mildly poisonous, look like those of a buckeye, giving the plant its name, but it isn't in the same family as buckeyes. From east to west, Mexican buckeye changes in appearance. In Houston it is a rapidly growing tree, with large pale pink flowers. But in Mc-

Kittrick Canyon, in the Guadalupe Mountains, it's a four-foot-tall shrub, with smaller, rosy-pink flowers. The difference is probably a matter of nutrition; Ray Pulaski of El Paso grew a Mexican buckeye from seed. In fifteen years it became a fifteen-foot-tree with a single five-inch-caliper trunk—without pruning!

282. Chisos rosewood
Vauquelinia angustifolia
The authors

281. **Latin Name** *Vaccinium arboreum*
Pronunciation vak-SIN-ee-um
ar-BOR-ee-um
Common Names FARKLEBERRY,
SPARKLEBERRY
Usual Height 12–15 feet, can reach 25 feet
Spacing 10–12 feet apart
Bloom Late spring; white; ½-inch bells;
fragrant
**Deciduous to almost evergreen, with leaves
turning red in fall**
Range Piney Woods, Post Oak Savannah,
and along coast south to Port Aransas
Virginia to Illinois to Gulf of Mexico
Soil Sand; acid; well drained
Dappled shade, part shade
Propagation Softwood cuttings in spring,
dormant hardwood cuttings

There is an exceptionally fine example of this tree
at Mercer Arboretum in Houston. It is twenty feet tall and
spaciously branched—and every spring it is hung with a
million tiny, white, fragrant bells. Farkleberry is a member of the heath family (which includes blueberries), so its
fruits look like little blueberries and are eaten by several
species of wintering birds. Your particular tree might be
deciduous, or it might be evergreen (perhaps I should say
"ever-red"). In the fall, farkleberry leaves turn a dramatic,
deep, rich red. They then fade to purple and might stay
around all winter, unless they get blown off by gusty
winds. In the summer the leaves are a shiny dark green
and have a thick, leathery feel. They can vary in length
from one to three inches.

282. **Latin Name** *Vauquelinia angustifolia*
Pronunciation vaw-kah-LIN-ee-ah
an'-gus-teh-FOLE-ee-ah
Common Names CHISOS ROSEWOOD,
GUAUYUL
Usual Height 9–15 feet, can reach 30 feet
Spacing 9–15 feet apart
Bloom Summer; white; 4- to 6-inch clusters;
fragrant
Evergreen
Range Chaparral and canyons of Chisos
and Dead Horse mountains in Trans-
Pecos
Northern Mexico
Soil Sand, loam, clay, caliche, limestone;
well drained
Part shade, full sun
Propagation Fresh seed

Our native rosewood has narrow leaves and big
clusters of flowers. It is actually a member of the rose
family, which means that on the one hand, it has the
sweet fragrance of roses, but on the other hand, it gets
fire blight and other nasty rose diseases. It can be used as
a large shrub for screening, as shown in the photo, or it
can be pruned into a small evergreen tree with intricate
branching. After the flowers have bloomed, you might
want to cut off the seed heads; they aren't particularly

283. Rusty blackhaw viburnum
Viburnum rufidulum
Doug Williams

283. Rusty blackhaw viburnum
Viburnum rufidulum
Benny J. Simpson

good-looking or important for feeding our feathered friends. Chisos rosewood has been found to be perfectly winter-hardy in Midland and Dallas, even during the awful winter of '83. So it could undoubtedly be useful farther north.

---

283. **Latin Name**   *Viburnum rufidulum*
Pronunciation   vye-BER-num
    roo-FID-yoo-lum
Common Name   RUSTY BLACKHAW
    VIBURNUM
Usual Height   12–15 feet, can reach 30 feet
Spacing   8–10 feet apart
Bloom   Late spring; white; 4- to 6-inch
    heads
Deciduous, with leaves turning red, mauve, purple, orange, and yellow in fall
Range   Open wooded areas in Piney
    Woods, Post Oak Woods, Blacklands,
    and Hill Country
    Virginia to Illinois to Gulf of Mexico
Soil   Sand, loam, clay, limestone; well
    drained
Dappled shade, part shade, full sun

Propagation   Fresh seed planted outdoors,
    semihardwood cuttings in fall

A rusty blackhaw viburnum with a four-inch-caliper trunk is quite mature and should be revered and treasured. This viburnum is slow-growing and hard to propagate—and always in demand. The leaves are a glossy, dark green in the summer and a wide range of warm hues in late fall. The flowers, which appear after the leaves are fully developed, are intensely white and seem to shine against the dark backdrop of the lustrous foliage. The fruits—the black haws—ripen in the fall and are big favorites with the birds. With south or west sun, and no pruning, rusty blackhaw's branches will arch gracefully down to the ground. But if you see one in the woods, it will be a small tree with a long bare trunk. An eastern viburnum, southern arrowwood (*V. dentatum*), has the same flowers, fruits, and red-to-wine fall colors but differs from rusty blackhaw in that it only likes sandy soils and prefers them moist.

Create-a-Woods Plan
Lot Size: 64' × 40'

When I first pointed out to my husband that we had a woods on our property, he looked at me in a funny way. "We have trees," he said, "but a woods means dozens of them. Acres of them! Doesn't it?"

Like a lot of people, he thought you can't enjoy your very own woods unless you have at least an acre. Our home is on far less land, yet we have an attractive woodsy area.

Ours runs alongside forty-odd feet of driveway and is only about twelve feet wide at one end and twenty at the other. It consists of two large shade trees, four understory trees, and a mixture of ground covers and woodland flowers. It gives great pleasure to us, our neighbors, our birds and squirrels—and our cats, who use this shaded spot to unwind from their "stressful" days.

I just came in from doing the spring weeding, and I think I have a fairly good idea of what the wildlife ate all winter. The cedar elm crop must have been particularly tasty. Other staples were hackberry, Japanese honeysuckle, yaupon holly, poison ivy, privet, Russian mulberry, Virginia creeper, and a sedge. I blame the squirrels for the oaks and pecans. I say "blame" because they bury the nuts, making them particularly hard to pull. I firmly believe that any one of our squirrels planted more acorns last year than any nurseryman in the state of Texas.

I finished this job in a little over an hour. I'll do it again in the fall. I never rake the leaves (they make an excellent mulch as they decompose). Every odd-numbered year we have the trees pruned professionally. I water if or when leaves droop. This is not a lot of work and trouble for a landscape that receives compliments all during the year from passing joggers.

Regions in Texas where a woods, as depicted in this plan, is a feasible landscape are Houston, Piney Woods, Post Oak, Blackland, Hill Country, and Valley. Of course, the trees used would be quite different for each one. Consult your regional plans for a tree list, and then follow the suggestions here for how to plant a woods if you want one but have only one or two trees—or none—to start with.

A woods is in three main layers. The canopy is the top layer, the tallest trees that shade everything below. The understory is made up of small trees and shrubs that tolerate or require shade. The ground cover is creeping plants, flowers, vines, and dead leaves.

Look at the plan. The smallish double circles show the trunks of the shade trees (I couldn't use large circles to indicate the spread of these trees without making the whole plan unreadable). Next are two different kinds of understory trees, for spring flowering and fall color. Evergreen trees are spaced for maximum privacy and backdrop. Closer to the woodland floor are large shrubs and some very small understory trees, then small shrubs and ferns, then lower-growing ground covers, and, finally, woodland flowers.

On the edge of the woods, you'll notice many dots. These indicate bird-planted saplings that are making a fencerow barrier on the west side of the yard, where heavy shade and privacy are desired.

The grid shown on the plan is in ten-foot squares, with one canopy tree in each square. However, these trees aren't evenly spaced, because that would look too contrived. I've placed them from two to eighteen feet apart, for a random, more natural look. It's hard to make yourself plant shade trees two feet apart, but that kind of clustering of the trunks is precisely what will make your woods effective.

In impenetrable woods, I've counted a consistent average of three or four understory trees or saplings in each ten-foot square, and fifteen to twenty shrubs or ground cover plants. The upper left-hand corner, where privacy is desired, reflects this density. Unless you are very rich or very impatient, plant the shade trees, evergreens, and small flowering understory, and then let the birds and squirrels plant the rest for you.

Actually, birds and squirrels are going to add copiously to all of your woods every year, and removing their unwanted offerings will be the bulk of your annual maintenance. Where beauty is more important than privacy, keep your woods cleared to maintain the density shown on the right-hand half of the plan. A desirable density here would be one understory tree for each shade tree. The trees should be pruned to a light, graceful look, and the woodland floor should be filled with ferns, flowering shrubs, flowers, bulbs, and so forth.

Planting

Choose very small container-grown trees, and plant them in the native soil. See the introduction to Chapter 9 (Shade Trees) for more details.

Important: Don't plant the shady ground covers, ferns, and flowers on the woodland floor until your trees are large enough to provide more than a half day of shade or dappled shade. When your trees are small, and plenty of sun gets through, the only easy-maintenance ground cover is grass. A meadow full of wildflowers is delightful. Most of the shrubs take sun as well as shade, so they can be planted immediately, but I'd hold off where they would make mowing the meadow difficult. Plant little bluestem, split-beard bluestem, Gulf muhly, sideoats grama, or buffalo grass. As the shade thickens, the grasses will recede and dwindle, leaving spaces for you to fill with the shade-loving flowers and ground covers.

Pruning

Woodland understory is typically open and airy. Even in the sunny developmental stages, don't hedge your shrubs. Let them develop naturally. If they seem too dense, you can thin them out by pick-pruning. Do the same with the ornamental trees. You want them to be artistically open and see-through, so cut out interior branches, but *never* cut off the end of a branch. If a branch obstructs a path, cut it off flush with the trunk.

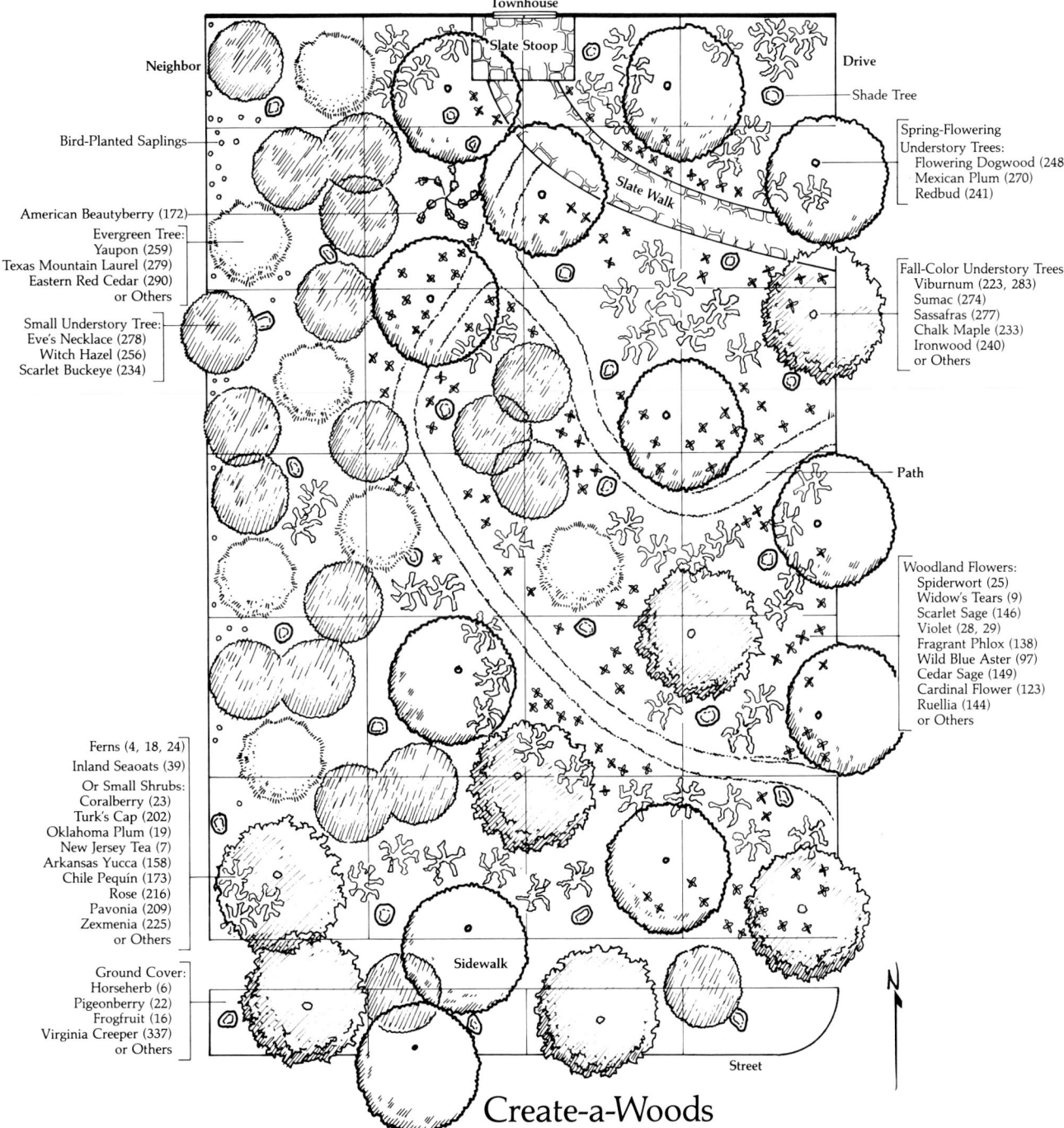

Townhouse

Slate Stoop

Neighbor

Drive

Shade Tree

Bird-Planted Saplings

Spring-Flowering
Understory Trees:
    Flowering Dogwood (248)
    Mexican Plum (270)
    Redbud (241)

Slate Walk

American Beautyberry (172)

Evergreen Tree:
    Yaupon (259)
Texas Mountain Laurel (279)
Eastern Red Cedar (290)
    or Others

Fall-Color Understory Trees:
    Viburnum (223, 283)
    Sumac (274)
    Sassafras (277)
    Chalk Maple (233)
    Ironwood (240)
    or Others

Small Understory Tree:
    Eve's Necklace (278)
    Witch Hazel (256)
Scarlet Buckeye (234)

Path

Woodland Flowers:
    Spiderwort (25)
    Widow's Tears (9)
    Scarlet Sage (146)
    Violet (28, 29)
    Fragrant Phlox (138)
    Wild Blue Aster (97)
    Cedar Sage (149)
    Cardinal Flower (123)
    Ruellia (144)
    or Others

Ferns (4, 18, 24)
Inland Seaoats (39)
Or Small Shrubs:
    Coralberry (23)
    Turk's Cap (202)
    Oklahoma Plum (19)
    New Jersey Tea (7)
    Arkansas Yucca (158)
    Chile Pequín (173)
    Rose (216)
    Pavonia (209)
    Zexmenia (225)
    or Others

Ground Cover:
    Horseherb (6)
    Pigeonberry (22)
    Frogfruit (16)
Virginia Creeper (337)
    or Others

Sidewalk

Street

N

Create-a-Woods

Paths

Woodland paths should be very informal and subtle so they blend into the woods and don't intrude. They can be mulched with pine needles, bark mulch (fine, not nuggets), pecan or ebony shells, other organic materials, crushed rock. Or you can just keep the paths mowed or trimmed. Or use them so frequently that your passing is sufficient to keep the soil compacted and encroaching branches at bay.

Lynn Lowrey, native plant nurseryman, and pianist James Dick, director and founder of the Festival-Institute at Round Top, designed and planted this woods about seven years before this picture was taken. Evergreens, canopy trees, and understory ornamentals are fairly evenly scattered throughout. Grass underneath is still appropriate at this stage, as not enough shade has developed to accommodate woodland ground covers. Photo by the authors.

EIGHT

Conifers

ONE of my biggest hopes in the area of landscaping is that more of you will become familiar with and start using our lovely native conifers. Why they aren't being used more often, when we have so many varieties in Texas, is a puzzle. But I have a few guesses, based mostly on observations and conversations with some of you around the state.

For one thing, native conifers share the stigma of all our native plants—familiarity, which breeds, if not contempt, at least indifference. Except in the Piney Woods and in the mountains of the Trans-Pecos, our most visible conifers are junipers. Eastern red cedar, Ashe juniper, and oneseed juniper are those most in abundance, often seen in vast natural stands, yet only rarely do we see them gracing some home landscape.

Now, if you have to stop and think a minute at the mention of junipers, I should add that you may know them as cedars. They aren't cedars, though. They're junipers of one kind or another. In fact, there are no genuine native cedars in the entire continental U.S. of A.

Loving junipers comes easily to me. I love their spicy smell, their shaggy bark, and their rugged, sheltering good looks. They are true evergreens. The berries of the females make vivid winter color, as well as tasty meals for birds, which roost and nest among the branches. Junipers are drought-tolerant and can grow in raw, newly cleared land. They're hardy and will probably outlast your house, growing more beautiful each year. Frankly, it always bowls me over when I meet people who don't like them. But such people exist.

Ranchers, I've heard, dislike junipers because "cattle won't eat them." Well, that's okay. That just means deer won't touch them either. Besides, how many residential landscapes have you seen that were designed with cows in mind?

Other people don't like them because of the bandwagon effect. (My husband calls it the lemming syndrome.) When you hear enough people bad-mouthing them, you assume they must be bad. Trouble is, the people who are saying negative things are doing it mostly because that's what they've heard from someone else.

So my message to you is, be brave. Take the plunge. Go against the tide of common wisdom, and plant a juniper or two in your yard. If your neighbors don't run you out of town, plant some more. Who knows? You might start a trend!

Junipers head an impressive list of native conifers. Many, I must admit, are comfortable only in their own back yards and don't do well in other regions. But some can thrive in numerous locales outside their natural habitats. Let's look at what our state offers in the way of conifers, and see what might be usable where you live.

Except for the aforementioned junipers, all Texas conifers are divided into two distinct groups: One is happy living in the High Country of the Trans-Pecos, while the other loves the Piney Woods of East Texas. Neither can tolerate the other's habitat.

The Trans-Pecos conifers are further divided into two subgroups. One is allied with the Rockies and needs cooler summers. The members of that group that are featured in this book are Rocky Mountain juniper, one-seed juniper, Colorado pinyon, Rocky Mountain ponderosa pine, and blue Douglas fir. Clearly, these are not good choices for Corpus Christi or Houston or Dallas, but they can be used in the High Plains as long as they get supplemental watering. They are often used in the mountains of New Mexico, Arizona, and Colorado.

The second Trans-Pecos subgroup is allied with Mexico and needs milder winters. The ones in the book from that group are Arizona cypress, alligator juniper, weeping juniper, and Mexican pinyon. These trees should be able to grow well in West Texas, the Hill Country, the Western Cross Timbers, and the Blacklands—wherever drainage is good and where they are winter-hardy. I say "should" because they are so seldom used in these areas; they're still virtually in an experimental stage.

The East Texas group is less complicated and is made up of shortleaf pine, longleaf pine, loblolly pine, eastern red cedar, and bald cypress (called *sabino* in Spanish, it gave its name to the Sabine River). These last two can be used all over the state as long as they get adequate water. In fact, the bald cypress is native to the Hill Country and is commonly seen there growing along streams and rivers.

An interesting sidelight is that each of these two major groups has a totally separate colony thriving in some other part of the state. Thus, we find East Texas loblollies in Bastrop State Park, southeast of Austin, some one hundred miles away from the main body of pines, and we find pinyon pines a good two hundred miles east of the High Country of the Trans-Pecos.

Why do they exist off by themselves? The loblollies simply grow wherever the soil is right for them. There are little fingers of acid sandy loam scattered between Conroe and Bastrop that contain these trees. Those at Bastrop are the farthest west and grow in an island surrounded by blackland prairie, so it's always dramatic when you come upon them.

As for the pinyon pines, back in the ice ages they were connected directly to the ones in the Trans-Pecos, making one vast continuous forest. The entire state was cooler and moister in those days. As the climate changed, the forests shrank, marooning small pockets in Edwards, Real, and other counties west of Lost Maples State Natural Area. It is a mystery why these still survive. The climate is so much hotter and drier there than they should be able to withstand. Apparently, these trees just decided they'd better adapt and get tougher or else.

Shortleaf and loblolly pines tower over a natural understory of dogwood and parsley hawthorn at Mercer Arboretum on the north side of Houston. Formal gardens are laid out on the edges of this woodland stand. Photo by the authors.

284. Arizona cypress
Cupressus arizonica var. *arizonica*
The authors

285. Ashe juniper
Juniperus ashei
The authors

284. **Latin Name** *Cupressus arizonica* var. *arizonica*
Pronunciation koo-PREH-sus
ah-reh-ZOHN-eh-kah
Common Name ARIZONA CYPRESS
Usual Height 30 feet, can reach 75 feet
Spacing 20 feet apart
Evergreen
Range Chisos Mountains (3,000–8,000 feet)
in Trans-Pecos
New Mexico, California, northern Mexico
Soil Sand, loam, clay; well drained
Full sun
Propagation Cuttings

This is probably the most widely used conifer in the state. It's fast-growing and therefore relatively short-lived (thirty to fifty years). The pleasantly aromatic foliage is a pale blue-green. When the tree is young, its branches grow all the way down to the ground, making it resemble a Christmas tree, but in old age the trunk is exposed and often unusually attractive. The rough outer bark scales off, exposing an inner bark that then goes through a rainbow of color changes: lime-green to tan to ocher to plum to red. Within the state this tree has been planted as far away from the Trans-Pecos mountains as East Texas, but where summers are hotter, it is never as beautiful as it is at home. The foliage looks thin and dusty gray, so I don't recommend it east of Dallas. This conifer is also one of the Mexican subgroup, so it is not winter-hardy in the far northern High Plains.

285. **Latin Name** *Juniperus ashei*
Pronunciation joo-NIP-er-us ASH-ee-eye
Common Names ASHE JUNIPER,
MOUNTAIN CEDAR
Usual Height 18 feet
Spacing 15 feet apart
Evergreen
Range Rocky soil in Edwards Plateau to
Fort Worth, Dallas, and Abilene
Missouri to Mexico
Soil Sand, loam, clay, limestone; well
drained
Part shade, full sun
Propagation Seed sown outdoors in fall

This is one of my favorite trees in the whole state. The big, thick, straight radiating branches start almost at ground level, so an old tree looks like it is multitrunked. The bark is wonderfully shaggy and peels off in strips, often six feet long. Which isn't to say you should go out and peel off a few! The peeling happens naturally, and the strips are then used by the rare golden-cheeked warblers to build their nests. (You can see the strips in the photo of the young tree.) The leaves are dark green and aromatic, and when the female is covered with large dark-blue fruits, the whole tree has a lovely blue-green color. Although shrubby when young, the full-grown tree is nothing less than majestic. These conifers are frequently found growing out of what appears to be solid limestone. It's often said that nothing will grow under one of these trees. Actually, their fallen needles create moist, acid organic matter in which unusual and coveted trees such as Texas madrone, Texas smoke tree, and silk-tassel tree germinate and grow; they rarely grow anywhere else. In addition,

286. Alligator juniper
Juniperus deppeana var. *deppeana*
The authors

287. Weeping juniper
Juniperus flaccida
The authors

two flowers—cedar sage and zexmenia—do exceptionally well in the needles. A big goodie is that Ashe juniper is immune to cedar-apple rust.

---

286. **Latin Name** *Juniperus deppeana* var. *deppeana*
Pronunciation joo-NIP-er-us
dep-ee-AY-nah
Common Name ALLIGATOR JUNIPER
Usual Height 15–20 feet, can reach 25 feet
Spacing 16 feet apart
Evergreen
Range Open rocky areas in mountains and foothills of Trans-Pecos
Arizona, New Mexico, Mexico
Soil Sand, loam, clay, limestone; well drained
Full sun
Propagation Seed sown outdoors in fall

The common name comes from the texture of the trunk; it looks like the hide of an alligator. This juniper is unusual in that the trunk is always exposed, and the branches never grow down to ground level. When it's still a sapling, the trunk resembles the scaly bark of an Arizona cypress. The foliage, especially of the females, is dark blue-green, and the fruits are copper-colored. Although slow-growing in the wild, alligator juniper is medium- to fast-growing if given water. It appears that this adaptable conifer is going to grow well over most of the state. Most alligator junipers have dark green needles, but some high up in the Davis Mountains have needles that are a soft steely gray.

287. **Latin Name** *Juniperus flaccida*
Pronunciation joo-NIP-er-us FLASS-eh-dah
Common Name WEEPING JUNIPER
Usual Height 20–30 feet
Spacing 15 feet apart
Evergreen
Range Forested or open rocky slopes of Chisos Mountains
Mexico
Soil Sand, loam, clay, igneous; acid or calcareous; well drained
Part shade, full sun
Propagation Seed from ripe fruits (fruits are reddish brown when ripe)

The only place in the United States where this tree grows natively is in the Chisos Mountains. You will spot these slow-growing, long-lived conifers in Big Bend National Park; several large specimens are close to the road that goes up to the lodge. They are easy to recognize because both the branches and the needles droop. But instead of looking limp and depressed, the tree has an overall grand and elegant appearance. This is another juniper that exposes its trunk rather than growing in the Christmas tree shape. It is winter-hardy at least as far north as Amarillo. For years this tree has been popular in the gardens of southern Europe and North Africa. I think it's high time it was used more widely here at home.

288. Oneseed juniper
Juniperus monosperma
Benny J. Simpson

289. Rocky Mountain juniper
Juniperus scopulorum
The authors

288. **Latin Name**   *Juniperus monosperma*
Pronunciation   joo-NIP-er-us
moh-noh-SPER-mah
Common Names   ONESEED JUNIPER,
CHERRYSTONE JUNIPER
Usual Height   18 feet
Spacing   10 feet apart
Evergreen
Range   Steep slopes and eroded breaks of
High Plains and Trans-Pecos
Northwest Oklahoma to Nevada to Mexico
Soil   Sand, loam, clay, caliche, limestone;
well drained
Part shade, full sun
Propagation   Seed sown outdoors in fall

Oneseed juniper is the most cold-hardy and drought-tolerant juniper in the state. When it is pruned to a single trunk and watered, it grows rapidly and looks fairly conventional. But it is most attractive when it grows slowly and naturally in the wild; there its gnarled, multi-trunked appearance speaks volumes about its hard life on the High Plains. For a landscape, I would try to prune a young tree so that it develops this kind of character. The female has bluish-black fruits that are eaten by quail, raccoons, rock squirrels, and several types of songbirds. Because of its need for mild summers, this important juniper should probably not be used in Texas outside the High Country of the Trans-Pecos and the High Plains.

289. **Latin Name**   *Juniperus scopulorum*
Pronunciation   joo-NIP-er-us
skohp-yoo-LOR-um
Common Name   ROCKY MOUNTAIN JUNIPER
Usual Height   36 feet
Spacing   12–15 feet apart
Evergreen
Range   In rocks and on breaks in
Guadalupe Mountains and High Plains
Western Canada to Arizona
Soil   Sand, loam, clay, caliche; well drained
Part shade, full sun
Propagation   Seed

Slow-growing and long-lived, this juniper usually has a short trunk that branches out close to the ground. It's like a broad shrub sitting on a short, stout trunk. Aside from this, it looks very much like eastern red cedar, which also has smooth, fibrous, shredding bark. The other chief difference is in the fruits, which take two years to ripen in Rocky Mountain juniper. The color of the fruits is hard to describe; they're a vivid blue but also hazy. If that sounds contradictory, then look at purple grapes in your grocery and you'll see what I mean. The bright color is there, but covered by a subtle, milky film.

290. Eastern red cedar
Juniperus virginiana
The authors

291. Shortleaf pine
Pinus echinata
The authors

blue-green, especially when they are laden with pale blue fruits. Of course, there have to be a few drawbacks to such an otherwise useful tree. It can get bagworms, spider mites, and juniper blight and can carry cedar-apple rust, which can harm your roses and hawthorns.

---

290. **Latin Name** *Juniperus virginiana*
Pronunciation joo-NIP-er-us ver-jin-ee-AY-nah
Common Names EASTERN RED CEDAR, VIRGINIA JUNIPER
Usual Height 30–40 feet
Spacing 20 feet apart
Evergreen
Range Dry sands and rocks from East Texas to Panhandle
Maine to Texas
Soil Sand, loam, clay, caliche, limestone; well drained
Dappled shade, part shade, full sun
Propagation Seed sown outdoors in fall, scarified and stratified seed

This juniper is not only the most adaptable one in the state but also the most varied, coming in an assortment of interesting shapes. You can get a tall, narrow one, shaped like a column; a drooping one, like weeping juniper; a broadly rounded one, with spreading branches that actually give shade; or one shaped like a pyramid. Bushy when young, they develop a single trunk with soft silvery bark around the age of ten. The foliage can be coarse- or fine-cut and can vary in color from gray to blue to dark green to light green. The males are most likely to be yellow-green, especially when full of pollen, and the females

291. **Latin Name** *Pinus echinata*
Pronunciation PYE-nus ek-eh-NAH-tah
Common Name SHORTLEAF PINE
Usual Height 50–70 feet
Spacing 12–15 feet apart
Evergreen
Range East Texas
Eastern U.S.
Soil Sand, sandy loam; acid; well drained
Part shade, full sun
Propagation Fresh untreated seed sown in fall

Shortleaf pine is reputed to be the most drought-tolerant of the East Texas pines. People tell me it's the best one to use if you're on sugar sand or on a dry hillside. However, I've seen loblolly pines growing in these same conditions around Palestine and acting every bit as drought-tolerant. The shortleaf looks a lot like the loblolly. In fact, they are sometimes so hard to tell apart, some people think they must interbreed. You know you've got a true shortleaf when you see extremely teensy pinecones all over the top of the tree. The needles are the shortest of those of the East Texas pines (two to four inches) and appear to grow in little tufts. This is a fairly slow-growing pine; it adds on only about a foot a year in the wild, although it will grow faster with watering.

292. Colorado pinyon
Pinus edulis
The authors

293. Longleaf pine
Pinus palustris
The authors

292. **Latin Name** *Pinus edulis*
Pronunciation PYE-nus ED-yoo-lus
Common Name COLORADO PINYON
Usual Height 10 feet, can reach 20 feet
Spacing 10–12 feet apart
Evergreen
Range Guadalupe Mountains
Oklahoma to Wyoming to California to
Mexico
Soil Sand, loam, clay, caliche; well drained
Part shade, full sun
Propagation Fresh untreated seed sown in
fall

Colorado pinyon is a short tree that makes a handsome accent in a courtyard, around a patio, or marking an entrance. There's something especially eye-catching about the way sunlight plays around the curving edges of the needles. It is one of three pinyon pines in Texas. These are our most drought-tolerant pines, and all are prized for their picturesque gnarled trunks. Colorado pinyon is the most cold-tolerant, and since it grows in a wide range, it is already available in the nursery trade. Mexican pinyon (*P. cembroides*), however, is the one most people prefer (assuming it's winter-hardy where they live) because of its rich blue-green color. It is found in the mountains of the Trans-Pecos, west to southeastern Arizona, and in northern Mexico. Our third pinyon, remote pinyon (*P. remota*), is found near Lost Maples on the Edwards Plateau. Some scientists lump it in with Mexican pinyon, but for landscaping purposes it's better to think of them as separate. Remote pinyon is the most heat-tolerant of the trio and probably the best one to experiment with in and around Austin and San Antonio. It's likely to be useful for other parts of the state as well. Lone Star Growers is propagating it. The pinyons can be dug up in the wild only if you can get an intact root ball as large as the tree itself—in rocky soil, that limits you to trees less than a foot tall.

293. **Latin Name** *Pinus palustris*
Pronunciation PYE-nus pal-US-triss
Common Name LONGLEAF PINE
Usual Height 80–100 feet
Spacing 30 feet apart or more
Evergreen
Range San Augustine, Jasper, Newton, and
Sabine counties
Gulf Coast from Virginia to Texas
Soil Sand, sandy loam; acid; seasonal poor
drainage okay
Full sun
Propagation Fresh untreated seed sown in
fall

If you're looking for stateliness, you want this pine. But don't worry about its getting too tall too soon; you've got a century or so before it reaches its full height. For the first seven years, longleaf pine looks like a large clump of evergreen grass. The bud that will form the trunk is lurking at ground level, building a deep root system. When the roots are established, the bud sprouts up six feet in just one year! After that, it will grow at a rate of a foot or so per year. This peculiar growth pattern came about to save the tree from prairie fires. In the Big Thicket it is still possible to see the natural habitat where these giants, widely spaced, tower over big-bluestem prairie (itself more than six feet high), with flowering dogwood and American holly as understory. Early settlers used these trees for building; the virgin timber was so hard and rich in resin that the lumber could last for generations without paint. This pine has to live in warm regions because its long needles, which hang like pom-poms, can hold so much ice that the weight snaps off the branches.

294. Rocky Mountain ponderosa pine
Pinus ponderosa var. *scopulorum*
The authors

295. Loblolly pine
Pinus taeda
Benny J. Simpson

294. **Latin Name** *Pinus ponderosa* var. *scopulorum*
Pronunciation PYE-nus pon-der-OH-sah
variety skohp-yoo-LOR-um
Common Name ROCKY MOUNTAIN
PONDEROSA PINE
Usual Height 60–70 feet
Spacing 25 feet apart
Evergreen
Range Mountains of the Trans-Pecos
Canada to northern Mexico
Soil Sand, loam, clay, limestone; well
drained
Full sun
Propagation Fresh untreated seed sown
in fall

This magnificent tree must be used in Texas at elevations above 3,000 feet, where nights get cool and summer days aren't so blazing hot. This means that residents in the High Country of the Trans-Pecos and the High Plains are the only Texans who get to use ponderosa pine. They must either choose seed or buy a plant propagated from our native stands, as our ponderosas have more drought and heat tolerance than the rest of this species. Ponderosa pine is at its most majestic (I've heard it can get nearly 250 feet tall) in the Pacific Northwest where temperatures never get Texas-hot. In Texas, it must be carefully placed with other trees around it to cool the air. Ground cover or grass beneath is a must, as reflected heat is a definite no-no. Regular watering, even in winter, is necessary. The tree grows rapidly at first but slows down with age. At least half the trunk is bare, giving you ample room to plant ornamental trees, shrubs, or flowers underneath. When the tree is about twenty years old, both male and female cones will appear on the same tree. The needles are blue-green or yellow-green, and unusually long—often six inches.

295. **Latin Name** *Pinus taeda*
Pronunciation PYE-nus tye-AY-dah
Common Name LOBLOLLY PINE
Usual Height 60 feet, can reach 110 feet
Spacing 12–15 feet apart
Evergreen
Range Piney Woods, Post Oak Savannah
New Jersey to Florida, west to Texas
Soil Sand, loam, gravel; acid; well drained
Part shade, full sun
Propagation Fresh untreated seed sown in
fall

Loblolly pine is the dominant component of the Piney Woods. Fast-growing and easy to establish, it is the one most East Texans think of first when the words "pine tree" are mentioned. As long as it's well drained, loblolly pine loves extra moisture and richer soils. After five years, it starts losing its lower branches and develops a strong, visible trunk. A few "odd" people, like my husband and me, have used the young loblolly as a Christmas tree. We like the way its free-form, widely spaced branches display our multishaped and multisized ornaments far better than more traditional trees. Although a cluster of loblollies gives off a wonderful piny scent, it's usually better to plant them in conjunction with oaks if you want understory, because little will grow under a bed of pine needles. A useful side to this is that the needles can be used effectively to form a weed-free path through a wooded area or between shady flower beds. Loblollies can also be used in the Eastern Cross Timbers in a watered yard, but they will not do well in dark clays.

296. Blue Douglas fir
Pseudotsuga menziesii var. *glauca*
Benny J. Simpson

297. Bald cypress
Taxodium distichum
The authors

296. **Latin Name** *Pseudotsuga menziesii* var. *glauca*
Pronunciation soo-DOH-tsoo-gah
men-zee-A-see-eye variety GLAW-kah
Common Name BLUE DOUGLAS FIR
Usual Height 15–25 feet
Spacing 8 feet apart
Evergreen
Range Trans-Pecos mountains
Western Canada to northern Mexico
Soil Sand, loam, limestone, igneous; well
drained
Part shade, full sun
Propagation Seed

Up in the Pacific Northwest the blue Douglas fir
can reach 150 feet, with a 5-foot diameter trunk, but here
at home it is a small, slow-growing tree. It just doesn't like
warm weather. In Dog Canyon it gets 25 feet tall, but it's
only 20 feet tall in McKittrick Canyon, a few miles south
(both canyons are in the Guadalupe Mountains), and only
15 feet tall two hundred miles farther south, at even lower
elevations in the Chisos Mountains of Big Bend National
Park. Our specimens have ascending branches and blue-
green leaves. Although the bark is thick, like that of pines,
you can't confuse the two, because the cones on the blue
Douglas fir sport rattails. A solitary tree has branches that
grow all the way down to the ground, and an almost perfect cone shape. But in a grove these firs self-prune, and
the trunks are bare. This tree requires more water than a
pinyon pine or a juniper but is about equal in needs to
Arizona cypress. It should be an especially fine ornamental tree for the High Plains.

297. **Latin Name** *Taxodium distichum*
Pronunciation tax-OH-dee-um DISS-tik-um
Common Name BALD CYPRESS
Usual Height 45 feet
Spacing 25 feet apart
**Deciduous, with leaves turning copper
in fall**
Range Along swamps and rivers from East
Texas to Uvalde
Eastern U.S. to Illinois
Soil Sand, loam, clay, limestone; poor
drainage okay
Part shade, full sun
Propagation Seed (remove resin, then sow
in fall or stratify)

Unlike all the other native conifers, this one loses
its leaves in the winter—hence the designation "bald."
The leaves look more like little feathers than needles. Because it is fast-growing and healthy and accommodates
well to small urban spaces and polluted air, it is popular
with landscapers. This is an ancient tree, known to the
dinosaurs. Some living specimens have been estimated to
be more than a thousand years old. The cypress is famous
for its "knees," which develop mostly in poorly drained
situations. On dry land, bald cypress is winter-hardy as
far north as Chicago, but it can suffer frozen roots in wet
areas north of the Red River. We also have an evergreen
version down in the Valley called Montezuma cypress
(*T. mucronatum*). It's not actually evergreen because, like
live oaks and southern magnolia, it sheds its leaves each
spring and then immediately grows new ones. Montezuma cypress is found mostly in Mexico; Texas is the
northernmost limit of its range. It's tall and pyramidal
in growth, with extremely fine feathery foliage. Not native to Texas since the Louisiana Purchase, pond cypress
(*T. ascendens*) is a smaller tree with thready, weeping
leaves. It grows well in the Houston area.

Mountain Garden Plan
Lot Size: 80′ × 120′

When I began designing this landscape, I specifically had in mind a country home in the High Country of the Trans-Pecos. This is probably the most dramatic and scenic part of the state, with a marvelous array of vegetation. The nice thing about this plan is that a somewhat reduced version can also be employed and enjoyed by people living on the High Plains—as long as they supply additional watering. These are the only regions in Texas that are cool enough in the summer to use conifers such as blue Douglas fir, Rocky Mountain juniper, weeping juniper, Colorado pinyon, and Rocky Mountain ponderosa pine. The plan would work well in Santa Fe, Albuquerque, Flagstaff, and the mountainous parts of Tucson too.

Beautiful, natural land in the High Country of the Trans-Pecos should be disturbed as little as possible. Allow it to heal itself from overgrazing or other abuses. Where you do need to augment the vegetation around your house, transplant seedlings from where you can spare them on your property. Or you can buy the plants I've indicated on this plan; they are among the most attractive and abundant of this region's natives. Either course is better than bringing in foreign material, which would look out of place and be poorly suited to the environment.

Except for Mohr oak, all of the plants on this plan can grow anywhere in the High Country. If you live near Alpine or Marfa, where the soils are igneous, use gray oaks (*Q. grisea*) and Emory oaks instead of Mohr oaks. Soils in the mountains of the Trans-Pecos are either igneous (volcanic) or sedimentary (limestone). The Glass Mountains and the Franklins have both limestone and igneous parts to them. The Davis and Chisos mountains are wholly igneous. The High Plains has sand or clay, both of which overlie caliche that is more closely allied to limestone mountains like the Guadalupes.

In this plan I've placed the drought-tolerant material outside the circular driveway. Oneseed junipers flank the entrance gates. Screening from the road is achieved by the grove of Mohr oaks (or gray or Emory oaks) and prairie flameleaf sumacs. A windbreak on the north and west is made up of oaks and the tough little silverleaf mountain mahogany. These trees can be quite drought-tolerant after they are well established. So can the soapberry, which is placed on the west side of the house, where it gets reflected heat from both the house and the driveway.

The bigtooth maple, chinquapin oak, Rocky Mountain ponderosa pine, blue Douglas fir, and Arizona cypress all grow quite well in High Country canyons, where they find running water, but if you don't happen to live in one, you'll have to continue watering these trees even after they're established. There just isn't enough rain to sustain them naturally. Rocky Mountain juniper, weeping juniper, pinyon pines, and alligator juniper are drought-tolerant in the High Country, but they would need occasional deep watering if used on the High Plains.

Three of these conifers—the blue Douglas fir, the Arizona cypress, and the Rocky Mountain juniper—grow much like a traditional Christmas tree, that is, with branches radiating from the trunk all the way down to the ground. They have been placed on the plan so they can grow this way, without being crowded at their bottoms.

The style of a home should fit with its environment, using materials such as native stone and wood. My choice for this plan is an adobe home. (See Dr. Barton Warnock's *Wildflowers of the Davis Mountains and the Marathon Basin, Texas* for a handsome example.) Driveways should be of crushed caliche, crushed granite, or gravel.

In the plan the land envelops the structure as naturally as possible. The native grass lawn is intended to be left unmowed, even around the house. This means that all rock outcroppings, and whatever grasses and flowers were there in the beginning, have been undisturbed. If you do need to start over on a lawn, choose one of the native lawn grasses—ear muhly, burro grass, blue grama, or buffalo grass. Plant seeds of flowers that bloom most abundantly near you in similar habitats.

I've given special attention to the front entrance. Have you ever been to a building and not been able to find the front door? It's a funny feeling. For the sake of first-time guests, I've marked the front door with some showy plantings. In this case, I started with four boulders of local stone. Then I added flowers for long-term color, such as zinnias and blackfoot daisies, a skeleton-leaf goldeneye (or pink plains penstemon for the High Plains), and a perennial buckwheat. Behind the largest boulder, I placed a bull muhly, but you could use some other bunchgrass such as two-flowered trichloris, sideoats grama, or, if you live on the High Plains, Indian ricegrass.

Since people normally want evergreens in the winter, I've placed a sotol under the chinquapin oak and a pinyon pine on the other side of the path. The Mexican pinyon from the Davis Mountains is prettiest; the Colorado pinyon is the most cold-hardy. The pinyon should be pruned high enough on the trunk to allow flowers and grasses to grow underneath.

Don't keep this entrance area too well groomed. You want it to look like nature was kind enough to give you an extra bounty of goodies by your front door.

Under the dining room windows on the protected east side of the house, special plantings continue. This is the most congenial spot to try a Texas madrone, but a surefire success would be a Mexican redbud with its spring pink flowers and crinkly leaves. Your choice. Prairie verbena and chocolate daisy provide more long-term color. In front of the blue Douglas fir, I've placed a small shrub for contrast. It could be the silvery, feathery sand sagebrush, starleaf Mexican orange, or scarlet bouvardia, depending on your soil and how mild your winters are.

Although the garage isn't shown on the plan, it is off the back of the drive, and the stepping-stones through the courtyard mark the main family entrance to the house. I have made the adobe wall fairly tall—six feet or so—to block as much north wind as possible. Of course, if you have a gorgeous view off in that direction, make it lower. The two "wings" at each end of the house effectively mask utility equipment.

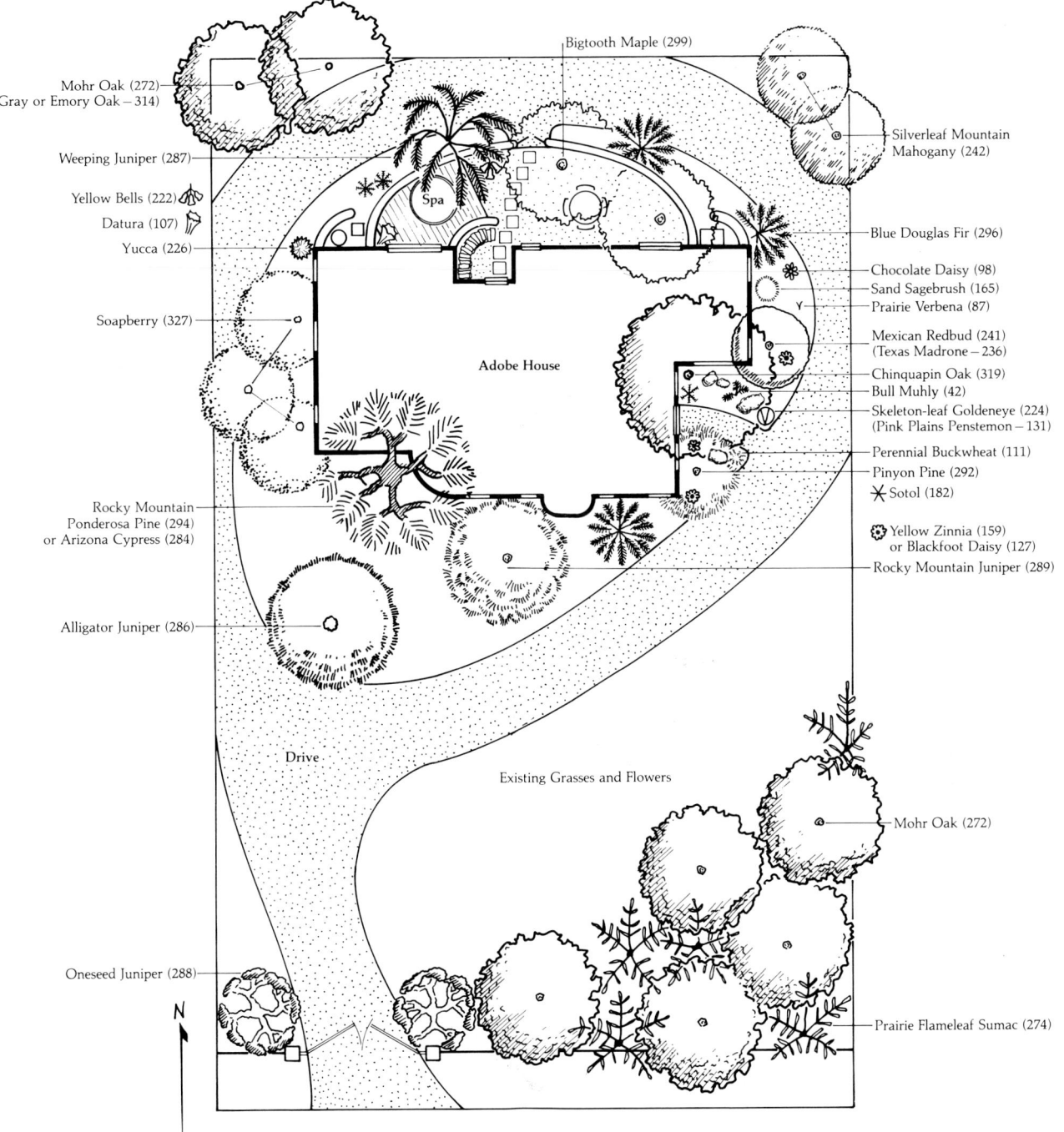

Mohr Oak (272)
(Gray or Emory Oak—314)

Bigtooth Maple (299)

Silverleaf Mountain
Mahogany (242)

Weeping Juniper (287)

Yellow Bells (222)
Datura (107)
Yucca (226)

Spa

Blue Douglas Fir (296)

Chocolate Daisy (98)
Sand Sagebrush (165)
Prairie Verbena (87)

Soapberry (327)

Adobe House

Mexican Redbud (241)
(Texas Madrone—236)
Chinquapin Oak (319)
Bull Muhly (42)
Skeleton-leaf Goldeneye (224)
(Pink Plains Penstemon—131)
Perennial Buckwheat (111)
Pinyon Pine (292)
Sotol (182)

Rocky Mountain
Ponderosa Pine (294)
or Arizona Cypress (284)

Yellow Zinnia (159)
or Blackfoot Daisy (127)
Rocky Mountain Juniper (289)

Alligator Juniper (286)

Drive

Existing Grasses and Flowers

Mohr Oak (272)

Oneseed Juniper (288)

N

Prairie Flameleaf Sumac (274)

Mountain Garden

The conifers of the Trans-Pecos can be enjoyed by people who live in the High Country and by those who live on the High Plains. This scene with pinyon pines (and a taller Afghan pine, from Afghanistan, of course) is at Burr Williams's Gone Native Nursery in Midland. In the foreground are chocolate daisies in a mixed meadow of buffalo grass and whatever else was growing there. The green mounds in front of the Gregg salvia are yellow zinnias, not yet in bloom. Photo by the authors.

The hot tub, or spa, is six feet in diameter and set into a redwood deck directly off the bedroom. A weeping juniper, planted on the outside of the wall, leans over it like a sheltering umbrella. A datura is tucked into the corner. Imagine lolling in the water, the stars overhead, and these large white trumpet-shaped blooms gleaming in the moonlight.

Where it's not decked, the court is paved with gravel to let all rain soak in for the benefit of the yellow bells (or pink plains penstemon for the High Plains) and the two bigtooth maples. Choose your maples in the fall when they turn, so that you end up with the coloring and timing you desire.

The Vaughn-Cone house in San Antonio lies in a grove of live oaks. In this picture, two understory trees—a redbud and a Texas persimmon—are also visible. The ground cover is a mixture of Asian jasmine and English ivy, to which Manuel Flores, owner of Native Design Nursery, has added drifts of Gregg salvia and purple lantana to create a vibrant yet elegant look. On other parts of the property, the natural understory of Texas mountain laurel, sumacs, kidneywood, yuccas, nolinas, perennials, and grasses has been left intact, with just enough pruning and clearing to enhance the most desirable items. In areas where this understory has been destroyed, Flores has added a rich array of flowers, shrubs, and understory trees to restore the natural beauty. Photo by the authors.

NINE

Shade Trees

WHEN we moved into our present home, there was a four-foot-tall bur oak in the front yard. At this writing, nine years later, it stands sixteen feet tall, with a four-inch-caliper trunk. Now, there are two ways you can respond to that statement: "Wow, a whole twelve feet in only nine years," or "Gee, only twelve feet after a whole nine years?"

Shade trees are not for the impatient. If you have some already well established on your land, terrific. But if, like many people moving into houses in subdivisions that have been denuded of trees, you have to plant a shade tree, don't sit around looking at your watch waiting for it to block the sun off your patio. This is a process that takes decades, not just years.

So why bother? I'm reminded of a story about a middle-aged woman who wanted to go back to school and get her degree. She told her husband that it would take four years. "Four years!" he exclaimed. "Do you know how old you'll be in four years?" His wife responded, "How old will I be in four years if I don't get the degree?"

Dallas landscape architect Michael Parkey told me an even more relevant tale. His grandfather planted a pecan tree when he was sixty years old. Everyone said he was crazy, but Michael says that when the old man was ninety, he was eating pecan pie.

A shade tree has to begin sometime. So don't waste a moment. Here are a few things to consider when you set out to establish one (or more) in your yard.

Your immediate impulse will be to run out to your neighborhood nursery and buy the biggest shade tree you can afford. You've just gained a bunch of years on that shade, right? Sorry, not true. Studies have proved that after five years or so, all else being equal, the smaller nursery tree (five-gallon size) will be as big òr bigger than that sixteen-footer you planted.

For example, let's take that bur oak in our front yard. If we'd bought it from a nursery at the size it was nine years ago, it would have cost us about $20. At its current size (four-inch caliper), it would have cost us in the area of $500—with a guarantee.

The guarantee is important because transplants of this size have a high mortality rate. No wonder. A tree can't be grown to that size in a pot; it has to be grown in the ground and then dug up. Extracting it from the ground chops off 95 percent of its root structure—and that's with a tree that's been nursery-grown. If it comes from the wild, it'll have a root structure that's two to five times larger, so the loss will be even greater. The trauma is extremely hard on the tree, and it has to expend all its energy the first five years or so just rebuilding those roots.

In the meantime, the $20 five-gallon tree is doing fine; its roots are intact, and it can channel all its nutrition into growth, not survival.

A specific case study, quoted by Dr. J. C. Raulston of North Carolina State University, involved planting a seven-foot flowering dogwood alongside one-foot seedlings. After only two years the seedlings had outgrown the seven-footer.

Another important point—the smaller trees will need watering for only two years. After that, they should be well established and will do well on whatever nature provides. On the other hand, a larger transplant will require lots of TLC for at least five years—if it lives that long.

If you got a guarantee from the nursery, they'll honor it. But the time of year has to be right for a successful transplant. Ideally, the replacement should not go in before the first fall rain or after the end of March. Summer transplants lose a lot of water from evaporation through their leaves, so they have a tougher time making it.

All shade trees do not grow at the same slow rate, and I'm not talking about slight variances. For instance, after ten years a hackberry will be twice the size of a live oak. But the hackberry will be dead in fifty years, while the slower-growing, and therefore harder-wooded oak will be around for centuries.

The faster-growing shade trees in this book are the maples, river birch, hackberry, ashes, sweetgum, cottonwood, soapberry, and American elm. The slow growers, which are longer-lived, are beech, southern magnolia, Texas palm, and most of the oaks.

These different growth rates make certain shade trees incompatible. For example, a Shumard red oak should not be planted next to a live oak. You'd think they would get along fine, but in fact they come from vastly different habitats. A Shumard is much faster-growing and competes with equally tall trees in creek bottoms. Live oaks, which get only two-thirds as high as a Shumard, are not used to sharing their canopy space; along the Gulf Coast and in the Hill Country they tend to be the big guys. As a result, a Shumard will soon shade out a live oak and turn it into a misshapen version of what it might have been.

Ultimate heights vary considerably, according to soil, climate, water, genetics, and just plain luck in being able to live so long. In this book I have tried to give you the usual heights for Texas. The literature gives height as the tallest tree recorded from some other source. When the species is native from Texas up to Canada and is listed as getting 150 feet tall, I strongly suspect that the 150-foot specimen was in Canada. Our trees tend not to get as tall as those in northern forests. We certainly had (unfortunately, past tense is accurate) some giants in the Big Thicket, and I've read that some old-timers estimated that longleaf pines got to be 150 feet tall. But if they did get that tall, it took centuries, which isn't relevant to your expectations in planting one in your yard. So in each entry the "Usual Height" figure indicates how tall the tree should be in fifty years or so.

Why should you care about fifty years down the road, you ask? Even if you're still around, chances are you won't still be living at that same address. The answer is that most of us plant trees with two goals in mind. First, we want something nice for now and for the near future. But we also want to leave something for posterity—something lasting and beautiful, so that one day our grandkids can look at it and say, "Hey, I remember when Gramps and Granny planted that oak. It wasn't any taller than I was." That's an elemental part of our makeup as human beings, and a nice one.

I also think about Highland Park, in Dallas. Way back in the 1920s, when that exclusive residential community was being developed, the builders weren't thinking fifty years ahead. So they put in a lot of hackberries. They grew reasonably fast, to satisfy the immediate landscape needs of the developers, and it wasn't until the late sixties that we discovered how short-sighted that approach had been. The hackberries died off in droves along the avenues and hurt the image of the neighborhood. Ah, but the live oaks, which were planted later by the homeowners themselves, looked magnificent. And will continue to do so for many more decades.

In my entries I also give you some idea of the growth rate of each tree. I say "some idea" because this is not an area of study that's loaded with absolutes. Growth rates—listed as slow, medium, and fast—are calculated either by observers in the wild or by people who have actually grown the trees. The problem is that the source books almost never indicate which observation the rates were based on. A tree that is termed slow-growing might grow quickly for you in your landscape with water and fertilizer. Or it might not.

Of course, fast growth is not necessarily a virtue. Trees that grow quickly also produce weaker or softer wood. You'll have to reach your own balance of conserving water and developing a tree with strong wood, or watering liberally and getting shade as fast as you can, but knowing that your tree is more vulnerable to high winds.

Another big decision you need to make in choosing shade trees has to do with fall color. You readers in the southern part of the state can skip the next few paragraphs because you don't get fall color. But about two thirds of the state does, although it will differ from year to year depending on the intensity and timing of the first blue norther in the fall. Trees of the same species vary considerably in how, when, and if they color. In some species, as many as half of the individuals may not color most years. Some are genetically programmed to color late and get caught in a freeze nine years out of ten. Some may not be programmed to color at all, ever.

The shade of turning can differ as well. For example, a red oak might turn red, maroon, burgundy, yellow, or brown. Red is the prettiest, but no nurseryman can guarantee you a red, because oaks must be grown from acorns. Even though the acorn was gathered from a brilliantly red tree, that's only half its parentage.

If you're buying a tree for its fall color, it's best to choose it in the fall while it is coloring. This is still not a guarantee, as young trees might change their habits as they mature, and trees in pots can feel the cold differently from trees in the ground. But at least you know your tree has the ability to color.

When planting a tree, work compost or well-rotted manure or mulch into the hole, or just replace the soil, leaving no air pockets. If you are transplanting a small native tree from similar soil, this latter method works amazingly well. Be careful to plant your tree at the same depth it is used to. If it's planted shallower, the top roots will dry out, and planting it too deep won't allow the top roots to breathe properly. If you have established trees in your yard, don't tamper with their soil levels, for the same reasons.

---

298. **Latin Name** *Acer barbatum* (*A. saccharum* var. *floridanum*)
Pronunciation AY-ser bar-BAY-tum
Common Names SOUTHERN SUGAR MAPLE, CADDO MAPLE
Usual Height 60 feet
Spacing 40–60 feet apart for specimen
Deciduous, with leaves turning cream, yellow, and salmon in fall
Range Along streams and in moist woodlands in Southeast Texas Southeastern U.S., Oklahoma
Soil Sand, loam, clay; moist, well drained
Part shade, full sun
Propagation Seed sown as soon as ripe

This is one of our prettiest coloring trees. The outer leaves start turning first, with the warm, glowing fall colors gradually spreading inward. As a result, you are often treated to the sight of several pastel shades—from cream to yellow to salmon—highlighted against a light green backdrop. This is the smaller, southern version of the sugar maple. It doesn't have adequate sap flow for maple syrup because our winters aren't cold enough. The owner of the tree in the photograph says that the colors are better in rainy autumns. This tree can color well as far south as Houston. If you live in Dallas or west to the High Plains, where these trees aren't native, you can use this maple if it has been propagated from the southern sugar maple of Oklahoma, called Caddo maple. Check this out with your nursery. Caddo maples have greater cold and drought tolerance and grow well in calcareous soils. Because maples give dense shade, it's extremely difficult to grow flowers or lawn beneath them, but you can use ground covers, as long as you fertilize them well. The fallen leaves make a fine mulch.

298. **Southern sugar maple**
Acer barbatum
The authors

299. Bigtooth maple
Acer grandidentatum
The authors

300. Trident maple
Acer rubrum var. *trilobum*
The authors

299. **Latin Name** *Acer grandidentatum*
Pronunciation AY-ser
gran-dee-den-TAH-tum
Common Name BIGTOOTH MAPLE
Usual Height 20–30 feet, can reach 48 feet
Spacing 16 feet apart
Fruit Summer; rose-colored; 1-inch samaras
**Deciduous, with leaves turning red and
gold in fall**
Range Moist canyons in Edwards Plateau
and Trans-Pecos mountains
Rocky Mountains, Wichita Mountains,
mountains in northern Mexico
Soil Sand, loam, clay, limestone;
calcareous; moist, well drained
Part shade, full sun
Propagation Seed fresh off tree

This maple is so gorgeous in McKittrick Canyon in the Guadalupe Mountains, and in Lost Maples on the Edwards Plateau, that Texans make pilgrimages at the end of each October to ooh and aah. Eight years ago scientists in Dallas and El Paso began experimenting with these maples to find the ones with the best fall color. They were dismayed to find that their maples weren't coloring at all. Since then, they've been trying to find out if this is because fall nights out of the canyons are too warm to trigger coloring or because the trees simply weren't old enough. Evidence is beginning to indicate that age might be the factor, as several colored for the first time last fall. However, anyone who doesn't live in the mountains or on the High Plains, where the fall nights are cold, should use maples propagated from those at Lost Maples or Fort Hood. Bigtooth maple grows quickly and well under cultivation, its only problem being that the leaves get damaged in late summer if you water often with salty water.

300. **Latin Name** *Acer rubrum* var. *drummondii*
Pronunciation AY-ser ROO-brum variety
drah-MUN-dee-eye
Common Names DRUMMOND RED MAPLE,
SWAMP MAPLE
Usual Height 100 feet
Spacing 30–40 feet apart
Bloom February to April, on males; red
Fruit March to June, on females; red;
1–1½ inches
**Deciduous, with leaves turning red, wine,
and orange in fall**
Range Swamps and alluvial forests in East
Texas
Eastern North America
Soil Sand, loam, clay; acid; poor drainage
okay
Part shade, full sun
Propagation Seed fresh off tree

Drummond red maple is the best maple to use in Houston, Beaumont, and moist places in East Texas. It grows down in the swamps with bald cypress or on sandy land with sweetgums and wax myrtles. It is a fast-growing, short-lived tree—which means you'll have to plant another one in fifty years. Not all Drummonds have good red flowers, red samaras (winged fruits), red stems on the leaves, or even red fall color. So growers have to select their seed carefully to have the most handsome specimens. Growth habits can vary too. Some of these maples are narrow and upright, while others are broad and spreading. Although I love the male flowers in the spring, I think the female fruits are equally colorful, and they last longer. It's a hard choice between the male and female of this species. Trident maple (*A. rubrum* var. *trilobum*) is a little more drought-tolerant and turns golden in the fall as often as red. The leaves are downy white on the undersides. Because of their fibrous root systems, it's hard to grow anything under either of these maples.

301. River birch
Betula nigra
The authors

302. Pecan
Carya illinoinensis
The authors

301. **Latin Name**   *Betula nigra*
Pronunciation   BET-yoo-lah NYE-grah
Common Name   RIVER BIRCH
Usual Height   30–50 feet, can reach 90 feet
Spacing   20–30 feet apart
**Deciduous, with leaves turning yellow in
fall**
Range   Streams and bottomlands in East
Texas
Eastern half of U.S.
Soil   Sand, loam, clay; acid; poor drainage
okay
Part shade, full sun
Propagation   Seed sown in fall

River birch is grown mostly for the beauty of it peeling, silvery, satiny bark and the salmon-pink trunk revealed beneath. But that's not all it has to offer. Its branches are languid and graceful and look lovely silhouetted against the setting sun. Because it thrives in poor drainage, it's especially good in the Houston-Beaumont area and around water gardens. But it can also grow well in any yard with ordinary watering. Very fast-growing, it should be around for thirty years or so. It's often multi-trunked, which just gives you more bark to enjoy. I often see it planted in front of windows, but because the trunks can get up to thirty inches in diameter, it shouldn't be placed close enough to a house to endanger the eaves. Friends in Houston tell me they can't count on fall color except every third year or so, when the nights get cold enough.

302. **Latin Name**   *Carya illinoinensis*
Pronunciation   KARE-ee-yah
ill-eh-noy-NEN-siss
Common Name   PECAN
Usual Height   50–60 feet
Spacing   50 feet apart
**Deciduous, with leaves sometimes turning
yellow in fall**
Range   Along streams and bottomlands
throughout Texas, mostly in Blackland
Prairies
Indiana to Iowa to Texas to Alabama
Soil   Sand, loam, clay, caliche; well drained
Full sun
Propagation   Seed, cuttings, budding,
grafting

This tree is usually the tallest one on the Blackland Prairies. It prefers deep, rich soils, but it isn't fussy. Usually one of the last of the big shade trees to get new spring leaves, it's one of the first to lose them. In the northern part of the state, it sometimes turns yellow in the fall. Native pecan nuts are usually tiny; you have to be patient to dig out enough meat for a decent-sized pie. Squirrels and blue jays love pecans. If you have two hundred pecan trees sprouting in your yard, it's because squirrels have buried them and then forgotten where. This is a nice symbiotic relationship. Mother Nature made pecans delicious to attract squirrels, and she made squirrels absentminded so pecans can continue to be propagated. (Which came first, the squirrel or the pecan?) In its native range the pecan is afflicted with galls, twig girdlers, aphids, borers, weevils, pecan scab, tent caterpillars, and webworms. It does a lot better outside its native range because all these pests haven't caught up to it.

303. Hackberry
Celtis laevigata
The authors

304. Anacua
Ehretia anacua
The authors

303. **Latin Name** *Celtis laevigata*
Pronunciation KELL-tis lah-vee-GAY-tah
Common Names HACKBERRY,
  TEXAS SUGARBERRY, PALO BLANCO
Usual Height 30–50 feet
Spacing 30 feet apart
**Deciduous, with leaves sometimes turning
  yellow in fall**
Range Eastern two thirds of Texas
  Virginia and Illinois to Gulf states and
    northeastern Mexico
Soil Sand, loam, clay, caliche; well drained
Part shade, full sun
Propagation Seed

Some people may be surprised to see this tree mentioned here. In Dallas it's considered a major weed! It has warty bark and warty leaves and comes up everywhere. But if you've ever seen it growing in South Texas, with attractive white patches on its smooth pale bark and with wart-free leaves, then you know that it can grow into one of our better shade trees. It is extremely drought-tolerant, because it stores water in the tissues of the trunk. It is shallow-rooted, so it responds to even a slight shower. If you water it, you will find it a fast grower, a boon to treeless yards and parking lots. Add the fact that it's a favorite feeding stop for birds, and you realize why this tree is so popular down in the Valley. If you have a freeze followed by a bright sunny day, the fruits ferment, and songbirds wintering over have one very long happy hour. Hackberries are short-lived; within thirty years or so they become infested with borers, fungus, and mistletoe.

304. **Latin Name** *Ehretia anacua*
Pronunciation eh-REE-shah
  ah-NOK-yoo-ah
Common Names ANACUA, SANDPAPER TREE
Usual Height 20–30 feet, can reach 45 feet
Spacing 20 feet apart
Bloom March, sporadically to November;
  white; 2- to 3-inch panicles; fragrant
Evergreen
Range Open forest, palm groves, and
  brushland from Austin to Valley
  Mexico
Soil Sand, loam, clay, caliche; well drained
Dappled shade, part shade, full sun
Propagation Fresh or stratified seed

Feel the leaves and you'll know why it's called sandpaper tree. It stands out in brush because of its large black-green oval leaves. In full bloom in the spring it looks like it's covered with snow. At these times it's also covered with honeybees. Like the live oak, it's not a true evergreen. New leaves come on every spring, but earlier than those of live oaks. Occasionally, new leaves (and sometimes old ones) will look a chlorotic yellow, but they always green up on their own. The fruits are yellow-orange, sometimes orange-red, quite sweet and juicy, and eaten by numerous birds and mammals, so you're likely to have an anacua planted for you. If you plant one yourself, it will need a lot of water to get established, but then it will be exceedingly drought-tolerant. Anacuas grow well as understory when young, but they eventually grow large enough to qualify as canopy trees. The trunk on an old anacua is unusual—it's like several corky corded trunks all bound together—and it has reddish flaking bark.

305. Beech
Fagus grandifolia var. *caroliniana*
The authors

306. Texas ash
Fraxinus texensis
The authors

305.   **Latin Name**   *Fagus grandifolia* var. *caroliniana*
Pronunciation   FAY-gus gran-deh-FOLE-ee-ah variety kare-oh-lin-ee-AY-nah
Common Name   BEECH
Usual Height   50–80 feet, can reach 100 feet or more
Spacing   50–70 feet apart
Deciduous, with leaves turning copper in fall
Range   Rich, moist forests in East Texas
Massachusetts to Gulf of Mexico
Soil   Rich sandy loam, clay-loam; acid; moist, well drained
Dappled shade, part shade, full sun
Taproot
Propagation   Stratified seed

The beech will never be used extensively in Texas; we have just a few special places that meet all its exacting requirements. If you have rich soil that stays moist but well drained, and you have some shade, then you probably have the ideal spot for this impressive tree. The young beech needs shade to develop, growing as an understory tree for approximately its first ten years. After about fifty years it can be categorized as massive. The trunk, which gets huge, is its chief beauty—very smooth and pale gray. The leaves are dark green and glossy. They turn to a gorgeous copper color in the fall and tend to hold on most of the winter. The roots are close to the surface—actually visible—and the shade is so dense that you shouldn't expect to have much of anything growing beneath it once it gains some height. It grows in the Big Thicket along with southern magnolia, white oak, and loblolly pines, with understory of redbud, fringe tree, two-winged silverbell, witch hazel, and piedmont azalea.

306.   **Latin Name**   *Fraxinus texensis*
Pronunciation   FRAX-eh-nus tex-EN-siss
Common Name   TEXAS ASH
Usual Height   30–45 feet
Spacing   20–30 feet apart
Deciduous, with leaves turning yellow, bronze, copper, pumpkin, tangerine, plum, mauve, dusty rose, and lime in fall
Range   Rocky slopes and lakeshores in Central and North Central Texas
Endemic to Texas
Soil   Sand, loam, clay, caliche, limestone; well drained
Part shade, full sun
Propagation   Seed sown in fall

Texas ash is exceptional in the fall, with redder shades on the outside and the yellows on the inside. The whole tree looks like a candle flame. It actually seems to glow—especially on a dark autumn day. It's fairly fast-growing, yet long-lived and healthy, with strong, hard wood. I think it's one of our best shade trees. The males have dark persistent flower clusters, and the females have pale fringes of fruit. Leaves might be either round or pointed. This is our most drought-tolerant ash. Some botanists consider it a variety of white ash (*F. americana*), and I would agree with that. The white ash, which grows on slopes or in stream bottoms in the eastern third of Texas, gets larger in every way but is otherwise quite similar. I've used it often in wooded landscapes and have had no trouble with scorched leaves or insect damage in the summer, like you'd find on Arizona or Mexican ashes. For some perverse reason, these latter two are our most frequently planted ashes, but even overwatered urban landscapes seem too dry for them. And they don't even have fall color.

307. Sweetgum
Liquidambar styraciflua
The authors

308. Southern magnolia
Magnolia grandiflora
The authors

307. **Latin Name** *Liquidambar styraciflua*
Pronunciation lik-wid-AM-ber
   stye-ruh-SIFF-loo-ah
Common Name SWEETGUM
Usual Height 50–60 feet, can reach 100 feet
   or more
Spacing 20–30 feet apart, can spread 60
   feet
**Deciduous, with leaves turning red, orange,
   burgundy, deep purple, and yellow in fall**
Range Swampy woods in East and South
   Central Texas
   Connecticut to Illinois, south to Central
   America
Soil Sand, loam, clay-loam; poor drainage
   okay in sand
Part shade, full sun
Propagation Fresh or stratified seed

Where sweetgum does best—in the moist, sandy soils of East Texas—it does so well that everybody hates it. The seedlings have to be weeded out constantly. It's considered trashy. And folks running around barefooted are forever treading on its spiky balls. Because of these negative feelings, people don't want to acknowledge the sweetgum's radiant fall colors. Each tree turns one or more of the bright, rich colors listed above. Ironically, in Dallas, people practically kill themselves trying to grow sweetgums. There they do fine if the soil is deep enough, but if they hit limestone, they turn chlorotic. Sweetgum is not one of our drought-tolerant trees; even in Dallas, where you can count on an average rainfall of 35 inches a year, it requires extra moisture. Those painful seedballs are often painted as decorations for Christmas ornaments, and about 25 species of birds eat the seeds. Sweetgum is fast-growing and long-lived. Buy your tree in the autumn

so you can choose the timing and color for the foliage, as some turn later than others, and the leaves may freeze and fall before turning red.

---

308. **Latin Name** *Magnolia grandiflora*
Pronunciation mag-NOH-lee-ah
   gran-deh-FLOR-ah
Common Name SOUTHERN MAGNOLIA
Usual Height 50 feet, rarely to 100 feet
Spacing 30 feet apart
Bloom May, occasionally in summer;
   creamy white; 6–9 inches; fragrant
Evergreen
Range Moist woods in East and Southeast
   Texas
   North Carolina to Gulf of Mexico
Soil Sand, loam, clay; acid or calcareous;
   moist, well drained
Part shade, full sun
Propagation Fresh seed sown in fall,
   stratified seed, semihardwood cuttings

The stately southern magnolia is redolent of the old South, with large glossy green leaves; huge, thick-petaled, and creamy white flowers up to 9 inches across; and bright red seeds. The flowers have a wonderful lemony fragrance. Since southern magnolia grows naturally in acid sands, it's surprising to find this tree growing on limestone, but it does very well there, as long as it has enough water. It also grows well in Houston's gumbo. Unpruned, the branches grow down to the ground, the whole tree becoming pyramidal in shape. The roots are up near the surface of the soil, and the shade is dense, making it almost impossible to grow anything underneath. If you have the space and the option, it's best not to prune off the lower branches.

309. Black gum
Nyssa sylvatica var. *sylvatica*
The authors

310. Texas ebony
Pithecellobium flexicaule
The authors

309. **Latin Name** *Nyssa sylvatica* var. *sylvatica*
Pronunciation NYE-sah sil-VAH-teh-kah
Common Names BLACK GUM, SOUR GUM, TUPELO, BLACK TUPELO
Usual Height 30–60 feet
Spacing 30 feet apart
Deciduous, with leaves turning red in fall
Range Swamps and sandy woodlands in East Texas
Maine to Gulf Coast, Mexico
Soil Sand, loam, clay; acid; poor drainage okay
Part shade, full sun
Propagation Fresh or stratified seed

Black gum is one of the best trees for fall color in the Houston area. Its red is a clear, strong, no-nonsense red, and the leaves are thin enough to let light shine through so that the tree glows. Black gum doesn't seem to need cold to trigger its fall color; actually, I've seen it in color in late summer, but I've been told that this color is due to a blight (which didn't seem to hurt the tree otherwise). It's slow-growing and fairly small, taking twenty years, under the best conditions, to become a shade tree. For a long time, you need to think of it as an ornamental tree, but not as understory—it likes lots of sun. It can be drought-tolerant in sand in its native area; it can also do well in gumbo or at the edge of a water garden. In fact, it can even grow well in shallow standing water. In that environment the trunk makes its famous bottle shape at the waterline.

310. **Latin Name** *Pithecellobium flexicaule*
Pronunciation pith-eh-sell-OH-bee-um flex-eh-CAW-lee
Common Names TEXAS EBONY, EBONY
Usual Height 25–30 feet
Spacing 20 feet apart
Bloom May to October; white; 1- to 2-inch spikes; fragrant
Fruit Usually present; brown; 4- to 6-inch pods containing red seeds
Evergreen
Range Valley north to Laredo and Corpus Christi
Mexico
Soil Sand, loam, clay, caliche; well drained
Part shade, full sun
Taproot
Propagation Scarified seed

Let's be honest right up front; ours is not a true botanically pure hardwood ebony. It's really a legume, like mesquites and green beans. The wood is dark—mahogany red to purple or brown—but certainly not black. I haven't a clue as to how it got its name, and neither do any of the references I've studied. But the thing nobody disputes is—it's gorgeous. Texas ebony can be dependably grown only in the Valley. In Corpus Christi, for example, it froze back to the roots in the Big Freeze of '83–'84, while it survived intact around Edinburg and McAllen. It's extremely drought-tolerant and, with mesquite and huisache, makes the canopy for the Valley. The leaves are dark green, the zigzag branches are spiny, and birds use the dense foliage for nesting. The trees are often multitrunked and might look brushy until quite old or

311. Cottonwood
Populus sp.
The authors

pruned. In fact, some people plant Texas ebony as a security hedge. It takes quite well to shearing (if you feel the overwhelming urge to do this). The blooms are white, fading to ivory, and you can smell their sweetness fifty feet away. Bees are very attracted to them.

311. **Latin Name** *Populus* spp.
 Pronunciation POP-yoo-lus species
 Common Names COTTONWOOD, ALAMO
 Usual Height 40–100 feet
 Spacing 50 feet apart
 Bloom March to June, on males; red or
  yellow catkins; 3–6 inches long
 Fruit March to June, on females; white
 **Deciduous, with leaves turning yellow in
  fall**
 Range Throughout Texas
  North America
 Soil Sand, loam, clay, caliche; well drained
 Part shade, full sun
 Propagation Fresh seed, semihardwood
  cuttings

Cottonwood is the biggest native shade tree they've got in West Texas. It's fast-growing and can last 150 years. It also has spectacular autumn coloring. I recall hearing a "cottonwood report" on the local news, directing folks out to a particularly lovely stand. Besides the color, people love the sound of the rustling leaves and the way they seem to spin and dance in a breeze. Some people also love the soft, white cottony fluffs that drift through the air like snow in slow motion and pile up in glistening drifts. Of course, other people hate the "snow" and grow only "cot-

tonless" cottonwoods, which are males. Other people call the cottonwood a trash tree. And they talk about how cottonwood roots are clever about finding water that's leaking out of plumbing and insinuating themselves into the conduits. Cottonwood can be used anywhere in the state. It's remarkably easy to establish; the Fort Davis corral was built out of cottonwood—and the posts sprouted! They became trees and are still thriving today.

312. **Latin Name** *Prosopis glandulosa*
 Pronunciation proh-SOH-pus
  lan-dyoo-LOH-sah
 Common Name HONEY MESQUITE
 Usual Height 20–30 feet
 Spacing 20–40 feet apart
 Bloom March to September; creamy white;
  2–3 inches long
 Deciduous
 Range Throughout Texas except Piney
  Woods
  Oklahoma to New Mexico to Mexico
 Soil Sand, loam, clay, caliche; well drained
 Full sun
 Taproot
 Propagation Fresh or scarified seed, root
  cuttings

Honey mesquite probably should have been named our state tree. It's quite abundant. Well pruned, as illustrated in the photo, it's a really good-looking tree. If you trim it up high, you'll show off its twisting multiple trunks, but if you let it grow down to the ground, the

312. Bright red mesquite beans
Prosopis glandulosa
Benny J. Simpson

312. Honey mesquite
Prosopis glandulosa
The authors

delicate foliage provides a handsome screen. Its shade is so light that even buffalo grass and flower gardens grow well underneath. It's ideal for a small yard, but I've seen it used effectively in masses in front of corporate offices. The branches are thorny, but nurseries could select a thornless variety from our native stock. I'd also like to see them make selections for bright red beans. Since mesquites flower and fruit over several months, red beans would greatly enhance the overall interest of this tree. Mesquites are deep-rooted and very drought-tolerant, but hard to transplant. You can buy only small mesquites; they won't grow until the taproot is in the ground. They respond well to watering, but they aren't fast growers. Honeybees are attracted to the sweet-smelling blossoms.

OAKS

Our American oaks began in central Mexico. We have approximately 250 species in the Western Hemisphere, and the lineage of every single one can probably be traced directly back to that land. Texas has the largest diversity of oaks in all the states—44 species and 2 varieties, by some expert accounts.

It's hard to identify a species of oak accurately, because the leaves can vary considerably, even on the same tree. Scholars get very technical and also very heated about the subject. There is a wonderful, and most likely apocryphal, tale about renowned Harvard professor Asa Gray (1810–1888), who asked each student in his class to gather an oak leaf for identification. Five of his students impishly got samples off the same big tree just outside the door. From them, Gray identified five "new species." The only accurate way to identify an oak is by knowing where the oak grew—and by the acorns and leaves. For accurate indentification, refer to *A Field Guide to Texas Trees,* by Benny J. Simpson (Texas Monthly Press).

Live oaks are so named because the leaves stay green all winter. In April the old leaves drop as new ones form, giving the tree a thin look for a week or so. Therefore, live oaks are not evergreen in the strict sense, but that is the easiest way to convey that they will be green in the winter.

One way to reduce the ultimate size of your oak is to let it form multiple trunks. Shumard red oak and Texas red oak are especially attractive with multiple trunks. The most common way to achieve this effect is to cut off the main stem at ground level when it is small and let three trunks come up and remain. Don't do this to coastal live oak; it may die! All oaks will sucker (send up baby trees from the roots) to some extent. Usually if the new shoots are cut or mown off, they are no problem. Oaks are fine trees—slow-growing, long-lived, the premier of shade trees.

To plant your own oak from an acorn, first choose an oak tree you particularly like that grows near you. The acorn is ripe when it will easily snap out of the cup. Always gather your acorn directly off the tree. As quickly as you can, plant it where you want it to grow. Keep it moist if it will be more than twelve hours before you can plant it.

---

313. **Latin Name**   *Quercus alba*
Pronunciation   KWER-kus AL-bah
Common Name   WHITE OAK
Usual Height   80–100 feet
Spacing   50–60 feet apart
Deciduous, with leaves turning wine-red to orange-red in fall
Range   Moist forests in East Texas
Eastern North America
Soil   Sand, loam, clay; acid; seasonal poor drainage okay
Part shade, full sun
Propagation   Fresh acorns

White oak is considered to be the best oak in East Texas for red fall color. The tints range from purply red to orangy red, so if you have a strong preference, choose your tree in the fall while it is coloring. Another desirable feature is the bark, which is off-white and flaky on a mature tree. A friend who is also a landscape architect further recommends this tree because it is "clean." That means it doesn't drop much deadwood or other tree debris. A slow to moderate grower, white oak is well adapted both to moist, rich sandy loams and to the black gumbo soils around Houston. Some white oaks share an unpopular characteristic with some Shumard red oaks— they hold their brown leaves all winter.

313. **White oak**
Quercus alba
Benny J. Simpson

314. Emory oak
Quercus emoryi
The authors

315. Escarpment live oak
Quercus fusiformis
The authors

314. **Latin Name** *Quercus emoryi*
Pronunciation KWER-kus em-OR-ee-eye
Common Name EMORY OAK
Usual Height 30–40 feet
Spacing 20–30 feet apart
Almost evergreen
Range Igneous Trans-Pecos mountains
Arizona, Mexico
Soil Sand, loam; acid; well drained
Part shade, full sun
Propagation Fresh acorns

The prettiest thing about this small live oak is the shape and configuration of the leaves. They're glossy, heavy in texture, and slightly scalloped along the edges, like a holly leaf, but not at all prickly. They're arranged on the branch in whorls, or star-shaped clusters. The bark is dark and thick and patterned like the back of an armadillo. Annual acorns are small and red and wear a yellow cap. Emory oak prefers deep soil and moisture. Since it grows only in the mountains at elevations above 5,000 feet and requires acid soil, it can probably be used in Texas only around Alpine or Fort Davis, and possibly in deep sands in the Panhandle if it gets supplemental water.

315. **Latin Name** *Quercus fusiformis* (*Q. virginiana* var. *fusiformis*)
Pronunciation KWER-kus fyoo-zee-FORM-iss
Common Name ESCARPMENT LIVE OAK
Usual Height 30–40 feet
Spacing 30–50 feet apart
Evergreen
Range Grand Prairie, Western Cross Timbers, Edwards Plateau, West Texas, Rio Grande Plains
Oklahoma to Mexico
Soil Sand, loam, clay, limestone; calcareous; well drained
Full sun
Propagation Fresh acorns

This is the most magnificent shade tree on the Edwards Plateau. Near Houston you'll find the coastal live oak. Everything in between is supposedly some combination of the two. Some botanists say the escarpment live oak is simply a variety of the coastal live oak. But the differences between the two, especially in a landscape sense, are distinct enough to warrant treating them separately in this book. Escarpment live oak is more drought-tolerant, handles Blackland Prairie clays, but not poor drainage, and is far more cold-hardy. Those that grow in the Quartz Mountains of Oklahoma are especially resistant to cold and should even be usable in the High Plains. I know they survived several days in a row of $-20°$ F with no damage. Escarpment live oak is resistant to cotton root rot, but when it has been stressed by drought, it is susceptible to live oak wilt and live oak decline. The acorns are fusiform (spindle-shaped).

316. Lacey oak, showing peach-colored new leaves
Quercus glaucoides
Benny J. Simpson

317. Bur oak
Quercus macrocarpa
The authors

316. **Latin Name** *Quercus glaucoides*
Pronunciation KWER-kus glaw-COY-deez
Common Name LACEY OAK
Usual Height 20–30 feet
Spacing 20–30 feet apart
Deciduous, with leaves turning peach-colored in fall
Range Limestone escarpments in Edwards Plateau
Northeastern Mexico
Soil Sand, loam, clay, caliche, limestone; well drained
Part shade, full sun
Propagation Fresh acorns

Lacey oak is on the smallish side, and if it's multi-trunked, it will be even smaller, making it a good selection for urban yards in the central portion of Texas—Blackland Prairies, Grand Prairie, and its native Edwards Plateau. Its chief beauty is its leaves, which come out a delicate peachy color in the spring, change to a soft blue-green in the summer, and then return to a rich, sunset peach in the autumn.

317. **Latin Name** *Quercus macrocarpa*
Pronunciation KWER-kus mak-roh-KAR-pah
Common Name BUR OAK
Usual Height 60–80 feet
Spacing 30–50 feet apart
Deciduous
Range Moist forests and along streams in eastern half of Texas
Eastern half of North America
Soil Sand, loam, clay, caliche, limestone; well drained
Part shade, full sun
Propagation Fresh acorns

This wonderful oak appears to grow anywhere in the state. In fact, bur oak is the most widely adaptive oak in the world. In the Midwest it's called the prairie oak, because it will quickly take over a fallow field in prairie soils. The farther south it grows, the bigger the acorns—in Texas they can get as long as two inches, and almost as fat. This tree is sometimes called mossy-cup oak, because of the mossy fringe around the edge of the acorn cup. In the central part of the state, bur oak stands out because of its especially large lobed leaves. Although you'll find the biggest bur oaks in the bottomlands (there was a famous hundred-foot giant, with a five- or six-foot-diameter trunk, at the Heard Natural Science Museum in McKinney), it will grow in the uplands and on thin soils. Bur oak is drought-resistant, long-lived, and reasonably fast-growing for an oak.

318. Swamp chestnut oak
Quercus michauxii
Doug Williams

319. Chinquapin oak
Quercus muhlenbergii
The authors

318. **Latin Name** *Quercus michauxii* (erroneously
 called *Q. prinus*)
 Pronunciation KWER-kus
 mee-SHOH-ee-eye
 Common Name SWAMP CHESTNUT OAK
 Usual Height 60–80 feet
 Spacing 30–50 feet apart
 Deciduous, with leaves turning red in fall
 Range Moist forests of East Texas and
 Houston
 Delaware to Missouri to Gulf of Mexico
 Soil Sand, loam, clay; acid; poor drainage
 okay
 Part shade, full sun
 Propagation Fresh acorns

Swamp chestnut oak is one of the premier oaks for
the Houston area; it tolerates poor drainage and grows
well in both gumbo and sandy areas. Most falls, it delivers
vibrant red color—always welcome in this part of the
state. It looks a little like chinquapin oak (the two are
closely related), but the leaves of swamp chestnut oak are
even larger and wider. It is a long-lived, slow-growing tree
with a narrow crown.

319. **Latin Name** *Quercus muhlenbergii*
 Pronunciation KWER-kus
 mew-len-BER-jee-eye
 Common Names CHINQUAPIN OAK,
 CHINKAPIN OAK
 Usual Height 40–60 feet
 Spacing 20–40 feet apart
 **Deciduous, with leaves turning parti-
 colored yellow with green and rust**
 Range Calcareous woods in Trans-Pecos,
 Hill Country, and Blacklands
 Calcareous woods in eastern two thirds of
 U.S., northern Mexico
 Soil Loam, clay, caliche, limestone;
 calcareous; well drained
 Part shade, full sun
 Propagation Fresh acorns

This oak got its name because the leaves resemble
those of the Allegheny chinquapin, a small tree found
in the eastern United States. In Dallas, chinquapin oak
grows in the bottomlands or on limestone slopes above
creeks, and it gets big! In this region the leaves are large,
sometimes broad like those of the Hill Country, and sometimes narrow like those in the Trans-Pecos. In the latter
two places the leaves and trees are always much smaller.
It's a beautiful tree, with a dark, glossy, almost lush look.
Usually tall and slender, old trees can sometimes get
"middle-age spread," forming a broad irregular crown.

320. Willow oak
Quercus phellos
The authors

321. Vasey oak
Quercus pungens var. *vaseyana*
Benny J. Simpson

320. **Latin Name** *Quercus phellos*
Pronunciation KWER-kus FELL-oss
Common Name WILLOW OAK
Usual Height 60 feet
Spacing 40–60 feet apart
Deciduous
Range Swamps and moist woods in East Texas and Houston
New York to Illinois to Gulf of Mexico
Soil Sand, loam, clay; acid; poor drainage okay
Part shade, full sun
Propagation Fresh acorns

Willow oak is for East Texas and Houston only. It likes lots of moisture. In fact, the one Andy shot for this book was in a foot or two of water. It likes the poor drainage in the Houston area so much, people there think it seeds out like a weed. Where this tree gets a lot of appreciation is in the pine and oak woods of East Texas. There it transplants easily, grows reasonably fast, and is considered a "clean" tree; it doesn't drop deadwood, and the leaves are so long and narrow there's not much to rake up. For these reasons, it's a good shade tree next to driveways and patios.

321. **Latin Name** *Quercus pungens* var. *vaseyana*
Pronunciation KWER-kus PUN-jenz variety vass-ee-AN-ah
Common Names VASEY OAK, SANDPAPER OAK
Usual Height 25–35 feet
Spacing 20–30 feet apart
Evergreen
Range Dry limestone hills near San Angelo and Del Rio, northwest to Guadalupe Mountains
Northeastern Mexico
Soil Sand, loam, clay, caliche, limestone; well drained
Part shade, full sun
Suckers
Propagation Fresh acorns

Vasey oak is a small, extremely drought-tolerant live oak. It's kin to the scrub oaks, and if it gets stressed enough, it can make a small thicket. Without watering in the Trans-Pecos, it only gets up to six feet tall. Use it as a small multitrunked tree in especially dry locations. It has been found to be fully winter-hardy all the way up to the Red River. Although it's not fully evergreen that far north, it tries real hard. The light green leaves are a little wavy on the edges, with tiny glands that emit a pleasant aroma when crushed.

322. **Shumard red oak**
Quercus shumardii
The authors

323. **Post oak**
Quercus stellata
The authors

322. **Latin Name** *Quercus shumardii* (*Q. shumardii* var. *shumardii*)
Pronunciation KWER-kus shoo-MAR-dee-eye
Common Name SHUMARD RED OAK
Usual Height 50 feet
Spacing 40 feet apart
Deciduous, with leaves turning red in fall
Range Moist forests and limestone upland woods in Blacklands, East Texas, Post Oak Woods, and Houston area Southeastern U.S.
Soil Sand, loam, clay, caliche, limestone; well drained
Part shade, full sun
Propagation Fresh acorns

The Shumard is probably our best red oak and can be used just about anywhere in Texas. Fairly fast-growing, with water and fertilizer, it is one of the last trees to sport fall color—it takes a few cold snaps to activate it, usually around late November. People often have a problem differentiating between the Shumard and the rest of the red oaks. In East Texas, two other oaks are often mistakenly marketed as Shumard, although most agree that the Shumard has a prettier leaf and shows better color. Some experts think that all red oaks that grow on limestone escarpment in the central part of the state are, in fact, Texas red oaks and not Shumards. However, Benny Simpson has given this matter a good deal of study and has concluded that the Shumard does indeed grow well on limestone—and often with very little soil. Still, identification is sticky, because the Shumard hybridizes with the Texas red oak. Some scientists now lump the two together.

323. **Latin Name** *Quercus stellata* (*Q. stellata* var. *stellata*)
Pronunciation KWER-kus stih-LAH-tah
Common Name POST OAK
Usual Height 40–50 feet
Spacing 30–40 feet apart
Deciduous, with leaves turning brown in fall
Range Dry, sandy woodlands in Cross Timbers and especially in Post Oak Savannah
Massachusetts to Kansas to Gulf of Mexico
Soil Sand; acid; well drained
Part shade, full sun
Propagation Fresh acorns

Each winter in North Texas the landscape is dominated by solid-looking stubby-branched oaks. To me, they always seem the same size, the same shape. These are the slow-growing post oaks, some of our most important and widespread trees. Most of the ones you see are one hundred to four hundred years old. If you own existing post oaks, leave them alone as much as possible. Their roots are extremely sensitive to disturbance. Compacting the soil, raising the soil level, paving over the roots, or overwatering all drive out the oxygen in the soil that is vital to their health. If you need to plant post oaks, you might have to start with acorns, although one grower told me that he'd planted fresh acorns in one-gallon containers and was selling eighteen-inch seedlings by the next spring. It is also possible, although difficult, to transplant specimens as large as twelve feet tall and four inches in caliper. Post oaks are usually found growing with the short-lived blackjack oaks (*Q. marilandica*). Post oak leaves are lobed and cross-shaped, and blackjack leaves are bell-shaped, complete with clapper. (Refer to the Post Oak Regional Description and Plan in Chapter 1 for more information about post oaks).

324. Texas red oak
Quercus texana
The authors

325. Avenue of coastal live oaks
Quercus virginiana
The authors

324. **Latin Name** *Quercus texana* (*Q. shumardii* var. *texana*)
Pronunciation KWER-kus tex-AN-ah
Common Names TEXAS RED OAK, SPANISH OAK, BUCKLEY OAK
Usual Height 15–30 feet
Spacing 15–30 feet apart
Deciduous, with leaves turning red in fall
Range Edwards Plateau
Endemic to Texas
Soil Loam, clay, limestone; well drained
Part shade, full sun
Propagation Fresh acorns

Texas red oak, in its pure form, is found west of Kerrville on the Edwards Plateau. North and east of there, it is probably genetically mixed with Shumard red oak and is now being considered a variety of that species. Both are drought-tolerant and grow on limestone, but Texas red oak is more drought-tolerant, as well as smaller and shorter-lived. It is also more likely to be multitrunked. Around Austin I've seen some beautiful specimens with attractive white patching on the trunks. The leaves are usually more slender than those of the Shumard, but not always. We have a third red oak in the Davis and Chisos mountains of the Trans-Pecos—Chisos red oak (*Q. gravesii*), which has smaller leaves that are not deeply indented. Its fall color can be either red or yellow. Because of its protected environment in the canyons, it can get taller (up to forty feet). It is often found growing with bigtooth maples and chinquapin oaks.

325. **Latin Name** *Quercus virginiana* (*Q. virginiana* var. *virginiana*)
Pronunciation KWER-kus ver-jin-ee-AY-nah
Common Names COASTAL LIVE OAK, SOUTHERN LIVE OAK
Usual Height 40–60 feet
Spacing 50–80 feet apart
Evergreen
Range Gulf Coast
Gulf and Atlantic coasts up to Virginia
Soil Sand, loam, clay; poor drainage okay
Full sun
Propagation Fresh acorns

Botanists see no difference between this oak and the escarpment live oak of the Hill Country, and in terms of how they look, they're right. They're both big, powerful-looking live oaks. But there's all the difference in the world in how they grow. The coastal live oak isn't nearly as drought-tolerant; around Houston, it lives in heavy clays, often in seasonal standing water, and is usually draped with Spanish moss. By the time you get to Aransas Pass, rainfall is low enough that it can grow only in deep sands, where its roots have access to deep-down moisture. One other difference: The coastal live oak isn't as cold-tolerant as its escarpment relative. All the live oaks growing between the Hill Country and the Gulf are hybrids of these two.

326. Texas palm
Sabal texana
The authors

327. Soapberry
Sapindus drummondii
The authors

326. **Latin Name** *Sabal mexicana (S. texana)*
Pronunciation SAY-bahl mex-eh-KAH-nah
Common Names TEXAS PALM,
    PALMA DI MICHAROS, MEXICAN PALM
Usual Height 45 feet
Spacing 12–15 feet apart
Bloom March to April; white; 7- to 8-foot
    stalks; fragrant
Evergreen
Range Flatlands by Rio Grande in Valley
    Mexico
Soil Sand, loam, clay; poor drainage okay
Part shade, full sun
Propagation Fresh or stratified seed

A palm that is winter-hardy as far north as Lake Livingston, Austin, and Del Rio should make a lot of people happy. Furthermore, this palm doesn't have any of those ugly spines on the leaf stems. So why isn't it used more often? For one thing, it's slow-growing. Like most Texas plants, Texas palm has an enormous root system and is extremely hard to transplant after it's a foot tall. It takes lots of water to establish and lots of time to become a mature tree—twenty to thirty years. However, the intermediate stages are extremely attractive. The three-foot blue-green fan-shaped leaves start out looking like palmetto leaves, pictured in Chapter 6. For about ten years, this handsome clump keeps getting bigger and bigger (to fifteen feet tall and just as wide), until gradually the trunk starts to appear at the base. The fruits (*micharos*) are dark purple and hang down in showy clusters. Little wonder that Mike Heep, in the Valley, says he can sell as many as he can grow—and then some.

327. **Latin Name** *Sapindus drummondii (S. sapon-*
    aria var. *drummondii*)
Pronunciation sah-PIN-dus
    druh-MUN-dee-eye
Common Names SOAPBERRY,
    WESTERN SOAPBERRY
Usual Height 10–50 feet
Spacing 12–20 feet apart
Bloom One week in May; white; 5- to
    10-inch panicles
Deciduous, with leaves turning yellow,
    lemon, gold, and pumpkin in fall
Range Throughout Texas
    Louisiana to Kansas to New Mexico,
    Mexico
Soil Sand, loam, clay, caliche, limestone;
    well drained
Part shade, full sun
Suckers
Propagation Scarified and stratified seed

If you found the usual height of ten to fifty feet (given above) a little bit puzzling, let me explain. Since soapberry grows throughout Texas, it is shaped by a wide variety of habitats. It is normally only ten to fifteen feet tall in the dry Trans-Pecos, but it often is as tall as forty feet in Corpus Christi and fifty feet in Dallas, where it gets more to drink. It's a fine shade tree in all these places, and one of the best in the state for dependable fall color; it even turns yellow in El Paso. The leaves look like small pecan leaves. The translucent amber fruits, which ripen in the fall, contain a substance called saponin, which is poisonous to people but not to bluebirds, who feast on the berries. Because of the saponin, the berries were used by early pioneers, and are still used today in Mexico, as laundry soap. Some people think that soapberry seeds out too much; they are probably confusing it with chinaberry, a small tree from Asia with purple flowers and opaque golden fruits. Both male and female soapberries have

328. American elm
Ulmus americana
The authors

329. Cedar elm
Ulmus crassifolia
The authors

flowers, with the male being the showier. When young, soapberry might sucker and form groves. If you keep the suckers cut off, they will eventually stop.

328. **Latin Name** *Ulmus americana*
   Pronunciation ULL-mus
      ah-mare-eh-KAH-nah
   Common Name AMERICAN ELM
   Usual Height 40–80 feet
   Spacing 30–60 feet apart
   Deciduous, with leaves turning lemon to gold in fall
   Range Along streams and rivers in eastern third of Texas
      From the Atlantic west to Rocky Mountains
   Soil Sand, loam, clay, limstone; moist, well drained
   Part shade, full sun
   Propagation Fresh seed, softwood cuttings

If you want a lot of shade in a hurry, this is one of the best fast growers in the state. It has distinctive V-shaped branching and looks great arching out over a house. The leaves look a lot like the popular Siberian elm. If you're planning to live a long time, don't confuse the two. The Siberian elm (also called Chinese or Asiatic elm) usually gets diseased and dies inside of fifty years, while the American elm can live well past three hundred years— that is, if it doesn't contract Dutch elm disease, which luckily doesn't seem to be a big problem in Texas. The seeds are small (less than half an inch long) and flat, which is good because a bumper crop is produced each spring, and a larger seed would make it harder to weed out seedlings in your garden. The root system is heavy and rambling, taking on sidewalks, flower beds, and sewer systems—and winning! The specimens we buy today in nurseries come from wetter, cooler climates northeast of Texas. In the near future, I hope, we'll be able to find more drought-tolerant stock propagated from our native stands.

329. **Latin Name** *Ulmus crassifolia*
   Pronunciation ULL-mus
      krass-eh-FOLE-ee-ah
   Common Name CEDAR ELM
   Usual Height 30–60 feet
   Spacing 20–30 feet apart
   Deciduous, with leaves turning yellow to gold in fall; evergreen in Valley
   Range Central and South Texas
      Mississippi to Arkansas to Texas
   Soil Sand, loam, clay, caliche, limestone; seasonal poor drainage okay
   Part shade, full sun
   Propagation Fresh seed

I love cedar elms because each one has its own unique shape. They are irregular, more tall than broad, with slightly drooping branches and tiny stiff leaves. You can always tell a cedar elm if you try to rub a leaf the wrong way. It's rough. The bark is also rough, with corky projections on the trunks of small nursery-size trees. Unlike the seeds of other elms, cedar elm seeds ripen and spread in the fall. This tree grows moderately fast and responds well to extra watering. It generally likes good drainage, but I know it can take standing water of less than a week's duration and will tolerate confined areas in medians and patios. It prefers calcareous soils, and is very drought-tolerant. In the Valley it is much shorter and more rounded in shape, with extremely dark evergreen leaves. If you live there or in San Antonio, you should propagate from locally grown stock, as the northern cedar elms might not be drought-tolerant enough for your region.

Church Landscape Plan
Lot Size: 320′ × 200′

Each year thousands of amateur gardeners find themselves faced with landscaping the property around their business establishment, their church, or some other community facility. Working in your own garden is one thing, but what do you do when confronted with a large-scale project?

Landscape architects are used to working on this scale, but often a church or small business just doesn't have the budget for all the services a good landscaper provides, such as site appraisal, design, overseeing the installation, maintenance, and so forth. In addition, you'll probably want a low-water-use design, one that is easy to mow and prune, is able to stand up to the wear and tear of several hundred people at one time, and looks terrific too!

To illustrate ways to meet these criteria with native plants, I chose a church. The plan shows a parking lot, easy-care street frontage, a formal entrance, a playground, and an inviting courtyard.

The first thing the public sees when driving by is the street frontage. There is usually a lot of it. So why not just put in a great big smooth, green lawn? For one thing, lawns need a lot of water and maintenance. That costs money, and economy is one of our criteria. Besides, it's boring.

I started my plan with some eye-catching, handsome trees. Not just one or two, here and there. If you've got a large tract of land, that can look pathetic. The trees need to be massed to show up properly. (The people at the Highway Department work on what might be called a grand scale. For them, a ground cover might be seven-foot-high smooth sumac covering one or two acres of embankment. Otherwise, it wouldn't be visible from a car driving by at 65 miles an hour.)

Here trees are grouped to form a narrow woodland surrounding the buildings. Trees are particularly appropriate around a church. Imagine yourself suddenly alone on an immense empty prairie—except for one solitary tree off in the distance. You'd head toward that tree, wouldn't you? Because it represents shade and shelter and a sense of place. Under a tree, you are no longer alone in infinity. And isn't that the sense you want to communicate about your church to people passing by?

The trees are clustered so they'll look substantial all year. In the spring, understory trees, such as plums and redbuds, will bloom. In the summer it will be cool and green beneath the canopy. In the fall, red, orange, and yellow leaves will provide color. And in the winter, there will be berries, junipers, or other evergreen trees and the sculptural patterns of branches to please the eye.

I've placed most of the colorful understory trees on the outer edges. Not only will this placement maximize the color, but it will keep the ground inside the woods shaded and barely visible. This makes maintaining a woodsy ground cover easier, as it will be well protected from drying winds and sunshine. Also, it will not be so visible that it need be kept in immaculate condition. Just prune out deadwood every now and then, and keep vines off the tree trunks, small trees, and shrubs.

From the woods to the street, I'd suggest buffalo grass or some other short turf grass suitable for your area. Seed the largest part in wildflowers to make a meadow, as is drawn on the plan. Another grass such as Gulf muhly or little bluestem could also be sown with the wildflowers.

The wildflowers will be lovely in the spring, but how far into the summer and fall this show of flowers will continue will depend on watering, soil type and depth, and region. Color also varies from year to year according to weather. The wildflower meadow should not be mowed before it loses its color and has set seed. Even if it is mowed as early as June 1, several weeks of mowing costs can be saved—along with the price of buying and applying poisons to keep the grass a pure monoculture. After it has been mowed, the meadow grass should be allowed to grow tall again. It should also be allowed to flower, because that gives the grass a soft, inviting look.

The only place that needs to be kept mowed is that bounded by the simple curve next to the street. Cutting one belt of grass while leaving the grass behind untouched is called contour mowing. It is useful for several reasons. It makes the meadow look planned and deliberate, even while the flowers are going to seed. It is more visually interesting, offering a contrast of textures between the mowed and unmowed sections. And it keeps streets and sidewalks clear, allowing full visibility for driving safety.

At the front edge of the woods, on the property line, is a thicket of trees and shrubs. In East Texas it might be composed of sassafras and New Jersey tea. Other places might use soapberry and aromatic sumac. Go for flowers and fall color rather than evergreens. The density should lead the eye back to the center of the property. A shrub thicket screens the parking lot from the street, and I've continued it around the parking lot to block the view of the adjacent property as well. Here it is combined with junipers, which provide a winter windbreak.

Thicket shrubs are smooth sumac (all Texas can use it, and it is guaranteed to sucker, but it requires occasional watering in most of the state), aromatic sumac, whitebrush, huisachillo, Havard oak, and dwarf wax myrtle. These shrubs will naturally spread to form a dense mass.

If you're on a small budget, plant them six to eight feet apart and they will fill in. If you plant at three-foot intervals, any shrub drought-tolerant for your area can be used. Thickets should not be hedged. Allow them to develop naturally. The only maintenance that is needed is to prune out deadwood.

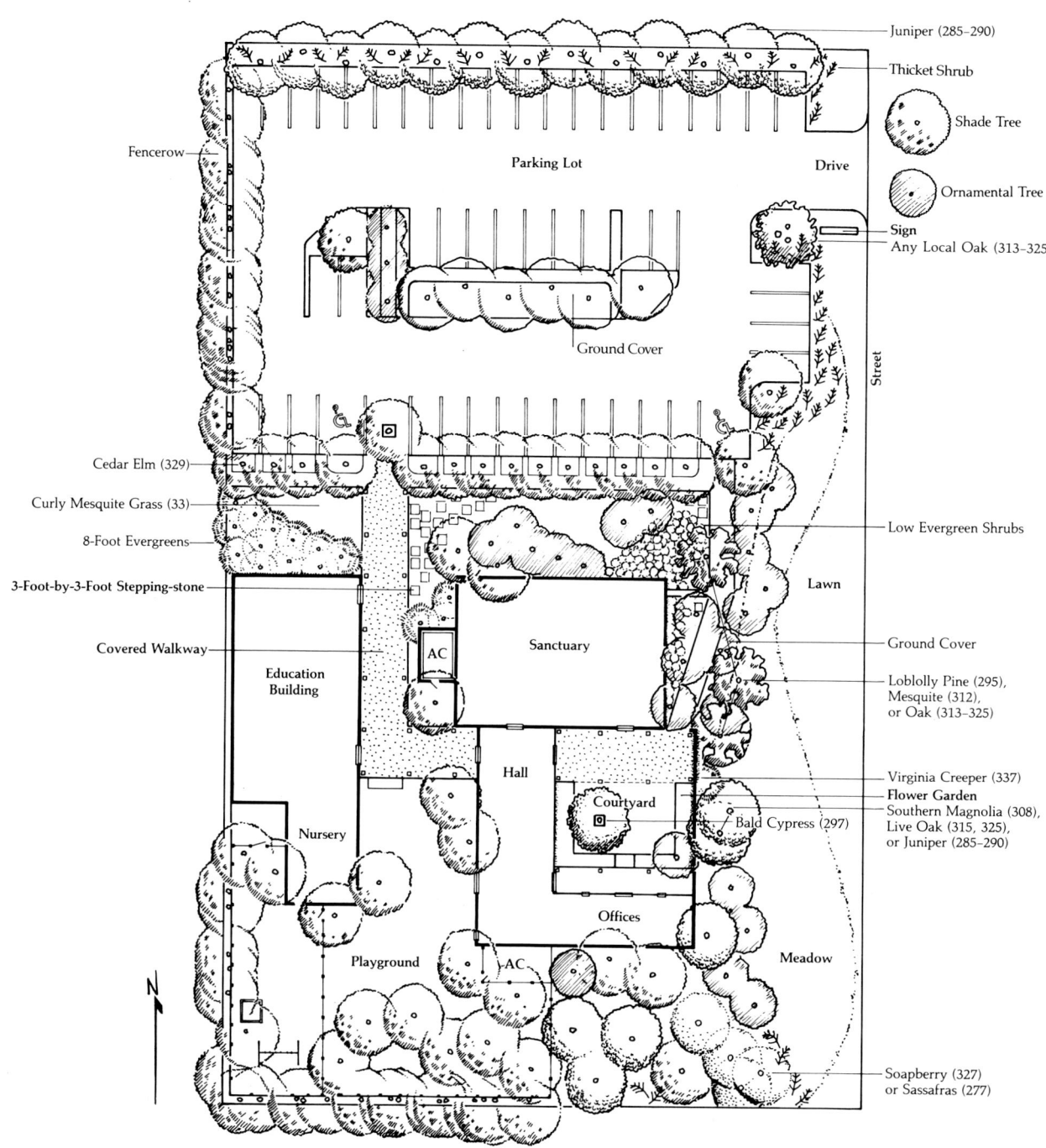

Juniper (285–290)

Thicket Shrub

Shade Tree

Ornamental Tree

Sign
Any Local Oak (313–325)

Fencerow

Parking Lot

Drive

Street

Ground Cover

Cedar Elm (329)

Curly Mesquite Grass (33)

8-Foot Evergreens

3-Foot-by-3-Foot Stepping-stone

Covered Walkway

Low Evergreen Shrubs

Lawn

Ground Cover

Loblolly Pine (295),
Mesquite (312),
or Oak (313–325)

Virginia Creeper (337)
Flower Garden
Southern Magnolia (308),
Live Oak (315, 325),
or Juniper (285–290)

Education
Building

AC

Sanctuary

Hall

Courtyard

Bald Cypress (297)

Nursery

Offices

Playground

AC

Meadow

Soapberry (327)
or Sassafras (277)

N

Church Landscape

Several flowering trees have been clustered there to give a big display of color. These don't have to be evergreen. Many of the ornamental trees have winter beauty in fruits, bark, or in the delicate tracery of their branches. If all the ornamental trees are of one kind, their impact will be much stronger visually. For instance, seven Texas redbuds here would be spectacular. Pruning these trees is crucial. Never cut the end of a branch. Keep the inside open by pick-pruning branches that grow toward the middle of the trees. Cut them off close to the main trunk or main branches.

The ground cover here could be curly mesquite grass in the early sunny years, but as the trees grow and cast more shade, a more shade-tolerant ground cover might be added. Where there are stepping-stones (you know people are going to cut the corners, so you might as well plan for it), curly mesquite grass, frogfruit, cherisse, silver ponyfoot, purple groundcherry, and horseherb are suitable choices.

Notice that on the east end, the last two ornamental trees direct your eye to the second path. They provide some height in contrast to the large planting of shrubs. All the shrubs should be the same and they should be allowed to grow together to form one solid, unpruned mass. The effect will echo the natural edges of the thickets, but it will be less than three feet high and evergreen. This gives year-round stability for the other parts of the design to play against. (Look on page oo for a list of evergreen shrubs under three feet.)

Along this walk are nine more ornamental trees, mixed with three large shade trees, to make a woodland walk. Here several different kinds of ornamental trees should be used so that something will always be blooming or turning color in the fall or holding bright berries.

On either side of the path, under the shrubs and on the shady side of the meadow, I've indicated ground covers. A mixture here would give more of a woodland feel and be more interesting. Ferns and New Jersey tea would be appropriate under East Texas pines. Coralberry, pink evening primrose, lazy daisy, and horseherb would look pretty under mesquites. On limestone, frogfruit, paleleaf or twisted-leaf yucca, white mistflower, cedar sage, and zexmenia could be used. Creeping barberry, New Mexico ponyfoot, and yellow columbine combine well in cooler parts of the state.

The east wall of the sanctuary (if it is not stained glass) would increase the woodsy feel if it were covered with Virginia creeper. In the fall its leaves turn a brilliant red, and its purple fruits feed many birds. Virginia creeper also covers the outside wall of the courtyard.

These two walls face the street. The vine will make the different parts of the building hold together visually, even if they were built at different times and of different materials. It will also convey a feeling of tradition, stability, and peace—qualities a church is supposed to have.

As the path ends, you enter a covered walkway as wide as the walkways on the other side of the building, but this one feels more like a porch, for it opens sideways onto the wedding courtyard. It looks across to a smaller covered walk that doubles as a porch for the church offices. Flowering vines growing up the columns give a feeling of intimacy and serenity.

Everyone knows that a parking lot needs to be functional. Few know that it can also be attractive. It takes just five extra feet of soil to be able to fit in shade trees and ground covers. I have also seen ornamental shrubs and flower gardens tucked in where the cars don't extend out beyond the pavement. The benefits of the shade trees are many. The parking lot radiates less heat, so cars don't get as hot in the summer, and the heat waves from the pavement don't slap you in the face and knock you over. Not as much heat is reflected into your building either, so air conditioning bills ought to be lower.

Trees that do especially well in parking lots are usually the same trees that can grow in floodplains. They are used to not being able to breathe through their roots, so having the roots covered by asphalt or pavement is no big deal to them. They also need to be able to adapt to dry, upland sites. From east to west, good choices are sweetgum, black gum, willow oak, white oak, coastal live oak, cedar elm, prairie flameleaf sumac, soapberry, cottonwood, and hackberry.

Do not use trees such as sycamore, Arizona ash, Mexican ash, and so on, because their leaves get scorched by midsummer every year. Avoid trees that bear squishy fruits, such as plums, or heavy fruits, such as female bois d'arcs. Avoid, if possible, trees that drop thorny branches capable of puncturing tires, such as mesquite and huisache.

The west end of the parking lot is a fencerow or hedgerow. Here is what you do if you need screening, and a chain link fence and a six-inch width of soil are all you have to work with. Let birds do the planting, and whatever they plant, let it grow thick. It should be kept pruned within three inches of the fence to a height of six to seven feet on the parking lot side. Poison ivy, ragweed, burs, tree-smothering vines, and anything else harmful should be removed. Otherwise it needs no maintenance whatsoever. It will get so thick that even in winter the fence will barely be visible.

Ground covers can be coarse, or low and neat, according to the scale needed. Fern acacia and artemesia are a good size for this parking lot. Under the trees by the walks, I'd recommend cherisse (other spiderworts will also do), pigeonberry, horseherb, flowers, and so on. Frogfruit is a good one to use if you find that feet continually stray off the walks into the planting areas.

As you approach the building from the parking lot, you'll notice that the landscaping becomes more evergreen and more structured. Between the educational building and the property line, I've massed tall evergreen shrubs to direct the eye and foot traffic to the broad covered walkway. (For a list of eight-foot evergreens, see page oo in the text accompanying the Shrub Garden Plan.) In front of the evergreens, an easy-care ground cover would be curly mesquite grass. Its rough texture is attractive whether green or tan, wildflowers can be planted in it, and it will take foot traffic and mowing if either is necessary.

In the area on the north side of the sanctuary, I've planted two shade trees for height. One wouldn't be a strong enough statement. They're

Buford TV in Tyler, Texas, wanted its offices to be completely surrounded by this beautiful woods, which lies on an ironstone hill in the Post Oak Savannah. Landscape architect Bryan Thompson removed invasive trash trees, greenbrier, and poison ivy and pruned the remaining post oak, blackjack and other oaks, elm, hackberry, black gum, flowering dogwood, rusty blackhaw viburnum, flameleaf sumac, wax myrtle, and other native trees not listed in this book, such as hickory and wild cherry. The ground cover is mostly Virginia creeper and fallen leaves. Each year, Thompson returns to supervise the pruning and to oversee the removal of invasive nonnative species such as mimosa and tallow. The sculpture is by James Surls. Photo by the authors.

planted close enough together so that their branches will soon overlap and form one visual mass.

The wedding courtyard reflects the four seasons, life's changes, and the processes of nature. Deciduous trees and flower beds, bare in the winter, hold seeds and the promise of new life. A profusion of spring blooms, more flowers and greenery in the summer, and bright autumn leaves complete the annual cycle. The atmosphere needs to be serene; this should be a haven, a place to sit and contemplate.

The five-foot borders around three sides of this courtyard are for flowering shrubs, perennials, and annuals. This area should be lush and colorful and will require regular watering and weeding. The large deciduous shade tree will cool the courtyard in the summer but allow sunlight to warm it in winter. A bald cypress would be a fine choice for this spot. The small ornamental tree should be chosen for year-round beauty and must be carefully pruned. My favorite candidates for perking up your winter landscape are possumhaw, Eve's necklace, and tornillo, with their attractive winter fruits; or Mexican plum, Texas persimmon, and paloverde—trees with uncommonly handsome barks.

The walls are covered with Virginia creeper, as on the outside, or with evergreen crossvine. The floor of the courtyard is paved. Stone, brick, or pavers with frogfruit or cherisse between the cracks would be charming, but if you have lots of people standing around here each Sunday, cement the materials, so the surface will be perfectly smooth and level. You don't want anyone stepping back and tripping on rough edges or getting a heel caught in a crack.

This leaves only the playgrounds to describe. The playground plantings are simple: trees for shade, and soft, sturdy buffalo grass. Be sure to use trees with nontoxic leaves and fruits, especially in the nursery playground. Where it is too shady for buffalo grass, bark mulch or gravel takes care of possible muddy spots. A shady playground is so much more comfortable in Texas than a sunny one. If there are existing tall trees, that's where to put the swing sets and teeter-totters. Additional trees can be planted everywhere else.

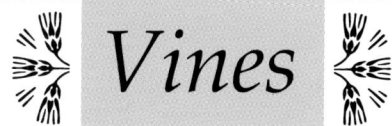 *Vines*

EVERYBODY knows what vines are, even little kids. They're those hanging ropes in the jungle that provide rapid transit for Tarzan. It may surprise you to know that we have vines that big in Texas—everywhere, in fact, except in the far western portions of the state.

However, these are the vines I'm leaving out of this chapter. Instead, I'd like to introduce (or reintroduce) you to a wide variety of smaller, more docile native vines that are infinitely better suited to home landscaping.

We'll look at vines that are evergreen, and vines that are deciduous; vines that climb, and vines that trail; vines that are woody, and vines that are annual. Some vines flower only when they are climbing, but a few others will bloom from a horizontal position. Some can climb up bricks or stone walls or can scale trees, while others climb only by twining; they must have something to twine around, such as a pole, string, or wire. I've grouped these vines according to their traits in the Walled Garden Plan description.

Vines are primarily used as greenery and color in confined, vertical spaces, such as on fences, walls, and trellises in courtyards and patios. Vines can look so gorgeous draped around pergolas and arbors that some people add those structures to their yards just for the colorful effect.

Some vines can be used as ground covers (Virginia creeper), and some do a great job of hiding an ugly fence (Carolina jessamine) or holding up the aged walls of a tumbledown garage (trumpet vine). Trumpet vine is also effective in holding eroding soil on a steep slope. Vines, however, are not without their faults. Some people fear that they will destroy the walls of their homes, and I have to admit there is some truth to this—but only if the walls are made of cheap brick. After all, look at Oxford University. Ivy has been clinging to those venerable buildings for centuries.

Vines can, however, damage roofs. This happens when their tiny tendrils insinuate themselves between the shingles and then grow big and fat. Trimming them off a foot or so under the eaves once a year suffices to keep this problem from developing.

The main thing that vines have in common is that they all love to have their roots cool and damp, which is why they do so well in and among rocks or in swamps. But they do need sun to bloom. If you have a choice, always plant your vines on the north or east side of a wall or fence, and let them drape over toward the sun.

If you must get vines established on the sunny south or west side of a house, where the soil gets hot, place a large rock over the roots to help keep them cool and moist.

This cascading trumpet vine blooms all summer and provides nectar for hummingbirds. Photo by the authors.

330. Crossvine
Bignonia capreolata
The authors

331. Trumpet vine
Campsis radicans
The authors

330. **Latin Name** *Bignonia capreolata*
    Pronunciation big-NOH-nee-ah
      kap-ree-oh-LAH-tah
    Common Name CROSSVINE
    Usual Height High-climbing, can reach
      70 feet
    Spacing 3 feet apart
    Bloom 7–10 days in spring; red and yellow;
      2 inches long
    Almost evergreen
    Range Woods, swamps, and creek bottoms
        in East Texas, along coast south to
        Victoria, and in North Central Texas
        New Jersey to Illinois to Gulf of Mexico
    Soil Sand, loam, clay, limestone; poor
      drainage okay
    Shade, dappled shade, part shade, full sun
    Propagation Seed, softwood cuttings, root
      cuttings

Although characterized as almost evergreen, crossvine acts like a true evergreen in Texas. This vine can grow thick fairly quickly—particularly in rich, moist soil. It even does well in lots of shade. At the end of its tendrils are three little claws that allow it to cling to bricks, stones, or fences, so you don't have to string up support wires for it. The hanging leaves are long and narrow, and the flowers, which are two-toned (brick-red and yellow), are so profuse when they bloom in the spring that they almost hide the vine itself. The blooming is timed to coincide with the annual hummingbird migration. This vine has been previously listed for East Texas only, but I've seen it growing wild on a limestone escarpment in a protected woodland at the Fort Worth Nature Center. I've also grown it successfully in blackland clays, so I'd bet that it would do well all over the state.

331. **Latin Name** *Campsis radicans*
    Pronunciation KAMP-siss RAD-eh-kanz
    Common Names TRUMPET VINE,
      TRUMPET CREEPER
    Usual Height 32 feet or more
    Spacing 3–4 feet apart
    Bloom June to September, continuously;
      red, yellow, or orange; 3–4 inches long
    Deciduous
    Range Eastern half of Texas
        Eastern half of U.S.
    Soil Sand, loam, clay, caliche, limestone;
      well drained
    Part shade, full sun
    Colonizes by suckers and self-layering
    Propagation Seed, stem or root cuttings

The late Carroll Abbott had a great answer when asked how high this vine can grow. "Three feet higher," he said, "than the highest object around." It can also sucker to such an extent that you can use it for erosion control. It climbs via aerial rootlets, which can be destructive to soft brick, aging mortar, and roofs. But it's terrific for hiding back fences, old garages, and tree stumps— places where you want lots of gorgeous summer color but you don't want to water. (West of the Cross Timbers, though, you'll have to give it periodic deep soakings.) It can also be used on wrought-iron balustrades and masonry walls. Plant it where the suckers can be controlled by mowing or by walkways or patios, and it can be an extremely easy-care vine. Most nurseries sell 'Madam Galen,' which is a cross between our native trumpet vine and one from China. Ours has smaller seedpods, and its flowers are narrower. The best thing about trumpet vine is that it never fails to attract hummingbirds.

332. Blue jasmine
Clematis crispa
The authors

333. Scarlet clematis
Clematis texensis
W. D. Bransford, National Wildflower
Research Center files

332.   **Latin Name**   *Clematis crispa*
Pronunciation   KLEM-ah-tus KRISS-pah
Common Name   BLUE JASMINE
Usual Height   Can reach 10 feet
Spacing   2 feet apart
Bloom   March to June (to October); blue,
pink, or lavender; 1–2 inches across
Dormant in winter
Range   Swamps and low woodlands from
East Texas to Victoria and Austin
Virginia to Illinois to Gulf states
Soil   Sand, loam, clay; poor drainage okay
Dappled shade, part shade
Propagation   Softwood cuttings in summer

Don't expect this short vine to climb very high on
walls or fences. In the Piney Woods Plan, I've used it on a
lattice, where its leaf stems twine around the framework.
With help like this, it can get as high as it can grow in one
season—maybe ten feet. Otherwise, it can be used effectively to sprawl over low structures, like the wings on
front steps, or a low wall around a patio. Or it can trail
over a planter box or large patio pot. It doesn't get tall,
because the stems grow fresh from the root each spring.
Almost as soon as they start growing, they sprout blooms.
I like the flowers a lot. What look like flower petals are
actually sepals that come in a range of pastel shades,
mostly lavender. The edges curl back and are ruffled, or
as they say in botanical circles, "crisped"—so now you
know how this vine got its Latin name. Blue jasmine will
grow in Houston's gumbo as well as East Texas sand.

333.   **Latin Name**   *Clematis texensis*
Pronunciation   KLEM-ah-tus tex-EN-siss
Common Name   SCARLET CLEMATIS
Usual Height   9 feet
Spacing   2 feet apart
Bloom   Spring and summer; red, rust,
maroon, or rose-pink; 1 inch
Dormant in winter
Range   Edwards Plateau
Endemic to Texas
Soil   Sand, loam, limestone; well drained
Shade, dappled shade, part shade
Propagation   Softwood cuttings

Scarlet clematis is a delicate little vine, hard to find
and hard to grow, but people love it and keep making the
effort. Its stems are often bare for the first two feet, and it
will bloom only on new growth climbing or clambering
over a trellis, tree, or shrub. It dies back to the ground
each year, so it never gets very big. The petals are actually thick leatherlike sepals, so this clematis is sometimes called scarlet leatherflower. The best-known and
most cold-hardy leatherflower is *C. pitcheri*. It comes in all
shades of purple and might be found in moist, shady
places throughout Texas, but mostly in the eastern half
of the state. The Trans-Pecos leatherflower is *C. filifera*,
which is also lavender or purple and fairly similar in appearance to *C. pitcheri*. Both look slightly like blue jasmine
without the ruffles. All three of the clematis featured on
this page appreciate moisture but, unlike blue jasmine,
cannot tolerate poor drainage. Their roots do best in
shaded, rocky, well-drained soil.

334. Carolina jessamine
Gelsemium sempervirens
The authors

335. Coral honeysuckle
Lonicera sempervirens
The authors

334. **Latin Name** *Gelsemium sempervirens*
Pronunciation jill-SEM-ee-um
sem-per-VYE-renz
Common Name CAROLINA JESSAMINE
Usual Height High-climbing
Spacing 6–8 feet apart
Bloom February to April; yellow; 1–1½
inches long; fragrant
Evergreen
Range Sunny woodlands in East Texas
Virginia to Arkansas to Gulf of Mexico
Soil Sand, loam, clay; poor drainage okay
Part shade, full sun
Propagation Cuttings

There are two big reasons why Carolina jessamine is our most popular native vine. It's evergreen, and it displays a cascade of yellow when it blooms. As far west as Midland it freezes back some and requires more watering than normal. Although naturally found in sandy loam, it grows extremely well in urban black clays. This vine climbs by twining. Besides its common use on fences and walls, it can also be used as a ground cover in the Piney Woods. It gets a bit too high to be walked through, but it won't climb the pines and is visually satisfactory for a large-scale landscape.

335. **Latin Name** *Lonicera sempervirens*
Pronunciation luh-neh-SARE-ah
sem-per-VYE-renz
Common Name CORAL HONEYSUCKLE
Usual Height High-climbing
Spacing 6–8 feet apart
Bloom Everblooming in mild weather; red;
2-inch clusters
Almost evergreen
Range Woods and thickets in East Texas
Eastern half of U.S.
Soil Sand, loam, clay, caliche; poor
drainage okay
Part shade, full sun
Propagation Softwood or semihardwood
cuttings in summer, layering

The question I get asked most often about this vine is, Does it take over your yard the way Japanese honeysuckle does? No. It's that ideal medium between being aggressive enough to grow well and being well behaved enough to make you happy you selected it. Its favorite habitat is where it gets sun all morning and shade in the afternoon. It will also take full sun all day, but if that's the case, you either have to water it more or have plenty of greenery or flowers growing beneath it to shade the roots. Rocks do a nice job of this, too. After it's established, it won't need any supplemental watering as long as it's in its natural range. Three to six soakings a year is normally adequate everywhere else in the state. Coral honeysuckle is a great vine for attracting birds; hummingbirds come to the blossoms in the spring, summer, and fall, and other birds are drawn to the bright red berries in the fall. I especially like this vine on an arbor or a pergola because it lets some sun in during the winter and because it isn't messy. It climbs by twining.

336. Snapdragon vine
Maurandya antirrhiniflora
The authors

337. Brilliant red fall color of Virginia creeper in the sun
Parthenocissus quinquefolia
The authors

336. **Latin Name** *Maurandya antirrhiniflora*
   Pronunciation maw-RAN-dee-ah
      an-teh-reh-NIFF-lor-ah
   Common Name SNAPDRAGON VINE
   Usual Height 3 feet or more
   Spacing 1–2 feet apart
   Bloom Spring to frost; purple; 1 inch across
   Dormant after frost, otherwise evergreen
   Range Shrubs, boulders, and dunes from
      southern coast to Trans-Pecos
      Texas to California to southern Mexico
   Soil Sand, loam, caliche, limestone; well
      drained; saline okay
   Dappled shade, part shade, full sun
   Propagation Seed

Snapdragon vine is a delicate little vine with small scattered flowers. You'd hardly call it showy; it's much better appreciated when viewed up close. I particularly like it trailing over the edge of a pot along with something else for height (damianita or bouvardia would be simpatico) or creeping out of a dry stone wall. It also makes a fine hanging basket. As you can see from its range, it isn't winter-hardy in most of Texas, but it grows so quickly from seed that it can be used as an annual everywhere else. The seed germinates in the spring, and the vine is blooming by mid-June. A similar snapdragon vine, *M. wislizenii*, is noted for its fruits, which look like little brown balloons. I've heard it called balloon-sepal snapdragon vine. It grows in deep sand or on limestone slopes in the Trans-Pecos, where it's classified as an annual or weak perennial. Ballon-sepal snapdragon vine blooms in spring and summer.

337. **Latin Name** *Parthenocissus quinquefolia*
   Pronunciation par-theh-noh-SISS-us
      kank-ah-FOLE-ee-ah
   Common Name VIRGINIA CREEPER
   Usual Height High-climbing
   Spacing 1 foot apart for ground cover,
      8 feet apart for walls
   **Deciduous, with leaves turning red, purple,
      or mauve in fall**
   Range Woods and rocky banks in eastern
      half of Texas
      Eastern half of U.S.
   P. inserta (*P. vitacea*) (Hiedra or Thicket
      Creeper)—western half of Texas; Canada
      to Wyoming south to Texas
   Soil Sand, loam, clay, caliche, limestone;
      well drained
   Shade, dappled shade, part shade, full sun
   Propagation Seed sown in fall,
      semihardwood cuttings, layering

"Quinquefolia" means "five leaves." That's good to know because it's one way you can tell this vine from poison ivy, which has three leaves. (Sometimes you'll find three leaflets at the base of very young Virginia creepers.) The stem's aerial rootlets have disks that fasten onto trees or masonry. This vine looks beautiful on a house, lush and green all spring and summer, brilliant red in the fall, and with black berries that songbirds enjoy in the winter. But it's vigorous, so keep it trimmed away from windows and roofs. An important use for it is as ground cover in our mid-Texas woods. There maintenance consists of pulling it off the trees each year. The fall color is mauve rather than red in this shady environment. Hiedra has the same vigor and brilliant red color of Virginia creeper but is even more drought-tolerant and likes more sun. It is not de-

338. Passionflower
Passiflora incarnata
The authors

339. Climbing prairie rose
Rosa setigera
The authors

structive, because it does not have aerial disks; it climbs by tendrils. The leaves are exceptionally beautiful—thick, shiny, and wavy-edged.

338. **Latin Name** *Passiflora incarnata*
Pronunciation pass-eh-FLOR-ah in-kar-NAH-tah
Common Names PASSIONFLOWER, MAYPOP
Usual Height 6 feet
Spacing 2–3 feet apart
Bloom May to August; lavender; 3 inches across
Dormant in winter
Range Eastern third of Texas Southeastern U.S., Bermuda
Soil Sand, loam; well drained
Dappled shade, part shade, full sun
Propagation Seed, cuttings

The flowers of this vine are unbelievably intricate and lovely. The name comes from the religious significance that some people find in the form of the flowers, with each part representing an aspect of the Passion at Easter time. This is one of those vines that starts fresh each year, so it never gets very big. It has tendrils for climbing but is often found sprawling along the ground, where it seems to bloom just as well as when it's up on a fence. If your passionflower is vigorous and rampant and can climb without your help, I'll bet the leaves are five-lobed rather than three. That means yours is naturalized from Asia. Our native is much better behaved. Passionflower belongs to a huge tropical family of five hundred species, most of which are in the Americas. In Texas we have seven of them. People in the Valley particularly love *P. foetida*. The name means it smells bad, but it looks great. These flowers are half the size of *P. incarnata*'s and much paler. The fruits are red, while *P. incarnata*'s are yellow.

339. **Latin Name** *Rosa setigera*
Pronunciation ROH-zah suh-TIJ-er-ah
Common Name CLIMBING PRAIRIE ROSE
Usual Height 9–15 feet
Spacing 4–8 feet apart
Bloom May; pink; 2–3 inches across
Deciduous, with leaves turning reddish in fall
Range Openings in pine and post oak forests and Blackland Prairies New York to Illinois to Gulf of Mexico
Soil Sand, loam, clay; calcareous; well drained
Part shade, full sun
Suckers
Propagation Seed, layering, dormant cuttings in January

Each May this rose is covered with deep-pink flowers that gradually fade to white, so that at the height of its glory it is covered with just about every shade of pink you can imagine. Like all species roses, it's very healthy. Just be sure the shiny leaves and reddish stems have plenty of air circulating around them. Its best use is on a pergola an arbor, or a lattice. Tie its long, limber branches (canes) to the structure. It is also beautiful growing in a tree; plant it three feet from the trunk on the windy side. Pruning is rarely necessary. If after several years your rose is getting too thick, prune out the older shoots and deadwood. Do this only right after the petals have dropped, as climbing prairie rose blooms on the previous season's growth. This rose has almost no thorns, and I've heard there's even a spineless variety. The fruits turn bright red and are decorative—at least until the birds have gobbled them up. There is a disadvantage: The plant suckers. Left alone, it can make an enormous rambling shrub. The most effective way to remove unwanted suckers is to pull them off where they join the root.

340. Texas wisteria
Wisteria macrostachya
The authors

340. **Latin Name** *Wisteria macrostachya*
Pronunciation wiss-TEER-ee-ah
mak-roh-STAY-kee-ah
Common Name TEXAS WISTERIA
Usual Height High-climbing
Spacing 3–6 feet apart
Bloom Late May; blue-violet; 4- to 6-inch
clusters; fragrant
Deciduous
Range Moist woods and banks in East and
Southeast Texas
Indiana and Illinois to Louisiana and Texas
Soil Sand, loam, clay; moist, well drained
Dappled shade, part shade, full sun
Propagation Cuttings

With a little attention, our native wisteria can be superior to the commonly used Asian species. By "attention," I mean care in selecting the cuttings for propagation (wisteria grown from seed might not bloom for ten to fifteen years). Be sure you see the blooms before taking your cuttings, so you'll get a good, rich color in the flowers. Like the Asian wisterias, ours has a pleasing fragrance, but in every other way our native is better. The leaves are dark green, shiny, and much prettier. The flowers appear after the leaves have come out, instead of on bare wood as with the Asian wisterias. And Texas wisteria is far less aggressive. It climbs by twining, so it will need support. You can use it in arbors or train it on a wall—in other words just about anywhere you'd use those other wisterias.

Walled Garden Plan
Lot Size: 40′ × 60′

This plan was inspired by the Old Rectory Garden just outside Oxford, England. The walled garden there is one small part of a vast estate, but it is so charming and memorable that I decided to try my hand at creating a Texas version.

My walled garden demonstrates an easy-care approach for a private, year-round outdoor living area. The plan shows how to use vines and other plants to decorate the walls without intruding out into the limited space of the courtyard. With beds no more than two feet deep anywhere, this courtyard can be lushly green and colorful. But it can also be easy to maintain,

Pot Plants:
12-Inch – A Columbine (94, 95) or Lila de los Llanos (93) G Pavonia (209)
16-Inch – B Hardy Hibiscus (117)   H Gregg Salvia (218)
              and Lanceleaf Coreopsis (106)   I Texas Lantana (196)
           C Mealy Blue Sage (148)   and Pink Evening Primrose (15)
              and Winecups (100)   J Blackfoot Daisy (127)
14-Inch – D Flame Acanthus (164)   K Turk's Cap (202)
           E Barbados Cherry (201)   L Scarlet Sage (146) or Cedar Sage (149)
           F Yucca (226)   M Scarlet Bouvardia (170)

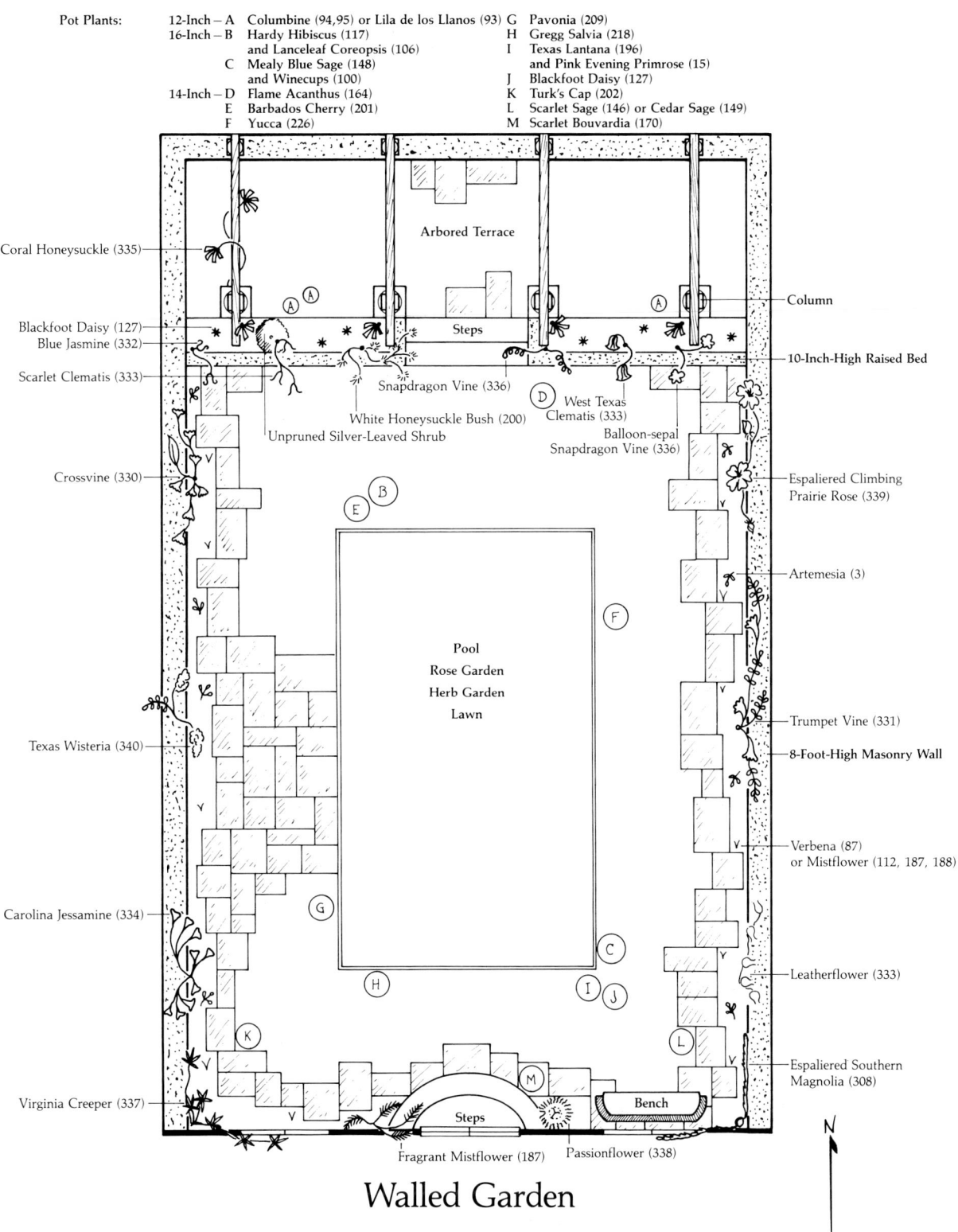

Coral Honeysuckle (335)

Arbored Terrace

Ⓐ Ⓐ

Ⓐ

Column

Blackfoot Daisy (127)
Blue Jasmine (332)

Steps

10-Inch-High Raised Bed

Scarlet Clematis (333)

Snapdragon Vine (336)

Ⓓ West Texas
Clematis (333)

White Honeysuckle Bush (200)
Unpruned Silver-Leaved Shrub

Balloon-sepal
Snapdragon Vine (336)

Crossvine (330)

Ⓔ Ⓑ

Ⓔ

Espaliered Climbing
Prairie Rose (339)

Artemesia (3)

Ⓕ

Pool
Rose Garden
Herb Garden
Lawn

Trumpet Vine (331)

Texas Wisteria (340)

8-Foot-High Masonry Wall

Verbena (87)
or Mistflower (112, 187, 188)

Carolina Jessamine (334)

Ⓖ

Ⓒ

Leatherflower (333)

Ⓗ

Ⓘ Ⓙ

Ⓚ

Ⓛ

Espaliered Southern
Magnolia (308)

Ⓜ

Bench

Virginia Creeper (337)

Steps

N

Fragrant Mistflower (187)   Passionflower (338)

Walled Garden

because there is little room for weeds to grow, yet it has lots of cool, damp places for roots to go.

To provide interest and color on the paved areas, I've grouped patio pots and filled them with plants and combinations of plants that have proven to be successful. Even though they've been double-potted, these plants, in full sun, require daily watering on hot summer days. If you don't want a daily watering chore but you do like the accents of color the pots provide, create open squares or rectangles between the paving stones to provide planting areas.

In this particular plan the south wall of the garden is formed by the house. The other three sides are surrounded by an 8-foot masonry wall 1½ feet thick. The focus at the back of the garden is an arbor on a raised platform and with an open roof nine feet overhead. This area could be used for dining, Sunday morning breakfasts, lounging, theatricals, and so forth. The platform, or terrace, is 1 foot high, 10 feet deep, and 37 feet long. Columns support an openwork roof of crisscrossed wood. The wood can be lumber, painted white or stained gray, or it can be saplings with the bark still on, treated with preservative. Vines—in this case coral honeysuckle—grow up on the roof to provide shade in the summer.

In front of the arbored terrace and flanking the steps are symmetrical raised beds, which are held by low retaining walls ten inches high and a foot wide. These walls are comfortable for sitting. The beds are only two feet deep to make weeding easier. I've indicated a coral honeysuckle at each column to climb onto the arbor. Along the edges are trailing vines, which should hang over these low walls at intervals.

The arrangement of the pavers is important. Note carefully how the pavers are staggered near the main walls. A straight line here would be tedious and lifeless. The pavers are all one to two and a half feet wide and two to three feet long. By placing them in this seemingly random format, pockets for plantings are created. Vines cover the walls, while low-growing flowers and shrubs should completely cover the ground and spill out over the pavers to further soften the edges and accent the ins and outs.

However, around the rectangle at the center of the courtyard, the pavers must make a straight line, or the whole design falls apart. The only other place I've set the pavers in a straight line is up against the house at the spot where I've placed a bench. The bench makes an accent point in the courtyard, and since there's no need to plant something here, there's no need to leave that open pocket of soil (which would only become a home for weeds anyway).

The dimensions of the rectangle on this plan are 17 feet by 28 feet. There are a lot of possibilities as to what could be done in this space. It can be lowered, raised, or remain at ground level. If the surface is lowered, it could be used as a small swimming pool, a large water lily pond (eighteen inches deep), or a reflecting pool, which can be even shallower. It could also be a bog garden (see the Water Garden Plan). If you have always wanted a rose garden or an herb garden, this would be an ideal spot. But you'd want to raise the bed to assure good drainage.

The west courtyard of the Plank garden in Midland is enclosed by stuccoed walls on all sides. The patio and paths of pink brick were designed by Bob and Dede Plank. The plantings, by Burr Williams, are in narrow margins and spill out over the brickwork. A West Texas clematis on a redwood trellis is flanked by pink evening primrose and lanceleaf coreopsis, backed by datura, yucca, and a naturalized shrub called bird-of-paradise (*Caesalpinia gilliesii*). In the foreground, the color is Indian blanket and Gregg salvia. The tree in the cutout is a nonnative goldenrain tree. Two other trees in this courtyard are a prairie flameleaf sumac and a Mexican elderberry (unseen in this photo). Photo by the authors.

At ground level this area could be a lawn, meadow, or parterre (see the Shrub Garden Plan). Less formally, it could be a kitchen garden, which is an attractive way to grow vegetables, fruits, and herbs all together. Or you might prefer a cutting garden, where long-lasting, long-stemmed flowers are grown to be cut and brought inside for floral arrangements.

It could also be a play area for small children or a teniquoit court (a version of lawn tennis played with rings and once popular as a deck game on cruise ships). If the garden were larger, it could accommodate a croquet lawn or a badminton court (20 feet by 44 feet).

The color scheme of this garden is restful—a subtle palette of silver and green foliage with purple or white flowers, accented with hot shades of red, orange, and pink.

As I was drawing this design, I envisioned the house, walls, and pavers of limestone. But sandstone, slate, tiles, scored and/or colored concrete, and so forth could be used as well, depending on your architectural style and the degree of formality you desire.

Because vines prefer their roots cool and moist, and because some parts of this garden would receive a lot of reflected heat, Houston (with its high humidity and gumbo soil) is probably the only place in the state where this garden might not need supplemental watering. The most drought-tolerant vines (trumpet vine, climbing prairie rose, and crossvine) are placed in the most heat-intensive spots.

The Virginia creeper in the corner next to the house is also drought-tolerant, but I placed it in that corner because it will take shade and because I like how it looks clinging to the walls of a house. It does need to be pruned off the roof and around windows, but that isn't an arduous task—usually one pruning per summer is enough.

Virginia creeper, crossvine, and trumpet vine all have the ability to climb on masonry. Coral honeysuckle, passionflower, Texas wisteria, Carolina jessamine, and the various clematis need wire or a trellis to twine around. Wires should be attached discreetly so we aren't aware of them. Trellises can be decorative in themselves and can be made of rustic branches, stained or painted lumber, or metal painted dark green or the color of the wall.

In the corner near the bench is an espaliered southern magnolia. Espaliering is done by attaching the supple branches of a young tree to walls and pruning them so that they lie flat against the wall. Here the magnolia is placed in a corner, and the branches form an evergreen cover. I have not tried it, but I'd bet this could also be done with yaupon holly, possumhaw, or wax myrtle. Trimming is done so that the window is framed by the foliage.

Beneath the vines, I'd suggest planting silvery artemesia if you have good drainage. Choose one with a pretty, fluffy blooming pattern, and let it go. For accents, spot in prairie verbena in hot sunny places and one of the mistflowers (either purple or white) in damp shady spots. Or fill the entire perimeter with perennials and annuals to make a colorful flower garden.

On the north side of the house, which is shady, I would let the passionflower trail on the ground instead of giving it something to climb on. Unlike some vines, it blooms well while supine. Also let the fragrant mistflower drape itself over the steps, as well as supporting it on the wall. Then I would plant winter annuals for color from frost through early spring. If you prefer, you could use any shade-loving ground cover appropriate to your area— ponyfoot, frogfruit, cherisse, horseherb, partridgeberry, or Christmas fern, for example.

The planters at the foot of the arbor are mostly filled with blackfoot daisy, which blooms at least nine months a year. If you have a sandy soil, the annual lazy daisy could be used. The trailing vines are all purple, except for the scarlet clematis. A passionflower could be used effectively here too. Just to break up the line of coral honeysuckle, white flowers, and purple trailers, there is a white honeysuckle bush trailing over the wall, which in old age might also climb the column. The unpruned silver-leaved shrub (which could be cenizo, silver agarito, sand sagebrush, or others) ties this bed in with the silvery foliage elsewhere. It also provides shade for the roots of the finicky scarlet clematis and a surface for it to clamber on.

Ferns, azaleas, iris, and spider lily from East Texas combine with Japanese evergreens, stepping stones, and carefully groomed bare earth to create this tranquil Japanese-style water garden designed by Kingscreek Landscaping of Dallas and the owners, Lorine and David Gibson. At the top left is a waterfall built of sandstone boulders. Sandstone also reinforces the sides of the earthbottomed pool and forms the two bridges. Although the pool is spring-fed, Lorine waters daily to keep the plantings fresh and to maintain a consistent water level. Photo by the authors.

 # *Water and Bog Plants*

WHEN some people think of Texas, they think of scorching summers and drying winds, water rationing, and burned-out crops, and they conclude that Texans should never have water gardens—only Xeriscapes. When you look at much of this state, it's hard to argue the point.

But, happily, there are parts of Texas where one finds abundant springs, streams, ponds, and bogs. More people than you might imagine have them on their property and use them as centerpieces for their landscapes.

Even if you don't have a naturally wet place on your land, a water garden is not out of the question. Most of the populations of Dallas, Corpus Christi, and Houston and its environs have to cope with poor drainage. They live on black clay, and black clay drains verrrry slowly. If you put western Xeriscape plants in that, they'd drown.

Many of the endemic plants in these areas can grow in standing water and also survive summers when the clay soil has shrunk, leaving great cracks in the ground. Since these flood-to-drought plants can be used in ordinary landscapes, as well as in water gardens, they are scattered throughout the book in their respective categories, but are grouped here in the Water Garden Plan.

Highlighted in this chapter are the water plants that need to be kept moist all year. There are two exceptions. Horsetail and swamp sunflower can grow well on land but are included here because a water or bog garden is their best use.

Horsetails are adaptable and aggressive and grow thickly, but they look peculiar and unsightly in a mass, so I wouldn't recommend them as a ground cover. Use them as water garden accents.

Swamp sunflower can be well behaved in a garden but looks almost gangly there. Besides, other yellow daisies are more desirable in a flower garden. The swamp sunflower's chief asset is the way it masses itself at the edge of water where there is mud all year. There it can make a dazzling sight.

Water plants are generally found in shallow water, on the banks of ponds or running water, or in any area that is consistently wet. The floating plants, like lotus and water lily, find eighteen inches to three feet of water optimum, although I've seen lotus rooted and thriving in water seven feet deep, and floating bladderwort in only nine inches of water.

Plants that grow on banks generally die back to the roots when the mud dries out, and they don't care to sit in water more than four to six inches deep. Most of these plants are shallow-rooted and travel by their roots extensively. Floodwater can drastically change a bank in a few hours.

The ability to reroot and grow quickly is more important than long-term stability.

Both open water and unstable banks are environments that are likely to have at least a half day of sun, if not full sun. Water plants, especially those with showy blooms, should have a minimum of six hours of sun to perform well. For a shady bog, use ferns and lizardtails, for example. (See the Water Garden Plan for specific suggestions.)

Now let's move on to some basic information on how to build and maintain a pond. Then I'll tell you how to plant and water a bog garden.

A pond can be concrete, metal, tiled, plastic-lined, or earthen. It can be diverted from a creek, spring-fed, filled with municipal water by a hose, or combinations of these. It can be formal or natural, large or small.

Guess where formal water gardens developed. In the Mideast—in the desert! They were designed many thousands of years ago as a part of irrigation systems that brought water from rivers to the homes of the rich. The lovely tradition of geometrically shaped tiled pools with clear water, fountains, and a few aesthetically placed water plants in pots or tubs then traveled with the Moors to Spain, then to Mexico, and on to us.

You can understand the strong appeal of such a garden in a hot and arid land. The sound of water trickling, the feel of it as you dip your hand in the pond . . . you feel cooler just thinking about it.

But wouldn't a water garden be unconscionable in, say, El Paso? Not really. As long as the pool is small and the fountain is a recirculating gurgle that doesn't blow into the wind and evaporate, the amount of water used can be carefully controlled (about as much as you'd use in one bath). The whole apparatus can be turned off and drained in a drought. The few water plants can be easily replaced.

If you have 40 to 50 inches of rainfall a year or have a spring on your property, consider the versatility of a natural earthen pond. An earthen pond can be any shape you like. It can have shelves and pockets artistically placed and hollowed out for iris, arrowhead, and other bog plants. The plants can be placed directly into the soil and weeded out at intervals.

A large pond dug in clay with a backhoe should hold water right away. A small one dug with a shovel usually needs a plastic liner at first, until the weight of the water has packed the clay sufficiently tight. Small holes should be cut in the plastic where the plants will go. Don't worry about having to remove the plastic at some future time; it will eventually rot away.

Those of you with lighter soils will always need a liner. Lay down a layer of organic material (grass, leaves, or newspaper, for example) under the plastic. As it decomposes in the absence of oxygen, it will form a tough, watertight layer called gley, which will resist leaks caused by punctures and greatly extend the life of your liner.

By nature, all water plants are aggressive. They are stopped only when the water is too deep, or not deep enough, to support them. If you want variety and control over your water plants without frequent weeding, place them in pots. Use terra cotta or black plastic pots that are ten or twelve inches across, less than six inches high, and without drainage holes.

The soil mix in the pots should be heavier than commercial potting soil and rich in clay-loam and manure. The organic material must be well rotted, or you will deplete the oxygen in the pond. If after several months you add commercial fertilizers to increase blooms, use those that are ammonium- or urea-based. Nitrates convert to nitrogen too quickly. Also, fill the last inch of the pot with gravel to keep your fish from nesting in the soil and partially digging up your plants in the process.

Tall plants can be placed at the correct depth right away. When you buy and pot small plants, you cannot set them on the bottom of the pond immediately. Their leaves need sunlight to make food. Pile up a stack of bricks and place the plants on top of it, starting with the leaves just an inch beneath the surface of the water. When the leaves have grown so that they are above the water, remove a brick and let them grow up to the air again. Continue doing this until they won't stretch anymore. Generally speaking, larger plants, like lotuses and water lilies, can go down deeper than plants like floating heart and bladderwort. All roots should be covered by at least two inches of water. Six to eighteen inches is better. Otherwise the roots will get too hot in the summer.

Submerged plants have the recommended depths indicated under *Soil*. If you are planting directly in the bottom of the pool, plant where the water is the right depth. If you are using a pot, measure from the top of the soil level in the pot.

To prevent the plants from freezing in the winter, lower the pots to the bottom of the pool. Covering the pool with plastic during a particularly hard frost helps keep the water warmer.

By their very nature, water gardens present several maintenance problems that you need to be aware of. The most prevalent problems are algae growing on the water and mosquito larvae hatching out. The solutions were worked out years ago, and they are really fairly simple.

Normally, all you need to do to keep algae and mosquitoes off of your pond is to keep the water moving, since they require still water to live and reproduce. There are several small recirculating pumps on the market that are easy to install. They can be hidden in the pool by an overturned flowerpot or some rocks. Let the water get cloudy and dense. It looks more natural that way, and it hides the pump better.

Clear plastic lines carry the water from one end of the pool to the other. Often some type of waterfall or fountain arrangement puts the water back in the pool, letting it pick up fresh oxygen on the way.

Another visually rewarding control for mosquitoes is goldfish. These splendid creatures can really make a water garden come alive with vibrant color and continual activity. Standard comets can be bought quite cheaply. More exotic ornamentals, such as koi (imperial Japanese carp) can run close to $200 for a pair of foot-long fish. The price may be more acceptable if you realize that they are not only incredibly gorgeous but also functional. If you are a purist, you can catch your own gambusia in a pond or ditch near you. These little top-water minnows are native all over Texas.

For a naturally functioning pond, get a bucket of scum with your native gambusia. Then, instead of messing with pumps, you can play with frogs and toads and occasionally weed out functional but unspectacular-looking water plants. Microscopic organisms that live in the scum are vital to the health of much of the pond life. The floating bladderwort, for instance, is actually carnivorous and can thrive only in a natural, earthen pond. If you enjoy watching a complete ecosystem at work, this kind of pond is the most rewarding.

Now I'd like to discuss the flowers that grow around the edges of the pond or can be used in a sunken garden called a bog garden. A bog garden does not necessarily have to coexist with a water garden. (See the Corpus Christi Plan for an example of one that does just fine all by itself.)

As demonstrated by Lilypons Water Gardens of Brookshire, Texas, a bog garden is a sunken bed, four inches or so below ground level, that has been stocked with water plants that don't need to float (narrowleaf cattails, crinum lily, arrowhead, powdery thalia, and so on) plus other flowers that are well adapted to poor drainage, such as cardinal flower, spider lily, and hibiscus. Fine bark mulch covers the bed to a depth of two inches, effectively holding in moisture. This mulch should be renewed once a year. Watering is done easily and efficiently by gentle flooding. Frequency, of course, is dictated by weather. Once a week in hot dry weather and once a month in winter are typical.

Design, prune, and weed as you would any other flower garden. For more specific ideas, see the Water Garden Plan at the end of this chapter. For help in placing flowers artistically in a bed, refer to the English Mixed Border Plan in Chapter 5, Perennials.

341. Lady fern
Athyrium filix-femina var. *asplenioides*
The authors

342. Buttonbush
Cephalanthus occidentalis
Edith Bettinger

341. **Latin Name** *Athyrium filix-femina* var. *asplenioides*
Pronunciation ah-THER-ee-um FEE-lix-FEM-eh-nah variety ass-plen-ee-OY-deez
Common Name LADY FERN
Usual Height 2–4 feet
Spacing 2 feet apart
Dormant in winter
Range Bogs, woods, swamps, wet thickets, and stream banks in Piney Woods, Coastal Prairies, and Post Oak Savannah, west to Georgetown
Eastern Massachusetts to Florida, Indiana to Texas
Soil Sand, loam, clay; acid or calcareous; moist, poor drainage okay
Shade, dappled shade, part shade
Colonizes by rhizomes
Propagation Root division

Anyone who has ever seen lady fern used as a ground cover back East will probably be surprised to see it listed here among water plants. The truth is, it likes to be moist all year, and the only way we can guarantee that condition here in Texas is to stick it in or near a bog. Lady fern is especially useful for cities with black clays, as it does not require acid sands the way many of our ferns do. Because the fronds are rather large and coarse, it does well where you want more height and texture than you'd get from wood fern (called river fern down in Austin and San Antonio). If lady fern is in an evenly moist area, it will be aggressive. If you want to use it only as an accent, surround it with higher, drier ground.

342. **Latin Name** *Cephalanthus occidentalis*
Pronunciation seff-ah-LAN-thus ok-seh-DEN-tal-iss
Common Name BUTTONBUSH
Usual Height Under 10 feet, can reach 45 feet
Spacing 6–8 feet apart
Bloom Summer; white or pale pink; 1- to 2-inch globes
Deciduous
Range Swamps, ponds, and margins of streams throughout Texas
Canada to Mexico
Soil Sand, loam, clay, limestone; moist, poor drainage okay, 0–12 inches underwater
Part shade, full sun
Propagation Seed, soft or hard root cuttings, root division

I like buttonbush! The bush (or small tree) is overwhelmed by balls of pale pink flowers that smell sweet and are always covered by bees and butterflies. In full sun, buttonbush can bloom solidly all summer; in shade, it'll bloom off and on from June to September. It will grow in shallow water, just a foot or so deep, or on land where it is always moist. It tends to stay shrubby in the water, but on the bank it will gradually develop into a tree with a twisty, gnarled trunk, which can be quite picturesque. The fruits grow in heavy, brown clusters and really aren't the plant's best quality—but they do attract more than 25 species of waterfowl.

343. Crinum lily
Crinum americanum
Dr. Harold Laughlin

344. Titi
Cyrilla racemiflora
The authors

343. **Latin Name** *Crinum americanum*
Pronunciation KRYE-num
ah-mare-eh-KAH-num
Common Names CRINUM LILY, SWAMP LILY
Usual Height 1–3 feet
Spacing 1–1½ feet apart
Bloom June to November; white;
3–4 inches long
Almost evergreen
Range Swamps and edges of water in
Southeast and coastal Texas
Florida to Georgia to Texas
Soil Sand, loam, clay; acid or calcareous;
moist, poor drainage okay, 0–6 inches
underwater
Shade, dappled shade, part shade, full sun
Colonizes by stoloniferous bulbs
(1–4 inches wide)
Propagation Bulbs

This plant is not fussy about the amount of sun or shade it gets; it's biggest asset is that it will give dependable color for a long time in deep shade where almost nothing else will bloom. The intensely fragrant flowers are quite large and bloom in isolated clusters. The leaves might remind you of an amaryllis—straplike, two to three inches wide, and three to four feet long. Nearly everyone who works with this plant raves about it. It freezes back to water level (or ground level) in the winter, but greens up again immediately, so you have leaves almost all year-round.

344. **Latin Name** *Cyrilla racemiflora*
Pronunciation kye-RILL-ah
ray-sem-eh-FLOR-ah
Common Names TITI (tye-tye),
LEATHERWOOD
Usual Height Under 30 feet
Spacing 10–15 feet apart
Bloom Late May; white; 4-6 inches; fragrant
Almost evergreen, with leaves turning rust-colored to red or yellow in fall
Range Bottomlands in Southeast Texas,
north to Davy Crockett National Forest
Coastal Virginia to Florida to Texas
Soil Sand, loam; acid; moist, poor drainage
okay, 0–6 inches underwater
Dappled shade, part shade, full sun
Might colonize to form a thicket
Propagation Root cuttings, softwood
cuttings

Titi is mostly used around shallow ponds, with buttonbush, viburnums, and wax myrtle. I also like it when it's surrounded by the lower-growing Virginia sweetspire. It looks shrubby for many years, but it eventually makes a slender tree with smooth cinnamon-colored trunks. The leaves are a lustrous dark green; in the fall, half remain green while the other half turn a rich, warm red. The look is very Christmasy. In the spring the leaves finally drop, and just as the new ones are unfurling, blooms appear as drooping white clusters. Bees are attracted to the sweet-smelling flowers. In the summer the fruits turn a mellow yellow-brown.

345. White-topped sedge
Dichromena colorata
The authors

346. Horsetail
Equisetum hyemale
The authors

345. **Latin Name** *Dichromena colorata*
Pronunciation dye-KROH-men-ah kuh-luh-RAT-ah
Common Name WHITE-TOPPED SEDGE
Usual Height 1–2 feet
Spacing 9 inches apart
Bloom Summer; white; bracts
Dormant in winter
Range Poorly drained areas from Gulf to Trans-Pecos
Virginia to Caribbean, eastern Mexico
Soil Sand, loam, clay; moist, poor drainage okay; saline okay; 0–6 inches underwater
Part shade, full sun
Colonizes by rhizomes
Propagation Root division

The white flowers of white-topped sedge are little tufts in the center of long, drooping bracts. Half of each bract is white, and the other half is green. It's the white part that makes this plant desirable—from a distance, it looks like a cluster of white stars on delicate slender stems. The foliage is dark green and grasslike, short and crowded down at the bottom. You can expect good color all summer from this plant. Place it along the edge of your water garden or in a bog garden. Bury it in a pot to keep it from spreading; sedges are fairly aggressive.

346. **Latin Name** *Equisetum hyemale*
Pronunciation eh-kweh-SEE-tum HYE-mah-lee
Common Names HORSETAIL, CANUELA
Usual Height 1–3 feet, can reach 9 feet
Spacing One is enough; 6-inch pot or larger
Evergreen
Range Moist places throughout Texas, most frequent in Blacklands and Edwards Plateau
U.S., Canada, Mexico, Eurasia
Soil Sand, loam, clay, limestone; poor drainage okay, 0–6 inches underwater
Dappled shade, part shade, full sun
Colonizes by rhizomes
Propagation Root division

Horsetail is extremely invasive, and if you think lack of water will slow it down, think again. I didn't put it in this chapter because it needs to be kept moist all the time, but because the only way you would want to use it is as a water plant. Always keep it contained in a pot, unless you need it to hold eroding banks on a large lake. You may be surprised to hear that this aggressive plant is often hard to get established—especially in heavy soils, where the roots seem to have trouble getting started. Another reason it is hard to start is that rabbits love it, which is odd since the tall, stiff stems are filled with silica; horsetail used to be called scouring rush and was once used to scrub out pots and pans. What I like about it is that it always attracts dragonflies; they lay their eggs on the stems. Use it on banks or in shallow water.

347. Swamp sunflower
Helianthus angustifolius
The authors

348. Waterleaf
Hydrolea ovata
The authors

347. **Latin Name** *Helianthus angustifolius*
Pronunciation hee-lee-AN-thus an-gus-teh-FOLE-ee-us
Common Name SWAMP SUNFLOWER
Usual Height 1½ feet
Spacing 1 foot apart
Bloom 7–10 days in October; yellow, with dark centers; 2 inches across
Dormant in winter
Range Moist places in East and Southeast Texas
New Jersey to Iowa, south to Florida and Texas
Soil Sand, loam, clay; acidity might be required; moist, poor drainage okay, 0–6 inches underwater
Part shade, full sun
Colonizes by rhizomes
Propagation Root division, seed

This sunflower could be used in a regular garden, along with perennials, in East Texas and Houston, but I find it usually too tall and gangly. A few have the genes to bunch into a thick bouquet six feet tall, which can look glorious at the back of a perennial border. But where this flower is most impressive and desirable is along low muddy lake edges. There it colonizes densely and attractively, making brilliant swaths of gold. In these muddy margins—never in more than six inches of water—it usually stays under two feet tall. If you have a lake or stock pond in East Texas, I don't see how you could pass up having this knockout sight every year. Swamp sunflower also does well in a bog garden.

348. **Latin Name** *Hydrolea ovata*
Pronunciation hye-DROH-lee-ah oh-VAY-tah
Common Names WATERLEAF, BLUE WATERLEAF
Usual Height 1½–3 feet
Spacing 6 inches apart, or 3 per 8-inch pot
Bloom August to October; blue (white); 1½ inches on spikes
Dormant in winter
Range Edges of ponds and streams in East and Southeast Texas
Louisiana, Texas, Mississippi, Arkansas
Soil Sand, loam, clay; acidity might be required; moist, poor drainage okay, 0–6 inches underwater
Part shade, full sun
Colonizes by rhizomes
Propagation Root division, seed

I was first attracted to this flower by its vivid sky-blue color, although some specimens can range from white to a deep royal blue. Waterleaf resides along the side of the water, where conditions are always moist. Despite its name, there doesn't seem to be anything particularly unusual about the leaves. They are smallish, oval, and fuzzy. The stem is a bit more distinctive, having spines that appear to be sharp but are really soft and flexible. This is one of those tall, spiky perennials that colonizes to form thick clumps. The flowers, which open midmorning and close before dark, start blooming in late summer and continue on up the stalk until well into October.

349. Chain fern
Lorinseria areolata
The authors

350. Yellow water lotus
Nelumbo lutea
The authors

349.   **Latin Name**   *Lorinseria areolata* (*Woodwardia*
      areolata)
      Pronunciation   lor-en-SER-ee-ah
      air-ee-oh-LAY-tah
      Common Name   CHAIN FERN
      Usual Height   1–2½ feet
      Spacing   1½ feet apart
      Dormant in winter
      Range   Bogs, swampy woods, and seepages
          in Piney Woods, Post Oak Savannah,
          and Houston area, south to Gonzales in
          Blackland Prairies
          Nova Scotia and Michigan, south to
          Florida and Texas
      Soil   Sand, loam, clay; acid or calcareous;
      moist, poor drainage okay
      Shade, dappled shade, part shade
      Colonizes by rhizomes
      Propagation   Root cuttings, root division

This is a well-mannered fern to use as a ground cover at the shady end of a pond. It's shorter than most species and not as aggressive as wood fern. New fronds are bronze in color but soon become green. Each plant has both fertile and infertile fronds; the fertile fronds have purple-brown stalks, which stand up stiff and tall in the middle of the clump. It's the sterile fronds on the outside that give the entire clump its soft look. Because chain fern is not picky about its soil, it should be a popular addition to the nursery trade's repertoire of ferns.

350.   **Latin Name**   *Nelumbo lutea*
      Pronunciation   neh-LUM-boh LOO-tee-ah
      Common Name   YELLOW WATER LOTUS
      Usual Height   1–1½ feet above water
      Spacing   1 per 19-inch container
      Bloom   Summer; yellow; 8–10 inches across
      Dormant in winter
      Range   Quiet water in eastern third of Texas
          Southern Ontario to Gulf of Mexico
      Soil   Any pond bottom; 4–12 inches
      underwater
      Full sun
      Colonizes by rhizomes
      Propagation   Seed, root division

Yellow water lotus flowers are dramatic. They're pale yellow, with rich gold centers. Although each lotus will give you many blooms all summer, the individual flowers last only two days. The petals open a couple of hours after sunup and close in the late afternoon, reopening the next day. The petals then drop off, and the yellow center turns green and starts to grow, gradually forming a decorative seed head that, when ripe and brown, is popular in floral arrangements. Each seed head is about the size of an adult's fist and has a flat top. Just imagine a moonscape, with seeds inside the craters. It's easy to tell this lotus from the water lilies in this chapter by looking at the leaves; these are perfectly round, while the water lily leaves are minus a pie-shaped wedge. Also, the lotus leaves often stick out of the water, as in the photo. Each leaf is more than a foot in diameter. Be careful to contain the lotus in a stout tub, as it is very aggressive.

351. **White water lily**
Nymphaea odorata
The authors

352. **Floating heart**
Nymphoides aquatica
Doug Williams

351. **Latin Name** *Nymphaea odorata*
Pronunciation nim-FEE-ah
oh-duh-RAH-tah
Common Name WHITE WATER LILY
Usual Height Flowers 3–6 inches above
water
Spacing 1 per 6–12 square feet of water
Bloom March to October; white; 4–7 inches
across; fragrant
Dormant in winter
Range Still, fresh water in Southeast Texas
Eastern Canada to Gulf of Mexico
Soil Any pond bottom; 6–18 inches
underwater
Full sun
Colonizes by rhizomes
Propagation Division of rhizomes in
March, when just leafing out

We have three native Texas water lilies, but the
white one is the most winter-hardy, has the most petals,
and has the added bonus of being fragrant. It's a comfortable size for almost any home water garden—the lily pads
range from three to ten inches across. It can be planted
directly into the bottom of an earthen pond and thinned
out every two or three years to keep it under control.
Monthly applications of bonemeal (wrapped in paper and
tucked into the soil by the roots) will keep the blooms
coming every month when the weather is warm. The flowers of all three lilies open in the morning and close in the
late afternoon. Blue water lily (*N. elegans*) has six-inch
flowers that are pale blue or lavender, and rarely pink. It
blooms only along the Gulf Coast, as does yellow water
lily (*N. mexicana*), sometimes called the banana lily. Its
flowers are three to five inches wide, but be warned—it
can propagate prolifically by stolons on the bottom of the
pond. All these water lilies do well in containers but will
have smaller blooms.

352. **Latin Name** *Nymphoides aquatica*
Pronunciation nim-FOY-deez
ah-KWAH-teh-kah
Common Name FLOATING HEART
Usual Height Floats on surface
Spacing 1 per 6-inch pot
Bloom May to September; white; ½ inch
across
Dormant in winter
Range Still, fresh water in East Texas
New Jersey to Gulf states
Soil Any pond bottom; 4–12 inches
underwater
Part shade, full sun
Propagation Seed, roots on leaves

Floating heart is the smallest of the native floating
plants in this book. If your water garden is the size of a
whiskey barrel, such as you might have in a small condo
patio, this floating plant is of the right scale. But I have
also seen it charmingly scattered like snowflakes over a
large earthen pond. The heart-shaped (sometimes kidney-
shaped) leaves are about six inches in diameter and are a
smooth, pale yellow-green, spongy and thick in texture,
and dark and pitted on the underside. The diminutive
white flowers spring from just under the cleft of the leaf,
where their roots are dangling. These roots (actually an
extra set) make floating heart aggressive in an earthen
pond. The original roots, in the soil, come from a tuber
that sends up a ten-inch-long stem.

353. Sensitive fern
Onoclea sensibilis
The authors

354. Cinnamon fern
Osmunda cinnamomea
The authors

353. **Latin Name** *Onoclea sensibilis*
Pronunciation oh-NAH-klee-ah sen-SIB-eh-lus
Common Names SENSITIVE FERN, BEAD FERN, SYMPATHY FERN
Usual Height 1–3 feet
Spacing 1–2 feet apart
Dormant in winter
Range Swamps, sandy bogs, and along streams in Piney Woods, Post Oak Savannah, and Houston area to north of Marble Falls and southeast of San Antonio
Canada to Gulf of Mexico
Soil Sand, loam, limestone seeps; moist, poor drainage okay
Shade, dappled shade, part shade, full sun
Colonizes by rhizomes
Propagation Root division

Sensitive fern gets its name because the fronds curl up slightly when touched. It's called bead fern because of the rounded spores that cluster thickly on the backside of the fertile fronds. This fern does best in well-drained soils that are kept evenly moist, which means sandy soils, where it can get both the moisture and oxygen its roots need. It will also grow in limestone seeps, but not in alkaline clays; the roots can't breathe in soil that tightly compacted. Unless it gets a rich soil with lots of organic matter mixed in, it will probably not grow more than a foot tall. Plant sensitive fern in deep shade and well-prepared soil, and it can get by with a weekly watering. Otherwise it can be used in Texas only in a bog garden or on the moist margins of a water garden.

354. **Latin Name** *Osmunda cinnamomea*
Pronunciation oz-MUN-dah sin-ah-MOH-mee-ah
Common Name CINNAMON FERN
Usual Height 2–3 feet
Spacing 2 feet apart
Dormant in winter
Range Moist or wet places from Piney Woods and Beaumont to a line east of Austin and San Antonio in Blacklands, one location in Uvalde County
Newfoundland to Florida and New Mexico
Soil Sand, loam, clay; acid or calcareous; moist, poor drainage okay
Shade, dappled shade, part shade
Rhizomes
Propagation Root division

This plant is called the cinnamon fern (no, the second *m* in the Latin name is not a typo) because the fertile fronds in the middle of the plant are cinnamon-colored at maturity. In fact, the fronds don't look like fronds at all; they're not leafy. As soon as the spores are ripe, they die back. This fern does best when it is in soppy, soupy mud, as Texas summers are hard on it. The roots are on the surface, which makes them vulnerable to drying out. One hot day can do them in. Cinnamon fern is a plant for someone who has the right wet environment; it's beautiful, but somewhat difficult to raise here. In cooler, moister climates, it gets five feet tall and colonizes, but don't expect that to happen in Texas.

355. Royal fern
Osmunda regalis var. *spectabilis*
The authors

356. Tuckahoe
Peltandra virginica
The authors

355. **Latin Name** *Osmunda regalis*
Pronunciation oz-MUN-dah REE-guh-lus
Common Name ROYAL FERN
Usual Height 4–6 feet
Spacing 3–4 feet apart
Dormant in winter
Range Piney Woods, Post Oak Savannah, Coastal Prairies south to Victoria, Blacklands near Austin
Canada to South America
Soil Sand, loam, clay, limestone; moist, poor drainage okay
Shade, dappled shade, part shade
Colonizes by rhizomes
Propagation Root division

Royal fern is a lot like cinnamon fern, except that royal fern is much larger and much better adapted to our summers. Also, its fertile fronds are more golden than cinnamon-colored, but you can judge that for yourself the next time you see them. Like most ferns, it can grow in full sun if it's in sufficiently wet soil, but it can get ratty in the summer. It's better to give it at least some shade. Its rhizomes are made of a substance called osmunda fiber, similar to tree fern fiber, which is compressed to make those stakes that hold up potted philodendrons. In poorly drained beds next to a house, in well-drained but well-watered woodland areas, and at shady ends of earthen ponds, this fern looks exotic, tropical, and dramatic.

356. **Latin Name** *Peltandra virginica*
Pronunciation pel-TAN-drah ver-JIN-eh-kah
Common Names TUCKAHOE, ARROW ARUM
Usual Height 1–2 feet
Spacing 1–2 feet apart, or 1 per pot
Bloom April to June; yellow; buried in leaves
Dormant in winter, after it is established
Range Swamps, bogs, and edges of water in East Texas
Canada to Gulf of Mexico
Soil Rich mud; 0–6 inches underwater
Shade, dappled shade, part shade
Subtuberous root
Propagation Root cuttings, seed

This small-scale, well-behaved water plant is suitable for any shady water garden. The leaves are usually shaped like arrowheads, about eight inches long and six inches wide, but the size and shape may vary a lot according to each individual plant's genetics. The flowers are not a significant part of this plant's allure; they are tiny and yellow and sit on a fingerlike protrusion (spadix) that is surrounded by a pale green leaflike shield called a spathe. The whole deal is buried among the leaves, so you have to hunt if you want to see it. The seeds, which are also light green or brown, are relished by wood ducks and other marsh fowl.

357. Pickerelweed
Pontederia cordata
The authors

358. Arrowhead
Sagittaria lancifolia
The authors

357. **Latin Name** *Pontederia cordata*
Pronunciation pon-teh-DARE-ee-ah
kor-DAH-tah
Common Name PICKERELWEED
Usual Height 2–3 feet
Spacing 6 inches apart, or 1 per 6-inch
container
Bloom June to September; lavender-blue;
6-inch spikes
Dormant in winter
Range Shallow water in East Texas
Eastern coastal Canada to Oklahoma,
Texas, and Gulf of Mexico
Soil Mud; 0–12 inches underwater
Dappled shade, part shade, full sun
Colonizes by rhizomes
Propagation Root division, even while in
bloom

I'm especially enthusiastic about this flower; it's probably our easiest-growing and most rewarding water plant. It will grow on ledges or along the edges of an earthen pond, in pots in shallow water, or in a bog garden. It blooms continuously all summer without extra feedings; the little flowers on the spike open over a period of days, keeping each spike in bloom about a week. Dragonflies are usually found in abundance on pickerelweed.

358. **Latin Name** *Sagittaria* spp.
Pronunciation sah-jeh-TARE-ee-ah species
Common Name ARROWHEAD
Usual Height 2–3 feet (1–4 feet)
Spacing 1 foot apart, or 1 per 6-inch
container
Bloom Spring to fall; white; 1–2 inches
across
Dormant in winter
Range Mud, marshes, and shallow water
throughout Texas
North America
Soil Mud; 0–12 inches underwater
Part shade, full sun
Colonizes by stolons
Propagation Root division anytime

We have nine arrowheads in Texas; all are white, all are useful, and all are long-blooming. Whichever one you find growing close to you is the best one to use. You might have a choice, in which case go with your own taste. Although they are all called arrowhead, only four of the nine have arrowhead-shaped leaves; the others have lance-shaped leaves. All have numerous three-petaled white blooms on leafless stalks. These plants are fairly aggressive, but they're perfect for getting a water garden started because they get established so quickly and bloom for such a long time.

359. Lizardtail
Saururus cernuus
The authors

360. Powdery thalia
Thalia dealbata
The authors

359. **Latin Name** *Saururus cernuus*
Pronunciation saw-ROO-rus SER-new-us
Common Names LIZARDTAIL, LIZARD'S-TAIL
Usual Height 1½–3 feet, when in bloom
Spacing 1 foot apart, or 1 per 6-inch container
Bloom April to August (most profuse in spring)
Dormant in winter
Range Standing water or mud in East and Southeast Texas
Southeastern Canada to Gulf of Mexico
Soil Mud; 0–6 inches underwater
Shade, dappled shade, part shade
Colonizes by rhizomes and stolons
Propagation Root division

I'm crazy about lizardtail. It's such a funny, endearing little plant, with long, thin stalks that lean over awkwardly and drooping fuzzy tails. Use it as a ground cover in shady, marshy areas or even on shady, well-watered slopes. It will go dormant in the summer if you don't keep it wet. You'll be amazed how profusely lizardtail blooms in the shade. In fact, I believe that crinum lily is the only other water plant that blooms so well without direct sunlight.

360. **Latin Name** *Thalia dealbata*
Pronunciation THAY-lee-ah dee-all-BAH-tah
Common Names POWDERY THALIA, WATER CANNA
Usual Height 6–8 feet, including flowers
Spacing 2 feet apart, or 1 per 19-inch tub
Bloom Summer and fall; purple, 4- to 6-inch spikes
Dormant in winter
Range Shallow water in East and Southeast Texas
Southeastern U.S.
Soil Mud; saline okay; 0–12 inches underwater
Part shade, full sun
Colonizes by rhizomes
Propagation Root division

Powdery thalia is a big plant, so if you don't have lots of room in your water or bog garden to let it spread out, contain it in a pot and enjoy it as a tall accent. It's also called water canna because the leaves look like those of the commonly cultivated cannas. (They're in the same family and are also fine water and bog garden options.) It's called powdery thalia because the leaves, stems, and flowers are all covered with a pale, filmy substance. For those of you who have to fill your water garden with public water that is heavy in salts, this plant shouldn't mind.

361. Meadow rue
Thalictrum sp.
The authors

362. Narrowleaf cattail
Typha angustifolia
The authors

up to six feet tall. One or two much shorter ones grow in Houston and Northeast Texas, and there is a Rocky Mountain meadow rue (*T. fendleri*) with deep-yellow flowers that grows in the Trans-Pecos.

361. **Latin Name** *Thalictrum* spp.
Pronunciation thah-LIK-trum species
Common Name MEADOW RUE
Usual Height 2–4 feet
Spacing 2 feet apart
Bloom 2 weeks in spring or summer; greenish white to yellow; ½ inch long
Dormant in winter
Range Cool, moist, shady places in East Texas, Houston, Post Oak Woods, Blackland woods, northern Panhandle, and Trans-Pecos
Canada to Texas
Soil Sandy loam, clay-loam; acid or calcareous; moist, poor drainage okay
Shade, dappled shade, part shade
Propagation Fresh seed, division of clumps

Meadow rue has delicate leaves and airy clusters of drooping flowers. There are no petals, just stamens or pistils, with the stamens on the male flowers being the showier. Usually male and female flowers are found on separate plants, but don't worry about which sex you're getting. You need both, planted in loose groups for a woodsy look. Let them seed out, so you maintain a good supply. Plant meadow rue among ferns, where its height and texture will lighten the scene. It can be used in moist woods as a woodland ground cover, on the damp edges of a water garden, or in a shady bog garden. The most common meadow rue is *T. dasycarpum*, which can get

362. **Latin Name** *Typha angustifolia*
Pronunciation TYE-fah an-gus-teh-FOLE-ee-ah
Common Name NARROWLEAF CATTAIL
Usual Height 7 feet
Spacing 1 per 12- to 19-inch pot
Bloom Summer; brown fruiting stalks; 6 inches
Dormant in winter
Range Coastal and saltwater marshes in South Texas
North and South America, Europe, Asia
Soil Mud; 0–12 inches underwater
Part shade, full sun
Colonizes by rhizomes
Propagation Root division

Never let narrowleaf cattail loose in your water or bog garden! It's extremely aggressive and can take over before you know it. Put it in a large, stout container that even Houdini couldn't get out of. So, now that you know this, why would you want to mess around with this plant in the first place? Because it makes a thick privacy screen or a tall accent. It grows seven feet high and densely. Despite its propensity to crowd out everything else, this is a very popular water plant. It grows anywhere, and it's ridiculously easy to establish; just drop it in the mud and walk away.

363. Floating bladderwort
Utricularia radiata
The authors

364. Virginia chain fern
Woodwardia virginica
Edith Bettinger

363. **Latin Name** *Utricularia radiata*
Pronunciation yoo-trik-yoo-LARE-ee-ah
ray-dee-AH-tah
Common Name FLOATING BLADDERWORT
Usual Height Floats are 2 inches above
water
Spacing 1 per square foot of water
Bloom March to July; yellow; 3 or 4
half-inch flowers per float, each float
2–3 inches wide
Dormant in winter
Range Still water or slow streams in East
Texas
Nova Scotia to Gulf of Mexico
Soil Acid; water 6–18 inches deep
Part shade, full sun
Colonizes by floats
Propagation Seed, floats

The silly-sounding name is really quite descriptive.
The whole plant floats, buoyed up by little bladders on
each of the radiating arms. It is usually anchored to submerged water plants such as fanwort (*Cabomba* spp.),
which can be harvested from almost any nearby pond or
purchased in pots. Floating bladderwort can live only in
an earthen pond that has been filled, not with tap water,
but with water from some pond that is rich in microorga-
nisms. This is because the bladderwort is a carnivore. Its
submerged leaves trap microscopic animal life, which are
then dissolved by enzymes and digested. It provides food
and shelter for fish and is occasionally eaten by waterfowl.
Bladderwort is extremely difficult to use and impossible to
buy. It's found most often in established ponds in sugar

sand. If it's been about a year since you added pond scum
to your water garden, if the water looks cloudy, and if
there appear to be numerous teensy beasties living in that
soup, then chances are good that it will have enough microscopic animal life to support a bladderwort. Scoop up
one or two bladderworts in a bucket of their own pond
water and transfer them immediately to your water garden—and keep your fingers crossed.

364. **Latin Name** *Woodwardia virginica*
Pronunciation wood-WAR-dee-ah
ver-JIN-eh-kah
Common Name VIRGINIA CHAIN FERN
Usual Height 1–2 feet
Spacing 1–2 feet apart
Dormant in winter
Range Bogs, swamps, and along streams
in Piney Woods, Post Oak Savannah,
and Houston area, west to an area in
Blackland Prairies east of Austin and
San Antonio
Eastern Canada to Gulf of Mexico and
Bermuda

Soil Sand, loam, clay; acid or calcareous; moist, poor drainage okay
Shade, dappled shade, part shade
Colonizes by rhizomes
Propagation Root division

In most of the eastern United States, this is one of the most common and adaptable native ferns. It is a large, coarse terrestrial that gets up to five feet tall and forms a dense ground cover in woods. In Texas, with our heat and high evaporation rates, it dies back when it gets too dry, so use it only in a shady bog garden. It is probably the most aggressive fern I'm covering in this book. The fronds grow almost like a thick mat all along its woody, ropelike, linear root system instead of radiating from one central point. The lustrous leafstalk of the fern (called a stipe) is dark at the base but often smooth and reddish above. New growth is bronze-colored. The plant is called chain fern not because it grows linearly but because of the pattern the spores form on the underside of the fronds.

Water Garden Plan
Lot Size: 40' × 60'

Water gardens conjure up images of elegant Italian villas overlooking the Mediterranean, palatial Beverly Hills mansions where the "beautiful people" live, or grand Southampton estates where guests stroll the grounds nonchalantly sipping Dom Perignon. In other words, the popular misconception is that if you want to have a water garden, you'd better be well-heeled.

In fact, almost anyone can enjoy a water garden; even a condo owner could create a small one in the patio area.

If you live in East Texas, or anywhere in, around, and between Houston and Dallas, this lush and extremely colorful plan is ideal for your water-holding clay soils. The plan is not appropriate for the entire state, however. It needs too much water to be practical in low-rainfall areas. If you happen to live in such a dry region, don't despair—you have other options. For instance, you can have a shallow birdbath pond (see the photo and caption for the Wildlife Garden Plan) or a small tiled fountain that burbles on a recycling system and holds two or three pots of water plants. (These water features have been included in the El Paso and Corpus Christi plans.)

If your property is characterized by poor drainage, a water garden can be as functional as it is beautiful. Have you noticed that your trees and flowers get mildewed? Or that drought-tolerant plants such as Gregg salvia, cenizo, and even coreopsis tend to rot? These are all signs of poor drainage, caused by clay soils, swales, runoff from uphill neighbors, or natural springs. This Water Garden Plan should give you some good ideas on how to make the most of these factors, so that poor drainage can be an asset, not a liability.

The high ground is at the top of the plan. The dry stream bed of gravel and river stone is designed to catch neighboring runoff and take it to where it can be of use. Starting at just below ground level, the stream bed narrows and deepens as it makes its way to the pond. Boulders, as well as the shallow banks, help break and direct the water into a foot-deep channel that sends it over a large stone and into the pond. During periods of heavy rain, you'll have a mini–Niagara Falls to enjoy.

The pond is lined with 4 mil black plastic sheets to hold the water. Eventually the plastic will rot away, but by then the weight of the water will have

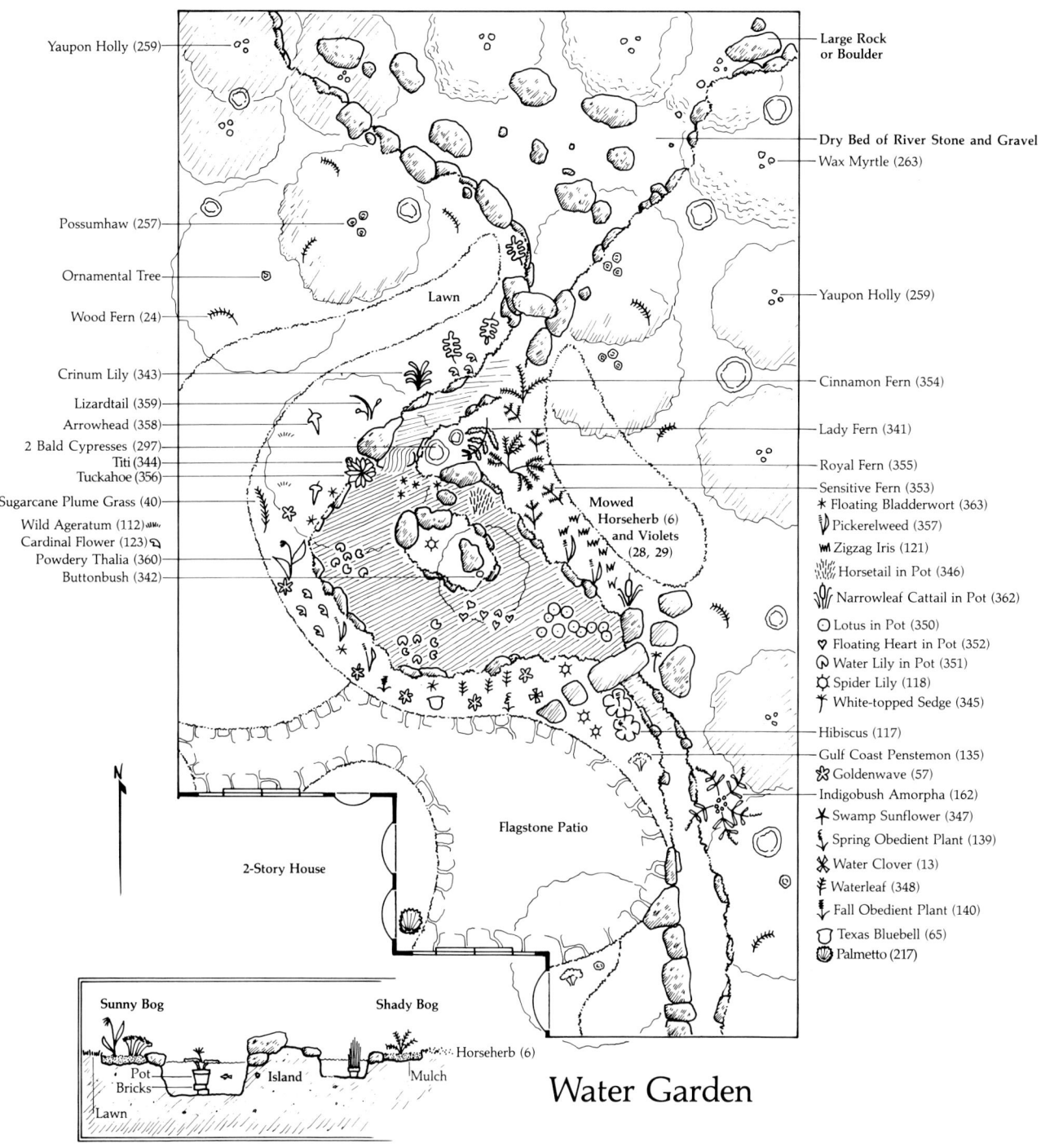

Yaupon Holly (259)

Large Rock or Boulder

Dry Bed of River Stone and Gravel
Wax Myrtle (263)

Possumhaw (257)

Ornamental Tree

Wood Fern (24)

Yaupon Holly (259)

Lawn

Crinum Lily (343)

Cinnamon Fern (354)

Lizardtail (359)
Arrowhead (358)

Lady Fern (341)

2 Bald Cypresses (297)
Titi (344)
Tuckahoe (356)

Royal Fern (355)

Sugarcane Plume Grass (40)

Sensitive Fern (353)
Floating Bladderwort (363)

Wild Ageratum (112)
Cardinal Flower (123)
Powdery Thalia (360)
Buttonbush (342)

Mowed
Horseherb (6)
and Violets
(28, 29)

Pickerelweed (357)
Zigzag Iris (121)
Horsetail in Pot (346)
Narrowleaf Cattail in Pot (362)
Lotus in Pot (350)
Floating Heart in Pot (352)
Water Lily in Pot (351)
Spider Lily (118)
White-topped Sedge (345)
Hibiscus (117)
Gulf Coast Penstemon (135)
Goldenwave (57)
Indigobush Amorpha (162)
Swamp Sunflower (347)
Spring Obedient Plant (139)
Water Clover (13)
Waterleaf (348)
Fall Obedient Plant (140)
Texas Bluebell (65)
Palmetto (217)

N

2-Story House

Flagstone Patio

Sunny Bog

Shady Bog

Horseherb (6)

Pot
Bricks

Island

Mulch

Lawn

Water Garden

packed the clay soil so tight that the pond will probably continue to hold water without it. The plastic is held in place and hidden at the edges by large rocks that line the sides of the pond.

After a heavy rain the pond level can rise to the tops of the rocks and cover the surrounding bog gardens. But the patio and lawn areas should never be under water. That's why I've indicated French drains, which run under the narrower dry stream bed below the pond to carry excess water to the street sewer. The drains start just under the stone footbridge at the bottom end of the pond.

Normally, the pond holds thirty inches of water. In the summer it needs to be watered to maintain that level. (Sometimes watering is unnecessary if you have a strong natural spring.) Water can be added by hose once or twice a week, but in this plan a "spaghetti" hose on the sprinkler system is hidden between the big rocks at the "waterfall" and runs constantly over the lower rock to feed the pond. Because Texas is so hot in the summer, evaporation losses run about one inch a week. With a pond this size, that translates to approximately 75 gallons a week.

In the pond is an island, about seven feet long and five feet wide. It is completely covered with spider lily and a buttonbush, which after many years will make a small gnarled tree. You can cross over to the island from the back side by way of a flat-topped boulder placed to make a stepping-stone. The water here is shallower, only about one foot deep, the perfect depth for floating bladderwort. (When Andy first heard that name, he immediately declared it, sight unseen, his favorite native plant!)

The water plants that I've set into this pond are those that float, with the exception of the horsetails. All, including the horsetails, are in containers. Otherwise any one of them might take over the whole pond. Keeping the plants contained gives you variety—more than one kind of water lily, a yellow water lotus, and floating hearts. The narrowleaf cattail is also in a pot, sunk into the mud of the bog garden.

The bog gardens in this plan are actually shelves or shallow ledges connected to the main pond. (See the introduction to this chapter for a definition of this type of bog garden.) To the eye, they look like flower gardens surrounding the pond. Where there is at least a half day of sun, they are very colorful, as seen in the photo of the Henschen garden.

The flowers are low-growing near the patio to allow a good view of the pond. Another vantage point is from the stone bridge that divides the pond from the lower dry stream bed. From there, you can walk over to a slightly raised area of mowed horseherb and violets, then to the stones that cross the upper dry stream bed, and over to the lawn. The view from here toward the house is full of contrasts. You are standing in a cool, shady woodland setting, looking toward a sunny vibrance of yellow and purple, with pink, white, red, maroon, or blue, according to the time of year.

The main spring color is the deep yellow of the maroon-centered swamp-loving goldenwave. Other spring blossoms are purple Gulf Coast penstemon, pink spring obedient plant, blue zigzag iris, and white spider lily.

Summer is bright with tall hibiscus (which might be red, pink, or white with a maroon throat) and the equally tall, lavender powdery thalia. The coreopsis continues to give spots of yellow, while the Texas bluebell and pickerelweed are purply blue and the arrowhead is white. All of these colors combine well with the flowers in the pond: pale yellow water lotuses, white floating hearts, and white (or yellow or blue) water lilies.

Fall can be even more spectacular. Bright yellow swamp sunflower holds together accents of brilliant red cardinal flower, wild ageratum, fall obedient plant, amazingly blue waterleaf, white-topped sedge, and sugarcane plume grass. In addition, hibiscus, pickerelweed, and powdery thalia continue to bloom, and the Gulf Coast penstemon usually blooms again.

Water clover covers the bog area like a low ground cover beneath and between the flowers. In mild climates, especially along the coast, it will provide a green cover all or most of the winter and will fill in any bare spots the rest of the year.

The shady parts are lush and ferny. A few flowers can blossom in here, though not as fulsomely as in partial sun. Crinum lily, lizardtail, and cardinal flower provide spots of color in the richly textured variety of ferns.

The lower wooded areas can stand an occasional flooding, as the canopy trees are indigenous to creeks in your area. Two understory trees are wax myrtle and yaupon holly, which should be allowed to grow shrublike to provide screening on the edges of the yard. Around the head of the pond, where there is a little more light, are three possumhaws, pruned into multi-trunked trees that provide vivid winter color.

Also on this plan are two ornamental trees, which could be plum, hawthorn, redbud, ironwood, witch hazel, or chalk maple, to name a few. Next to the one in the lower right-hand corner, by the dry stream bed and opposite the patio, is the strange little shrub-tree call indigobush amorpha. It has spikes of purple flowers with orange stamens and an airy way of growing. It should be allowed to droop over the stream bed. Beneath the trees are wood ferns, which need to be watered deeply during hot dry spells.

Around the house are evergreen ferns, the evergreen Gulf Coast penstemon, and palmettos.

The overall effect of this plan is luxuriant, but with somewhat of a split personality. The scene is intense and almost tropical, with vivid color around the pond, yet at the same time it is cool and elegant, with ferny woods as the backdrop.

Martha Henschen designed and dug this plastic-lined pond out of Houston's gumbo. It has shelves and pockets to hold hibiscus and iris, and a deep portion for floating water plants. After filling it from the tap, she added a bucket of ditch water rich with pond life and gambusia, a small native fish vital to natural pond functioning. She dug up about one square foot of soil from the bank, and it produced a bounty of varied plants that grew from dormant seed. Most of the flowers were specially bought. In bloom when we took this photo in early June are black-eyed Susan, goldenwave, and a naturalized verbena, *V. rigida*, all planted on the muddy banks. Earlier, there was spring obedient plant and iris. Later, there will be hibiscus, arrowhead, pickerelweed, white-topped sedge, and water lilies; in the fall, wild ageratum and swamp sunflower. Photo by the authors.

TWELVE

Who's Who in Native Plant Landscaping

A number of individuals and organizations have contributed greatly to our knowledge of how to use Texas native plants in landscapes. Here is a brief description of those who are well known statewide for their invaluable contributions.

INDIVIDUALS

Carroll Abbott is sometimes called the Father of Texas Wildflowers. He persuaded the Texas Legislature to declare the fourth Saturday in April as Wildflower Day, the day he and the president of Texas Woman's University started celebrating in 1981 with lectures and an awards luncheon. He founded the Native Plant Society of Texas as well as Green Horizons, a mail-order wildflower seed and native plant book business in Kerrville, and wrote a little book sold by Green Horizons called *How to Know and Grow Texas Wildflowers.* He frequently gave slide-show lectures on wildflowers and native plants and issued a quarterly publication, *Texas Wildflower Newsletter,* which served as the newsletter of the Native Plant Society of Texas until his death in 1984.

Geyata Ajilvsgi, author of *Wildflowers of Texas* and *Wildflowers of the Big Thicket, East Texas, and Western Louisiana,* is currently working on two other books, on butterflies and the plants they eat. Her work is known for its fine scholarship and photography.

Lady Bird Johnson has long been an advocate for the use and preservation of wildflowers. A native Texan, she founded the National Wildflower Research Center in 1983 to educate the public about the beauty and usefulness of wildflowers all over the United States.

Marshall Johnston, professor of botany at the University of Texas at Austin, coauthored *Manual of the Vascular Plants of Texas* with D. S. Correll. He is currently working on a multivolume treatise on all the useful wild plants in Texas.

Lynn Lowrey, landscape designer and founder of the Lowrey Nursery in Conroe, has worked in the Houston area for many years and has trained many of the leaders in the field today. He also spent several years discovering and selecting plants for Lone Star Growers to propagate for landscapers like you. He travels in both Texas and Mexico in his search for the most beautiful and useful native landscape plant material.

Jill Nokes, the author of *How to Grow Native Plants of Texas and the Southwest,* is a frequent lecturer on native plants and has written numerous articles on the subject. She is currently in charge of the new gardens and trail walks at the Trail House at the Austin Nature Center.

Benny J. Simpson is our foremost lecturer on native plants. He specializes in woody plants (trees and shrubs) and is author of *A Field Guide to Texas Trees,* the first comprehensive book on Texas trees to use photographs. He is in charge of a project with the Texas Agricultural Experiment Station to test and select native plants for the landscape trade. He has gone on many scouting expeditions with Lynn Lowrey and Dr. Barton Warnock.

John Thomas, founder of WildSeed, Inc., has developed machinery to plant and harvest wildflowers on a large scale so that native Texas wildflower seed can be available at reasonable cost and in sufficient quantity for consumer use. He often lectures on the subject and does many projects for highway departments and for large commercial landscapes.

Barton H. Warnock, retired professor of botany at Sul Ross State University, has written three books on the flora of the Trans-Pecos. His aesthetic observations have been of incalculable help to Benny Simpson and Lynn Lowrey in their selection of plants from the Trans-Pecos. He manages a demonstration shrub garden on private land in Marathon.

ORGANIZATIONS

Containerized Plants (Route 5, Box 143, Brenham, TX 77833, 409-836-4293) is a wholesale and retail native plant nursery, allied with the Antique Rose Emporium. Demonstration gardens are open 8:30–5 Monday through Friday. Owner Michael Shoup listed 90 natives plus many other adapted plants in his 1987 catalog and each year the list gets longer.

Lone Star Growers (7960 Cagnon Road, Box 220, San Antonio, TX 78227, 512-677-8020) is the largest wholesale producer of native plants in the state and has a section devoted to experimentation and development in this field. Its 1987 catalog listed nearly 115 Texas native species plus numerous natives from Mexico and other adapted species.

National Wildflower Research Center (2600 FM 973 North, Austin, TX 78725, 512-929-3600), a nonprofit organization, issues a journal and a bimonthly newsletter, holds seminars, tests wildflower mixes, leads tours, and is developing a data bank of growers, nurseries, species suitable for different areas, and more. Lists from the data bank are sent on request. During April and May, call 512-929-3607 for a recorded message detailing where to find the most spectacular Texas wildflowers each week.

Native Plant Project (c/o P.O. Box 8124, Weslaco, TX 78596) is the equivalent of the Native Plant Society of Texas for the Rio Grande Valley and espouses the same goals. It publishes a sometimes monthly newsletter called *Sabal* and is working on several public projects.

Native Plant Society of Texas (1204 S. Trinity Street, Decatur, TX 76234) is a nonprofit organization composed of grass-roots native-plant enthusiasts. Its purpose is to educate, preserve, and encourage the use of native Texas plants (not only wildflowers but also shrubs, trees, vines, and grasses) in landscaping and other activities beneficial to man, such as dyes and medicine. It issues a bimonthly newsletter and holds an annual program in October. Each region conducts field trips, lectures, and other activities related to native plants.

Native Prairies Association of Texas (7575 Wheatland Road, Dallas, TX 75249) is a nonprofit organization that was formed by Madge Gatlin (now Madge M. Lindsey) and Dr. Geoffrey Stanford in 1984 to study remnants of tallgrass prairie and to develop ways to maintain and restore these vanishing habitats. It publishes a bimonthly newsletter and holds an annual meeting in January. It also conducts numerous field trips and work sessions throughout the year.

Texas Department of Agriculture (P.O. Box 12847, Austin, TX 78711), under the direction of Commissioner Jim Hightower, has been solidly supporting state efforts to grow native plants commercially. It publishes a free directory of wholesale and retail nurseries that sell trees and other native ornamentals.

Texas Natural Heritage Program (Texas Parks and Wildlife Department, 4200 Smith School Road, Austin, TX 78744, 512-389-4997) was formed in 1983 as a joint project of the General Land Office and the Nature Conservancy. It computerizes and maps data on the existence, characteristics, and distribution of plants, animals, and man-managed natural communities in Texas. It is also involved with the study and protection of endangered species of plants and animals.

Texas Nature Celebration (312 Canyon Ridge Drive, Richardson, TX 75080, 214-644-0778) is producing a video program designed for use in the Texas school system as a resource tool in teaching Texas natural history and ecology. Sponsors include the Native Plant Society of Texas, Texas Natural Heritage Program, Lone Star Chapter of the Sierra Club, and Texas State Teachers Association.

WildSeed, Inc. (P.O. Box 308, Eagle Lake, TX 77434, 713-578-7800), sows, harvests, and sells Texas wildflower seed. You may order bulk seed directly from WildSeed or buy packaged seed from numerous retail outlets. It often has small quantities of seed not listed in its catalog, so don't hesitate to make a special request. Most of its business is turnkey jobs from growing to sowing for Texas state highway and other mammoth-sized projects.

 # *Public Native Landscapes*

Most public gardens in Texas use native shade trees, but more frequently now, they are using our native flowering plants. Occasionally a garden is purely native, even endemic, but usually natives are mixed in with anything else that grows well. Besides conventional gardens, there are nature centers with preserved, reconstructed, or managed habitats, such as meadows, prairies, and woods, and there are experiment stations with test plots and gardens. I have listed here places that already have gardens installed or are in advanced planning stages with available funding, so they should be completed by the time this book is in your hands.

There are also many state, city, county, national, and foundation sponsored parks and refuges, most of which preserve native habitat and have handouts on how to identify the most eye-catching plants. These are found on most state maps and are not listed here unless they have special landscaping.

The listings below are organized by nearest city. "Daily" means seven days a week.

Abilene

Abilene Zoological Garden, Nelson Park, Texas Highway 36 at Loop 322, 915-672-9771. 10–5 daily. Fee.

Alpine

Chihuahuan Desert Research Institute, Texas Highway 118 north of Alpine, 915-837-8370. Desert gardens and a small nursery.

Austin

National Wildflower Research Center, 2600 FM 973 North, 512-929-3600. Free. Wildflower test plots.

Texas Department of Agriculture, Stephen F. Austin State Office Building, Seventeenth and Colorado streets. Landscaping on the south and east sides of the building is with native and naturalized plants.

Trail House at Austin Nature Center, 2416 Barton Springs Road. Garden, pond, exhibits, greenhouse, and trail walks planned.

Zilker Park, Barton Springs Road, 512-477-6511. 6–10 daily. Free. Xeriscape garden in Zilker Botanical Gardens.

Corpus Christi

Corpus Christi Botanical Garden, on Staples beyond Oso Creek, 512-993-7551. Fee. Formal gardens and trail walks planned.

Welder Wildlife Refuge, U.S. 77, 8 miles north-east of Sinton, 512-364-2643. By appointment or periodic field days. A foundation for the study of wildlife management.

Dallas

Dallas Arboretum and Botanical Garden, 8525 Garland Road, near White Rock Lake, 214-327-8263. 10–5 Tuesday through Sunday. Fee. Many endemic trees, and plans for a native flower garden and meadow.

Dallas Garden Center, Fair Park, 214-428-7476. Outside gardens always open. Free. Some natives.

Dallas Nature Center, 7575 Wheatland Road, near Joe Pool Lake, 214-296-1955. Open during daylight hours. Free. New native plant gardens and trails.

Heard Natural Science Museum, FM 1378 off Texas Highway 5, 5 miles south of McKinney, 214-542-5012. 9–5 Tuesday through Saturday, 1–5 Sunday. Free. Managed prairie.

Texas Agricultural Experiment Station, 17360 Coit Road, just north of Campbell Road, 214-231-5362. 8–5 Monday through Friday. Free. Native experimental plantings.

El Paso

Texas A&M Experiment Station, 1380 A&M Circle (off Interstate 10 and U.S. 80), 915-859-9111. 8–5 Monday through Friday. Free. All-endemic experimental gardens.

Wilderness Park Museum, 2000 Transmountain Road, 915-755-4332. Native plant and cactus garden.

Fort Worth

Fort Worth Nature Center and Refuge, Texas Highway 199, 817-237-1111. 8–5 Monday through Friday, 9–5 Saturday and Sunday. Free. No formal plantings, but a managed meadow and prairie, and both escarpment and riparian woodlands.

Fort Worth Water Department, Rolling Hills Demonstration Garden, 817-870-8220. Always open. Free. Xeriscape garden.

Fort Worth Zoo, University off Interstate 30, 817-870-7050. 9–5 daily. Pioneer landscapes and nature walk planned.

Houston

Armand Bayou Nature Center, 8600 Bay Area Boulevard in Clear Lake, 713-474-2551. 9–5 Tuesday through Sunday. Free. Bog garden and native plant nursery.

Houston Arboretum, 4501 Woodway, Memorial Park, 713-681-8433. 8:30–6 daily. Free. Water and bog garden, woods, prairie.

Mercer Arboretum, 22306 Aldine-Westfield Road in Humble, 713-443-8731. 8–5 daily. Free. Formal gardens; theme gardens specializing in native irises, ferns, and so on.

Langtry

Judge Roy Bean Visitor Center, Loop 25 off Texas Highway 90, 915-291-3340. 8–5 daily. Free. Landscape and gardens using native plants indigenous to the area.

Lubbock

Texas Tech University, Ranching Heritage Center, Fourth and Indiana, 806-742-2498. 9–4:30 Monday through Saturday, 1–4:30 Sunday (to 8:30 in summer). Fee.

San Antonio

San Antonio Botanical Center, 555 Funston, 512-821-5115. 9–6 Wednesday through Sunday. Fee. Extensive formal mixed-native gardens plus all-native plantings for Hill Country, South Texas, and East Texas. New conservatory to house natives from Valley and Mexico. A Xeriscape garden bordering the parking lot uses drought-tolerant natives and other adapted plants.

Valley

Gladys Porter Zoo, Ringgold and Sixth, Brownsville, 512-546-2177. Daily 10 a.m. until one hour before dusk. Fee. Native plants are the settings for the animals.

Santa Ana Wildlife Refuge, U.S. 281 on the Rio Grande near McAllen, ½ mile east of FM 907, 512-787-3079. 9–4:30 daily. Free. Indigenous landscaping in parking lot and around building entrance.

Bibliography

Abbott, Carroll. *How to Know and Grow Texas Wildflowers*. Kerrville, Tex.: Green Horizons Press (500 Thompson Drive, Kerrville, TX 78028), 1979.

Ajilvsgi, Geyata. *Wildflowers of the Big Thicket, East Texas, and Western Louisiana*. College Station: Texas A&M University Press, 1979.

————. *Wildflowers of Texas*. Bryan, Tex.: Shearer Publishing, 1984.

American Medical Association. *AMA Handbook of Poisonous and Injurious Plants*. Chicago: Chicago Review Press, 1985.

Beales, Peter. *Classic Roses*. New York: Holt, Rinehart and Winston, 1985.

Brown, Clair A. *Wildflowers of Louisiana and Adjoining States*. Baton Rouge: Louisiana State University Press, 1972.

Coombes, Allen J. *Dictionary of Plant Names*. Portland, Oregon: Timber Press, 1985.

Correll, Donovan Stewart, and Marshall Conring Johnston. *Manual of the Vascular Plants of Texas*. Vol. 6 of Contributions from Texas Research Foundation: A Series of Botanical Studies, edited by Cyrus Longworth Lundell. Richardson, Tex.: University of Texas at Dallas, 1979.

Duffield, Mary Rose, and Warren D. Jones. *Plants for Dry Climates*. Tucson, Arizona: H. P. Books, 1981.

Enquist, Marshall. *Wildflowers of the Texas Hill Country*. Austin, Tex.: Lone Star Botanical, 1987.

Fort Worth Nature Center and Refuge. *Checklist of Wild Flowering Plants*. Fort Worth, Tex.

Geiser, Samuel Wood. *Horticulture and Horticulturists in Early Texas*. Dallas: University Press in Dallas, Southern Methodist University, 1945.

————. *Naturalists of the Frontier*. Dallas: University Press in Dallas, Southern Methodist University, 1948.

Gould, F. W., and T. W. Box. *Grasses of the Texas Coastal Bend*. College Station: Texas A&M University Press, 1965.

Greene, A. C. *A Personal Country*. College Station: Texas A&M University Press, 1969.

Hargreaves, Dorothy, and Bob Hargreaves. *Tropical Blossoms of the Caribbean*. Kailua, Hawaii: Hargreaves Company (Box 895, Kailua, HI 96734), 1960.

————. *Tropical Trees*. Kailua, Hawaii: Hargreaves Company (Box 895, Kailua, HI 96734), 1965.

Heminway, Jessie. *Plants of the Southwest* seed catalog, 1987. Available from 1812 Second St., Santa Fe, NM 87501.

Huey, Edith Lancaster. *Ozark Wild Flowers II*. Little Rock, Ark.: Wood Brothers Agency, 1978.

James, Wilma Roberts. *Know Your Poisonous Plants*. Happy Camp, Calif.: Naturegraph Publishers, 1973.

Lyndon B. Johnson School of Public Affairs. *Preserving Texas' Natural Heritage*. Austin: LBJ School of Public Affairs, University of Texas, 1978.

Jones, F. B., C. M. Rowell, and M. C. Johnston. *Flora of the Texas Coastal Bend*. Sinton, Tex.: Rob and Bessie Welder Wildlife Foundation, 1975.

Judy, Susan. "Scientist Develops Water Lilies for Texas." *Texas Gardener Magazine*, May–June 1987.

Kartesz, J., and R. Kartesz. *Synonymized Checklist of the Vascular Flora of the United States, Canada, and Greenland*. Vol. 2 of *The Biota of North America*. Chapel Hill: University of North Carolina Press, 1980.

Lewis, George W., and James F. Miller. *Identification and Control of Weeds in Southern Ponds*. Athens, Ga.: University of Georgia, 1984.

Native Plant Society of New Mexico. *Proceedings of the Southwestern Native Plant Symposium*, Albuquerque, 1987.

Native Plant Society of Texas, South Texas Region. *A Plant List for Bexar County, Texas*. 1986. Available from 85 Campden Circle, San Antonio, TX 78218.

Natural Vegetation Committee, Arizona Chapter, Soil Conservation Society of America. *Landscaping With Native Arizona Plants*. Tucson: University of Arizona Press, 1973.

Nokes, Jill. *How to Grow Native Plants of Texas and the Southwest*. Austin, Tex.: Texas Monthly Press, 1986.

North Carolina Wild Flower Preservation Society, *Native Plant Propagation Handbook*. Chapel Hill: 1977.

O'Kennon, Lou Ellen, and Robert O'Kennon. *Texas Wildflower Portraits*. Austin, Tex.: Texas Monthly Press, 1987.

Phillips, Judith. *Southwestern Landscaping With*

Native Plants. Santa Fe: Museum of New Mexico Press, 1987.

Rickett, Harold William. *Wild Flowers of the United States.* Vol. 3, pts. 1 and 2. New York: McGraw-Hill Book Co., 1969.

Rock and Water Gardens. Time-Life Encyclopedia of Gardening. Alexandria, Va.: Time-Life Books, 1979.

Rose, Francis L., and Russell W. Standtmann. *Wildflowers of the Llano Estacado.* Dallas: Taylor Publishing Co., 1986.

Rowell, Chester M. *A Guide to the Identification of Plants Poisonous to Livestock of Western Texas.* San Angelo, Tex.: Angelo State University (San Angelo, TX 76909).

Russell, Steve. *Natural History Guide to Armand Bayou Nature Center.* Houston: Armand Bayou Nature Center.

Schmutz, Ervin M., Barry N. Freeman, and Raymond E. Reed. *Livestock Poisoning Plants of Arizona.* Tucson: University of Arizona Press, 1968.

Sharpe, Patricia, and Robert S. Weddle. *Texas.* Texas Monthly Guidebooks. Austin, Tex.: Texas Monthly Press, 1982.

Shinners, Lloyd H. *Shinners' Spring Flora.* Dallas: Southern Methodist University Herbarium (Dallas, TX 75275), 1958.

Stupka, Arthur, with Donald H. Robinson. *Wildflowers in Color.* New York: Harper and Row, 1965.

Taylor, M., and C. Hill. *Hardy Plants Introduced to Britain by 1799.* Hatfield, Herts.: Hatfield House, Great Britain.

The Texas Almanac. Dallas: Dallas Morning News, 1986.

Vines, Robert A. *Trees, Shrubs, and Woody Vines of the Southwest.* Austin: University of Texas Press, 1960.

———. *Trees of North Texas.* Austin: University of Texas Press, 1982.

Warnock, Barton H. *Wildflowers of the Big Bend Country, Texas.* Alpine, Tex.: Sul Ross State University, 1970.

———. *Wildflowers of the Guadalupe Mountains and the Sand Dune Country, Texas.* Alpine, Tex.: Sul Ross State University, 1974.

———. *Wildflowers of the Davis Mountains and Marathon Basin, Texas.* Alpine, Tex.: Sul Ross State University, 1977.

Wasowski, Andy. *Texas Land: Uses and Abuses.* Dallas: Triland Corp., 1986.

Wasowski, Sally, and Julie Ryan. *Landscaping With Native Texas Plants.* Austin, Tex.: Texas Monthly Press, 1985.

Whitcomb, Carl E. *Know It and Grow It: A Guide to the Identification and Use of Landscape Plants.* Vol. 2. Stillwater, Okla.: Lacebark Publications, 1983.

Wills, Mary Motz, and Irwin, Howard S. *Roadside Flowers of Texas.* Austin, Tex.: University of Texas Press, 1961.

Wyman, Donald. *Wyman's Gardening Encyclopedia.* New York: Macmillan Publishing Co., 1971.

Index

Page numbers in italics refer to illustrations and photographs.